THE
SPECTATOR

THE
SPECTATOR

J. HUGHES ESQ.

G. Knell. r Eq: Bar Pinx 1718. G. Vander Gucht Sculp

JOHN HUGHES
From the engraving by G. van der Gucht after the portrait by Sir
Godfrey Kneller (Hughes's *Poems on Several Occasions*, 1735)

THE
SPECTATOR

EDITED
WITH AN INTRODUCTION
AND NOTES BY
DONALD F. BOND

VOLUME IV

OXFORD
AT THE CLARENDON PRESS
1965

Oxford University Press, Amen House, London E.C.4

GLASGOW NEW YORK TORONTO MELBOURNE WELLINGTON
BOMBAY CALCUTTA MADRAS KARACHI LAHORE DACCA
CAPE TOWN SALISBURY NAIROBI IBADAN
KUALA LUMPUR HONG KONG

PRINTED IN GREAT BRITAIN
AT THE UNIVERSITY PRESS, OXFORD
BY VIVIAN RIDLER
PRINTER TO THE UNIVERSITY

CONTENTS

CONTENTS

VOLUME III

VOLUME IV

VOLUME V

*Quantum a rerum turpitudine abes, tantum Te a verborum
libertate sejungas.*

Tull.

IT is a certain Sign of an ill Heart to be inclin'd to Defamation.
They who are harmless and innocent, can have no Gratification
that way; but it ever arises from a Neglect of what is laudable in
a Man's self, and an Impatience of seeing it in another. Else why
should Virtue provoke? Why should Beauty displease in such a
Degree, that a Man given to Scandal never lets the Mention of
either pass by him without offering something to the Diminution
of it? A Lady the other Day at a Visit being attack'd somewhat
rudely by one, whose own Character has been very roughly treated,
answer'd a great deal of Heat and Intemperance very calmly, *Good
Madam, spare me, who am none of your Match; I speak Ill of no body, and
it is a new thing to me to be spoken Ill of.* Little Minds think Fame consists in the Number of Votes they have on their Side among the
Multitude, whereas it is really the inseparable Follower of good and
worthy Actions. Fame is as natural a Follower of Merit, as a Shadow
is of a Body. It is true, when Crowds press upon you, this Shadow
cannot be seen, but when they separate from around you, it will
again appear. The Lazy, the Idle, and the Froward, are the Persons
who are most pleas'd with the little Tales which pass about the
Town to the Disadvantage of the rest of the World. Were it not for
the Pleasure of speaking Ill, there are Numbers of People who are
too lazy to go out of their own Houses, and too ill-natur'd to open
their Lips in Conversation. It was not a little diverting the other
Day to observe a Lady reading a Post-Letter, and at these Words,
*After all her Airs, he has heard some Story or other, and the Match is broke
off,* give Orders in the Midst of her Reading, *Put to the Horses.* That
a young Woman of Merit has miss'd an advantageous Settlement,
was News not to be delay'd, lest some Body else should have given
her malicious Acquaintance that Satisfaction before her. The Unwillingness to receive good Tidings is a Quality as inseparable from
a Scandal Bearer, as the Readiness to divulge bad. But, alas, how

---

[1] *Motto.* Cicero, *Pro M. Caelio*, 3. 8: You should be as careful of your words, as
your actions; and as far from speaking, as from doing ill.

wretchedly low and contemptible is that State of Mind, that cannot be pleas'd but by what is the Subject of Lamentation. This Temper has ever been in the highest Degree odious to gallant Spirits. The *Persian* Soldier, who was heard reviling *Alexander* the Great, was well admonished by his Officer; *Sir, You are paid to fight against* Alexander, *and not to rail at him*.[1]

Cicero in one of his Pleadings, defending his Client from general Scandal, says very handsomely, and with much Reason, *There are many who have particular Engagements to the Prosecutor: There are many who are known to have Ill-will to him for whom I appear; there are many who are naturally addicted to Defamation, and envious of any Good to any Man, who may have contributed to spread Reports of this Kind: For nothing is so swift as Scandal, nothing is more easily sent abroad, nothing receiv'd with more Welcome, nothing diffuses it self so universally. I shall not desire, that if any Report to our Disadvantage has any Ground for it, you would overlook or extenuate it: But if there be any thing advanced without a Person who can say whence he had it, or which is attested by one who forgot who told him it, or who had it from one of so little Consideration that he did not then think it worth his Notice, all such Testimonies as these, I know, you will think too slight to have any Credit against the Innocence and Honour of your Fellow-Citizen*.[2] When an ill Report is traced, it very often vanishes among such as the Orator has here recited. And how despicable a Creature must that be, who is in Pain for what passes among so frivolous a People? There is a Town in *Warwickshire* of good Note, and formerly pretty famous for much Animosity and Dissention, the chief Families of which have now turned all their Whispers, Backbitings, Envies, and private Malices, into Mirth and Entertainment, by means of a peevish old Gentlewoman, known by the Title of the Lady *Bluemantle*. This Heroine had for many Years together outdone the whole Sisterhood of Gossips in Invention, quick Utterance, and unprovoked Malice. This good Body is of a lasting Constitution, though extremely decay'd in her Eyes, and decrepid in her Feet. The two Circumstances of being always at Home from her Lameness, and very attentive from her Blindness, make her Lodgings the Receptacle of all that passes in Town, Good or Bad; but for the latter, she seems to have the better Memory. There is another Thing to be noted of her, which is, That as it is usual with old

---

[1] A familiar story, related of Memnon, the general of Darius's army (Plutarch, *Moralia* 174C). Bayle quotes it at least twice: art. William Bedell, Remark E; and art. Memnon, Remark C.

[2] Cicero, *Oratio pro Cnaeo Plancio*, 23. 57.

People, she has a livelier Memory of Things which pass'd when she was very young, than of late Years. Add to all this, that she does not only not love any Body, but she hates every Body. The Statue in *Rome*[1] does not serve to vent Malice half so well, as this old Lady does to disappoint it. She does not know the Author of any thing that is told her, but can readily repeat the Matter it self; therefore, though she exposes all the whole Town, she offends no one Body in it. She is so exquisitely restless and peevish, that she Quarrels with all about her, and sometimes in a Freak will instantly change her Habitation. To indulge this Humour, she is led about the Grounds belonging to the same House she is in, and the Persons to whom she is to remove, being in the Plot, are ready to receive her at her own Chamber again. At stated Times, the Gentlewoman at whose House she supposes she is at the Time, is sent for to quarrel with, according to her common Custom: When they have a Mind to drive the Jest, she is immediately urged to that Degree, that she will board in a Family with which she has never yet been; and away she will go this Instant, and tell them all that the rest have been saying of them. By this Means she has been an Inhabitant of every House in the Place without stirring from the same Habitation; and the many Stories which every Body furnishes her with to favour that Deceit, make her the general Intelligencer of the Town of all that can be said by one Woman against another. Thus groundless Stories die away, and sometimes Truths are smothered under the general Word: When they have a Mind to discountenance a thing, Oh! that is in my Lady *Bluemantle's* Memoirs.

  Whoever receives Impressions to the Disadvantage of others without Examination, is to be had in no other Credit for Intelligence than this good Lady *Bluemantle*, who is subjected to have her Ears imposed upon for want of other Helps to better Information. Add to this, that other Scandal-bearers suspend the Use of these Faculties which she has lost, rather than apply them to do Justice to their Neighbours; and I think, for the Service of my fair Readers, to acquaint them, that there is a voluntary Lady *Bluemantle* at every Visit in Town.   T

---

[1] For the statue of Pasquin see No. 23 (vol. i).

No. 428

[STEELE]

Friday, July 11, 1712[1]

Occupet extremum Scabies . . .

Hor.

IT is an impertinent and unreasonable Fault in Conversation, for one Man to take up all the Discourse. It may possibly be objected to me my self, that I am guilty in this Kind, in entertaining the Town every Day, and not giving so many able Persons who have it more in their Power, and as much in their Inclination, an Opportunity to oblige Mankind with their Thoughts. Besides, said one whom I over-heard the other Day, why must this Paper turn altogether upon Topicks of Learning and Morality? Why should it pretend only to Wit, Humour, or the like? Things which are useful only to amuse Men of Literature and superior Education. I would have it consist also of all things which may be necessary or useful to any Part of Society, and the mechanick Arts should have their Place as well as the liberal. The Ways of Gain, Husbandry, and Thrift, will serve a greater Number of People, than Discourses upon what was well said or done by such a Philosopher, Heroe, General, or Poet. I no sooner heard this Critick talk of my Works, but I minuted what he had said; and from that Instant resolved to enlarge the Plan of my Speculations, by giving Notice to all Persons of all Orders, and each Sex, that if they are pleased to send me Discourses, with their Names and Places of Abode to them, so that I can be satisfied the Writings are authentick, such their Labours shall be faithfully inserted in this Paper. It will be of much more Consequence to a Youth in his Apprenticeship, to know by what Rules and Arts such a one became Sheriff of the City of *London*, than to see the Sign of one of his own Quality with a Lion's Heart in each Hand. The World indeed is enchanted with romantick and improbable Atchievements, when the plain Path to respective Greatness and Success in the Way of Life a Man is in, is wholly overlooked. Is it possible that a young Man at present could pass his Time better, than in reading the History of Stocks, and knowing by what secret Springs they have such sudden Ascents and Falls in the same Day? Could he be better conducted in his Way to Wealth, which is the great Article of Life, than in a Treatise dated from *Change-Alley*[2] by

[1] *Motto.* Horace, *Ars poetica*, 417: The Devil take the hindmost!
[2] See No. 155 (vol. ii).

an able Proficient there? Nothing certainly could be more useful, than to be well instructed in his Hopes and Fears; to be diffident when others exalt, and with a secret Joy buy when others think it their Interest to sell. I invite all Persons who have any thing to say for the profitable Information of the Publick, to take their Turns in my Paper: They are welcome, from the late noble Inventor of the Longitude,[1] to the humble Author of Strops for Razors.[2] If to carry Ships in Safety, to give Help to People tost in a troubled Sea, without knowing to what Shore they bear, what Rocks to avoid, or what Coast to pray for in their Extremity, be a worthy Labour, and an Invention that deserves a Statue; at the same Time, he who has found a Means to let the Instrument which is to make your Visage less horrid,[3] and your Person more smug,[4] easy in the Operation, is worthy of some kind of good Reception: If things of high Moment meet with Renown, those of little Consideration, since of any Consideration, are not to be despised. In order that no Merit may lie hid, and no Art unimprov'd, I repeat it, that I call Artificers, as well as Philosophers, to my Assistance in the Publick Service. It would be of great Use, if we had an exact History of the Successes of every great Shop within the City-Walls, what Tracts of Land have been

[1] It is not known who is referred to here. John Flamsteed, the official 'astronomical observer', was the author of *Historia coelestis*, which in an edition by Edmond Halley was published, against Flamsteed's wishes, in 1712. In 1714 Sir Isaac Newton appeared before a committee of the House of Commons to give evidence regarding several projects which had been put forward for determining the longitude. (One was by Addison's friend William Whiston.) As a result of this investigation, Parliament offered a reward for an exact way of measuring the longitude; the newspapers of 1714 contain many advertisements of pamphlets on the subject.

[2] Rival advertisements of strops for razors appear constantly in the newspapers of this period. Addison had written in *Tatler* 224, apropos of polemical advertisements: 'The Inventors of Strops for Razors have written against one another this Way for several Years, and that with great Bitterness.' One type was sold only at John's Coffee-house in Swithin's Alley near the Royal Exchange, another (Reynolds's Strops) at Sam's Coffee-house in Ludgate Street, while 'Jacob's Famous Strops' could be had only at Jacob's Coffee-house behind the Royal Exchange. One of the best known was advertised in No. 394 (and in Nos. 423, 431, and 449) as follows:

The Famous Original Venetian Strops, neatly fix'd on Boards, now brought to the highest Perfection, so as vastly to exceed all others, and for polishing and setting Razors, Penknives, Lancets, &c. are not to be parallel'd, being much more durable and smooth, never growing rough by using, but setting Razors, &c. with greater Fineness and Exactness than any other sort possible can. Price 1s. each . . ., sold only at Mr. Allcrafts, a Toy-shop, at the Blue-Coat-Boy, against the Royal-Exchange in Cornhill, Mr. Paiston's a Stationer, at the May-Pole in the Strand, and at Mr. Cooper's, a Toy-shop, the Corner of Charles-Court, near York-Buildings in the Strand.

[3] Horrid, in the literal sense of 'shaggy, rough'.
Here used in the former literal sense of 'smooth, sleek'.

purchased by a constant Attendance within a Walk of Thirty Foot. If it could also be noted in the Equipage of those who are ascended from the Successful Trade of their Ancestors into Figure and Equipage, such Accounts would quicken Industry in the Pursuit of such Acquisitions, and discountenance Luxury in the Enjoyment of them.

To diversify these kind of Informations, the Industry of the Female World is not to be unobserv'd: She to whose Houshold-Virtues it is owing, that Men do Honour to her Husband, should be recorded with Veneration; she who has wasted his Labours, with Infamy. When we are come into Domestick Life in this manner, to awaken Caution and Attendance to the main Point, it would not be amiss to give now and then a Touch of Tragedy, and describe that most dreadful of all Humane Conditions, the Case of Bankrupcy; how Plenty, Credit, Chearfulness, full Hopes, and easy Possessions, are in an Instant turned into Penury, faint Aspects, Diffidence, Sorrow, and Misery; how the Man, who with an open Hand the Day before could administer to the Extremities of others, is shunn'd to Day by the Friend of his Bosom. It would be useful to shew how just this is on the Negligent, how lamentable on the Industrious. A Paper written by a Merchant, might give this Island a true Sense of the Worth and Importance of his Character: It might be visible from what he could say, That no Soldier entring a Breach adventures more for Honour, than the Trader does for Wealth to his Country. In both Cases the Adventurers have their own Advantage, but I know no Cases wherein every Body else is a Sharer in the Success.

It is objected by Readers of History, That the Battles in those Narrations are scarce ever to be understood. This Misfortune is to be ascribed to the Ignorance of Historians in the Methods of drawing up, changing the Forms of a Batallia,[1] and the Enemy retreating from, as well as approaching to, the Charge. But in the Discourses from the Correspondents whom I now invite, the Danger will be of another Kind; and it is necessary to caution them only against using Terms of Art,[2] and describing Things that are familiar to them in Words unknown to their Readers. I promise my self a great Harvest of new Circumstances, Persons, and Things from this Proposal; and a World, which many think they are well acquainted with, discovered as wholly new. This Sort of Intelligence will give a lively

---

[1] I.e. the order of battle.   [2] Cf. No. 297 (vol. iii).

Image of the Chain and mutual Dependance of Humane Society, take off impertinent Prejudices, enlarge the Minds of those, whose Views are confin'd to their own Circumstances; and, in short, if the Knowing in several Arts, Professions, and Trades will exert themselves, it cannot but produce a new Field of Diversion, an Instruction more agreeable than has yet appear'd.   T

No. 429

[STEELE]

Saturday, July 12, 1712[1]

> *. . . Populumque falsis dedocet uti*
> *Vocibus . . .*

Mr. SPECTATOR,

'SINCE I gave an Account of an agreeable Set of Company which were gone down into the Country, I have received Advices from thence, that the Institution of an Infirmary for those who should be out of Humour, has had very good Effects.[2] My Letters mention particular Circumstances of two or three Persons, who had the good Sense to retire of their own Accord, and notified that they were withdrawn, with the Reasons of it, to the Company, in their respective Memorials.

The *Memorial of Mrs.* Mary Dainty, *Spinster*,

Humbly sheweth,

"THAT conscious of her own Want of Merit, accompanied with a Vanity of being admired, she had gone into Exile of her own accord.

"She is sensible, that a vain Person is the most insufferable Creature living in a well-bred Assembly.

"That she desired, before she appeared in publick again, she might have Assurances, that, tho' she might be thought handsome, there might not more Address or Compliment be paid to her, than to the rest of the Company.

---

[1] *Motto.* Horace, *Odes*, 2. 2. 19-21:
> From cheats of Words the Crowd she brings
> To real Estimate of things. CREECH.

[2] No. 424 (vol. iii).

"That she conceived it a Kind of Superiority, that one Person should take upon him to commend another.

"Lastly, That she went into the Infirmary, to avoid a particular Person who took upon him to profess an Admiration of her.

"She therefore pray'd, that to applaud out of due place, might be declared an Offence, and punished in the same Manner with Detraction, in that the latter did but report Persons defective, and the former made them so.

All which is submitted, &c."

'There appeared a Delicacy and Sincerity in this Memorial very uncommon, but my Friend informs me, that the Allegations of it were groundless, insomuch that this Declaration of an Aversion to being praised, was understood to be no other than a secret Trap to purchase it, for which Reason it lies still on the Table unanswered.

The humble Memorial of the Lady Lydia Loller,

Sheweth,

"THAT the Lady *Lydia* is a Woman of Quality; married to a private Gentleman.

"That she finds her self neither well nor ill.

"That her Husband is a Clown.

"That Lady *Lydia* cannot see Company.

"That she desires the Infirmary may be her Apartment during her stay in the Country.

"That they would please to make merry with their Equals.

"That Mr. *Loller* might stay with them if he thought fit."

'It was immediately resolved, that Lady *Lydia* was still at *London*.

The Humble Memorial of Thomas Sudden, *Esq; of the* Inner-Temple,

Sheweth,

"THAT Mr. *Sudden* is conscious that he is too much given to Argumentation.

"That he talks loud.

"That he is apt to think all Things Matter of Debate.

"That he stay'd behind in *Westminster-Hall*, when the late Shake of the Roof[1] happen'd, only because a Council of the other Side asserted it was coming down.

---

[1] This has not been identified.

"That he cannot for his Life consent to any thing.

"That he stays in the Infirmary to forget himself.

"That as soon as he has forgot himself, he will wait on the Company."

'His Indisposition was allowed to be sufficient to require a Cessation from Company.

The Memorial of Frank Jolly,

Sheweth,

"THAT he hath put himself into the Infirmary, in regard[1] he is sensible of a certain rustick Mirth, which renders him unfit for polite Conversation.

"That he intends to prepare himself by Abstinence and thin Diet to be one of the Company.

"That at present he comes into a Room as if he were an Express from Abroad.

"That he has chosen an Apartment with a matted Anti-Chamber, to practise Motion without being heard.

"That he bows, talks, drinks, eats, and helps himself before a Glass, to learn to act with Moderation.

"That by reason of his luxuriant Health, he is oppressive to Persons of compos'd Behaviour.

"That he is endeavouring to forget the Word *Pshaw*, *Pshaw*.

"That he is also weaning himself from his Cane.

"That when he has learnt to live without his said Cane, he will wait on the Company, *&c.*"

The Memorial of John Rhubarb, *Esq*;

Sheweth,

."THAT your Petitioner has retired to the Infirmary, but that he is in perfect good Health, except that he has by long Use, and for want of Discourse, contracted an Habit of Complaint that he is sick.

"That he wants for nothing under the Sun, but what to say; and therefore has fallen into this unhappy Malady of complaining that he is sick.

"That this Custom of his makes him, by his own Confession, fit only for the Infirmary, and therefore he has not waited for being sentenced to it.

---

[1] Here used in the obsolete sense, 'because, inasmuch as'. The last example in *OED* is dated 1821.

"That he is conscious there is nothing more improper than such a Complaint in good Company, in that they must pity, whether they think the Lamenter ill or not; and that the Complainant must make a silly Figure, whether he is pity'd or not.

"Your Petitioner humbly prays, that he may have Time to know how he does, and he will make his Appearance."

'The *Valetudinarian* was likewise easily excused; and this Society being resolv'd not only to make it their Business to pass their Time agreeably for the present Season, but also to commence such Habits in themselves as may be of Use in their future Conduct in general, are very ready to give into a fancied or real Incapacity to join with their Measures, in order to have no Humourist, proud Man, impertinent or sufficient Fellow, break in upon their Happiness. Great Evils seldom happen to disturb Company, but Indulgence in Particularities of Humour, is the Seed of making half our Time hang in Suspence, or waste away under real Discomposures.

'Among other Things it is carefully provided, that there may not be disagreeable Familiarities. No one is to appear in the publick Rooms undress'd, or enter abruptly into each other's Apartment without Intimation. Every one has hitherto been so careful in his Behaviour, that there has but one Offender in ten Days' Time been sent into the Infirmary, and that was for throwing away his Cards at Whist.[1]

'He has offer'd his Submission in the following Terms.

  The humble Petition of Jeoffry Hotspur, *Esq*;

Sheweth,

"THOUGH the Petitioner swore, stamp'd, and threw down his Cards, he has all imaginable Respect for the Ladies, and the whole Company.

"That he humbly desires it may be consider'd in the Case of Gaming, there are many Motives which provoke to Disorder.

"That the Desire of Gain, and the Desire of Victory, are both thwarted in Losing.

"That all Conversations in the World have indulged Humane Infirmity in this Case.

"Your Petitioner therefore most humbly prays, that he may be restored to the Company, and he hopes to bear ill Fortune with

---

[1] See Nos. 72 (vol. i), 245 (vol. ii).

a good Grace for the future, and to demean himself so as to be no more than chearful^a when he wins, than grave when he loses." '

T

No. 430
[STEELE]

Monday, July 14, 1712[1]

Quære peregrinum vicinia rauca reclamat.
Hor.

SIR,

' AS you are Spectator-General, you may with Authority censure whatsoever looks ill, and is offensive to the Sight; the worst Nusance of which Kind, methinks, is the scandalous Appearance of Poor in all Parts of this wealthy City. Such miserable Objects affect the compassionate Beholder with dismal Ideas, discompose the Chearfulness of his Mind, and deprive him of the Pleasure that he might otherwise take in surveying the Grandeur of our Metropolis. Who can without Remorse see a disabled Sailor, the Purveyor of our Luxury, destitute of Necessaries? Who can behold an honest Soldier that bravely withstood the Enemy, prostrate and in Want amongst his Friends? It were endless to mention all the Variety of Wretchedness, and the numberless Poor, that not only singly, but in Companies, implore your Charity. Spectacles of this Nature every where occur; and it is unaccountable, that amongst the many lamentable Cries that infest this Town, your Comptroller-General[2] should not take Notice of the most shocking, *viz.* those of the Needy and Afflicted. I can't but think he wav'd it meerly out of good Breeding, choosing rather to stifle his Resentment, than upbraid his Countrymen with Inhumanity; however, let not Charity be sacrific'd to Popularity, and if his Ears were deaf to their Complaints, let not your Eyes overlook their Persons. There are, I know, many Impostors among them.[3] Lameness and Blindness are

^a more than chearful] more chearful *Fol. Corrected in Errata (No. 430)*

---

[1] *Motto.* Horace, *Epistles,* 1. 17. 62.
The Crowd replies,
Go seek a Stranger to believe thy Lyes. CREECH.

[2] See No. 251 (vol. ii).
[3] Advertisements headed 'To prevent People being impos'd upon by Beggars' are frequent in the newspapers. They give information that such and such a pretender has been taken into the Workhouse in Bishops-gate Street.

THE SPECTATOR

certainly very often acted; but can those that have their Sight and
Limbs, employ them better than in knowing whether they are
counterfeited or not? I know not which of the two misapplies his
Senses most, he who pretends himself blind to move Compassion,
or he who beholds a miserable Object without pitying it. But in
order to remove such Impediments, I wish, Mr. SPECTATOR, you
would give us a Discourse upon Beggars, that we may not pass by
true Objects of Charity, or give to Impostors. I looked out of my
Window the other Morning earlier than ordinary, and saw a blind
Beggar, an Hour before the Passage he stands in is frequented, with
a Needle and Thread, thriftily mending his Stockings: My Astonishment was still greater, when I beheld a lame Fellow, whose Legs
were too big to walk within an Hour after, bring him a Pot of Ale.
I will not mention the Shakings, Distortions, and Convulsions
which many of them practise to gain an Alms; but sure I am, they
ought to be taken Care of in this Condition, either by the Beadle or
the Magistrate. They, it seems, relieve their Posts according to
their Talents: There is the Voice of an old Woman never begins to
beg till nine in the Evening, and then she is destitute of Lodging,
turned out for want of Rent, and has the same ill Fortune every
Night in the Year. You should employ an Officer to hear the Distress of each Beggar that is constant at a particular Place, who is
ever in the same Tone, and succeeds because his Audience is continually changing, tho' he does not alter his Lamentation. If we
have nothing else for our Money, let us have more Invention to be
cheated with. All which is submitted to your Spectatorial Vigilance;
and I am,

SIR,
Your most humble Servant.'

SIR,

'I WAS last *Sunday* highly transported at our Parish-Church;[1] the
Gentleman in the Pulpit pleaded movingly in Behalf of the poor
Children, and they for themselves much more forcibly by singing
an Hymn; and I had the Happiness to be a Contributor to this little
religious Institution of Innocents, and I am sure I never dispos'd of

[1] Cf. No. 380 (vol. iii). A letter signed M. S. (Lillie, ii. 296–9) encloses a hymn by
the poet-laureate, Mr. Tate, 'sung at the Church of St. George, Southwark, on
Sunday November the 9th, 1712. by the children of the charity-school there'. The
correspondent pleads for more attention to the charity-schools, 'a concern of such
publick benefit, that it ought not to be overlooked by the Spectator of Great-
Britain'.

Money more to my Satisfaction and Advantage. The inward Joy I find in my self, and the Good-will I bear to Mankind, make me heartily wish these pious Works may be encouraged, that the present Promoters may reap the Delight, and Posterity the Benefit of them. But whilst we are building this beautiful Edifice, let not the old Ruins remain in View to sully the Prospect: Whilst we are cultivating and improving this young hopeful Offspring, let not the ancient and helpless Creatures be shamefully neglected. The Crowds of Poor, or pretended Poor, in every Place, are a great Reproach to us, and eclipse the Glory of all other Charity. It is the utmost Reproach to Society, that there should be a poor Man unreliev'd, or a poor Rogue unpunished. I hope you will think no Part of Humane Life out of your Consideration, but will, at your Leisure, give us the History of Plenty and Want, and the natural Gradations towards them, calculated for the Cities of *London* and *Westminster*.

I am, SIR,

Your most Humble Servant,

T. D.'

Mr. SPECTATOR,

'I BEG you would be pleas'd to take Notice of a very great Indecency, which is extremely common, though, I think, never yet under your Censure. It is, Sir, the strange Freedoms some ill-bred marry'd People take in Company: The unseasonable Fondness of some Husbands, and the ill-tim'd Tenderness of some Wives. They talk and act, as if Modesty was only fit for Maids and Batchelors, and that too before both. I was once, Mr. SPECTATOR, where the Fault I speak of was so very flagrant, that, (being, you must know, a very bashful Fellow, and several young Ladies in the Room) I protest, I was quite out of Countenance. *Lucina*,[1] it seems, was breeding, and she did nothing but entertain the Company with a Discourse upon the Difficulty of Reckoning to a Day, and said, She knew those who were certain to an Hour; then fell a laughing at a silly unexperienc'd Creature, who was a Month above her Time. Upon her Husband's coming in, she put several Questions to him; which he not caring to resolve, Well, cries *Lucina*, I shall have 'em all at Night—— But, lest I should seem guilty of the very Fault I write against, I shall only intreat Mr. SPECTATOR to correct such Misdemeanors.

[1] Lucina was the goddess who presided over the birth of children.

For higher of the Genial Bed by far,
And with mysterious Reverence I deem.[1]
I am, SIR,
Your Humble Servant,
T. Meanwell.'
T

No. 431   *Tuesday, July* 15, 1712[2]
[STEELE]

Quid Dulcius hominum generi a Natura datum est quam
sui cuique liberi?

Tull.

I HAVE lately been casting in my Thoughts the several Unhappinesses of Life, and comparing the Infelicities of old Age to those of Infancy. The Calamities of Children are due to the Negligence or Misconduct of Parents, those of Age to the past Life which led to it. I have here the History of a Boy and Girl to their Wedding-Day, and think I cannot give the Reader a livelier Image of the insipid way which time uncultivated passes, than by entertaining him with their authentick Epistles, expressing all that was remarkable in their Lives, till the Period of their Life above-mentioned. The Sentence at the Head of this Paper, which is only a warm Interrogation, *What is there in Nature so dear as a Man's own Children to him?* is all the Reflection I shall at present make on those who are negligent or cruel in the Education of them.

Mr. SPECTATOR,

'I AM now entering into my One and Twentieth Year, and do not know that I had one Day's thorough Satisfaction since I came to Years of any Reflection, till the Time they say others lose their Liberty, the Day of my Marriage. I am Son to a Gentleman of a very great Estate, who resolved to keep me out of the Vices of the Age; and in Order to it, never let me see any Thing that he thought could give me the least Pleasure. At Ten Years old I was put to a Grammar-

[1] Milton, *Paradise Lost*, viii. 598–9 ('Though higher').
[2] *Motto.* Cicero, *Oratio post reditum ad Quirites*, 1. 2: What is there in nature dearer than a man's own children to him?

School, where my Master received Orders every Post to use me very severely, and have no Regard to my having a great Estate. At Fifteen I was removed to the University, where I lived, out of my Father's great Discretion, in scandalous Poverty and Want, till I was big enough to be married, and I was sent for to see the Lady who sends you the Underwritten. When we were put together, we both consider'd that we could not be worse than we were in taking one another, and out of a Desire of Liberty entered into Wedlock. My Father says I am now a Man, and may speak to him like another Gentleman.

I am,

SIR,

Your most humble Servant,

Richard Rentfree.'

Mr. SPEC.

'I GREW tall and wild at my Mother's, who is a gay Widow, and did not care for shewing me till about two Years and a half ago; at which time my Guardian Uncle sent me to a Boarding-School, with Orders to contradict me in nothing, for I had been misused enough already. I had not been there above a Month, when, being in the Kitchin, I saw some Oatmeal on the Dresser; I put two or three Corns in my Mouth, lik'd it, stole a Handful, went into my Chamber, chew'd it, and for two Months after never fail'd taking Toll of every Pennyworth of Oatmeal that came into the House: But one Day playing with a Tobacco-pipe between my Teeth, it happen'd to break in my Mouth, and the spitting out the Pieces left such a delicious Roughness on my Tongue, that I could not be satisfied till I had champ'd up the remaining Part of the Pipe. I forsook the Oatmeal, and stuck to the Pipes three Months, in which Time I had dispenc'd with 37 foul Pipes, all to the Boles: They belong'd to an old Gentleman, Father to my Governess——He lock'd up the clean ones. I left off eating of Pipes, and fell to licking of Chalk.[1] I was soon tir'd of this; I then nibbled all the red Wax of our last Ball-Tickets, and three Weeks after the black Wax from the Burying-Tickets of the old Gentleman. Two Months after this

---

[1] There are frequent references in the literature of the time to these tastes of young girls. In Shadwell's *Scowrers* (v. i) 'Green-Sickness Maids now dream of Clay and Lime'. Among the questions proposed in the *British Apollo* (29 Mar. 1710) is the following: 'What is the Reason that the Female-Sex, and more especially Girls, are so subject to eat Chalk, Lime, Cinders, &c.?' Cf. also the *Visions of Quevedo*, trans. L'Estrange (9th ed., 1702), p. 97.

I liv'd upon Thunder-bolts,[1] a certain long, round, blueish Stone, which I found among the Gravel in our Garden. I was wonderfully delighted with this; but Thunder-bolts growing scarce, I fasten'd Tooth and Nail upon our Garden-Wall, which I stuck to almost a Twelve-month, and had in that Time peel'd and devour'd half a Foot toward our Neighbour's Yard. I now thought my self the happiest Creature in the World, and, I believe in my Conscience, I had eaten quite through, had I had it in my Chamber; but now I became lazy, and unwilling to stir, and was oblig'd to seek Food nearer Home. I then took a strange Hankering to Coals; I fell to scranching[2] 'em, and had already consum'd, I am certain, as much as would have dress'd my Wedding-Dinner, when my Uncle came for me home. He was in the Parlour with my Governess when I was call'd down. I went in, fell on my Knees, for he made me call him Father; and when I expected the Blessing I ask'd, the good Gentleman, in a Surprize, turns himself to my Governess, and asks, Whether this (pointing to me) was his Daughter? This (added he) is the very Picture of Death. My Child was a plump-fac'd, hale, fresh-colour'd Girl; but this looks as if she were half-starv'd, a meer Skeleton. My Governess, who is really a good Woman, assur'd my Father I had wanted for nothing; and withal told him I was continually eating some Trash or other, and that I was almost eaten up with the Green-Sickness,[3] her Orders being never to cross me. But this magnified[4] but little with my Father, who presently, in a Kind of Pett, paying for my Board, took me home with him. I had not been long at home, but one *Sunday* at Church (I shall never forget it) I saw a young neighbouring Gentleman that pleas'd me hugely; I lik'd him of all Men I ever saw in my Life, and began to wish I could be as pleasing to him. The very next Day he came, with his Father, a visiting to our House: We were left alone together, with Directions on both Sides to be in Love with one another, and in three Weeks Time we were marry'd. I regain'd my former Health and Complexion, and am now as happy as the Day is long. Now, Mr. SPEC. I desire you would find out some Name for these craving Damsels, whether dignified or distinguish'd under some or all of

[1] A term 'locally applied to various stones, fossils, or mineral concretions' (*OED*).
[2] Scranch, i.e. crunch. Marked *Obs. exc. dial.* by *OED*.
[3] 'An anaemic disease which mostly affects young women about the age of puberty and gives a pale or greenish tinge to the complexion' (*OED*).
[4] Johnson defines this as 'a cant word for *to have effect*'. This is the earliest example in *OED*.

the following Denominations, (to wit) *Trash-eaters*, *Oatmeal-chewers*, *Pipe-champers*, *Chalk-lickers*, *Wax-nibblers*, *Coal-Scranchers*, *Wall-peelers*, or *Gravel-diggers:* And, good Sir, do your utmost Endeavour to prevent (by exposing) this unaccountable Folly, so prevailing among the young ones of our Sex, who may not meet with such sudden good Luck as,

SIR,

Your constant Reader,

And very Humble Servant,

Sabina Green,

Now Sabina Rentfree.'

T

No. 432
[STEELE]

Wednesday, July 16, 1712[1]

Inter strepit anser olores.
Virg.

Mr. SPECTATOR,   Oxford, *July* 14.[a]

'ACCORDING to a late Invitation in one of your Papers[2] to every Man who pleases to write, I have sent you the following short Dissertation against the Vice of being prejudiced.

Your most Humble Servant.

'MAN is a sociable Creature, and a Lover of Glory; whence it is, that when several Persons are united in the same Society, they are studious to lessen the Reputation of others, in order to raise their own. The Wise are content to guide the Springs in Silence, and rejoice in Secret at their regular Progress: To prate and triumph is the Part allotted to the Trifling and Superficial: The Geese were providentially ordained to save the *Capitol*.[3] Hence it is, that the Invention of Marks and Devices to distinguish Parties, is owing to the *Beaux* and *Belles* of this Island. Hats moulded into different

[a] *July* 14.] *June* 10. *Fol.*

[1] *Motto.* Virgil, *Eclogues*, 9. 36 (altered):
But gabble like a Goose, amidst the Swan-like Quire. DRYDEN.
[2] No. 428.
[3] According to legend, when the Gauls occupied Rome in 390 B.C., it was the cries of geese which awakened Manlius Capitolinus and enabled him to repulse an attack on the Capitol. Cf. Ovid, *Metamorphoses*, 2. 538; Livy, *History*, 5. 47. 4.

Cocks[1] and Pinches,[2] have long bid mutual Defiance; Patches have been set against Patches in Battle-Array;[3] Stocks have risen or fallen in Proportion to Head-Dresses;[4] and Peace or War been expected, as the *White* or the *Red* Hood hath prevail'd.[5] These are the Standard-Bearers in our contending Armies, the Dwarfs and Squires who carry the Impresses[6] of the Giants or Knights, not born to fight themselves, but to prepare the Way for the ensuing Combat.

'It is Matter of Wonder to reflect how far Men of weak Understanding and strong Fancy are hurried by their Prejudices, even to the believing that the whole Body of the adverse Party are a Band of Villains and Dæmons. Foreigners complain, that the *English* are the proudest Nation under Heaven.[7] Perhaps they too have their Share; but, be that as it will, general Charges against Bodies of Men is the Fault I am writing against. It must be own'd, to our Shame, that our common People, and most who have not travell'd, have an irrational Contempt for the Language, Dress, Customs, and even the Shape and Minds of other Nations. Some Men, otherwise of Sense, have wonder'd that a great Genius should spring out of *Ireland*;[8] and think you mad in affirming, that fine Odes have been written in *Lapland*.[9]

'This Spirit of Rivalship, which heretofore reign'd in the Two Universities, is extinct, and almost over betwixt College and College: In Parishes and Schools the Thirst of Glory still obtains. At the Seasons of Foot-ball and Cock-fighting, these little Republicks reassume their national Hatred to each other. My Tenant in the Country is verily perswaded, that the Parish of the Enemy hath not one honest Man in it.

'I always hated Satyrs against Woman, and Satyrs against Man;[10] I am apt to suspect a Stranger who laughs at the Religion of *The Faculty*:[11] My Spleen rises at a dull Rogue, who is severe upon Mayors and Aldermen; and was never better pleased than with a Piece of Justice executed upon the Body of a Templer, who was very arch upon Parsons.

[1] Cf. No. 129 (vol. ii).
[2] A pinch is a bend or fold in the brim of a hat. Cf. *OED*, where quotations range from 1593 to 1860.　　　　[3] See No. 81 (vol. i).
[4] No. 98 (vol. i).　　　　　　　　　　[5] No. 265 (vol. ii).
[6] I.e. emblems or devices.
[7] See No. 407 (vol. iii).
[8] Contemporary readers would probably take this as a tribute to Swift.
[9] A reference to the poems translated in Nos. 366 and 406 (vol. iii).
[10] The same point is made by Addison at the end of No. 209 (vol. ii).
[11] The popular term for the medical profession.

'The Necessities of Mankind require various Employments; and whoever excells in his Province is worthy of Praise. All Men are not educated after the same Manner, nor have all the same Talents. Those who are deficient deserve our Compassion, and have a Title to our Assistance. All cannot be bred in the same Place; but in all Places there arise, at different Times, such Persons as do Honour to their Society, which may raise Envy in little Souls, but are admir'd and cherish'd by generous Spirits.

'It is certainly a great Happiness to be educated in Societies of great and eminent Men. Their Instructions and Examples are of extraordinary Advantage. It is highly proper to instill such a Reverence of the governing Persons, and Concern for the Honour of the Place, as may spur the growing Members to worthy Pursuits and honest Emulation: But to swell young Minds with vain Thoughts of the Dignity of their own Brotherhood, by debasing and villifying all others, doth them a real Injury. By this means I have found that their Efforts have become languid, and their Prattle irksome, as thinking it sufficient Praise that they are Children of so illustrious and ample a Family. I should think it a surer, as well as more generous Method, to set before the Eyes of Youth such Persons as have made a noble Progress in Fraternities less talk'd of; which seem tacitly to reproach their Sloth, who loll so heavily in the Seats of mighty Improvement: Active Spirits hereby would enlarge their Notions, whereas by a servile Imitation of one, or perhaps two, admired Men in their own Body, they can only gain a secondary and derivative kind of Fame. These Copies of Men, like those of Authors or Painters, run into Affectations of some Oddness, which perhaps was not disagreeable in the Original, but sits ungracefully on the narrow-soul'd Transcriber.

'By such early Corrections of Vanity, while Boys are growing into Men, they will gradually learn not to censure superficially; but imbibe those Principles of general Kindness and Humanity, which alone can make them easie to themselves, and beloved by others.

'Reflections of this Nature have expunged all Prejudices out of my Heart, insomuch, that tho' I am a firm Protestant, I hope to see the Pope and Cardinals without violent Emotions; and tho' I am naturally grave, I expect to meet good Company at *Paris*.

I am, SIR,
Your Obedient Servant.'

Mr. SPECTATOR,

'I FIND you are a general Undertaker, and have by your Correspondents or self an Insight into most things; which makes me apply my self to you at present in the sorest Calamity that ever befel Man. My Wife has taken something ill of me, and has not spoke one Word, good or bad, to me, or any Body in the Family, since *Friday* was Sevennight. What must a Man do in that Case? Your Advice would be a great Obligation to,

SIR,

Your most humble Servant,

Ralph Thimbleton.'

Mr. SPECTATOR,

'WHEN you want a Trifle to fill up a Paper, in inserting this you will lay an Obligation on

Your humble Servant,

Olivia.

July 15*th*,
1712.

Dear Olivia,

' "IT is but this Moment I have had the Happiness of knowing to whom I am oblig'd for the Present I receiv'd the second of *April.* I am heartily sorry it did not come to Hand the Day before; for I can't but think it very hard upon People to lose their Jest, that offer at one but once a Year. I congratulate my self however upon the Earnest given me of something further intended in my Favour; for I am told, that the Man who is thought worthy by a Lady to make a Fool of, stands fair enough in her Opinion to become one Day her Husband. Till such Time as I have the Honour of being sworn, I take Leave to subscribe my self,

Dear Olivia,

Your Fool Elect,

Nicodemuncio." '

T

> *Perlege Mæonio cantatas carmine Ranas,*
> *Et frontem nugis solvere disce meis.*
>   Mart.

THE Moral World, as consisting of Males and Females, is of a mixt Nature, and filled with several Customs, Fashions and Ceremonies, which would have no place in it, were there but *One* Sex. Had our Species no Females in it, Men would be quite different Creatures from what they are at present; their Endeavours to please the opposite Sex, polishes and refines them out of those Manners which are most natural to them, and often sets them upon modelling themselves, not according to the Plans which they approve in their own Opinions, but according to those Plans which they think are most agreeable to the Female World. In a word, Man would not only be an unhappy, but a rude unfinished Creature, were he conversant with none but those of his own Make.

Women, on the other side, are apt to form themselves in every thing with regard to that other half of reasonable Creatures, with whom they are here blended and confused; their Thoughts are ever turned upon appearing amiable to the other Sex; they talk, and move, and smile, with a design upon us; every Feature of their Faces, every part of their Dress is filled with Snares and Allurements. There would be no such Animals as Prudes or Coquets in the World, were there not such an Animal as Man. In short, it is the Male that gives Charms to Womankind, that produces an Air in their Faces, a Grace in their Motions, a Softness in their Voices, and a Delicacy in their Complections.

As this mutual Regard between the two Sexes tends to the Improvement of each of them, we may observe that Men are apt to degenerate into rough and brutal Natures, who live as if there were no such things as Women in the World; as on the contrary, Women, who have an Indifference or Aversion for their Counter-parts in Human Nature, are generally Sower and Unamiable, Sluttish and Censorious.

---

[1] *Motto.* Martial, *Epigrams,* 14. 183:
> See martial Frogs in Homer's lofty Vein,
> And learn to smile on my more trifling Strain.

I am led into this train of Thoughts by a little Manuscript which is lately fallen into my Hands, and which I shall communicate to the Reader, as I have done some other curious Pieces of the same Nature, without troubling him with any Enquiries about the Author of it. It contains a summary Account of two different States which bordered upon one another. The one was a Commonwealth of *Amazons*, or Women without Men; the other was a Republick of Males that had not a Woman in their whole Community.[1] As these two States bordered upon one another, it was their way, it seems, to meet upon their Frontiers at a certain Season of the Year, where those among the Men who had not made their Choice in any former Meeting, associated themselves with particular Women, whom they were afterwards obliged to look upon as their Wives in every one of these yearly Rencounters. The Children that sprung from this Alliance, if Males, were sent to their respective Fathers; if Females, continued with their Mothers. By means of this Anniversary Carnival, which lasted about a Week, the Commonwealths were recruited from time to time, and supplied with their respective Subjects.

These two States were engaged together in a perpetual League, Offensive and Defensive, so that if any Foreign Potentate offered to attack either of them, both the Sexes fell upon him at once, and quickly brought him to Reason. It was remarkable that for many Ages this Agreement continued inviolable between the two States, notwithstanding, as was said before, they were Husbands and Wives; but this will not appear so wonderful if we consider that they did not live together above a Week in a Year.

In the Account which my Author gives of the Male Republick, there were several Customs very remarkable. The Men never shaved their Beards, or pared their Nails above once in a Twelvemonth, which was probably about the time of the great Annual Meeting

[1] The story related here recalls that of the Amazons and Scythians in Herodotus, *History*, 4. 110-16. Travel accounts from South America may have revived interest in the word. Captain Woodes Rogers, *A Cruising Voyage round the World* (1712), p. 59, writes of the River of the Amazons:

'Twas call'd *Amazons*, not because of any Nation of Virago's, who as some fancy are govern'd by a Queen, and have no Commerce with our Sex; but at certain times, when they make an Appointment with the Males of neighbouring Nations, and if they prove with Child, keep the Daughters and send away the Sons, as the *Greeks* fabled of their *Amazons*. But the true Reason of the Name is, that the *Spaniards*, who first discover'd it, were told of such a terrible barbarous Nation of Women by some of the Natives, on purpose to frighten them, and that they did actually on several places of this River find their Women as fierce and warlike as the Men; it being their Custom to follow their Husbands, &c. to War, on purpose to animate them, and to share in their Fate. . . .

upon their Frontiers. I find the Name of a Minister of State in one part of their History, who was fined for appearing too frequently in clean Linnen; and of a certain great General who^a was turned out of his Post for Effeminacy, it having been proved upon him by several credible Witnesses that he washed his Face every Morning.[1] If any Member of the Commonwealth had a soft Voice, a smooth Face, or a supple Behaviour, he was banished into the Commonwealth of Females, where he was treated as a Slave, dressed in Petticoats, and set a Spinning. They had no Titles of Honour among them, but such as denoted some Bodily Strength or Perfection, as such an one *the Tall*, such an one *the Stocky*, such an one *the Gruff*. Their publick Debates were generally managed with Kicks and Cuffs, insomuch that they often came from the Council Table with broken Shins, black Eyes and Bloody Noses. When they would reproach a Man in the most bitter Terms, they would tell him his Teeth were white, or that he had a fair Skin, and a soft Hand. The greatest Man I meet with in their History, was one who could lift Five hundred weight, and wore such a Prodigious Pair of Whiskers as had never been seen in the Commonwealth before his Time. These Accomplishments it seems had rendered him so popular, that if he had not died very seasonably, it is thought he might have enslaved the Republick. Having made this short Extract out of the History of the Male Commonwealth, I shall look into the History of the neighbouring State which consisted of Females, and if I find any thing in it, will not fail to Communicate it to the Publick.

C

^a who] that *Fol.*

---

[1] The French translation of the *Spectator* (by D. Mortier, Amsterdam, 1725) notes this as an allusion to the fall of Godolphin and Marlborough.

No. 434
[ADDISON]

Friday, July 18, 1712[1]

> *Quales Threiciæ cùm flumina Thermodoontis*
> *Pulsant, & pictis bellantur Amazones armis:*
> *Seu circum Hippolyten, seu cùm se Martia curru*
> *Penthesilea refert, magnoque ululante tumultu*
> *Fœminea exultant lunatis agmina peltis.*
>
> Virg.

HAVING carefully perused the Manuscript I mentioned in my Yesterday's Paper, so far as it relates to the Republick of Women, I find in it several Particulars which may very well deserve the Reader's Attention.

The Girls of Quality, from six to twelve Years old, were put to Publick Schools, where they learned to Box and play at Cudgels, with several other Accomplishments of the same Nature; so that nothing was more usual than to see a little Miss returning Home at Night with a broken Pate, or two or three Teeth knocked out of her Head. They were afterwards taught to ride the great Horse,[2] to Shoot, Dart, or Sling, and listed into several Companies, in order to perfect themselves in Military Exercises. No Woman was to be married till she had killed her Man. The Ladies of Fashion used to play with young Lions instead of Lap-dogs, and when they made any Parties of Diversion, instead of entertaining themselves at Ombre or Piquet, they would Wrestle and pitch the Bar for a whole Afternoon together. There was never any such thing as a Blush seen, or a Sigh heard, in the Commonwealth. The Women never dressed but to look terrible, to which end they would sometimes after a Battel paint their Cheeks with the Blood of their Enemies.

---

[1] *Motto.* Virgil, *Aeneid*, 11. 659–63:

> So march'd the *Thracian Amazons* of old,
> When *Thermodon* with bloody Billows rowl'd:
> Such Troops as these in shining Arms were seen;
> When *Theseus* met in Fight their Maiden Queen.
> Such to the Field *Penthisilea* led,
> From the fierce Virgin when the *Grecians* fled:
> With such, return'd Triumphant from the War;
> Her Maids with Cries attend the lofty Carr:
> They clash with manly force their Moony Shields;
> With Female Showts resound the *Phrygian* Fields. DRYDEN.

[2] The Great Horse (French, *Grand Cheval*), the war-horse or charger used in battle and tournament, 1466–1700 (*OED*).

For this Reason likewise the Face which^a had the most Scars was looked upon as the most beautiful. If they found Lace, Jewels, Ribbons, or any Ornaments in Silver or Gold, among the Booty which they had taken, they used to dress their Horses with it, but never entertained a Thought of wearing it themselves. There were particular Rights and Privileges allowed to any Member of the Commonwealth, who was a Mother of three Daughters.[1] The Senate was made up of old Women; for by the Laws of the Country none was to be a Councellor of State that was not past Child-bearing. They used to boast their^b Republick had continued Four thousand Years, which is altogether improbable, unless we may suppose, what I am very apt to think, that they measured their Time by *Lunar* Years.[2]

There was a great Revolution brought about in this Female Republick, by means of a Neighbouring King, who had made War upon them several Years with various Success, and at length over-threw them in a very great Battel. This Defeat they ascribe to several Causes; some say that the Secretary of State having been troubled with the Vapours, had committed some fatal Mistakes in several Dispatches about that Time. Others pretend, that the first Minister being big with Child, could not attend the Publick Affairs, as so great an Exigency of State required; but this I can give no manner of Credit to, since it seems to contradict a Fundamental Maxim in their Government, which I have before mentioned. My Author gives the most probable Reason of this great Disaster; for he affirms, that the General was brought to Bed, or (as others say) Miscarried the very Night before the Battel: However it was, this signal Overthrow obliged them to call in the Male Republick to their Assistance; but notwithstanding their Common Efforts to repulse the Victorious Enemy, the War continued for many Years before they could entirely bring it to a happy Conclusion.

The Campaigns which both Sexes passed together made them so well acquainted with one another, that at the end of the War they did not care for parting. In the beginning of it they lodged in separate Camps, but afterwards as they grew more familiar, they pitched their Tents promiscuously.

From this time the Armies being Chequered with both Sexes,

^a which] that *Fol.*   ^b boast their] boast that their *Fol.*

[1] An allusion to the *Jus trium liberorum* (see No. 203, vol. ii).
[2] The lunar year consists of twelve lunar months, or about 354½ days.

they polished apace. The Men used to invite their Fellow-Soldiers into their Quarters, and would dress their Tents with Flowers and Boughs, for their Reception. If they chanced to like one more than another, they would be cutting her Name in the Table, or Chalking out her Figure upon a Wall, or talking of her in a kind of rapturous Language, which[a] by degrees improved into Verse and Sonnet. These were as the first Rudiments of Architecture, Painting and Poetry among this Savage People. After any Advantage over the Enemy, both Sexes used to Jump together and make a Clattering with their Swords and Shields, for Joy, which in a few Years produced several Regular Tunes and Sett Dances.

As the two Armies romped on[b] these Occasions, the Women complained of the thick bushy Beards and long Nails of their Confederates, who thereupon[c] took care to prune themselves into such Figures as were most pleasing to their Female Friends and Allies.

When they had taken any Spoils from the Enemy, the Men would make a Present of every thing that was Rich and Showy to the Women whom they most admired, and would frequently dress the Necks, or Heads, or Arms of their Mistresses, with any thing which they thought appeared Gay or Pretty. The Women observing that the Men took delight in looking upon 'em, when they were adorned with such Trappings and Gugaws, set their Heads at Work to find out new Inventions, and to out-shine one another in all Councils of War or the like solemn Meetings. On the other Hand, the Men observing how the Womens Hearts were set upon Finery, begun to Embellish themselves and look as agreeably as they could in the Eyes of their Associates. In short, after a few Years conversing together, the Women had learnt to Smile, and the Men to Ogle, the Women grew Soft, and the Men Lively.

When they had thus insensibly formed one another, upon the finishing of the War, which concluded with an entire Conquest of their common Enemy, the Colonels in one Army married the Colonels in the other; the Captains in the same manner took the Captains to their Wives: The whole Body of Common Soldiers were matched, after the Example of their Leaders. By this means the two Republicks incorporated with one another, and became the most Flourishing and Polite Government in the Part of the World which they Inhabited.   C

[a] which] that *Fol.*   [b] romped on] romped together on *Fol.*   [c] thereupon] immediately *Fol.*

Nec duo sunt at forma duplex, nec fœmina dici
Nec puer ut possint, neutrumque & utrumque videntur.
Ovid.

MOST of the Papers I give[a] the Publick are written on Subjects that never vary, but are for ever fixt and immutable. Of this kind are all my more Serious Essays and Discourses; but there is another sort of Speculations, which I consider as Occasional Papers, that take their Rise from the Folly, Extravagance, and Caprice of the present Age. For I look upon my self as one set to watch the Manners and Behaviour of my Countrymen and Contemporaries, and to mark down every absurd Fashion, ridiculous Custom, or affected Form of Speech that makes its Appearance in the World, during the Course of these my Speculations. The Petticoat no sooner begun to swell, but I observed its Motions. The Party-patches had not time to muster themselves before I detected them. I had Intelligence of the Coloured Hood the very first time it appeared in a Publick Assembly.[2] I might here mention several other the like Contingent[3] Subjects, upon which I have bestowed distinct Papers. By this Means I have so effectually quashed those Irregularities which gave Occasion to 'em, that I am afraid Posterity will scarce have a sufficient Idea of them to Relish those Discourses which were in no little Vogue at the time when they were written. They will be apt to think that the Fashions and Customs I attacked, were some Fantastick Conceits of my own, and that their Great-Grandmothers cou'd not be so whimsical as I have represented them. For this Reason, when I think on the Figure my several Volumes of Speculations will make about a Hundred Years hence, I consider them as so many Pieces of old Plate, where the Weight will be regarded, but the Fashion lost.

[a] I give] which I give *Fol.*

---

[1] *Motto.* Ovid, *Metamorphoses,* 4. 378–9:
Both bodies in a single body mix,
A single body with a double sex.

[2] The petticoat, the party-patches, the coloured hood, were dealt with in Nos. 81 (vol. i), 127, and 265 (vol. ii).

[3] I.e. touching each other, tangential (1570–1703, *OED*).

Among the several Female Extravagancies I have[a] already taken Notice of, there is one which[b] still keeps its Ground. I mean that of the Ladies who dress themselves in a Hat and Feather, a Riding-coat and a Perriwig; or at least tie up their Hair in a Bag or Ribbond, in imitation of the smart Part of the opposite Sex. As in my Yester-day's Paper I gave an Account of the Mixture of two Sexes in one Commonwealth, I shall here take notice of this Mixture of two Sexes in one Person. I have already shewn my Dislike of this Immodest Custom more than once;[1] but in Contempt of every thing I have hitherto said, I am informed that the Highways about this great City are still very much infested with these Female Cavaliers.

I remember when I was at my Friend Sir ROGER DE COVERLY's about this time Twelve-month, an Equestrian Lady of this Order appeared upon the Plains which lay at a distance from his House. I was at that time walking in the Fields with my old Friend; and as his Tenants ran out on every side to see so strange a Sight, Sir ROGER asked one of them who came by us what it was? To which the Country Fellow reply'd, 'Tis a Gentlewoman, saving your Worship's Presence, in a Coat and Hat. This produced a great deal of Mirth at the Knight's House, where we had a Story at the same time of another of his Tenants, who meeting this Gentleman-like Lady on the High-way, was asked by her *whether that was* Coverly-Hall, the Honest Man seeing only the Male part of the Querist, replied, *Yes, Sir*; but upon the second Question, *whether Sir* ROGER DE COVERLY *was a Married Man*, having dropped his Eye upon the Petticoat, he chang'd his Note into *No Madam*.

Had one of these Hermaphrodites appeared in *Juvenal*'s Days, with what an Indignation should we have seen her described by that excellent Satyrist. He would have represented her in her Riding Habit, as a greater Monster than the Centaur. He would have called for Sacrifices, or Purifying Waters, to expiate the Appearance of such a Prodigy. He would have Invoked the Shades of *Portia* or *Lucretia*, to see into what the *Roman* Ladies had transformed themselves.

For my own part, I am for treating the Sex with greater Tender-ness, and have all along made use of the most gentle Methods to bring them off from any little Extravagance, into which they are sometimes unwarily fallen: I think it however absolutely necessary

[a] I have] which I have *Fol.*   [b] which] that *Fol.*

[1] See especially Nos. 104 (vol. i) and 331 (vol. iii).

to keep up the Partition between the two Sexes, and to take Notice of the smallest Encroachments which[a] the one makes upon the other. I hope therefore that I shall not hear any more Complaints on this Subject. I am sure my She-Disciples who peruse these my daily Lectures, have profited but little by them, if they are capable of giving into such an Amphibious Dress. This I should not have mentioned, had not I lately met one of these my Female Readers in *Hide-Park*, who looked upon me with a masculine Assurance, and cocked her Hat full in my Face.

For my part, I have one general Key to the Behaviour of the Fair Sex. When I see them singular in any Part of their Dress, I conclude it is not without some Evil Intention; and therefore question not but the Design of this strange Fashion is to smite more effectually their Male Beholders. Now to set them right in this Particular, I would fain have them consider with themselves whether we are not more likely to be struck by a Figure entirely Female, than with such an one as we may see every Day in our Glasses: Or, if they please, let them reflect upon their own Hearts, and think how they would be affected should they meet a Man on Horseback, in his Breeches and Jack-boots, and at the same time dressed up in a Commode[1] and a Night-raile.[2]

I must observe that this Fashion was first of all brought to us from *France*, a Country which[b] has Infected all the Nations of *Europe* with its Levity. I speak not this in derogation of a whole People, having more than once found fault with those[c] general Reflections which[d] strike at Kingdoms or Common-wealths in the Gross: a piece of Cruelty, which an ingenious Writer of our own compares to that of *Caligula*, who wished the *Roman* People had all but one Neck, that he might behead them at a Blow.[3] I shall therefore only Remark, that as Liveliness and Assurance are in a peculiar manner the Qualifications of the *French* Nation, the same Habits and Customs will not give the same Offence to that People, which they produce among those of our own Country. Modesty is our distinguishing Character,[4] as Vivacity is theirs: And when this our National Virtue

<hr>

a which] that *Fol.*   b which] that *Fol.*   c those] these *Fol.*
d which] that *Fol.*

<hr>

[1] See No. 98 (vol. i).
[2] No. 63 (vol. i).
[3] This is referred to earlier in Nos. 16 (vol. i) and 246 (vol. ii).
[4] Cf. Nos. 104 (vol. i) and 407 (vol. iii), where modesty is noted as the characteristic English virtue.

appears in that Female Beauty, for which our *British* Ladies are celebrated above all others in the Universe, it makes up the most amiable Object that the Eye of Man can possibly behold.

C[1]

No. 436

Monday, July 21, 1712[2]

[STEELE]

. . . Verso pollice vulgi
Quemlibet occidunt Populariter.

Juv.

BEING a Person of insatiable Curiosity, I could not forbear going on *Wednesday* last[3] to a Place of no small Renown for the Gallantry of the lower Order of *Britons*, namely, to the Bear-Garden at *Hockley in the* Hole;[4] where (as a whitish brown Paper, put into my Hands in the Street, inform'd me) there was to be a Tryal of

[1] Two letters in Lillie refer to this number. The first (ii. 299–300), signed Audacia, is dated 22 July:

By your exclaiming against our riding in habits, you have mightily offended us who take delight in that exercise, and who expected, that if you had taken any notice of that fashion, you would have spoken in its commendation, and shewn (as you ought to have done) yourself proud that we women should be fond of appearing like you men in any thing. As for my part, you shall never persuade me but that either envy or fear occasioned your writing that paper. You was either angry that we should rival you in your own persons, or else afraid that as we had already got all to the breeches, we should in a little time, wear them too.

But, Sir, to let you see how little I regard your advice, I think fit to acquaint you, that I shall be in Hide-park to morrow in the evening, where, if I happen to meet you, I shall certainly repeat the affront before given you, and cock my hat in defiance.

The second, undated, is signed Tom Jockey (ii. 303) and begins:

I am commanded to tell you, that whilst you was a tatler no acceptions could be taken, for your title gave you authority to prate; but as spectator, you ought to hear, see, and say nothing, especially in what regards the fair sex. . . .

[2] *Motto.* Juvenal, *Satires*, 3. 36–37 (altered):

Where influenc'd by the Rabble's bloody Will,
With Thumbs bent back, they popularly kill. DRYDEN.

[3] The match is advertised in the *Daily Courant* of 15 July 1712:

A Tryall of Skill to be fought at the Bear-Garden in Hockley in the Hole, to Morrow being Wednesday the 16th of July, at 2 of the Clock precisely, between James Miller, Serjeant, (lately come from the Frontiers in Portugal) Master of the Noble Science of Defence, and Timothy Buck, Master of the said Science.

[4] Hockley in the Hole was properly the name of a street south-west of the New River water-works near Clerkenwell Green, but had come to stand for the bear-garden located there. See Nos. 31 (vol. i) and 141 (vol. ii), and *Tatlers* 28 and 134. Uffenbach (*London in 1710*, pp. 88–91) describes a match there on 2 July 1710, and stresses the brutality of this 'truly English amusement'.

Skill to be exhibited between Two Masters of the Noble Science of Defence, at Two of the Clock precisely. I was not a little charm'd with the Solemnity of the Challenge, which ran thus:

I James Miller,[1] *Serjeant, (lately come from the Frontiers of* Portugal) *Master of the Noble Science of Defence, hearing in most Places where I have been of the great Fame*[2] *of* Timothy Buck *of* London, *Master of the said Science, do invite him to meet me, and exercise at the several Weapons following,* viz.

Back-Sword,	Single Falchon,
Sword and Dagger,	Case of Falchons,
Sword and Buckler,	Quarter-Staff.[3]

If the generous Ardour in *James Miller* to dispute the Reputation of *Timothy Buck,* had something resembling the old Heroes of Romance, *Timothy Buck* return'd Answer in the same Paper with the like Spirit, adding a little Indignation at being challenged, and seeming to condescend to fight *James Miller,* not in regard to *Miller* himself, but in that, as the Fame went out, he had fought *Parks* of *Coventry.* The Acceptance of the Combat ran in these Words:

I Timothy Buck *of* Clare-Market,[4] *Master of the Noble Science of Defence, hearing he did fight Mr.* Parkes *of* Coventry,[5] *will not fail*

[1] This is the first reference I have found to Miller. According to Nichols he was 'a man of vast athletic accomplishments', who 'was advanced afterwards to the rank of a captain in the British army, and did notable service in Scotland under the Duke of Cumberland in 1745'.

[2] The 'great fame' of Timothy Buck is attested by numerous advertisements in the newspapers of 1710–12, in which he is announced as fighting with Adam Wood, William Emerson of Norwich, John Terrewest, and John Sparks (or Parkes) of Coventry.

[3] For sword-play and other sports see Ashton, i. 315–23. 'This sword-fighting, however, was seeing its last days, and was, in the next reign, to be superseded by pugilistic encounters' (p. 319).

[4] Clare-Market, a small open space a little south-west of Lincoln's Inn Fields, 'by some called New Market' (Hatton, p. 18).

[5] He is called 'Parkes of Coventry' in all the contemporary advertisements (1711–24), although his name appears as Sparks in his epitaph in 'the Great Church-yard, Coventry', as quoted in *Gentleman's Magazine,* 1786, Supp., p. 1141:

TO the memory of Mr. John SPARKS,
A native of this city.
He was a man of a mild disposition,
A gladiator by profession,
Who, after having fought 350 battles,
In the principal parts of Europe,
With honour and applause,
At length quitting the stage, sheathed his sword,
And with Christian resignation
Submitted to the Grand Victor,
In the 52d year of his age,
Anno Salutis 1733.

(God willing) to meet this fair Inviter at the Time and Place appointed, desiring a clear Stage and no Favour.

Vivat Regina.

I shall not here look back on the Spectacles of the *Greeks* and *Romans* of this Kind, but must believe this Custom took its Rise from the Ages of Knight-Errantry; from those who lov'd one Woman so well, that they hated all Men and Women else; from those who would fight you, whether you were or were not of their Mind; from those who demanded the Combat of their Contemporaries, both for admiring their Mistress or discommending her. I cannot therefore but lament, that the terrible Part of the ancient Fight is preserv'd, when the amorous Side of it is forgotten. We have retain'd the Barbarity, but lost the Gallantry of the old Combatants. I could wish, methinks, these Gentlemen had consulted me in the Promulgation of the Conflict. I was obliged by a fair young Maid, whom I understood to be called *Elizabeth Preston*,[1] Daughter of the Keeper of the Garden, with a Glass of Water; whom I imagined might have been, for Form's sake, the general Representative of the Lady fought for, and from her Beauty the proper *Amarillis* on these Occasions. It wou'd have ran better in the Challenge; *I* James Miller, *Serjeant, who have travell'd Parts abroad, and came last from the Frontiers of* Portugal, *for the Love of* Elizabeth Preston, *do assert, That the said* Elizabeth is the Fairest of Women. Then the Answer; *I* Timothy Buck, *who have stay'd in* Great Britain *during all the War in Foreign Parts, for the Sake of* Susanna Page, *do deny that* Elizabeth Preston *is so fair as the said* Susanna Page. Let *Susanna Page* look on, and I desire of *James Miller* no Favour.

This would give the Battle quite another Turn; and a proper Station for the Ladies, whose Complexion was disputed by the Sword, would animate the Disputants with a more gallant Incentive than the Expectation of Money from the Spectators; tho' I would not have that neglected, but thrown to that Fair One, whose Lover was approved by the Donor.

Yet, considering the Thing wants such Amendments, it was carry'd with great Order.[2] *James Miller* came on first, preceded by

---

[1] The Prestons were keepers of the bear-garden. According to Ashton (i. 297) Christopher Preston was attacked and killed by one of his own bears in 1709. The satire on Pope entitled *Æsop at the Bear-Garden* (1715) was professedly written by 'Mr. Preston', the bear-marshal at Hockley in the Hole (G. Sherburn, *Early Career of Alexander Pope*, p. 136).

[2] The ceremonial of the bear-garden is alluded to in Defoe's *Defence of the Allies and*

two disabled Drummers, to shew, I suppose, that the Prospect of maimed Bodies did not in the least deter him. There ascended with the daring *Miller* a Gentleman, whose Name I could not learn, with a dogged Air, as unsatisfy'd that he was not Principal. This Son of Anger lowr'd at the whole Assembly, and weighing himself as he march'd around from Side to Side, with a stiff Knee and Shoulder, he gave Intimations of the Purpose he smother'd till he saw the Issue of this Encounter. *Miller* had a blue Ribband ty'd round the Sword-Arm; which Ornament I conceive to be the Remain[1] of that Custom of wearing a Mistress's Favour on such Occasions of old.

Miller is a Man of six Foot eight Inches Height, of a kind but bold Aspect, well-fashion'd, and ready of his Limbs; and such a Readiness as spoke his Ease in them, was obtain'd from a Habit of Motion in Military Exercise.

The Expectation of the Spectators was now almost at its Height, and the Crowd pressing in, several active Persons thought they were placed rather according to their Fortune than their Merit, and took it in their Heads to prefer themselves from the open Area, or Pitt, to the Galleries. This Dispute between Desert and Property brought many to the Ground,[2] and raised others in proportion to the highest Seats by Turns for the Space of ten Minutes, till *Timothy Buck* came on, and the whole Assembly giving up their Disputes, turn'd their Eyes upon the Champions. Then it was that every Man's Affection turn'd to one or the other irresistibly. A judicious Gentleman near me said, *I could, methinks, be* Miller's *Second, but I had rather have* Buck *for mine. Miller* had an audacious Look, that took the Eye; *Buck* a perfect Composure, that engaged the Judgment. *Buck* came on in a plain Coat, and kept all his Air till the Instant of Engaging; at which Time he undress'd to his Shirt, his Arm adorn'd with a Bandage of red Ribband. No one can describe the sudden Concern in the whole Assembly; the most tumultuous Crowd in

---

the Late Ministry, a pamphlet published by J. Baker in 1712, in answer to Swift's *Conduct of the Allies*. Swift's pamphlet is described as entering the stage 'like a Gladiator at the Bear-garden, with a great Flourish, Brandishing its Weapons, carrying a fine Feather in its Hat, the Shirt and Hair tied up with Ribbands, a bright Weapon in its Hand *in Terrorem*, and the like; so it comes ushered in by the Shouts and Huzza's of the Rabble, who, according to Custom, always attend it' (p. 2).

[1] 'A survival; a relic of some obsolete custom or practice . . . Now *rare*' (*OED*).

[2] The unruliness of the mob at the bear-garden is often referred to. An advertisement in the *Daily Courant* of 18 Aug. 1711, of a combat between John Terrewest and Thomas Soon 'the bold Welshman', announces: 'A peculiar Care will be taken towards the Suppression of the Mobb in the Gallerys that no Gentleman shall be molested. . . .'

Nature was as still and as much engaged, as if all their Lives depended on the first Blow. The Combatants met in the Middle of the Stage, and shaking Hands as removing all Malice, they retired with much Grace to the Extremities of it; from whence they immediately faced about, and approached each other, *Miller* with an Heart full of Resolution, *Buck* with a watchful untroubled Countenance; *Buck* regarding principally his own Defence, *Miller* chiefly thoughtful of annoying his Opponent. It is not easy to describe the many Escapes and imperceptible Defences between two Men of quick Eyes and ready Limbs; but *Miller*'s Heat laid him open to the Rebuke of the calm *Buck*, by a large Cut on the Forehead. Much Effusion of Blood covered his Eyes in a Moment, and the Huzzas of the Crowd undoubtedly quickened the Anguish. The Assembly was divided into Parties upon their different ways of Fighting; while a poor Nymph in one of the Galleries apparently suffered for *Miller*, and burst into a Flood of Tears. As soon as his Wound was wrapped up, he came on again with a little Rage, which still disabled him further. But what brave Man can be wounded into more Patience and Caution? The next was a warm eager Onset, which ended in a decisive Stroke on the left Leg of *Miller*. The Lady in the Gallery, during this second Strife, covered her Face; and for my Part, I could not keep my Thoughts from being mostly employed on the Consideration of her unhappy Circumstance that Moment, hearing the Clash of Swords, and apprehending Life or Victory concerned her Lover in every Blow, but not daring to satisfy her self on whom they fell. The Wound was exposed to the View of all who could delight in it, and sowed up on the Stage. The surly Second of *Miller* declared at this Time, that he would that Day Fortnight fight Mr. *Buck* at the same Weapons, declaring himself the Master of the renowned *Gorman*;[1] but *Buck* denied him the Honour of that couragious Disciple, and asserting that he himself had taught that Champion, accepted the Challenge.

There is something in Nature very unaccountable on such Occasions, when we see the People take a certain painful Gratification in beholding these Encounters. Is it Cruelty that administers this Sort of Delight? or is it a Pleasure which is taken in the Exercise of Pity? It was methought pretty remarkable, that the Business of the

---

[1] Timothy Gorman is mentioned in *Tatler* 31 and in the Epilogue to Lansdowne's *Jew of Venice*. He is advertised to appear against Timothy Buck on 8 July 1713 'at the Bear-Garden in Marrow-Bone-Fields the Backside of Soho-Square at the Boarded House near Tyburn Road' (*Daily Courant*, 6 July).

Day being a Trial of Skill, the Popularity did not run so high as one would have expected on the Side of *Buck*. Is it that People's Passions have their Rise in Self-love, and thought themselves (in Spite of all the Courage they had) liable to the Fate of *Miller*, but could not so easily think of themselves qualified like *Buck*?

Tully speaks of this Custom with less Horrour than one would expect, tho' he confesses it was ..nuch abused in his Time, and seems directly to approve of it under its first Regulations, when Criminals only fought before the People. *Crudele Gladiatorum spectaculum & inhumanum nonnullis videri solet; & haud scio annon ita sit ut nunc fit; cum vero sontes ferro depugnabant, auribus fortasse multa, oculis quidem nulla, poterat esse fortior contra dolorem & mortem disciplina.*[1] *The Shows of Gladiators may be thought barbarous and inhumane, and I know not but it is so as it is now practised; but in those Times when only Criminals were Combatants, the Ear perhaps might receive many better Instructions, but it is impossible that any thing which affects our Eyes, should fortify us so well against Pain and Death.*   T

No. 437   *Tuesday, July 22, 1712*[2]
[STEELE]

> *Tune Impune hæc facias? Tune hic homines adolescentulos*
> *Imperitos rerum, eductos libere, in fraudem illicis?*
> *Sollicitando, & pollicitando eorum animos lactas?*
> *Ac meritricios amores nuptiis conglutinas?*
>
> Ter. And.

THE other Day pass'd by me in her Chariot a Lady, with that pale and wan Complexion, which we sometimes see in young People, who are fallen into Sorrow and private Anxiety of Mind, which antedate Age and Sickness. It is not three Years ago since she was gay, airy, and a little towards Libertine in her Carriage; but, methought, I easily forgave her that little Insolence, which she so severely pays for in her present Condition. *Favilla*, of whom I am speaking, is marry'd to a sullen Fool with Wealth: Her Beauty and

[1] Cicero, *Tusculan Disputations*, 2. 17. 41. (For *annon* read *an*; and for *multa* read *multae*.)

[2] *Motto.* Terence, *Andria*, 910–13: Shall you escape with impunity? Are you laying snares here for young men, of a liberal education but unacquainted with the world, and duping them by force of importunity and promises? Are you cementing affairs with courtesans by marriage?

Merit are lost upon the Dolt, who is insensible of Perfection in any thing. Their Hours together are either painful or insipid: The Minutes she has to her self in his Absence, are not sufficient to give Vent at her Eyes to the Grief and Torment of his last Conversation. This poor Creature was sacrific'd with a Temper (which, under the Cultivation of a Man of Sense, would have made the most agreeable Companion) into the Arms of this loathsome Yoak-fellow by *Sempronia*.[1] *Sempronia* is a good Lady, who supports her self in an affluent Condition, by contracting Friendship with rich young Widows and Maids of plentiful Fortunes at their own Disposal, and bestowing her Friends upon Worthless indigent Fellows; on the other Side, she ensnares inconsiderate and rash Youths of great Estates into the Arms of vitious Women. For this Purpose, she is accomplished in all the Arts which can make her acceptable at impertinent Visits; she knows all that passes in every Quarter, and is well acquainted with all the favourite Servants, Busy-bodies, Dependants, and poor Relations of all Persons of Condition in the whole Town. At the Price of a good Sum of Money, *Sempronia*, by the Instigation of *Favilla*'s Mother, brought about the Match for the Daughter, and the Reputation of this which is apparently, in point of Fortune, more than *Favilla* could expect, has gain'd her the Visits and frequent Attendance of the Crowd of Mothers, who had rather see their Children miserable in great Wealth, than the Happiest of the Race of Mankind in a less conspicuous State of Life. When *Sempronia* is so well acquainted with a Woman's Temper and Circumstance, that she believes Marriage would be acceptable to her, and advantageous to the Man who shall get her; her next Step is to look out for some one, whose Condition has some secret Wound in it, and wants a Sum, yet, in the Eye of the World, not unsuitable to her. If such is not easily had, she immediately adorns a worthless Fellow with what Estate she thinks convenient, and adds as great a Share of good Humour and Sobriety as is requisite: After this is setled, no Importunities, Arts, and Devices are omitted to hasten the Lady to her Happiness. In the general indeed she is a Person of so strict Justice, that she marries a poor Gallant to a rich Wench, and a Moneyless Girl to a Man of Fortune. But then she has no manner of Conscience in the Disparity, when she has a Mind to impose a poor

---

[1] Sempronia, the profligate wife of D. Junius Brutus, took part in Catiline's conspiracy without her husband's knowledge. See Sallust, *Bellum Catilinae*, 25, 40. In No. 45 (vol. i) Sempronia is the name given to the woman addicted to French fashions.

Rogue or one of an Estate; she has no Remorse in adding to it, that he is illiterate, ignorant, and unfashion'd; but makes those Imperfections Arguments of the Truth of his Wealth; and will, on such an Occasion, with a very grave Face, charge the People of Condition with Negligence in the Education of their Children. Exception being made t'other Day against an ignorant Booby of her own Cloathing, whom she was putting off for a rich Heir, *Madam*, said she, *you know there is no making Children who know they have Estates attend their Books.*

Sempronia, by these Arts, is loaded with Presents, importun'd for her Acquaintance, and admir'd by those who do not know the first Taste of Life, as a Woman of exemplary good Breeding. But sure, to murder and to rob are less Iniquities, than to raise Profit by Abuses, as irreparable as taking away Life; but more grievous, as making it lastingly unhappy. To rob a Lady at Play of Half her Fortune, is not so ill, as giving the whole and her self to an unworthy Husband. But *Sempronia* can administer Consolation to an unhappy Fair at Home, by leading her to an agreeable Gallant elsewhere. She can then preach the general Condition of all the Married World, and tell an unexperienced young Woman the Methods of softning her Affliction, and laugh at her Simplicity and Want of Knowledge, with an *Oh! my Dear, you will know better.*

The Wickedness of *Sempronia*, one would think, should be superlative; but I cannot but esteem that of some Parents equal to it; I mean such as sacrifice the greatest Endowments and Qualifications to base Bargains. A Parent who forces a Child of a liberal and ingenious Spirit into the Arms of a Clown or a Blockhead, obliges her to a Crime too odious for a Name. It is in a Degree the unnatural Conjunction of rational and brutal Beings. Yet what is there so common, as the bestowing an accomplished Woman with such a Disparity. And I could name Crowds who lead miserable Lives, for want of Knowledge in their Parents, of this Maxim, that good Sense and good Nature always go together. That which is attributed to Fools, and call'd good Nature, is only an Inability of observing what is faulty, which turns in Marriage, into a Suspicion of every thing as such, from a Consciousness of that Inability.

Mr. SPECTATOR,

'I AM intirely of your Opinion[1] with Relation to the Equestrian Females, who affect both the Masculine and Feminine Air at the

[1] See No. 435.

same time; and cannot forbear making a Presentment against another Order of them who grow very numerous and powerful; and since our Language is not very capable of good compound Words, I must be contented to call them only the *Naked Shoulder'd*.[1] These Beauties are not contented to make Lovers wherever they appear, but they must make Rivals at the same time. Were you to see *Gatty*[2] walk the *Park* at high Mall,[3] you would expect those who followed her and those who met her could immediately draw their Swords for her. I hope, Sir, you will provide for the future, that Women may stick to their Faces for doing any future Mischief, and not allow any but direct Traders in Beauty to expose more than the fore Part of the Neck, unless you please to allow this After-Game[4] to those who are very defective in the Charms of the Countenance. I can say, to my Sorrow, the present Practice is very unfair, when to look back is Death; and it may be said of our Beauties, as a great Poet did of Bullets,

They kill and wound like Parthians *as they fly*.[5]

I submit this to your Animadversion; and am, for the little while I have left,

Your humble Servant,
the languishing PHILANTHUS.

'P. S. *Suppose you mended my Letter, and made a Simile about the Porcupine, but I submit that also.*'

T

[1] In *Tatler* 215 a Petition of the Company of Linen drapers complained that 'there has of late prevailed among the Ladies so great an Affectation of Nakedness, that they have not only left the Bosom wholly bare, but lowered their Stays some Inches below the former Mode'.

[2] An abbreviation of Gertrude. See No. 515.

[3] The time of greatest resort in the Mall, formed on the analogy of 'high noon', 'high time', &c. (*OED*). A similar form is 'high Change' in No. 69 (vol. i).

[4] 'A second game played in order to reverse or improve the issues of the first; hence "The scheme which may be laid or the expedients which are practised after the original game has miscarried; methods taken after the first turn of affairs"— Johnson' (*OED*). Cf. Addison's *Cato*, III. vii. 1–2:

> Our first design, my friend, has prov'd abortive;
> Still there remains an after-game to play.

[5] The 'great poet' is Dennis, and the line is from his poem 'Upon our Victory at Sea', in his *Miscellanies* (1693), p. 13:

> Bullets amain, unseen by mortal Eye,
> Fly in whole Legions thro' the darkned Sky,
> And kill and wound, like Parthians, as they fly.

The poem was published in the *Gentleman's Journal*, June 1692; the lines quoted above appear on p. 3.

> ... *Animum rege qui nisi paret*
> *Imperat* ...
>
> Hor.

IT is a very common Expression, That such a one is very good-natur'd, but very passionate. The Expression indeed is very good-natur'd, to allow passionate People so much Quarter: But I think a passionate Man deserves the least Indulgence imaginable. It is said, it is soon over; that is, all the Mischief he does is quickly dispatch'd, which, I think, is no great Recommendation to Favour. I have known one of these good-natur'd passionate Men say in a mix'd Company, even to his own Wife or Child, such Things as the most inveterate Enemy of his Family would not have spoke, even in Imagination. It is certain, that quick Sensibility is inseparable from a ready Understanding; but why should not that good Understanding call to it self all its Force on such Occasions, to master that sudden Inclination to Anger. One of the greatest Souls now in the World is the most subject by Nature to Anger, and yet so famous from a Conquest of himself this Way, that he is the known Example when you talk of Temper and Command of a Man's self.[2] To contain the Spirit of Anger, is the worthiest Discipline we can put our selves to. When a Man has made any Progress this way, a frivolous Fellow in a Passion, is to him as contemptible as a froward Child. It ought to be the Study of every Man, for his own Quiet and Peace. When he stands combustible and ready to flame upon every thing that touches him, Life is as uneasie to himself as it is to all about him. *Syncropius* leads, of all Men living, the most ridiculous Life; he is ever offending, and begging Pardon. If his Man enters the Room without what he sent for, *That Blockhead*, begins he—*Gentlemen, I ask your Pardon; but Servants now-a-days*—The wrong Plates are laid, they are thrown into the Middle of the Room; his Wife stands by in Pain for him, which he sees in her Face, and answers as if he had heard all she was thinking; *Why, what the Devil! Why don't you*

---

[1] *Motto.* Horace, *Epistles*, I. 2. 62–63.
> Curb thy soul,
> And check thy rage, which must be rul'd or rule. CREECH.

[2] The 1789 edition, followed by all later editors, identifies this as a reference to Lord Somers.

take Care to give Orders in these Things? His Friends sit down to a taste-less Plenty of every thing, every Minute expecting new Insults from his impertinent Passions. In a Word, to eat with, or visit *Syncropius*, is no other than going to see him exercise his Family, exercise their Patience, and his own Anger.

It is monstrous that the Shame and Confusion in which this good-natur'd angry Man must needs behold his Friends while he thus lays about him, does not give him so much Reflection as to create an Amendment. This is the most scandalous Disuse of Reason imaginable; all the harmless Part of him is no more than that of a Bull-Dog, they are tame no longer than they are not offended. One of these good-natur'd angry Men shall, in an Instant, assemble together so many Allusions to secret Circumstances, as are enough to dissolve the Peace of all the Families and Friends he is acquainted with, in a Quarter of an Hour, and yet the next Moment be the best natur'd Man in the whole World. If you would see Passion in its Purity, without Mixture of Reason, behold it represented in a mad Hero, drawn by a mad Poet. *Nat. Lee* makes his *Alexander* say thus:

> *Away, begon, and give a Whirlwind Room,*
> *Or I will blow you up like Dust! Avaunt;*
> *Madness but meanly represents my Toil,*
> *Eternal Discord!*
> *Fury! Revenge! Disdain and Indignation!*
> *Tear my swoln Breast, make way for Fire and Tempest.*
> *My Brain is burst, Debate and Reason quench'd;*
> *The Storm is up, and my hot bleeding Heart*
> *Splits with the Rack, while Passions, like the Wind,*
> *Rise up to Heav'n, and put out all the Stars.*[1]

Every passionate Fellow in Town talks half the Day with as little Consistency, and threatens Things as much out of his Power.

The next disagreeable Person to the outragious Gentleman, is one of a much lower Order of Anger, and he is what we commonly call a peevish Fellow. A peevish Fellow is one who has some Reason in himself for being out of Humour, or has a natural Incapacity for Delight, and therefore disturbs all who are happier than himself with Pishes and Pshaws, or other well-bred Interjections, at every thing that is said or done in his Presence. There should be Physick

---

[1] Lee, *The Rival Queens*, III. i. (The words are spoken by Roxana, not by Alexander.) Steele omits a line and a half after the third line. In the next to last line, for *Wind* read *Winds*.

mix'd in the Food of all which these Fellows eat in good Company. This Degree of Anger passes, forsooth, for a Delicacy of Judgment, that won't admit of being easily pleas'd: But none above the Character of wearing a peevish Man's Livery, ought to bear with his ill Manners. All Things among Men of Sense and Condition should pass the Censure, and have the Protection, of the Eye of Reason.

No Man ought to be tolerated in an habitual Humour, Whim, or Particularity of Behaviour, by any who do not wait upon him for Bread. Next to the peevish Fellow is the Snarler. This Gentleman deals mightily in what we call the Irony, and as these sort of People exert themselves most against those below them, you see their Humour best, in their Talk to their Servants. That is so like you, you are a fine fellow, thou art the quickest Head-piece, and the like. One would think the Hectoring, the Storming, the Sullen, and all the different Species and Subordinations of the Angry should be cured, by knowing they live only as pardoned Men, and how pityful is the Condition of being only suffered? But I am interrupted by the Pleasantest Scene of Anger and the Disappointment of it that I have ever known, which happen'd while I was yet Writing, and I overheard as I sat in the Back-room at a *French* Booksellers.[1] There came into the Shop a very learned Man with an erect Solemn Air, and tho' a Person of great Parts otherwise, slow in understanding any thing which makes against himself. The Composure of the faulty Man, and the whimsical perplexity of him that was justly angry, is perfectly New: After turning over many Volumes, said the Seller to the Buyer, *Sir, you know I have long asked you to send me back the first Volume of French Sermons I formerly lent you;* Sir, said the Chapman,[2] I have often looked for it but cannot find it; It is certainly lost, and I know not to whom I lent it, it is so many Years ago; *then Sir, here is the other Volume, I'll send you home that, and please to pay for both.* My Friend, reply'd he, can'st thou be so Senseless as not to know that one Volume is as imperfect in my Library as your Shop. *Yes, Sir, but it is you have lost the first Volume, and to be short I will be Paid.* Sir, answer'd the Chapman, you are a Young Man, your Book is lost,

---

[1] 'This Scene passed in the shop of Mr. Vaillant, now of Mr. Elmsly, in the Strand; and the subject of it was (for it is still in remembrance) a volume of Massillon's "Sermons"' (Nichols). Paul Vaillant was a French refugee who conducted a book-shop over against Bedford House in the Strand, carried on later by his sons Paul and Isaac.

[2] I.e. purchaser or customer. *OED* marks this usage as *Obs.* or *dial.*; the last quotation is dated 1807.

and learn by this little Loss to bear much greater Adversities, which you must expect to meet with. *Yes, Sir, I'll bear when I must, but I have not lost now, for I say you have it and shall Pay me.* Friend you grow Warm, I tell you the Book is lost, and I foresee in the Course even of a prosperous Life, that you will meet Afflictions to make you Mad, if you cannot bear this Trifle. *Sir, there is in this Case no need of bearing, for you have the Book.* I say, Sir, I have not the Book, but your Passion will not let you hear enough to be informed that I have it not. Learn Resignation of your self to the Distresses of this Life: Nay do not fret and fume, it is my Duty to tell you that you are of an impatient Spirit, and an impatient Spirit is never without Woe. *Was ever any thing like this?* Yes, Sir, there have been many things like this. The Loss is but a Trifle, but your Temper is Wanton, and incapable of the least Pain; therefore let me advise you, be Patient, the Book is lost, but do not you for that reason lose your self.

T

No. 439   *Thursday, July 24, 1712*[1]

[ADDISON]

Hi narrata ferunt aliò: mensuraque ficti
Crescit; & auditis aliquid novus adjicit auctor.

Ov.

OVID describes the Palace of Fame as situated in the very Center of the Universe, and perforated with so many Windows and Avenues as gave her the Sight of every thing that was done in the Heavens, in the Earth, and in the Sea.[2] The Structure of it was contrived in so admirable a manner, that it Eccho'd every Word which was spoken in the whole Compass of Nature; so that the Palace, says the Poet, was always filled with a confused Hubbub of low dying Sounds, the Voices being almost spent and worn out before they arrived at this General Rendezvous of Speeches and Whispers.

[1] *Motto.* Ovid, *Metamorphoses*, 12. 57–58:
Some carry Tales; each in the telling grows,
And every Author adds to what he knows.

[2] *Metamorphoses*, 12. 39–63.

I consider Courts with the same regard to the Governments which they superintend, as *Ovid's* Palace of Fame, with regard to the Universe. The Eyes of a watchful Minister run through the whole People. There is scarce a Murmur or Complaint, that does not reach his Ears. They have News-Gatherers and Intelligencers distributed into their several Walks and Quarters, who bring in their respective Quotas, and make them acquainted with the Discourse and Conversation of the whole Kingdom or Common-wealth where they are Employed. The wisest of Kings, alluding to these Invisible and unsuspected Spies who[a] are planted by Kings and Rulers over their Fellow-Citizens, as well as to those Voluntary Informers that are buzzing about the Ears of a great Man, and making their Court by such secret Methods of Intelligence, has given us a very prudent Caution: *Curse not the King no not in thy Thought, and Curse not the Rich in thy Bed-chamber: For a Bird of the Air shall carry the Voice, and that which hath Wings shall tell the matter.*[1]

As it is absolutely necessary for Rulers to make use of other Peoples Eyes and Ears, they should take particular Care to do it in such a manner, that it may not bear too hard on the Person whose Life and Conversation are enquired into. A Man who is capable of so infamous a Calling as that of a Spy, is not very much to be relied upon. He can have no great Ties of Honour, or Checks of Conscience, to restrain him in those covert Evidences, where the Person accused has no Opportunity of vindicating himself. He will be more industrious to carry that which is grateful, than that which is true. There will be no Occasion for him, if he does not hear and see things worth Discovery; so that he naturally inflames every Word and Circumstance, aggravates what is faulty, perverts what is good, and misrepresents what is indifferent. Nor is it to be doubted but that such ignominious Wretches let their private Passions into these their clandestine Informations, and often wreak their particular Spite or Malice against the Person whom they are set to watch. It is a pleasant Scene enough, which an *Italian* Author describes between a Spy, and a Cardinal who[b] employed him.[2] The Cardinal is represented as minuting down every thing that is told him. The Spie begins with a Low Voice, Such an one, the Advocate,

---

[a] who] that *Fol.*   [b] who] that *Fol.*

[1] Eccles. x. 20.   [2] Possibly a recollection of the scene in Molière's *L'Avare* (III, i). between Harpagon and his servant Maître Jacques.

whispered to one of his Friends, within my hearing, that your Eminence was a very great Poultron; and after having given his Patron time to take it down, adds, that another called him a Mercenary Rascal in a Publick Conversation. The Cardinal replies Very well, and bids him go on. The Spie proceeds, and loads him with Reports of the same Nature, till the Cardinal rises in great Wrath, calls him an Impudent Scoundrel, and kicks him out of the Room.

It is observed of great and heroic Minds, that they have not only shewn a particular Disregard to those unmerited Reproaches which have been cast upon 'em, but have been altogether free from that Impertinent Curiosity of Enquiring after them, or the poor Revenge of resenting them. The Histories of *Alexander* and *Cæsar* are full of this kind of Instances. Vulgar Souls are of a quite contrary Character. *Dionysius*, the Tyrant of *Sicily*, had a Dungeon which was a very curious Piece of Architecture; and of which, as I am informed, there are still to be seen some Remains in that Island.[1] It was called *Dionysius*'s *Ear*, and built with several little Windings and Labyrinths in the form of a real Ear. The Structure of it made it a kind of whispering Place, but such a one as gathered the Voice of him who[a] spoke into a Funnel, which was placed at the very Top of it. The Tyrant used to lodge all his State Criminals, or those whom he supposed to be engaged together in any Evil Designs upon him, in this Dungeon. He had at the same time an Apartment over it, where he used to apply himself to the Funnel, and by that means over-hear every thing that was whispered in the Dungeon. I believe one may venture to affirm, that a *Cæsar* or an *Alexander* would rather have died by the Treason, than have used such disingenuous Means for the detecting of it.

A Man, who in ordinary Life is very Inquisitive after every thing which[b] is spoken ill of him, passes his Time but very indifferently. He is wounded by every Arrow that is shot at him, and puts it in the Power of every insignificant Enemy to disquiet him. Nay, he will suffer from what has been said of him, when it is forgotten by those

---

[a] who] that *Fol.*   [b] which] that *Fol.*

---

[1] Dionysius the Elder was tyrant of Syracuse in the fourth century B.C. The dungeon was one of the quarries used by the Syracusans after their victory in 413 B.C. to imprison the captured Athenians. This one, with a contracting size toward the top, seems to have been given the name 'Ear of Dionysius' by the painter Caravaggio at the beginning of the seventeenth century. See A. J. C. Hare, *Cities of Southern Italy and Sicily* (Edinburgh, 1883), p. 444.

who said or heard it. For this Reason I could[a] never bear one of those Officious Friends, that would[b] be telling every malicious Report, every idle Censure that passed[c] upon me. The Tongue of Man is so petulant, and his Thoughts so variable, that one should not lay too great a stress upon any present Speeches and Opinions. Praise and Obloquy proceed very frequently out of the same Mouth upon the same Person, and upon the same Occasion. A generous Enemy will sometimes bestow Commendations, as the dearest Friend cannot sometimes refrain from speaking Ill. The Man who is indifferent in either of these respects, gives his Opinion at random, and praises or disapproves as he finds himself in Humour.

I shall conclude this Essay with Part of a Character which is finely drawn by the Earl of *Clarendon*, in the first Book of his History, and which[d] gives us the lively Picture of a great Man teizing himself with an absurd Curiosity.[1]

'He had not that Application and Submission, and Reverence for the Queen, as might have been expected from his Wisdom and Breeding; and often crossed her Pretences and Desires with more Rudeness than was natural to him. Yet he was impertinently sollicitous to know what her Majesty said of him in private, and what Resentments she had towards him. And when by some Confidents, who had their Ends upon him from those Offices, he was informed of some bitter Expressions fallen from her Majesty, he was so exceedingly afflicted and tormented with the Sense of it, that sometimes by passionate Complaints and Representations to the King; sometimes by more dutiful Addresses and Expostulations with the Queen, in bewailing his Misfortune; he frequently exposed himself, and left his Condition worse than it was before, and the Eclaircisment commonly ended in the Discovery of the Persons from whom he had receiv'd his most secret Intelligence.'　　　　C

---

[a] could] shou'd *Fol.*　　　[b] would] will *Fol.*　　　[c] passed] passes *Fol.*　　　and which] which *Fol.*

---

[1] Clarendon, *History of the Rebellion* (Oxford, 1843), book i, p. 21 (a character of Lord Treasurer Weston, Earl of Portland).

No. 440   *Friday, July 25, 1712*[1]
ADDISON]

Vivere si rectè nescis, discede peritis.

Hor.

I HAVE already given my Reader an Account of a Sett of merry
Fellows, who are passing their Summer together in the Country,
being provided of a great House, where there is not only a convenient Apartment for every particular Person, but a large Infirmary
for the Reception of such of them as are any way Indisposed, or out
of Humour.[2] Having lately received a Letter from the Secretary of
this Society, by Order of the whole Fraternity, which acquaints me
with their Behaviour during the last Week, I shall here make a Present of it to the Publick.

Mr. SPECTATOR,

'W E are glad to find that you approve the Establishment which
we have here made for the retrieving of good Manners and
agreeable Conversation, and shall use our best Endeavours so to
improve our selves in this our Summer Retirement, that we may
next Winter serve as Patterns to the Town. But to the end that this
our Institution may be no less Advantageous to the Publick than
to our selves, we shall communicate to you one Week of our Proceedings, desiring you at the same time, if you see any thing faulty
in them, to favour us with your Admonitions. For you must know,
Sir, that it has been proposed among us to chuse you for our Visitor,
to which I must further add, that one of the College having declared
last Week, he[a] did not like the *Spectator* of the Day, and not being
able to assign any just Reasons for such his Dislike, he was sent to
the Infirmary, *Nemine contradicente.*

'On *Monday* the Assembly was in very good Humour, having
received some Recruits of *French* Claret that Morning; when unluckily, towards the middle of the Dinner, one of the Company
swore at his Servant in a very rough manner, for having put too
much Water in his Wine. Upon which the President of the Day,
who is always the Mouth of the Company, after having convinced

---

a he] that he *Fol.*

[1] *Motto.* Horace, *Epistles,* 2. 2. 213. If you cannot live aright, make wayſ or the
wise.
[2] See Nos. 424 (vol. iii), 429.

him of the Impertinence of his Passion, and the Insult it had made upon the Company, ordered his Man to take him from the Table, and convey him to the Infirmary. There was but one more sent away that Day; this was a Gentleman who is reckoned by some Persons one of the greatest Wits, and by others one of the greatest Boobys about Town. This you will say is a strange Character, but what makes it stranger yet, it is a very true one, for he is perpetually the Reverse of himself, being always merry or dull to Excess. We brought him hither to divert us, which he did very well upon the Road, having lavished away as much Wit and Laughter upon the Hackney Coach-man, as might have served him during his whole Stay here, had it been duly managed. He had been lumpish[1] for two or three Days, but was so far connived at, in hopes of Recovery, that we dispatched one of the briskest Fellows among the Brother-hood into the Infirmary, for having told him at Table he[a] was not merry. But our President observing that he indulged himself in this long Fit of Stupidity, and construing it as a Contempt of the College, order'd him to retire into the Place prepared for such Companions. He was no sooner got into it, but his Wit and Mirth return'd upon him in so violent a manner, that he shook the whole Infirmary with the Noise of it, and had so good an Effect upon the rest of the Patients, that he brought them all out to Dinner with him the next Day.

'On *Tuesday* we were no sooner sat down, but one of the Company complained that his Head aked; upon which another asked him, in an insolent manner, what he did there then; this insensibly grew into some warm Words; so that the President, in order to keep the Peace, gave directions to take them both from the Table, and lodge them in the Infirmary. Not long after, another of the Company telling us, he knew by a Pain in his Shoulder that we should have some Rain, the President order'd him to be removed, and placed as a Weather-glass in the Apartment above-mentioned.

'On *Wednesday* a Gentleman having received a Letter written in a Woman's Hand, and changing Colour twice or thrice as he read it, desired leave to retire into the Infirmary. The President consented, but denied him the use of Pen, Ink and Paper till such time as he had slept upon it. One of the Company being seated at the lower end of

---

[a] he] that he *Fol.*

[1] 'low-spirited, dejected, melancholy. *Obs.*' (*OED*). In No. 518 Tom Tweer speaks of 'a lumpish, down-cast look'.

the Table, and discovering his secret Discontent, by finding fault with every Dish that was served up, and refusing to Laugh at any thing that was said, the President told him, that he found he was in an uneasie Seat, and desired him to accommodate himself better in the Infirmary. After Dinner a very honest Fellow chancing to let a Punn fall from him, his Neighbour cry'd out, *to the Infirmary*; at the same time pretending to be Sick at it, as having the same Natural Antipathy to a Punn, which some have to a Cat.[1] This produced a long Debate. Upon the whole the Punnster was Acquitted, and his Neighbour sent off.

'On *Thursday* there was but one Delinquent. This was a Gentleman of strong Voice, but weak Understanding. He had unluckily engaged himself in a Dispute with a Man of excellent Sense, but of a modest Elocution. The Man of Heat replied to every Answer of his Antagonist with a louder Note than ordinary, and only raised his Voice when he should have enforced his Argument. Finding himself at length driven to an Absurdity, he still reasoned in a more clamorous and confused manner, and to make the greater Impression upon his Hearers, concluded with a loud Thump upon the Table. The President immediately ordered him to be carried off, and dieted with Water-gruel, till such time as he should be sufficiently weakened for Conversation.

'On *Friday* there passed very little remarkable, saving only, that several Petitions were read of the Persons in Custody, desiring to be released from their Confinement, and vouching for one another's good Behaviour for the future.

'On *Saturday* we receiv'd many Excuses from Persons who had found themselves in an unsociable Temper, and had voluntarily shut themselves up. The Infirmary was indeed never so full as on this Day, which I was at some loss to account for, till upon my going Abroad I observed that it was an Easterly Wind.[2] The Retirement of most of my Friends has given me Opportunity and Leisure of writing you this Letter, which I must not conclude without assuring you, that all the Members of our College, as well those who are under Confinement, as those who are at Liberty, are your very humble Servants, tho' none more than,

&c.'

C

[1] Cf. Nos. 538, 609.
[2] For this as a cause of melancholy see No. 241 (vol. ii).

Si fractus illabatur orbis
Impavidum ferient ruinæ.
Hor.

MAN, considered in himself, is a very helpless and a very
wretched Being. He is subject every Moment to the greatest
Calamities and Misfortunes. He is beset with Dangers on all sides,
and may become unhappy by numberless Casualties, which he
could not foresee, nor have prevented, had he foreseen them.

It is our Comfort, while we are obnoxious to so many Accidents,
that we are under the Care of one who directs Contingencies, and
has in his Hands the Management of every Thing that is capable of
annoying or offending us; who knows the Assistance we stand in
need of, and is always ready to bestow it on those who ask it of him.

The natural Homage, which such a Creature bears to so infinitely
Wise and Good a Being, is a firm Reliance on him for the Blessings
and Conveniencies of Life, and an habitual Trust in him for Deliverance out of all such Dangers and Difficulties as may befall us.

The Man, who always lives in this Disposition of Mind, has not
the same dark and melancholly Views of Human Nature, as he who
considers himself abstractedly from this Relation to the Supreme
Being. At the same time that he reflects upon his own Weakness and
Imperfection, he comforts himself with the Contemplation of those
Divine Attributes, which are employed for his Safety and his Welfare. He finds his want of Foresight made up by the Omniscience of
him who is his Support. He is not sensible of his own want of
Strength, when he knows that his Helper is Almighty. In short, the
Person who has a firm Trust on the Supreme Being is Powerful in
his Power, Wise by *his* Wisdom, Happy by *his* Happiness. He reaps
the Benefit of every Divine Attribute, and loses his own Insufficiency
in the Fullness of infinite Perfection.

To make our Lives more easy to us, we are commanded to put
our Trust in him, who is thus able to relieve and succour us; the

---

[1] *Motto.* Horace, *Odes*, 3. 3. 7–8:
> Should the whole Frame of Nature round him break,
> In Ruin and Confusion huri'd,
> He, unconcern'd, would hear the mighty Crack,
> And stand secure amidst a falling World. ADDISON (in No. 615).

Divine Goodness having made such a Reliance a Duty, notwith-standing we should have been miserable had it been forbidden us.

Among several Motives, which might be made use of to recom-mend this Duty to us, I shall only take notice of those that follow.

The first and strongest is, that we are promised, He will not fail those who put their Trust in him.

But without considering the Supernatural Blessing which accom-panies this Duty, we may observe that it has a natural Tendency to its own Reward, or in other words, that this firm Trust and Confidence in the great Disposer of all Things, contributes very much to the getting clear of any Affliction, or to the bearing it man-fully. A Person who believes he has his Succour at hand, and that he acts in the sight of his Friend, often exerts himself beyond his Abilities, and does Wonders that are not to be matched by one who is not animated with such a Confidence of Success. I could produce Instances from History of Generals, who out of a Belief that they were under the Protection of some invisible Assistant, did not only encourage their Soldiers to do their utmost, but have acted them-selves beyond what they would have done, had they not been inspired by such a Belief. I might in the same manner shew how such a Trust in the Assistance of an Almighty Being, naturally pro-duces Patience, Hope, Chearfulness, and all other Dispositions of Mind that alleviate those Calamities which we are not able to remove.

The Practice of this Virtue administers great Comfort to the Mind of Man in times of Poverty and Affliction, but most of all in the Hour of Death. When the Soul is hovering in the last Moments of its Separation,[a] when it is just entring on another State of Exist-ence, to converse with Scenes, and Objects, and Companions that are altogether new, what can support her under such tremblings of Thought, such Fear, such Anxiety, such Apprehensions, but the casting of all her Cares upon him who first gave her Being, who has conducted her through one Stage of it, and will be always with her to Guide and Comfort her in her Progress[b] through Eternity?

David has very beautifully represented this steady Reliance on God Almighty in his twenty third Psalm, which is a kind of *Pastoral* Hymn, and filled with those Allusions which are usual in that kind of Writing. As the Poetry is very exquisite, I shall present my Reader with the following Translation of it.

[a] Separation,] Dissolution, *Fol.*   [b] Progress] Passage *Fol.*

I.

The Lord my Pasture shall prepare,
And feed me with a Shepherd's Care:
His Presence shall my Wants supply,
And guard me with a watchful Eye;
My Noon-day Walks he shall attend,
And all my midnight Hours defend.

II.

When in the sultry Glebe I faint,
Or on the thirsty Mountain pant;
To fertile Vales and dewy Meads,
My weary wand'ring Steps he leads;
Where peaceful Rivers soft and slow,
Amid the verdant Landskip flow.

III.

Tho' in the Paths of Death I tread,
With gloomy Horrors over-spread;
My steadfast Heart shall fear no Ill,
For thou, O Lord, art with me still;
Thy friendly Crook shall give me Aid,
And guide me through the dreadful Shade.

IV.

Tho' in a bare and rugged Way,
Through devious lonely Wilds I stray,
Thy Bounty shall my Pains beguile:
The barren Wilderness shall smile
With sudden Greens and Herbage crown'd,
And Streams shall murmur all around.[1]

C

---

[1] 'The author's devout turn of mind, and exquisite taste, mutually assisted each other in composing these divine hymns, of which we have several specimens in the course of the Spectator. As the sentiments are highly poetical in themselves, and taken, for the most part, from inspired scripture, his true judgment suggested to him, that the splendour of them was best preserved in a pure and simple expression: and the fervour of his piety, made that simplicity, pathetic' (Hurd).

No. 442
[STEELE]

Monday, July 28, 1712[1]

Scribimus Indocti Doctique . . .

Hor.

I DO not know whether I enough explained my self to the World, when I invited all Men to be assistant to me in this my Work of Speculation;[2] for I have not yet acquainted my Readers, that besides the Letters and valuable Hints I have from Time to Time received from my Correspondents, I have by me several curious and extraordinary Papers sent with a Design (as no one will doubt when they are publish'd) that they might be printed entire, and without any Alteration, by way of *Spectator*. I must acknowledge also, that I my self being the first Projector of the Paper, thought I had a Right to make them my own, by dressing them in my own Stile, by leaving out what wou'd not appear like mine, and by adding whatever might be proper to adapt them to the Character and Genius of my Paper, with which it was almost impossible these cou'd exactly correspond, it being certain that hardly two Men think alike, and therefore so many Men so many *Spectators*. Besides, I must own my Weakness for Glory is such, that if I consulted that only, I might be so far sway'd by it, as almost to wish that no one could write a *Spectator* besides my self; nor can I deny, but upon the first Perusal of those Papers, I felt some secret Inclinations of ill Will towards the Persons who wrote them. This was the Impression I had upon the first reading them; but upon a late Review (more for the Sake of Entertainment than Use) regarding them with another Eye than I had done at first, (for by converting them as well as I cou'd to my own Use, I thought I had utterly disabled them from ever offending me again as *Spectators*) I found my self mov'd by a Passion very different from that of Envy; sensibly touch'd with Pity, the softest and most generous of all Passions, when I reflected what a cruel Disappointment the Neglect of those Papers must needs have been to the Writers, who impatiently long'd to see them appear in Print, and who, no Doubt, triumph'd to themselves in the Hopes of having a Share with me in the Applause of the Publick; a Pleasure so great,

---

[1] *Motto.* Horace, *Epistles*, 2. 1. 117:
And skilful, or unskilful, all must write. CREECH.

[2] No. 428.

that none but those who have experienc'd it can have a Sense of it. In this Manner of viewing those Papers, I really found I had not done them Justice, there being something so extremely natural and peculiarly good in some of them, that I will appeal to the World whether it was possible to alter a Word in them without doing them a manifest Hurt and Violence; and whether they can ever appear rightly, and as they ought, but in their own native Dress and Colours: And therefore I think I shou'd not only wrong them, but deprive the World of a considerable Satisfaction, shou'd I any longer delay the making them publick.

After I have publish'd a few of these *Spectators*, I doubt not but I shall find the Success of them to equal, if not surpass, that of the best of my own. An Author should take all Methods to humble himself in the Opinion he has of his own Performances. When these Papers appear to the World, I doubt not but they will be followed by many others; and I shall not repine, tho' I my self shall have left me but very few Days to appear in Publick: But preferring the general Weal and Advantage to any Considerations of my self, I am resolv'd for the Future to publish any *Spectator* that deserves it, entire, and without any Alteration; assuring the World (if there can be Need of it) that it is none of mine; and if the Authors think fit to subscribe their Names, I will add them.

I think the best way of promoting this generous and useful Design, will be by giving out Subjects or Themes of all Kinds whatsoever, on which (with a Preamble of the extraordinary Benefit and Advantage that may accrue thereby to the Publick) I will invite all manner of Persons, whether Scholars, Citizens, Courtiers, Gentlemen of the Town or Country, and all Beaux, Rakes, Smarts,[1] Prudes, Coquets, Housewives, and all Sorts of Wits, whether Male or Female, and however distinguish'd, whether they be True-Wits, Whole, or Half-Wits, or whether Arch, Dry, Natural, Acquir'd, Genuine, or Deprav'd Wits; and Persons of all Sorts of Tempers and Complexions, whether the Severe, the Delightful, the Impertinent, the Agreeable, the Thoughtful, Busy, or Careless; the Serene or Cloudy, Jovial or Melancholy, Untowardly or Easy; the Cold, Temperate, or Sanguine; and of what Manners or Dispositions soever, whether the Ambitious or Humble-minded, the Proud or Pitiful, Ingenuous or Base-minded, Good or Ill-natur'd, Publick-spirited or Selfish; and

---

[1] 'One who affects smartness in dress, manners, or talk' (*OED*). This is the first quotation of the word in this sense in *OED*.

under what Fortune or Circumstance soever, whether the Contented or Miserable, Happy or Unfortunate, High or Low, Rich or Poor (whether so thro' Want of Money, or Desire of more), Healthy or Sickly, Marry'd or Single; nay, whether Tall or Short, Fat or Lean; and of what Trade, Occupation, Profession, Station, Country, Faction, Party, Perswasion, Quality, Age or Condition soever, who have ever made Thinking a Part of their Business or Diversion, and have any thing worthy to impart on these Subjects to the World, according to their several and respective Talents or Genius's, and as the Subject given out hits their Tempers, Humours, or Circumstances, or may be made profitable to the Publick by their particular Knowledge or Experience in the Matter propos'd, to do their utmost on them by such a Time; to the End they may receive the inexpressible and irresistible Pleasure of seeing their Essays allow'd of and relish'd by the rest of Mankind.

I will not prepossess the Reader with too great Expectation of the extraordinary Advantages which must redound to the Publick by these Essays, when the different Thoughts and Observations of all Sorts of Persons, according to their Quality, Age, Sex, Education, Professions, Humours, Manners and Conditions, &c. shall be set out by themselves in the clearest and most genuine Light, and as they themselves wou'd wish to have them appear to the World.

The Thesis *propos'd for the present Exercise of the Adventurers to write* Spectators, *is* MONEY, *on which Subject all Persons are desired to send in their Thoughts within Ten Days after the Date hereof.* T[1]

---

[1] Letters on the subject of money written in response to this number and not used by Steele are printed in Lillie (ii. 281–5, 315–18).

Tuesday, July 29, 1712[1]

Sublatam ex oculis Quærimus invidi.

Hor.

Camilla *to the* SPECTATOR.[2]

Mr. SPECTATOR,   *Venice, July* 10. N. S.

'I TAKE it extremely ill, that you do not reckon conspicuous Persons of your Nation are within your Cognizance, tho' out of the Dominions of *Great-Britain.* I little thought in the green Years of my Life, that I should ever call it an Happiness to be out of dear *England;* but as I grew to Woman, I found my self less acceptable in Proportion to the Encrease of my Merit. Their Ears in *Italy* are so differently formed from the Make of yours in *England,* that I never come upon the Stage, but a general Satisfaction appears in every Countenance of the whole People. When I dwell upon a Note, I behold all the Men accompanying me with Heads enclining, and falling of their Persons on one Side, as dying away with me. The Women too do Justice to my Merit, and no ill-natur'd worthless Creature cries, *The vain Thing,* when I am wrapp'd up in the Performance of my Part, and sensibly touch'd with the Effect my Voice has upon all who hear me. I live here distinguished, as one whom Nature has been liberal to in a graceful Person, an exalted Mein, and Heavenly Voice. These Particularities in this strange Country, are Arguments for Respect and Generosity to her who is possess'd

---

[1] *Motto.* Horace, *Odes,* 3. 24. 32:

But when gone
Wish and gaze after her with longing Eyes.

[2] This letter, which recalls Steele's satirical portrait in *Tatler* 20, purports to come from Mrs. Catherine Tofts, the very successful singer of Italian opera in England and the creator of the role of Camilla in Buononcini's opera. Cibber (*Apology,* chap. xii) wrote that 'the beauty of her fine proportioned figure, and exquisitely sweet, silver tone of her voice, with that peculiar, rapid swiftness of her throat, were perfections not to be imitated by art or labour' (Everyman's Library ed., p. 199). She seems to have lost her reason and retired from the stage early in 1709, while still at the height of her career. She was married to Joseph Smith, the art collector and consul at Venice, and here she lived (as described in this letter) in retirement, although the *Daily Courant* of 25 Apr. 1712 quotes a dispatch from Venice that 'Mrs. Tofts hath been much applauded here for her fine Singing, wherein she hath succeeded all the excellent Voices on the Stage of Venice'. According to Sir John Hawkins's *General History of the Science and Practice of Music* (1776), v. 153, 'she dwelt sequestered from the world in a remote part of the house, and had a large garden to range in, in which she would frequently walk, singing and giving way to that innocent frenzy which had seized her in the earlier part of her life'. She died at Venice in 1756 and is buried there (Grove's *Dictionary of Music*).

of them. The *Italians* see a thousand Beauties I am sensible I have no Pretence to, and abundantly make up to me the Injustice I received in my own Country, of disallowing me what I really had. The Humour of Hissing, which you have among you, I do not know any thing of; and their Applauses are utter'd in Sighs, and bearing a Part at the Cadences of Voice with the Persons who are performing. I am often put in Mind of those complaisant Lines of my own Countryman, when he is calling all his Faculties together to hear *Arabella*;

> Let all be hush'd, each softest Motion cease,
> Be ev'ry loud tumultuous Thought at Peace;
> And ev'ry ruder Gasp of Breath
> Be calm, as in the Arms of Death:
> And thou, most fickle, most uneasy Part,
> Thou restless Wanderer, my Heart,
> Be still; gently, ah! gently leave,
> Thou busy, idle Thing, to heave.
> Stir not a Pulse; and let my Blood,
> That turbulent, unruly Flood,
>   Be softly staid:
> Let me be all but my Attention dead.[1]

The whole City of *Venice* is as still when I am singing, as this polite Hearer was to Mrs. *Hunt*. But when they break that Silence, did you know the Pleasure I am in, when every Man utters his Applause, by calling me aloud the *Dear Creature*, the *Angel*, the *Venus*; *What Attitude she moves with!*—*Hush, she sings again!* We have no boisterous Wits who dare disturb an Audience, and break the publick Peace meerly to shew they dare. Mr. SPECTATOR, I write this to you thus in Haste, to tell you I am very much at Ease here, that I know nothing but Joy; and I will not return, but leave you in *England* to hiss all Merit of your own Growth off the Stage. I know, Sir, you were always my Admirer, and therefore I am yours,

Camilla.

'*P. S.* I am ten times better dress'd than ever I was in *England*.'

Mr. SPECTATOR,

'THE Project in yours of the 11th Instant,[2] of furthering the Correspondence and Knowledge of that considerable Part of

---

[1] The first stanza (omitting four lines at the end) of Congreve's ode, 'On Mrs. Arabella Hunt Singing: Irregular Ode' (1692).   [2] No. 428.

Mankind, the Trading World, cannot but be highly commendable. Good Lectures to young Traders may have very good Effects on their Conduct: But beware you propagate no false Notions of Trade; let none of your Correspondents impose on the World, by putting forth base Methods in a good Light, and glazing them over with improper Terms. I would have no Means of Profit set for Copies to others, but such as are laudable in themselves. Let not Noise be call'd Industry, nor Impudence Courage. Let not good Fortune be imposed on the World for good Management, nor Poverty be call'd Folly; impute not always Bankrupcy to Extravagance, nor an Estate to Foresight: Niggardliness is not good Husbandry, nor Generosity Profusion.

'*Honestus* is a well-meaning and judicious Trader, hath substantial Goods, and trades with his own Stock; husbands his Money to the best Advantage, without taking all Advantages of the Necessities of his Workmen, or grinding the Face of the Poor. *Fortunatus* is stock'd with Ignorance, and consequently with Self-Opinion; the Quality of his Goods cannot but be suitable to that of his Judgment. *Honestus* pleases discerning People, and keeps their Custom by good Usage; makes modest Profit by modest Means, to the decent Support of his Family: whilst *Fortunatus* blustering always, pushes on, promising much, and performing little, with Obsequiousness offensive to People of Sense; strikes at all, catches much the greater Part; raises a considerable Fortune by Imposition on others, to the Discouragement and Ruin of those who trade in the same Way.

'I give here but loose Hints, and beg you to be very circumspect in the Province you have now undertaken: If you perform it successfully, it will be a very great Good; for nothing is more wanting, than that Mechanick Industry were set forth with the Freedom and Greatness of Mind which ought always to accompany a Man of a liberal Education.

From my Shop under the   *Your humble Servant,*
Royal-Exchange, July 14.   R. C.'

Mr. SPECTATOR,   *July* 24, 1712.

'NOTWITHSTANDING the repeated Censures that your Spectatorial Wisdom has passed upon People more remarkable for Impudence than Wit, there are yet some remaining, who pass with the giddy Part of Mankind for sufficient Sharers of the latter, who have nothing but the former Qualification to recommend them. Another timely Animadversion is absolutely necessary; be pleased therefore once for all to let these Gentlemen know, that there is neither Mirth nor good Humour in hooting a young Fellow out of Countenance; nor that it will ever constitute a Wit, to conclude a tart Piece of Buffoonry with a *what makes you blush?* Pray please to inform them again, That to speak what they know is shocking, proceeds from ill Nature, and a Sterility of Brain; especially when the Subject will not admit of Raillery, and their Discourse has no Pretension to Satyr but what is in their Design to disoblige. I should be very glad too if you would take Notice, that a daily Repetition of the same over-bearing Insolence is yet more insupportable, and a Confirmation of very extraordinary Dulness. The sudden Publication of this, may have an Effect upon a notorious Offender of this Kind, whose Reformation would redound very much to the Satisfaction and Quiet of

Your most humble Servant,

F. B.'[1]

T

No. 444   *Wednesday, July 30, 1712*[2]
[STEELE]

Parturiunt montes.
Hor.

IT gives me much Despair in the Design of reforming the World by my Speculations, when I find there always arise, from one Generation to another, successive Cheats and Bubbles, as naturally as Beasts of Prey, and those which are to be their Food. There is hardly a Man in the World, one would think, so ignorant, as not to know that the ordinary quack Doctors, who publish their great Abilities in little brown Billets, distributed to all who pass by, are to a Man Impostors and Murderers; yet such is the Credulity of the Vulgar, and the Impudence of these Professors, that the Affair still

[1] 'Francis Beasniffe, uncle to the present Recorder of Hull, is said to have been the author of this last letter' (Nichols).

[2] *Motto.* Horace, *Ars poetica*, 139: The mountains are in labour.

In the Folio sheets the motto was line 138 from the same poem, . . . *Dignum tanto feret hic promissor hiatu?* (What will this boaster produce in keeping with such mouthing?)—later used as motto for No. 550.

goes on, and new Promises of, what was never done before are made every Day. What aggravates the Jest is, that even this Promise has been made as long as the Memory of Man can trace it, and yet nothing performed, and yet still prevails. As I was passing along to Day, a Paper given into my Hand by a Fellow without a Nose tells us as follows what good News is come to Town, to wit, that there is now a certain Cure for the *French* Disease,[1] by a Gentleman just come from his Travels.

In Russel-Court,[2] *over-against the* Cannon-Ball, *at the* Surgeon's Arms *in* Drury-lane, *is lately come from his Travels a Surgeon who hath practised Surgery and Phisick both by Sea and Land these* 24 *Years. He (by the Blessing) cures the* Yellow Gandice, Green Sickness, Scurvey, Dropsy, Surfeits, long Sea Voyages, Campains, *and* Womens Miscarriages, Lying-In, &c. *as some People that has been lame these* 30 *Years can testify; in short, he cureth all Diseases incident to Men, Women, or Children.*[a]

If a Man could be so indolent as to look upon this Havock of the Humane Species, which is made by Vice and Ignorance, it would be a good ridiculous Work to comment upon the Declaration of this accomplish'd Traveller. There is something unaccountably taking among the Vulgar in those who come from a great Way off. Ignorant People of Quality, as many there are of such, doat excessively this Way; many Instances of which every Man will suggest to himself without my Enumeration of them. The Ignorants of lower Order,

---

a *Children.*] Children. *He hath a Chimical Medicine for all Veneral Malidies whatever;* 3 *Doses of it infallibly cures the most malignant Clap, whether old or new, taking away its Cause;* 7 *Doses of it perfectly eradicates the most confirm'd and stubborn Pox, tho' of the longest Date; for it immediately, as soon as taken into the Body, finds out and unites it self with the Veneral Poyson, in what Part or Parts soever lurking, and presently overcomes and destroys its Principle, carrying off clearly the Recrements of the Tint. In slight Claps, or where the Infection is but just taken,* 1 *Dose frequently carries of the Cause, and at once effects the Cure; and mild Poxes,* 3 *Doses, but even in the worst, seldom more than* 3 *Doses in a Clap, and* 7 *in a Pox is requir'd, tho' the first be attended with Scalding, Cordee, Shankers, Blubo's, &c. and the latter with vehement Pains, Ulcers, Sores, Blotches, &c. even in those Cases the* 1st *Dose always eases, and* 3 *in Claps,* 7th *in Poxes cures, and that without the least Hazard, or Danger of Relapse. Note, For the Good of the Publick, come to his Chamber he bleedeth for* 3 d. *and attends there from* 8 *to* 12, *and from* 2 *till* 6. Fol.[3]

---

[1] A popular term in English for venereal diseases, used as early as 1598 (OED).

[2] For Russel Court see No. 2 (vol. i).

[3] This passage, which appears only in the Folio sheets, reproduces both the illiterate spelling and the specific names of some of the manifestations of venereal disease. Recrements of the Tint, i.e. refuse or dross of the taint. Shankers is an obsolete spelling of chancres, the ulcer occurring in venereal diseases. Blubo is apparently an error for bubo.

who cannot, like the upper Ones, be profuse of their Money to those recommended by coming from a Distance, are no less complaisant than the others, for they venture their Lives from the same Admiration.

The Doctor is lately come from his Travels, and has *practised* both by Sea and Land, and therefore cures the *Green-Sickness, long Sea Voyages, Campains, and Lying-in*. Both by Sea and Land!—I will not answer for the Distempers called *Sea-Voyages and Campains*; but I dare say, those of Green-Sickness and Lying-in might be as well taken Care of if the Doctor had stay'd a-shore. But the Art of managing Mankind, is only to make them stare a little, to keep up their Astonishment, to let nothing be familiar to them, but ever to have something in your Sleeve, in which they must think you are deeper than they are. There is an ingenious Fellow, a Barber, of my Acquaintance, who, besides his broken Fiddle and a dry'd Sea-Monster, has a Twine-Cord, strain'd with two Nails at each End, over his Window, and the Words *Rainy, Dry, Wet*, and so forth, written, to denote the Weather according to the Rising or falling of the Cord. We very great Scholars are not apt to wonder at this: But I observed a very honest Fellow, a Chance-Customer, who sate in the Chair before me to be shaved, fix his Eye upon this miraculous Performance during the Operation upon his Chin and Face. When those and his Head also were clear'd of all Incumbrances and Excrescences, he look'd at the Fish, then at the Fiddle, still grubling[1] in his Pockets, and casting his Eye again at the Twine, and the Words writ on each Side; then alter'd his Mind as to Farthings, and gave my Friend a Silver Six-pence. The Business, as I said, is to keep up the Amazement; and if my Friend had had only the Skeleton and Kitt,[2] he must have been contented with a less Payment. But the Doctor we were talking of, adds to his long Voyages the Testimony of some People *that has been thirty Years lame*. When I received my Paper, a sagacious Fellow took one at the same time, and read till he came to the Thirty Years Confinement of his Friends, and went off very well convinc'd of the Doctor's Sufficiency. You have many of these prodigious Persons, who have had some extraordinary Accident at their Birth, or a great Disaster in some Part of their Lives. Any thing, however foreign from the Business the People want of you, will convince them of your Ability in that you profess. There is

[1] Gruble, i.e. to grope. The last quotation in *OED* is dated 1719.
[2] A small fiddle.

a Doctor in *Mouse-Alley*,[1] near *Wapping*, who sets up for curing Cataracts, upon the Credit of having, as his Bill sets forth, lost an

[1] There was formerly a Mouse Alley in Upper East Smithfield, later Dean Street. It was removed for the formation of St. Katherine's Dock and the adjacent warehouses in 1827. William Wadd (*Nugae chirurgicae*, 1824, p. 72) identifies the quack as the popular oculist, Roger Grant, for whom see No. 472. Advertisements in the *British Apollo* (3 Apr. 1710, &c.), however, show that Grant was living in St. Christopher's Churchyard, behind the Royal Exchange. There are no advertisements for Grant in the *Spectator*, although there are frequent claims for various medical quacks. Among these are Dr. Maynwaringe, at the Moor's Head in Baldwin's Garden, by Gray's Inn, who advertises the cure of 'Internal Apostems, Ulcers, Fistula's, Cancers, Consumptive Wastings, External Cancerous Tumors, or Ulcers cancerated, Scrofulous Tumors, called King's-Evil, Rheumatism, Gout, and such like' (Nos. 426, 431, 436); Richard Moose of Ipswich, who has 'great Success in the Cure of the Gout and Rheumatism', to be heard of at St. Paul's Coffee-house every forenoon and 'at Mr. Richard Bayly's, a Surgeon, in the Middle of Arundel-street near St. Clement's Church in the Strand at all other Times' (Nos. 378, 380); Dr. Greenfield, 'a College Physician', who cuts for the stone and resides 'at the Golden-Wheat-Sheaf in the Old Bayly' (Nos. 352, 362); Paul Protier, 'who hath been mentioned in the Gazette these twenty Years for curing all sorts of Ruptures in Men, Women, and Children, for which he maketh Steel Trusses of an extraordinary Invention'; he 'liveth at the Golden Ball in Cecill street in the Strand' and 'cureth also the a la Mode Disease with all its Symptoms' (No. 240); Thomas Fern, Chyrurgeon, 'who has cur'd several Hundreds of the King's Evil, and all kind of Leprous as well as Scrofulous Humours, for above Twenty Years', and lives in Grange Court near Lincoln's Inn (Nos. 542, 544, 547); Susanna Kirleus, daughter of 'that Eminent Doctor Tho. Kirleus', who 'with his famous Pills and Drink cures the secret Disease, and all Ulcers, Sores, Swellings, Kings Evil, Scabs, Itch, . . .' without the use of mercury; she lives at the Glass Lanthorn in Plough Yard in Gray's Inn Lane and 'gives her Advice in Distempers, to all that write or come to her, gratis' (Nos. 331, 341); Robert Norris, at the Pestle and Mortar near the Middle of Hatton Garden, who offers to treat lunatics (Nos. 602, 603, 604); Mr. Vickers, 'the Clergyman, who cures the King's Evil', and who lives in Sherburn Lane near Lombard Street (No. 361); and several anonymous practitioners, including 'A Regular Physician that has travelled and seen as much of the Venereal Practice, both here and Abroad, as perhaps any one' and who informs the public of a Panacea which is 'as innocent as Bread, agreeable to the Taste, and requires no Confinement'. 'He has left it to be disposed of at Mr. Lovel's at the Sign of the Patten and Perriwig over-against Great Suffolk-street near Charing-cross, at a Guinea a Pot' (Nos. 464, 469, 476, 482, 488, 493, 538).

Many of the nostrums advertised bear the name of the apothecary or quack who 'discovered' them. Among these are 'Mr. Bowden's Issue-Pease and Plaisters', sold by him at the Plough and Harrow, the first House in Chancery Lane next Fleet Street (No. 544); 'Dr. Byfield's Sal Oleosum Vollatile', sold at his House in Salisbury Court near Fleet Street (No. 226, &c., sixteen times in all); 'Doctor Coleburt's most famous Elixir, and Salt of Lemmons' (No. 156); Dr. Tyson's Apoplectick Snuff (No. 348); 'the famous Antirheumatick Tincture, of the late most experienced Chymist Mr. Geo. Wilson', now sold by his widow at her House in Well Yard, near St. Bartholomew's Hospital (Nos. 516, 544); 'the most celebrated Elixir Salutis, commonly call'd Daffy's Elixir' (Nos. 157, 287, 355, 367, 416); a medicine prepared 'by Mr. Perronet, surgeon, at his house in Dyot-street near Bloomsbury', of help to children in teething (No. 117, &c., eleven times in all); 'the Magisterial Gout Pills and Tincture' and 'the famous Drops to prevent Miscarriage', prepared by T. Higgs, Apothecary at the Pestle and Mortar, on Clerkenwell Green (Nos. 301, 305, 308, 312, 318); and others. It is against the background of these medical advertisements in the *Spectator* and the newspapers of the time that Steele's satirical essay is to be read.

Eye in the Emperor's Service. His Patients come in upon this, and he shews the Muster-Roll, which confirms that he was in his Imperial Majesty's Troops; and he puts out their Eyes with great Success. Who would believe that a Man should be a Doctor for the Cure of bursten Children, by declaring that his Father and Grand-father were both bursten?[1] But *Charles Ingoltson*, next Door to the *Harp* in *Barbacan*,[2] has made a pretty Penny[3] by that Asseveration. The Generality go upon their first Conception, and think no further; all the rest is granted. They take it, that there is something un-common in you, and give you Credit for the rest. You may be sure it is upon that I go, when sometimes, let it be to the Purpose or not, I keep a *Latin* Sentence in my Front; and I was not a little pleased when I observed one of my Readers say, casting his Eye on my Twentieth Paper, *More* Latin *still? What a prodigious Scholar is this Man!* But as I have here taken much Liberty with this learned Doctor, I must make up all I have said by repeating what he seems to be in Earnest in, and honestly to promise to those who will not receive him as a great Man; to wit, That from *Eight till Twelve, and from Two till Six, he attends for the Good of the Publick to bleed for Three Pence.*   T[4]

No. 445   *Thursday, July 31, 1712*[5]
[ADDISON]

Tanti non es ais. Sapis, Luperce.
Mart.

THIS is the Day on which many eminent Authors will prob-ably Publish their Last Words.[6] I am afraid that few of our

---

[1] Cf. Beaumont and Fletcher, *The Scornful Lady*, v. iii:

> My eldest boy is half a rogue already:
> He was born bursten; and, your worship knows,
> That is a pretty step to men's compassion.

[2] Barbican. See No. 41 (vol. i).
[3] This is the earliest quotation in *OED* in illustration of the phrase (s.v. *pretty*).
[4] Lillie (ii. 322–8) contains a letter from M. N., on quacks. The writer has made a collection of their 'sanatory manifesto's, whereby I have had the opportunity of observing the grounds of their several pretensions . . .'.
[5] *Motto*. Martial, *Epigrams*, I. 117. 18: You say you are not worth it; you're wise, Lupercus, when you say so.
[6] On the following day, 1 Aug., the new Stamp Act (10 Anne, cap. 19) came into

Weekly Historians, who are Men that above all others delight in War,[1] will be able to subsist under the Weight of a Stamp, and an approaching Peace. A Sheet of Blank Paper that must have this new Imprimatur clapt upon it, before it is qualified to Communicate any thing to the Publick, will make its way in the World but very heavily. In short, the Necessity of carrying a Stamp, and the Improbability of notifying a Bloody Battel will, I am afraid, both concur to the sinking of those thin Folios, which have every other Day retailed to us the History of *Europe* for several Years last past. A Facetious Friend of mine, who loves a Pun, calls this present Mortality among Authors, *The Fall of the Leaf.*

I remember, upon Mr. *Baxter*'s Death,[2] there was Published a Sheet of very good Sayings, inscribed, *The last Words of Mr.* Baxter. The Title sold so great a Number of these Papers, that about a Week after, there came out a second Sheet inscribed, *More last Words of Mr.* Baxter. In the same manner, I have Reason to think, that several Ingenious Writers, who have taken their Leave of the Publick, in farewel Papers, will not give over so, but intend to appear again, tho' perhaps under another Form, and with a different Title. Be that as it will, it is my Business, in this place, to give an Account of my own Intentions, and to acquaint my Reader with the Motives by which I Act, in this great Crisis of the Republick of Letters.[3]

I have been long debating in my own Heart, whether I should throw up my Pen, as an Author that is cashiered by the Act of Parliament, which is to Operate within these Four and Twenty

effect; included in a general bill levying duties on soap, paper, parchment, silk, &c., it imposed a tax of one halfpenny on each half-sheet, and a shilling for every advertisement. Swift writes to Stella on 7 Aug.: 'The Observator is fallen, the Medleys are jumbled together with the Flying-post, the Examiner is deadly sick, the Spectator keeps up, and doubles its price. I know not how long it will hold. Have you seen the red Stamp the Papers are marqued with. Methinks it is worth a halfpenny the stamping it' (*Journal to Stella*, ed. H. Williams, p. 554). The *Spectator* in fact met the tax by raising its price to twopence; other papers adopted similar expedients, the *Daily Courant*, for example, advancing from one penny to three halfpence.

[1] This refers, of course, to the peace treaty pending with France, but the phrase had much currency, owing to the famous sermon of the Bishop of St. Asaph, William Fleetwood—a sermon which he had prepared for delivery before the House of Lords on the general Fast Day (16 Jan. 1712), defending the necessity of the war. The Tory ministry adjourned the House beyond the day fixed for the sermon, so that it was not delivered, but it was published by Samuel Buckley on 19 Jan., *A Sermon on the Fast-Day, January 16, 1711–12, against such as delight in war* (advertisement in *Daily Courant*), to the vexation of the Tories.

[2] Richard Baxter died 8 Dec. 1691.

[3] An early use of this phrase. The first example in *OED* is from Addison's *Dialogue on Medals*, published in 1721.

Hours, or whether I should still persist in laying my Speculations, from Day to Day, before the Publick. The Argument which prevails with me most on the first side of the Question is, that I am informed by my Bookseller he must raise the Price of every single Paper to Two-pence, or that he shall not be able to pay the Duty of it. Now as I am very desirous my Readers should have their Learning as cheap as possible, it is with great Difficulty that I comply with him in this Particular.

However, upon laying my Reasons together in the Balance, I find that those which plead for the Continuance of this Work have much the greater Weight. For, in the First place, in recompence for the Expence to which this will put my Readers, it is to be hoped they may receive from every Paper so much Instruction, as will be a very good Equivalent. And, in order to this, I would not advise any one to take it in, who, after the Perusal of it, does not find himself Two-pence the wiser, or the better Man for it; or who, upon Examination, does not believe that he has had Two penny-worth of Mirth or Instruction for his Mony.

But I must confess there is another Motive which prevails with me more than the former. I consider that the Tax on Paper was given for the Support of the Government; and as I have Enemies, who are apt to pervert every thing I do or say, I fear they wou'd ascribe the laying down my Paper, on such an occasion, to a Spirit of Malecontentedness, which I am resolved none shall ever justly upbraid me with. No, I shall glory in contributing my utmost to the Weal Publick; and if my Country receives Five or Six Pounds a-Day[1] by my Labours, I shall be very well pleased to find my self so useful a Member. It is a receiv'd Maxim, that no Honest Man shou'd enrich himself by Methods that are prejudicial to the Community in which he lives, and by the same Rule I think we may pronounce the Person to deserve very well of his Country-men, whose Labours bring more into the Publick Coffers, than into his own Pocket.

Since I have mentioned the Word Enemies, I must explain my self so far as to acquaint my Reader, that I mean only the insignificant Party Zealots on both sides; Men of such poor narrow Souls, that they are not capable of thinking on any thing but with an Eye to Whig or Tory. During the Course of this Paper, I have been accused by these despicable Wretches of Trimming, Time-serving,

---

[1] This would suggest a daily circulation of 2,400 or 2,880 numbers.

Personal Reflection, secret Satire, and the like. Now, tho' in these my Compositions, it is visible to any Reader of Common Sense, that I consider nothing but my Subject, which is always of an Indifferent Nature; how is it possible for me to write so clear of Party, as not to lie open to the Censures of those who will be applying every Sentence, and finding out Persons and Things in it which it has no regard to?

Several Paltry Scribblers and Declaimers have done me the Honour to be dull upon me in Reflections of this Nature; but notwithstanding my Name has been sometimes traduced by this contemptible Tribe of Men, I have hitherto avoided all Animadversions upon 'em. The truth of it is, I am afraid of making them appear considerable by taking notice of them, for they are like those Imperceptible Insects which are discover'd by the Microscope, and cannot be made the Subject of Observation without being magnified.

Having mentioned those few who have shewn themselves the Enemies of this Paper, I shou'd be very ungrateful to the Publick, did not I at the same time testifie my Gratitude to those who are its Friends, in which number I may reckon many of the most distinguished Persons of all Conditions, Parties and Professions in the Isle of *Great Britain*. I am not so vain as to think this Approbation is so much due to the Performance as to the Design. There is, and ever will be, Justice enough in the World, to afford Patronage and Protection for those who endeavour to advance Truth and Virtue, without regard to the Passions and Prejudices of any particular Cause or Faction. If I have any other Merit in me, it is that I have new-pointed all the Batteries of Ridicule. They have been generally planted against Persons who have appeared Serious rather than Absurd; or at best, have aimed rather at what is Unfashionable than what is Vicious. For my own part, I have endeavoured to make nothing Ridiculous that is not in some measure Criminal. I have set up the Immoral Man as the Object of Derision: In short, if I have not formed a new Weapon against Vice and Irreligion, I have at least shewn how that Weapon may be put to a right use, which has so often fought the Battels of Impiety and Prophaneness.   C

No. 446
[ADDISON]

Friday, August 1, 1712[1]

Quid deceat, quid non; quò Virtus, quò ferat Error.

Hor.

SINCE two or three Writers of Comedy who are now living have taken their Farewell of the Stage,[2] those who succeed them finding themselves incapable of rising up to their Wit, Humour and good Sense, have only imitated them in some of those loose unguarded Strokes, in which they complied with the corrupt Taste of the more Vicious Part of their Audience. When Persons of a low Genius attempt this kind of Writing, they know no Difference between being Merry and being Lewd. It is with an Eye to some of these degenerate Compositions that I have written the following Discourse.[3]

Were our *English* Stage but half so virtuous as that of the *Greeks* or *Romans*, we should quickly see the Influence of it in the Behaviour of all the Politer Part of Mankind. It would not be fashionable to ridicule Religion, or its Professors; the Man of Pleasure would not be the compleat Gentleman; Vanity would be out of Countenance, and every Quality which is Ornamental to Human Nature, wou'd meet with that Esteem which is due to it.

If the *English* Stage were under the same Regulations the *Athenian* was formerly, it would have the same Effect that had, in recommending the Religion, the Government, and Publick Worship of its Country. Were our Plays subject to proper Inspections and Limitations, we might not only pass away several of our vacant Hours in the highest Entertainments; but should always rise from them wiser and better than we sat down to them.

It is one of the most unaccountable things in our Age, that the Lewdness of our Theatre should be so much complained of, so well exposed, and so little redressed. It is to be hoped, that some time or other we may be at leisure to restrain the Licentiousness of the Theatre, and make it contribute its Assistance to the Advancement

---

[1] *Motto.* Horace, *Ars poetica*, 308:

What fit, what not, what excellent or ill. ROSCOMMON.

[2] Congreve, Vanbrugh, and Wycherley may well be intended, who had taken 'their farewell of the stage' some time ago—Congreve with *The Way of the World* in 1700 and *The Judgment of Paris* in 1701, Vanbrugh with *The Mistake* in 1706, and Wycherley with *The Plain Dealer* in 1677.

[3] Cf. Nos. 51 and 65 (vol. i).

of Morality, and to the Reformation of the Age. As Matters stand at present, Multitudes are shut out from this noble Diversion, by reason of those Abuses and Corruptions that accompany it. A Father is often afraid that his Daughter should be ruined by those Entertainments, which were invented for the Accomplishment and Refining of Human Nature. The *Athenian* and *Roman* Plays were written with such a regard to Morality, that *Socrates* used to frequent the one, and *Cicero* the other.

It happened once indeed, that *Cato* dropped into the *Roman* Theatre, when the *Floralia* were to be represented; and as in that Performance, which was a kind of Religious Ceremony, there were several indecent Parts to be acted, the People refused to see them whilst *Cato* was present. *Martial* on this Hint made the following Epigram, which we must suppose was applied to some grave Friend of his, that had been accidentally present at some such Entertainment.

> *Nosses jocosæ dulce cum sacrum Floræ,*
> *Festosque lusus, & licentiam vulgi,*
> *Cur in Theatrum Cato severe venisti?*
> *An Ideo tantum veneras, ut exires?*[1]

> *Why dost thou come, great Censor of thy Age,*
> *To see the loose Diversions of the Stage?*
> *With awful Countenance and Brow severe,*
> *What in the Name of Goodness dost thou here?*
> *See the mixt Crowd! how Giddy, Lewd and Vain!*
> *Didst thou come in but to go out again?*

An Accident of this Nature might happen once in an Age among the *Greeks* or *Romans*; but they were too wise and good to let the constant Nightly Entertainment be of such a Nature, that People of the most Sense and Virtue could not be at it. Whatever Vices are represented upon the Stage, they ought to be so marked and branded by the Poet, as not to appear either laudable or amiable in the Person who is tainted with them. But if we look into the *English* Comedies abovementioned, we would think they were formed upon a quite contrary Maxim, and that this Rule, tho' it held good upon the Heathen Stage, was not to be regarded in Christian Theatres. There is another Rule likewise, which was observed by Authors of

---

[1] Martial, *Epigrams*, 1. 1–4. The translation is Addison's.

Antiquity, and which these Modern Genius's have no regard to, and that was never to chuse an improper Subject for Ridicule. Now a Subject is improper for Ridicule, if it is apt to stir up Horrour and Commiseration rather than Laughter. For this Reason, we do not find any Comedy in so polite an Author as *Terence*, raised upon the Violations of the Marriage Bed. The Falshood of the Wife or Husband has given Occasion to noble Tragedies, but a *Scipio* or a *Lelius* would have looked upon Incest or Murder to have been as proper Subjects for Comedy.[1] On the contrary, Cuckoldom is the Basis of most of our Modern Plays. If an Alderman appears upon the Stage, you may be sure it is in order to be Cuckolded. An Husband that is a little grave or elderly, generally meets with the same Fate. Knights and Baronets, Country-Squires, and Justices of the *Quorum*,[2] come up to Town for no other Purpose. I have seen Poor *Dogget* Cuckolded in all these Capacities.[3] In short, our *English* Writers are as frequently severe upon this Innocent unhappy Creature, commonly known by the Name of a Cuckold, as the Ancient Comick Writers were upon an eating Parasite, or a vain-glorious Soldier.

At the same time the Poet so contrives Matters,[a] that the two Criminals are the Favourites of the Audience. We sit still, and wish well to them through the whole Play, are pleased when they meet with proper Opportunities, and out[b] of humour when they are disappointed. The truth of it is, the accomplished Gentleman upon the *English* Stage, is the Person that is familiar with other Mens Wives, and indifferent to his own; as the Fine Woman is generally a Composition of Sprightliness and Falshood. I do not know whether it proceeds from Barrenness of Invention, Depravation of Manners, or Ignorance of Mankind; but I have often wondered that our ordinary Poets cannot frame to themselves the Idea of a Fine Man who[c] is not a Whore-master, or of a Fine Woman that is not a Jilt.

I have sometimes thought of compiling a System of Ethics out of the Writings of these corrupt Poets, under the Title of *Stage Morality*. But I have been diverted from this Thought, by a Project which

---

[a] contrives Matters,] contrives his Matters, *Fol.*   [b] and out] and are out *Fol.*
[c] who] that *Fol.*

---

[1] The friendship between Scipio Africanus the Younger and Laelius, both men of culture and unimpeachable morals, is commemorated in Cicero's dialogue, *Laelius: De Amicitia.*
[2] See No. 2 (vol. i).
[3] Doggett had played Fondle-Wife, in *The Old Batchelor* of Congreve, at Drury Lane on 13 May—a role which he had created.

has been executed by an Ingenious Gentleman of my Acquaintance. He has composed, it seems, the History of a young Fellow, who has taken all his Notions of the World from the Stage, and who has directed himself in every Circumstance of his Life, and Conversation, by the Maxims and Examples of the Fine Gentle-man in *English* Comedies. If I can prevail upon him to give me a Copy of this new-fashioned Novel, I will bestow on it a Place in my Works, and question not but it may have as good an Effect upon the Drama, as *Don Quixote* had upon Romance.   C

No. 447

[ADDISON]

Saturday, August 2, 1712[1]

φημὶ πολυχρονίην μελέτην ἔμμεναι, φίλε· καὶ δὴ
ταύτην ἀνθρώποισι τελεύτῶσαν φύσιν εἶναι.

THERE is not a Common-Saying which has a better turn of Sense in it, than what we often hear in the Mouths of the Vulgar, that Custom is a second Nature.[2] It is indeed able to form the Man anew, and to give him Inclinations and Capacities altogether different from those he was born with. Dr. *Plot*,[3] in his History of *Staffordshire*, tells us of an Ideot that chancing to live within the Sound of a Clock, and always amusing himself with counting the Hour of the Day whenever the Clock struck, the Clock being

---

[1] *Motto.* Evenus Parius (Winterton's *Poetae Minores Graeci*, ed. 1677, p. 469):

> For Custom of some date, my Friend, foregoes
> Its proper Shape, and second Nature grows.

[2] Apperson traces the proverb back in this form to the early fifteenth century.

[3] Robert Plot (*Natural History of Stafford-shire*, Oxford, 1686, p. 303) quotes the anecdote from Thomas Willis, *De anima brutorum*, part i, cap. 16:

> Next the imperfections of the *body*, follow those of the *mind*; which are so much greater as the *Soule* is more noble than the *body*: those who are void of *understanding* being more helpless and miserable; than such as are either *lame*, *deaf*, or *blind*. Yet even these sometimes have such natural *assistances*, that they can performe things scarce attainable by the quickest parts or most solid understandings. Whereof Dr. *Willis* gives us a most remarkable *instance*, of a certain *Foole* who having been long used to repeat the *strokes* of a *Clock* near which he lived with a loud voice; comeing after to live where there was none, yet retained so strong *impressions* of it, that he could exactly distinguish the *horary distances* and would personate so many *strokes* of the *Clock* with a loud voice as oft as an hour past, successively increasing the *number* of each hour, according as the time required; from which he could not be diverted, by any sort of business they could set him about: being become in a manner a natural *living* Clock, so strongly had *Custom* wrought this upon him.

spoiled by some Accident, the Ideot continued to strike and count the Hour without the help of it,[a] in the same manner as he had done when it was entire. Tho' I dare not vouch for the Truth of this Story, it is very certain that Custom has a Mechanical Effect upon the Body, at the same time that it has a very extraordinary Influence upon the Mind.

I shall in this Paper consider one very remarkable Effect which Custom has upon Human Nature; and which, if rightly observed, may lead us into very useful Rules of Life. What I shall here take notice of in Custom, is its wonderful Efficacy in making every thing pleasant to us. A Person who is addicted to Play or Gaming, tho' he took but little delight in it at first, by degrees contracts so strong an Inclination towards it, and gives himself up so entirely to it, that it seems the only End of his Being. The Love of a retired or a busie Life will grow upon a Man insensibly, as he is conversant in the one or the other, 'till he is utterly unqualified for relishing that to which he has been for some time disused. Nay, a Man may Smoak, or Drink, or take Snuff, 'till he is unable to pass away his Time without it; not to mention how our Delight in any particular Study, Art, or Science, rises and improves in proportion to the Application which we bestow upon it. Thus what was at first an Exercise, becomes at length an Entertainment. Our Employments are changed into our Diversions. The Mind grows fond of those Actions she is accustomed to, and is drawn with Reluctancy from those Paths in which she has been used to walk.

Not only such Actions as were at first Indifferent to us, but even such as were Painful, will by Custom and Practice become pleasant. Sir *Francis Bacon* observes in his Natural Philosophy, that our Taste is never pleased better than with those things which at first created a Disgust in it.[1] He gives particular Instances of Claret, Coffee, and other Liquors, which the Palate seldom approves upon the first

[a] of it,] of the Clock, *Fol.*

[1] Bacon discusses coffee in *Sylva Sylvarum* (7th ed., 1658, p. 155) but does not make this point. Earlier (p. 66) he discusses satiety and appetite in certain foods:

To give the reason of the *Distaste* of *Satiety*, and of the *Pleasure* in *Novelty*; and to distinguish not only in Meats and Drinks, but also in Motions, Loves, Company, Delights, Studies, what they be that *Custome* maketh more gratefull; And what more tedious; were a large Field. But for *Meats*, the Cause is *Attraction*, which is quicker, and more excited towards that which is new, than towards that whereof there remaineth a Relish by former use. And (generally) it is a Rule, that whatsoever is somewhat Ingrate at first, is made Gratefull by *Custome*. But whatsoever is too Pleasing at first, groweth quickly to *satiate*.

Taste; but when it has once got a Relish of them, generally retains it for Life. The Mind is constituted after the same manner, and after having habituated her self to any particular Exercise or Employment, not only loses her first Aversion towards it, but conceives a certain Fondness and Affection for it. I have heard one of the greatest Genius's this Age has produced, who had been trained up in all the Polite Studies of Antiquity, assure me, upon his being obliged to search into several Rolls and Records, that notwithstanding such an Employment was at first very dry and irksome to him, he at last took an incredible Pleasure in it, and preferred it even to the reading of *Virgil* or *Cicero*.[1] The Reader will observe, that I have not here considered Custom as it makes things easie, but as it renders them delightful; and tho' others have often made the same Reflections, it is possible they may not have drawn those Uses from it, with which I intend to fill the remaining Part of this Paper.

If we consider attentively this Property of Human Nature, it may instruct us in very fine Moralities. In the first place, I would have no Man discouraged with that kind of Life or Series of Action, in which the Choice of others, or his own Necessities, may have engaged him. It may perhaps be very disagreeable to him at first; but Use and Application will certainly render it not only less painful, but pleasing and satisfactory.

In the second place, I would recommend to every one that admirable Precept which *Pythagoras* is said to have given to his Disciples, and which that Philosopher must have drawn from the Observation I have enlarged upon. *Optimum, vitæ genus eligito, nam consuetudo faciet jucundissimum*, Pitch upon that Course of Life which is the most Excellent, and Custom will render it the most Delightful.[2] Men, whose Circumstances will permit them to chuse their own way of Life, are inexcusable if they do not pursue that which their Judgment tells them is the most laudable. The Voice of Reason is more to be regarded than the Bent of any present Inclination, since, by the Rule above-mentioned, Inclination will at length come over to Reason, though we can never force Reason to comply with Inclination.

[1] Nichols, followed by later editors, identifies this as a reference to Francis Atterbury, but I have found no confirmation of this.

[2] A maxim frequently cited—by Bacon, essay 'Of Parents and Children'; by Jeremy Taylor, *Holy Dying* (Bohn ed., p. 340); by Tillotson, sermons 6 and 29; &c. In André Dacier's *Life of Pythagoras* (1707), p. 64, it is quoted: 'Chuse always the Way that seems best; how rough and difficult soever it be, Custom will render it easie and agreeable.'

In the third place, this Observation may teach the most sensual and irreligious Man, to overlook those Hardships and Difficulties which are apt to discourage him from the Prosecution of a Virtuous Life. *The Gods*, said *Hesiod*, *have placed Labour before Virtue, the way to her is at first rough and difficult, but grows more smooth and easie the further you advance in it*.[1] The Man who proceeds in it, with Steadiness and Resolution, will in a little time find, that *her Ways are Ways of Pleasantness, and that all her Paths are Peace*.[2]

To enforce this Consideration, we may further observe, that the Practice of Religion will not only be attended with that Pleasure, which naturally accompanies those Actions to which we are habituated, but with those Supernumerary Joys of Heart, that rise from the Consciousness of such a Pleasure, from the Satisfaction of acting up to the Dictates of Reason, and from the Prospect of an happy Immortality.

In the fourth place, we may learn from this Observation which we have made on the Mind of Man, to take particular Care, when we are once settled in a regular Course of Life, how we too frequently indulge our selves in any the most innocent Diversions and Entertainments, since the Mind may insensibly fall off from the Relish of virtuous Actions, and, by degrees, exchange that Pleasure which it takes in the Performance of its Duty, for Delights of a much more inferior and unprofitable Nature.

The last Use which I shall make of this remarkable Property in Human Nature, of being[a] delighted with those Actions to which[b] it is accustomed, is to shew how absolutely necessary it is for us to gain Habits of Virtue in this Life, if we would enjoy the Pleasures of the next. The State of Bliss we call Heaven will not be capable of affecting those Minds, which are not thus qualified for it; we must, in this World, gain a Relish of Truth and Virtue, if we would be able to taste that Knowledge and Perfection, which are to make us happy in the next. The Seeds of those spiritual Joys and Raptures, which are to rise up and flourish in the Soul to all Eternity, must be planted in her, during this her present State of Probation. In short, Heaven is not to be looked upon only as the Reward, but as the natural Effect of a religious Life.

On the other Hand, those evil Spirits, who, by long Custom, have

---

[a] of being] to be *Fol.*   [b] to which] with which *Fol.*

---

[1] *Works and Days*, I. 287-90.   Prov. iii. 17.

contracted in the Body Habits of Lust and Sensuality, Malice and Revenge, an Aversion to every thing that is good, just or laudable, are naturally seasoned and prepared for Pain and Misery. Their Torments have already taken root in them, they cannot be happy when divested of the Body, unless we may suppose, that Providence will, in a manner, create them anew, and work a Miracle in the Rectification of their Faculties. They may, indeed, taste a kind of malignant Pleasure in those Actions to which they are accustomed, whilst in this Life, but when they are removed from all those Objects which are here apt to gratifie them, they will naturally become their own Tormentors, and cherish in themselves those painful Habits of Mind which are called, in Scripture[a] Phrase, the Worm[b] which never dies.[1] This Notion of Heaven and Hell is so very conformable to the Light of Nature, that it was discovered by several of the most exalted Heathens. It has been finely improved by many Eminent Divines of the last Age, as in particular by Arch-Bishop *Tillotson* and Dr. *Sherlock*,[2] but there is none who has raised such noble Speculations upon it, as Dr. *Scott*, in the First Book of his Christian Life, which is one of the finest and most rational Schemes of Divinity that is written in our Tongue, or in any other.[3] That Excellent Author has shewn how every particular Custom and Habit of Virtue will, in its own Nature, produce the Heaven, or a State of Happiness, in him who shall hereafter practise it: As on the contrary, how every Custom or Habit of Vice will be the natural Hell of him in whom it subsists.   C

---

[a] in Scripture] in the Scripture *Fol.*   [b] the Worm] that Worm *Fol.*

---

[1] Mark ix. 44.

[2] Tillotson, Sermons 8, 13, 131. William Sherlock's *Practical Discourse concerning Death* appeared in 1689; his *Practical Discourse concerning a Future Judgment* in 1692; both were frequently reprinted.

[3] Dr. John Scott (1639–95), rector of St. Peter-le-Poor and later (1691) of St. Giles in the Fields. He held a canonry of St. Paul's from 1685 till his death. *The Christian Life* was first published in 1681 and ran through many editions.

No. 448
[STEELE]

Monday, August 4, 1712[1]

Fœdius hoc aliquid quandoque audebis.
Juv.

THE first Steps towards Ill are very carefully to be avoided, for Men insensibly go on when they are once entered, and do not keep up a lively Abhorrence of the least Unworthiness. There is a certain frivolous Falshood that People indulge themselves in, which ought to be had in greater Detestation than it commonly meets with: What I mean is a Neglect of Promises made on small and indifferent Occasions, such as Parties of Pleasure, Entertainments, and sometimes Meetings out of Curiosity in Men of like Faculties to be in each other's Company. There are many Causes to which one may assign this light Infidelity. *Jack Sippet* never keeps the Hour he has appointed to come to a Friends to Dinner, but he is an insignificant Fellow who does it out of Vanity. He could never, he knows, make any Figure in Company, but by giving a little Disturbance at his Entry, and therefore takes Care to drop in when he thinks you are just seated. He takes his Place after having discomposed every Body, and desires there may be no Ceremony; then does he begin to call himself the saddest Fellow, in disappointing so many Places as he was invited to elsewhere. It is the Fop's Vanity to name Houses of better Chear, and to acquaint you that he chose yours out of ten Dinners which he was obliged to be at that Day. The last Time I had the Fortune to eat with him, he was imagining how very fat he should have been had he eaten all he had ever been invited to. But it is impertinent to dwell upon the Manners of such a Wretch as obliges all whom he disappoints, tho' his Circumstances constrain them to be civil to him. But there are those that every one would be glad to see, who fall into the same detestable Habit. It is a merciless thing, that any one can be at Ease, and suppose a Set of People who have a Kindness for him, at that Moment waiting out of Respect to him, and refusing to taste their Food or Conversation with the utmost Impatience. One of these Promisers sometimes shall make his Excuses for not coming at all, so late that half the Company have only to lament, that they have neglected Matters of Moment to meet him whom they find a Trifler.

---

[1] *Motto.* Juvenal, *Satires*, 2. 82: Much greater guilt in time you'll dare to venture on.

They immediately repent for the Value they had for him; and such Treatment repeated, makes Company never depend upon his Promise any more; so that he often comes at the Middle of a Meal, where he is secretly slighted by the Persons with whom he eats, and cursed by the Servants, whose Dinner is delayed by his prolonging their Master's Entertainment. It is wonderful, that Men guilty this Way, could never have observed, that the whiling Time,[1] the gathering together, and waiting a little before Dinner, is the most awkardly passed away of any Part in the four and twenty Hours. If they did think at all, they would reflect upon their Guilt, in lengthening such a Suspension of agreeable Life. The constant offending this Way, has, in a Degree, an Effect upon the Honesty of his Mind who is guilty of it, as common Swearing is a kind of habitual Perjury: It makes the Soul unattentive to what an Oath is, even while it utters it at the Lips. *Phocion* beholding a wordy Orator while he was making a magnificent Speech to the People full of vain Promises, *Methinks,* said he, *I am now fixing my Eyes upon a Cypress Tree; it has all the Pomp and Beauty imaginable in its Branches, Leaves, and Height, but alas it bears no Fruit.*[2]

Tho' the Expectation which is raised by impertinent Promisers is thus barren, their Confidence, even after Failures, is so great, that they subsist by still promising on. I have heretofore discoursed of the insignificant Liar, the Boaster, and the Castle-builder,[3] and treated them as no ill-designing Men, (tho' they are to be placed among the frivolously false ones) but Persons who fall into that Way purely to recommend themselves by their Vivacities; but indeed I cannot let heedless Promisers, tho' in the most minute Circumstances, pass with so slight a Censure. If a Man should take a Resolution to pay only Sums above an hundred Pounds, and yet contract with different People Debts of five and ten, how long can we suppose he will keep his Credit? This Man will as long support his good Name in Business, as he will in Conversation, who without Difficulty makes Assignations which he is indifferent whether he keeps or not.

I am the more severe upon this Vice, because I have been so unfortunate as to be a very great Criminal my self. Sir ANDREW

---

[1] For 'whiling' as participial adjective (of time: passing tediously, tedious) this quotation and the one in No. 522 are the only examples in *OED*.

[2] Plutarch, *Life of Phocion*, 752 AB (also *Moralia*, 188D).

[3] The liar and boaster are dealt with in No. 136 (vol. ii), the castle-builder in No. 167 (vol. ii).

FREEPORT, and all other my Friends, who are scrupulous to Promises of the meanest Consideration imaginable from an Habit of Virtue that Way, have often upbraided me with it. I take Shame upon my self for this Crime, and more particularly for the greatest I ever committed of the Sort, that when as agreeable a Company of Gentlemen and Ladies as ever were got together, and I forsooth, Mr. SPECTATOR, to be of the Party with Women of Merit, like a Booby as I was, mistook the Time of Meeting, and came the Night following. I wish every Fool who is negligent in this Kind, may have as great a Loss as I had in this; for the same Company will never meet more, but are dispersed into various Parts of the World, and I am left under the Compunction that I deserve, in so many different Places to be called a Trifler.

This Fault is sometimes to be accounted for, when desirable People are fearful of appearing precious and reserv'd by Denials; but they will find the Apprehension of that Imputation will betray them into a childish Impotence of Mind, and make them promise all who are so kind to ask it of them. This leads such soft Creatures into the Misfortune of seeming to return Overtures of Good-will with Ingratitude. The first Steps in the Breach of a Man's Integrity are much more important than Men are aware of. The Man who scruples breaking his Word in little Things, would not suffer in his own Conscience so great Pain for Failures of Consequence, as he who thinks every little Offence against Truth and Justice a Disparagement. We should not make any thing we our selves disapprove habitual to us, if we would be sure of our Integrity.

I remember a Falshood of the trivial Sort, tho' not in relation to Assignations, that exposed a Man to a very uneasy Adventure. *Will Trap* and *Jack Stint* were Chamber-fellows in the *Inner-Temple* about 25 Years ago. They one Night sate in the Pit together at a Comedy, where they both observed and liked the same young Woman in the Boxes. Their Kindness for her enter'd both Hearts deeper than they imagined. *Stint* had a good Faculty at writing Letters of Love, and made his Address privately that Way; while *Trap* proceeded in the ordinary Course, by Money and her Waiting-Maid. The Lady gave them both Encouragement, receiving *Trap* into the utmost Favour and answering at the same time *Stint*'s Letters, and giving him Appointments at third Places. *Trap* began to suspect the Epistolary Correspondence of his Friend, and discovered also that *Stint* opened all his Letters which came to their common Lodgings, in order to form his own Assignations. After much Anxiety and Restlesness, *Trap* came to a Resolution, which he thought would break off their Commerce with one another without any hazardous Explanation. He therefore writ a Letter in a feign'd Hand to Mr. *Trap* at his Chambers in the *Temple*. *Stint*, according to Custom, seized and open'd it, and was not a little surpriz'd to find the Inside directed to himself, when, with great Perturbation of Spirit, he read as follows:

Mr. *Stint*,

'YOU have gain'd a slight Satisfaction at the Expence of doing a very heinous Crime. At the Price of a faithful Friend you have obtain'd an inconstant Mistress. I rejoice in this Expedient I have thought of to break my Mind to you, and tell you, You are a base Fellow, by a Means which does not expose you to the Affront except you deserve it. I know, Sir, as criminal as you are, you have still Shame enough to avenge your self against the Hardiness of any one that should publickly tell you of it. I therefore, who have received so many secret Hurts from you, shall take Satisfaction with Safety to my self. I call you Base, and you must bear it, or acknowledge it; I triumph over you that you cannot come at me; nor do I think it dishonourable to come in Armour to assault him, who was in Ambuscade when he wounded me.

'What need more be said to convince you of being guilty of the basest Practice imaginable, than that it is such as has made you liable to be treated after this Manner, while you your self cannot in your own Conscience but allow the Justice of the Upbraidings of

Your Injur'd Friend,

Ralph Trap.'

T

No. 449
[STEELE]

Tuesday, August 5, 1712[1]

... Tibi scriptus, Matrona, libellus.

Mart.

WHEN I reflect upon my Labours for the Publick, I cannot but observe, that Part of the Species, of which I profess my self a Friend and Guardian, is sometimes treated with Severity; that is, there are in my Writings many Descriptions given of ill Persons, and not yet any direct Encomium made of those who are good.[2] When I was convinced of this Error, I could not but immediately call to Mind several of the Fair Sex of my Acquaintance, whose Characters deserve to be transmitted to Posterity in Writings which will long out-live mine: But I do not think that a Reason why I should not give them their Place in my Diurnal as long as it will last. For the Service therefore of my Female Readers, I shall single out some Characters of Maids, Wives and Widows, which deserve the Imitation of the Sex. She who shall lead this small illustrious Number of Heroines shall be the amiable Fidelia.

Before I enter upon the particular Parts of her Character, it is necessary to preface, that she is the only Child of a decrepid Father, whose Life is bound up in hers. This Gentleman has used Fidelia from her Cradle with all the Tenderness imaginable, and has view'd her growing Perfections with the Partiality of a Parent, that soon thought her accomplished above the Children of all other Men, but never thought she was come to the utmost Improvement of which she her self was capable. This Fondness has had very happy Effects upon his own Happiness, for she reads, she dances, she sings, uses her Spinet and Lute to the utmost Perfection: And the Lady's Use of all these Excellencies, is to divert the old Man in his easy Chair, when he is out of the Pangs of a Chronical Distemper. Fidelia is now in the twenty third Year of her Age; but the Application of many Lovers, her vigorous Time of Life, her quick Sense of all that is truly gallant and elegant in the Enjoyment of a plentiful Fortune, are not able to draw her from the Side of her good old Father. Certain it is, that there is no Kind of Affection so pure and angelick as

---

[1] Motto. Martial, Epigrams, 3. 68. 1: A book compil'd for the modest matron's eyes.
[2] Mr. Spectator had published an outstanding encomium in No. 302 (vol. iii), the character of Emilia, by Hughes.

that of a Father to a Daughter. He beholds her both with, and without Regard to her Sex. In Love to our Wives there is Desire, to our Sons there is Ambition; but in that to our Daughters, there is something which there are no Words to express. Her Life is designed wholly domestick, and she is so ready a Friend and Companion, that every thing that passes about a Man, is accompanied with the Idea of her Presence. Her Sex also is naturally so much exposed to Hazard, both as to Fortune and Innocence, that there is, perhaps, a new Cause of Fondness arising from that Consideration also. None but Fathers can have a true Sense of these Sort of Pleasures and Sensations; but my Familiarity with the Father of *Fidelia*, makes me let drop the Words which I have heard him speak, and observe upon his Tenderness towards her.

Fidelia on her Part, as I was going to say, as accomplish'd as she is, with all her Beauty, Wit, Air, and Mien, employs her whole Time in Care and Attendance upon her Father. How have I been charmed to see one of the most beauteous Women the Age has produced on her Knees helping on an old Man's Slipper. Her filial Regard to him is what she makes her Diversion, her Business, and her Glory. When she was asked by a Friend of her deceased Mother to admit of the Courtship of her Son, she answer'd, That she had a great Respect and Gratitude to her for the Overture in Behalf of one so near to her, but that during her Father's Life, she would admit into her Heart no Value for any thing that should interfere with her Endeavour to make his Remains of Life as happy and easy as could be expected in his Circumstances. The Lady admonished her of the Prime of Life with a Smile; which *Fidelia* answered with a Frankness that always attends unfeigned Virtue. *It is true, Madam, there is to be sure very great Satisfactions to be expected in the Commerce of a Man of Honour, whom one tenderly loves; but I find so much Satisfaction in the Reflection, how much I mitigate a good Man's Pains, whose Welfare depends upon my Assiduity about him, that I willingly exclude the loose Gratifications of Passion for the solid Reflections of Duty. I know not whether any Man's Wife, would be allow'd, and (what I still more fear) I know not whether I, a Wife, should be willing, to be as officious[1] as I am at present about my Parent.* The happy Father has her Declaration that she will not marry during his Life, and the Pleasure of seeing that Resolution not uneasy to her. Were one to paint filial Affection in its utmost Beauty, he could not have a more lively Idea of it than in beholding

---

[1] See No. 108 (vol. i).

Fidelia serving her Father at his Hours of Rising, Meals, and Rest.

When the general Crowd of female Youth are consulting their Glasses, preparing for Balls, Assemblies, or Plays; for a young Lady, who could be regarded among the foremost in those Places, either for her Person, Wit, Fortune, or Conversation, and yet contemn all these Entertainments, to sweeten the heavy Hours of a decrepid Parent, is a Resignation truly heroick. *Fidelia* performs the Duty of a Nurse with all the Beauty of a Bride; nor does she neglect her Person, because of her Attendance on him, when he is too ill to receive Company, to whom she may make an Appearance.

Fidelia, who gives him up her Youth, does not think it any great Sacrifice to add to it the Spoiling of her Dress. Her Care and Exactness in her Habit, convince her Father of the Alacrity of her Mind; and she has of all Women the best Foundation for affecting the Praise of a seeming Negligence. What adds to the Entertainment of the good old Man is, that *Fidelia*, where Merit and Fortune cannot be overlook'd by Epistolary Lovers, reads over the Accounts of her Conquests, plays on her Spinet the gayest Airs, (and while she is doing so, you would think her formed only for Gallantry) to intimate to him the Pleasures she despises for his Sake.

Those who think themselves the Patterns of good Breeding and Gallantry, would be astonished to hear, that in those Intervals when the old Gentleman is at Ease, and can bear Company, there are at his House, in the most regular Order, Assemblies of People of the highest Merit; where there is Conversation without Mention of the Faults of the Absent, Benevolence between Men and Women without Passion, and the highest Subjects of Morality treated of as natural and accidental Discourse: All which is owing to the Genius of *Fidelia*, who at once makes her Father's Way to another World easy, and her self capable of being an Honour to his Name in this.

Mr. SPECTATOR,

'I WAS the other Day at the *Bear-Garden*,[1] in hopes to have seen your short Face; but not being so fortunate, I must tell you by way of Letter, That there is a Mystery among the Gladiators which has escaped your Spectatorial Penetration. For being in a Box at an Ale-house, near that renowned Seat of Honour above-mentioned, I over-heard two Masters of the Science agreeing to quarrel on the next Opportunity. This was to happen in the Company of a Set of

---

[1] See No. 436.

the Fraternity of Basket-Hilts, who were to meet that Evening. When this was settled, one asked the other, Will you give Cuts, or receive? The other answered, Receive. It was replied, Are you a passionate Man? No, provided you cut no more nor no deeper than we agree. I thought it my Duty to acquaint you with this, that the People may not pay their Money for Fighting and be cheated.

Your humble Servant,
Scabbard Rusty.'

T

No. 450   *Wednesday, August 6, 1712*[1]
[STEELE]

> *. . . Quærenda pecunia primum*
> *Virtus post nummos.*

Mr. SPECTATOR,[2]
' ALL Men, through different Paths, make at the same common thing, *Money*; and it is to her we owe the Politician, the Merchant, and the Lawyer; nay, to be free with you, I believe to that also we are beholden for our *Spectator*. I am apt to think, that could we look into our own Hearts, we should see Money ingraved in them in more lively and moving Characters than Self-Preservation; for who can reflect upon the Merchant hoisting Sail in a doubtful Pursuit of her, and all Mankind sacrificing their Quiet to her, but must perceive that the Characters of Self-Preservation (which were doubtless originally the brightest) are sullied, if not wholly defaced; and that those of Money (which at first was only valuable as a Mean to Security) are of late so brightened, that the Characters of Self-Preservation, like a less Light set by a greater, are become almost imperceptible? Thus has Money got the upper Hand of what all Mankind formerly thought most dear, *viz.* Security; and I wish

[1] *Motto.* Horace, *Epistles*, I. I. 53–54 (altered):
> Gold must first be sought,
> Then Virtue. CREECH.

[2] The letter, whether contributed, or written by Steele, is designed as an answer to the request made in No. 442.

I could say she had here put a Stop to her Victories; but, alass! common Honesty fell a Sacrifice to her. This is the Way Scholastick Men talk of the greatest Good in the World; but I, a Tradesman, shall give you another Account of this Matter in the plain Narrative of my own Life. I think it proper, in the first Place, to acquaint my Readers, that since my setting out in the World, which was in the Year 1660, I never wanted Money; having begun with an indifferent good Stock in the Tobacco Trade, to which I was bred; and by the continual Successes it has pleased Providence to bless my Endeavours with, am at last arrived at what they call a *Plumb*.[1] To uphold my Discourse in the Manner of your Wits or Philosophers, by speaking fine things, or drawing Inferences, as they pretend, from the Nature of the Subject, I account it vain; having never found any thing in the Writings of such Men, that did not savour more of the Invention of the Brain, or what is stiled Speculation, than of sound Judgment or profitable Observation. I will readily grant indeed, that there is what the Wits call Natural in their Talk; which is the utmost those curious Authors can assume to themselves, and is indeed all they endeavour at, for they are but lamentable Teachers. And what, I pray, is Natural? That which is Pleasing and Easy: And what are Pleasing and Easy? Forsooth, a new Thought or Conceit dressed up in smooth quaint Language, to make you smile and wag your Head, as being what you never imagined before, and yet wonder why you had not; meer frothy Amusements! fit only for Boys or silly Women to be caught with.

'It is not my present Intention to instruct my Readers in the Methods of acquiring Riches, that may be the Work of another Essay; but to exhibit the real and solid Advantages I have found by them in my long and manifold Experience: nor yet all the Advantages of so worthy and valuable a Blessing, (for who does not know or imagine the Comforts of being warm[2] or living at Ease? and that Power and Preheminence are their inseparable Attendants?) but only to instance the great Supports they afford us under the severest Calamities and Misfortunes; to shew that the Love of them is a special Antidote against Immorality and Vice, and that the same does likewise naturally dispose Men to Actions of Piety and Devotion: All which I can make out by my own Experience, who think

---

[1] A plum is defined in the 1789 edition as 'a cant word used by commercial people, to signify an £100,000'. The earliest quotation in *OED* is dated 1689–1702.
[2] See No. 242 (vol. ii).

my self no ways particular from the rest of Mankind, nor better nor worse by Nature than generally other Men are.

'In the Year 1665, when the Sickness was, I lost by it my Wife and two Children, which were all my Stock. Probably I might have had more, considering I was married between 4 and 5 Years; but finding her to be a teeming Woman, I was careful, as having then little above a Brace of thousand Pounds to carry on my Trade and maintain a Family with. I loved them as usually Men do their Wives and Children, and therefore could not resist the first Impulses of Nature on so wounding a Loss; but I quickly rouzed my self, and found Means to alleviate, and at last conquer my Affliction, by reflecting how that she and her Children having been no great Expence to me, the best Part of her Fortune was still left; that my Charge being reduced to my self, a Journeyman, and a Maid, I might live far cheaper than before; and that being now a childless Widower, I might perhaps marry a no less deserving Woman, and with a much better Fortune than she brought, which was but 800 *l*. And to convince my Readers that such Considerations as these were proper and apt to produce such an Effect, I remember it was the constant Observation at that deplorable Time, when so many Hundreds were swept away daily, that the Rich ever bore the Loss of their Families and Relations far better than the Poor; the latter having little or nothing before-hand, and living from Hand to Mouth, placed the whole Comfort and Satisfaction of their Lives in their Wives and Children, and were therefore inconsolable.

'The following Year happened the Fire; at which Time, by good Providence, it was my Fortune to have converted the greatest Part of my Effects into ready Money, on the Prospect of an extraordinary Advantage which I was preparing to lay Hold on. This Calamity was very terrible and astonishing, the Fury of the Flames being such, that whole Streets, at several distant Places, were destroyed at one and the same Time, so that (as it is well known) almost all our Citizens were burnt out of what they had. But what did I then do? I did not stand gazing on the Ruins of our noble Metropolis; I did not shake my Head, wring my Hands, sigh, and shed Tears; I considered with my self what cou'd this avail; I fell a plodding what Advantages might be made of the ready Cash I had, and immediately bethought my self that wonderful Pennyworths might be bought of the Goods that were saved out of the Fire. In short, with about 2000 *l*. and a little Credit, I bought as much Tobacco as raised my Estate to the Value of 10000 *l*. I then *looked on the Ashes of our City, and the Misery of its late Inhabitants, as an Effect of the just Wrath and Indignation of Heaven towards a sinful and perverse People.*[1]

'After this I married again, and that Wife dying, I took another; but both proved to be idle Baggages; the first gave me a great deal of Plague and Vexation by her Extravagancies, and I became one of the By-words of the City. I knew it would be to no manner of Purpose to go about to curb the Fancies and Inclinations of Women, which fly out the more for being restrain'd; but what I cou'd I did. I watch'd her narrowly, and by good Luck found her in the Embraces (for which I had two Witnesses with me) of a wealthy Spark of the Court-end of the Town; of whom I recover'd 15000 Pounds, which made me Amends for what she had idly squander'd, and put a Silence to all my Neighbours, taking off my Reproach by the Gain they saw I had by it. The last died about two Years after I marry'd her, in Labour of three Children. I conjecture they were begotten by a Country Kinsman of hers, whom, at her Recommendation, I took into my Family, and gave Wages to as a Journey-man. What this Creature expended in Delicacies and high Diet with her Kinsman (as well as I could compute by the Poulterers, Fishmongers, and Grocers Bills) amounted in the said two Years to One hundred eighty six Pounds, four Shillings, and five Pence Half-penny. The fine Apparel, Bracelets, Lockets, and Treats, *&c.* of the other, according to the best Calculation, came in three Years and about three Quarters to Seven hundred forty four Pounds, seven Shillings and nine Pence. After this I resolved never to marry more, and found I had been a Gainer by my Marriages, and the Damages granted me for the Abuses of my Bed, (all Charges deducted) Eight thousand three hundred Pounds within a Trifle.

'I come now to shew the good Effects of the Love of Money on the Lives of Men towards rendring them honest, sober, and religious. When I was a young Man, I had a Mind to make the best of my Wits, and over-reach'd a Country Chap[2] in a Parcel of unsound Goods; to whom, upon his upbraiding, and threatning to expose me for it, I return'd the Equivalent of his Loss; and upon his good Advice, wherein he clearly demonstrated the Folly of such Artifices,

---

[1] This looks like a quotation, but I have not identified it.
[2] i.e. chapman, purchaser, customer. According to *OED* the word came into vulgar use in the end of the sixteenth century, but it is rare in books, even in the dramatists, before 1700. It is not recognized by Johnson, but is in Bailey's Dictionary (1731).

which can never end but in Shame, and the Ruin of all Correspondence, I never after transgress'd. Can your Courtiers, who take Bribes, or your Lawyers or Physicians in their Practice, or even the Divines who intermeddle in worldly Affairs, boast of making but one Slip in their Lives, and of such a thorough and lasting Reformation? Since my coming into the World I do not remember I was ever overtaken in Drink, save nine times, one at the Christening of my first Child, thrice at our City Feasts, and five times at driving of Bargains. My Reformation I can attribute to nothing so much as the Love and Esteem of Money; for I found my self to be extravagant in my Drink, and apt to turn Projector, and make rash Bargains. As for Women, I never knew any, except my Wives: For my Reader must know, and it is what he may confide in as an excellent Recipe, That the Love of Business and Money is the greatest Mortifier of inordinate Desires imaginable, as employing the Mind continually in the careful Oversight of what one has, in the eager Quest after more, in looking after the Negligences and Deceits of Servants, in the due Entring and Stating of Accounts, in hunting after Chaps, and in the exact Knowledge of the State of Markets; which Things whoever thoroughly attends, will find enough and enough to employ his Thoughts on every Moment of the Day: So that I cannot call to Mind, that in all the Time I was a Husband, which, off and on, was about twelve Years, I ever once thought of my Wives but in Bed. And, lastly, for Religion, I have ever been a constant Churchman, both Forenoons and Afternoons on *Sundays*, never forgetting to be thankful for any Gain or Advantage I had had that Day; and on *Saturday* Nights, upon casting up my Accounts, I always was grateful for the Sum of my Week's Profits, and at *Christmas* for that of the whole Year. It is true perhaps, that my Devotion has not been the most fervent; which, I think, ought to be imputed to the Evenness and Sedateness of my Temper, which never would admit of any Impetuosities of any Sort: And I can remember, that in my Youth and Prime of Manhood, when my Blood ran brisker, I took greater Pleasure in Religious Exercises than at present, or many Years past, and that my Devotion sensibly declined as Age, which is dull and unweildy, came upon me.

'I have, I hope, here proved, that the Love of Money prevents all Immorality and Vice; which if you will not allow, you must, that the Pursuit of it obliges Men to the same Kind of Life as they would follow if they were really virtuous: Which is all I have to say at present, only recommending to you, that you would think of it, and turn ready Wit into ready Money as fast as you can. I conclude,

Your Servant,

Ephraim Weed.'

T

No. 451

Thursday, August 7, 1712[1]

[ADDISON]

> . . . *Jam sævus apertam*
> *In rabiem cœpit verti jocus, & per honestas*
> *Ire minax impunè domos* . . .

THERE is nothing so scandalous to a Government, and detestable in the Eyes of all good Men, as Defamatory Papers and Pamphlets; but at the same time there is nothing so difficult to tame, as a Satyrical Author. An angry Writer, who cannot[a] appear in Print, naturally vents his Spleen in Libels and Lampoons. A gay old Woman, says the Fable, seeing all her Wrinkles represented in a large Looking-glass, thew it upon the Ground in a Passion, and broke it into a thousand Pieces; but as she was afterwards surveying the Fragments with a spiteful kind of Pleasure, she could not forbear uttering her self in the following Soliloquy. What have I got by this revengeful Blow of mine, I have only multiplied my Deformity, and see an hundred ugly Faces, where before I saw but one.[2]

It has been proposed, *to oblige every Person that writes a Book, or a Paper, to swear himself the Author of it, and enter down in a Publick Register his Name and Place of Abode.*

This, indeed, would have effectually suppressed all printed Scandal, which generally appears under borrowed Names, or under none

---

 a cannot] can't *Fol.*

---

[1] *Motto.* Horace, *Epistles*, 2. 1. 148–50 (altered):

> At last they shew'd their Teeth, and sharply bit,
> And *Raillery* usurpt the Place of *Wit.*
> Good Persons were abus'd, and suffer'd wrong,
> They loudly talkt, no Law to curb their Tongue. CREECH.

[2] Cf. Burton, *Anatomy of Melancholy*, II. iii. 7: 'And, as *Praxiteles* did by his glass, when he saw a scurvy face in it, break it in pieces: but for that one, he saw many more as bad in a moment. . . .'

at all. But it is to be feared, that such an Expedient would not only destroy Scandal, but Learning. It would operate promiscuously, and root up the Corn and Tares, together. Not to mention some of the most Celebrated Works of Piety, which have proceeded from Anonymous Authors, who have made it their Merit to convey to us so great a Charity in secret. There are few Works of Genius that come out at first with the Author's Name. The Writer generally makes a Tryal of them in the World before he owns them; and, I believe, very few, who are capable of Writing, would set Pen to Paper, if they knew, before Hand, that they must not publish their Productions but on such Conditions. For my own part, I must declare the Papers I present the Publick are like Fairy Favours, which shall last no longer than while the Author is concealed.[1]

That which makes it particularly difficult to restrain these Sons of Calumny and Defamation is, that all Sides are equally guilty of it, and that every dirty Scribler is countenanced by great Names, whose Interests he propagates by such vile and infamous Methods. I have never yet heard of a Ministry, who have inflicted an exemplary Punishment on an Author that has supported their Cause with Falshood and Scandal, and treated, in a most cruel manner, the Names of those who have been look'd upon as their Rivals and Antagonists. Would a Government set an everlasting Mark of their Displeasure upon one of those infamous Writers, who makes his Court to them by tearing to Pieces the Reputation of a Competitor, we should quickly see an End put to this Race of Vermin, that are a Scandal to Government, and a Reproach to Human Nature. Such a Proceeding would make a Minister of State shine in History, and would fill all Mankind with a just Abhorrence of Persons[a] who should treat him unworthily, and employ against him those Arms which he scorn'd to make use of against his Enemies.

I cannot think that any one will be so unjust as to imagine what I have here said, is spoken with a Respect to any Party or Faction. Every one who has in him the Sentiments either of a Christian or a Gentleman, cannot but be highly offended at this wicked and ungenerous Practice which is so much in use among us at present, that it is become a kind of National Crime, and[b] distinguishes us

---

[a] of Persons] of those Persons *Fol*.   [b] and] which *Fol*.

---

[1] 'These Fayery favours are lost when not concealed' (Dryden, *Spanish Friar*, II. 21, quoted in *OED*).

from all the Governments that lie about us. I cannot but look upon the finest Strokes of Satyr which are aimed at particular Persons, and which are supported even with the Appearances of Truth, to be the Marks of an evil Mind, and highly Criminal in themselves. Infamy, like other Punishments, is under the direction and distribution of the Magistrate, and not of any private Person. Accordingly we learn from a Fragment of *Cicero*, that tho' there were[a] very few Capital Punishments in the twelve Tables, a Libel or Lampoon which took away the good Name of another, was to be punished by Death.[1] But this is far from being our Case. Our Satyr is nothing but Ribaldry, and *Billingsgate*. Scurrility passes for Wit; and he who can call Names in the greatest Variety of Phrases, is looked upon to have the shrewdest Pen. By this means the Honour of Families is ruin'd, the highest Posts and greatest Titles are rendered cheap and vile in the Sight of the People; the noblest Virtues, and most exalted Parts, exposed to the Contempt of the Vicious and the Ignorant. Should a Foreigner, who knows nothing of our private Factions, or one who is to act his part in the World, when our present Heats and Animosities are forgot, should, I say, such an one form to himself a Notion of the greatest Men of all Sides in the *British* Nation, who are now living, from the Characters which are given them in some or other of those abominable Writings which are daily Published among us, what a Nation of Monsters must we appear![b]

As this cruel Practice tends to the utter Subversion of all Truth and Humanity among us, it deserves the utmost Detestation and Discouragement of all who have either the Love of their Country, or the Honour of their Religion, at Heart. I would therefore earnestly recommend it to the Consideration of those who deal in these pernicious Arts of Writing; and of those who take pleasure in the Reading of them. As for the first, I have spoken of them in former Papers, and have not stuck to rank them with the Murderer and Assassin. Every honest Man sets as high a Value upon a good Name, as upon Life it self; and I cannot but think that those who privily assault the one, would destroy the other, might they do it with the same Secrecy and Impunity.

As for Persons who take Pleasure in the reading and dispersing of such detestable Libels, I am afraid they fall very little short of the

---

[a] were] are *Fol.*   [b] appear!] appear. *Fol.*

---

[1] Cicero, *De republica*, 4. 10. 12.

Guilt of the first Composers. By a Law of the Emperors *Valentinian* and *Valens*, it was made Death for any Person not only to write a Libel, but if he met with one by chance, not to tear or burn it. But because I would not be thought singular in my Opinion of this matter, I shall conclude my Paper with the Words of Monsieur *Bayle*, who was a Man of great Freedom of Thought, as well as of exquisite Learning and Judgment.[1]

'I cannot imagine, that a Man who disperses a Libel is less desirous of doing Mischief than the Author himself. But what shall we say of the Pleasure which a Man takes in the reading of a Defamatory Libel? Is it not an heinous Sin in the Sight of God? We must distinguish in this point. This Pleasure is either an agreeable Sensation we are affected with, when we meet with a witty Thought which is well expressed, or it is a Joy which we conceive from the Dishonour of the Person who is defamed. I will say nothing to the first of these Cases; for perhaps some would think that my Morality is not severe enough, if I should affirm that a Man is not Master of those agreeable Sensations, any more than of those occasioned by Sugar or Honey when they touch his Tongue; but as to the second, every one will own that Pleasure to be a heinous Sin. The Pleasure in the first case is of no continuance; it prevents our Reason and Reflection, and may be immediately follow'd by a secret Grief, to see our Neighbour's Honour blasted. If it does not cease immediately, it is a Sign that we are not displeased with the Ill-nature of the Satyrist, but are glad to see him defame his Enemy by all kinds of Stories; and then we deserve the Punishment to which the Writer of the Libel is subject. I shall here add the Words of a Modern Author.[2] *St.* Gregory *upon excommunicating those Writers who had dishonoured* Castorius, *does not except those who read their Works; because,* says he, *if Calumnies have always been the delight of the Hearers, and a gratification of those Persons who have no other Advantage over honest Men, is not he who takes Pleasure in reading them as guilty as he who composed them?* It is an uncontested Maxim, that they who approve an Action would certainly do it if they could; that is, if some reason of Self-love did not hinder them. There is no difference, says *Cicero*, between advising a Crime, and approving it when committed.[3] The *Roman* Law confirmed this

---

[1] Addison quotes, with a few verbal changes, a portion of the final paragraph of Bayle's 'Dissertation concerning defamatory libels', appended to the *Dictionary* (London, 1710, vol. iv, p. xxvi).

[2] Clavigny de saint Honorine, *Usage des livres suspects*, pp. 41–42 (Bayle's note).

[3] *Philippics*, 2. 12. 29.

Maxim, having subjected the Approvers and Authors of this Evil to the same Penalty. We may therefore conclude, that those who are pleased with reading Defamatory Libels, so far as to approve the Authors and Dispersers of them, are as guilty as if they had composed them; for if they do not write such Libels themselves, it is because they have not the Talent of Writing, or because they will run no Hazard.'

The Author produces other Authorities to confirm his Judgment in this Particular.   C

No. 452   *Friday, August 8, 1712*[1]
[ADDISON; POPE]

Est natura Hominum Novitatis avida.
Plin. apud Lill.

THERE is no Humour in my Countrymen, which I am more enclined to wonder at, than their general Thirst after News. There are about half a Dozen Ingenious Men, who live very plentifully upon this Curiosity of their Fellow-Subjects. They all of them receive the same Advices from abroad, and very often in the same Words; but their way of Cooking it is so different, that there is no Citizen, who has an Eye to the Publick Good, that can leave the Coffee-house with Peace of Mind, before he has given every one of them a Reading. These several Dishes of News are so very agreeable to the Palate of my Countrymen, that they are not only pleased with them when they are served up hot, but when they are again set cold before them, by those penetrating Politicians who oblige the Publick with their Reflections and Observations upon every Piece of Intelligence that is sent us from abroad. The Text is given us by one Sett of Writers, and the Comment by another.

But notwithstanding we have the same Tale told us in so many different Papers, and if Occasion requires in so many Articles of the same Paper; Notwithstanding in a scarcity of Foreign Posts we hear the same Story repeated, by different Advices from *Paris, Brussels,*

---

[1] *Motto.* Pliny the Elder, *Natural History,* 12. 5. Quoted in Lilly's Latin Grammar, where it is cited in illustration of the genitive after adjectives (ed. 1759, p. 77): Human nature is greedy for novelty.

the *Hague*, and from every great Town in *Europe*; Notwithstanding the Multitude of Annotations, Explanations, Reflections, and various Readings which it passes through, our Time lies heavy on our Hands till the Arrival of a fresh Mail: We long to receive further Particulars, to hear what will be the next Step, or what will be the Consequences of that which has been already taken. A Westerly Wind keeps the whole Town in Suspence, and puts a stop to Conversation.

This general Curiosity has been raised and inflamed by our late Wars, and, if rightly directed, might be of good use to a Person who has such a Thirst awakened in him. Why should not a Man, who takes Delight in reading every thing that is new, apply himself to History, Travels, and other Writings of the same kind, where he will find perpetual Fuel for his Curiosity, and meet with much more Pleasure and Improvement, than in these Papers of the Week?[a] An honest Tradesman, who languishes a whole Summer in expectation of a Battel, and perhaps is balked at last, may here meet with half a dozen in a Day. He may read the News of a whole Campain, in less time than he now bestows upon the Products of any single Post. Fights, Conquests and Revolutions lie thick together. The Reader's Curiosity is raised and satisfied every Moment, and his Passions disappointed or gratified, without being detained in a State of Uncertainty from Day to Day, or lying at the Mercy of Sea and Wind.[b] In short, the Mind is not here kept in a perpetual Gape after Knowledge, nor punished with that Eternal Thirst, which is the Portion of all our Modern News-mongers and Coffee-house Politicians.

All Matters of Fact, which a Man did not know before, are News to him; and I do not see how any Haberdasher in *Cheapside* is more concerned in the present Quarrel of the Cantons,[1] than he was in that of the League.[2] At least, I believe every one will allow me, it is of more Importance to an *Englishman* to know the History of his Ancestors, than that of his Contemporaries, who live upon the Banks of the *Danube* or the *Borysthenes*.[3] As for those who are of another

---

[a] Week?] Week. *Fol.*   [b] Sea and Wind.] Sea, or Wind. *Fol.*

---

[1] This dispute between the cantons of Zürich and Bern on the one hand, and the five Roman Catholic cantons who took the part of the Abbot of St. Gall on the other, is referred to again in No. 481. The London newspapers contain frequent references to the quarrel in the spring and summer of 1712.
[2] The Holy League, formed in the Roman Catholic interest in 1576 with the Guise family at its head, opposed Henry of Navarre.
[3] The ancient name for the Dnieper.

Mind, I shall recommend to them the following Letter, from[a] a Projector, who is willing to turn a Penny by this remarkable Curiosity of his Countrymen.[1]

Mr. SPECTATOR,

'YOU must have observed, that Men who frequent Coffeehouses, and delight in News, are pleased with every thing that is Matter of Fact, so it be what they have not heard before. A Victory, or a Defeat, are equally agreeable to them. The shutting of a Cardinal's Mouth pleases them one Post, and the opening of it another.[2] They are glad to hear the *French* Court is removed to *Marli,* and are afterwards as much delighted with its Return to *Versailles.*[3] They read the Advertisements with the same Curiosity as the Articles of Publick News; and are as pleased to hear of a Pyebald Horse that is stray'd out of a Field near *Islington,* as of a whole Troop that has been engaged in any Foreign Adventure. In short, they have a Relish for every thing that is News, let the matter of it be what it will; or to speak more properly, they are Men of a Voracious Appetite, but no Taste. Now, Sir, since the great Fountain of News, I mean the War, is very near being dried up; and since these Gentlemen have contracted such an inextinguishable Thirst after it; I have taken their Case and my own into Consideration, and have thought of a Project which may turn to the Advantage of us both. I have Thoughts of Publishing a daily Paper, which shall comprehend in it all the most remarkable Occurrences in[b] every little Town, Village and Hamlet, that lie within ten Miles of *London,* or in other Words, within the Verge of the Penny-Post.[4] I have pitched upon this Scene of Intelligence for two Reasons; first, because the Carriage of Letters will be very cheap; and secondly, because I may receive them every Day. By this means my Readers will have their News fresh and fresh,[5] and many worthy Citizens, who cannot Sleep with

---

[a] from] which comes from *Fol.*   [b] in] that pass in *Fol.*

---

[1] For Pope's authorship of this letter see No. 457.

[2] In the secret consistory held at the consecration of a cardinal, the Pope closes the mouth of the new cardinal, as a symbol of the discretion he must observe; later he opens the cardinal's mouth, again to symbolize the cardinal's privilege and duty of expressing his opinion and voting. The *London Gazette* of 19 June 1712 quotes a dispatch from Venice, 10 June, N.S.: 'They write from Rome, that on the Thirtieth of the last Month, the Pope performed the Ceremony of shutting the Mouth of four new Cardinals, who were then in Town.'

[3] See No. 305 (vol. iii).   [4] See No. 148 (vol. ii).

[5] *OED* notes this reduplication of the word as common at this time.

any Satisfaction at present, for want of being informed how the World goes, may go to Bed contentedly, it being my Design to put out my Paper every Night at nine a Clock precisely. I have already established Correspondencies in these several Places, and received very good Intelligence.[1]

'By my last Advices from *Knights-bridge* I hear that a Horse was clapped into the Pound on the third Instant, and that he was not released when the Letters came away.

'We are inform'd from *Pankridge*, that a dozen Weddings were lately celebrated in the Mother Church of that Place, but are referred to their next Letters for the Names of the Parties concerned.[2]

'Letters from *Brompton* advise, That the Widow *Blight* had received several Visits from *John Milldew*, which affords great matter of Speculation in those Parts.

'By a Fisherman which lately touched at *Hammersmith*, there is Advice from *Putney*, that a certain Person well known in that Place, is like to lose his Election for Church-warden; but this being Boat News, we cannot give entire Credit to it.

'Letters from *Paddington* bring little more, than that *William Squeak*, the Sow-gelder, passed through that Place the 5th Instant.

'They advise from *Fulham*, that things remained there in the same State they were. They had Intelligence, just as the Letters came away, of a Tub of excellent Ale just set abroach at *Parsons Green*; but this wanted confirmation.

'I have here, Sir, given you a Specimen of the News with which I intend to entertain the Town, and which, when drawn up regularly in the form of a News Paper, will, I doubt not, be very acceptable to many of those Publick-Spirited Readers, who take more delight in acquainting themselves with other Peoples Business than their own. I hope a Paper of this kind, which lets us know what is done near home, may be more useful to us, than those which are filled with Advices from *Zug* and *Bender*,[3] and make some Amends for that Dearth of Intelligence, which we may justly apprehend from times of Peace. If I find that you receive this Project favourably, I will

---

[1] This is the earliest quotation in *OED* to illustrate the obsolete meaning of *correspondency*, ' a corresponding agency'.

[2] The old church of St. Pancras in the Fields was at this time a fashionable place for weddings.

[3] Zug was one of the Roman Catholic Swiss cantons (cf. paragraph 4 of this number). Bender is the modern Tighina, in Bessarabia; here Charles XII of Sweden took refuge with the Grand Vizier in 1711.

shortly trouble you with one or two more; and in the mean time am, most worthy Sir, with all due Respect,

Your most obedient,
and most humble Servant.'

C

No. 453
[ADDISON]

Saturday, August 9, 1712[1]

Non usitatâ nec tenui ferar
Pennâ . . .

Hor.

THERE is not a more pleasing Exercise of the Mind than Gratitude. It is accompanied with such an inward Satisfaction, that the Duty is sufficiently rewarded by the Performance. It is not like the Practice of many other Virtues, difficult and painful, but attended with so much Pleasure, that were there no positive Command which enjoin'd it, nor any Recompence laid up for it hereafter, a Generous Mind wou'd indulge in it, for the natural Gratification that accompanies it.

If Gratitude is due from Man to Man, how much more from Man to his Maker? The Supream Being does not only confer upon us those Bounties which proceed more immediately from his Hand, but even those Benefits which are convey'd to us by others. Every Blessing we enjoy, by what Means soever it may be deriv'd upon us, is the Gift of him who is the great Author of Good, and Father of Mercies.

If Gratitude, when exerted towards one another, naturally produces a very pleasing Sensation in the Mind of a Grateful Man; it exalts the Soul into Rapture, when it is employ'd on this great Object of Gratitude; on this Beneficent Being who has given us every thing we already possess, and from whom we expect every thing we yet hope for.

Most of the Works of the Pagan Poets were either direct Hymns to their Deities, or tended indirectly to the Celebration of their

[1] *Motto.* Horace, *Odes,* 2. 20. 1–2:
No weak, no common Wing shall bear
My rising Body thro the Air. CREECH.

respective Attributes and Perfections. Those who are acquainted with the Works of the *Greek* and *Latin* Poets which are still extant, will upon Reflection find this Observation so true, that I shall not enlarge upon it. One wou'd wonder that more of our Christian Poets have not turned their Thoughts this way, especially if we consider, that our Idea of the Supreme Being is not only Infinitely more Great and Noble than what could possibly enter into the Heart of an Heathen, but filled with every thing that can raise the Imagination, and give an Opportunity for the Sublimest Thoughts and Conceptions.

Plutarch tells us of a Heathen who[a] was singing an Hymn to *Diana*, in which he celebrated her for her delight in Human Sacrifices, and other Instances of Cruelty and Revenge; upon which a Poet who was present at this piece of Devotion, and seems to have had a truer Idea of the Divine Nature, told[b] the Votary by way of reproof, that in recompence for his Hymn, he heartily wished he might have a Daughter of the same Temper with the Goddess he celebrated. It was indeed impossible to write the Praises of one of those false Deities, according to the Pagan Creed, without a mixture of Impertinence and Absurdity.[1]

The *Jews*, who before the Times of Christianity were the only People that had the Knowledge of the True God, have set the Christian World an Example how they ought to employ this Divine Talent of which I am speaking. As that Nation produced Men of great Genius, without considering them as Inspired Writers, they have transmitted to us many Hymns and Divine Odes, which excell those that are deliver'd down to us by the Ancient *Greeks* and *Romans* in the Poetry, as much as in the Subject to which it was consecrated. This I think might easily be shewn, if there were occasion for it.

[c]I have already communicated to the Publick some Pieces of Divine Poetry, and as they have met with a very favourable Reception, I shall from time to time publish any Work of the same Nature which has not yet appeared in Print, and may be acceptable to my Readers.[c]

---

[a] who] that *Fol.*   [b] Nature, told] Nature, (I think it was *Epicharmus*) told *Fol.*
[c-c] I have . . . Readers.] I have already obliged the Publick with some Pieces of Divine Poetry which have fallen into my Hands, and as they have met with the Reception which they deserved, I shall from time to time communicate any Work of the same Nature which has not appeared in Print, and may be acceptable to my Readers. *Fol.*

---

[1] 'How to study poetry', *Moralia*, 22A. The story is also told in Plutarch's 'Superstition', *Moralia*, 170AB. The singer was Timotheus, and the poet Cinesias.

I.

WHEN all thy Mercies, O my God,
My rising Soul surveys;
Transported with the View, I'm lost
In Wonder, Love, and Praise:

II.

O how shall Words with equal Warmth
The Gratitude declare
That glows within my Ravish'd Heart!
But Thou canst read it there.

III.

Thy Providence my Life sustain'd
And all my Wants redrest,
When in the silent Womb I lay,
And hung upon the Breast.

IV.

To all my weak Complaints and Cries
Thy Mercy lent an Ear,
Ere yet my feeble Thoughts had learnt
To form themselves in Pray'r.

V.

Unnumber'd Comforts to my Soul
Thy tender Care bestow'd,
Before my Infant Heart conceiv'd
From whom those Comforts flow'd.

VI.

When in the slipp'ry Paths of Youth
With heedless Steps I ran,
Thine Arm unseen convey'd me safe
And led me up to Man;[a]

---

[a] *Man;*] Man. Fol.

VII.

Through hidden Dangers, Toils, and Deaths,
* It gently clear'd my Way,*
And through the pleasing Snares of Vice,
* More to be fear'd than they.*

VIII.

When worn with Sickness oft hast Thou
* With Health renew'd my Face,*
And when in Sins and Sorrows sunk
* Revived my Soul with Grace.*

IX.

Thy bounteous Hand with worldly Bliss
* Has made my Cup run o'er,*
And in a kind and faithful Friend
* Has doubled all my Store.*

X.

Ten thousand thousand precious Gifts
* My Daily Thanks employ,*
Nor is the least a chearful Heart,
* That tastes those Gifts with Joy.*

XI.

Through ev'ry Period of my Life
* Thy Goodness I'll pursue,*
And after Death in distant Worlds
* The glorious Theme renew.*

XII.

When Nature fails, and Day and Night
* Divide thy Works no more,*
My Ever-grateful Heart, O Lord,
* Thy Mercy shall adore.*

XIII.

Through all Eternity to Thee
A joyful Song I'll raise,
For oh! Eternity's too short
To utter all thy Praise.[1]

C

No. 454   *Monday, August* 11, 1712[2]
[STEELE]

Sine me, Vacivom tempus ne quod dem mihi Laboris.
Ter. Heau.

IT is an inexpressible Pleasure to know a little of the World, and be of no Character or Significancy in it. To be ever unconcerned, and ever looking on new Objects with an endless Curiosity, is a Delight known only to those who are turned for Speculation: Nay they who enjoy it, must value things only as they are the Objects of Speculation, without drawing any worldly Advantage to themselves from them, but just as they are what contribute to their Amusement, or the Improvement of the Mind. I lay one Night last Week at *Richmond*; and being restless, not out of Dissatisfaction, but a certain busy Inclination one sometimes has, I arose at Four in the Morning, and took Boat for *London,* with a Resolution to rove by Boat and Coach for the next Four and twenty Hours, till the many different Objects I must needs meet with should tire my Imagination, and give me an Inclination to a Repose more profound than I was at that Time capable of. I beg People's Pardon for an odd Humour I am guilty of, and was often that Day, which is saluting any Person whom I like, whether I know him or not. This is a Particularity would be tolerated in me, if they considered that the greatest Pleasure I know I receive at my Eyes, and that I am obliged to an agreeable Person for coming abroad into my View, as another is for a Visit of Conversation at their own Houses.

---

[1] F. E. Hutchinson, in his edition of the poems of George Herbert (Oxford, 1941, p. 529), notes the similarity to the last two lines of Herbert's 'Praise (II)':

> Ev'n eternitie is too short
>   To extoll thee.

[2] *Motto.* Terence, *Heautontimorumenos* 90: Give me leave to allow myself no respite from labour.

The Hours of the Day and Night are taken up in the Cities of *London* and *Westminster* by People as different from each other as those who are born in different Centuries. Men of Six a Clock give Way to those of Nine, they of Nine to the Generation of Twelve, and they of Twelve disappear, and make Room for the fashionable World, who have made Two a Clock the Noon of the Day.

When we first put off from Shore, we soon fell in with a Fleet of Gardiners bound for the several Market-Ports of *London*; and it was the most pleasing Scene imaginable to see the Chearfulness with which those industrious People ply'd their Way to a certain Sale of their Goods. The Banks on each Side are as well peopled, and beautified with as agreeable Plantations, as any Spot on the Earth; but the *Thames* it self, loaded with the Product of each Shore, added very much to the Landskip. It was very easy to observe by their Sailing, and the Countenances of the ruddy Virgins who were Supercargoes, the Parts of the Town to which they were bound. There was an Air in the Purveyors for *Covent-Garden*, who frequently converse with Morning Rakes, very unlike the seemly Sobriety of those bound for *Stocks-Market*.[1]

Nothing remarkable happen'd in our Voyage; but I landed with Ten Sail of Apricock Boats at *Strand-Bridge*,[2] after having put in at *Nine-Elmes*,[3] and taken in Melons, consign'd by Mr. *Cuffe* of that Place, to *Sarah Sewell* and Company, at their Stall in *Covent-Garden*. We arriv'd at *Strand-Bridge* at Six of the Clock, and were unloading; when the Hackney-Coachmen of the foregoing Night took their Leave of each other at the *Dark-House*,[4] to go to Bed before the Day was too far spent. Chimney-Sweepers pass'd by us as we made up to the Market, and some Raillery happen'd between one of the Fruit-Wenches and those black Men, about the Devil and *Eve*, with Allusion to their several Professions. I could not believe any Place more entertaining than *Covent-Garden*; where I strolled from one Fruit-Shop to another, with Crowds of agreeable young Women around me, who were purchasing Fruit for their respective Families.

---

[1] Stocks Market, on the site of the Mansion House, took its name from a pair of stocks for punishing criminals which formerly stood there (Hatton, p. 79). It contained a marble equestrian statue of Charles II, given by Sir Robert Viner. In 1737 it was removed to make way for the Mansion House.

[2] Strand Bridge, a landing-place at the foot of Strand Lane, just east of Somerset House.

[3] On the south bank of the Thames, between Battersea and Vauxhall.

[4] A dark house was formerly a place of confinement for a madman (1590–1687, *OED*). Harben (*Dictionary of London*) lists two 'Dark House Lanes' leading down to the Thames.

It was almost Eight of the Clock before I could leave that Variety of Objects. I took Coach and followed a young Lady, who tripped into another just before me, attended by her Maid. I saw immediately she was of the Family of the *Vainloves*. There are a sett of these, who of all things affect the Play of *Blindman's-Buff*, and leading Men into Love for they know not whom, who are fled they know not where.[1] This Sort of Woman is usually a janty Slattern; she hangs on her Cloaths, plays her Head, varies her Posture, and changes Place incessantly; and all with an Appearance of striving at the same time to hide her self, and yet give you to understand she is in Humour to laugh at you. You must have often seen the Coachmen make Signs with their Fingers as they drive by each other, to intimate how much they have got that Day. They can carry on that Language to give Intelligence where they are driving. In an Instant my Coachman took the Wink to pursue, and the Lady's Driver gave the Hint that he was going through *Long-Acre*[2] towards St. *James*'s: While he whipp'd up *James-street*,[3] we drove for *King-street*,[4] to save the Pass at St. *Martin*'s-*Lane*. The Coachmen took Care to meet, justle, and threaten each other for Way, and be intangled at the End of *Newport-street* and *Long-Acre*.[5] The Fright, you must believe, brought down the Lady's Coach Door, and obliged her, with her Mask off, to enquire into the Bustle, when she sees the Man she would avoid. The Tackle of the Coach-Window is so bad she cannot draw it up again, and she drives on sometimes wholly discovered, and sometimes half escaped, according to the Accident of Carriages in her Way. One of these Ladies keeps her Seat in an Hackney-Coach as well as the best Rider does on a managed Horse. The laced Shooe of her Left Foot, with a careless Gesture, just appearing on the opposite Cushion, held her both firm, and in a proper Attitude to receive the next Jolt.

As she was an excellent Coach-Woman, many were the Glances at each other which we had for an Hour and an Half in all Parts of the Town by the skill of our Drivers; till at last my Lady was conveniently lost with Notice from her Coachman to ours to make off,

---

[1] Cf. No. 245 (vol. ii).   [2] No. 250.

[3] James Street was a broad but short thoroughfare leading north from the Great Piazza in Covent Garden to Long Acre.

[4] King Street extended west from the north-west corner of Covent Garden to the junction of New Street with Rose Street. New Street in turn joined St. Martin's Lane, at 'the pass'.

[5] Newport Street ran westward from the end of Long Acre at St. Martin's Lane to the end of Poster Street.

and he should hear where she went. This Chace was now at an End, and the Fellow who drove her came to us, and discovered that he was ordered to come again in an Hour, for that she was a Silk-Worm.[1] I was surprized with this Phrase, but found it was a Cant among the Hackney Fraternity for their best Customers, Women who ramble twice or thrice a Week from Shop to Shop, to turn over all the Goods in Town without buying any thing. The Silk-Worms are, it seems, indulged by the Tradesmen; for tho' they never buy, they are ever talking of new Silks, Laces and Ribbands, and serve the Owners in getting them Customers, as their common Dunners do in making them pay.[2]

The Day of People of Fashion began now to break, and Carts and Hacks[3] were mingled with Equipages of Show and Vanity; when I resolved to walk it out of Cheapness; but my unhappy Curiosity is such, that I find it always my Interest to take Coach, for some odd Adventure among Beggars, Ballad Singers, or the like, detains and throws me into Expence. It happen'd so immediately; for at the Corner of *Warwick-street*,[4] as I was listning to a new Ballad, a ragged Rascal, a Beggar who knew me, came up to me, and began to turn the Eyes of the good Company upon me, by telling me he was extreme poor, and should die in the Streets for want of Drink, except I immediately would have the Charity to give him Six-pence to go into the next Ale-house and save his Life. He urged, with a melancholy Face, that all his Family had died of Thirst. All the Mob have Humour, and two or three began to take the Jest; by which Mr. *Sturdy* carried his Point, and let me sneak off to a Coach. As I drove along, it was a pleasing Reflection to see the World so prettily chequer'd since I left *Richmond*, and the Scene still filling with Children of a new Hour. This Satisfaction encreased as I moved towards the City; and gay Signs, well disposed Streets, magnificent publick Structures, and wealthy Shops, adorn'd with contented Faces,

---

[1] 'A woman given to frequenting drapers' shops and examining goods without buying' (*OED*). This is the only quotation given to illustrate this meaning. Cf. Swift's 'Description of a City Shower' in *Tatler* 238:

> To Shops in Crowds the daggled Females fly,
> Pretend to cheapen Goods, but nothing buy.

[2] Dunner, a solicitor for debts. *OED* gives one quotation earlier than this, from the *Dictionary of the Canting Crew* (a. 1700).

[3] Hack, a vehicle plying for hire; a hackney coach or carriage. Now only U.S. (*OED*).

[4] Hatton (p. 86) mentions two, one near Golden Square, the other on the south side of Charing Cross. In *Tatler* 99 the Company of Upholders indicate that they have a back door into Warwick Street.

made the Joy still rising till we came into the Centre of the City, and Centre of the World of Trade, the *Exchange* of *London*.[1] As other Men in the Crowds about me were pleased with their Hopes and Bargains, I found my Account in observing them, in Attention to their several Interests. I, indeed, look'd upon my self as the richest Man that walk'd the *Exchange* that Day; for my Benevolence made me share the Gains of every Bargain that was made. It was not the least of the Satisfactions in my Survey, to go up Stairs,[2] and pass the Shops of agreeable Females; to observe so many pretty Hands busy in the Foldings of Ribbands, and the utmost Eagerness of agreeable Faces in the Sale of Patches, Pins, and Wires, on each Side the Counters, was an Amusement, in which I should longer have indulged my self, had not the dear Creatures called to me to ask what I wanted, when I could not answer, only *To look at you*. I went to one of the Windows which opened to the Area below, where all the several Voices lost their Distinction, and rose up in a confused Humming; which created in me a Reflection that could not come into the Mind of any but of one a little too studious; for I said to my self, with a kind of Pun in Thought, *What Nonsense is all the Hurry of this World to those who are above it?* In these, or not much wiser Thoughts, I had like to have lost my Place at the Chop-House; where every Man, according to the natural Bashfulness or Sullenness of our Nation, eats in a publick Room a Mess of Broth, or Chop of Meat, in dumb Silence, as if they had no Pretence to speak to each other on the Foot of being Men, except they were of each other's Acquaintance.

I went afterwards to *Robin*'s,[3] and saw People who had din'd with me at the Five-penny Ordinary just before, give Bills for the Value of large Estates; and could not but behold with great Pleasure, Property lodged in, and transferr'd in a Moment from such as would never be Masters of half as much as is seemingly in them, and given from them every Day they live. But before Five in the Afternoon I left the City, came to my common Scene of *Covent-Garden*, and pass'd the Evening at *Will*'s in attending the Discourses of several Sets of People, who reliev'd each other within my Hearing on the Subjects of Cards, Dice, Love, Learning and Politicks.[4] The last

---

[1] Evidently the Royal Exchange (see No. 69, vol. i).
[2] The shops were on the upper floor surrounding the Exchange (cf. i. 293, n. 3).
[3] Robin's Coffee-house, in Exchange Alley, much patronized by the merchants about Change. The other two were Garraway's and Jonathan's.
[4] See No. 1 (vol. i).

Subject kept me till I heard the Streets in the Possession of the Bell-man, who had now the World to himself, and cry'd, *Past Two of Clock.* This rous'd me from my Seat, and I went to my Lodging, led by a Light,[1] whom I put into the Discourse of his private Oeconomy, and made him give me an Account of the Charge, Hazard, Profit and Loss of a Family that depended upon a Link, with a Design to end my trivial Day with the Generosity of Six pence, instead of a third Part of that Sum. When I came to my Chamber I writ down these Minutes; but was at a Loss what Instruction I should propose to my Reader from the Enumeration of so many insignificant Matters and Occurrences; and I thought it of great Use, if they could learn with me to keep their Minds open to Gratification, and ready to receive it from any thing it meets with. This one Circumstance will make every Face you see give you the Satisfaction you now take in behold-ing that of a Friend; will make every Object a pleasing one; will make all the Good which arrives to any Man, an Encrease of Happi-ness to your self.

T

No. 455

Tuesday, August 12, 1712[2]

[STEELE]

> ... *Ego Apis Matinæ*
> *More modoque*
> *Grata Carpentis thyma per laborem*
> *Plurimum* ...

THE following Letters have in them Reflections, which will seem of Importance both to the Learned World and to Domes-tick Life. There is in the first an Allegory so well carry'd on, that it cannot but be very pleasing to those[a] who have a Taste of good Writing; and the other Billets may have their Use in common Life.

a those] these *Fol.*

1 Here used for *linkman* (the only example in *OED*).
2 *Motto.* Horace, *Odes,* 4. 2. 27–30:
> I like a *Bee* with toil and pain
> Fly humbly o're the flowry Plain. CREECH.

Mr. SPECTATOR,

'   AS I walked t'other Day in a fine Garden, and observ'd the great
        Variety of Improvements in Plants and Flowers beyond what
they otherwise would have been, I was naturally led into a Reflection upon the Advantages of Education, or moral culture; how many
good Qualities in the Mind are lost, for want of the like due Care in
nursing and skilfully managing them; how many Virtues are choak'd,
by the Multitude of Weeds which are suffer'd to grow among them;
how excellent Parts are often starved and useless, by being planted
in a wrong Soil; and how very seldom do these moral Seeds produce
the noble Fruits which might be expected from them, by a Neglect
of proper Manuring, necessary Pruning, and an artful Management
of our tender Inclinations and first Spring of Life. These obvious
Speculations made me at length conclude, that there is a Sort of
vegetable Principle in the Mind of every Man when he comes into
the World. In Infants the Seeds lie buried and undiscovered, till after
a While they sprout forth in a kind of rational *Leaves*, which are
Words; and in a due Season the *Flowers* begin to appear in Variety
of beautiful Colours, and all the gay Pictures of youthful Fancy and
Imagination; at last the Fruit knits and is form'd, which is green,
perhaps, first, and soure, unpleasant to the Taste, and not fit to be
gather'd; till ripen'd by due Care and Application, it discovers it
self in all the noble Productions of Philosophy, Mathematicks, close
Reasoning, and handsome Argumentation: And these Fruits, when
they arrive at a just Maturity, and are of a good Kind, afford the
most vigorous Nourishment to the Minds of Men. I reflected further
on the intellectual Leaves beforementioned, and found almost as
great a Variety among them as in the vegetable World. I could
easily observe the smooth shining *Italian* Leaves; the nimble *French*
Aspen, always in Motion; the *Greek* and *Latin* Ever-greens, the
Spanish Myrtle, the *English* Oak, the *Scotch* Thistle, the *Irish* Sham-
brogue, the prickly *German* and *Dutch* Holly, the *Polish* and *Russian*
Nettle, besides a vast Number of Exoticks imported from *Asia*,
Africk, and *America*. I saw several barren Plants, which bore only
Leaves, without any Hopes of Flower or Fruit: The Leaves of some
were fragrant and well-shap'd, of others ill-scented and irregular.
I wonder'd at a Set of old whimsical Botanists, who spent their
whole Lives in the Contemplation of some withered *Ægyptian, Cop-
tick, Armenian,* or *Chinese* Leaves, while others made it their Business
to collect in voluminous Herbals all the several Leaves of some one

Tree. The Flowers afforded a most diverting Entertainment, in a wonderful Variety of Figures, Colours and Scents; however, most of them wither'd soon, or at best are but *Annuals*. Some profess'd Florists make them their constant Study and Employment, and despise all Fruit; and now and then a few fanciful People spend all their Time in the Cultivation of a single Tulip, or a Carnation: But the most agreeable Amusement seems to be the well chusing, mixing, and binding together these Flowers, in pleasing Nosegays to present to Ladies. The Scent of *Italian* Flowers is observ'd, like their other Perfume, to be too strong, and to hurt the Brain; that of the *French* with glaring, gaudy Colours, yet faint and languid; *German* and *Northern* Flowers have little or no Smell, or sometimes an unpleasant one. The Ancients had a Secret to give a lasting Beauty, Colour, and Sweetness to some of their choice Flowers, which flourish to this Day, and which few of the Moderns can effect. These are becoming enough and agreeable in their Season, and do often hansomely adorn an Entertainment; but an Overfondness of them seems to be a Disease. It rarely happens to find a Plant vigorous enough, to have (like an Orange-Tree) at once beautiful shining Leaves, fragrant Flowers, and delicious nourishing Fruit.

SIR, yours, &c.'

Dear SPEC. *August* 6, 1712.

'YOU have given us in your *Spectator* of *Saturday* last, a very excellent Discourse upon the Force of Custom, and its wonderful Efficacy in making every thing pleasant to us.[1] I cannot deny but that I received above Two-penny-worth of Instruction from your Paper, and in the General was very well pleased with it; but I am, without a Compliment, sincerely troubled that I cannot exactly be of your Opinion, That it makes every thing pleasing to us. In short, I have the Honour to be yoked to a young Lady, who is, in plain *English*, for her Standing, a very eminent Scold. She began to break her Mind very freely both to me and to her Servants about two Months after our Nuptials; and tho' I have been accustomed to this Humour of hers this three Years, yet, I do not know what's the Matter with me, but I am no more delighted with it than I was at the very first. I have advised with her Relations about her, and they all tell me that her Mother and her Grandmother before her were both taken much after the same Manner; so that since it runs in the

---

[1] No. 447.

Blood, I have but small Hopes of her Recovery. I should be glad to have a little of your Advice in this Matter: I wou'd not willingly trouble you to contrive how it may be a Pleasure to me; if you will but put me in a Way that I may bear it with Indifference, I shall rest satisfied.

Dear SPEC.

Your very humble Servant.

'*P. S.* I must do the poor Girl the Justice to let you know, that this Match was none of her own chusing, (or indeed of mine either;) in Consideration of which I avoid giving her the least Provocation; and indeed we live better together than usually Folks do who hated one another when they were first joyn'd. To evade the Sin against Parents, or at least to extenuate it, my Dear rails at my Father and Mother, and I curse hers for making the Match.'

Mr. SPECTATOR,

'I LIKE the Theme you lately gave out extremely,[1] and should be as glad to handle it as any Man living: But I find my self no better qualified to write about Money, than about my Wife; for, to tell you a Secret, which I desire may go no further, I am Master of neither of those Subjects.

Aug. 8. 1712

Yours,

Pill Garlick.'[2]

Mr. SPECTATOR,

'I DESIRE you would print this in *Italick*, so as it may be generally taken Notice of. It is designed only to admonish all Persons, who speak either at the Bar, Pulpit, or any publick Assembly whatsoever, how they discover their Ignorance in the Use of Similies. There are in the Pulpit it self, as well as other Places such gross Abuses in this Kind, that I give this Warning to all I know, I shall bring them for the Future before your Spectatorial Authority. On *Sunday* last, one, who shall be nameless, reproving several of his Congregation for standing at Prayers, was pleased to say, *One would think*, like the Elephant, *you had no Knees*: Now I myself saw an Elephant in

---

[1] No. 442.
[2] An appellation given first to a 'pilled' or bald head, ludicrously likened to a peeled head of garlic, and then to a bald-headed man; from the seventeenth century applied in a ludicrously contemptuous or mock-pitiful way, 'poor creature'. Now *dial.* in various shades of meaning (*OED*).

Bartholomew-Fair kneel down to take on his Back the ingenious Mr. *William Penkethman*.[1]

Your most humble Servant.'

T

No. 456　　　　　　*Wednesday, August 13, 1712*[2]

[STEELE]

> *De quo libelli in celeberrimis locis proponuntur*
> *Huic ne perire quidem tacite conceditur.*
> Tull.

OTWAY, in his Tragedy of *Venice preserv'd*, has described the Misery of a Man, whose Effects are in the Hands of the Law, with great Spirit. The Bitterness of being the Scorn and Laughter of base Minds, the Anguish of being insulted by Men harden'd beyond the Sense of Shame or Pity, and the Injury of a Man's Fortune being wasted, under Pretence of Justice, are excellently aggravated in the following Speech of *Pierre* to *Jaffeir*.

> *I pass'd this very Moment by thy Doors,*
> *And found them guarded by a Troop of Villains,*
> *The Sons of publick Rapine, were destroying.*
> *They told me by the Sentence of the Law,*
> *They had Commission to seize all thy Fortune:*
> *Nay more,* Priuli's *cruel Hand had sign'd it.*
> *Here stood a Ruffian with a horrid Face,*
> *Lording it o'er a Pile of massy Plate,*
> *Tumbled into a Heap for publick Sale.*
> *There was another making villanous Jests*
> *At thy Undoing: He had ta'en Possession*
> *Of all thy antient most domestick Ornaments;*
> *Rich Hangings intermix'd and wrought with Gold;*
> *The very Bed, which on thy Wedding-Night*

---

[1] Penkethman's use of an elephant is referred to in *Tatler* 20. 'Like that merry Fellow Pinkethman on an Elephant' is one of the similes in *A Second Tale of a Tub* (1715), by Thomas Burnet and George Duckett (p. 211).
[2] *Motto.* Cicero, *Pro Publio Quinctio*, 15. 50: The man whose conduct is publicly arraigned, is not suffered even to be undone quietly.

Receiv'd thee to the Arms of Belvidera,
The Scene of all thy Joys, was violated
By the coarse Hands of filthy Dungeon Villains,
And thrown amongst the common Lumber.[1]

Nothing indeed can be more unhappy than the Condition of Bankrupcy. The Calamity which happens to us by ill Fortune, or by the Injury of others, has in it some Consolation; but what arises from our own Misbehaviour or Error, is the State of the most exquisite Sorrow. When a Man considers not only an ample Fortune, but even the very Necessaries of Life, his Pretence to Food it self, at the Mercy of his Creditors, he cannot but look upon himself in the State of the Dead, with his Case thus much worse, that the last Office is perform'd by his Adversaries, instead of his Friends. From this Hour the cruel World does not only take Possession of his whole Fortune, but even of every thing else, which had no Relation to it. All his indifferent Actions have new Interpretations put upon them; and those whom he has favour'd in his former Life, discharge themselves of their Obligations to him, by joyning in the Reproaches of his Enemies. It is almost incredible that it should be so; but it is too often seen that there is a Pride mix'd with the Impatience of the Creditor, and there are who would rather recover their own by the Downfal of a prosperous Man, than be discharged to the common Satisfaction of themselves and their Creditors. The wretched Man, who was lately Master of Abundance, is now under the Direction of others; and the Wisdom, Oeconomy, good Sense and Skill in humane Life before, by reason of his present Misfortune, are of no Use to him in the Disposition of any thing. The Incapacity of an Infant or a Lunatick, is design'd for his Provision and Accommodation; but that of a Bankrupt, without any Mitigation in respect of the Accidents by which it arrived, is calculated for his utter Ruin, except there be a Remainder ample enough after the Discharge of his Creditors, to bear also the Expence of rewarding those by whose Means the Effect of all his Labours was transferred from him. This Man is to look on and see others giving Directions upon what Terms and Conditions his Goods are to be purchased, and all this usually done not with an Air of Trustees to dispose of his Effects, but Destroyers to divide and tear them to Pieces.

There is something sacred in Misery to great and good Minds;

---

[1] *Venice Preserv'd,* i. 232–49.

for this Reason all wise Law-givers have been extremely tender how they let loose even the Man who has Right on his Side, to act with any Mixture of Resentment against the Defendant. Virtuous and modest Men, though they be used with some Artifice, and have it in their Power to avenge themselves, are slow in the Application of that Power, and are ever constrained to go into rigorous Measures. They are careful to demonstrate themselves not only Persons injur'd, but also that to bear it longer would be a Means to make the Offender injure others, before they proceed. Such Men clap their Hands upon their Hearts, and consider what it is to have at their Mercy the Life of a Citizen. Such would have it to say to their own Souls, if possible, That they were merciful when they could have destroy'd, rather than when it was in their Power to have spared a Man, they destroy'd. This is a Due to the common Calamity of Humane Life, due in some measure to our very Enemies. They who scruple doing the least Injury, are cautious of exacting the utmost Justice.

Let any one who is conversant in the Variety of Humane Life reflect upon it, and he will find the Man who wants Mercy has a Taste of no Enjoyment of any Kind. There is a natural Disrelish of every thing which is good in his very Nature, and he is born an Enemy to the World. He is ever extremely partial to himself in all his Actions, and has no Sense of Iniquity but from the Punishment which shall attend it. The Law of the Land is his Gospel, and all his Cases of Conscience are determined by his Attorney. Such Men know not what it is to gladden the Heart of a miserable Man, that Riches are the Instruments of serving the Purposes of Heaven or Hell, according to the Disposition of the Possessor. The Wealthy can torment or gratify all who are in their Power, and chuse to do one or other as they are affected with Love or Hatred to Mankind. As for such who are insensible of the Concerns of others, but merely as they affect themselves, these Men are to be valued only for their Mortality, and as we hope better Things from their Heirs. I could not but read with great Delight a Letter from an eminent Citizen, who has fail'd, to one who was intimate with him in his better Fortune, and able by his Countenance to retrieve his lost Condition.

SIR,

'IT is in vain to multiply Words and make Apologies for what is never to be defended by the best Advocate in the World, the Guilt of being Unfortunate. All that a Man in my Condition can do or say, will be received with Prejudice by the Generality of Mankind, but I hope not with you: You have been a great Instrument in helping me to get what I have lost, and I know (for that Reason as well as Kindness to me) you cannot but be in Pain to see me undone. To shew you I am not a Man incapable of bearing Calamity, I will, though a poor Man, lay aside the Distinction between us, and talk with the Frankness we did when we were nearer to an Equality: As all I do will be received with Prejudice, all you do will be looked upon with Partiality. What I desire of you, is, that you, who are courted by all, would smile upon me who am shunned by all. Let that Grace and Favour which your Fortune throws upon you, be turned to make up the Coldness and Indifference that is used towards me. All good and generous Men will have an Eye of Kindness for me for my own Sake, and the rest of the World will regard me for yours. There is an happy Contagion in Riches, as well as a destructive one in Poverty; the Rich can make rich without parting with any of their Store, and the Conversation of the Poor make Men poor, though they borrow nothing of them. How this is to be accounted for I know not; but Mens Existimation[1] follows us according to the Company we keep. If you are what you were to me, you can go a great Way towards my Recovery; if you are not, my good Fortune, if ever it returns, will return by slower Approaches.

I am, SIR,

Your affectionate Friend,
and humble Servant.'

This was answered with a Condescension that did not, by long impertinent Professions of Kindness, insult his Distress, but was as follows.

Dear Tom,

'I AM very glad to hear that you have Heart enough to begin the World a second Time. I assure you, I do not think your numerous Family at all diminished (in the Gifts of Nature for which I have ever so much admired them) by what has so lately happened to you. I shall not only countenance your Affairs with my Appearance for you, but shall accommodate you with a considerable Sum at common Interest for three Years. You know I could make more of it; but I have so great a Love for you, that I can wave Opportunities

---

[1] An obsolete form of *estimation*. This is the last quotation in *OED* for this word.

of Gain to help you: For I do not care whether they say of me after I am dead, that I had an Hundred or Fifty thousand Pounds more than I wanted when I was living.

Your obliged humble Servant.'

T

No. 457   *Thursday, August* 14, 1712[1]
[ADDISON; POPE]

> . . . *Multa & præclara minantis.*
> Hor.

I SHALL this Day lay before my Reader a Letter, written by the same Hand with that of last *Friday*, which contained Proposals for a Printed News-Paper, that should take in the whole Circle of the Penny-Post.[2]

SIR,

'THE kind Reception you gave my last *Friday*'s Letter, in which I broached my Project of a News Paper, encourages me to lay before you two or three more; for, you must know, Sir, that we look upon you to be the *Lowndes* of the learned World, and cannot think any Scheme practicable or rational before you have approved of it, tho' all the Mony we raise by it is on our own Funds, and for our private Use.[3]

'I have often thought that a *News-Letter of Whispers*, written every Post, and sent about the Kingdom, after the same manner as that of Mr. *Dyer*, Mr. *Dawkes*, or any other Epistolary Historian, might be highly gratifying to the Publick, as well as beneficial to the Author.[4] By Whispers I mean those Pieces of News which are communicated as Secrets, and which bring a double Pleasure to the

[1] *Motto.* Horace, *Satires*, 2. 3. 9:
And yet you seem'd to promise something great. CREECH.

[2] No. 452.

[3] William Lowndes was Secretary to the Treasury from 1695 until his death in 1724; although a Whig, he managed to survive the Tory victories of 1710. For his services to the government in putting the Revolution on a sound financial basis see Trevelyan, ii. 163–4.

[4] For John Dyer see No. 43 (vol. i). The newsletter of Ichabod Dawks, of which the first number was issued on 4 Aug. 1696, was printed on writing-paper in script

Hearer; first, as they are private History, and in the next place, as they have always in them a Dash of Scandal. These are the two chief Qualifications in an Article of News, which[a] recommend it, in a more than ordinary manner, to the Ears of the Curious. Sickness of Persons in high Posts, Twilight Visits paid and received by Ministers of State, Clandestine Courtships and Marriages, Secret Amours, Losses at Play, Applications for Places, with their respective Successes or Repulses, are the Materials in which I chiefly intend to deal. I have two Persons, that are each of them the Representative of a Species, who are to furnish me with those Whispers which I intend to convey to my Correspondents. The first of these is *Peter Hush*, descended from the Ancient Family of the *Hushes*.[1] The other is the old Lady *Blast*, who has a very numerous Tribe of Daughters in the two great Cities of *London* and *Westminster*. *Peter Hush* has a whispering Hole in most of the great Coffee-houses about Town. If you are alone with him in a wide Room, he carries you up into a Corner of it, and speaks in your Ear. I have seen *Peter* seat himself in a Company of seven or eight Persons, whom he never saw before in his Life; and after having looked about to see there was no one that over-heard him, has communicated to them in a low Voice, and under the Seal of Secrecy, the Death of a great Man in the Country, who was perhaps a Fox-hunting the very moment this Account was giving of him. If upon your entring into a Coffee-house you see

[a] which] that *Fol.*

---

type, with a blank space left for correspondence. It continued until perhaps 1716. Both news-writers are mentioned in *Tatler* 18:

I remember Mr. *Dyer*, who is justly look'd upon by all the Fox-hunters in the Nation as the greatest Statesman our Country has produc'd, was particularly famous for dealing in Whales; insomuch that in Five Months Time . . . he brought Three into the Mouth of the River *Thames*. . . . The judicious and wary Mr. *I. Dawks* hath all along been the Rival of this great Writer, and got himself a Reputation from Plagues and Famine, by which, in those Days, he destroy'd as great Multitudes, as he has lately done by the Sword. In every Dearth of News, *Grand Cairo* was sure to be unpeopled.

[1] During the summer of 1712 the *Flying Post* caused considerable vexation to the Tory government by the publication of letters entitled 'The Present State of Fairy Land: in a Letter from 'Squire Hush, an eminent Citizen of Fickle-Burrough to the King of Slave-onia'. These letters, signed Bob Hush, were made up of ironical praise of Louis XIV and wry comments on the decay of the Protestant interest in Great Britain. The printer of the paper, William Hurt, was committed to Newgate on 2 Sept. and the writer, George Ridpath, on 8 Sept. The letters are reprinted in the *Political State of Great Britain*, Sept. 1712, pp. 196–214. Ridpath there is called 'the only *Whigg*-Writer, who since the Restraint put upon the Press by the Stamps, took upon him to encounter the *Examiner*, *Post Boy*, and other *Tory*-Papers . . .' (p. 214). See also the *Post Boy* of 9 Sept. Ridpath has a long vindication of his articles in the *Flying Post* of 11 Sept.

a Circle of Heads bending over the Table, and lying close by one another, it is ten to one but my Friend *Peter* is among them. I have known *Peter* publishing the Whisper of the Day by eight a Clock in the Morning at *Garraway*'s, by twelve at *Will*'s, and before two at the *Smyrna*.[1] When *Peter* has thus effectually launched a Secret, I have been very well pleased to hear People whispering it to one another at second Hand, and spreading it about as their own; for you must know, Sir, the great Incentive to Whispering is the Ambition which every one has of being thought in the Secret, and being looked upon as a Man who has Access to greater People than one would imagine. After having given you this Account of *Peter Hush*, I proceed to that vertuous Lady, the old Lady *Blast*, who is to communicate to me the private Transactions of the Crimp Table,[2] with all the *Arcana* of the fair Sex. The Lady *Blast*, you must understand, has such a particular Malignity in her Whisper, that it blights like an Easterly Wind, and withers every Reputation that it breaths upon. She has a particular knack at making private Weddings, and last Winter married above five Women of Quality to their Footmen. Her Whisper can make an innocent young Woman big with Child, or fill an healthful young Fellow with Distempers that are not to be named. She can turn a Visit into an Intrigue, and a distant Salute into an Assignation. She can beggar the Wealthy, and degrade the Noble. In short, she can whisper Men Base or Foolish, Jealous or Ill-natured, or, if occasion requires, can tell you the Slips of their Great Grandmothers, and traduce the Memory of honest Coachmen that have been in their Graves above these hundred Years. By these, and the like helps, I question not but I shall furnish out a very handsom News Letter. If you approve my Project, I shall begin to Whisper by the very next Post, and question not but every one of my Customers will be very well pleased with me, when he considers that every Piece of News I send him is a Word in his Ear, and lets him into a Secret.

'Having given you a Sketch of this Project, I shall, in the next place, suggest to you another for a Monthly Pamphlet, which I shall likewise submit to your Spectatorial Wisdom. I need not tell you, Sir, that there are several Authors in *France*, *Germany* and *Holland*, as well as in our own Country, who[a] Publish every Month, what

[a] who] that *Fol.*

---

[1] For Garraway's, see No. 138 (vol. ii); Will's, No. 1; The Smyrna, No. 305 (vol. iii).   [2] See No. 323 (vol. iii).

they call *An Account of the Works of the Learned,* in which they give us an Abstract of all such Books as are Printed in any Part of *Europe.*[1] Now, Sir, it is my Design to Publish every Month, *An Account of the Works of the Unlearned.* Several late Productions of my own Country-men, who many of them make a very Eminent Figure in the Illiterate World, Encourage me in this Undertaking. I may, in this Work, possibly make a Review of several Pieces which have appeared in the Foreign *Accounts* above-mentioned, tho' they ought not to have been taken Notice of in Works which bear such a Title. I may, like-wise, take into Consideration such Pieces as appear, from time to time, under the Names of those Gentlemen who Compliment one another, in Publick Assemblies, by the Title of the *Learned Gentle-men.* Our Party-Authors will also afford me a great Variety of Sub-jects, not to mention Editors, Commentators, and others, who are often Men of no Learning, or what is as bad, of no Knowledge. I shall not enlarge upon this Hint; but if you think any thing can be made of it, I shall set about it with all the Pains and Application that so useful a Work deserves.

> *I am ever,*
> *Most Worthy Sir,* &c.'[2]
>
> C

[1] The *History of the Works of the Learned; Or, An Impartial Account of Books lately printed in all Parts of Europe* was published from 1699 to 1712 and contained reviews —principally long excerpts—of learned books, in science, philosophy, religion, &c. The monthly issues for the early part of 1711 are advertised in No. 104.

[2] It is possible that Pope is the author of this letter. In a letter dated only 23 Oct., Pope, speaking of Scriblerian projects, writes to Gay:

> Dr. *Swift* much approves what I proposed even to the very title, which I design shall be, *The Works of the Unlearned,* published monthly, in which whatever Book appears that deserves praise, shall be depreciated Ironically, and in the same manner that modern Critics take to undervalue Works of Value, and to commend the high Productions of *Grubstreet.*

In *The Early Career of Alexander Pope* (p. 75) Professor Sherburn offers cogent reasons for dating the letter 1712, but in his edition of Pope's *Correspondence* he places it in the year 1713, the date assigned to it by Elwin–Courthope. Whichever date is accepted, one can argue that Pope is recalling the proposal which he originally made in *Spectator* 457, or that he is presenting as his own something which he had read and still subconsciously recalled from the *Spectator*—or that the similarity in phrasing is pure coincidence. If No. 457 is by Pope—it is included by Norman Ault in vol. i of the *Prose Works* of Pope—then the authorship of the letter in No. 452 must also be assigned to Pope, since Steele says that the letter which occupies most of No. 457 was 'written by the same Hand with that of last Friday'.

$$Ai\delta\grave{\omega}\varsigma\ \delta'\ o\grave{\upsilon}\kappa\ \grave{\alpha}\gamma\alpha\theta\acute{\eta}\qquad\text{Hes.}$$

$$\ldots\ Pudor\ malus\ \ldots\qquad\text{Hor.}$$

I COULD not but Smile at the Account, that was Yesterday given me of a modest young Gentleman, who being invited to an Entertainment, though he was not used to drink, had not the Confidence to refuse his Glass in his Turn, when on a sudden he grew so flustered, that he took all the Talk of the Table into his own Hands, abused every one of the Company,[a] and flung a Bottle at the Gentleman's Head who[b] treated him. This has given me Occasion to reflect upon the ill Effects of a vicious Modesty, and to remember the saying of *Brutus*, as it is quoted by *Plutarch*, that *the Person has had but an ill Education, who has not been taught to deny any thing*.[2] This false kind of Modesty has, perhaps, betrayed both Sexes into as many Vices as the most abandoned Impudence, and is the more inexcusable to Reason, because it acts to gratifie others rather than it self, and is punished with a kind of Remorse, not only like other vicious Habits when the Crime is over, but even at the very time that it is committed.

Nothing is more amiable than true Modesty, and nothing is more contemptible than the false. The one guards Virtue, the other betrays it. True Modesty is ashamed to do any thing that is repugnant to the Rules of right Reason: False Modesty is ashamed to do any thing that is opposite to the Humour of the Company.[c] True Modesty avoids every thing that is criminal, false Modesty every thing that is unfashionable. The latter is only a general undetermined Instinct; the former is that Instinct, limited and circumscribed by the Rules of Prudence and Religion.

We may conclude that Modesty to be false and vicious, which engages a Man to do any thing that is ill or indiscreet, or which

[a] of the Company,] that was present, *Fol.*   [b] who] that *Fol.*   [c] of the Company.] of Company. *Fol.*

---

[1] *Motto.* Hesiod, *Works and Days*, 1. 317: An evil shame. Horace, *Epistles*, 1. 16. 24: False modesty. Only the phrase from Horace appeared as motto in the Folio sheets.
[2] Plutarch, *Life of Marcus Brutus*, 6. 9; 'Of Bashfulness' (*Moralia*, 530A).

restrains him from doing any that is of a contrary Nature. How many Men, in the common Concerns of Life, lend Sums of Mony which[a] they are not able to spare, are Bound for Persons whom they have but little Friendship for, give Recommendatory Characters of Men whom they are not acquainted with, bestow Places on those whom they do not esteem, live in such a manner as they themselves do not approve, and all this meerly because they have not the Confidence[b] to resist Solicitation, Importunity or Example?

Nor does this false Modesty expose us only to[c] such Actions as are indiscreet, but very often to such as are highly criminal. When Xenophanes[d] was called timorous, because he would not venture his Mony in a Game at Dice: *I confess*, said he, *that I am exceeding timorous, for I dare not do an ill thing.*[1] On the contrary, a Man of vicious Modesty complies with every thing, and is only fearful of doing what may look singular in the Company where he is engaged. He falls in with the Torrent, and lets himself go to every Action or Discourse, however unjustifiable in its self, so it be in Vogue among the present Party. This, though one of the most common, is one of the most ridiculous Dispositions in Human Nature, that Men should not be ashamed of speaking or acting in a dissolute or irrational manner, but that one who is in their Company should be ashamed of governing himself by the Principles of Reason and Virtue.

In the second place we are to consider false Modesty, as it restrains a Man from doing what is good and laudable. My Reader's own Thoughts will suggest to him many Instances and Examples under this Head. I shall only dwell upon one Reflection, which I cannot make without a Secret Concern. We have in *England* a particular Bashfulness in every thing that regards Religion. A well-bred Man is obliged to conceal any Serious Sentiment of this Nature, and very often to appear a greater Libertine than he is, that he may keep himself in Countenance among the Men of Mode. Our Excess of Modesty makes us shame-faced in all the Exercises of Piety and Devotion. This Humour prevails upon us daily; insomuch, that at many well-bred Tables, the Master of the House is so very Modest

---

[a] whihc] that *Fol.*   [b] the Confidence] a Confidence *Fol.*   [c] us only to] us to *Fol.*   [d] *Xenophanes*] *Xenophon Fol.*

---

[1] Plutarch, 'Of Bashfulness' (*Moralia*, 530F). See Bayle, art. 'Xenophanes', concluding sentences.

a Man, that he has not the Confidence to say Grace at his own Table: A Custom which[a] is not only practised by all the Nations about us, but was never omitted by the Heathens themselves. *English* Gentlemen who Travel into Roman Catholick Countries, are not a little surprized to meet with People of the best Quality kneeling in their Churches, and engaged in their private Devotions, tho' it be not at the Hours of Publick Worship. An Officer of the Army, or a Man of Wit and Pleasure in those Countries, would be afraid of passing not only for an Irreligious, but an Ill-bred Man, should he be seen to go to Bed, or sit down at Table, without offering up his Devotions on such Occasions. The same Show of Religion appears in all the Foreign Reformed Churches, and enters so much into their Ordinary Conversation, that an *Englishman* is apt to term them Hypocritical and Precise.

This little Appearance of a Religious Deportment in our Nation, may proceed in some measure from that Modesty which is natural to us, but the great occasion of it is certainly this. Those Swarms of Sectaries that over-ran the Nation in the time of the great Rebellion, carried their Hypocrisie so high, that they had converted our whole Language into a Jargon of Enthusiasm; insomuch that upon the Restoration Men thought they could not recede too far from the Behaviour and Practice of those Persons, who had made Religion a Cloak to so many Villanies. This led them into the other Extream, every Appearance of Devotion was looked upon as Puritannical, and falling into the Hands of the Ridiculers who flourished in that Reign, and attacked every thing that was Serious, it has ever since been out of Countenance among us. By this means we are gradually fallen into that Vicious Modesty which has in some measure worn out from among us the Appearance of Christianity in Ordinary Life and Conversation, and which distinguishes us from all our Neighbours.[b]

Hypocrisie cannot indeed be too much detested, but at the same time is to be preferred to open Impiety. They are both equally destructive to the Person who is possessed with[c] them; but in regard to others, Hypocrisie is not so pernicious as bare-faced Irreligion. The due Mean to be observed is to be sincerely Virtuous, and at the same time to let the World see we are so. I do not know a more dreadful Menace in the Holy Writings, than that which is

---

[a] which] that *Fol.*   [b] our Neighbours.] the Nations that lie about us. *Fol.*
[c] with] of *Fol.*

pronounced against those who have this perverted Modesty, to be ashamed before Men in a Particular of such unspeakable Importance.[1]

C[a]

No. 459

[ADDISON]

Saturday, August 16, 1712[2]

... quicquid dignum sapiente bonoque est.

Hor.

RELIGION may be considered under two General Heads. The first comprehends what we are to believe, the other what we are to practise. By those things which we are to believe, I mean whatever is revealed to us in the Holy Writings, and which we could not have obtained the Knowledge of by the Light of Nature; by the things which we are to practise, I mean all those Duties to which we are directed by Reason or Natural Religion. The First of these I shall distinguish by the Name of Faith, the Second by that of Morality.

If we look into the more Serious Part of Mankind, we find many who lay so great a Stress upon Faith, that they neglect Morality; and many who build so much upon Morality, that they do not pay a due Regard to Faith. The perfect Man should be defective in neither of these Particulars, as will be very evident to those who consider the Benefits which arise from each of them, and which I shall make the Subject of this Day's Paper.

Notwithstanding this general Division of Christian Duty into Morality and Faith, and that they have both their peculiar Excellencies, the first has the Pre-eminence in several Respects.

First, Because the greatest part of Morality (as I have stated the Notion of it,) is of a fixt Eternal Nature, and will endure when Faith shall fail, and be lost in Conviction.

Secondly, Because a Person may be qualified to do greater Good to Mankind, and become more beneficial to the World, by Morality, without Faith, than by Faith without Morality.

---

[a] *No. 458 unsigned in Fol.*

[1] Matt. x. 33.
[2] *Motto.* Horace, *Epistles*, 1. 4. 5:
What befits the Wise and Good. CREECH.

Thirdly, Because Morality gives a greater Perfection to human Nature, by quieting the Mind, moderating the Passions, and advancing the Happiness of every Man in his private Capacity.

Fourthly, Because the Rule of Morality is much more certain than that of Faith, all the Civilized Nations of the World agreeing in the great Points of Morality, as much as they differ in those of Faith.

Fifthly, Because Infidelity is not of so malignant a Nature as Immorality, or, to put the same Reason in another Light, because it is generally owned, there may be Salvation for a virtuous Infidel, (particularly in the Case of Invincible Ignorance[1]) but none for a vicious Believer.

Sixthly, Because Faith seems to draw its Principal, if not all its Excellency, from the Influence it has upon Morality; as we shall see more at large, if we consider wherein consists the Excellency of Faith, or the Belief of Revealed Religion; and this I think is,

First, In explaining, and carrying to greater Heights, several Points of Morality.

Secondly, In furnishing new and stronger Motives to enforce the Practice of Morality.

Thirdly, In giving us more amiable Ideas of the Supreme Being, more endearing Notions of one another, and a truer State of our selves, both in regard to the Grandeur and Vileness of our Natures.

Fourthly, By shewing us the Blackness and Deformity of Vice, which in the Christian System is so very great, that he who is possessed of all Perfection and the Sovereign Judge of it, is represented by several of our Divines as hating Sin to the same degree that he loves the Sacred Person who was made the Propitiation of it.

Fifthly, In being the ordinary and prescribed Method of making Morality effectual to Salvation.

I have only touched on these several Heads, which every one who[a] is conversant in Discourses of this Nature will easily enlarge upon in his own Thoughts, and draw Conclusions from them which may be useful to him in the Conduct of his Life. One I am sure is so obvious, that he cannot miss it, namely that a Man cannot be perfect in his Scheme of Morality, who does not strengthen and support it with that of the Christian Faith.

---

[a] who] that *Fol.*

---

[1] In medieval theology *Ignorantia invincibilis*, 'an ignorance the means of overcoming which are not possessed by the ignorant person himself'. See *OED* for quotations of the phrase from the seventeenth century.

Besides this, I shall lay down two or three other Maxims which I think we may deduce from what has been said,

First, That we should be particularly cautious of making any thing an Article of Faith, which does not contribute to the Confirmation or Improvement of Morality.

Secondly, That no Article of Faith can be true and authentick, which[a] weakens or subverts the practical part of Religion, or what I have hitherto called Morality.

Thirdly, That the greatest Friend of Morality, or Natural Religion, cannot possibly apprehend any Danger from embracing Christianity, as it is preserved pure and uncorrupt in the Doctrines of our National Church.

There is likewise another Maxim which I think may be drawn from the foregoing Considerations, which is this, that we should in all dubious Points consider any ill Consequences that may arise from them, supposing they should be Erroneous, before we give up our Assent to them.

For Example, In that disputable Point of Persecuting Men for Conscience Sake, besides the imbittering their Minds with Hatred, Indignation, and all the Vehemence of Resentment, and ensnaring them to profess what they do not believe; we cut them off from the Pleasures and Advantages of Society, afflict their Bodies, distress their Fortunes, hurt their Reputations, ruin their Families, make their Lives painful, or put an End to them. Sure when I see such dreadful Consequences rising from a Principle, I would be as fully convinced of the truth of it, as of a Mathematical Demonstration, before I would venture to act upon it, or make it a Part of my Religion.

In this Case the Injury done our Neighbour is plain and evident, the Principle that puts us upon doing it, of a dubious and disputable Nature. Morality seems highly violated by the one, and whether or no a Zeal for what a Man thinks the true System of Faith may justifie it, is very uncertain. I cannot but think, if our Religion produces Charity as well as Zeal, it will not be for shewing it self by such Cruel Instances. But, to conclude with the Words of an Excellent Author, *We have just enough Religion to make us hate, but not enough to make us love one another.*[1]   C[2]

---

[a] which] that *Fol.*

[1] Swift, *Thoughts on Various Subjects,* 1706 (*Prose Works,* ed. H. Davis, i. 241).

[2] The position in this essay is close to that of John Scott, *The Christian Life,* part ii, chap. i, sect. 3, 'Moral Good the Main of Religion' (ed. 1700, part ii, pp. 41–70).

[STEELE; PARNELL]

Decipimur Specie Recti . . .
Hor.

OUR Defects and Follies are too often unknown to us; nay, they are so far from being known to us, that they pass for Demonstrations of our Worth. This makes us easy in the Midst of them, fond to shew them, fond to improve in them, and to be esteem'd for them. Then it is that a thousand unaccountable Conceits, gay Inventions, and extravagant Actions must afford us Pleasures, and display us to others in the Colours which we our selves take a Fancy to glory in: And indeed there is something so amusing for the Time in this State of Vanity and ill-grounded Satisfaction, that even the wiser World has chosen an exalted Word to describe its Enchantments, and call'd it *the Paradise of Fools.*

Perhaps the latter Part of this Reflection may seem a false Thought to some, and bear another Turn than what I have given; but it is at present none of my Business to look after it, who am going to confess that I have been lately amongst them in a Vision.

Methought I was transported to a Hill, green, flowery, and of an easy Ascent. Upon the broad Top of it resided squint-ey'd *Errour* and popular *Opinion* with many Heads; two that dealt in Sorcery, and were famous for bewitching People with the Love of themselves. To these repair'd a Multitude from every Side, by two different Paths which lead towards each of them. Some who had the most assuming Air went directly of themselves to *Errour*, without expecting a Conductor; others of a softer Nature went first to popular *Opinion*, from whence, as she influenc'd and engag'd them with their own Praises, she deliver'd them over to his Government.

When we had ascended to an open Part of the Summit where *Opinion* abode, we found her entertaining several who had arriv'd before us. Her Voice was pleasing; she breath'd Odours as she spoke: She seem'd to have a Tongue for every one; every one thought he heard of something that was valuable in himself, and expected a Paradise which she promis'd as the Reward of his Merit. Thus were

---

[1] *Motto.* Horace, *Ars poetica*, 25:
Deluded by a seeming Excellence. ROSCOMMON.

The allegory of the Palace of Vanity is by Thomas Parnell and is reprinted in his *Poems on Several Occasions* (1722), pp. 183–90.

we drawn to follow her, till she shou'd bring us where it was to be bestow'd: And it was observable, that all the Way we went, the Company was either praising themselves for their Qualifications, or one another for those Qualifications which they took to be conspicuous in their own Characters, or dispraising others for wanting theirs, or vying in the Degrees of them.

At last we approach'd a Bower, at the Entrance of which *Errour* was seated. The Trees were thick-woven, and the Place where he sat artfully contriv'd to darken him a little. He was disguis'd in a whitish Robe, which he had put on, that he might appear to us with a nearer Resemblance to *Truth*: And as she has a Light whereby she manifests the Beauties of Nature to the Eyes of her Adorers, so he had provided himself with a magical Wand, that he might do something in Imitation of it, and please with Delusions. This he lifted solemnly, and muttering to himself, bid the Glories which he kept under Enchantment to appear before us. Immediately we cast our Eyes on that Part of the Sky to which he pointed, and observ'd a thin blue Prospect, which clear'd up as Mountains in a Summer Morning when the Mists go off, and the Palace of *Vanity* appear'd to Sight.

The Foundation hardly seem'd a Foundation, but a Set of curling Clouds, which it stood upon by magical Contrivance. The Way by which we ascended was painted like a Rainbow; and as we went, the Breeze that play'd about us bewitch'd the Senses. The Walls were guilded all for Show; the lowest Set of Pillars were of the slight fine *Corinthian* Order, and the Top of the Building being rounded, bore so far the Resemblance of a Bubble.

At the Gate the Travellers neither met with a Porter, nor waited till one shou'd appear; every one thought his Merits a sufficient Passport, and pressed forward. In the Hall we met with several Phantomes, that rov'd amongst us, and rang'd the Company according to their Sentiments. There was decreasing *Honour*, that had nothing to show in but an old Coat of his Ancestors Atchievements: There was *Ostentation*, that made himself his own constant Subject, and *Gallantry* strutting upon his Tiptoes. At the upper End of the Hall stood a Throne, whose Canopy glitter'd with all the Riches that Gayety could contrive to lavish on it; and between the guilded Arms sat *Vanity*, deck'd in the Peacock's Feathers, and acknowledg'd for another *Venus* by her Votaries. The Boy who stood beside her for a *Cupid*, and who made the World to bow before her, was call'd *Self-*

Conceit. His Eyes had every now and then a Cast inwards, to the Neglect of all Objects about him; and the Arms which he made use of for Conquest, were borrow'd from those against whom he had a Design. The Arrow which he shot at the Soldier, was fledg'd from his own Plume of Feathers; the Dart he directed against the Man of Wit, was wing'd from the Quills he writ with; and that which he sent against those who presum'd upon their Riches, was headed with Gold out of their Treasuries: He made Nets for Statesmen from their own Contrivances; he took Fire from the Eyes of Ladies, with which he melted their Hearts; and Lightning from the Tongues of the Eloquent, to enflame them with their own Glories. At the Foot of the Throne sat three false Graces, *Flattery*, with a Shell of Paint, *Affectation* with a Mirrour to practise at, and *Fashion* ever changing the Posture of her Cloaths. These apply'd themselves to secure the Conquests which *Self-Conceit* had gotten, and had each of them their particular Polities. *Flattery* gave new Colours and Complections to all things, *Affectation* new Airs and Appearances which, as she said, were not vulgar, and *Fashion* both conceal'd some home Defects, and added some foreign external Beauties.

As I was reflecting upon what I saw, I heard a Voice in the Crowd, bemoaning the Condition of Mankind, which is thus manag'd by the Breath of *Opinion*, deluded by *Errour*, fir'd by *Self-Conceit*, and given up to be train'd in all the Courses of *Vanity*, till *Scorn* or *Poverty* come upon us. These Expressions were no sooner handed about, but I immediately saw a general Disorder, till at last there was a Parting in one Place, and a grave old Man, decent and resolute, was led forward to be punish'd for the Words he had utter'd. He appear'd inclin'd to have spoken in his own Defence, but I cou'd not observe that any one was willing to hear him. *Vanity* cast a scornful Smile at him, *Self-Conceit* was angry, *Flattery*, who knew him for *Plain-dealing*, put on a Vizard, and turn'd away, *Affectation* toss'd her Fan, made Mouths, and call'd him *Envy* or *Slander*, and *Fashion* would have it, that at least he must be *Ill Manners*. Thus slighted and despised by all, he was driven out for abusing People of Merit and Figure; and I heard it firmly resolv'd, that he should be used no better wherever they met with him hereafter.

I had already seen the Meaning of most part of that Warning which he had given, and was considering how the latter Words should be fulfill'd, when a mighty Noise was heard without, and the Door was blackned by a numerous Train of Harpies crowding in upon us. *Folly* and *Broken Credit* were seen in the House before they enter'd, *Trouble, Shame, Infamy, Scorn* and *Poverty* brought up the Rear. *Vanity*, with her *Cupid* and *Graces*, disappear'd; her Subjects ran into Holes and Corners; but many of them were found and carry'd off (as I was told by one who stood near me) either to Prisons or Cellars, Solitude, or little Company, the mean Arts or the viler Crafts of Life. But these, added he with a disdainful Air, are such who would fondly live here, when their Merits neither matched the Lustre of the Place, nor their Riches its Expences. We have seen such Scenes as these before now; the Glory you saw will all return when the Hurry is over. I thank'd him for his Information, and believing him so incorrigible as that he would stay till it was his Turn to be taken, I made off to the Door, and overtook some few, who, though they would not hearken to *Plain-Dealing*, were now terrified to good purpose by the Example of others: But when they had touch'd the Threshold, it was a strange Shock to them to find that the Delusion of *Errour* was gone, and they plainly discern'd the Building to hang a little up in the Air without any real Foundation. At first we saw nothing but a desperate Leap remain'd for us, and I a thousand times blam'd my unmeaning Curiosity that had brought me into so much Danger. But as they began to sink lower in their own Minds, methought the Palace sunk along with us, till they were arriv'd at the due Point of *Esteem* which they ought to have for themselves; then the Part of the Building in which they stood touched the Earth, and we departing out, it retir'd from our Eyes. Now, whether they who stay'd in the Palace were sensible of this Descent, I cannot tell; it was then my Opinion that they were not. However it be, my Dream broke up at it, and has given me Occasion all my Life to reflect upon the fatal Consequences of following the Suggestions of *Vanity*.

Mr. SPECTATOR,

'I WRITE to you to desire, that you would again touch upon a certain Enormity, which is chiefly in Use among the politer and better-bred Part of Mankind; I mean the Ceremonies, Bows, Courtsies, Whisperings, Smiles, Winks, Nods, with other familiar Airs of Salutation, which take up in our Churches so much Time, that might be better employ'd, and which seem so utterly inconsistent with the Duty and true Intent of our entring into those Religious

Assemblies.[1] The Resemblance which this bears to our indeed proper Behaviour in Theatres, may be some Instance of its Incongruity in the above-mention'd Places. In *Roman* Catholick Churches and Chappels abroad, I my self have observ'd, more than once, Persons of the first Quality, of the nearest Relation, and intimatest Acquaintance, passing by one another unknowing as it were, and unknown, and with so little Notices of each other, that it look'd like having their Minds more suitably and more solemnly engaged; at least it was an Acknowledgment that they ought to have been so. I have been told the same even of the *Mahometans*, with relation to the Propriety of their Demeanour in the Conventions of their erroneous Worship: And I cannot but think either of them sufficient and laudable Patterns for our Imitation in this Particular.

'I cannot help upon this Occasion remarking on the excellent Memories of those Devotionists, who upon returning from Church shall give a particular Account how two or three hundred People were dress'd; a Thing, by reason of its Variety, so difficult to be digested and fix'd in a Head, that 'tis a Miracle to me how two poor Hours of Divine Service can be Time sufficient for so elaborate an Undertaking, the Duty of the Place too being jointly and, no doubt, oft pathetically perform'd along with it. Where it is said in Sacred Writ, that *the Woman ought to have a Covering on her Head, because of the Angels,*[2] that last Word is by some thought to be metaphorically used, and to signify young Men. Allowing this Interpretation to be right, the Text may not appear to be wholly foreign to our present Purpose.

'When you are in a Disposition proper for writing on such a subject, I earnestly recommend this to you, and am

SIR, your very humble Servant.'

T

---

[1] The *Spectator* had already commented on ill behaviour in church, in Nos. 50, 259, 270, and 284.
[2] 1 Cor. xi. 10.

No. 461   *Tuesday, August* 19, 1712[1]
[STEELE; WATTS]

> . . . *Sed non Ego credulus illis.*
> Virg.

FOR Want of Time to substitute something else in the Room of them, I am at present obliged to publish Compliments above my Desert in the following Letters. It is no small Satisfaction, to have given Occasion to ingenious Men to employ their Thoughts upon sacred Subjects, from the Approbation of such Pieces of Poetry as they have seen in my *Saturday*'s Papers. I shall never publish Verse on that Day but what is written by the same Hand; yet shall I not accompany those Writings with *Eulogiums*, but leave them to speak for themselves.

For the SPECTATOR,

Mr. SPECTATOR,

'YOU very much promote the Interests of Virtue, while you reform the Taste of a prophane Age, and perswade us to be entertain'd with Divine Poems. While we are distinguish'd by so many thousand Humours, and split into so many different Sects and Parties, yet Persons of every Party, Sect, and Humour are fond of conforming their Taste to yours. You can transfuse your own Relish of a Poem into all your Readers, according to their Capacity to receive; and when you recommend the pious Passion that reigns in the Verse, we seem to feel the Devotion, and grow proud and pleas'd inwardly, that we have Souls capable of relishing what the SPECTATOR approves.

'Upon reading the Hymns that you have publish'd in some late Papers, I had a Mind to try Yesterday whether I could write one. The 114th *Psalm* appears to me an admirable Ode, and I began to turn it into our Language. As I was describing the Journey of *Israel* from *Egypt*, and added the Divine Presence amongst them, I perceiv'd a Beauty in the *Psalm* which was entirely new to me, and which I was going to lose; and that is, that the Poet utterly conceals the Presence of God in the Beginning of it, and rather lets a possessive Pronoun go without a Substantive, than he will so much as

---

[1] *Motto.* Virgil, *Eclogues*, 9. 34:
  But I discern their Flatt'ry from their Praise. DRYDEN.
The first word of the motto was omitted in the Folio sheets.

mention any thing of Divinity there. Judah *was his Sanctuary, and* Israel *his Dominion or Kingdom.* The Reason now seems evident, and this Conduct necessary: For if God had appear'd before, there could be no Wonder why the Mountains should leap and the Sea retire; therefore that this Convulsion of Nature may be brought in with due Surprize, his Name is not mention'd till afterward, and then with a very agreeable Turn of Thought God is introduced at once in all his Majesty. This is what I have attempted to imitate in a Translation without Paraphrase, and to preserve what I could of the Spirit of the sacred Author.

'If the following Essay be not too incorrigible, bestow upon it a few Brightenings from your Genius, that I may learn how to write better, or to write no more.

Your daily Admirer and humble Servant, &c.'

PSALM CXIV.[1]

I.

WHEN Israel, *freed from* Pharoah's *Hand,*
Left the proud Tyrant and his Land,
The Tribes with chearful Homage own
Their King, and Judah *was his Throne.*

II.

Across the Deep their Journey lay,
The Deep divides to make them Way;
The Streams of Jordan *saw, and fled*
With backward Current to their Head.

---

[1] The paraphrase is reprinted in the first edition of Isaac Watts's *The Psalms of David imitated in the Language of the New Testament, and apply'd to the Christian State and Worship* (1719), pp. 299–300, where it is given the title 'Miracles attending *Israel*'s Journey'. The only revisions made are in line 7 ('*Jordan* beheld their March and fled'), line 8 ('to his Head'), and line 24 ('confess the Lord'). Following the paraphrase is a note which sets forth some of the ideas in paragraph 2 of the letter:

This Psalm appears to me an admirable Ode, but if I had introduced the *Presence of God* into the Camp of *Israel* removing from *Egypt,* as all my Predecessors have done, I had lost the Divine Beauty of the Psalm: For had God appeared at first, there could be no Wonder why *the Mountains should leap,* and *the Sea retire;* therefore that this Convulsion of Nature may be brought in with due Surprize, the Sacred Poet conceals his Name till afterward, and then with a very agreeable Turn of Thought *God* is introduced at once in all his Majesty. This is what I have attempted to imitate, and to preserve what I could of the Spirit of the inspired Author.

III.

The Mountains shook like frighted Sheep,
Like Lambs the little Hillocks leap;
Not Sinai on her Base could stand,
Conscious of Sovereign Power at hand.

IV.

What Power cou'd make the Deep divide?
Make Jordan backward roll his Tide?
Why did ye leap, ye little Hills?
And whence the Fright that Sinai feels?

V.

Let every Mountain, every Flood
Retire, and know th' approaching God,
The King of Israel: See him here;
Tremble thou Earth, adore and fear.

VI.

He thunders, and all Nature mourns;
The Rock to standing Pools he turns;
Flints spring with Fountains at his Word,
And Fires and Seas confess their Lord.

Mr. SPECTATOR,

'THERE are those who take the Advantage of your putting an Half-penny Value upon your self above the rest of our daily Writers, to defame you in publick Conversation, and strive to make you unpopular upon the Account of the said Half-penny.[1] But if I were you, I would insist upon that small Acknowledgment for the superior Merit of yours, as being a Work of Invention. Give me Leave therefore to do you Justice, and say in your Behalf what you cannot your self, which is, That your Writings have made Learning a more necessary Part of good Breeding than it was before you appear'd: That Modesty is become fashionable, and Impudence stands in need of some Wit, since you have put them both in their proper Lights. Prophaneness, Lewdness, and Debauchery are not now Qualifications, and a Man may be a very fine Gentleman, tho' he is neither a Keeper nor an Infidel.

[1] No. 445.

'I would have you tell the Town the Story of the *Sibyls,* if they deny giving you Two-pence. Let them know, that those sacred Papers were valued at the same rate after two Thirds of them were destroy'd, as when there was the whole Set. There are so many of us who will give you your own Price, that you may acquaint your Non-Conformist Readers, That they shall not have it, except they come in within such a Day, under Three-pence. I don't know but you might bring in the *Date Obolum Bellisario* with a good Grace.[1] The Witlings come in Clusters to two or three Coffee-houses which have left you off, and I hope you will make us, who fine to your Wit, merry with their Characters who stand out against it.

I am your most humble Servant.

'*P. S.* I have lately got the ingenious Authors of Blacking for Shooes,[2] Powder for colouring the Hair,[3] Pomatum for the Hands,[4]

---

[1] Belisarius (d. A.D. 565), the great Byzantine general, is said to have been forced to beg for charity in his old age. 'That he was deprived of his eyes, and reduced by envy to beg his bread, "Give a penny to Belisarius the general!" is a fiction of later times, which has obtained credit, or rather favour, as a strange example of the vicissitudes of fortune' (Gibbon, *Decline and Fall,* ed. Bury, 1898, iv. 429–30). For the history of the phrase see Karl Krumbacher, *Geschichte der byzantinischen Litteratur,* 2. Aufl., 1897, pp. 825–7 (= von Müller, *Handbuch,* IX. i).

[2] First advertised in No. 108 and twenty-six times thereafter (through No. 545), all in numbers printed by Buckley:

The famous Spanish Blacking for Gentlemens Shoes, that ever was Invented or Used; it making them always look like New, never Daubs the Hands in putting on, or Soils the Stockings in wearing; neither has it the ordinary Gloss of German-Balls, or the intolerable noisome stink of Size, but [is of] an agreeable Scent. It indeed makes the Shoes look extreamly Neat and mightily preserves the Leather: All that use it Admire it, and those that once try it, will never use any thing else. Sold for 1s. 6d. the Pot, with Directions, (which will last 3 or 4 Months) only at Mr. John Hannam's, a Toyshop, at the 3 Angels near Foster-Lane in Cheapside.

[3] The following advertisement appears in Nos. 344, 347, 348, 353, 499, and 500:

The Gentlewoman who liv'd 20 Years in Raquet-Court, and 7 Years in Crane-Court, Fleet-street, and has served most of the Quality in England, Scotland and Ireland, also the East and West Indies, with the most excellent Curiosities for preserving the Face, Hands and Teeth, in present Beauty; for colouring red or grey Hair to a lovely brown or black, a Cosmatick that certainly takes away the Spots and Marks remaining after the Small-Pox, with many other rare Secrets in Physick, is now removed to her own House the upper End of Wine-Office-Court in Gough Square next Door to the Sun-dial on the Left hand, where you may be furnished with all things as formerly, and all prepared with her own Hand. She is to be spoken with every Day from 9 to 12, and from 2 till 8 at Night. She has a House in Lawrence-street near the Church in Chelsea to be Lett or sold. . . . Enquire at Mrs. Maddox's over-against the Cross-Keys in Chelsea, or at her House in Wine-Office-Court as above directed.

[4] One of the popular advertisements (in Nos. 25, 48, &c.) reads:

A most Incomparable Paste for the Hands, far exceeding any thing ever yet in Print: It makes them Delicately white, sleeke and plump; fortifies them against the Scorching heat of the Fire or Sun, and Sharpness of the Wind. A Hand cannot

Cosmetick for the Face,[1] to be your constant Customers; so that your Advertisements will as much adorn the outward Man, as your Paper[a] does the inward.' T

No. 462   *Wednesday, August 20, 1712*[2]
[STEELE]

Nil ego prætulerim Jucundo sanus amico.

Hor.

PEOPLE are not aware of the very great Force which Pleasantry in Company has upon all those with whom a Man of that Talent converses. His Faults are generally over-look'd by all his Acquaintance, and a certain Carelessness that constantly attends all his Actions, carries him on with greater Success, than Diligence and Assiduity does others who have no Share of this Endowment. *Dacinthus* breaks his Word upon all Occasions both trivial and important; and when he is sufficiently railed at for that abominable

[a] Paper] Papers *Fol.*

be so spoil'd but the use of it will recover them. Sold only at Mr. Allcrafts Toyshop, over against the Royal Exchange, at 1s. 6d. a pot, with directions. . . .

[1] The 'Chrystal Cosmetick approv'd of by the worthy Dr. Paul Chamberline', which 'takes off all Morphews, Pimples and Freckles', is frequently advertised (Nos. 25, 48, &c.). It is sold

at Mr. Allcrofts over-against the Royal Exchange, Cornhill, Mr. Jackson's the Corner of Wood-Street, Cheapside; formerly sold at the Comb, but now removed to the Seven Stars under St. Dunstans Church, Fleet-Street, Mrs. Bracknocks at the upper end of St. James's Street, Piccadillie.

There is also the 'Britannick Beautifier: Or, the greatest Cleanser of the Skin in Nature' (Nos. 400, 438, 480), sold 'at 2s. a Bottle, at Mrs. Dring's, a Picture shop, next Door to the Leg-Tavern in Fleet-street, and at Mr. Halsey's, Bookseller, at the Plough and Harrow near the Royal-Exchange in Cornhill'. Another popular advertisement (Nos. 124, 143, &c.) is that of 'The famous Bavarian Red Liquor':

Which gives such a delightful blushing Colour to the Cheeks of those that are White or Pale, that it is not [to] be distinguished from a natural fine Complexion, nor perceived to be artificial by the nearest Friend. Is nothing of Paint, or in the least hurtful, but good in many Cases to be taken inwardly. It renders the Face delightfully handsome and beautiful; is not subject to be rubb'd off like Paint, therefore cannot be discovered by the nearest Friend. It is certainly the best Beautifier in the World. Is sold only at Mr. Payn's Toyshop, at the Angel and Crown in St. Paul's Church-yard near Cheapside, at 3s. 6d. a Bottle, with Directions.

[2] *Motto.* Horace, *Satires*, I. 5. 44 (altered):

A Friend's the dearest thing a Man can have. CREECH.

Steele had used this also as the motto for No. 100.

Quality, they who talk of him end with, *After all he is a very pleasant Fellow*. *Dacinthus* is an ill-natured Husband, and yet the very Women end their Freedom of Discourse upon his Subject, *But after all he is very pleasant Company*. *Dacinthus* is neither in point of Honour, Civility, good Breeding, or good Nature unexceptionable, and yet all is answer'd, *For he is a very pleasant Fellow*. When this Quality is conspicuous in a Man who has, to accompany it, manly and virtuous Sentiments, there cannot certainly be any thing which can give so pleasing Gratification as the Gayety of such a Person; but when it is alone, and serves only to gild a Crowd of ill Qualities, there is no Man so much to be avoided as your pleasant Fellow. A very pleasant Fellow shall turn your good Name to a Jest, make your Character contemptible, debauch your Wife or Daughter, and yet be receiv'd by the rest of the World with Welcome where-ever he appears. It is very ordinary with those of this Character to be attentive only to their own Satisfactions, and have very little Bowels for the Concerns or Sorrows of other Men; nay, they are capable of purchasing their own Pleasures at the Expence of giving Pain to others. But they who do not consider this Sort of Men thus carefully, are irresistibly expos'd to his Insinuations. The Author of the following Letter carries the Matter so high, as to intimate that the Liberties of *England* have been at the Mercy of a Prince merely as he was of this pleasant Character.

Mr. SPECTATOR,

'THERE is no one Passion which all Mankind so naturally give into as Pride, nor any other Passion which appears in such different Disguises: It is to be found in all Habits and all Complections. Is it not a Question, Whether it does more Harm or Good in the World? And if there be not such a Thing as what we may call a vertuous and laudable Pride?

'It is this Passion alone, when misapply'd, that lays us so open to Flatterers; and he who can agreeably condescend to sooth our Humour or Temper, finds always an open Avenue to our Soul; especially if the Flatterer happen to be our Superior.

'One might give many Instances of this in a late *English* Monarch, under the Title of, *The Gayeties of King* Charles II. This Prince was by Nature extremely familiar, of very easy Access, and much delighted to see and be seen; and this happy Temper, which in the highest Degree gratified his Peoples Vanity, did him more Service with his loving Subjects than all his other Virtues, tho' it must be confess'd he had many. He delighted, tho' a mighty King, to give and take a Jest, as they say; and a Prince of this fortunate Disposition, who were inclined to make an ill Use of his Power, may have any thing of his People, be it never so much to their Prejudice. But this good King made generally a very innocent Use, as to the Publick, of this ensnaring Temper; for, 'tis well known, he pursued Pleasure more than Ambition: He seem'd to glory in being the first Man at Cock-matches, Horse-races, Balls, and Plays; he appeared highly delighted on those Occasions, and never fail'd to warm and gladden the Heart of every Spectator. He more than once dined with his good Citizens of *London* on their Lord-Mayor's Day, and did so the Year that Sir *Robert Viner* was Mayor.[1] Sir *Robert* was a very loyal Man, and if you will allow the Expression, very fond of his Sovereign; but what with the Joy he felt at Heart for the Honour done him by his Prince, and thro' the Warmth he was in with continual toasting Healths to the royal Family, his Lordship grew a little fond of His Majesty, and entered into a Familiarity not altogether so graceful in so publick a Place. The King understood very well how to extricate himself on all kind of Difficulties, and with an Hint to the Company to avoid Ceremony, stole off, and made towards his Coach, which stood ready for him in *Guild-Hall* Yard: But the Mayor liked his Company so well, and was grown so intimate, that he pursued him hastily, and catching him fast by the Hand, cry'd out with a vehement Oath and Accent, *Sir, you shall stay and take t'other Bottle.* The airy Monarch look'd kindly at him over his Shoulder, and with a Smile and graceful Air, (for I saw him at the Time, and do now) repeated this Line of the old Song;

He that's drunk is as great as a King.[2]

and immediately return'd back and complied with his Landlord.

'I give you this Story, Mr. SPECTATOR, because, as I said, I saw

---

[1] Sir Robert Viner became Lord Mayor in 1674. A broadside in the Luttrell collection in the British Museum, entitled 'The Kings Entertainment at Guild-Hall or, Londons Option in Fruition' (1674), is addressed to Sir Robert Viner, Lord Mayor.

[2] The refrain of a popular song. In Shadwell's *Miser* (III. ii) the 'catch in four parts' begins:

Come, lay by your Cares, and hang up your Sorrow;
Drink on, he's a Sot that e'er thinks on to-Morrow;
Good Store of good Claret supplies ev'ry thing,
And the Man that is drunk, is as great as a King.

Cf. also D'Urfey's *Comical History of Don Quixote*, part iii (III. ii).

the Passage; and I assure you it's very true, and yet no common one; and when I tell you the Sequel, you will say I have yet a better Reason for't.[1] This very Mayor afterwards erected the Statue of his merry Monarch in *Stocks-Market*, and did the Crown many and great Services; and it was owing to this Humour of the King, that his Family had so great a Fortune shut up in the Exchequer of their pleasant Sovereign. The many good-natur'd Condescensions of this Prince are vulgarly known; and it is excellently said of him by a great Hand which writ his Character, *That he was not a King a Quarter of an Hour together in his whole Reign.*[2] He would receive Visits even from Fools and half Mad-men, and at Times I have met with People who have box'd, fought at Back-Sword, and taken Poison before King *Charles* II. In a Word, he was so pleasant a Man, that no one could be sorrowful under his Government. This made him capable of baffling, with the greatest Ease imaginable, all Suggestions of Jealousy, and the People could not entertain Notions of any thing terrible in him, whom they saw every way agreeable. This Scrap of the familiar Part of that Prince's History I thought fit to send you, in Compliance to the Request you lately made to your Correspondents.

I am,

SIR,

Your most humble Servant.

T

[1] I have found no verification of this anecdote, although it is often cited by writers on Charles II. The author of the article on Viner in *DNB* makes the impossible statement that Steele himself 'witnessed the occurrence'.

[2] See 'A Character of Charles II', by John Sheffield, Duke of Buckinghamshire (*Works*, 1726, ii. 57).

No. 463   *Thursday, August 21, 1712*[1]
[ADDISON]

Omnia quæ sensu volvuntur vota diurno
Pectore sopito reddit amica quies.
Venator defessa toro cùm membra reponit
   Mens tamen ad sylvas & sua lustra redit.
Judicibus lites, aurigæ somnia currus,
Vanaque nocturnis meta cavetur equis.
Me quoque Musarum studium sub nocte silenti
   Artibus assuetis sollicitare solet.

                                          Claud.

I WAS lately entertaining my self with comparing *Homer*'s Ballance,[2] in which *Jupiter* is represented as weighing the Fates of *Hector* and *Achilles*, with a Passage of *Virgil*,[a] wherein that Deity is introduced as weighing the Fates of *Turnus* and *Æneas*.[3] I then considered, how the same way of thinking prevailed in the Eastern Parts of the World, as in those noble Passages of Scripture, wherein we are told, that the great King of *Babylon*, the Day before his Death, had been weighed in the Ballance, and been found wanting.[4] In other Places of the Holy Writings, the Almighty is described as weighing the Mountains in Scales,[5] making the weight for the Winds,[6] knowing the Ballancings of the Clouds,[7] and, in others, as weighing the Actions of Men,[8] and laying their Calamities together in a Ballance.[9] *Milton*, as I have observed in a former Paper,[10] had an Eye to several of these foregoing Instances, in that beautiful Description[b] wherein

---

[a] with a Passage of *Virgil*,] with that of *Virgil*, Fol.   [b] Description] Passage *Fol.*

---

[1] *Motto.* Claudian, 27 (*Panegyricus de Sexto Consulatu Honorii Augusti*: Praefatio), 1–6, 11–12:

> Whate'er Delights employ our waking Sense,
> The same does Fancy to our Dreams dispence.
> The Hunter when weigh'd down to rest by Toil,
> Sports in his Slumbers and pursues the Spoil:
> Racers and Charioteers in Dreams make speed,
> And Judges sum up Evidence in Bed.
> My self so close to my gay Studies keep,
> That oft I am composing in my Sleep.

[2] *Iliad*, 8. 68–72.   [3] *Aeneid*, 12. 725–7.
[4] Dan. v.   [5] Isa. xl. 12.   [6] Job xxviii. 25.
[7] Job xxxvii. 16.   [8] 1 Sam. ii. 3.
[9] Job vi. 2.   [10] No. 321.

he represents the Arch-Angel and the Evil Spirit as addressing themselves for the Combat, but parted by the Ballance which appeared
in the Heavens, and weighed the Consequences of such a Battel.

> *Th' Eternal to prevent such horrid fray*
> *Hung forth in Heav'n his golden Scales, yet seen*
> *Betwixt Astrea and the Scorpion Sign,*
> *Wherein all things created first he weigh'd,*
> *The pendulous round Earth with ballanc'd Air*
> *In counterpoise, now ponders all events,*
> *Battels and Realms; in these he put two weights*
> *The sequel each of parting and of fight,*
> *The latter quick up flew, and kickt the beam;*
> *Which* Gabriel *spying, thus bespake the Fiend.*

> Satan *I know thy strength, and thou know'st mine,*
> *Neither our own but giv'n; what folly then*
> *To boast what Arms can do, since thine no more*
> *Than Heav'n permits, nor mine, though doubled now*
> *To trample thee as mire: for proof look up,*
> *And read thy lot in yon cœlestial Sign,*
> *Where thou art weigh'd and shown, how light, how weak,*
> *If thou resist. The Fiend look'd up, and knew*
> *His mounted Scale aloft; nor more, but fled*
> *Murm'ring, and with him fled the shades of night.*[1]

These several amusing[2] Thoughts having taken Possession of my
Mind some time before I went to sleep, and mingling themselves
with my ordinary Ideas, raised in my Imagination a very odd kind
of Vision. I was, methought, replaced in my Study, and seated in
my Elbow Chair, where I had indulged the foregoing Speculations,
with my Lamp burning by me, as usual. Whilst I was here meditating on several Subjects of Morality, and considering the Nature
of many Virtues and Vices, as Materials for those Discourses with
which I daily entertain the Publick, I saw, methought, a Pair of
Golden Scales hanging by a Chain of the same Mettal over the Table
that stood before me; when, on a sudden, there were great Heaps
of Weights thrown down on each side of them. I found, upon
examining these Weights, they shewed the Value of every thing
that is in Esteem among Men. I made an Essay of them, by putting

---

[1] *Paradise Lost*, iv. 996–1015.   [2] See No. 321 (vol. iii).

the Weight of Wisdom in one Scale, and that of Riches in another; upon which the latter, to shew its comparative Lightness, immediately *flew up and kickt the Beam*.

But, before I proceed, I must inform my Reader, that these Weights did not exert their Natural Gravity, till they were laid in the Golden Ballance, insomuch that I could not guess which was light or heavy, whilst I held them in my Hand. This I found by several Instances, for upon my laying a Weight in one of the Scales, which was inscribed by the Word *Eternity*; tho' I threw in that of Time, Prosperity, Affliction, Wealth, Poverty, Interest, Success, with many other Weights, which in my Hand seemed very ponderous, they were not able to stir the opposite Ballance, nor could they have prevailed, though assisted with the Weight of the Sun, the Stars, and the Earth.

Upon emptying the Scales, I laid several Titles and Honours, with Pomps, Triumphs, and many Weights of the like Nature, in one of them, and seeing a little glittering Weight lie by me, I threw it accidentally into the other Scale, when, to my great Surprize, it proved so exact a Counterpoise, that it kept the Ballance in an Equilibrium. This little glittering Weight was inscribed upon the Edges of it with the Word *Vanity*. I found there were several other Weights which were equally Heavy, and exact Counterpoises to one another; a few of them I tried, as Avarice and Poverty, Riches and Content, with some others.

There were likewise several Weights that were of the same Figure, and seemed to Correspond with each other, but were entirely different when thrown into the Scales; as Religion and Hypocrisie, Pedantry and Learning, Wit and Vivacity, Superstition and Devotion, Gravity and Wisdom, with many others.

I observed one particular Weight lettered on both sides, and upon applying my self to the Reading of it, I found on one side, written, *In the Dialect of Men*, and underneath it, *CALAMITIES*; on the other side was written, *In the Language of the Gods*, and underneath, *BLESSINGS*. I found the intrinsick Value of this Weight to be much greater than I imagined, for it over-powered Health, Wealth, Good Fortune, and many other Weights, which were much more ponderous in my Hand than the other.

There is a Saying among the *Scotch*, that an Ounce of Mother is worth a Pound of Clergy[1]; I was sensible of the Truth of this Saying, when I saw the difference between the Weight of Natural Parts, and

[1] The earliest example of this proverb in Apperson is dated 1690.

that of Learning. The Observation which I made upon these two Weights opened to me a new Field of Discoveries, for notwithstanding the weight of Natural Parts was much heavier than that of Learning, I observed that it weighed an hundred times heavier than it did before, when I put Learning into the same Scale with it. I made the same Observation upon Faith and Morality; for notwithstanding the latter out-weighed the former separately, it received a thousand times more additional weight from its Conjunction with the former, than what it had by it self.[1] This odd Phænomenon shewed it self in other Particulars, as in Wit and Judgment, Philosophy and Religion, Justice and Humanity, Zeal and Charity, Depth of Sense and Perspicuity of Stile, with innumerable other Particulars, too long to be mentioned in this Paper.

As a Dream seldom fails of dashing Seriousness with Impertinence, Mirth with Gravity, methought I made several other Experiments of a more ludicrous Nature, by one of which I found that an *English* Octavo was very often heavier than a *French* Folio; and by another, that an old *Greek* or *Latin* Author weighed down a whole Library of Moderns. Seeing one of my *Spectators* lying by me, I laid it into one of the Scales, and flung a two-penny Piece into the other. The Reader will not enquire into the Event, if he remembers the first Tryal which I have recorded in this Paper. I afterwards threw both the Sexes into the Ballance; but as it is not for my Interest to disoblige either of them, I shall desire to be excused from telling the Result of this Experiment. Having an Opportunity of this Nature in my Hands, I could not forbear throwing into one Scale the Principles of a Tory, and in the other those of a Whig; but as I have all along declared this to be a Neutral Paper, I shall likewise desire to be silent under this Head also, though upon examining one of the Weights, I saw the Word *TEKEL* Engraven on it in Capital Letters.

I made many other Experiments, and tho'[a] I have not room for them all in this Day's Speculation, I may perhaps reserve them for another. I shall[b] only add, that upon my awaking I was sorry to find my Golden Scales vanished, but resolved for the future to learn this Lesson from them, not to despise or value any Things for their

---

^a and tho'] *8vo*; and though *12mo*; but as *Fol.*   ^b another. I shall] another; and shall *Fol.*

---

[1] Cf. No. 459.

Appearances, but to regulate my Esteem and Passions towards them according to their real and intrinsick Value.

C

No. 464   *Friday, August 22, 1712*[1]
[ADDISON]

> *Auream quisquis mediocritatem*
> *Diligit, tutus caret obsoleti*
> *Sordibus tecti, caret invidendâ*
> *Sobrius aulâ. . . .*
>
>   Horat.

I AM wonderfully pleased when I meet with any Passage in an old *Greek* or *Latin* Author, that is not blown upon, and which[a] I have never met with in a Quotation. Of this kind is a Beautiful Saying in *Theognis*. *Vice is cover'd by Wealth, and Virtue by Poverty*; or to give it in the Verbal Translation, *Among Men there are some who have their Vices concealed by Wealth, and others who have their Virtues concealed by Poverty.*[2] Every Man's Observation will supply him with Instances of Rich Men, who have several Faults and Defects that are overlooked, if not entirely hidden, by means of their Riches; and, I think, we cannot find a more Natural Description of a Poor Man, whose Merits are lost in his Poverty, than that in the Words of the Wise Man. *There was a little City, and few Men within it; and there came a great King against it, and besieged it, and built great Bulwarks against it: Now there was found in it a poor Wise Man, and he, by his Wisdom, delivered the City; yet no Man remembered that same poor Man. Then said I, Wisdom is better than Strength; nevertheless, the poor Man's Wisdom is despised, and his Words are not heard.*[3]

---

[a] which] that *Fol.*

---

[1] *Motto.* Horace, *Odes*, 2. 10. 5–8:

    To those that choose the golden Mean:
    The Waves are smooth, the Skies serene;
    They want the baseness of the Poor's retreat,
    And envy'd Houses of the Great. CREECH.

[2] Theognis, *Elegies*, 1. 1061–2.   [3] Eccles. ix. 14–16.

The middle Condition seems to be the most advantageously situated for the gaining of Wisdom. Poverty turns our Thoughts too much upon the supplying of our Wants, and Riches upon enjoying our Superfluities; and, as *Cowley* has said in another Case, *It is hard for a Man to keep a steady Eye upon Truth, who is always in a Battel or a Triumph.*[1]

If we regard Poverty and Wealth, as they are apt to produce Virtues or Vices in the Mind of Man, one may observe, that there is a Set of each of these growing out of Poverty, quite different from that which rises out of Wealth. Humility and Patience, Industry and Temperance, are very often the good Qualities of a poor Man. Humanity and Good-nature, Magnanimity, and a Sense of Honour, are as often the Qualifications of the Rich. On the contrary, Poverty is apt to betray a Man into Envy, Riches into Arrogance. Poverty is too often attended with Fraud, vicious Compliance, Repining, Murmur and Discontent. Riches expose a Man to Pride and Luxury, a foolish Elation of Heart, and too great a Fondness for the present World. In short, the middle Condition is most eligible to the Man who would improve himself in Virtue; as I have before shown, it is the most advantageous for the gaining of Knowledge.[2] It was upon this Consideration that *Agur* founded his Prayer, which for the Wisdom of it is recorded in Holy Writ. *Two things have I required of thee, deny me them not before I dye. Remove far from me Vanity and Lies; give me neither Poverty, nor Riches; feed me with Food convenient for me. Lest I be full and deny thee, and say, who is the Lord? or least I be poor and steal, and take the name of my God in vain.*[3]

I shall fill the remaining Part of my Paper with a very pretty[a] Allegory, which is wrought into a Play by *Aristophanes* the *Greek* Comedian.[4] It seems originally designed as a Satyr upon the Rich, though, in some Parts of it, 'tis like the foregoing Discourse, a kind of Comparison between Wealth and Poverty.

Chremylus, who was an old and a Good Man, and withal exceeding Poor, being desirous to leave some Riches to his Son, consults the

[a] pretty] beautiful *Fol.*

---

[1] Cowley, *To the Royal Society*, 107–8:
>   For who on things remote can fix his sight,
>   That's alwayes in a Triumph, or a Fight?

[2] Cf. No. 287 (vol. iii).

[3] Prov. xxx. 7–9.   [4] *Plutus*, produced in 388 B.C.

Oracle of *Apollo* upon the Subject. The Oracle bids him follow the first Man he should see upon his going out of the Temple. The Person he chanced to see was to Appearance an old sordid Blind Man, but upon his following him from Place to Place, he at last found by his own Confession, that he was *Plutus* the God of Riches, and that he was just come out of the House of a Miser. *Plutus* further told him, that when he was a Boy he used to declare, that as soon as he came to Age he wou'd distribute Wealth to none but vertuous and just Men; upon which *Jupiter*, considering the pernicious Consequences of such a Resolution, took his Sight away from him, and left him to strole about the World in the Blind Condition wherein *Chremylus* beheld him. With much ado *Chremylus* prevailed upon him to go to his House, where he met an old Woman in a tattered Raiment, who had been his Guest for many Years, and whose Name was *Poverty*. The old Woman refusing to turn out so easily as he would have her, he threatned to banish her not only from his own House, but out of all *Greece*, if she made any more Words upon the Matter. *Poverty* on this Occasion pleads her Cause very notably, and represents to her old Landlord, that should she be driven out of the Country, all their Trades, Arts and Sciences would be driven out with her; and that if every one was Rich, they would never be supplied with those Pomps, Ornaments and Conveniencies of Life which made Riches desirable. She likewise represented to him the several Advantages which she bestowed upon her Votaries, in regard to their Shape, their Health, and their Activity, by preserving them from Gouts, Dropsies, Unweildiness and Intemperance. But whatever she had to say for her self, she was at last forced to troop off. *Chremylus* immediately considered how he might restore *Plutus* to his Sight; and in order to it conveyed him to the Temple of *Esculapius*, who was famous for Cures and Miracles of this Nature. By this means the Deity recovered his Eyes, and begun to make a right use of them, by enriching every one that was[a] distinguished by Piety towards the Gods, and Justice towards Men;[b] and at the same time by taking away his Gifts from the Impious and Undeserving. This produces several merry Incidents, 'till in the last Act *Mercury* descends with great Complaints from the Gods, that since the Good Men were grown Rich they had received no Sacrifices, which is confirmed by a Priest of *Jupiter*, who enters with a Remonstrance, that since this late Innovation he was reduced to

[a] was] were *Fol.*   [b] Men;] Man; *Fol.*

a Starving Condition, and could not live upon his Office. *Chremylus*, who in the beginning of the Play was Religious in his Poverty, concludes it with a Proposal which was relished by all the Good Men who were now grown Rich as well as himself, that they should carry *Plutus* in a Solemn Procession to the Temple, and Install him in the place of *Jupiter*. This Allegory instructed the *Athenians* in two Points; first, as it vindicated the Conduct of Providence in its ordinary Distributions of Wealth; and in the next place, as it showed the great Tendency of Riches to corrupt the Morals of those who possessed them.[a]

C

No. 465   *Saturday, August 23, 1712*[1]
[ADDISON]

> *Quâ ratione queas traducere leniter ævum:*
> *Nè te semper inops agitet vexetque cupido;*
> *Nè pavor & rerum mediocriter utilium Spes.*
>   Hor.

HAVING endeavoured in my last *Saturday*'s Paper to shew the great Excellency of Faith, I shall here consider what are the proper Means of strengthning and confirming it in the Mind of Man. Those who delight in reading Books of Controversie, which[b] are written on both sides of the Question in Points of Faith, do very seldom arrive at a fixed and settled Habit of it. They are one Day entirely convinced of its important Truths, and the next meet with something that shakes and disturbs them. The Doubt which[c] was laid revives again, and shews it self in new Difficulties, and that generally for this Reason, because the Mind which is perpetually tost in Controversies and Disputes, is apt to forget the Reasons

---

[a] possessed them.] were possessed of them. *Fol.*   [b] which] that *Fol.*   [c] which] that *Fol.*

---

[1] *Motto.* Horace, *Epistles* 1. 18. 97–99:
     How thou may'st live, how spend thine Age in Peace,
     Lest fierce desire, still poor, disturb thine Ease;
     Or Fears should shake, or Cares thy Mind abuse,
     Or ardent hope for things of little use. CREECH.

which had once set it at rest, and to be disquieted with any former Perplexity, when it appears in a new Shape, or is started by a different Hand. As nothing is more laudable than an Enquiry after Truth, so nothing is more irrational than to pass away our whole Lives, without determining our selves one way or other in those Points which are of the last Importance to us. There are indeed many things from which we may with-hold our Assent; but in Cases by which we are to regulate our Lives, it is the greatest Absurdity to be wavering and unsettled, without closing with that Side which appears the most safe and the most[a] probable. The first Rule therefore which I shall lay down is this, that when by Reading or Discourse we find our selves thoroughly convinced of the Truth of any Article, and of the Reasonableness of our Belief in it, we should never after suffer our selves to call it into question. We may perhaps forget the Arguments which occasioned our Conviction, but we ought to remember the Strength they had with us, and therefore still to retain the Conviction which they once produced. This is no more than what we do in every common Art or Science, nor is it possible to act otherwise, considering the Weakness and Limitation of our Intellectual Faculties. It was thus, that *Latimer,* one of the[b] glorious Army of Martyrs who introduced the Reformation in *England,* behaved himself in that great Conference which was managed between the most learned among the Protestants and Papists in the Reign of Queen *Mary.*[1] This venerable old Man knowing how his Abilities were impaired by Age, and that it was impossible for him to recollect all those Reasons which had directed him in the Choice of his Religion, left his Companions who were in the full Possession of their Parts and Learning, to baffle and confound their Antagonists by the Force of Reason. As for himself he only repeated to his Adversaries the Articles in which he firmly believed, and in the Profession of which he was determined to die. It is in this manner that the Mathematician proceeds upon Propositions which he has once demonstrated, and tho' the Demonstration may have slipt out of his Memory, he builds upon the Truth, because he knows it was demonstrated. This Rule is absolutely necessary for weaker Minds, and in some measure for Men of the greatest Abilities; but to these last I would propose, in the second place, that they should lay up

a and the most] and most *Fol.*   b the] that *Fol.*

1 The account here follows that of Bishop Gilbert Burnet, *History of the Reformation of the Church of England* (1681), ii. 283.

in their Memories, and always keep by them in a readiness, those Arguments which appear to them of the greatest Strength, and which cannot be got over by all the Doubts and Cavils of Infidelity.

But, in the third place, there is nothing which strengthens Faith more than Morality. Faith and Morality naturally produce each other. A Man is quickly convinced of the Truth of Religion, who finds it is not against his Interest that it should be true. The Pleasure he receives at present, and the Happiness which he promises himself from it hereafter, will both dispose him very powerfully to give Credit to it, according to the ordinary Observation that *we are easie to believe what we wish*. It is very certain, that a Man of sound Reason cannot forbear closing with Religion upon an impartial Examination of it; but at the same time it is as certain, that Faith is kept alive in us, and gathers Strength from Practice more than from Speculation.

There is still another Method which is more Persuasive than any of the former, and that is an habitual Adoration of the Supreme Being, as well in constant Acts of Mental Worship, as in outward Forms. The Devout Man does not only believe, but feels there is a Deity. He has actual Sensations of him; his Experience concurs with his Reason; he sees him more and more in all his Intercourses with him, and even in this Life almost loses his Faith in Conviction.

The last Method which I shall mention for the giving Life to a Man's Faith, is frequent Retirement from the World, accompanied with religious Meditation. When a Man thinks of any thing in the Darkness of the Night, whatever deep Impressions it may make in his Mind, they are apt to vanish as soon as the Day breaks about him. The Light and Noise of the Day, which are perpetually solliciting his Senses, and calling off his Attention, wear out of his Mind the Thoughts that imprinted themselves in it, with so much Strength, during the Silence and Darkness of the Night. A Man finds the same difference as to[a] himself in a Crowd and in a Solitude; the Mind is stunned and dazzled amidst that variety of Objects which[b] press upon her in a great City: She cannot apply her self to the Consideration of those things which are of the utmost Concern to her. The Cares or Pleasures of the World strike in with every Thought, and a Multitude of vicious Examples give a kind of Justification to our Folly.[c] In our Retirements every thing disposes us to be serious. In

---

[a] as to] in *Fol.*   [b] which] that *Fol.*   [c] and ... Folly.] as a Multitude of vicious Examples gives us a kind of Justification in our Folly. *Fol.*

Courts and Cities we are entertained with the Works of Men, in the Country with those of God. One is the Province of Art, the other of Nature. Faith and Devotion naturally grow in the Mind of every reasonable Man, who sees the Impressions of Divine Power and Wisdom in every Object on which he casts his Eye. The Supream Being has made the best Arguments for his own Existence, in the Formation of the Heavens and the Earth, and these are Arguments which a Man of Sense cannot forbear attending to, who is out of the Noise and Hurry of Human Affairs. *Aristotle* says, that should a Man live under Ground, and there converse with Works of Art and Mechanism, and should afterwards be brought up into the open Day, and see the several Glories of the Heav'n and Earth, he would immediately pronounce them the Works of such a Being as we define God to be.[1] The Psalmist has very beautiful Strokes of Poetry to this purpose, in that exalted Strain, *The Heavens declare the Glory of God: And the Firmament sheweth his handy Work. One Day telleth another: and one Night certifieth another. There is neither Speech nor Language: but their Voices are heard among them. Their Sound is gone out into all Lands: and their Words into the Ends of the World.*[2] As such a bold and sublime manner of Thinking furnishes[a] very noble Matter for an Ode, the Reader may see it wrought into the following one.

I.

The Spacious Firmament on high,
With all the blue Etherial Sky,
And spangled Heav'ns, a Shining Frame,
Their great Original proclaim:
Th'unwearied Sun, from day to day,
Does his Creator's Pow'r display,
And publishes to every Land
The Work of an Almighty Hand.

II.

Soon as the Evening Shades prevail,
The Moon takes up the wondrous Tale,
And nightly to the listning Earth
Repeats the Story of her Birth:

[a] furnishes] furnishes out *Fol.*

---

[1] Aristotle, in the lost treatise *De Philosophia*, quoted by Cicero, *Of the Nature of the Gods*, 2. 37. 95.
[2] Ps. xix. 1–4 (Prayer Book version).

Whilst all the Stars that round her burn,
And all the Planets, in their turn,
Confirm the Tidings as they rowl,
And spread the Truth from Pole to Pole.

III.

What though, in solemn Silence, all
Move round the dark terrestrial Ball?
What tho' nor real Voice nor Sound
Amid their radiant Orbs be found?
In Reason's Ear they all rejoice,
And utter forth a glorious Voice,
For ever singing, as they shine,
'The Hand that made us is Divine'.

C

No. 466   *Monday, August 25, 1712*[1]

[STEELE]

. . . Vera incessu patuit Dea.
Virg.

WHEN *Æneas*, the Hero of *Virgil*, is lost in the Wood, and a perfect Stranger in the Place on which he is landed, he is accosted by a Lady in an Habit for the Chase.[2] She enquires of him, Whether he has seen pass by that Way any young Woman dress'd as she was? Whether she were following the Sport in the Wood, or any other way employ'd, according to the Custom of Huntresses. The Hero answers with the Respect due to the beautiful Appearance she made, tells her, He saw no such Person as she enquir'd for; but intimates, that he knows her to be of the Deities, and desires she would conduct a Stranger. Her Form from her first Appearance manifested she was more than mortal; but tho' she was certainly a Goddess, the Poet does not make her known to be the Goddess of *Beauty* till she moved: All the Charms of an agreeable Person are then in their highest Exertion, every Limb and Feature appears with

---

[1] *Motto.* Virgil, *Aeneid,* I. 405:
           And by her graceful Walk a Goddess shows.

[2] *Aeneid,* I. 314 ff.

its respective Grace. It is from this Observation, that I cannot help being so passionate an Admirer as I am of good Dancing.[1] As all Art is an Imitation of Nature, this is an Imitation of Nature in its highest Excellence, and at a Time when she is most agreeable. The Business of Dancing is to display Beauty, and for that Reason all Distortions and Mimickries, as such, are what raise Aversion instead of Pleasure: But Things that are in themselves excellent, are ever attended with Imposture and false Imitation. Thus, as in Poetry there are laborious Fools who write Anagrams and Acrosticks, there are Pretenders in Dancing, who think meerly to do what others cannot, is to excel.[2] Such Creatures should be rewarded like him who had acquired a Knack of throwing a Grain of Corn through the Eye of a Needle, with a Bushel to keep his Hand in Use.[3] The Dancers[a] on our Stages are very faulty in this Kind; and what they mean by writhing themselves into such Postures, as it would be a Pain for any of the Spectators to stand in, and yet hope to please those Spectators, is unintelligible. Mr. *Prince* has a Genius, if he were encouraged, would prompt them to better Things.[4] In all the Dances he invents, you see he keeps close to the Characters he represents. He does not hope to please by making his Performers move in a Manner in which no one else ever did, but by Motions proper to the Characters he represents. He gives to Clowns and Lubbards[5] clumsy Graces, that is, he makes them practise what they would think Graces: And I have seen Dances of his, which might give Hints that would be useful to a comick Writer. These Performances have pleas'd the Taste of such as have not Reflection enough to know their Excellence, because they are in Nature; and the distorted Motions of others have offended those, who could not form Reasons to themselves for their Displeasure, from their being a Contradiction to Nature.

When one considers the inexpressible Advantage there is in arriving at some Excellence in this Art, it is monstrous to behold it so much neglected. The following Letter has in it something very natural on the Subject.

[a] Dancers] *1723*; Dancing *Fol., 8vo, 12mo*

[1] See Nos. 334, 370, 376 (vol. iii).   [2] See No. 60 (vol. i).
[3] The incident is quoted in Bayle, art. 'Macedonia', Remark Q. Montaigne (*Essays*, I. liv, 'Of Vain Subtilties') quotes it after discussing typographical poems and other 'frivolous Subtilties' (trans. Cotton, 1685, i. 603–4).
[4] The 'last New Morrice-Dance by Mr. Prince and others' is announced for performance at Drury Lane on 5 Aug.
[5] This form is marked by *OED* as obsolete except *Sc.* and *north. dial.*

Mr. SPECTATOR,

'I AM a Widower with but one Daughter; she was by Nature much enclined to be a Romp, and I had no Way of educating her, but commanding a young Woman, whom I entertain'd to take Care of her, to be very watchful in her Care and Attendance about her. I am a Man of Business, and oblig'd to be much abroad. The Neighbours have told me, that in my Absence our Maid has let in the spruce[1] Servants in the Neighbourhood to Junketings, while my Girl play'd and romped even in the Street. To tell you the plain Truth, I catched her once, at eleven Years old, at Chuck-Farthing,[2] among the Boys. This put me upon new Thoughts about my Child, and I determin'd to place her at a Boarding-School, and at the same Time gave a very discreet young Gentlewoman her Maintenance at the same Place and Rate, to be her Companion. I took little Notice of my Girl from Time to Time, but saw her now and then in good Health, out of Harm's way, and was satisfied. But by much Importunity, I was lately prevailed with to go to one of their Balls. I cannot express to you the Anxiety my silly Heart was in, when I saw my Romp, now fifteen, taken out: I never felt the Pangs of a Father upon me so strongly in my whole Life before; and I could not have suffered more, had my whole Fortune been at Stake. My Girl came on with the most becoming Modesty I had ever seen, and casting a respectful Eye, as if she feared me more than all the Audience, I gave a Nod, which, I think, gave her all the Spirit she assumed upon it, but she rose properly to that Dignity of Aspect. My Romp, now the most graceful Person of her Sex, assumed a Majesty which commanded the highest Respect; and when she turned to me, and saw my Face in Rapture, she fell into the prettiest Smile, and I saw in all her Motion that she exulted in her Father's Satisfaction. You, Mr. SPECTATOR, will, better than I can tell you, imagine to your self all the different Beauties and Changes of Aspect in an accomplished young Woman, setting forth all her Beauties with a Design to please no one so much as her Father. My Girl's Lover can never know half the Satisfaction that I did in her that Day. I could not possibly have imagined, that so great Improvement could have been wrought by an Art that I always held in it self ridiculous and

---

[1] I.e. brisk, smart, lively. The last quotation in *OED* in this sense is dated 1749.

[2] A game in which coins were pitched at a mark and then tossed at a hole by the player who came nearest the mark and who won all that alighted in the hole. See Strutt, *Sports and Pastimes* (2nd ed., 1810), p. 343.

contemptible There is, I am convinced, no Method like this, to give young Women a Sense of their own Value and Dignity; and I am sure there can be none so expeditious to communicate that Value to others. As for the flippant insipidly Gay and wantonly Forward, whom you behold among Dancers, that Carriage is more to be attributed to the perverse Genius of the Performers, than imputed to the Art it self. For my Part, my Child has danced her self into my Esteem, and I have as great an Honour for her as ever I had for her Mother, from whom she derived those latent good Qualities which appear'd in her Countenance when she was dancing; for my Girl, tho' I say it my self, shew'd in one Quarter of an Hour the innate Principles of a modest Virgin, a tender Wife, a generous Friend, a kind Mother, and an indulgent Mistress. I'll strain hard but I will purchase for her an Husband suitable to her Merit. I am your Convert in the Admiration of what I thought you jested when you recommended; and if you please to be at my House on *Thursday* next, I make a Ball for my Daughter, and you shall see her dance, or, if you will do her that Honour, dance with her.

I am, Sir,

Your most humble Servant,

Philipater.'

I have some Time ago[1] spoken of a Treatise written by Mr. *Weaver* on this Subject, which is now, I understand, ready to be published.[2] This Work sets this Matter in a very plain and advantageous Light; and I am convinced from it, that if the Art was under proper Regulations, it would be a mechanick way of implanting insensibly in Minds not capable of receiving it so well by any other Rules, a Sense of good Breeding and Virtue.

Were any one to see *Marianne* Dance, let him be never so sensual a Brute, I defy him to entertain any Thoughts but of the highest Respect and Esteem towards her.[3] I was shew'd last Week a Picture in a Lady's Closet, for which she had an hundred different Dresses,

---

[1] No. 334 (vol. iii).
[2] It is advertised in No. 476 (5 Sept. 1712):

This Day is Published,

An Essay towards a History of Dancing, in which the whole Art and its various Excellencies are in some Measure explain'd. Containing the several Sorts of Dancing. Antique and Modern, Serious, Scenical, Grotesque, &c. With the Use of it as an Exercise, Qualification, Diversion, &c. Spartam quam nactus est, hanc ornat. Printed for Jacob Tonson at Shakespear's Head over-against Catherine Street in the Strand.

[3] 'Probably Mrs. Bicknell' (Nichols).

that she could clap on round the Face, on purpose to demonstrate the force of Habits in the diversity of the same Countenance. Motion, and change of Posture and Aspect, has an Effect no less surprising on the Person of *Mariamne* when she Dances.

Chloe is extreamly pretty, and as silly as she is pretty. This Ideot has a very good Ear, and a most agreeable Shape; but the folly of the Thing is such, that it Smiles so impertinently, and affects to please so sillily, that while she Dances you see the Simpleton from Head to Foot. For you must know (as trivial as this Art is thought to be,) no one ever was a good Dancer, that had not a good Understanding. If this be a Truth, I shall leave the Reader to Judge from that Maxim, what Esteem they ought to have for such Impertinents as fly, hop, caper, tumble, twirl, turn round, and jump over their Heads, and, in a Word, play a thousand Pranks which many Animals can do better than a Man, instead of performing to Perfection what the humane Figure only is capable of performing.

It may perhaps appear odd, that I, who set up for a mighty Lover, at least, of Virtue, should take so much Pains to recommend what the soberer Part of Mankind look upon to be a Trifle; but, under Favour of the soberer Part of Mankind, I think they have not enough considered this Matter, and for that Reason only disesteem it. I must also, in my own Justification say, that I attempt to bring into the Service of Honour and Virtue every Thing in Nature that can pretend to give elegant Delight. It may possibly be proved, that Vice is in it self destructive of Pleasure, and Virtue in it self conducive to it. If the Delights of a free Fortune were under proper Regulations, this Truth would not want much Argument to support it; but it would be obvious to every Man, that there is a strict Affinity between all Things that are truly laudable and beautiful, from the highest Sentiment of the Soul, to the most indifferent Gesture of the Body.   T

No. 467   *Tuesday, August 26, 1712*[1]

> ... *Quodcunque meæ poterunt Audere Camœnæ*
> *Seu Tibi par poterunt, seu, quod spes abnuit ultra;*
> *Sive minus; certeque canent minus; omne vovemus*
> *Hoc tibi; nec tanto careat mihi nomine Charta.*
>
> Tibull. ad Messalam.

THE Love of Praise is a Passion deeply fix'd in the Mind of every extraordinary Person, and those who are most affected with it, seem most to partake of that Particle of the Divinity which distinguishes Mankind from the inferior Creation. The supreme Being it self is most pleased with Praise and Thanksgiving; the other Part of our Duty is but an Acknowledgment of our Faults, whilst this is the immediate Adoration of his Perfections. 'Twas an excellent Observation, That we then only despise Commendation when we cease to deserve it;[2] and we have still extant two Orations of *Tully* and *Pliny*,[3] spoken to the greatest and best Princes of all the *Roman* Emperors, who, no Doubt, heard with the greatest Satisfaction, what even the most disinterested Persons, and at so large a Distance of Time, cannot read without Admiration. *Cæsar* thought his Life consisted in the Breath of Praise, when he profess'd he had liv'd long enough for himself when he had for his Glory;[4] others have sacrific'd themselves for a Name which was not to begin till they were dead, giving away themselves to purchase a Sound which was not to commence till they were out of hearing: But by Merit and superior Excellencies not only to gain, but, whilst living, to enjoy a great and universal Reputation, is the last Degree of Happiness which we can hope for here. Bad Characters are dispers'd

---

[1] *Motto.* Tibullus, *Elegies*, 4. 1. 24–27:

> Whate'er my Genius dares attempt to write,
> Or whether worthy your judicious Sight;
> Or whether Joys beneath your Taste I sing,
> (Beyond that noble Taste no Muse can wing)
> All I devote or to your Praise or Scorn,
> That such a Patron may my Page adorn.

[2] This has not been identified.

[3] For Cicero's praise of Caesar see the oration *Pro Marcello*, delivered 46 B.C. The only surviving speech of Pliny the younger is the panegyric which he delivered in A.D. 100 in praise of the reforms of Trajan.

[4] *Se satis vel ad naturam, vel ad gloriam vixisse.* Cicero, *Pro Marcello*, 8. 25. This is also cited in No. 256 (vol. ii) and in the dedication to vol. iv of the first collected editions 8vo and 12mo.

abroad with Profusion, I hope for Example Sake, and (as Punishments are design'd by the Civil Power) more for the deterring the Innocent, than the chastising the Guilty. The Good are less frequent, whether it be that there are indeed fewer Originals of this Kind to copy after, or that, thro' the Malignity of our Nature, we rather delight in the Ridicule than the Virtues we find in others. However, it is but just, as well as pleasing, even for Variety, sometimes to give the World a Representation of the bright Side of humane Nature, as well as the dark and gloomy! The Desire of Imitation may, perhaps, be a greater Incentive to the Practice of what is good, than the Aversion we may conceive at what is blameable; the one immediately directs you what you shou'd do, whilst the other only shews you what you shou'd avoid: And I cannot at present do this with more Satisfaction, than by endeavouring to do some Justice to the Character of *Manilius*.[1]

It wou'd far exceed my present Design, to give a particular Description of *Manilius* thro' all the Parts of his excellent Life: I shall now only draw him in his Retirement, and pass over in Silence the various Arts, the courtly Manners, and the undesigning Honesty by which he attained the Honours he has enjoy'd, and which now give a Dignity and Veneration to the Ease he does enjoy. 'Tis here that he looks back with Pleasure on the Waves and Billows thro' which he has steered to so fair an Haven; he is now intent upon the Practice of every Virtue, which a great Knowledge and Use of Mankind has discovered to be the most useful to them. Thus in his private domestick Employments he is no less glorious than in his publick; for 'tis in Reality a more difficult Task to be conspicuous in a sedentary inactive Life, than in one that is spent in Hurry and Business; Persons engag'd in the latter, like Bodies violently agitated, from the Swiftness of their Motion have a Brightness added to them, which often vanishes when they are at Rest; but if it then still remain, it must be the Seeds of intrinsick Worth that thus shine out without any foreign Aid or Assistance.

His Liberality in another might almost bear the Name of Profusion; he seems to think it laudable even in the Excess, like that

---

[1] Nichols, followed by later editors, identifies Manilius as Lord Cowper. William Cowper, created Baron Cowper in 1706, presided at the trial of Sacheverell in 1710 and voted for his condemnation. He resigned his seal of office as Lord Chancellor in September 1710 and devoted himself to the opposition. He was reappointed after the accession of George I. He resigned in 1718 and died in 1723. Steele had dedicated the third volume of the *Tatler* to him.

River which most enriches when it overflows:[1] But *Manilius* has too perfect a Taste of the Pleasure of doing good, ever to let it be out of his Power; and for that Reason he will have a just Oeconomy, and a splendid Frugality at home, the Fountain from whence those Streams should flow which he disperses abroad. He looks with Disdain on those who propose their Death as the Time when they are to begin their Munificence; he will both see and enjoy (which he then does in the highest Degree) what he bestows himself; he will be the living Executor of his own Bounty, whilst they who have the Happiness to be within his Care and Patronage at once, pray for the continuation of his Life, and their own good Fortune. No one is out of the reach of his Obligations; he knows how, by proper and becoming Methods, to raise himself to a Level with those of the highest Rank; and his good Nature is a sufficient Warrant against the want of those who are so unhappy as to be in the very lowest. One may say of him, as *Pindar* bids his Muse say of *Theron.*

> *Swear, that* Theron *sure has sworn,*
> *No one near him shou'd be Poor.*
> *Swear that none e'er had such a graceful Art,* ⎫
> *Fortune's Free-Gifts as freely to impart,* ⎬
> *With an unenvious Hand, and an unbounded Heart.*[2] ⎭

Never did *Atticus* succeed better in gaining the universal Love and Esteem of all Men, nor steer with more Success betwixt the Extreams of two contending Parties.[3] 'Tis his peculiar Happiness, that while he espouses neither with an intemperate Zeal, he is not only admir'd, but, what is a more rare and unusual Felicity, he is belov'd and caress'd by both; and I never yet saw any Person, of whatsoever Age or Sex, but was immediately struck with the Merit of *Manilius.* There are many who are acceptable to some particular Persons, whilst the rest of Mankind look upon them with Coldness and Indifference; but he is the first whose entire good Fortune it is ever to please and to be pleased, where-ever he comes to be admir'd, and where-ever he is absent to be lamented. His Merit fares like the Pictures of *Raphael,* which are either seen with Admiration by all, or at least no one dare own he has no Taste for a Composition which has received so universal an Applause.[4] Envy and Malice find it

---

[1] The Nile.
[2] Cowley's version of the *Second Olympique Ode,* 175–9.
[3] See No. 385 (vol. iii).   [4] No. 226 (vol. ii).

against their Interest to indulge Slander and Obloquy. 'Tis as hard for an Enemy to detract from, as for a Friend to add to his Praise. An Attempt upon his Reputation is a sure lessening of one's own; and there is but one Way to injure him, which is to refuse him his just Commendations, and be obstinately silent.

It is below him to catch the Sight with any Care of Dress; his outward Garb is but the Emblem of his Mind, it is genteel, plain, and unaffected; he knows that Gold and Embroidery can add nothing to the Opinion which all have of his Merit, and that he gives a Lustre to the plainest Dress, whilst 'tis impossible the richest should communicate any to him. He is still the principal Figure in the Room: He first engages your Eye, as if there were some Point of Light which shone stronger upon him than on any other Person.

He puts me in mind of a Story of the famous *Bussy d'Amboise*, who at an Assembly at Court, where every one appear'd with the utmost Magnificence, relying upon his own superior Behaviour, instead of adorning himself like the rest, put on that Day a plain Suit of Cloaths, and dress'd all his Servants in the most costly gay Habits he could procure:[1] The Event was, that the Eyes of the whole Court were fix'd upon him, all the rest look'd like his Attendants, whilst he alone had the Air of a Person of Quality and Distinction.

Like *Aristippus*, whatever Shape or Condition he appears in, it still sits free and easy upon him;[2] but in some Part of his Character, 'tis true, he differs from him; for as he is altogether equal to the Largeness of his present Circumstances, the Rectitude of his Judgment has so far corrected the Inclinations of his Ambition, that he will not trouble himself with either the Desires or Pursuits of any thing beyond his present Enjoyments.

A thousand obliging Things flow from him upon every Occasion, and they are always so just and natural, that it is impossible to think he was at the least Pains to look for them. One would think it were the Dæmon of good Thoughts that discovered to him those Treasures, which he must have blinded others from seeing, they lay so directly in their Way. Nothing can equal the Pleasure is taken in hearing him speak, but the Satisfaction one receives in the Civility and Attention he pays to the Discourse of others. His Looks are a silent Commendation of what is good and praise-worthy, and a

---

[1] Saint-Evremond, 'A Letter to the Dutchess of Mazarin', tells this story (*Works*, 1714, ii. 131–2).
[2] Horace, *Epistles*, I. 17. 23.

secret Reproof to what is licentious and extravagant. He knows how to appear free and open without Danger of Intrusion, and to be cautious without seeming reserved. The Gravity of his Conversation is always enlivened with his Wit and Humour, and the Gayety of it is temper'd with something that is instructive, as well as barely agreeable. Thus with him you are sure not to be merry at the Expence of your Reason, nor serious with the Loss of your good Humour; but, by a happy Mixture in his Temper, they either go together, or perpetually succeed each other. In fine, his whole Behaviour is equally distant from Constraint and Negligence, and he commands your Respect, whilst he gains your Heart.

There is in his whole Carriage such an engaging Softness, that one cannot perswade one's self he is ever actuated by those rougher Passions, which, wherever they find Place, seldom fail of shewing themselves in the outward Demeanour of the Persons they belong to: But his Constitution is a just Temperature[1] between Indolence on one Hand and Violence on the other. He is mild and gentle, wherever his Affairs will give him Leave to follow his own Inclinations; but yet never failing to exert himself with Vigour and Resolution in the Service of his Prince, his Country, or his Friend. Z[2]

No. 468   *Wednesday, August 27, 1712*[3]
[STEELE]

Erat Homo ingeniosus, acutus, acer, & qui plurimum &
salis haberet & fellis, nec candoris minus.

Plin. Epist.

MY Paper is in a Kind a Letter of News, but it regards rather what passes in the World of Conversation than that of Business. I am very sorry that I have at present a Circumstance before me, which is of very great Importance to all who have a Relish for Gayety, Wit, Mirth, or Humour; I mean the Death of

[1] Here used in the obsolete sense of a moderate position between opposites, a middle course. This is the last quotation for this meaning in *OED*.

[2] This number has been attributed, by Nichols and others, to Hughes. It is not, however, in Duncombe's list. It is claimed for Pope by Ault. See Introduction, pp. xlix–l.

[3] *Motto.* Pliny, *Epistles*, 3. 21: He was an ingenious, acute, and sharp man, one who had much salt and satire in him, and no less good humour.

poor *Dick Eastcourt*.[1] I have been obliged to him for so many Hours of Jollity, that it is but a small Recompence, tho' all I can give him, to pass a Moment or two in Sadness for the Loss of so agreeable a Man. Poor *Eastcourt*! the last Time I saw him, we were plotting to shew the Town his great Capacity for acting in its full Light, by introducing him as dictating to a Set of young Players, in what Manner to speak this Sentence, and utter t'other Passion——He had so exquisite a Discerning of what was defective in any Object before him, that in an Instant he could shew you the ridiculous Side of what would pass for beautiful and just, even to Men of no ill Judgment, before he had pointed at the Failure. He was no less skilful in the Knowledge of Beauty; and, I dare say, there is no one who knew him well, but can repeat more well-turned Compliments, as well as smart Repartees, of Mr. *Eastcourt*'s, than of any other Man in *England*. This was easily to be observed in his inimitable Faculty of telling a Story, in which he would throw in natural and unexpected Incidents, to make his Court to one Part, and rally the other Part of the Company: Then he would vary the Usage he gave them, according as he saw them bear kind or sharp Language. He had the Knack to raise up a pensive Temper, and mortify an impertinently gay one, with the most agreeable Skill imaginable. There are a thousand things which crowd into my Memory, which make me too much concerned to tell on about him. *Hamlet* holding

---

[1] Richard Estcourt (1668–1712), described in *Tatler* 51 as '*Tom Mirrour*, the Comical Actor', is referred to in Nos. 264, 358, and 370. He was buried at St. Paul's, Covent Garden, on the day this number was issued. Some of his famous roles were Bayes in *The Rehearsal*, Falstaff in *Henry IV*, Ned Blunt in *The Committee*, and Sir Joslin Jolly in *She Wou'd if She Cou'd*. Shortly before his death he had taken the part of the Friar in *The Spanish Fryar* (15 May), that of Serjeant Kite in *The Recruiting Officer* (10 June), and that of Palmer in *Love in a Tub* (12 June), all at Drury Lane. *A Letter from Dick Estcourt, the Comedian, to the Spectator*, is the title of a pamphlet published by J. Baker in 1713. In the form of a letter dated 'Brandipolis, Octob. 1712', it purports to describe the activities of Godolphin, Hoadly, Dodwell, and others in the underworld.

I promised you before my Departure to these Regions to communicate any Thing of Moment that occurr'd to me in my Journey, or any of the Remarkable Transactions of this Place, that might entertain you or your Gay Friend, *Will. Honeycomb.* . . . The Wise and Ingenious SPECTATOR has contributed more by his Speculations to the advancing of Virtue and Morality, and given a greater Check to the growing Vices of the Times, than all the Endeavours of United Societies with florid Sermons and pompous Feasts. This *Great Man* (like the Physician that gilds the bitter Pill, to recommend it the better to the Palate) pleased us where he gave us Pain; and Instructions combined with Wit and Humour will never fail to meet with the desired Success. The Design of this Pamphlet is not to reflect on those who claim by their Decease the most favourable Scrutiny of their Actions, but by shewing Vice in its Native Dress of Shame and Contempt, to deter the Living from imitating the Deceased Patrons of it.

up the Skull which the Grave-digger threw to him, with an Account that it was the Head of the King's Jester, falls into very pleasing Reflections, and cries out to his Companion,

Alas, poor Yorick! *I knew him,* Horatio, *a Fellow of infinite Jest, of most excellent Fancy; he hath born me on his Back a thousand times: And how abhorred my Imagination is now, my Gorge rises at it. Here hung those Lips that I have kiss'd I know not how oft. Where be your Gibes now, your Gambols, your Songs, your Flashes of Merriment, that were wont to set the Table on a Roar: No one now to mock your own Jeerings, quite chop-fallen! Now get you to my Lady's Chamber, and tell her, Let her paint an Inch thick, to this Favour she must come. Make her laugh at that.*[1]

It is an Insolence natural to the Wealthy, to affix, as much as in them lies, the Character of a Man to his Circumstances. Thus it is ordinary with them to praise faintly the good Qualities of those below them, and say it is very extraordinary in such a Man as he is, or the like, when they are forced to acknowledge the Value of him whose Lowness upbraids their Exaltation. It is to this Humour only, that it is to be ascribed, that a quick Wit in Conversation, a nice Judgment upon any Emergency that could arise, and a most blame-less inoffensive Behaviour, could not raise this Man above being received only upon the Foot of contributing to Mirth and Diversion. But he was as easy under that Condition, as a Man of so excellent Talents was capable; and since they would have it, that to divert was his Business, he did it with all the seeming Alacrity imaginable, tho' it stung him to the Heart that it was his Business. Men of Sense, who could taste his Excellencies, were well satisfied to let him lead the Way in Conversation, and play after his own Manner; but Fools, who provoked him to Mimickry, found he had the Indigna-tion to let it be at their Expence who called for it, and he would shew the Form of conceited heavy Fellows as Jests to the Company at their own Request, in Revenge for interrupting him from being a Companion to put on the Character of a Jester.

What was peculiarly excellent in this memorable Companion, was, that in the Accounts he gave of Persons and Sentiments, he did not only hit the Figure of their Faces and Manner of their Gestures, but he would in his Narrations fall into their very Way of Thinking, and this when he recounted Passages, wherein Men of the best Wit were concerned, as well as such wherein were repre-

[1] *Hamlet*, v. i. 202 ff.

sented Men of the lowest Rank of Understanding. It is certainly as great an Instance of Self-love to a Weakness, to be impatient of being mimick'd, as any can be imagined. There were none but the Vain, the Formal, the Proud, or those who were incapable of amending their Faults, that dreaded him; to others he was in the highest Degree pleasing; and I do not know any Satisfaction of any indifferent Kind I ever tasted so much, as having got over an Impatience of seeing my self in the Air he could put me when I have displeased him. It is indeed to his exquisite Talent this way, more than any Philosophy I could read on the Subject, that my Person is very little of my Care; and it is indifferent to me what is said of my Shape, my Air, my Manner, my Speech, or my Address. It is to poor *Eastcourt* I chiefly owe, that I am arrived at the Happiness of thinking nothing a Diminution to me, but what argues a Depravity of my Will.

It has as much surpriz'd me as any thing in Nature, to have it frequently said, That he was not a good Player: But that must be owing to a Partiality for former Actors in the Parts in which he succeeded them, and judging by Comparison of what was liked before rather than by the Nature of the Thing.[1] When a Man of his Wit and Smartness could put on an utter Absence of common Sense in his Face, as he did in the Character of *Bullfinch* in the *Northern Lass*, and an Air of insipid Cunning and Vivacity in the Character of *Pounce* in the *Tender Husband*, it is Folly to dispute his Capacity and Success, as he was an Actor.[2]

Poor *Eastcourt!* let the Vain and Proud be at Rest; thou wilt[a] no more disturb their Admiration of their dear selves, and thou art no longer to drudge in raising the Mirth of Stupids, who know nothing of thy Merit, for thy Maintenance.

It is natural for the Generality of Mankind to run into Reflections upon our Mortality, when Disturbers of the World are laid at Rest, but to take no Notice when they who can please and divert are pulled from us: But for my Part, I cannot but think the Loss of such Talents as the Man of whom I am speaking was Master of, a more

---

[a] thou wilt] *M*; they will *all edd.*

[1] Cibber, after praising Estcourt's skill in mimicry, thought he was 'upon the whole, a languid, unaffecting actor' (*Apology*, chap. iv, Everyman ed., p. 65).

[2] Bullfinch is one of the two justices in *The Northern Lass*, by Richard Brome. Estcourt took this part in performances at Drury Lane on 13 Feb. and 31 Dec. 1711. Pounce is the lawyer in Steele's comedy, *The Tender Husband*, and was played by Estcourt on 11 Jan. and 10 May 1711. (The Epilogue in this play was also spoken by Estcourt.) I have no record of either of these plays being performed from Jan. to Sept. 1712.

melancholy Instance of Mortality, than the Dissolution of Persons of never so high Characters in the World, whose Pretensions were that they were noisy and mischievous.

But I must grow more succinct, and, as a SPECTATOR, give an Account of this extraordinary Man, who, in his Way, never had an equal in any Age before him, or in that wherein he lived. I speak of him as a Companion, and a Man qualified for Conversation. His Fortune exposed him to an Obsequiousness towards the worst Sort of Company, but his excellent Qualities rendered him capable of making the best Figure in the most refin'd. I have been present with him among Men of the most delicate Taste a whole Night, and have known him (for he saw it was desired) keep the Discourse to himself the most Part of it, and maintain his good Humour with a Countenance, in a Language so delightful, without Offence to any Person or Thing upon Earth, still preserving the Distance his Circumstances obliged him to; I say, I have seen him do all this in such a charming Manner, that I am sure none of those I hint at will read this, without giving him some Sorrow for their abundant Mirth, and one Gush of Tears for so many Bursts of Laughter. I wish it were any Honour to the pleasant Creature's Memory, that my Eyes are too much suffused to let me go on——[a]   T

---

[a] *The following final paragraph in Fol. was omitted in 8vo and 12mo:*[1]

It is a Felicity his Friends may rejoyce in, that he had his Senses, and used them as he ought to do, in his last Moments. It is remarkable, that his Judgment was in its calm Perfection to the utmost Article; for when his Wife, out of her Fondness, desired she might send for a certain illiterate Humourist, (whom he has accompanied in a thousand mirthful Moments, and whose Insolence makes Fools think he assumes from conscious Merit) he answered, *Do what you please, but he won't come near me.* Let poor *Eastcourt's* Negligence about this Message, convince the Unwary of a triumphant Empyrick's Ignorance and Inhumanity.[2]

---

[1] This omitted passage was 'apparently levelled at Dr. Radcliffe' (Nichols). Dr. John Radcliffe (1650–1714), who seems to have neglected Estcourt in his last hours, had been ridiculed by Steele in *Tatlers* 44, 47, and 67, for his falling in love with one of his patients. He died unmarried in 1714, leaving the greater part of his wealth to charity, including the erection of an infirmary and other benefactions to science at Oxford.

[2] A letter signed Eliz. M. (Lillie, ii. 336–7) praises this tribute to Estcourt.

He had the art of preserving a due respect and modest regard to our sex, though when so elated, that it could hardly be expected from him. He was merry without scurrility, and satyrical without offence, the best comforter upon any melancholy accident, not by set speeches so often ill-timed, but by first entering into our passions he led us insensibly into his own. As to his acting, the least of his good qualities, he could, like the poet in Scarroon, have acted a whole play himself: I have heard him on the stage in Dublin, in the compass of one scene, speak in the key of all the eminent actors in this town.

[ADDISON]

Detrahere aliquid alteri, & hominem hominis incommodo
suum augere commodum, magis est contra naturam,
quam mors, quam paupertas, quam dolor, quam cætera
quæ possunt aut corpori accidere, aut rebus externis.

                                       Tull.

I AM perswaded there are few Men, of generous Principles, who
would seek after great Places, were it not rather to have an
Opportunity in their Hands of obliging their particular Friends, or
those whom they look upon as Men of Worth, than to procure
Wealth and Honour for themselves. To an honest Mind the best
Perquisites of a Place are the Advantages it gives a Man of doing
Good.

Those who are under the great Officers of State, and are the
Instruments by which they act, have more frequent Opportunities[a]
for the Exercise of Compassion, and Benevolence, than their Superiors
themselves. These Men know every little Case that is to come before
the Great Man, and if they are possessed with honest Minds, will
consider Poverty as a Recommendation in the Person who applies
himself to them, and make the Justice of his Cause the most powerful Sollicitor in his behalf. A Man of this Temper, when he is in a
Post of Business, becomes a Blessing to the Publick: He patronizes
the Orphan and the Widow, assists the Friendless, and guides the
Ignorant: He does not reject the Persons Pretensions, who does not
know how to explain them, or refuse doing a good Office for a Man,
because he cannot pay the Fee of it. In short, tho' he regulates himself in all his Proceedings by Justice and Equity, he finds a thousand
Occasions for all the good-natured Offices of Generosity[b] and Compassion.

A Man is unfit for such a Place[c] of Trust, who is of a sower

---

[a] more frequent Opportunities] generally greater Conveniencies *Fol.*   [b] finds
. . . Generosity] finds a thousand Opportunities of exercising his Generosity *Fol.*
[c] a Place] an Office *Fol.*

---

[1] *Motto.* Cicero, *De Officiis*, 3. 5. 21 (altered): To take away any thing wrongfully
from any man, or to make my Own Fortune by the empoverishing of another, is
more Contrary to *Nature*, than Death, Beggary, Pain; or whatever else can befall
a man's Body, or Estate. L'ESTRANGE.

untractable Nature, or has any other Passion that makes him uneasie to those who approach him. Roughness of Temper is apt to discountenance the Timorous or Modest. The proud Man discourages those from approaching him, who are of a mean Condition, and who most want his Assistance. The impatient Man will not give himself time to be informed of the matter that lies before him. An Officer with one or more or these unbecoming Qualities, is sometimes looked upon as a proper Person to keep off Impertinence and Solicitation from his Superior; but this is a kind of Merit, that can never attone for the Injustice which may very often arise from it.

There are two other vicious Qualities which render a Man very unfit for such a Place of Trust. The first of these is a Dilatory Temper, which commits innumerable Cruelties without Design. The Maxim which several have laid down for a Man's Conduct in ordinary Life, should be inviolable with a Man in Office, never to think of doing that to Morrow which may be done to Day.[1] A Man who defers doing what ought to be done, is guilty of Injustice so long as he defers it. The Dispatch of a good Office is very often as beneficial to the Sollicitor as the good Office it self. In short, if a Man compared the Inconveniencies which another suffers by his Delays, with the trifling Motives and Advantages which he himself may reap by such a Delay, he would never be guilty of a Fault which very often does an irreparable Prejudice to the Person who depends upon him, and which might be remedied with little[a] Trouble to himself.

But in the last place, there is no Man so improper to be employed in Business, as he who is in any degree capable of Corruption; and such an one is the Man, who upon any Pretence whatsoever receives more than what is the stated and unquestioned Fee of his Office. Gratifications, Tokens of Thankfulness, Dispatch Mony, and the like specious Terms, are the Pretences under which Corruption very frequently shelters it self. An honest Man will however look on all these Methods as unjustifiable, and will enjoy himself better in a moderate Fortune that is gained with Honour and Reputation, than in an overgrown Estate that is canker'd with the Acquisitions of Rapine and Exaction. Were all our Offices discharged with such an inflexible Integrity, we should not see Men in all Ages, who grow

[a] little] so little *Fol.*

---

[1] Cf. No. 283 (vol. iii), where Budgell calls this an Italian proverb. It is to be found in English as early as the fourteenth century (Apperson).

up to exorbitant Wealth with the Abilities which are to be met with in an ordinary Mechanick. I cannot but think that such a Corruption proceeds chiefly from Mens employing the first that offer themselves, or those who have the Character of shrewd worldly Men, instead of searching out such as have had a liberal Education, and have been trained up in the Studies of Knowledge and Virtue.

It has been observed, that Men of Learning who take to Business, discharge it generally with greater Honesty than Men of the World. The chief Reason for it I take to be as follows. A Man that has spent his Youth in Reading, has been used to find Virtue extolled, and Vice stigmatized. A Man that has past his Time in the World, has often seen Vice triumphant, and Virtue discountenanced. Extortion, Rapine and Injustice, which are branded with Infamy in Books, often give a Man a Figure in the World; while several Qualities which are celebrated in Authors, as Generosity, Ingenuity and Good-Nature, impoverish and ruin him. This cannot but have a proportionable Effect on Men, whose Tempers and Principles are equally Good and Vicious.

There would be at least this Advantage in employing Men of Learning and Parts in Business, that their Prosperity would set more gracefully on them, and that we should not see many worthless Persons shot up into the greatest Figures of Life.　　　C

No. 470　　　　　　　　*Friday, August 29, 1712*[1]
[ADDISON]

> *Turpe est difficiles habere nugas,*
> *Et stultus est labor ineptiarum.*
> Mart.

I HAVE been very often disappointed of late Years, when upon examining the new Edition of a Classick Author, I have found above half the Volume taken up with Various Readings.[2] When I

---

[1] *Motto.* Martial, *Epigrams*, 2. 86. 9–10 (altered): It is not good to make Difficulties out of mere nothing: and it is the part of a Fool to labour about Fooleries.

[2] Nichols interpreted this satire as having special reference to the edition of the *Pervigilium Veneris* published at The Hague in 1712, a work which was later ridiculed in the well-known *Chef d'Œuvre d'un Inconnu* of Thémiseul de Saint-Hyacinthe in 1714. It is hardly necessary, of course, to limit this essay to a parody of any particular work, since it expresses perfectly the attitude toward textual criticism shared by all the

have expected to meet with[a] a Learned Note upon a doubtful Passage in a *Latin* Poet, I have only been informed, that such or such Ancient Manuscripts for an *et* write an *ac*, or of some other notable Discovery of the like Importance. Indeed, when a different Reading gives us a different Sense, or a new Elegance in an Author, the Editor[1] does very well in taking Notice of it; but when he only entertains us with the several ways of Spelling the same Word, and gathers together the various Blunders and Mistakes of twenty or thirty different Transcribers, they only take up the Time of the learned Reader, and puzzle the Minds of the Ignorant. I have often fancied with myself how enraged an old *Latin* Author would be, should he see the several Absurdities in Sense and Grammar, which are imputed to him by some or other of these Various Readings. In one he speaks Nonsense; in another makes use of a Word that was never heard of: And indeed,[b] there is scarce a Solecism in Writing which the best Author is not guilty of, if we may be at Liberty to read him in the Words of some Manuscript, which the laborious Editor has thought fit to examine in the Prosecution of his Work.

I question not but the Ladies and pretty Fellows will be very curious to understand what it is that I have been hitherto talking of. I shall therefore give them a Notion of this Practice, by endeavouring to write after the manner of several Persons who make an eminent Figure in the Republick of Letters. To this end we will

---

[a] meet with] find *Fol.*   [b] And indeed,] In short, *Fol.*

---

wits and gentlemen of the time. Addison is simply showing here what he can do in the vein of the Scriblerians. If, as Spence reports, Addison liked the Scriblerus Club 'very well, and was not disinclined to come in to it', this essay could well be a trial contribution. If any specific edition is referred to here it is very likely Bentley's Horace. In 1712 Lintott began publishing, in 24 sixpenny parts (the first 17 dated 1712, the others 1713), 'The Odes of Horace in Latin and English; with a Translation of Dr. Bentley's Notes, to which are added, Notes upon Notes, Done in the Bentleian Stile and Manner', and published in two volumes in 1713 as *The Odes, Epodes, and Carmen Seculare of Horace, in Latin and English; with a Translation of Dr. Ben-ley's Notes . . . By several Hands*. The comment on the 19th Ode of the second Book (in part x, p. 31) is exactly in the style of Addison's essay:

In this *Ode* the Dr. makes a horrid Pother about the spelling of some proper Names; much Ink is spilt, many Pages consum'd, several old Parchments and Copies dusted, Commentators and Criticks quoted and confuted, various Lections settled, Indexes and Lexicons turn'd over, and a great deal of *Latin* and *Greek* squander'd away; and all to prove whether we must read, *Thyas* or *Thias*, or *Thuas*, or *Thyias*; . . . whereas all this is just to as much purpose, as if a Critick should write a Book, to prove *K* to be the first Letter in the spelling of *Calendar*.

[1] This is the first example in *OED* of the word used in the modern sense, 'one who prepares the literary work of another person for publication; also one who prepares an edition of any literary work'.

suppose, that the following Song is an old Ode[a] which I present to the Publick in a new Edition, with the several Various Readings which I find of it in former Editions, and in Ancient Manuscripts. Those who cannot relish the various Readings, will perhaps[b] find their Account in the Song, which never before appeared in Print.

> *My Love was fickle once and changing,*
> *Nor e'er would settle in my Heart;*
> *From Beauty still to Beauty ranging,*
> *In ev'ry Face I found a Dart.*

> *'Twas first a Charming Shape enslav'd me;*
> *An Eye then gave the fatal Stroke:*
> *'Till by her Wit Corinna sav'd me,*
> *And all my former Fetters broke.*

> *But now a long and lasting Anguish*
> *For Belvidera I endure;*
> *Hourly I Sigh and hourly Languish,*
> *Nor hope to find the wonted Cure.*

> *For here the false unconstant Lover,*
> *After a thousand Beauties shown;*
> *Does new surprising Charms discover,*
> *And finds Variety in One.*

Various Readings.

Stanza the First, Verse the First. *And changing.*] The *and* in some Manuscripts is written thus, *&*, but that in the *Cotton* Library writes it in three distinct Letters.

Verse the Second. *Nor e'er would.*] *Aldus*[1] reads it *ever would*; but as this would hurt the Metre, we have restored it to its genuine Reading, by observing that *Synæresis*[2] which had been neglected by ignorant Transcribers.

Ibid. *In my Heart.*] *Scaliger,*[3] and others, *on my Heart.*

Song is an old Ode] Song, which by the way is a beautiful Descant upon a single Thought, like the Compositions of the best Ancient Lyrick Poets, I say we will suppose this Song is an old Ode *Fol.*   [b] perhaps] however *Fol.*

---

[1] Aldus Manutius, the Elder (*c.* 1450–1515), founder of the famous Aldine press at Venice *c.* 1490. Aldus Manutius, the Younger (1547–97), was his grandson.
[2] 'Contraction, especially of two vowels into a diphthong or a simple vowel' (*OED*).
[3] Either Julius Caesar Scaliger (1484–1558) or his son, Joseph Justus Scaliger (1540–1609), who brought out numerous editions of Latin writers. It is more likely the

Verse the Fourth. *I found a Dart*.] The *Vatican* Manuscript for *I* reads *it*, but this must have been the Hallucination of the Transcriber, who probably mistook the Dash of the *I*. for a *T*.

Stanza the Second, Verse the Second. *The fatal Stroke*.] *Scioppius*,[1] *Salmasius*,[2] and many others, for *the* read *a*, but I have stuck to the usual Reading.

Verse the Third. *Till by her Wit*.] Some Manuscripts have it *his Wit*, others *your*, others *their Wit*. But as I find *Corinna* to be the Name of a Woman in other Authors, I cannot doubt but it should be *her*.

Stanza the Third, Verse the First. *A long and lasting Anguish*.] The *German* Manuscript reads *a lasting Passion*, but the Rhyme will not admit it.

Verse the Second. *For Belvidera I endure*.] Did not all the Manuscripts reclaim,[3] I should change *Belvidera* into *Pelvidera*; *Pelvis*[4] being used by several of the Ancient Comick Writers for a Looking-Glass, by which means the Etymology of the Word is very visible, and *Pelvidera* will signifie a Lady who often looks in her Glass, as indeed she had very good reason, if she had all those Beauties which our Poet here ascribes to her.

Verse the Third. *Hourly I sigh and hourly languish*.] Some for the Word *hourly* read *dayly*, and others *nightly*; the last has great Authorities of its side.

Verse the Fourth. *The wonted Cure*.] The Elder *Stevens* reads *wanted Cure*.[5]

Stanza the Fourth, Verse the Second. *After a thousand Beauties*.] In several Copies we meet with a *Hundred Beauties*, by the usual Errour of the Transcribers, who probably omitted a Cypher, and had not taste enough to know, that the Word *Thousand* was ten times a greater Compliment to the Poet's Mistress than an *Hundred*.

Verse the Fourth. *And finds Variety in one*.] Most of the Ancient

---

elder, who is frequently referred to in the satirical edition of Bentley's Horace of 1712–13.

[1] Caspar Schoppe (1576–1649), the German scholar and Catholic controversialist, author of *De arte critica, Grammatica philosophica*, and other works.

[2] Claude de Saumaise (1588–1653), the French classical scholar and professor at Leyden, author of many learned works, including a commentary on the *Polyhistor* of Solinus.

[3] I.e. exclaim, protest. 'Now *rare*' (*OED*).

[4] Pelvis (*Lat.*, basin, laver).

[5] Robert Estienne, or Stephanus (1503–59), produced a series of *editiones principes* of Greek authors in the early sixteenth century, and also the Greek Testament (1550).

Manuscripts have it *in two*. Indeed so many of them concur in this last Reading, that I am very much in doubt whether it ought not to take place. There are but two Reasons which incline me to the Reading, as I have Published it; First because the Rhime, and Secondly because the Sense is preserv'd by it. It might likewise proceed from the Oscitancy[1] of Transcribers, who, to dispatch their Work the sooner, used to write all Numbers in Cypher, and seeing the Figure 1 followed by a little Dash of the Pen, as is customary in old Manuscripts, they perhaps mistook the Dash for a second Figure, and by casting up both together composed out of them the Figure 2. But this I shall leave to the Learned, without determining any thing in a matter of so great Uncertainty.   C

No. 471   *Saturday, August 30, 1712*[2]

[ADDISON]

'Εν ἐλπίσιν χρὴ τοὺς σοφοὺς ἔχειν βίον.   Euripid.

THE *Time present* seldom affords sufficient Employment to the Mind of Man. Objects of Pain or Pleasure, Love or Admiration, do not lie thick enough together in Life to keep the Soul in constant Action, and supply an immediate Exercise to its Faculties. In order, therefore, to remedy this Defect, that the Mind may not want Business, but always have Materials for thinking, she is endowed with certain Powers, that can recall what is passed, and anticipate what is to come.

That wonderful Faculty, which we call the Memory, is perpetually looking back, when we have nothing present to entertain us. It is like those Repositories in several Animals, that are filled with Stores of their former Food, on which they may ruminate when their present Pasture fails.

As the Memory relieves the Mind in her vacant Moments, and prevents any Chasms of Thought by Ideas[a] of what is *past*, we have other Faculties that agitate and employ her upon what *is to come*. These are the Passions of Hope and Fear.

[a] prevents . . . Ideas] fills up the Chasms of Thought with Ideas *Fol.*

[1] A learned word for 'drowsiness, such as is manifested by yawning' (*OED*).
[2] *Motto*. Euripides, *Ino*, Fragment 7: The Wise should employ their Life in future Hope.

By these two Passions we reach forward into Futurity, and bring up to our present Thoughts Objects that lie hid in the remotest Depths of Time. We suffer Misery, and enjoy Happiness, before they are in Being; we can set the Sun and Stars forward, or lose sight of them by wandring into those retired Parts of Eternity, when the Heavens and Earth shall be no more.

By the way, who can imagine that the Existence of a Creature is to be circumscribed by Time, whose Thoughts are not? But I shall, in this Paper, confine my self to that particular Passion which goes by the Name of Hope.

Our Actual Enjoyments are so few and transient, that Man would be a very miserable Being, were he not endowed with this Passion, which gives him a Taste of those good Things that may possibly come into his Possession. *We should hope for every thing that is good,* says the old Poet *Linus, because there is nothing which may not be hoped for, and nothing but what the Gods are able to give us.*[1] Hope quickens all the still[a] Parts of Life, and keeps the Mind awake in her most Remiss and Indolent Hours. It gives habitual Serenity and good Humour. It is a kind of Vital Heat in the Soul, that cheers and gladdens her, when she does not attend to it. It makes Pain easie, and Labour pleasant.

Besides these several Advantages which rise from *Hope*, there is another which is none of the least, and that is, its great Efficacy in preserving us from setting too high a Value on present Enjoyments. The Saying of *Cæsar* is very well known.[2] When he had given away all his Estate in Gratuities among his Friends, one of them asked what he had left for himself; to which that great Man replied, *Hope*. His Natural Magnanimity hindered him from prizing what he was certainly possessed of, and turned all his Thoughts upon something more valuable that he had in View. I question not but every Reader will draw a Moral from this Story, and apply it to himself without my Direction.

The old Story of *Pandora*'s Box (which many of the Learned believe was formed among the Heathens upon the Tradition of the Fall of Man)[3] shews us how deplorable a State they thought the

[a] still] dead *Fol.*

[1] Stobaeus, *Florilegium,* 110. 1 (Winterton, p. 467).
[2] An error for Alexander. See Plutarch, *Life of Alexander,* 15. 2.
[3] Burton (*Anatomy of Melancholy,* I. 1. i. 1) refers to the similarity between the two stories.

present Life without Hope. To set forth the utmost Condition of Misery they tell us, that our Forefather, according to the Pagan Theology, had a great Vessel presented him by *Pandora*: Upon his lifting up the Lid of it, says the Fable, there flew out all the Calamities and Distempers incident to Men, from which, 'till that time, they had been altogether exempt. *Hope*, who had been enclosed in the Cup with so much bad Company, instead of flying off with the rest, stuck so close to the Lid of it, that it was shut down upon her.

I shall make but two Reflections upon what I have hitherto said. First, that no kind of Life is so happy as that which is full of Hope, especially when the Hope is well grounded, and when the Object of it is of an exalted kind, and in its Nature proper to make the Person happy who enjoys it. This Proposition must be very evident to those who consider how few are the present Enjoyments of the most happy Man, and how insufficient to give him an entire Satisfaction and Acquiescence in them.

My next Observation is this, that a Religious Life is that which most abounds in a well-grounded Hope, and such an one as is fixed on Objects that are capable of making us entirely happy. This Hope in a Religious Man, is much more sure and certain than the Hope of any Temporal Blessing, as it is strengthned not only by Reason, but by Faith. It has at the same time its Eye perpetually fixed on that State, which implies in the very Notion of it the most full and the most compleat Happiness.

I have before shewn how the Influence of Hope in general sweetens Life, and makes our present Condition supportable, if not pleasing; but a Religious Hope has still greater Advantages. It does not only bear up the Mind under her Sufferings, but makes her rejoice in them, as they may be the Instruments of procuring her the great and ultimate End of all her Hope.

Religious Hope has likewise this Advantage above any other kind of Hope, that it is able to revive the *dying* Man, and to fill his Mind not only with secret Comfort and Refreshment, but sometimes with Rapture and Transport. He triumphs in his Agonies, whilst the Soul springs forward with Delight to the great Object which she has always had in view, and leaves the Body with an expectation of being re-united to her in a glorious and joyful Resurrection.

I shall conclude this Essay with those emphatical Expressions of a lively Hope, which the Psalmist made use of in the midst of those Dangers and Adversities which surrounded him, for the following

Passage had its present and personal, as well as its future and pro-phetick Sense. *I have set the Lord always before me: because he is at my right hand I shall not be moved. Therefore my heart is glad, and my Glory rejoiceth: my flesh also shall rest in hope. For thou wilt not leave my Soul in Hell, neither wilt thou suffer thine holy One to see Corruption. Thou wilt shew me the path of life: in thy presence is fulness of joy, at thy right hand there are pleasures for evermore.*[1]

C

No. 472
[STEELE]

Monday, September 1, 1712[2]

> ... *Voluptas*
> *Solamenque mali* ...
> Virg.

I RECEIVED some time ago a Proposal, which had a Preface to it, wherein the Author discoursed at large of the innumerable Ob-jects of Charity in a Nation, and admonish'd the Rich, who were afflicted with any Distemper of Body, particularly to regard the Poor in the same Species of Affliction, and confine their Tenderness to them, since it is impossible to assist all who are presented to them. The Proposer had been relieved from a Malady in his Eyes by an Operation perform'd by Sir *William Read*;[3] and being a Man of Condition, had taken a Resolution to maintain three poor blind Men during their Lives, in Gratitude for that great Blessing. This

---

[1] Ps. xvi. 8–11.

[2] *Motto.* Virgil, *Aeneid*, 3. 660–1:

This onely Solace his hard Fortune sends. DRYDEN.

[3] 'Surely you have heard of him', Swift writes to Stella, 11 Apr. 1711. 'He has been a mountebank, and is the queen's oculist: he makes admirable punch, and treats you in gold vessels' (*Journal to Stella*, ed. Williams, p. 240). In Jan. 1705 Read advertised that he had restored to sight between 1,600 and 1,700 who were blind of cataracts (*Daily Courant*, 1 Jan.), and in the following July he was knighted by Queen Anne 'as a Mark of Her Royal Favour for his great Services done in curing great Numbers of Seamen and Soldiers of Blindness, Gratis' (*Daily Courant*, 30 July 1705). He advertises in the *Gazette* of 5 Jan. 1710 that he cures 'Her Majesty's Seamen and Soldiers gratis'; he offers to couch the poor of cataracts gratis, and also to take off wens, to cure wry necks or hare-lips, 'tho' never so deformed' (*Tatler* 147, 18 Mar. 1710); and claims to cure cancers (*Post Boy*, 5 Dec. 1710). A testimonial to the cure of one Elizabeth Milfris, in the parish of St. John of Wapping, of blindness, performed by Lady Read under Sir William's directions, is printed among the advertisements in Nos. 21 and 25. An advertisement in No. 502 advises that he has returned from Norfolk and Suffolk to his house in Durham-yard in the Strand, and lists a number

Misfortune is so very great and unfrequent, that, one would think, an Establishment for all the Poor under it might be easily accomplished, with the Addition of a very few others to those Wealthy who are in the same Calamity. However, the Thought of the Proposer arose from a very good Motive, and the parcelling of our selves out, as called to particular Acts of Beneficence, would be a pretty Cement of Society and Virtue. It is the ordinary Foundation for Mens holding a Commerce with each other, and becoming familiar, that they agree in the same Sort of Pleasure; and sure it may also be some Reason for Amity, that they are under one common Distress. If all the Rich who are lame in the Gout, from a Life of Ease, Pleasure, and Luxury, would help those few who have it without a previous Life of Pleasure, and add a few of such laborious Men, who are become lame from unhappy Blows, Falls, or other Accidents of Age or Sickness; I say, would such gouty Persons administer to the Necessities of Men disabled like themselves, the Consciousness of such a Behaviour would be the best Julep, Cordial, and Anodine in the feverish, faint, and tormenting Vicissitudes of that miserable Distemper. The same may be said of all other, both bodily and intellectual Evils. These Classes of Charity would certainly bring down Blessings upon an Age and People; and if Men were not petrify'd with the Love of this World, against all Sense of the Commerce which ought to be among them, it would not be an unreasonable Bill for a poor Man in the Agony of Pain, aggravated by Want and Poverty, to draw upon a sick Alderman after this Form.

Mr. Basil Plenty,
SIR,

> *YOU have the Gout and Stone, with Sixty thousand Pounds Sterling; I have the Gout and Stone, not worth one Farthing: I shall pray for you, and desire you would pay the Bearer Twenty Shillings for Value received from,*

SIR,

Cripple-Gate,[1]   Your humble Servant,
  Aug. 29. 1712.   *Lazarus Hopeful.*

of cures performed by him. After the death of Queen Anne he was continued 'sworn Oculist and Operator of the Eyes in Ordinary' to George I (*Post Boy*, 13 Jan. 1715), and died at Rochester on 24 May 1715 (*Post Boy*, 26 May).

[1] The ancient structure of stone with towers, just outside the city wall on the north, and west of Bethlehem Hospital.

The Reader's own Imagination will suggest to him the Reasonableness of such Correspondences, and diversify them into a thousand Forms; but I shall close this as I began upon the Subject of Blindness.[1] The following Letter seems to be written by a Man of Learning, who is return'd to his Study after a Suspence[2] of an Ability to do so. The Benefit he reports himself to have received, may well claim the handsomest Encomium he can give the Operator.

Mr. SPECTATOR,

'RUMINATING lately on your admirable Discourses[3] on the *Pleasures of the Imagination,* I began to consider to which of our Senses we are obliged for the greatest and most important Share of those Pleasures; and I soon concluded that it was to the *Sight*: That is the Sovereign of the Senses, and Mother of all the Arts and Sciences, that have refined the Rudeness of the uncultivated Mind to a Politeness that distinguishes the fine Spirits from the barbarous *Goût* of the *great* Vulgar and the *small.*[4] The Sight is the obliging Benefactress, that bestows on us the most transporting Sensations that we have from the various and wonderful Products of Nature. To the Sight we owe the amazing Discoveries of the Height, Magnitude, and Motion of the Planets; their several Revolutions about their common Centre of Light, Heat, and Motion, the *Sun.* The *Sight* travels yet farther to the fix'd Stars, and furnishes the Understanding with solid Reasons to prove, that each of them is a *Sun* moving on its own Axis, in the Centre of its own Vortex or Turbillion,[5] and performing the same Offices to its dependant Planets, that our glorious Sun does to this. But the Enquiries of the *Sight* will not be stopp'd here, but make their Progress through the immense Expanse to the *Milky Way,* and there divide the blended Fires of the *Galaxy* into infinite and different Worlds, made up of distinct Suns, and their peculiar Equipages of Planets; till unable to pursue this Track any farther, it deputes the Imagination to go on to new Discoveries, till it fill the unbounded Space with endless Worlds.

[1] 'A benevolent Institution in favour of Blind People, and Swift's *Hospital,* seem to have originated from this Paper, certainly from the Principles of humanity stated in it' (Nichols).

[2] I.e. deferment, delay. Cf. No. 284 (vol. iii).

[3] Nos. 411–21.

[4] For Cowley's 'great Vulgar' see No. 114 (vol. i).

[5] Both words are used in older theories of the universe, particularly that of Descartes, to describe a whirling mass of cosmic matter. This is the earliest example in *OED* of the second word (correctly *tourbillion*).

'The *Sight* informs the Statuary's Chizel with Power to give Breath to liveless Brass and Marble, and the Painter's Pencil to swell the flat Canvas with moving Figures actuated by imaginary Souls. Musick indeed may plead another Original, since *Jubal*,[1] by the different Falls of his Hammer on the Anvil, discovered by the Ear the first rude Musick that pleas'd the Antediluvian Fathers; but then the *Sight* has not only reduc'd those wilder Sounds into artful Order and Harmony, but conveys that Harmony to the most distant Parts of the World without the Help of Sound. To the *Sight* we owe not only all the Discoveries of Philosophy, but all the divine Imagery of Poetry, that transport the intelligent Reader of *Homer*, *Milton*, and *Virgil*.

'As the Sight has polish'd the World, so does it supply us with the most grateful and lasting Pleasure. Let Love, let Friendship, paternal Affection, filial Piety, and conjugal Duty, declare the Joys the *Sight* bestows on a Meeting after Absence. But it would be endless to enumerate all the Pleasures and Advantages of *Sight*; every one that has it, every Hour he makes use of it, finds them, feels them, enjoys them.

'Thus as our greatest Pleasures and Knowledge are deriv'd from the Sight, so has Providence been more curious in the Formation of its Seat, the Eye, than of the Organs of the other Senses. That stupendious[2] Machine is compos'd in a wonderful Manner of Muscles, Membranes, and Humours. Its Motions are admirably directed by the Muscles; the Perspicuity[3] of the Humours transmit the Rays of Light; the Rays are regularly refracted by their Figure; the black Lining of the Sclerotes[4] effectually prevents their being confounded by Reflection. It is wonderful indeed to consider how many Objects the Eye is fitted to take in at once, and successively in an Instant, and at the same Time to make a Judgment of their Position, Figure, and Colour. It watches against our Dangers, guides our Steps, and lets in all the visible Objects, whose Beauty and Variety instruct and delight.

'The Pleasures and Advantages of Sight being so great, the Loss must be very grievous; of which *Milton*, from Experience, gives the

---

[1] Gen. iv. 21.

[2] According to *OED* this was the accepted spelling until the latter part of the seventeenth century, 'when the correct *stupendous* began to be used'.

[3] I.e. transparency, translucency. The last quotation in *OED* in this sense is dated 1750.

[4] 'The hard outer coat of the posterior part of the eyeball, forming the white of the eye' (*OED*).

most sensible Idea, both in the third Book of his *Paradise lost*, and in his *Sampson Agonistes*.

To Light in the former.

> ... *Thee I revisit safe,*
> *And feel thy sovereign vital Lamp; but thou*
> *Revisit'st not these Eyes, that roul in vain*
> *To find thy piercing Ray, but find no Dawn.*[1]

And a little after.

> *Seasons return, but not to me returns*
> *Day, or the sweet Approach of Ev'n and Morn,*
> *Or Sight of vernal Bloom, or Summer's Rose,*
> *Or Flocks or Herds, or humane Face divine;*
> *But Cloud instead, and ever-during Dark*
> *Surround me: From the chearful Ways of Men*
> *Cut off; and for the Book of Knowledge fair,*
> *Presented with an universal Blank*
> *Of Nature's Works, to me expung'd and raz'd,*
> *And Wisdom at one Entrance quite shut out.*[2]

Again, in *Sampson Agonistes*.

> ... *But Chief of all,*
> *O Loss of Sight! of thee I most complain;*
> *Blind among Enemies! O worse than Chains,*
> *Dungeon, or Beggery, or decrepid Age!*
> *Light, the prime Work of God, to me's extinct,*
> *And all her various Objects of Delight*
> *Annull'd* ...

> ... *Still as a Fool,*
> *In Power of others, never in my own.*
> *Scarce half I seem to live, dead more than Half:*
> *O dark! dark! dark! amid the Blaze of Noon!*
> *Irrecoverably dark, total Eclipse,*
> *Without all Hopes of Day!*[3]

'The Enjoyment of Sight then being so great a Blessing, and the Loss of it so terrible an Evil, how excellent and valuable is the Skill of that Artist which can restore the former, and redress the latter?

---

[1] *Paradise Lost*, iii. 21–24. (Line 24, 'and find'.)
[2] Ibid. 41–50. (Line 42, 'Ev'n or Morn'; line 46, 'Surrounds'.)
[3] *Samson Agonistes*, 66–72, 77–82. (Line 82, 'hope'.)

My frequent Perusal of the Advertisements in the publick News-Papers (generally the most agreeable Entertainment they afford) has presented me with many and various Benefits of this Kind done to my Countrymen by that skilful Artist Dr. *Grant*, Her Majesty's Occulist Extraordinary, whose happy Hand has brought and restor'd to Sight several Hundreds in less than Four Years.[1] Many have received Sight by his means who came blind from their Mother's Womb, as in the famous Instance of *Jones* of *Newington*. I my self have been cured by him of a Weakness in my Eyes next to Blindness, and am ready to believe any thing that is reported of his Ability this way; and know that many, who could not purchase his Assistance with Money, have enjoy'd it from his Charity. But a List of Particulars would swell my Letter beyond its Bounds, what I have said being sufficient to comfort those who are in the like Distress, since they may conceive Hopes of being no longer miserable in this Kind, while there is yet alive so able an Oculist as Dr. *Grant*.

I am

The SPECTATOR'*s humble Servant,*

Philanthropus.'

T

[1] 'Mr. Roger Grant having cured great Numbers in Her Majesty's Service, who have laboured under Distempers in the Eyes, is sworn Occulist and Operator in Extraordinary to Her Majesty' (*Gazette*, 28 Sept. 1710). After the death of Sir William Read he was appointed 'Oculist in Ordinary to George I' (*Flying Post*, 25 June). According to William Wadd (*Nugae chirurgicae*, 1824, p. 72) Grant had been a soldier in the service of the Emperor, where he had lost one eye. 'As he had this misfortune, he thought no better recompense could be given him than the privilege of enlightening those of other persons. Elated with this idea he returned to Great Britain in the reign of Queen Anne, and commenced *doctor* in Mouse Alley, Wapping. . . .'

In the summer of 1709 Grant gained considerable publicity because of his supposed cure of one William Jones of Newington, Surrey, on 29 June. (Steele, who seems to have believed that this was a genuine cure, printed a circumstantial account of the affair in *Tatler* 55.) On 10 Sept. a pamphlet was published by Timothy Childe exposing Grant's methods; it is entitled *A Full and True Account of a Miraculous Cure, of a Young Man in Newington, that was born blind, and was in five minutes brought to perfect sight*. When Jones and his mother tried to get the minister of the parish church to sign a certificate of the cure, 'for then they should have the Cure *Gratis*', the clergyman declined; forgery was then resorted to, and the certificate was duly published in the *Daily Courant* of 29 July. In the certificate Grant is said to be living in St. Christopher's Court behind the Royal Exchange. The pamphlet describes him as an illiterate man, bred up either as a cobbler or as a tinker. 'But besides this Gift of Curing, to give him his Due, he has another as extraordinary, of Preaching. This Talent he powerfully exercises, to the Admiration of all his Hearers, in a Congregation of *Anabaptists*' (p. 13). See also the *Daily Courant* of 24 Aug. Further testimonials to his cures appear in the newspapers of 1710 (*Post-Man*, 23 Mar.; *British Apollo*, 3 Apr., &c.). The case of William Jones is brought up again and an affidavit of his cure published in the *Post-Man* of 10 and 15 Aug. 1710. There are no advertisements for Grant in the *Spectator*.

No. 473
[STEELE]

Quid? si quis vultu torvo ferus & pede nudo
Exiguæque togæ simulet textore Catonem;
Virtutemne repræsentet moresque Catonis?

Hor.

To the SPECTATOR.

SIR,

'I AM now in the Country, and employ most of my Time in reading, or thinking upon what I have read. Your Paper comes
constantly down to me, and it affects me so much, that I find my
Thoughts run into your Way; and I recommend to you a Subject
upon which you have not yet touched, and that is the Satisfaction
some Men seem to take in their Imperfections, I think one may call
it glorying in their Insufficiency; a certain great Author is of Opinion
it is the contrary to Envy, tho' perhaps it may proceed from it.[2]
Nothing is so common, as to hear Men of this Sort speaking of themselves, add to their own Merit (as they think) by impairing it, in
praising themselves for their Defects, freely allowing they commit
some few frivolous Errors, in order to be esteemed Persons of uncommon Talents and great Qualifications. They are generally pro-
fessing an injudicious Neglect of Dancing, Fencing, and Riding, as
also an unjust Contempt for Travelling and the modern Languages;
as for their Part (say they) they never valued or troubled their Head
about them. This panegyrical Satyr on themselves certainly is
worthy of your Animadversion. I have known one of these Gentlemen think himself obliged to forget the Day of an Appointment,
and sometimes even that you spoke to him; and when you see 'em,
they hope you'll pardon 'em, for they have the worst Memory in
the World. One of 'em started up t'other Day in some Confusion,
and said, Now I think on't, I'm to meet Mr. *Mortmain* the Attorney
about some Business, but whether it is to Day or to Morrow, faith,
I can't tell: Now to my certain Knowledge he knew his Time to a

---

[1] *Motto.* Horace, *Epistles*, I. 19. 12–14:
　　Suppose a Man the coarsest Gown should wear,
　　No Shoes, his Forehead rough, his look severe,
　　And Ape great *Cato* in his Form and Dress:
　　Must He his Vertues and his Mind express? CREECH.

[2] La Bruyère, *Les Caractères*, chap. xi ('De l'homme').

Moment, and was there accordingly. These forgetful Persons have, to heighten their Crime, generally the best Memories of any People, as I have found out by their remembering sometimes through Inadvertency. Two or three of 'em that I know can say most of our modern Tragedies by Heart. I asked a Gentleman the other Day that is famous for a good Carver, (at which Acquisition he is out of Countenance, imagining it may detract from some of his more essential Qualifications) to help me to something that was near him; but he excused himself, and blushing told me, Of all things he cou'd never carve in his Life; tho' it can be proved upon him, that he cuts up, disjoints, and uncases with incomparable Dexterity. I wou'd not be understood as if I thought it laudable for a Man of Quality and Fortune to rival the Acquisitions of Artificers, and endeavour to excel in little handy Qualities; No, I argue only against being ashamed at what is really Praiseworthy. As these Pretences to Ingenuity shew themselves several Ways, you'll often see a Man of this Temper ashamed to be clean, and setting up for Wit only from Negligence in his Habit. Now I am upon this Head, I can't help observing also upon a very different Folly proceeding from the same Cause. As these above-mention'd arise from affecting an Equality with Men of greater Talents from having the same Faults, there are others who would come at a Parallel with those above them, by possessing little Advantages which they want. I heard a young Man not long ago, who has Sense, comfort himself in his Ignorance of *Greek*, *Hebrew*, and the *Orientals*:[1] At the same Time that he published his Aversion to these Languages, he said that the Knowledge of 'em was rather a Diminution than an Advancement of a Man's Character, tho' at the same Time I know he languishes and repines he is not Master of them himself. Whenever I take any of these fine Persons, thus detracting from what they don't understand, I tell them I will complain to you, and say I am sure you will not allow it an Exception against a thing, that he who contemns it is an Ignorant in it.

I *am*,

SIR,

Your most humble Servant,

S. P.'

---

[1] I.e. the Oriental languages. *OED* gives quotations from 1680 to *a*. 1734.

Mr. SPECTATOR,

'I AM a Man of a very good Estate, and am honourably in Love. I hope you will allow, when the ultimate Purpose is honest, there may be, without Trespass against Innocence, some Toying by the Way. People of Condition are perhaps too distant and formal on those Occasions; but, however that is, I am to confess to you, that I have writ some Verses to attone for my Offence. You profess'd Authors are a little severe upon us, who write like Gentlemen: But if you are a Friend to Love, you will insert my Poem. You cannot imagine how much Service it will do me with my Fair one, as well as Reputation with all my Friends, to have something of mine in the *Spectator.* My Crime was, that I snatch'd a Kiss, and my Poetical Excuse as follows:

I.

ªBellinda, *see from yonder Flowers*
The Bee flies loaded to its Cell;
Can you perceive what it devours?
Are they impair'd in Shew or Smell?

II.

So, tho' I robb'd you of a Kiss,
Sweeter than their Ambrosial Dew,
Why are you angry at my Bliss?
Has it at all impoverish'd you?

III.

'Tis by this Cunning I contrive,
In spight of your unkind Reserve,
To keep my famish'd Love alive,
*Which you inhumanly would starve.*ª [1]

I am,
SIR,
Your humble Servant,
Timothy Stanza.'

ª⁻ª *Indentation thus in 8vo, 12mo; lines not indented in Fol.*

---

[1] This poem is not included in Miss Blanchard's edition of Steele's *Occasional Verse* (Oxford, 1952), but is briefly discussed among the 'poems of doubtful authorship' (p. 114).

SIR,   *Aug.* 23. 1712.
'HAVING a little Time upon my Hands, I cou'd not think of
bestowing it better, than in writing an Epistle to the
SPECTATOR, which I now do, and am
                              SIR,
                              Your humble Servant,
                              Bob Short.

'P. S. If you approve of my Stile, I am likely enough to become
your Correspondent. I desire your Opinion of it. I design it for that
Way of Writing called by the Judicious the *Familiar.*'

                                                            T

No. 474   *Wednesday, September* 3, 1712[1]
[STEELE]

            Asperitas agrestis & inconcinna.
                              Hor.

Mr. SPECTATOR,
'BEING of the Number of those that have lately retired from the
Center of Business and Pleasure, my Uneasiness in the Country where I am, arises rather from the Society than the Solitude of it.
To be oblig'd to receive and return Visits from and to a Circle of
Neighbours, who through Diversity of Age or Inclinations, can
neither be entertaining or serviceable to us, is a vile Loss of Time,
and a Slavery from which a Man should deliver himself, if possible:
For why must I lose the remaining Part of my Life, because they
have thrown away the former Part of theirs? It is to me an insupportable Affliction, to be tormented with the Narrations of a Set of
People, who are warm in their Expressions, of the quick Relish of
that Pleasure, which their Dogs and Horses have a more delicate
Taste of. I do also in my Heart detest and abhor that damnable
Doctrine and Position of the Necessity of a Bumper, though to one's
own Toast; for tho' 'tis pretended these deep Potations[a] are used

---

[a] Potations] *Aitken*; Politicians *all edd.*

[1] *Motto.* Horace, *Epistles*, 1. 18. 6: A clownish roughness, and inelegant.

only to inspire Gaiety, they certainly drown that Chearfulness
which would survive a moderate Circulation. If at these Meetings
it were left to every Stranger either to fill his Glass according to his
own Inclination, or to make his Retreat when he finds he has been
sufficiently obedient to that of others, these Entertainments would
be govern'd with more good Sense, and consequently with more
good Breeding, than at present they are. Indeed where any of the
Guests are known to measure their Fame or Pleasure by their Glass,
proper Exhortations might be used to these to push their Fortunes
in this Sort of Reputation; but where 'tis unseasonably insisted on
to a modest Stranger, this Drench may be said to be swallow'd with
the same Necessity, as if it had been tender'd in the Horn for that
Purpose,[1] with this aggravating Circumstance, that it distresses the
Entertainer's Guest in the same Degree as it relieves his Horses.

'To attend without Impatience an Account of Five-barr'd Gates,
double Ditches and Precipices, and to survey the Orator with desiring Eyes, is to me extremely difficult, but absolutely necessary to
be upon tolerable Terms with him: But then the occasional Burst-
ings out into Laughter is of all other Accomplishments the most
requisite. I confess at present I have not that Command of these
Convulsions, as is necessary to be good Company; therefore I beg
you would publish this Letter, and let me be known all at once for
a queer Fellow, and avoided. It is monstrous to me, that we, who
are given to Reading and calm Conversation, should ever be visited
by these Roarers:[2] But they think they themselves, as Neighbours,
may come into our Rooms with the same Right that they and their
Dogs hunt in our Grounds.

'Your Institution of Clubs I have always admir'd, in which you
constantly endeavour'd the Union of the metaphorically Defunct,[3]
that is, such as are neither serviceable to the busy and enterprizing
Part of Mankind, nor entertaining to the Retir'd and Speculative.
There should certainly therefore, in each County, be establish'd a
Club of the Persons whose Conversations I have describ'd, who for
their own private, as also the publick Emolument, should exclude,
and be excluded all other Society. Their Attire should be the same
with their Huntsmens, and none should be admitted into this green

---

[1] 'A horn is used to administer potions to horses' (Nichols).
[2] I.e. roisterers. The last example of this word in *OED* is from *Tatler* 40.
[3] The *Tatler*, in its early numbers, had made much of those who were dead to all
good purposes, and drew up imaginary 'bills of mortality' of the metaphorically
defunct.

Conversation-Piece,[1] except he had broke his Collar-Bone thrice. A broken Rib or two might also admit a Man without the least Opposition. The President must necessarily have broken his Neck, and have been taken up dead once or twice: For the more Maims this Brotherhood shall have met with, the easier will their Conversation flow and keep up; and when any one of these vigorous Invalids had finish'd his Narration of the Collar-Bone, this naturally would introduce the History of the Ribs. Besides, the different Circumstances of their Falls and Fractures, would help to prolong and diversify their Relations. There should also be another Club of such Men, who have not succeeded so well in maiming themselves, but are however in the constant Pursuit of these Accomplishments. I would by no means be suspected by what I have said to traduce in general the Body of Fox-hunters; for whilst I look upon a reasonable Creature full Speed after a Pack of Dogs, by way of Pleasure, and not of Business, I shall always make honourable Mention of it.

'But the most irksome Conversation of all others I have met with in the Neighbourhood, has been among two or three of your Travellers, who have overlook'd Men and Manners, and have pass'd through *France* and *Italy* with the same Observation that the Carriers and Stage-Coachmen do through *Great-Britain*; that is, their Stops and Stages have been regulated according to the Liquor they have met with in their Passage. They indeed remember the Names of abundance of Places, with the particular Fineries of certain Churches: But their distinguishing Mark, is certain Prettinesses of foreign Languages, the Meaning of which they could have better express'd in their own. The Entertainment of these fine Observers *Shakespear* has described to consist

> *In talking of the* Alps *and* Appennines,
> *The* Pyrenæan, *and the River* Po.

And then concludes with a Sigh,

> *Now this is worshipful Society.*[2]

'I would not be thought in all this to hate such honest Creatures

---

[1] 'A kind of *genre* painting representing a group of figures.' This is the first example in *OED*.
[2] *King John*, I. i. 202–3, 205 ('And talking . . . But this . . .').

as Dogs; I am only unhappy that I cannot partake in their Diversions. But I love them so well, as Dogs, that I often go with my Pockets stuffed with Bread to dispense my Favours, or make my way thro' them at Neighbours Houses. There is in particular a young Hound of great Expectation, Vivacity, and Enterprize, that attends my Flights where-ever he spies me. This Creature observes my Countenance, and behaves himself accordingly. His Mirth, his Frolick, and Joy upon the Sight of me has been observed, and I have been gravely desired not to encourage him so much, for it spoils his Parts; but I think he shews them sufficiently in the several Boundings, Friskings, and Scourings, when he makes his Court to me: But I foresee in a little Time he and I must keep Company with one another only, for we are fit for no other in these Parts. Having inform'd you how I do pass my Time in the Country where I am, I must proceed to tell you how I would pass it, had I such a Fortune as would put me above the Observance of Ceremony and Custom.

'My Scheme of a Country Life then should be as follows. As I am happy in three or four very agreeable Friends, these I would constantly have with me; and the Freedom we took with one another at School and the University, we would maintain and exert upon all Occasions with great Courage. There should be certain Hours of the Day to be employed in Reading, during which Time it should be impossible for any one of us to enter the other's Chamber, unless by Storm. After this we would communicate the Trash or Treasure we had met with, with our own Reflections upon the Matter; the Justness of which we would controvert with good-humour'd Warmth, and never spare one another out of that complaisant Spirit of Conversation, which makes others affirm and deny the same Matter in a Quarter of an Hour. If any of the neighbouring Gentlemen, not of our Turn, should take it in their Heads to visit me, I should look upon these Persons in the same Degree Enemies to my particular State of Happiness, as ever the *French* were to that of the Publick, and I would be at an annual Expence in Spies to observe their Motions. Whenever I should be surpriz'd with a Visit, as I hate Drinking, I would be brisk in swilling Bumpers, upon this Maxim, That 'tis better to trouble others with my Impertinence, than to be troubled my self with theirs. The Necessity of an Infirmary makes me resolve to fall into that Project; and as we should be but five, the Terrors of an involuntary Separation, which our Number can't so well admit of, would make us exert our selves, in

Opposition to all the Particulars mentioned in your Institution of that equitable Confinement.[1] This my Way of Life I know would subject me to the Imputation of a morose, covetous, and singular Fellow. These and all other hard Words, with all Manner of insipid Jests, and all other Reproach, would be Matter of Mirth to me and my Friends: Besides, I would destroy the Application of the Epithets Morose and Covetous, by a yearly Relief of my undeservedly necessitous Neighbours, and by treating my Friends and Domesticks with an Humanity that should express the Obligation to lie rather on my Side; and as for the Word Singular, I was always of Opinion every Man must be so, to be what one would desire him.

Your very humble Servant,

J. R.'[2]

Mr. SPECTATOR,

' ABOUT two Years ago I was called upon by the younger Part of a Country Family, by my Mother's Side related to me, to visit Mr. *Campbell*[3] the dumb Man; for they told me that That was chiefly what brought them to Town, having heard Wonders of him in *Essex*. I, who always wanted Faith in Matters of that Kind, was not easily prevailed on to go, but least they should take it ill, I went with 'em; when, to my Surprize, *Mr. Campbell* related all their past Life, (in short, had not he been prevented, such a Discovery wou'd have come out, as would have ruin'd the next Design of their coming to Town, *viz.* buying Wedding-Cloaths.) Our Names— tho' he never heard of us before—and we endeavour'd to conceal— were as familiar to him as to ourselves. To be sure, Mr. SPECTATOR, he is a very learned and wise Man. Being impatient to know my Fortune, having paid my Respects in a Family *Jacobus*,[4] he told me (after his Manner) among several other things, that in a Year and nine Months I should fall ill of a new Feaver, be given over by my

¹ See Nos. 424 (vol. iii), 429, 440.

² 'This Letter was probably written by Steele's fellow collegian and friend, the Rev. Mr. Richard Parker. This accomplished scholar was for many years Vicar of Embleton, in Northumberland, a living in the gift of Merton College, where he and Steele lived in the most cordial familiarity. Not relishing the rural sports of Bamboroughshire, he declined the interchange of visits with most of the hospitable gentlemen in his neighbourhood; who, invigorated by their diversions, indulged in copious meals, and were apt to be vociferous in their mirth, and over importunate with their guests, to join in their conviviality' (Nichols).

³ See No. 31 (vol. i).

⁴ A gold coin, issued in the reign of James I, valued at 20 to 24 shillings. Miege (1707) gives the value as 25s. 6d., and says that the Jacobus and the Broad Piece are 'now kept close by the Curious, which makes few of 'em to be seen abroad' (p. 243).

Physicians, but shou'd with much Difficulty recover: That the first Time I took the Air afterwards, I shou'd be address'd to by a young Gentleman of a plentiful Fortune, good Sense, and a generous Spirit. *Mr.* SPECTATOR, he is the purest[1] Man in the World, for all he said is come to pass, and I am the happiest She in *Kent*. I have been in quest of Mr. *Campbell* these three Months, and can't find him out: Now hearing you are a dumb Man too, I thought you might correspond, and be able to tell me something; for I think my self highly obliged to make his Fortune as he has mine. 'Tis very possible your Worship, who has Spies all over this Town, can inform me how to send to him: If you can, I beseech you be as speedy as possible, and you will highly oblige

Your constant Reader and Admirer,
Dulcibella Thankley.'

Ordered, That the Inspector I employ about Wonders,[2] enquire at the *Golden Lion,* opposite to the *Half-Moon* Tavern in *Drury-Lane,* into the Merit of this silent Sage, and report accordingly.[3]

T

No. 475
[ADDISON]

Thursday, September 4, 1712[4]

> . . . *quæ res in se neque Consilium neque modum
> Habet ullum, eam consilio regere non potes.*
>
> Ter.

IT is an old Observation, which has been made of Politicians who would rather ingratiate themselves with their Soveraign, than promote his real Service, That they accommodate their Councils to his Inclinations, and advise him to such Actions only as his Heart is naturally set upon. The Privy-Councellor of one in Love must

---

[1] A slang term much in use at this time, in the general sense of 'fine, excellent' Now *rare* or *Obs.* (*OED*).

[2] Mr. Spectator does not refer to this officer elsewhere.

[3] The Golden Lion does not figure in advertisements in the *Spectator*. Duncan Campbell's house was in Drury Lane.

[4] *Motto.* Terence, *Eunuchus,* 57–58: The thing that in itself has neither measure nor consideration counsel cannot rule.

observe the same Conduct, unless he would forfeit the Friendship of the Person who desires his Advice. I have known several odd Cases of this Nature. *Hipparchus* was going to marry a common Woman, but being resolved to do nothing without the Advice of his Friend *Philander*, he consulted him upon the Occasion. *Philander* told him his Mind freely, and represented his Mistress to him in such strong Colours, that the next Morning he received a Challenge for his Pains, and before Twelve a Clock was run through the Body by the Man who had asked his Advice. *Celia* was more prudent on the like Occasion; she desired *Leonilla* to give her Opinion freely upon a young Fellow, who made his Addresses to her. *Leonilla*, to oblige her, told her with great Frankness, that she looked upon him as one of the most worthless—*Celia*, foreseeing what a Character she was to expect, begged her not to go on, for that she had been privately married to him above a Fortnight. The truth of it is, a Woman seldom asks Advice before she has bought her Wedding Cloaths. When she has made her own Choice, for form's sake she sends a *Conge d'elire* to her Friends.[1]

If we look into the secret Springs and Motives that set People at work in these Occasions, and put them upon asking Advice, which they never intend to take, I look upon it to be none of the least That they are incapable of keeping a Secret which is so very pleasing to them. A Girl longs to tell her Confident, that she hopes to be married in a little time, and, in order to talk of the pretty Fellow that dwells so much in her Thoughts, asks her very gravely, what she would advise her to in a Case of so much Difficulty. Why else shou'd *Melissa*, who had not a Thousand Pound in the World, go into every Quarter of the Town to ask her Acquaintance whether they would advise her to take *Tom Townly*, that made his Addresses to her with an Estate of Five Thousand a Year? 'Tis very pleasant, on this Occasion, to hear the Lady propose her Doubts, and to see the Pains she is at to get over them.

I must not here omit a Practice that is in Use among the vainer Part of our own Sex, who will often ask a Friend's Advice, in relation to a Fortune whom they are never likely to come at. WILL HONEYCOMB, who is now on the Verge of Threescore, took me aside not long since, and asked me in his most serious Look, whether I

---

[1] *Congé d'élire*, 'permission to elect', the letter sent by the government signifying royal permission to a monastic body or cathedral chapter, to fill a vacant see or abbacy by election—in practice to accept the choice of the Sovereign.

would advise him to marry my Lady *Betty Single*, who, by the way, is one of the greatest Fortunes about Town. I stared him full in the Face upon so strange a Question; upon which he immediately gave me an Inventory of her Jewels and Estate, adding, that he was resolved to do nothing, in a matter of such Consequence, without my Approbation. Finding he would have an Answer, I told him, if he could get the Lady's Consent, he had mine. This is about the Tenth Match which, to my Knowledge, WILL has consulted his Friends upon, without ever opening his Mind to the Party her self.

I have been engaged in this Subject by the following Letter, which comes to me from some notable young Female Scribe, who, by the Contents of it, seems to have carried Matters so far, that she is ripe for asking Advice; but as I would not lose her Good-Will, nor forfeit the Reputation which I have with her for Wisdom, I shall only communicate the Letter to the Publick, without returning any Answer to it.

Mr. SPECTATOR,

'NOW, Sir, the thing is this: Mr. *Shapely* is the prettiest Gentleman about Town. He is very Tall, but not too Tall neither. He Dances like an Angel. His Mouth is made I don't know how, but 'tis the prettiest that I ever saw in my Life. He is always Laughing, for he has an infinite deal of Wit. If you did but see how he rowls his Stockins! He has a thousand pretty Fancies, and I am sure, if you saw him, you wou'd like him. He is a very good Scholar, and can talk *Latin* as fast as *English*. I wish you cou'd but see him Dance. Now you must understand poor Mr. *Shapely* has no Estate, but how can he help that, you know? And yet my Friends are so unreasonable as to be always teizing me about him, because he has no Estate. But, I am sure, he has that that is better than an Estate, for he is a Good-natured, Ingenious, Modest, Civil, Tall, Well-bred, Handsome Man, and I am obliged to him for his Civilities ever since I saw him. I forgot to tell you, that he has black Eyes, and looks upon me now and then, as if he had Tears in them. And yet my Friends are so unreasonable, that they wou'd have me be uncivil to him. I have a good Portion which they can't hinder me of, and I shall be Fourteen on the Twenty Ninth Day of *August* next, and am therefore willing to settle in the World as soon as I can, and so is Mr. *Shapely*. But every Body I advise with here is poor Mr. *Shapely*'s Enemy. I desire, therefore, you will give me your Advice, for I know

you are a wise Man; and if you advise me well, I am resolved to
follow it. I heartily wish you cou'd see him Dance, and am,

SIR,

Your most humble Servant,

B. D.

'He loves your *Spectators* mightily.'[1]

C

No. 476   *Friday, September 5, 1712*[2]

[ADDISON]

. . . lucidus Ordo.

Hor.

AMONG my Daily-Papers, which I bestow on the Publick, there
are some which are written with Regularity and Method, and
others that run out into the Wildness of those Compositions, which
go by the Name of *Essays*. As for the first, I have the whole Scheme
of the Discourse in my Mind, before I set Pen to Paper. In the other

---

[1] This letter is highly praised by Saintsbury in his *History of English Prose Rhythm*
(1912), p. 251.

Lillie (ii. 328–9) prints a supplementary letter from B. D.:

    I do not know what you mean, Sir, but I will assure you I take it very ill at
your hands to be served thus by you in a matter of so much consequence to me,
that instead of giving me your advice as a friend (as I consulted you) only to
publish my letter without telling me you would not lose my good-will forsooth;
and I do not know what nonsense about your wisdom, as if you was so much wiser
than other folks, I warrent ye; but I'll tell you I don't care a fig for you nor your
spectators neither, for I will have him in spight of your teeth; and let my friends
say what they will. I know you design to banter me out on't by all your stuff
there before-hand, but I an't such a fool neither; for Mr. Shapely is a very pretty
man, and loves me dearly, and I don't care a pin what all the world can say, for
I could live with him upon bread and water, that I could. Alass! you are not so
mighty wise as you take your self to be; for I am sure if Mr. Shapely had a mind
to it, he could make better spectators than you do a great deal, that he could; for
he says the prettiest things, and writes the sweetest letters, better than ever you
did in all your life, you old Put you: and now I think I am even with you; nay,
more, I am not

Your humble servant,

B. D.

    P. S. But hold, pray, what is it you mean by calling such names as scribe, Sir?
I do not understand your calling a lady scribe, Sir. Now if you were not an old
fellow, Mr. Shapely should challenge you for—O! he's below! I won't write
another word.

[2] *Motto.* Horace, *Ars poetica*, 41:

His *Method* will be clear. CREECH.

kind of Writing, it is sufficient that I have several Thoughts on a Subject, without troubling my self to range them in such order, that they may seem to grow out of one another, and be disposed under the proper Heads. *Seneca* and *Montaigne* are Patterns for Writing in this last Kind, as *Tully* and *Aristotle* excel in the other. When I read an Author of Genius, who[a] writes without Method, I fancy my self in a Wood that abounds with a great many noble Objects, rising among one another in the greatest Confusion and Disorder. When I read a Methodical Discourse, I am in a regular Plantation, and can place my self in its several Centers, so as to take a view of all the Lines and Walks that are struck from them. You may ramble in the one a whole Day together, and every Moment discover something or other that is new to you, but when you have done you will have but a confused imperfect Notion of the Place; in the other, your Eye commands the whole Prospect, and gives you such an Idea of it, as is not easily worn out of the Memory.

Irregularity and want of Method are only supportable in Men of great Learning or Genius, who are often too full to be exact, and therefore chuse to throw down their Pearls in Heaps before the Reader, rather than be at the Pains of stringing them.

Method is of Advantage to a Work, both in respect to the Writer and the Reader. In regard to the first, it is a great help to his Invention. When a Man has plann'd his Discourse, he finds a great many Thoughts rising out of every Head, that do not offer themselves upon the general Survey of a Subject. His Thoughts are at the same time more intelligible, and better discover their Drift and Meaning, when they are placed in their proper Lights, and follow one another in a regular Series, than when they are thrown together without Order and Connexion. There is always an Obscurity in Confusion, and the same Sentence that wou'd have enlightened the Reader in one Part of a Discourse, perplexes him in another. For the same Reason likewise every Thought in a Methodical Discourse shews its self in its greatest Beauty, as the several Figures in a piece of Painting receive new Grace from their Disposition in the Picture. The Advantages of a Reader from a Methodical Discourse, are correspondent with those of the Writer. He comprehends every thing easily, takes it in with Pleasure, and retains it long.

Method is not less requisite in ordinary Conversation, than in

[a] who] that *Fol.*

Writing, provided a Man would talk to make himself understood. I, who hear a Thousand Coffee-house Debates every Day, am very sensible of this want of Method in the Thoughts of my honest Countrymen. There is not one Dispute in Ten, which is managed in those Schools of Politicks, where, after the three first Sentences, the Question is not entirely lost. Our Disputants put me in mind of the Skuttle Fish,[1] that when he is unable to extricate himself, blackens all the Water about him, till he becomes invisible. The Man who does not know how to methodize his Thoughts, has always, to borrow a Phrase from the Dispensary, *a barren Superfluity of Words*.[2] The Fruit is lost amidst the Exuberance of Leaves.

Tom Puzzle is one of the most Eminent Immethodical Disputants of any that has fallen under my Observation. *Tom* has read enough to make him very Impertinent: His Knowledge is sufficient to raise Doubts, but not to clear them. It is pity that he has so much Learning, or that he has not a great deal more. With these Qualifications *Tom* sets up for a Free-thinker, finds a great many things to blame in the Constitution of his Country, and gives shrewd Intimations that he does not believe another World. In short, *Puzzle* is an Atheist as much as his Parts will give him leave. He has got about half a Dozen common-place Topicks, into which he never fails to turn the Conversation, whatever was the Occasion of it: Tho' the Matter in Debate be about *Doway* or *Denain*,[3] it is ten to one but half his Discourse runs upon the Unreasonableness of Bigottry and Priest-craft. This makes Mr. *Puzzle* the Admiration of all those[a] who have less Sense than himself, and the Contempt of all those who have more. There is none in Town whom *Tom* dreads so much as my Friend *Will Dry*. *Will*, who is acquainted with *Tom's* Logick, when he finds him running off the Question, cuts him short, with a *What then? we allow all this to be true, but what is it to our present Purpose?* I have known *Tom* eloquent half an Hour together, and triumphing, as he thought, in the Superiority of the Argument,

---

[a] of all those] of those Fol.

[1] A common eighteenth-century spelling of *cuttle-fish*.
[2] *The Dispensary*, by Samuel Garth, ii. 94–95:
> Hourly his learn'd impertinence affords
> A barren superfluity of words.

[3] Douai, one of the four fortress towns captured by the Allies in 1710, capitulated to Marlborough and Prince Eugene on 14 June 1710. At Denain, on 24 July N.S. 1712, Villars outmanœuvred Prince Eugene and inflicted on him a crushing defeat; the French thereupon recaptured Douai.

when he has been non-plus'd, on a sudden, by Mr. *Dry's* desiring him to tell the Company, what it was that he endeavoured to prove. In short, *Dry* is a Man of a clear methodical Head, but few Words, and gains the same Advantages over *Puzzle*, that a small Body of regular Troops would gain over a numberless undisciplined Militia.

C

No. 477   *Saturday, September 6, 1712*[1]
[ADDISON]

> . . . *An me ludit amabilis*
> *Insania? audire & videor pios*
> *Errare per lucos, amœnæ*
> *Quos & aquæ subeunt & auræ.*
>   Hor.[a]

SIR,

'HAVING lately read your Essay on the Pleasures of the Imagination,[2] I was so taken with your Thoughts upon some of our *English* Gardens, that I cannot forbear troubling you with a Letter upon that Subject. I am one, you must know, who am looked upon as an Humorist in Gardening. I have several Acres about my House, which I call my Garden, and which a Skillful Gardener would not know what to call. It is a Confusion of Kitchin and Parterre, Orchard and Flower Garden, which lie so mixt and interwoven with one another, that if a Foreigner, who had seen nothing of our Country, should be conveyed into my Garden at his first landing, he would look upon it as a natural Wilderness, and

Motto. Hor. *om. Fol.*

---

[1] *Motto.* Horace, *Odes*, 3. 4. 5–8:

> Or airy Frenzies cheat
> My Mind well pleas'd with the Deceit!
> I seem to hear, I seem to move,
> And wander thro' the happy Grove,
> Where smooth Springs flow, and murm'ring Breeze
> Does wanton through the waving Trees. CREECH.

The letter which makes up this number may have been sent in by a correspondent, but in style and subject-matter it is like Addison's best work.

[2] Nos. 411–21 (vol. iii), especially No. 414.

one of the uncultivated Parts of our Country. My Flowers grow up in several Parts of the Garden in the greatest Luxuriancy and Profusion. I am so far from being fond of any particular one, by reason of its Rarity, that if I meet with any one in a Field which pleases me, I give it a Place in my Garden. By this means, when a Stranger walks with me, he is surprized to see several large Spots of Ground covered with Ten thousand different Colours, and has often singled out Flowers that he might have met with under a common Hedge, in a Field, or in a Meadow, as some of the greatest Beauties of the Place. The only Method I observe in this Particular, is to range in the same Quarter the Products of the same Season, that they may make their Appearance together, and compose a Picture of the greatest Variety. There is the same Irregularity in my Plantations, which run into as great a Wildness as their Natures will permit. I take in none that do not naturally rejoice in the Soil, and am pleased when I am walking in a Labyrinth of my own raising, not to know whether the next Tree I shall meet with is an Apple or an Oak, an Elm or a Pear-tree. My Kitchin has likewise its particular Quarters assigned it; for besides the wholesome Luxury which that Place abounds with, I have always thought a Kitchin-garden a more pleasant Sight, than the finest Orangerie, or artificial Green-house. I love to see every thing in its Perfection, and am more pleased to survey my Rows of Coleworts and Cabbages, with a thousand nameless Pot-herbs, springing up in their full Fragrancy and Verdure, than to see the tender Plants of Foreign Countries kept alive by artificial Heats, or withering in an Air and Soil that are not adapted to them. I must not omit, that there is a Fountain rising in the upper Part of my Garden, which forms a little wandring Rill, and administers to the Pleasure as well as the Plenty of the Place. I have so conducted it, that it visits most of my Plantations, and have taken particular Care to let it run in the same manner as it would do in an open Field, so that it generally passes through Banks of Violets and Primroses, Plats of Willow, or other Plants, that seem to be of its own producing. There is another Circumstance, in which I am very particular, or, as my Neighbours call me, very whimsical: As my Garden invites into it all the Birds of the Country, by offering them the Conveniency of Springs and Shades, Solitude and Shelter, I do not suffer any one to destroy their Nests in the Spring, or drive them from their usual Haunts in Fruit time. I value my Garden more for being full of Blackbirds than Cherries, and very frankly give them Fruit for their Songs. By this means I have always the Musick of the Season in its Perfection, and am highly delighted to see the Jay or the Thrush hopping about my Walks, and shooting before my Eye across the several little Glades and Allies that I pass through. I think there are as many Kinds of Gardening, as of Poetry; Your Makers of Parterres and Flower-Gardens, are Epigrammatists and Sonneteers in this Art. Contrivers of Bowers and Grotto's, Treillages[1] and Cascades, are Romance Writers. *Wise* and *London*[2] are our Heroick Poets, and if, as a Critick, I may single out any Passage of their Works to commend, I shall take Notice of that Part in the upper Garden at *Kensington,* which was at first nothing but a Gravel-Pitt.[3] It must have been a fine Genius for Gardening, that could have thought of forming such an unsightly Hollow into so beautiful an *Area,* and to have hit the Eye with so uncommon and agreeable a Scene, as that which it is now wrought into. To give this particular Spot of Ground the greater Effect, they have made a very pleasing Contrast; for as on one side of the Walk you see this hollow Basin, with its several little Plantations lying so conveniently under the Eye of the Beholder; on the other side of it there appears a seeming Mount, made up of Trees rising one higher than another, in Proportion as they approach the Center. A Spectator, who has not heard this Account of it, would think this Circular Mount was not only a real one, but that it had been actually scooped out of that hollow Space, which I have before mentioned. I never yet met with any one who had walked in this Garden, who was not struck with that Part of it which I have here mentioned. As for my self, you will find, by the Account which I have already given you, that my Compositions in Gardening are altogether after the *Pindarick* manner,

---

[1] Lattice-work or trellis. Only one example earlier than this (1698) is cited by *OED.*

[2] See No. 5 (vol. i).

[3] Cf. Thomas Tickell, *Kensington* (1722):

> That hollow space where now, in living rows
> Line above line the yew's sad verdure grows,
> Was, ere the planter's hand its beauty gave,
> A common pit, a rude unfinished cave.

As Addison says, this area had at first been 'nothing but a gravel-pit', lying to the north and west of Kensington Palace. It is described, with illustrations, in David Green, *Gardener to Queen Anne: Henry Wise (1653–1738) and the Formal Garden* (Oxford University Press, 1956), pp. 75–76. When Wise made the sunk garden described in this paper, writes Mr. Green, 'it was something daring and unprecedented; although symmetry was strictly respected. At the least it showed original thought and at the most it might be counted an early "imperfect essay" in what would now be called landscape gardening' (p. 76).

and run into the beautiful Wildness of Nature, without affecting the nicer Elegancies of Art.[1] What I am now going to mention will, perhaps, deserve your Attention more than any thing I have yet said. I find that in the Discourse which I spoke of at the beginning of my Letter, you are against filling an *English* Garden with Ever-Greens, and indeed I am so far of your Opinion, that I can by no means think the Verdure of an Ever-Green comparable to that which shoots out Annually, and cloaths our Trees in the Summer Season. But I have often wondered that those who are like my self, and love to live in Gardens, have never thought of contriving a *Winter Garden*,[2] which should consist of such Trees only as never cast their Leaves. We have very often little Snatches of Sunshine, and Fair Weather, in the most uncomfortable Parts of the Year, and have frequently several Days in *November* and *January*, that are as agreeable as any in the finest Months. At such times, therefore, I think there could not be a greater Pleasure, than to walk in such a *Winter Garden* as I have proposed. In the Summer Season the whole Country blooms, and is a kind of Garden, for which reason we are not so sensible of those Beauties, that at this time may be every where met with; but when Nature is in her Desolation, and presents us with nothing but bleak and barren Prospects, there is something unspeakably cheerful in a Spot of Ground, which is covered with Trees that smile amidst all the Rigors of Winter, and give us a View of the most gay Season, in the midst of that which is the most dead and melancholy. I have so far indulged my self in this Thought, that I have set apart a whole Acre of Ground for the executing of it. The Walls are covered with Ivy instead of Vines. The Laurel, the Hornbeam, and the Holly, with many other Trees and Plants of the same Nature, grow so thick in it, that you cannot imagine a more lively Scene. The glowing Redness of the Berries, with which they are hung at this time, vies with the Verdure of their Leaves, and are apt to inspire the Heart of the Beholder with that vernal Delight,

---

[1] After praising the work of Wise at Kensington Addison goes on to describe the more natural kind of garden which was eventually to supplant the formal tradition of Le Nôtre, Wise, and others. Green (p. 184) writes:

Inasmuch as they delighted those they were made for, Wise's gardens were undoubtedly a success. It was no fault of his that, just as tapestry had had its day before Marlborough's campaigns had been woven into the hangings for Blenheim, so Addison was tolling the knell of the formal garden [in *Spectator* 477] while its supreme example—Blenheim's Great Parterre—had yet to be completed.

[2] A garden of plants that flourish in winter, such as evergreens. This is the first example in *OED* of this combination.

which you have somewhere taken notice of in your former Papers.[1] It is very pleasant, at the same time, to see the several Kinds of Birds retiring into this little Green Spot, and enjoying themselves among the Branches and Foliage, when my great Garden, which I have before mentioned to you, does not afford a single Leaf for their Shelter.

'You must know, Sir, that I look upon the Pleasure which we take in a Garden, as one of the most innocent Delights in Humane Life. A Garden was the Habitation of our First Parents before the Fall. It is naturally apt to fill the Mind with Calmness and Tranquility, and to lay all its turbulent Passions at rest. It gives us a great Insight into the Contrivance and Wisdom of Providence, and suggests innumerable Subjects for Meditation. I cannot but think the very Complacency and Satisfaction which a Man takes in these Works of Nature, to be a laudable, if not a virtuous Habit of Mind. For all which Reasons, I hope you will pardon the Length of my present Letter.

> *I am,*
> *SIR, &c.'*
> C

No. 478   *Monday, September 8, 1712*[2]
[STEELE]

> . . . *Usus*
> *Quem penes Arbitrium est, & Jus & norma* . . .

Mr. SPECTATOR,

'IT happened lately, that a Friend of mine, who had many things to buy for his Family, wou'd oblige me to walk with him to the Shops. He was very nice in his Way, and fond of having every thing shewn, which at first made me very uneasy; but as his Humour still continu'd, the things which I had been staring at along with him

---

[1] No. 393 (vol. iii).
[2] *Motto.* Horace, *Ars poetica*, 71–72:
    Use is the Judge, the Law, and Rule of Speech. ROSCOMMON.

began to fill my Head, and led me into a Set of amusing Thoughts concerning them.

'I fancy'd it must be very surprizing to any one who enters into a Detail of Fashions, to consider how far the Vanity of Mankind has laid it self out in Dress, what a prodigious Number of People it maintains, and what a Circulation of Money it occasions. Providence in this Case makes use of the Folly which we will not give up, and it becomes instrumental to the Support of those who are willing to labour. Hence it is, that Fringe-Makers, Lace-Men, Tire-Women, and a Number of other Trades, which would be useless in a simple State of Nature, draw their Subsistence; tho' it is seldom seen that such as these are extremely rich, because their original Fault of being founded upon Vanity, keeps them poor by the light Inconstancy of its Nature. The Variableness of Fashion turns the Stream of Business, which flows from it now into one Channel, and anon into another; so that different Sets of People sink or flourish in their Turns by it.

'From the Shops we retir'd to the Tavern, where I found my Friend express so much Satisfaction for the Bargains he had made, that my moral Reflections (if I had told them,) might have pass'd for a Reproof; so I chose rather to fall in with him, and let the Discourse run upon the use of Fashions.

'Here we remembred how much Man is govern'd by his Senses, how livelily he is struck by the Objects which appear to him in an agreeable Manner, how much Cloaths contribute to make us agreeable Objects, and how much we owe it to our selves that we should appear so.

'We considered Man as belonging to Societies; Societies as form'd of different Ranks, and different Ranks distinguished by Habits, that all proper Duty or Respect might attend their Appearance.

'We took notice of several Advantages which are met with in the Occurrences of Conversation. How the bashful Man has been sometimes so rais'd, as to express himself with an Air of Freedom, when he imagines that his Habit introduces him to Company with a becoming manner: And again, how a Fool in fine Cloaths shall be suddenly heard with Attention, till he has betrayed himself; whereas a Man of Sense appearing with a Dress of Negligence, shall be but coldly received, till he be prov'd by Time, and established in a Character. Such Things as these we cou'd recollect to have happen'd to our own Knowledge so very often, that we concluded the Author had his Reasons, who advises his Son to go in Dress rather above his Fortune than under it.[1]

'At last the Subject seem'd so considerable, that it was propos'd to have a Repository builded for Fashions, as there are Chambers for Medals and other Rarities. The Building may be shap'd as that which stands among the Pyramids, in the Form of a Woman's Head. This may be rais'd upon Pillars, whose Ornaments shall bear a just Relation to the Design. Thus there may be an Imitation of Fringe carv'd in the Base, a Sort of Appearance of Lace in the Frize;[2] and a Representation of curling Locks, with Bows of Riban sloping over them, may fill up the Work of the Cornish.[3] The Inside may be divided into two Apartments, appropriated to each Sex. The Apartments may be fill'd with Shelves, on which Boxes are to stand as regularly as Books in a Library. These are to have Folding-Doors, which being open'd, you are to behold a Baby[4] dress'd out in some Fashion which has flourish'd, and standing upon a Pedestal, where the Time of its Reign is mark'd down. For its further Regulation let it be order'd, that every one who invents a Fashion shall bring in his Box, whose Front he may at Pleasure have either work'd or painted with some amorous or gay Device, that, like Books with gilded Leaves and Covers, it may the sooner draw the Eyes of the Beholders. And to the End that these may be preserv'd with all due Care, let there be a Keeper appointed, who shall be a Gentleman qualify'd with a competent Knowledge in Cloaths; so that by this Means the Place will be a comfortable Support for some Beau who has spent his Estate in dressing.

'The Reasons offer'd by which we expected to gain the Approbation of the Publick, were as follows.

'First, That every one who is considerable enough to be a Mode,[5] and has any Imperfection of Nature or Chance, which it is possible to hide by the Advantage of Cloaths, may, by coming to this Repository, be furnish'd her self, and furnish all who are under the same Misfortune, with the most agreeable Manner of concealing it; and that on the other Side, every one who has any Beauty in Face or Shape, may be also furnish'd with the most agreeable Manner of shewing it.

[1] Francis Osborne, *Advice to a Son*, part ii, sect. 36. Cited also in No. 150 (vol. ii).
[2] I.e. frieze, or decorative part of the entablature.
[3] The old spelling of *cornice*.   [4] A doll. See No. 277 (vol. ii).
[5] 'One who sets or displays the fashion.' This is the first example in *OED* of the word in this sense.

'Secondly, That whereas some of our young Gentlemen who Travel, give us great reason to suspect that they only go abroad to make or improve a fancy for Dress, a Project of this nature may be a means to keep them at Home, which is in effect the keeping of so much Money in the Kingdom. And perhaps the Ballance of fashion in *Europe*, which now leans upon the side of *France*, may be so alter'd for the future, that it may become as common with *Frenchmen* to come to *England* for their finishing stroke of Breeding, as it has been for *Englishmen* to go to *France* for it.

'Thirdly, Whereas several great Scholars, who might have been otherwise useful to the World, have spent their time in studying to describe the Dresses of the Ancients from dark Hints, which they are feign to interpret and support with much Learning, it will from henceforth happen that they shall be freed from the trouble, and the World from useless Volumes. This Project will be a Registry to which Posterity may have recourse for the clearing such obscure Passages as tend that way in Authors, and therefore we shall not for the future submit ourselves to the learning of Etymology, which might perswade the Age to come, that the Farthingal was worn for cheapness, or the Furbeloe for warmth.

'Fourthly, Whereas they who are old themselves, have often a way of railing at the extravagance of Youth, and the whole Age in which their Children live; it is hoped that this ill Humour will be much suppress'd, when we can have Recourse to the Fashions of their Times, produce them in our Vindication, and be able to shew that it might have been as expensive in Queen *Elizabeth*'s Time only to wash and quill a Ruff,[1] as it is now to buy Cravats or Neck-Handkerchiefs.[2]

'We desire also to have it taken Notice of, That because we would shew a particular Respect to Foreigners, which may induce them to perfect their Breeding here in a Knowledge which is very proper for pretty Gentlemen, we have conceived the Motto for the House in the Learned Language. There is to be a Picture over the Door, with a Looking-Glass and a Dressing-Chair in the Middle of it: Then on one Side are to be seen, above one another, Patch-Boxes, Pin-Cushions, and little Bottles; on the other, Powder-Bags, Puffs, Combs, and Brushes; beyond these, Swords with fine Knots, whose

---

[1] To quill: 'To form into small cylindrical plaits or folds resembling a quill.' The first example in *OED*.
[2] The first example in *OED* of this combination.

Points are hidden, and Fans almost closed, with the Handles down-ward, are to stand out interchangeably from the Sides, till they meet at the Top, and form a Semi-circle over the rest of the Figures: Beneath all, the Writing is to run in this pretty sounding manner:

Adeste, o quotquot sunt, Veneres, Gratiæ, Cupidines,
En vobis adsunt in promptu
Faces, Vincula, Spicula,
Hinc eligite, sumite, regite.[1]

I *am, Sir,*
Your most humble Servant,
A. B.'

The Proposal of my Correspondent I cannot but look upon as an ingenious Method of placing Persons (whose Parts make them ambitious to exert themselves in frivolous Things) in a Rank by themselves. In order to this, I would propose, That there be a Board of Directors of the Fashionable Society; and because it is a Matter of too much Weight for a private Man to determine alone, I should be highly obliged to my Correspondents if they would give in Lists of Persons qualified for this Trust. If the chief Coffee-houses, the Conversations of which Places are carry'd on by Persons, each of whom has his little Number of Followers and Admirers, would name from among themselves two or three to be inserted, they shou'd be put up with great Faithfulness. Old Beaus are to be preferr'd in the first Place; but as that Sect, with relation to Dress, is almost extinct, it will, I fear, be absolutely necessary to take in all Time-Servers, properly so deem'd; that is, such as, without any Conviction of Conscience, or View of Interest, change with the World, and that meerly from a Terror of being out of Fashion. Such, also, who from Facility of Temper, and too much Obsequiousness, are vitious against their Will, and follow Leaders whom they do not approve, for Want of Courage to go their own Way, are capable Persons for this Superintendency. Those who are loth to grow old, or would do any thing contrary to the Course and Order of Things out of Fond-ness to be in Fashion, are proper Candidates. To conclude, those who are in Fashion without apparent Merit, must be suppos'd to

[1] Nichols translates:

> All ye Venuses, Graces, and Cupids, attend:
> See, prepared to your hands,
> Darts, torches, and bands:
> Your weapons here choose, and your empire extend.

have latent Qualities, which would appear in a Post of Direction, and therefore are to be regarded in forming these Lists. Any who shall be pleas'd, according to these, or what further Qualifications may occur to himself, to send a List, is desired to do it within Fourteen Days after this Date.

N. B. *The Place of the Physician to this Society, according to the last mentioned Qualification, is already engaged.*

T[1]

No. 479   *Tuesday, September 9, 1712*[2]

[STEELE]

. . . Dare Jura maritis.
Hor.

MANY are the Epistles I every Day receive from Husbands, who complain of Vanity, Pride, but above all Ill-nature, in their Wives. I cannot tell how it is, but I think I see in all their Letters that the Cause of their Uneasiness is in themselves; and indeed I have hardly ever observed the married Condition unhappy, but from want of Judgment or Temper in the Man. The Truth is, we generally make Love in a Stile, and with Sentiments very unfit for ordinary Life: They are half Theatrical, half Romantick. By this Means we raise our Imaginations to what is not to be expected in humane Life; and because we did not before-hand think of the Creature we were enamoured of as subject to Dishumour,[3] Age, Sickness, Impatience, or Sullenness, but altogether considered her as the Object of Joy, humane Nature it self is often imputed to her as her particular Imperfection or Defect.

I take it to be a Rule proper to be observed in all Occurrences of Life, but more especially in the domestick or matrimonial Part of it, to preserve always a Disposition to be pleased. This cannot be supported but by considering things in their right Light, and as Nature has formed them, and not as our own Fancies or Appetites

---

[1] A dream vision inspired by this paper is printed in Lillie (ii. 332–5), with a request for appointment as 'chief architect to the society mentioned in your paper'.

[2] *Motto.* Horace, *Ars poetica*, 398: To prescribe Laws for Husbands. This had been used as Motto for No. 236 (vol. ii).

[3] See No. 424 (vol. iii).

would have them. He then who took a young Lady to his Bed, with no other Consideration than the Expectation of Scenes of Dalliance, and thought of her (as I said before) only as she was to administer to the Gratification of Desire; as that Desire flags, will, without her Fault, think her Charms and her Merit abated: From hence must follow Indifference, Dislike, Peevishness, and Rage. But the Man who brings his Reason to support his Passion, and beholds what he loves as liable to all the Calamities of humane Life both in Body and Mind, and even at the best, what must bring upon him new Cares and new Relations; such a Lover, I say, will form himself accordingly, and adapt his Mind to the Nature of his Circumstances. This latter Person will be prepared to be a Father, a Friend, an Advocate, a Steward for People yet unborn, and has proper Affections ready for every Incident in the Marriage-State. Such a Man can hear the Cries of Children with Pity instead of Anger; and when they run over his Head, he is not disturbed at their Noise, but is glad of their Mirth and Health. *Tom Trusty* has told me, that he thinks it doubles his Attention to the most intricate Affair he is about, to hear his Children, for whom all his Cares are applied, make a Noise in the next Room: On the other Side, *Will Sparkish* cannot put on his Perriwig, or adjust his Cravat at the Glass, for the Noise of those damn'd Nurses and squawling Brats; and then ends with a gallant Reflection upon the Comforts of Matrimony, runs out of the Hearing, and drives to the Chocolate-house.

According as the Husband is disposed in himself, every Circumstance of his Life is to give him Torment or Pleasure. When the Affection is well placed, and supported by the Considerations of Duty, Honour, and Friendship, which are in the highest Degree engaged in this Alliance, there can nothing arise in the common Course of Life, or from the Blows or Favours of Fortune, in which a Man will not find Matters of some Delight unknown to a single Condition.

He that sincerely loves his Wife and Family, and studies to improve that Affection in himself, conceives Pleasure from the most indifferent things; while the married Man who has not bid adieu to the Fashions and false Gallantries of the Town, is perplexed with every thing around him. In both these Cases Men cannot, indeed, make a sillier Figure, than in repeating such Pleasures and Pains to the rest of the World; but I speak of them only, as they sit upon those who are involved in them. As I visit all Sorts of People, I cannot indeed but smile, when the good Lady tells her Husband what extraordinary things the Child spoke since he went out. No longer than Yesterday I was prevailed with to go home with a fond Husband; and his Wife told him, that his Son, of his own Head, when the Clock in the Parlour struck Two, said Pappa would come home to Dinner presently. While the Father has him in a Rapture in his Arms, and is drowning him with Kisses, the Wife tells me he is but just four Year old. Then they both struggle for him, and bring him up to me, and repeat his Observation of two a Clock. I was called upon by Looks upon the Child, and then at me, to say something; and I told the Father, that this Remark of the Infant of his coming home, and joyning the Time with it, was a certain Indication that he would be a great Historian and Chronologer. They are neither of them Fools, yet received my Compliment with great Acknowledgment of my Prescience. I fared very well at Dinner, and heard many other notable Sayings of their Heir, which would have given very little Entertainment to one less turn'd to Reflection than I was; but it was a pleasing Speculation to remark on the Happiness of a Life, in which Things of no Moment give Occasions of Hope, Self-Satisfaction, and Triumph. On the other Hand, I have known an ill-natur'd Coxcomb, who was hardly improved in any thing but Bulk, for want of this Disposition, silence the whole Family, as a Set of silly Women and Children, for recounting Things which were really above his own Capacity.

When I say all this, I cannot deny but there are perverse Jades that fall to Mens Lots, with whom it requires more than common Proficiency in Philosophy to be able to live. When these are join'd to Men of warm Spirits, without Temper or Learning, they are frequently corrected with Stripes; but one of our famous Lawyers is of Opinion, That this ought to be used sparingly.[1] As I remember those are his very Words; but as it is proper to draw some spiritual Use out of all Afflictions, I should rather recommend to those who are visited with Women of Spirit, to form themselves for the World by Patience at home. *Socrates*, who is by all Accounts the undoubted Head of the Sect of the Hen-peck'd, own'd and acknowledg'd that he ow'd great part of his Virtue to the Exercise which his useful Wife constantly gave it. There are several good Instructions may be drawn from his wise Answers to People of less Fortitude than himself on her Subject. A Friend, with Indignation, ask'd how so

[1] Henry de Bracton, *De legibus*, i. 10. Cf. No. 482.

good a Man could live with so violent a Creature? He observ'd to him, *That they who learn to keep a good Seat on Horseback, mount the least manageable they can get, and when they have master'd them, they are sure never to be discomposed on the Backs of Steeds less restive.* At several Times, to different Persons, on the same Subject, he has said, *My dear Friend, you are beholden to* Xantippe *that I bear so well your flying-out in a Dispute.* To another, *My Hen clacks very much, but she brings me Chickens. They that live in a trading Street, are not disturbed at the Passage of Carts.*[1] I would have, if possible, a wise Man be contented with his Lot, even with a Shrew; for tho' he cannot make her better, he may, you see, make himself better by her Means.

But instead of pursuing my Design of displaying Conjugal Love in its natural Beauties and Attractions, I am got into Tales to the Disadvantage of that State of Life. I must say therefore that I am verily perswaded, that whatever is delightful in humane Life, is to be enjoyed in greater Perfection in the marry'd, than in the single Condition. He that has this Passion in Perfection, in Occasions of Joy can say to himself, besides his own Satisfaction, *How happy will this make my Wife and Children?* Upon Occurrences of Distress or Danger can comfort himself, *But all this while my Wife and Children are safe.* There is something in it that doubles Satisfactions, because others participate them; and dispels Afflictions, because others are exempt from them. All who are married without this Relish of their Circumstance, are either in a tasteless Indolence and Negligence, which is hardly to be attain'd, or else live in the hourly Repetition of sharp Answers, eager Upbraidings, and distracting Reproaches. In a Word, the married State, with and without the Affection suitable to it, is the compleatest Image of Heaven and Hell we are capable of receiving in this Life.　　　　　　　　　　　　T

---

[1] Xenophon, *Symposium*, 2. 10; Diogenes Laertius, *Lives of the Philosophers*, 2. 37.

Responsare cupidinibus, contemnere honores
Fortis, & in se ipso totus, teres atque rotundus.
                                                    Hor.

THE other Day looking over those old Manuscripts, of which
I have formerly given some Account, and which relate to the
Character of the mighty *Pharamond* of *France*, and the close Friendship between him and his Friend *Eucrate*;[2] I found, among the Letters
which had been in the Custody of the latter, an Epistle from a
Country Gentleman to *Pharamond*, wherein he excuses himself from
coming to Court. The Gentleman, it seems, was contented with his
Condition, had formerly been in the King's Service, but at the
writing the following Letter, had, from Leisure and Reflection,
quite another Sense of things than that which he had in the more
active Part of his Life.

                    Monsieur Chezluy *to* Pharamond.
Dread Sir,
'I HAVE from your own Hand (enclosed under the Cover of Mr.
Eucrate of your Majesty's Bed-chamber) a Letter which invites
me to Court. I understand this great Honour to be done me out
of Respect and Inclination to me, rather than Regard to your own
Service: For which Reason I beg Leave to lay before your Majesty
my Reasons for declining to depart from Home; and will not doubt
but, as your Motive in desiring my Attendance was to make me
an happier Man, when you think that will not be effected by my
Remove, you will permit me to stay where I am. Those who have
an Ambition to appear in Courts, have ever an Opinion, that their
Persons or their Talents are particularly formed for the Service or
Ornament of that Place; or else are hurried by downright Desire
of Gain, or what they call Honour, to take upon themselves whatever the Generosity of their Master can give them Opportunities

---

[1] *Motto.* Horace, *Satires*, 2. 7. 85–86:
> Who's proof against the Charms of vain Delight,
> Whom feeble Fortune strives in vain to wound,
> So closely gathered in a perfect Round. CREECH.

[2] See Nos. 76, 84, 97 (vol. i).

to grasp at. But your Goodness shall not be thus imposed upon by me: I will therefore confess to you, that frequent Solitude, and long Conversation with such who know no Arts which polish Life, have made me the plainest Creature in your Dominions. Those less Capacities of moving with a good Grace, bearing a ready Affability to all around me, and acting with Ease before many, have quite left me. I am come to that, with Regard to my Person, that I consider it only as a Machine I am obliged to take Care of, in order to enjoy my Soul in its Faculties with Alacrity; well remembering, that this Habitation of Clay will in a few Years be a meaner Piece of Earth than any Utensil about my House. When this is, as it really is, the most frequent Reflection I have, you will easily imagine how well I should become a Drawing-Room: Add to this, What shall a Man without Desires do about the generous *Pharamond?* Monsieur *Eucrate* has hinted to me, that you have Thoughts of distinguishing me with Titles. As for my self, in the Temper of my present Mind, Appellations of Honour would but embarrass Discourse, and new Behaviour towards me perplex me in every Habitude of Life. I am also to acknowledge to you, that my Children, of whom your Majesty condescended to enquire, are all of them mean both in their Persons and Genius. The Estate my eldest Son is Heir to, is more than he can enjoy with a good Grace. My Self-love will not carry me so far, as to impose upon Mankind the Advancement of Persons (meerly for their being related to me) into high Distinctions, who ought for their own Sakes, as well as that of the Publick, to affect Obscurity. I wish, my generous Prince, as it is in your Power to give Honours and Offices, it were also to give Talents suitable to them: Were it so, the noble *Pharamond* would reward the Zeal of my Youth with Abilities to do him Service in my Age.

'Those who accept of Favour without Merit, support themselves in it at the Expence of your Majesty. Give me Leave to tell you, Sir, this is the Reason that we in the Country hear so often repeated the Word *Prerogative*. That Part of your Law which is reserved in your self for the readier Service and Good of the Publick, slight Men are eternally buzzing in our Ears to cover their own Follies and Miscarriages. It would be an Addition to the high Favour you have done me, if you would let *Eucrate* send me word how often, and in what Cases you allow a Constable to insist upon the Prerogative. From the highest to the lowest Officer in your Dominions, something of their own Carriage they would exempt from Examination under the Shelter of the Word *Prerogative*. I would fain, most noble *Phara-mond*, see one of your Officers assert your Prerogative by good and gracious Actions. When is it used to help the Afflicted, to rescue the Innocent, to comfort the Stranger? Uncommon Methods, apparently undertaken to attain worthy Ends, would never make Power invidious. You see, Sir, I talk to you with the Freedom your noble Nature approves in all whom you admit to your Conversation.

'But to return to your Majesty's Letter, I humbly conceive, that all Distinctions are useful to Men only as they are to act in Publick; and it would be a romantick Madness for a Man to be a Lord in his Closet. Nothing can be honourable to a Man apart from the World, but the Reflection upon worthy Actions; and he that places Honour in a Consciousness of Well-doing, will have but little Relish for any outward Homage that is paid him, since what gives him Distinction to himself, cannot come within the Observation of his Beholders. Thus all the Words of Lordship, Honour, and Grace, are only Repetitions to a Man that the King has ordered him to be called so; but no Evidences that there is any thing in himself that would give the Man who applies to him those Ideas, without the Creation of his Master.

'I have, most Noble *Pharamond*, all Honours and all Titles in your own Approbation; I triumph in them as they are your Gift, I refuse them as they are to give me the Observation of others. Indulge me, my Noble Master, in this Chastity[1] of Renown; let me know my self in the Favour of *Pharamond*, and look down upon the Applause of the People.

I am,
In all Duty and Loyalty,
Your Majesty's most obedient
Subject and Servant,
Jean Chezluy.'[2]

[1] This figurative use of the word is marked *Obs.* by *OED*; the last quotation is dated 1762–9.

[2] A correspondent in Lillie (ii. 338–42) signing himself R. Middle-Thought, 15 Sept. 1712, objects to this letter as too extreme:

> They who are naturally inclined to such vices, are such adamants, that no such tool as a pen is will touch them. . . . Therefore . . . let me desire you on this, at your own time, and in your own words (which are a great advantage to every thing they recommend) to write nearer to practical truth, and let the world know from your spectatorial wisdom (what generally speaking they will always think) that riches, honours, and power are very good things, and that they who desire them desire good things.

SIR,

'I NEED not tell you with what Disadvantages Men of low Fortunes and great Modesty come into the World, what wrong Measures their Diffidence of themselves, and Fear of offending, often obliges them to take, and what a Pity it is that their greatest Vertues and Qualities, that should soonest recommend them, are the main Obstacle in the Way of their Preferment.

'This, Sir, is my Case; I was bred at a Country School, where I learn'd *Latin* and *Greek*. The Misfortunes of my Family forced me up to Town, where a Profession of the politer Sort has protected me against Infamy and Want. I am now Clerk to a Lawyer, and, in Times of Vacancy and Recess from Business, have made my self Master of *Italian* and *French*; and though the Progress I have made in my Business has gain'd me Reputation enough for one of my Standing, yet my Mind suggests to me every Day, that it is not upon that Foundation I am to build my Fortune.

'The Person I have my present Dependance upon, has it in his Nature, as well as his Power, to advance me, by recommending me to a Gentleman that is going beyond Sea in a publick Employment. I know the Printing this Letter would point me out to those I want Confidence to speak to, and I hope it is not in your Power to refuse making any Body happy.

Septemb. 9.   *Yours,* &c.

1712.   M. D.'[1]

                                                        T

---

[1] 'This letter was written by Mr. Robert Harper of Lincoln's Inn, an eminent conveyancer. Steele omitted some parts of it, and made some alterations in it; at least the author's original draft of it in his letter-book, communicated to the Annotator by the Rev. Mr. Harper of the British Museum, is somewhat different. This letter was sent to the Spect. Aug. 9, 1712, as appears from the author's autograph endorsement' (Nichols). Aitken (viii. 412) states that Harper's letter-book was at that time in the possession of Dr. Grosart and that the original of this letter contains the postscript: 'I know the printing this letter would point me out to those I want confidence to speak to, and I hope it is not in your power to refuse making anybody happy.'

No. 481
[ADDISON]

Thursday, September 11, 1712[1]

. . . *uti non*
Compositum meliùs cum Bitho Bacchius, in jus
Acres procurrunt . . .

Hor.

IT is sometimes pleasant enough to consider the different Notions, which different Persons have of the same thing. If Men of low[a] Condition very often set a value on things, which are not prized by those who are in an higher Station of Life, there are many things these esteem which are in no value among Persons of an inferiour Rank. Common People are, in particular, very much astonished, when they hear of those solemn Contests and Debates, which are made among the Great upon the Punctilio's of a Publick Ceremony, and wonder to hear that any Business of Consequence should be retarded by those little Circumstances, which they represent to themselves as trifling and insignificant. I am mightily pleased with a Porter's Decision[2] in one of Mr. *Southern's* Plays, which is founded upon that fine Distress of a Virtuous Woman's marrying a second Husband, while her first was yet living. The first Husband, who was supposed to have been dead, returning to his House after a long Absence, raises a noble Perplexity for the Tragick Part of the Play. In the mean while the Nurse and the Porter conferring upon the Difficulties that would ensue in such a Case, Honest *Sampson* thinks the Matter may be easily decided, and solves it very judiciously, by the old Proverb, that if his first Master be still living, *The Man must have his Mare again*. There is nothing in my Time which has so much surprized and confounded the greatest part of my honest Countrymen, as the present Controversie between Count *Rechteren* and Monsieur *Mesnager*, which employs the wise Heads of so many Nations, and holds all the Affairs of *Europe* in Suspense.[3]

of low] of a low *Fol.*

----

[1] *Motto.* Horace, *Satires*, 1. 7. 19–21:
　　　Not *Byth* and *Bacchus* were a Match so fair,
　　　Began their Suit; away to Court they run. CREECH.
[2] In Southern's *The Fatal Marriage, or the Innocent Adultery* (last given at Drury Lane on 5 Feb.), v. i. The part of Sampson, the porter, was taken by Underhill.
[3] The dispute between M. de Mesnager, the French plenipotentiary, and Count

205

Upon my going into a Coffee-house Yesterday, and lending an Ear to the next Table, which was encompassed with a Circle of Inferior Politicians, one of them, after having read over the News very attentively, broke out into the following Remarks: I am afraid, says he, this unhappy Rupture between the Footmen at *Utrecht* will retard the Peace of Christendom. I wish the Pope may not be at the Bottom of it. His Holiness has a very good Hand at fomenting a Division, as the poor *Suisse Cantons* have lately Experienced to their cost.[1] If Monsieur *What d'ye call him*'s Domesticks will not come to an Accommodation, I do not know how the Quarrel can be ended, but by a Religious War.

Why truly, says a *Wiseacre* that sate by him, were I as the King of *France*, I would scorn to take part with the Footmen of either side: Here's all the Business of *Europe* stands still, because Monsieur *Mesnager*'s Man has had his Head broke. If Count *Rectrum* had given

de Rechteren, plenipotentiary of the Dutch States, at Utrecht, which threatened to disrupt the entire peace negotiations, fills many columns of the English newspapers in Aug. and Sept. 1712. According to the *Flying Post* of 19 Aug. the servants of M. de Mesnager twice hissed at and jeered the Count de Rechteren and his domestics as they passed by Mesnager's house after the French victory at Denain on 24 July (cf. No. 476), whereupon

the Count has done himself Justice, by making his Servants Thresh those of M. Mesnager; so that most part of them are Lame. While the Count and Mesnager were walking together in the Mall, one of the Monsieur's Servants came running to him in a bloody Pickle, to tell him what had happen'd; upon which Mesnager dema[n]ded Satisfaction of the Count, who told him very frankly, that what was done was by his Order, and that he was ready to give him immediate Satisfaction: But when the Dutchman put his Hand to his Sword, the Monsieur sneak'd off. The French Plenipotentiaries threaten to leave Utrecht upon this Affront; but the Venetian Ministers and the Pope's Nuncio disswade them from it.

A longer account, from the Tory point of view, appears in the *Post Boy* of 21 Aug. Shortly before this number of the *Spectator* appeared, Mesnager's relation of the affair was published verbatim in the *Daily Courant* (8 Sept.) and in the *Flying Post* on the following day (occupying the entire number). The affair dragged on at length and ended with Count de Rechteren's resignation as plenipotentiary and an apology to the French king (*Daily Courant*, 22 Oct.). On 18 Sept. was published:

An Enquiry into the Real Interest of Princes in the Persons of their Ambassadors, and how far the Petty Quarrels of Ambassadors, or the Servants and Dependents of Ambassadors one among another, ought to be Resented by their Principals. With an Essay on what Satisfaction it is necessary to Give or Take in such Cases. Impartially applied to the Affairs of Monsieur Menager, and the Count de Rechteren, Plenipotentiaries at Utrecht. Sold by J. Baker at the Black-Boy in Pater-Noster-Row. Price 3d. (Advertisement in *Daily Courant*.

[1] The quarrel between the Protestant and the Roman Catholic cantons is dealt with at length in the newspapers in the summer of 1712. The *Daily Courant* on 22 July reported that the cantons of Schwyz, Unterwalden, and Zug had rejected the proposed truce. 'This they have done at the Perswasion and by the Intrigues of the Pope's Nuncio, who went busily from Canton to Canton.' The quarrel is mentioned in No. 452.

them a Pot of Ale after it, all would have been well, without any of this Bustle; but they say he's a warm Man, and does not care to be made Mouths at.

Upon this, one, that had held his Tongue hitherto, began[a] to exert himself; declaring, That he was very well pleased, the Plenipotentiaries of our Christian Princes took this matter into their serious Consideration; for that Lacqueys were never so saucy and pragmatical,[1] as they are now-a-days, and that he should be glad to see them taken down in the Treaty of Peace, if it might be done without prejudice to the Publick[b] Affairs.

One, who sate at the other End of the Table, and seemed to be in the Interests of the *French* King, told them, that they did not take the Matter right, for that his most Christian Majesty did not resent this Matter because it was an Injury done to Monsieur *Mesnager's* Footmen; for, says he, what are Monsieur *Mesnager's* Footmen to him? but because it was done to his Subjects; now, says he, let me tell you, it would look very odd for a Subject of *France* to have a Bloody Nose, and his Soveraign not to take Notice of it. He is obliged, in Honour, to defend his People against Hostilities; and if the *Dutch* will be so insolent to a Crowned Head, as, in any wise, to cuff or kick those who are under *His* Protection, I think he is in the right to call them to an Account for it.

This Distinction set the Controversie upon a new Foot, and seemed to be very well approved by most that heard it, till a little warm Fellow, who declared himself a Friend to the House of *Austria*, fell most unmercifully upon his *Gallic* Majesty, as Encouraging his Subjects to make Mouths at their Betters, and afterwards screening them from the Punishment that was due to their Insolence. To which he added, that the *French* Nation was so addicted to Grimace, that if there was not a stop put to it at the General Congress, there would be no walking the Streets for them in a time of Peace, especially if they continued Masters of the *West Indies*. The little Man proceeded with a great deal of Warmth, declaring, that if the Allies were of his Mind, he would oblige the *French* King to burn his Gallies, and tolerate the Protestant Religion in his Dominions, before he would Sheath his Sword. He concluded with calling Monsieur *Mesnager* an Insignificant Prig.[2]

[a] began] begun *Fol.*   [b] to the Publick] to Publick *Fol.*

---

[1] I.e. conceited, self-important. Now *rare* (*OED*).   [2] See No. 403 (vol. iii).

The Dispute was now growing very Warm, and one does not know where it wou'd have ended, had not a young Man of about One and Twenty, who seems to have been brought up with an Eye to the Law, taken the Debate into his Hand, and given it, as his Opinion, that neither Count *Rechteren,* nor Monsieur *Mesnager,* had behaved themselves right in this Affair. Count *Rechteren,* says he, shou'd have made Affidavit that his Servants had been affronted, and then Monsieur *Mesnager* would have done him Justice, by taking away their Liveries from 'em, or some other way that he might have thought the most proper; for let me tell you, if a Man makes a Mouth at me, I am not to knock the Teeth out of it for his Pains. Then again, as for Monsieur *Mesnager,* upon his Servants being beaten, why! he might have had his Action of Assault and Battery. But as the Case now stands, if you will have my Opinion, I think they ought to bring it to Referees.

I heard a great deal more of this Conference, but I must confess with little Edification; for all I could learn at last from these honest Gentlemen was, that the Matter in Debate was of too high a Nature for such Heads as theirs, or mine, to Comprehend.

O

No. 482   *Friday, September 12, 1712*[1]
[ADDISON]

Floriferis ut apes in saltibus omnia libant.
Lucr.

WHEN I have published any single Paper that falls in with the Popular Taste, and pleases more than ordinary, it always brings me in a great return of Letters. My *Tuesday's* Discourse, wherein I gave several Admonitions to the Fraternity of the *Henpeck'd,* has already produced me very many Correspondents; the Reason I cannot guess at, unless it be that such a Discourse is of general Use, and every married Man's Money. An honest Tradesman, who dates his Letter from *Cheapside,* sends me Thanks in the Name of a Club, who, he tells me, meet as often as their Wives will

[1] *Motto.* Lucretius, *De rerum natura,* 3. 11:
As Bees suck Sweets from every Flower.

give them leave, and stay together till they are sent for home. He informs me, that my Paper has administered great Consolation to their whole Club, and desires me to give some further Account of *Socrates*, and to acquaint them in whose Reign he lived, whether he was a Citizen or a Courtier, whether he buried *Xantippe*, with many other particulars: for that by his Sayings he appears to have been a very Wise Man and a good Christian. Another, who writes himself *Benjamin Bamboo*, tells me, that being coupled with a Shrew, he had endeavoured to tame her by such lawful Means as those which I mentioned in my last *Tuesday*'s Paper, and that in his Wrath he had often gone further than *Bracton*[1] allows in those Cases; but that for the future he was resolved to bear it like a Man of Temper and Learning, and consider her only as one who lives in his House to teach him Philosophy. *Tom Dapperwit* says, that he agrees with me in that whole Discourse, excepting only the last Sentence, where I affirm the married State to be either an Heaven or an Hell. *Tom* has been at the Charge of a Penny upon this occasion, to tell me that by his Experience it is neither one nor the other, but rather that middle kind of State commonly known by the Name of *Purgatory*.

The fair Sex have likewise obliged me with their Reflections upon the same Discourse. A Lady, who calls her self *Euterpe*, and seems a Woman of Letters, asks me whether I am for establishing the *Salick* Law in every Family, and why it is not fit that a Woman who has Discretion and Learning should sit at the Helm, when the Husband is weak and illiterate? Another, of a quite contrary Character, subscribes her self *Xantippe*, and tells me, that she follows the Example of her Name-sake, for being married to a Bookish Man, who has no Knowledge of the World, she is forced to take their Affairs into her own Hands, and to spirit him up[2] now and then, that he may not grow musty, and unfit for Conversation.

After this Abridgement of some Letters which are come to my Hands upon this occasion, I shall publish one of them at large.

Mr. SPECTATOR,

'YOU have given us a lively Picture of that kind of Husband who comes under the Denomination of the Henpeck'd; but I do not remember that you have ever touched upon one that is of the quite different Character, and who, in several Places of

---

[1] See No. 479.   [2] See No. 299 (vol. iii).

England, goes by the Name of a Cott-Quean.[1] I have the Misfortune to be joined for Life with one of this Character, who in reality is more a Woman than I am.[a] He was bred up under the Tuition of a Tender Mother, till she had made him as good an Housewife as her self. He could preserve Apricots, and make Gellies, before he had been two Years out of the Nursery. He was never suffered to go abroad, for fear of catching Cold; when he should have been hunting down a Buck, he was by his Mother's Side learning how to Season it, or put it in Crust; and was making Paper Boats with his Sisters, at an Age when other young Gentlemen are crossing the Seas, or travelling into Foreign Countries. He has the whitest Hand that you ever saw in your Life, and raises Paste better than any Woman in *England*. These Qualifications make him a sad Husband: He is perpetually in the Kitchin, and has a thousand Squabbles with the Cookmaid. He is better acquainted with the Milk Score, than his Steward's Accounts. I fret to Death when I hear him find fault with a Dish that is not dressed to his liking, and instructing his Friends that dine with him in the best Pickle for a Wallnut, or Sawce for an Haunch of Venison. With all this, he is a very good-natured Husband, and never fell out with me in his Life but once, upon the over-roasting of a Dish of Wild Fowl. At the same time I must own I would rather he was a Man of a rough Temper, that would treat me harshly sometimes, than of such an effeminate busie Nature in a Province that does not belong to him. Since you have given us the Character of a Wife who wears the Breeches, pray say something of a Husband that wears the Petticoat. Why should not a Female Character be as ridiculous in a Man, as a Male Character in one of our Sex?

I am, &c.'

O

---

[a] than I am.] than my self. *Fol.*

---

[1] A man that acts the housewife. The last quotation in *OED* is dated 1825.

Saturday, September 13, 1712[1]

> *Nec Deus intersit nisi dignus vindice nodus*
> *Inciderit . . .*
>
> Hor.

WE cannot be guilty of a greater Act of Uncharitableness, than to interpret the Afflictions which befall our Neighbours, as *Punishments* and *Judgments*. It aggravates the Evil to him who suffers, when he looks upon himself as the Mark of Divine Vengeance, and abates the Compassion of those towards him, who regard him in so dreadful a Light. This Humour, of turning every Misfortune into a Judgment, proceeds from wrong Notions of Religion, which, in its own Nature, produces Good-will towards Men, and puts the mildest Construction upon every Accident that befalls them. In this Case, therefore, it is not Religion that sowers a Man's Temper, but it is his Temper that sowers his Religion: People of gloomy unchearful Imaginations, or of envious malignant Tempers, whatever kind of Life they are engaged in, will discover their natural Tincture of Mind in all their Thoughts, Words, and Actions. As the finest Wines have often the Taste of the Soil, so even the most religious Thoughts often draw something, that is particular, from the Constitution of the Mind in which they arise. When Folly or Superstition strike in with this natural Depravity of Temper, it is not in the Power, even of Religion it self, to preserve the Character of the Person who is possessed with it, from appearing highly absurd and ridiculous.

An old Maiden Gentlewoman, whom I shall conceal under the Name of *Nemesis*, is the greatest Discoverer of Judgments that I have met with. She can tell you what Sin it was that set such a Man's House on Fire, or blew down his Barns. Talk to her of an unfortunate young Lady that lost her Beauty by the Small Pox, she fetches a deep Sigh, and tells you, that when she had a fine Face she was always looking on it in her Glass. Tell her of a Piece of good Fortune that has befallen one of her Acquaintance, and she wishes it may prosper with her; but her Mother used one of her Neices very

---

[1] *Motto.* Horace, *Ars poetica*, 191–2:
> Never presume to make a God appear,
> But for a Business worthy of a God. ROSCOMMON.

Addison had used this before as the motto of No. 315.

barbarously. Her usual Remarks turn upon People who had great Estates, but never enjoyed them, by reason of some Flaw in their own, or their Forefather's Behaviour. She can give you the Reason why such an one died Childless: Why such an one was cut off in the Flower of his Youth: Why such an one was Unhappy in her Marriage: Why one broke his Leg on such a particular Spot of Ground, and why another was killed with a Back-sword, rather than with any other kind of Weapon. She has a Crime for every Misfortune that can befall any of her Acquaintance, and when she hears of a Robbery that has been made, or a Murder that has been committed, enlarges more on the Guilt of the suffering Person, than on that of the Thief, or the Assassin. In short, she is so good a Christian, that whatever happens to her-self is a Tryal, and whatever happens to her Neighbours, is a Judgment.

The very Description of this Folly, in ordinary Life, is sufficient to expose it; but when it appears in a Pomp and Dignity of Stile, it is very apt to amuse[1] and terrify the Mind of the Reader. *Herodotus* and *Plutarch* very often apply their Judgments as impertinently as the old Woman I have before mentioned, though their manner of relating them makes the Folly it self appear venerable. Indeed, most Historians, as well Christian as Pagan, have fallen into this idle Superstition, and spoken of ill Successes, unforeseen Disasters, and terrible Events, as if they had been let into the Secrets of Providence, and made acquainted with that private Conduct by which the World is governed.[2] One would think several of our own Historians in particular, had many Revelations of this Kind made to them. Our old *English* Monks seldom let any of their Kings depart in Peace, who had endeavoured to diminish the Power or Wealth of which the Ecclesiasticks were in those times possessed. *William* the Conqueror's Race generally found their Judgments in the *New Forest*, where their Father had pulled down Churches and Monastries.[3] In short, read one of the Chronicles, written by an Author of this

---

[1] 'To cause to "muse" or stare; to confound, distract, bewilder, puzzle' (*OED*). The last quotation in *OED* in this sense is dated 1741.
[2] 'Successes' is here used in the archaic sense of good or bad fortune. Quotations in *OED* range from 1590 to 1764.
[3] Cf. Guy Miege, *Present State of Great Britain* (1707), pp. 10–11:

William the Conqueror was so taken with *New-Forest*, that to enlarge it, he caused several Towns and Villages, with 36 Parish Churches, to be demolished. Which Sacrilege was not left unpunished. For two of his Sons, namely *Richard* and *William*, besides *Robert* his Grandson, lost strangely their Lives in this very Forest.

Sir Richard Baker, in his *Chronicle*, also describes this as a 'pregnant example of Gods Judgment' (ed. 1684, p. 37).

Frame of Mind, and you would think you were reading an History of the Kings of *Israel* or *Judah*, where the Historians were actually inspired, and where, by a particular Scheme of Providence, the Kings were distinguished by Judgments or Blessings, according as they promoted Idolatry, or the Worship of the true God.

I cannot but look upon this manner of judging upon Misfortunes, not only to be very uncharitable, in regard to the Person whom they befall, but very presumptuous in regard to him who is supposed to inflict them. It is a strong Argument for a State of Retribution hereafter, that in this World vertuous Persons are very often unfortunate, and vicious Persons prosperous, which is wholly repugnant to the Nature of a Being, who appears infinitely wise and good in all his Works, unless we may suppose that such a promiscuous and undistinguishing Distribution of Good and Evil, which was necessary for carrying on the Designs of Providence in this Life, will be rectified and made amends for in another. We are not, therefore, to expect that Fire should fall from Heaven in the ordinary Course of Providence;[a] nor when we see triumphant Guilt, or depressed Virtue in particular Persons, that Omnipotence will make bare its Holy Arm in the Defence of the one, or Punishment of the other.[1] It is sufficient, that there is a Day set apart for the hearing and requiting of both, according to their respective Merits.

The Folly of ascribing Temporal Judgments to any particular Crimes, may appear from several Considerations. I shall only mention two: First, that, generally speaking, there is no Calamity or Affliction, which is supposed to have happened, as a Judgment, to a vicious Man, which does not sometimes happen to Men of approved Religion and Virtue. When *Diagoras*, the Atheist, was on board one of the *Athenian* Ships, there arose a very violent Tempest; upon which the Mariners told him, that it was a just Judgment upon them for having taken so impious a Man on Board. *Diagoras* begged them to look upon the rest of the Ships, that were in the same Distress, and asked them whether or no *Diagoras* was on board every Vessel in the Fleet.[2] We are all involved in the same Calamities, and subject to the same Accidents; and when we see any one of the Species under any particular Oppression, we should look upon it as

---

[a] Providence;] Providence *Fol.*

---

[1] Isa. lii. 10.
[2] Cicero, *De natura deorum*, 3. 37. 89. Bayle cites this (art. 'Diagoras', Remark I).

arising from the common Lot of Human Nature, rather than from the Guilt of the Person who suffers.

Another Consideration, that may check our Presumption in putting such a Construction upon a Misfortune is this, That it is impossible for us to know what are Calamities, and what are Blessings. How many Accidents have passed for Misfortunes, which have turned to the Welfare and Prosperity of the Persons in whose Lot they have fallen? How many Disappointments have, in their Consequences, saved a Man from Ruin? If we could look into the Effects of every thing, we might be allowed to pronounce boldly upon Blessings and Judgments; but for a Man to give his Opinion of what he sees but in part, and in its Beginnings, is an unjustifiable Piece of Rashness and Folly. The Story of *Biton* and *Cleobis,* which was in great Reputation among the Heathens, for we see it quoted by all the Ancient Authors, both *Greek* and *Latin,* who have written upon the Immortality of the Soul, may teach us a Caution in this Matter.[1] These two Brothers, being the Sons of a Lady who was Priestess to *Juno,* drew their Mother's Chariot to the Temple at the time of a great Solemnity, the Persons being absent who by their Office were to have drawn her Chariot on that Occasion. The Mother was so transported with this Instance of filial Duty, that she petitioned her Goddess to bestow upon them the greatest Gift that could be given to Men, upon which they were both cast into a deep Sleep, and the next Morning found dead in the Temple. This was such an Event, as would have been construed into a Judgment, had it happened to the two Brothers after an Act of Disobedience, and would doubtless have been represented as such by any Ancient Historian, who had given us an Account of it.

O

---

[1] Herodotus, *History,* 1. 31; Plutarch, *Life of Solon,* 27. 5, and 'A Letter to Apollonius' (*Moralia,* 108F).

Neque cuiquam tam statim clarum ingenium est, ut possit emergere; nisi illi materia, occasio, fautor etiam, commendatorque contingat.

Plin. Epist.

Mr. SPECTATOR,

'OF all the young Fellows who are in their Progress thro' any Profession, none seem to have so good a Title to the Protection of the Men of Eminence in it as the modest Man;[2] not so much because his Modesty is a certain Indication of his Merit, as because 'tis a certain Obstacle to the producing of it. Now, as of all Professions this Virtue is thought to be more particularly unnecessary in that of the Law than in any other, I shall only apply my self to the Relief of such who follow this Profession with this Disadvantage. What aggravates the Matter is, that those Persons, who, the better to prepare themselves for this Study, have made some Progress in others, have, by addicting themselves to Letters, encreased their natural Modesty, and consequently heighten'd the Obstruction to this Sort of Preferment; so that every one of these may emphatically be said to be such a one as *laboureth and taketh Pains, and is still the more behind.*[3] It may be a Matter worth discussing then, Why that which made a Youth so amiable to the Ancients, should make him appear so ridiculous to the Moderns? and, Why in our Days there should be Neglect, and even Oppression of young Beginners, instead of that Protection which was the Pride of theirs? In the Profession spoken of, 'tis obvious to every one whose Attendance is requir'd at *Westminster-Hall*, with what Difficulty a Youth of any Modesty has been permitted to make an Observation, that could in no wise detract from the Merit of his Elders, and is absolutely necessary for the advancing his own. I have often seen one of these not only molested in his Utterance of something very pertinent, but even plunder'd of his Question, and by a strong Serjeant shoulder'd out

---

[1] *Motto.* Pliny, *Epistles*, 6. 23 (altered): Nor has any one so clear a genius as to rise from obscurity immediately, unless scope, opportunity, and a patron assist him in it.

[2] In the character of Nestor (Sir Christopher Wren) in *Tatler* 52 Steele had earlier shown modesty as an obstacle to the producing of merit.

[3] Ecclesiasticus II. II.

of his Rank, which he has recovered with much Difficulty and Confusion. Now as great Part of the Business of this Profession might be dispatch'd by one that perhaps

> . . . *abest virtute diserti*
> *Messalæ, nec scit quantum Causellius Aulus.* Hor.[1]

so I can't conceive the Injustice done to the Publick, if the Men of Reputation in this Calling would introduce such of the young ones into Business, whose Application to this Study will let them into the Secrets of it, as much as their Modesty will hinder them from the Practice: I say, it would be laying an everlasting Obligation upon a young Man, to be introduc'd at first only as a Mute, till by this Countenance, and a Resolution to support your good Opinion conceiv'd of him in his Betters, his Complection shall be so well settled, that the Litigious of this Island may be secure of his obstreperous Aid. If I might be indulged to speak in the Stile of a Lawyer, I would say, That any one about thirty Years of Age, might make a common Motion to the Court with as much Elegance and Propriety as the most aged Advocates in the Hall.

'I can't advance the Merit of Modesty by any Argument of my own so powerfully, as by enquiring into the Sentiments the greatest among the Ancients of different Ages entertain'd upon this Virtue. If we go back to the Days of *Solomon*, we shall find Favour a necessary Consequence to a shame-fac'd Man. *Pliny*, the greatest Lawyer and most elegant Writer of the Age he liv'd in, in several of his Epistles is very sollicitous in recommending to the Publick some young Men of his own Profession; and very often undertakes to become an Advocate, upon Condition that some one of these his Favourites might be joyn'd with him, in order to produce the Merit of such, whose Modesty otherwise would have suppress'd it. It may seem very marvelous to a sawcy Modern, that *Multum sanguinis, multum verecundiæ, multum sollicitudinis in ore; To have the Face first full of Blood, then the Countenance dashed with Modesty, and then the whole Aspect as of one dying with Fear, when a Man begins to speak;*[2] should be esteem'd by *Pliny* the necessary Qualifications of a fine Speaker. *Shakespear* also has

---

[1] Horace, *Ars poetica*, 370–1 ('Cascellius').

> May want *Messala*'s pow'rful Eloquence,
> Or be less read than deep *Cascellius*. ROSCOMMON.

[2] Pliny, *Epistles*, 5. 17.

express'd himself in the same favourable Strains of Modesty when he says,

> ... *In the Modesty of fearful Duty*
> *I read as much as from the ratling Tongue*
> *Of sawcy and audacious Eloquence* . . .[1]

'Now since these Authors have profess'd themselves for the modest Man, even in the utmost Confusions of Speech and Countenance, why should an intrepid Utterance and a resolute Vociferation thunder so successfully in our Courts of Justice? and why shou'd that Confidence of Speech and Behaviour, which seems to acknowledge no Superior, and to defy all Contradiction, prevail over that Deference and Resignation with which the modest Man implores that favourable Opinion which the other seems to command.

'As the Case at present stands, the best Consolation that I can administer to those who cannot get into that Stroke of Business[2] (as the Phrase is) which they deserve, is to reckon every particular Acquisition of Knowledge in this Study as a real Increase of their Fortune; and fully to believe, that one Day this imaginary Gain, will certainly be made out by one more substantial. I wish you would talk to us a little on this Head, you would oblige,

SIR,
Your most humble Servant.'

The Author of this Letter is certainly a Man of good Sense; but I am perhaps particular in my Opinion on this Occasion; for I have observed, that, under the Notion of Modesty, Men have indulged themselves in a spiritless Sheepishness, and been for ever lost to themselves, their Families, their Friends, and their Country. When a Man has taken Care to pretend to nothing but what he may justly aim at, and can execute as well as any other, without Injustice to any other; it is ever want of Breeding or Courage, to be browbeaten or elbow'd out of his honest Ambition. I have said often, Modesty must be an Act of the Will, and yet it always implies Self-Denial:[3] For if a Man has an ardent Desire to do what is laudable in him to perform, and, from an unmanly Bashfulness, shrinks away, and lets his Merit languish in Silence, he ought not to be angry at

---

[1] *A Midsummer-Night's Dream*, v. i. 101–3.
[2] This is the earliest example in *OED* of *stroke*, in the sense of 'a large or considerable amount of work, business, trade'.
[3] In *Tatler* 52 Steele had discussed modesty as 'a voluntary Quality, and the Effect of good Sense', and in *Tatler* 217 the difference between true and false modesty.

the World that a more unskilful Actor succeeds in his Part, because he has not Confidence to come upon the Stage himself. The Generosity my Correspondent mentions of *Pliny,* cannot be enough applauded. To cherish the Dawn of Merit, and hasten its Maturity, was a Work worthy a Noble *Roman* and a liberal Scholar. That Concern which is described in the Letter, is to all the World the greatest Charm imaginable; but then the modest Man must proceed, and shew a latent Resolution in himself; for the Admiration of his Modesty, arises from the Manifestation of his Merit. I must confess, we live in an Age wherein a few empty Blusterers carry away the Praise of Speaking, while a Crowd of Fellows over-stock'd with Knowledge are run down by them. I say Over-stock'd, because they certainly are so as to their Service of Mankind, if from their very Store they raise to themselves Ideas of Respect, and Greatness of the Occasion, and I know not what, to disable themselves from explaining their Thoughts. I must confess, when I have seen *Charles Frankair* rise up with a commanding Mein, and Torrent of handsome Words, talk a Mile off the Purpose, and drive down twenty bashful Boobies of ten times his Sense, who at the same Time were envying his Impudence and despising his Understanding, it has been Matter of great Mirth to me; but it soon ended in a secret Lamentation, that the Fountains of every thing Praise-worthy in these Realms, the Universities, should be so muddied with a false Sense of this Virtue, as to produce Men capable of being so abused. I will be bold to say, that it is a ridiculous Education which does not qualify a Man to make his best Appearance before the greatest Man and the finest Woman to whom he can address himself. Were this judiciously corrected in the Nurseries of Learning, pert Coxcombs would know their Distance: But we must bear with this false Modesty in our young Nobility and Gentry, till they cease at *Oxford* and *Cambridge* to grow dumb in the Study of Eloquence.

T

Nihil tam firmum est, cui periculum non sit, etiam ab Invalido.

Quint. Curt.

Mr. SPECTATOR,

'MY Lord *Clarendon* has observ'd, *that few Men have done more Harm than those who have been thought to be able to do least; and there cannot be a greater Error, than to believe a Man whom we see qualified with too mean Parts to do Good, to be therefore incapable of doing Hurt. There is a Supply of Malice, of Pride, of Industry, and even of Folly, in the Weakest, when he sets his Heart upon it, that makes a strange Progress in Mischief.*[2] What may seem to the Reader the greatest Paradox in the Reflection of the Historian, is, I suppose, that Folly which is generally thought incapable of contriving or executing any Design, should be so formidable to those whom it exerts it self to molest. But this will appear very plain, if we remember that *Solomon* says, *It is as Sport to a Fool to do Mischief;*[3] and that he might the more emphatically express the calamitous Circumstances of him that falls under the Displeasure of this wanton Person, the same Author adds further, that *A Stone is heavy, and the Sand weighty, but a Fool's Wrath is heavier than them both.*[4] It is impossible to suppress my own Illustration upon this Matter, which is, That as the Man of Sagacity bestirs himself to distress his Enemy by Methods probable and reducible to Reason, so the same Reason will fortify his Enemy to elude these his regular Efforts; but your Fool projects, acts, and concludes with such notable Inconsistence, that no regular Course of Thought can evade or counterplot his prodigious Machinations. My Frontispiece, I believe, may be extended to imply, that several of our Misfortunes arise from Things, as well as Persons, that seem of very little Consequence. Into what tragical Extravagancies does *Shakespear* hurry *Othello* upon the Loss of an Handkerchief only? and what Barbarities does *Desdemona* suffer from a slight Inadvertency in regard to this fatal Trifle? If the Schemes of all the enterprizing Spirits were to be carefully examined, some intervening Accident, not considerable enough to occasion any Debate upon, or give 'em any Apprehension

---

[1] *Motto.* Quintus Curtius, *History of Alexander*, 7. 8. 15: Nothing is so secure as to be free from danger, even from what is weaker.

[2] Clarendon, *History of the Rebellion* (Oxford, 1843), book iii, p. 79.

[3] Prov. x. 23.   [4] Prov. xxvii. 3.

of ill Consequence from it, will be found to be the Occasion of their ill Success, rather than any Error in Points of Moment and Difficulty, which naturally engaged their maturest Deliberations. If you go to the Levee of any great Man, you will observe him exceeding gracious to several very insignificant Fellows; and this upon this Maxim, That the Neglect of any Person must arise from the mean Opinion you have of his Capacity to do you any Service or Prejudice; and that this calling his Sufficiency in Question must give him Inclination, and where this is, there never wants Strength or Opportunity to annoy you. There is no Body so weak of Invention, that can't aggravate or make some little Stories to vilify his Enemy; and there are very few but have good Inclinations to hear 'em, as 'tis infinite Pleasure to the Majority of Mankind to level a Person superior to his Neighbours. Besides, in all Matters of Controversy, that Party which has the greatest Abilities labours under this Prejudice, that he will certainly be supposed, upon Account of his Abilities, to have done an Injury, when perhaps he has received one. It would be tedious to enumerate the Strokes that Nations and particular Men have suffer'd from Persons very contemptible.

'I think *Henry* IV. of *France*, so formidable to his Neighbours, could no more be secur'd against the resolute Villany of *Ravillac*,[1] than *Villiers*, Duke of *Buckingham*, could be against that of *Felton*.[2] And there is no incens'd Person so destitute, but can provide himself with a Knife or a Pistol, if he finds Stomach to apply 'em. That Things and Persons of no Moment should give such powerful Revolutions to the Progress of those of the greatest, seems a providential Disposition to baffle and abate the Pride of humane Sufficiency; as also, to engage the Humanity and Benevolence of Superiors to all below 'em, by letting them into this Secret, That the Stronger depends upon the Weaker.

I am,

SIR,

Your very Humble Servant.'

Dear Sir,   *Temple, Paper-Buildings.*[3]

'I RECEIVED a Letter from you some Time ago, which I should have answered sooner, had you inform'd me in yours to what

[1] François Ravaillac was a Roman Catholic fanatic who assassinated Henri IV of France in 1610.
[2] John Felton, an army officer, assassinated the Duke of Buckingham (23 Aug. 1628), because the latter had refused to give him command of a company.
[3] The Paper Buildings were erected in 1607 and rebuilt after the Fire, described

Part of this our Island I might have directed my Impertinence; but having been let into the Knowledge of that Matter, this handsome Excuse is no longer serviceable. My Neighbour *Prettyman* shall be the Subject of this Letter; who falling in with the SPECTATOR's Doctrine concerning the Month of *May*, began from that Season to dedicate himself to the Service of the Fair in the following Manner.[1] I observed at the Beginning of the Month he bought him a new Night-gown, either Side to be worn outwards, both equally gorgeous and attractive; but till the End of the Month I did not enter so fully into the Knowledge of his Contrivance, as the Use of that Garment has since suggested to me. Now you must know that all new Cloaths raise and warm the Bearer's Imagination into a Conceit of his being a much finer Gentleman than he was before, banishing all Sobriety and Reflection, and giving him up to Gallantry and Amour. Inflam'd therefore with this way of thinking, and full of the Spirit of the Month of *May*, did this merciless Youth resolve upon the Business of Captivating. At first he confin'd himself to his Room only, now and then appearing at his Window in his Night-gown, and practising that easy Posture which expresses the very Top and Dignity of Languishment. It was pleasant to see him diversify his Loveliness, sometimes obliging the Passengers only with a Side-Face, with a Book in his Hand; sometimes being so generous as to expose the Whole in the Fullness of its Beauty; at other Times, by a judicious throwing back his Perriwig, he would throw in his Ears. You know he is that Sort of Person which the Mob call a handsome jolly Man;[2] which Appearance can't miss of Captives in this Part of the Town. Being emboldened by daily Success, he leaves his Room with a Resolution to extend his Conquests; and I have apprehended him in his Night-gown smiting in all Parts of this Neighbourhood.

'This I, being of an amorous Complection, saw with Indignation, and had Thoughts of purchasing a Wig in these Parts; into which, being at a greater Distance from the Earth, I might have thrown a very liberal Mixture of white Horse-hair, which would make a fairer, and consequently a handsomer Appearance, while my

---

by Hatton (p. 693) as 'a noble Pile of spacious pleasant Chambers, at the North end whereof are finely painted, appearing like so many Statues, the Figures of the 4 Cardinal Virtues . . .'.

[1] See Nos. 365, 395 (vol. iii).

[2] Here used in the colloquial sense of 'healthy and well-developed; of large make and fine appearance' (*OED*).

Situation would secure me against any Discoveries. But the Passion to the handsome Gentleman, seems to be so well fixed to that Part of the Building, that it will be extremely difficult to divert it to mine; so that I'm resolved to stand boldly to the Complection of my own Eye-brow, and prepare me an immense Black-Wig of the same sort of Structure with that of my Rival. Now, tho' by this I shall not, perhaps, lessen the Number of the Admirers of his Complection, I shall have a fair Chance to divide the Passengers by the irresistable Force of mine.

'I expect sudden Dispatches from you, with Advice of the Family you are in now, how to deport my self upon this so delicate a Conjuncture; with some comfortable Resolutions in Favour of the handsome black Man against the handsome fair one.

I am,

SIR,

Your most humble Servant,

C

'N. B. *He who writ this is a black Man two Pair of Stairs; the Gentleman of whom he writes is fair, and one Pair of Stairs.*'

Mr. SPECTATOR,

'I ONLY say, that it is impossible for me to say how much I am

Yours,

Robin Shorter.

'P. S. I shall think it a little hard, if you do not take as much Notice of this Epistle as you have of the ingenious Mr. *Short*'s.[1] I am not afraid to let the World see which is the deeper Man of the two.'

ADVERTISEMENT.

London, September 15.

Whereas a young Woman on Horseback, in an Equestrian Habit, on the 13th Instant in the Evening, met the SPECTATOR *within a Mile and an Half of this Town, and flying in the Face of Justice, pulled off her Hat, in which there was a Feather, with the Mein and Air of a young Officer, saying at the same Time your Servant Mr.* SPEC. *or Words to that Purpose; This is to give Notice, that if any Person can discover the Name,*

---

[1] See No. 473.

and Place, and Abode of the said Offender, so as she can be brought to Justice, the Informant shall have all fitting Encouragement.[1]

T

No. 486   Wednesday, September 17, 1712[2]
[STEELE]

> Audire est operæ pretium procedere recte
> Qui mæchos non vultis . . .
>
>   Hor.

Mr. SPECTATOR,

'THERE are very many of my Acquaintance Followers of *Socrates*, with more particular Regard to that Part of his Philosophy which we, among our selves, call his *Domesticks*, under which Denomination, or Title, we include all the Conjugal Joys and Sufferings. We have indeed, with very great Pleasure, observed the Honour you do the whole Fraternity of the Hen-peck'd, in placing that illustrious Man at our Head;[3] and it does in a very great measure baffle the Raillery of pert Rogues, who have no Advantage above us, but in that they are single. But when you look about into the Crowd of Mankind, you will find the Fair Sex reign with greater Tyranny over Lovers than Husbands. You shall hardly meet one in a thousand who is wholly exempt from their Dominion, and those that are so are capable of no Taste of Life, and breathe and walk about the Earth as Insignificants.[4] But I am going to desire your further Favour in Behalf of our harmless Brotherhood, and hope you will shew in a true Light the unmarried Hen-peck'd as well as you have done Justice to us, who submit to the Conduct of our Wives. I am very particularly acquainted with one who is under entire Submission to a kind Girl, as he calls her; and tho' he

---

[1] Advertisement. Whereas a young woman . . . Cf. No. 435.
[2] *Motto.* Horace, *Satires*, I. 2. 37–38:

> Now you that wish these base *Adulterers* ill,
> And Punishment as bad as is their Will;
> Must needs be pleas'd. . . .   CREECH.

Steele had used this before as motto for No. 274 (vol. ii).
[3] See Nos. 479, 482.
[4] 'An unimportant or contemptible person' (*OED*). The first quotation in *OED* is from *Tatler* 247; the latest is dated 1816.

knows I have been Witness both to the ill Usage he has received from her, and his Inability to resist her Tyranny, he still pretends to make a Jest of me for a little more than ordinary Obsequiousness to my Spouse. No longer than *Tuesday* last he took me with him to visit his Mistress; and he having, it seems, been a little in Disgrace before, thought by bringing me with him she would constrain her self, and insensibly fall into general Discourse with him; and so he might break the Ice, and save himself all the ordinary Compunctions and Mortifications she used to make him suffer before she would be reconciled after any Act of Rebellion on his Part. When we came into the Room, we were received with the utmost Coldness; and when he presented me as Mr. Such-a-one, his very good Friend, she just had Patience to suffer my Salutation; but when he himself, with a very gay Air, offered to follow me, she gave him a thundering Box on the Ear, called him pitiful poor-spirited Wretch, how durst he see her Face? His Wig and Hat fell on different Parts of the Floor. She seized the Wig too soon for him to recover it, and kicking it down Stairs, threw her self into an opposite Room, pulling the Door after her with a Force, that you would have thought the Hinges would have given Way. We went down, you must think, with no very good Countenances; and as we sneaked off, and were driving home together, he confessed to me that her Anger was thus highly raised, because he did not think fit to fight a Gentleman who had said she was what she was; but, says he, a kind Letter or two, or fifty Pieces, will put her in Humour again. I asked him why he did not part with her; he answered, he loved her with all the Tenderness imaginable, and she had too many Charms to be abandoned for a little Quickness of Spirit. Thus does this illegitimate Hen-peck'd overlook the Hussy's having no Regard to his very Life and Fame, in putting him upon an infamous Dispute about her Reputation; yet has he the Confidence to laugh at me, because I obey my poor Dear in keeping out of Harm's Way, and not staying too late from my own Family, to pass through the Hazards of a Town full of Ranters[1] and Debauchees. You that are a Philosopher should urge in our Behalf, that when we bear with a froward Woman, our Patience is preserved, in Consideration that a Breach with her might be a Dishonour to Children who are descended from us, and whose Concern makes us tolerate a thousand Frailties, for Fear they should

---

[1] I.e. rakes. *OED* gives quotations from 1654 to 1828.

redound[1] Dishonour upon the Innocent. This and the like Circum-stances, which carry with them the most valuable Regards of humane Life, may be mentioned for our long Suffering; but in the Case of Gallants, they swallow ill Usage from one to whom they have no Obligation, but from a base Passion which it is mean to indulge, and which it would be glorious to overcome.

'These Sort of Fellows are very numerous, and some have been conspicuously such without Shame; nay, they have carried on the Jest in the very Article of Death, and, to the Diminution of the Wealth and Happiness of their Families, in Bar of those honourably near to them, have left immense Wealth to their Paramours. What is this but being a Cully in the Grave! Sure this is being Hen-peck'd with a Vengeance! But without dwelling upon these less frequent Instances of eminent Cullyism,[2] what is there so common as to hear a Fellow curse his Fate that he cannot get rid of a Passion to a Jilt, and quote an Half-Line out of a Miscellany Poem to prove his Weakness is natural. If they will go on thus, I have nothing to say to it; but then let them not pretend to be free all this while, and laugh at us poor married Patients.

'I have known one Wench in this Town carry an haughty Dominion over her Lovers so well, that she has at the same time been kept by a Sea-Captain in the *Streights*,[3] a Merchant in the City, a Country Gentleman in *Hampshire*, and had all her Correspondences managed by one she kept for her own Uses. This happy Man (as the Phrase is) used to write very punctually every Post Letters for the Mistress to transcribe. He would sit in his Night-Gown and Slippers, and be as grave giving an Account, only changing Names, that there was nothing in these idle Reports they had heard of such a Scoundrel as one of the other Lovers was; and how could he think she could condescend so low, after such a fine Gentleman as each of them? For the same Epistle said the same thing to and of every one of them. And so Mr. Secretary and his Lady went to Bed with great Order.

'To be short, Mr. SPECTATOR, we Husbands shall never make the Figure we ought in the Imaginations of young Men growing up in the World, except you can bring it about that a Man of the Town shall be as infamous a Character as a Woman of the Town.

---

[1] Here used in the obsolete sense of 'reflect (honour, blame, etc.) upon a person'. This is the last quotation in *OED* in this sense.
[2] The only example in *OED* of this nonce-word.
[3] I.e. the Bermudas.

But of all that I have met in my Time, commend me to[1] *Betty Duall*: She is the Wife of a Sailor, and the kept Mistress of a Man of Quality; she dwells with the latter during the Sea-faring of the former. The Husband asks no Questions, sees his Apartments furnished with Riches not his, when he comes into Port, and the Lover is as joyful as a Man arrived at his Haven when the other puts to Sea. *Betty* is the most eminently victorious of any of her Sex, and ought to stand recorded the only Woman of the Age in which she lives, who has possess'd at the same Time two Abused and two Contented. . . .'   T

No. 487   *Thursday, September 18, 1712*[2]
[ADDISON]

. . . cùm prostrata sopore
Urget membra quies, & mens sine pondere ludit.
                                                          Petr.

THO' there are many Authors, who have written on Dreams, they have generally considered them only as Revelations of what has already happened in distant Parts of the World, or as Presages of what is to happen in future Periods of Time.[3]

I shall consider this Subject in another Light, as Dreams may give us some Idea of the great Excellency of an Human Soul, and some Intimations of its Independency on Matter.

In the first Place, our Dreams are great Instances of that Activity which is Natural to the Humane Soul, and which it is not in the Power of Sleep to deaden or abate. When the Man appears tired and worn out with the Labours of the Day, this active Part in his Composition is still busie and unwearied. When the Organs of Sense want their due Repose and necessary Reparations, and the Body is no longer able to keep pace with that spiritual Substance to which it is united, the Soul exerts her self in her several Faculties, and

---

[1] 'A colloquial expression, serious or ironical, of choice or preference' (*OED*). This is the earliest example quoted.

[2] *Motto.* Petronius Arbiter, from a poem found in one MS. of the *Satyricon*:
    While sleep oppresses the tir'd limbs, the mind
    Plays without weight, and wantons unconfin'd.
See Petronius, Poems, 31. 3–4, in *Poetae Latini Minores*, ed. E. Baehrens, vol. iv (Leipzig, 1882), p. 110.

[3] Cf. Bayle, art. 'Junianus Majus', Remark D ('A Reflection on Dreams').

continues in Action 'till her Partner is again qualified to bear her Company. In this case Dreams look like the Relaxations and Amusements of the Soul, when she is disencumbered of her Machine, her Sports and Recreations, when she has laid her Charge asleep.

In the Second Place, Dreams are an Instance of that Agility and Perfection which is natural to the Faculties of the Mind, when they are disengaged from the Body. The Soul is clogged and retarded in her Operations, when she acts in Conjunction with a Companion that is so heavy and unwieldy in its Motions. But in Dreams it is wonderful, to observe with what a Sprightliness and Alacrity she exerts her self. The slow of Speech make unpremeditated Harangues, or converse readily in Languages that they are but little acquainted with. The Grave abound in Pleasantries, the Dull in Repartees, and Points of Wit. There is not a more painful Action of the Mind, than Invention; yet in Dreams it works with that Ease and Activity, that we are not sensible when the Faculty is employed. For Instance, I believe every one, some time or other, Dreams that he is reading Papers, Books or Letters, in which Case the Invention prompts so readily, that the Mind is imposed upon, and mistakes its own Suggestions for the Compositions of another.

I shall, under this Head, quote a Passage out of the *Religio Medici*, in which the ingenious Author gives an Account of himself in his dreaming, and his waking Thoughts. *We are somewhat more than our selves in our Sleeps, and the Slumber of the Body seems to be but the waking of the Soul. It is the Ligation[1] of Sense, but the Liberty of Reason, and our waking Conceptions do not match the Fancies of our Sleeps. At my Nativity my Ascendant was the watery Sign of Scorpius: I was born in the Planetary Hour of Saturn, and, I think, I have a Piece of that Leaden Planet in me. I am no way facetious, nor disposed for the Mirth and Galliardize[2] of Company; yet in one Dream I can compose a whole Comedy, behold the Action, apprehend the Jests, and laugh my self awake at the Conceits thereof. Were my Memory as faithful as my Reason is then fruitful, I would never Study but in my Dreams; and this time also would I chuse for my Devotions; but our grosser Memories have then so little hold of our abstracted Understandings, that they forget the Story, and can only relate to our awaked Souls, a confused and broken Tale of that that has passed. . . . Thus it is*

---

[1] I.e. binding fast, suspension (of faculties). The latest quotation in OED is dated 1684.

[2] 'Gaiety, mirth, revelry. *arch.*' (OED).

*observed that Men sometimes, upon the Hour of their Departure, do speak
and reason above themselves, for then the Soul beginning to be freed from the
Ligaments of the Body, begins to reason like her self, and to discourse in a
Strain above Mortality.*[1]

We may likewise observe in the third Place, that the Passions
affect the Mind with greater Strength when we are a-sleep, than
when we are awake. Joy and Sorrow give us more vigorous Sensations of Pain or Pleasure at this time, than at any other. Devotion
likewise, as the excellent Author above-mentioned has hinted, is
in a very particular manner heightned and inflamed, when it rises
in the Soul at a time that the Body is thus laid at Rest. Every Man's
Experience will inform him in this matter, though it is very probable, that this may happen differently in different Constitutions.
I shall conclude this Head with the two following Problems, which
I shall leave to the Solution of my Reader. Supposing a Man always
happy in his Dreams, and miserable in his waking Thoughts, and
that his Life was equally divided between them, whether would
he be more happy or miserable? Were a Man a King in his Dreams,
and a Beggar awake, and dreamt as consequentially, and in as
continued unbroken Schemes as he thinks when awake, whether
he would be in reality a King or a Beggar, or rather whether he
wou'd not be both?

There is another Circumstance which methinks gives us a very
high Idea of the Nature of the Soul, in regard to what passes in
Dreams, I mean that innumerable multitude and variety of Ideas
which then arise in her. Were that active watchful Being only
conscious of her own Existence at such a time, what a painful
Solitude would her Hours of Sleep be? Were the Soul sensible of
her being alone in her sleeping Moments, after the same manner
that she is sensible of it while awake, the time would hang very
heavy on her, as it often actually does when she Dreams that she
is in such a Solitude;

> . . . *Semperque relinqui*
> *Sola sibi, semper longam incomitata videtur*
> *Ire viam . . .*[2]   Virg.

[1] *Religio Medici*, part ii, paragraph 12 (Everyman's Library ed., pp. 84–85).
[2] *Aeneid*, 4. 466–8:

> She seems alone,
> To wander in her Sleep, thro ways unknown,
> Guideless and dark. . . .   DRYDEN.

Addison had used these lines as the motto for No. 241 (vol. ii).

But this Observation I only make by the way. What I would here remark is that wonderful Power in the Soul, of producing her own Company on these Occasions. She converses with numberless Beings of her own Creation, and is transported into ten thousand Scenes of her own raising. She is herself the Theatre, the Actors, and the Beholder. This puts me in mind of a Saying which I am infinitely pleased with, and which *Plutarch* ascribes to *Heraclitus*, *That all Men whilst they are awake are in one common World; but that each of them, when he is asleep, is in a World of his own.*[1] The waking Man is conversant in the World of Nature, when he sleeps he retires to a private World that is particular to himself. There seems something in this Consideration that intimates to us a Natural Grandeur and Perfection in the Soul, which is rather to be admired than explained.

I must not omit that Argument for the Excellency of the Soul, which I have seen quoted out of *Tertullian*, namely, its Power of Divining in Dreams.[2] That several such Divinations have been made, none can question who believes the Holy Writings, or who has but the least degree of a common Historical Faith, there being innumerable Instances of this Nature in several Authors, both Ancient and Modern, Sacred and Prophane. Whether such dark Presages, such Visions of the Night proceed from any latent Power in the Soul, during this her State of Abstraction, or from any Communication with the Supreme Being, or from any Operation of Subordinate Spirits, has been a great Dispute among the Learned; the matter of Fact is I think incontestable, and has been looked upon as such by the greatest Writers, who have been never suspected either of Superstition or Enthusiasm.

I do not suppose, that the Soul in these Instances is entirely loose and unfettered from the Body: It is sufficient, if she is not so far sunk, and immersed in Matter, nor intangled and perplexed in her Operations, with such Motions of Blood and Spirits, as when she actuates the Machine in its waking Hours. The Corporeal Union is slackned enough to give the Mind more play. The Soul seems gathered within her self, and recovers that Spring which is broke and weakned, when she operates more in concert with the Body.

The Speculations I have here made, if they are not Arguments, they are at least strong Intimations, not only of the Excellency of

---

[1] Plutarch, 'On superstition' (*Moralia*, 166C).
[2] Tertullian, *De anima*, 46. See Bayle, art. 'Achillea', Remark C.

an Humane Soul, but of its Independance on the Body; and if they do not prove, do at least confirm these two great Points, which are established by many other Reasons that are altogether unanswerable.   O[1]

No. 488   *Friday, September 19, 1712*[2]
[ADDISON]

Quanti emptæ? parvo. Quanti ergo? octo assibus. Eheu!
Hor.

I FIND, by several Letters which I receive daily, that many of my Readers would be better pleased to pay Three Half-Pence for my Paper, than Two-Pence.[3] The ingenious *T. W.*[4] tells me, that I have deprived him of the best Part of his Breakfast, for that, since the Rise of my Paper, he is forced every Morning to drink his Dish of Coffee by it self, without the Addition of the *Spectator*, that used to be better than Lace[5] to it. *Eugenius* informs me very obligingly, that he never thought he should have disliked any Passage in my Paper, but that of late there have been two Words in every one of them, which he could heartily wish left out, *viz. Price Two-Pence.* I have a Letter from a Soap-boyler, who condoles with me very affectionately, upon the necessity we both lie under of setting an higher Price on our Commodities, since the late Tax has been laid upon them, and desiring me, when I write next on that Subject, to speak a Word or two upon the present Duties on Castle-Soap.[6] But there is none of these my Correspondents, who

---

[1] A letter signed S. T. and dated 11 Oct. 1712 (Lillie, ii. 343–6) praises this paper and speculates further as to why fancy, memory, and the passions remain active in sleep.

[2] *Motto.* Horace, *Satires*, 2. 3. 156:

What doth it cost? Not much upon my word.
How much pray? Why Two Groats: *Two Groats! Oh Lord!* CREECH.

[3] See No. 445.

[4] 'Dr. Thomas Walker, head master of the Charterhouse-School, whose scholars Addison and Steele had been.' The Doctor was head-master 49 years, and died June 12, 1728, in the 81st year of his age' (Nichols).

[5] Here brandy or rum, in 'laced coffee'. Cf. No. 317 (vol. iii).

[6] Owing to the heavy expenses of the war, the government was deeply in debt and the Commons had imposed increased charges on many articles, such as candles, beer, coal, and soap. Rival claims for making the best 'English Barrell'd White Soap' appear in No. 443 (Thomas Vincent, at the Three Doves in Marrowbone-street, at the Upper-End of St. James's Hay-Market) and No. 547 (William Cowpland, Soapmaker, at the 3 Pidgeons and Crown in the Old Bailey, near Ludgate).

writes with a greater turn of good Sense and Elegance of Expression, than the generous *Philomedes*, who advises me to value every *Spectator* at Six Pence, and promises that he himself will engage for above an Hundred of his Acquaintance, who shall take it in at that Price.[1]

Letters from the Female World are likewise come to me, in great Quantities, upon the same Occasion, and as I naturally bear a great Deference to this Part of our Species, I am very glad to find that those, who approve my Conduct in this Particular, are much more numerous than those who condemn it. A large Family of Daughters have drawn me up a very handsome Remonstrance, in which they set forth, that their Father having refused to take in the *Spectator*, since the additional Price was set upon it, they offered him unanimously to 'bate him the Article of Bread and Butter in the Tea Table Account, provided the *Spectator* might be served up to them every Morning as usual. Upon this the old Gentleman, being pleased, it seems, with their Desire of improving themselves, has granted them the Continuance both of the *Spectator* and their Bread and Butter; having given particular Orders, that the Tea Table shall be set forth every Morning with its Customary Bill of Fare, and without any manner of Defalcation. I thought my self obliged to mention this Particular, as it does Honour to this worthy Gentleman; and if the young Lady *Lætitia*, who sent me this Account, will acquaint me with his Name, I will insert it at length in one of my Papers, if he desires it.

I should be very glad to find out any Expedient that might alleviate the Expence which this my Paper brings to any of my Readers, and, in order to it, must propose two Points to their Consideration. First, that if they retrench any the smallest Particular in their ordinary Expence, it will easily make up the Half Penny a Day, which we have now under Consideration. Let a Lady sacrifice but a single Ribband to her Morning Studies, and it will be sufficient: Let a Family burn but a Candle a Night less than the usual Number, and they may take in the *Spectator* without Detriment to their private Affairs.

In the next Place, if my Readers will not go to the Price of buying my Papers by Retail, let them have Patience, and they may buy them in the Lump, without the Burthen of a Tax upon them. My Speculations, when they are sold single, like Cherries upon the

[1] Philomedes, i.e. laughter-loving. Cf. No. 341 (vol. iii).

Stick, are Delights for the Rich and Wealthy; after some time they come to Market in greater Quantities, and are every ordinary Man's Mony. The truth of it is, they have a certain Flavour at their first appearance, from several Accidental Circumstances of Time, Place and Person, which they may lose if they are not taken early; but in this case every Reader is to consider, whether it is not better for him to be half a Year behind hand with the fashionable and polite part of the World, than to strain himself beyond his Circumstances. My Bookseller has now about Ten Thousand of the Third and Fourth Volumes,[1] which he is ready to publish, having already disposed of as large an Edition both of the First and Second Volume. As he is a Person whose Head is very well turned to his Business, he thinks they would be a very proper Present to be made to Persons at Christenings, Marriages, Visiting Days, and the like joyful Solemnities, as several other Books are frequently given at Funerals.[2] He has printed them in such a little portable Volume, that many of them may be rang'd together upon a single Plate, and is of Opinion, that a Salver of *Spectators* would be as acceptable an Entertainment to the Ladies, as a Salver of Sweetmeats.

I shall conclude this Paper with an Epigram lately sent to the Writer of the *Spectator*, after having returned my Thanks to the ingenious Author of it.

SIR,

'HAVING heard the following Epigram very much commended, I wonder that it has not yet had a place in any of your Papers; I think the Suffrage of our Poet Laureat should not be overlooked, which shows the Opinion he entertains of your Paper, whether the Notion he proceeds upon be true or false. I make bold to convey it to you, not knowing if it has yet come to your Hands.'

On the SPECTATOR.

By Mr. *TATE.*[3]

. . . aliusque & idem

Nasceris . . .[4]   *Hor.*

WHEN first the Tatler *to a Mute was turn'd,*

Great Britain *for her Censor's Silence mourn'd.*

---

[1] These volumes were published in November 1712.
[2] For 'visiting days' see No. 24 (vol. i).

[*For notes 3 and 4 see opposite page.*

Robb'd of his sprightly Beams she wept the Night,
Till the Spectator *rose, and blaz'd as bright.*
So the first Man the Sun's first setting view'd,
And sigh'd, till circling Day his Joys renew'd;
Yet doubtful how that Second Sun to name,
Whether a bright Successor, or the same.
So we: but now from this Suspence are freed, ⎫
Since all agree, who both with Judgment read, ⎬
'Tis the same Sun, and does himself succeed. ⎭

O

No. 489   *Saturday, September 20, 1712*[1]

[ADDISON]

. . . Βαθυῤῥείταο μέγα σθένος 'Ωκεανοῖο.
Hom.

SIR,

'UPON Reading your *Essay*, concerning the Pleasures of the Imagination,[2] I find, among the three Sources of those Pleasures which you have discovered, that[a] *Greatness* is one. This has suggested to me the Reason why, of all Objects that I have ever seen, there is none which affects my Imagination so much as the Sea or Ocean. I cannot see the Heavings of this prodigious Bulk of Waters, even in a Calm, without a very pleasing Astonishment; but when it is worked up in a Tempest, so that the Horison on every side is nothing but foaming Billows and floating Mountains, it is impossible to describe the agreeable Horrour that rises from such

---

[a] discovered, that] discovered, *Fol.*

[1] *Motto.* Homer, *Iliad*, 21. 195:
    The mighty force of the deep-flowing sea.
[2] Nos. 411–21 (vol. iii).

[3] Nahum Tate was at this time the Poet Laureate, having been appointed in 1692. He died on 30 July 1715, and was succeeded by Nicholas Rowe. The poem was printed a month later in Curll's *Tunbridge Miscellany* (published 21 Oct.), as 'An Epigram on the Spectator', without Tate's name and without the motto from Horace. The only textual change is in line 10, which reads 'Since all must own, who Both with Judgment read'.
[4] Horace, *Carmen Saeculare*, 10–11. (You rise afresh, another, and yet the same.)

a Prospect. A troubled Ocean, to a Man who sails upon it, is, I think, the biggest Object that he can see in Motion, and consequently gives his Imagination one of the highest Kinds of Pleasure that can arise from Greatness. I must confess, it is impossible for me to survey this World of fluid Matter, without thinking on the Hand that first poured it out, and made a proper Channel for its Reception. Such an Object naturally raises in my Thoughts the Idea of an Almighty Being, and convinces me of his Existence, as much as a Metaphisical Demonstration. The Imagination prompts the Understanding, and by the Greatness of the sensible Object, produces in it the Idea of a Being who is neither circumscribed by Time nor Space.

'As I have made several Voyages upon the Sea I have often been tossed in Storms, and on that occasion have frequently reflected on the Descriptions of them in ancient Poets. I remember *Longinus* highly recommends one in *Homer*, because the Poet has not amused himself with little Fancies upon the Occasion, as Authors of an inferiour Genius, whom he mentions, had done, but because he has gathered together those Circumstances which are the most apt to terrifie the Imagination, and which really happen in the raging of a Tempest.[1] It is for the same Reason, that I prefer the following Description of a Ship in a Storm, which the Psalmist has made, before any other I have ever met with. *They that go down to the Sea in Ships, that do Business in great Waters: These see the Works of the Lord, and his Wonders in the Deep. For he commandeth and raiseth the stormy Wind, which lifteth up the Waters thereof. They mount up to the Heaven, they go down again to the Depths, their Soul is melted because of trouble. They reel too and fro, and stagger like a drunken Man, and are at their Wits end. Then they cry unto the Lord in their trouble, and he bringeth them out of their Distresses. He maketh the Storm a Calm, so that the Waves thereof are still. Then they are glad, because they be quiet; so he bringeth them unto their desired Haven.*[2]

'By the way, how much more comfortable, as well as rational, is this System of the Psalmist, than the Pagan Scheme in *Virgil*, and other Poets, where one Deity is represented as raising a Storm, and another as laying it.[3] Were we only to consider the Sublime in this Piece of Poetry, what can be nobler than the Idea it gives us, of the Supreme Being thus raising a Tumult among the Elements, and

[1] *On the Sublime*, 10. 3. [2] Ps. cvii. 23–30.
[3] *Aeneid*, 1. 50–156.

recovering them out of their Confusion; thus troubling and be-calming Nature?

'Great Painters do not only give us Landskips of Gardens, Groves, and Meadows, but very often employ their Pencils upon Sea-Pieces: I could wish you would follow their Example. If this small Sketch may deserve a Place among your Works, I shall accompany it with a Divine Ode, made by a Gentleman upon the Conclusion of his Travels.'

I.

HOW are Thy Servants blest, O Lord!
  How sure is their Defence!
Eternal Wisdom is their Guide,
  Their Help Omnipotence.

II.

In foreign Realms, and Lands remote,
  Supported by Thy Care,
Through burning Climes I pass'd unhurt,
  And breath'd in tainted Air.

III.

Thy Mercy sweetned ev'ry Soil,
  Made ev'ry Region please;
The hoary Alpine *Hills it warm'd,*
  And smooth'd the Tyrrhene *Seas:*

IV.

Think, O my Soul, devoutly think,
  How with affrighted Eyes
Thou saw'st the wide extended Deep
  In all its Horrors rise!

V.

Confusion dwelt in ev'ry Face,
  And Fear in ev'ry Heart;
When Waves on Waves, and Gulphs in Gulphs,
  O'ercame the Pilot's Art.

VI.

Yet then from all my Griefs, O Lord,
Thy Mercy set me free,
Whilst in the Confidence of Pray'r
My Soul took hold on Thee;

VII.

For tho' in dreadful Whirles we hung
High on the broken Wave,
I knew Thou wert not slow to Hear,
Nor Impotent to Save:

VIII.

The Storm was laid, the Winds retir'd,
Obedient to thy Will;
The Sea, that roar'd at Thy Command,
At Thy Command was still.

IX.

In midst of Dangers, Fears, and Death,
Thy Goodness I'll adore,
And praise Thee for Thy Mercies past;
And humbly hope for more:

X.

My Life, if Thou preserv'st my Life,
Thy Sacrifice shall be;
And Death, if Death must be my Doom,
Shall join my Soul to Thee.[1]

O

[1] The following note appeared in the folio edition:

ADVERTISEMENT.

The Author of the Spectator *having received the Pastoral Hymn in his 441st Paper, set to Musick by one of the most Eminent Composers of our own Country, and by a Foreigner, who has not put his Name to his ingenious Letter, thinks himself obliged to return his Thanks to those Gentlemen for the Honour they have done him.*

Domus & placens Uxor.

Hor.

I HAVE very long entertained an Ambition to make the Word *Wife* the most agreeable and delightful Name in Nature. If it be not so in it self, all the wiser Part of Mankind from the Beginning of the World to this Day has consented in an Error: But our Unhappiness in *England* has been, that a few loose Men of Genius for Pleasure, have turned it all to the Gratification of ungoverned Desires, in Despite of good Sense, Form, and Order; when, in Truth, any Satisfaction beyond the Boundaries of Reason, is but a Step towards Madness and Folly. But is the Sense of Joy and Accomplishment of Desire no Way to be indulged or attained? and have we Appetites given us to be at all gratify'd? Yes certainly. Marriage is an Institution calculated for a constant Scene of as much Delight as our Being is capable of. Two Persons who have chosen each other out of all the Species, with Design to be each other's mutual Comfort and Entertainment, have in that Action bound themselves to be good-humour'd, affable, discreet, forgiving, patient, and joyful, with Respect to each other's Frailties and Perfections, to the End of their Lives. The Wiser of the Two (and it always happens one of them is such) will, for her or his own Sake, keep things from Outrage with the utmost Sanctity. When this Union is thus preserv'd (as I have often said) the most indifferent Circumstance administers Delight. Their Condition is an endless Source of new Gratifications. The marry'd Man can say, If I am unacceptable to all the World beside, there is one, whom I entirely love, that will receive me with Joy and Transport, and think her self obliged to double her Kindness and Caresses of me from the Gloom with which she sees me over-cast. I need not dissemble the Sorrow of my Heart to be agreeable there, that very Sorrow quickens her Affection.

This Passion towards each other, when once well fixed, enters into the very Constitution, and the Kindness flows as easily and silently as the Blood in the Veins. When this Affection is enjoyed in the most sublime Degree, unskilful Eyes see nothing of it; but

[1] *Motto.* Horace, *Odes,* 2. 14. 21–22:
    Thy Lands and House and pleasing Wife. CREECH.

when it is subject to be changed, and has an Allay in it that may make it end in Distaste, it is apt to break into Rage, or overflow into Fondness, before the rest of the World.

Uxander and *Viramira* are amorous and young, and have been married these two Years; yet do they so much distinguish each other in Company, that in your Conversation with the dear things you are still put to a Sort of Cross-Purposes. Whenever you address your self in ordinary Discourse to *Viramira*, she turns her Head another Way, and the Answer is made to the dear *Uxander*: If you tell a merry Tale, the Application is still directed to her Dear; and when she should commend you, she says to him, as if he had spoke it, That is, my Dear, so pretty—— This puts me in Mind of what I have somewhere read in the admired Memoirs of the famous *Cervantes*, where, while honest *Sancho Pança* is putting some necessary humble Question concerning *Rozinante*, his Supper, or his Lodgings, the Knight of the Sorrowful Countenance is ever improving the harmless lowly Hints of his Squire to poetical Conceit, Rapture, and Flight, in Contemplation of the dear *Dulcinea* of his Affections.[1]

On the other Side, *Dictamnus* and *Moria* are ever squabbling, and you may observe them all the Time they are in Company in a State of Impatience. As *Uxander* and *Viramira* wish you all gone, that they may be at Freedom for Dalliance, *Dictamnus* and *Moria* wait your Absence, that they may speak their harsh Interpretations on each other's Words and Actions during the Time you were with them.

It is certain, that the greater Part of the Evils attending this Condition of Life arises from Fashion. Prejudice in this Case is turned the wrong Way, and instead of expecting more Happiness than we shall meet with in it, we are laughed into a Prepossession, that we shall be disappointed if we hope for lasting Satisfactions.

With all Persons who have made good Sense the Rule of Action, Marriage is described as the State capable of the highest humane Felicity. *Tully* has Epistles full of affectionate Pleasure, when he writes to his Wife or speaks of his Children.[2] But above all the Hints of this Kind I have met with in Writers of ancient Date, I am pleased with an Epigram of *Martial*, in Honour of the Beauty of his

---

[1] This also provides the subject of the opening scene in D'Urfey's *Comical History of Don Quixote*, part i (1694).
[2] Cicero, *Epistulae ad Familiares*, 14.

Wife *Cleopatra*.[1] Commentators say it was written the Day after his Wedding Night. When his Spouse was retired to the Bathing-room in the Heat of the Day, he, it seems, came in upon her when she was just going into the Water. To her Beauty and Carriage on this Occasion we owe the following Epigram, which I shewed my Friend WILL. HONEYCOMB in *French*, who has translated it as follows, without understanding the Original. I expect it will please the *English* better than the *Latin* Reader.

> *When my bright Consort, now nor Wife nor Maid,*
> *Asham'd and wanton, of Embrace afraid,*
> *Fled to the Streams, the Streams my Fair betray'd.*
> *To my fond Eyes she all transparent stood,*
> *She blush'd, I smil'd at the slight covering Flood.*
> *Thus through the Glass the lovely Lilly glows,*
> *Thus through the ambient Gem shines forth the Rose.*
> *I saw new Charms, and plung'd to seize my Store,*
> *Kisses I snatch'd, the Waves prevented more.*

My Friend would not allow that this luscious[2] Account could be given of a Wife, and therefore used the Word *Consort*, which, he learnedly said, would serve for a Mistress as well, and give a more Gentlemanly Turn to the Epigram. But, under Favour of him and all other such fine Gentlemen, I cannot be perswaded but that the Passion a Bridegroom has for a virtuous young Woman, will, by little and little, grow into Friendship, and then it is ascended to an higher Pleasure than it was in its first Fervour. Without[3] this happens, he is a very unfortunate Man who has enter'd into this State, and left the Habitudes of Life he might have enjoy'd with a faithful Friend. But when the Wife proves capable of filling serious as well as joyous Hours, she brings Happiness unknown to Friendship it self. *Spencer* speaks of each Kind of Love with great Justice, and attributes the highest Praise to Friendship; and indeed there is no disputing that Point, but by making that Friendship take its Place between two married Persons.[4]

---

[1] Martial, *Epigrams* 4. 22.

[2] I.e. voluptuous, wanton. The last example in *OED* in this sense is dated 1815.

[3] For the use of this word as conjunction see No. 48 (vol. i).

[4] *Faerie Queene*, IV. ix. 1, 2. (Lines 106-7: 'Or raging fire of loue to woman kind, / Or zeale of friends combynd with vertues meet.' Line 109: 'Me seemes the gentle hart . . . .') Burton, *Anatomy of Melancholy*, III. i. 3, quotes these two stanzas in illustration of friendship, with the same variations in text as here.

Hard is the Doubt, and difficult to deem,
When all three Kinds of Love together meet,
And do dispart the Heart with Power extreme,
Whether shall weigh the Ballance down; to wit,
The dear Affection unto Kindred sweet,
Or raging Fire of Love to Womenkind,
Or Zeal of Friends, combin'd by Virtues meet.
But, of them all, the Band of virtuous Mind,
Methinks the gentle Heart should most assured bind.

For natural Affection soon doth cease,
And quenched is with Cupid's greater Flame;
But faithful Friendship doth them both suppress,
And them with mastering Discipline doth tame,
Through Thoughts aspiring to eternal Fame.
For as the Soul doth rule the Earthly Mass,
And all the Service of the Body frame;
So Love of Soul doth Love of Body pass
No less than perfect Gold surmounts the meanest Brass.

T

No. 491

[STEELE]

Tuesday, September 23, 1712[1]

. . . Digna satis fortuna revisit.

Virg.

IT is common with me to run from Book to Book to exercise my Mind with many Objects, and qualify my self for my daily Labours. After an Hour spent in this loitering Way of reading, something will remain to be Food to the Imagination. The Writings that please me most on such Occasions are Stories, for the Truth of which there is good Authority. The Mind of Man is naturally a Lover of Justice, and when we read a Story wherein a Criminal is overtaken, in whom there is no Quality which is the Object of Pity, the Soul enjoys a certain Revenge for the Offence done to its Nature in the wicked Actions committed in the preceding Part of the History.

[1] *Motto.* Virgil, *Aeneid*, 3. 318:
    Returning Fortune with Desert has blest.

This will be better understood by the Reader from the following Narration it self, than from any thing which I can say to introduce it.

WHEN *Charles* Duke of *Burgundy*, sirnamed *The Bold*, reigned over spacious Dominions now swallowed up by the Power of *France*, he heaped many Favours and Honours upon *Claudius Rhynsault*, a *German*, who had served him in his Wars against the Insults of his Neighbours.[1] A great Part of *Zealand* was at that Time in Subjection to that Dukedom. The Prince himself was a Person of singular Humanity and Justice. *Rhynsault*, with no other real Quality than Courage, had Dissimulation enough to pass upon his generous and unsuspicious Master for a Person of blunt Honesty and Fidelity, without any Vice that could biass him from the Execution of Justice. His Highness prepossessed to his Advantage, upon the Decease of the Governour of his chief Town of *Zealand*, gave *Rhynsault* that Command. He was not long seated in that Government, before he cast his Eyes upon *Sapphira*, a Woman of exquisite Beauty, the Wife of *Paul Danvelt*, a wealthy Merchant of the City under his Protection and Government. *Rhynsault* wa ʿ a Man of a warm Constitution, and violent Inclination to Women, and not unskilled in the soft Arts which win their Favour. He knew what it was to enjoy the Satisfactions which are reaped from the Possession of Beauty, but was an utter Stranger to the Decencies, Honours, and Delicacies that attend the Passion towards them in elegant Minds. However he had so much of the World, that he had a great Share of the Language which usually prevails upon the weaker Part of that Sex, and he could with his Tongue utter a Passion with which his Heart was wholly untouched. He was one of those brutal Minds which can be gratified with the Violation of Innocence and Beauty, without the least Pity, Passion, or Love to that with which they are so much delighted. Ingratitude is a Vice inseparable to a lustful Man; and the Possession of a Woman by him who has no Thought but allaying a Passion painful to himself, is necessarily followed by Distaste and Aversion. *Rhynsault* was resolved to accomplish his Will on the Wife of *Danvelt*, left no Arts untried to get into a Familiarity at her House; but she knew his Character and Disposition too well, not to shun all Occasions that might ensnare her into his Conversation. The Governour despairing of

---

[1] The story is told in Bayle, art. 'Burgundy (Charles, Duke of)', Remark N.

Success by ordinary Means, apprehended and imprisoned her Husband, under Pretence of an Information that he was guilty of a Correspondence with the Enemies of the Duke, to betray the Town into their Possession. This Design had its desired Effect; and the Wife of the unfortunate *Danvelt*, the Day before that which was appointed for his Execution, presented her self in the Hall of the Governour's House, and as he passed through the Apartment, threw her self at his Feet, and holding his Knees, beseeched his Mercy. *Rhynsault* beheld her with a dissembled Satisfaction, and assuming an Air of Thought and Authority, he bid her arise, and told her she must follow him to his Closet; and asking her whether she knew the Hand of the Letter he pulled out of his Pocket, went from her, leaving this Admonition aloud, *If you would save your Husband, you must give me an Account of all you know without Prevarication; for every Body is satisfied he was too fond of you to be able to hide from you the Names of the rest of the Conspirators, or any other Particulars whatsoever.* He went to his Closet, and soon after the Lady was sent for to an Audience. The Servant knew his Distance when Matters of State were to be debated; and the Governour, laying aside the Air with which he had appeared in Publick, began to be the Supplicant, to rally an Affliction, which it was in her Power easily to remove. She easily perceiv'd his Intention, and, bathed in Tears, began to deprecate so wicked a Design, and relieve an innocent Man from his Imprisonment. Lust, like Ambition, takes in all the Faculties of the Mind and Body into its Service and Subjection. Her becoming Tears, her honest Anguish, the Wringing of her Hands, and the many Changes of her Posture and Figure in the Vehemence of Speaking, were but so many Attitudes in which he beheld her Beauty, and further Incentives of his Desire. All Humanity was lost in that one Appetite, and he signified to her in so many plain Terms, That he was unhappy till he had possess'd her, and nothing less should be the Price of her Husband's Life; and she must, before the following Noon, pronounce the Death or Enlargement of *Danvelt*. After this Notification, when he saw *Sapphira* enough again distracted to make the Subject of their Discourse to common Eyes appear different from what it was, he called Servants to conduct her to the Gate. Loaded with insupportable Affliction, she immediately repairs to her Husband, and having signify'd to his Goalers, That she had a Proposal to make to her Husband from the Governour, she was left alone with him, reveal'd to him all that had pass'd, and represented the endless Conflict she was in between Love to his Person, and Fidelity to his Bed. It is easy to imagine the sharp Affliction this honest Pair was in upon such an Incident in Lives not used to any but ordinary Occurrences. The Man was bridled by Shame from speaking what his Fear prompted upon so near an Approach of Death; but let fall Words that signify'd to her, He should not think her polluted, though she had not yet confess'd to him that the Governour had violated her Person, since he knew her Will had no Part in the Action. She parted from him with this oblique Permission to save a Life he had not Resolution enough to resign for the Safety of his Honour.

The next Morning the unhappy *Sapphira* attended the Governour, and being led into a remote Apartment, submitted to his Desires. *Rhynsault* commended her Charms, claim'd a Familiarity after what pass'd between them, and with an Air of Gayety, in the Language of a Gallant, bid her return, and take her Husband out of Prison: But, continued he, my Fair One must not be offended that I have taken Care he should not be an Interruption to our future Assignations. These last Words foreboded what she found when she came to the Goal, her Husband executed by the Order of *Rhynsault*.

It was remarkable, that the Woman, who was full of Tears and Lamentations during the whole Course of her Affliction, utter'd neither Sigh or Complaint, but stood fixed with Grief at this Consummation of her Misfortunes. She betook her self to her Abode, and, after having in Solitude paid her Devotions to him who is th' Avenger of Innocence, she repair'd privately to Court. Her Person, and a certain Grandeur of Sorrow negligent of Forms, gain'd her Passage into the Presence of the Duke her Sovereign. As soon as she came into the Presence, she broke forth into the following Words, *Behold, O mighty Charles, a Wretch weary of Life, though it has always been spent with Innocence and Virtue. It is not in your Power to redress my Injuries, but it is to avenge them. And if the Protection of the Distressed, the Punishment of Oppressors, is a Task worthy a Prince, I bring the Duke of Burgundy ample Matter for doing Honour to his own great Name, and wiping Infamy off of mine.*

When she had spoke this, she deliver'd the Duke a Paper reciting her Story. He read it with all the Emotions that Indignation and Pity could raise in a Prince jealous of his Honour in the Behaviour of his Officers, and Prosperity of his Subjects.

Upon an appointed Day *Rhynsault* was sent for to Court, and in the Presence of a few of the Council, confronted by *Sapphira*, the Prince asking, *Do you know that Lady?* *Rhynsault*, as soon as he could recover his Surprize, told the Duke he would marry her, if his Highness would please to think that a Reparation. The Duke seem'd contented with his Answer, and stood by during the immediate Solemnization of the Ceremony. At the Conclusion of it he told *Rhynsault*, *Thus far you have done as constrain'd by my Authority: I shall not be satisfy'd of your kind Usage of her, without you sign a Gift of your whole Estate to her after your Decease.* To the Performance of this also the Duke was a Witness. When these two Acts were executed, the Duke turned to the Lady, and told her, It now remains for me to put you in quiet Possession of what your Husband has so bountifully bestowed on you; and ordered the immediate Execution of *Rhynsault*. T

No. 492   *Wednesday, September 24, 1712*[1]

[STEELE]

Quicquid est boni moris Levitate extinguitur.

Sen.

Dear Mr. SPECTATOR,   *Tunbridge, Sept.* 18.

'I AM a young Woman of Eighteen Years of Age, and, I do assure you, a Maid of unspotted Reputation, founded upon a very careful Carriage in all my Looks, Words, and Actions. At the same time I must own to you, that it is with much Constraint to Flesh and Blood that my Behaviour is so strictly irreproachable; for I am naturally addicted to Mirth, to Gayety, to a free Air, to Motion, and Gadding. Now what gives me a great deal of Anxiety, and is some Discouragement in the Pursuit of Virtue, is, that the young Women who run into greater Freedoms with the Men are more taken Notice of than I am. The Men are such unthinking Sots, that they do not prefer her who restrains all her Passions and Affections, and keeps much within the Bounds of what is lawful, to her who goes to the utmost Verge of Innocence, and parlies at the very

---

[1] *Motto.* Seneca, *Naturales Quaestiones*, 7. 31. 2 (altered):
Whatsoever remains of good is drowned in levity.

Brink of Vice, whether she shall be a Wife or a Mistress. But I must appeal to your Spectatorial Wisdom, who, I find, have passed very much of your Time in the Study of Woman, whether this is not a most unreasonable Proceeding. I have read somewhere, that *Hobbes* of *Malmesbury* asserts, That continent Persons have more of what they contain, than those who give a Loose to their Desires.[1] According to this Rule, let there be equal Age, equal Wit, and equal good Humour, in the Woman of Prudence, and her of Liberty: What Stores has he to expect who takes the former? What Refuse must he be contented with who chuses the latter? Well, but I sate down to write to you to vent my Indignation against several pert Creatures who are address'd to and courted in this Place, while poor I, and two or three like me, are wholly unregarded.

'Every one of these affect gaining the Hearts of your Sex: This is generally attempted by a particular Manner of carrying themselves with Familiarity. *Glycera* has a dancing Walk, and keeps Time in her ordinary Gate. *Chloe*, her Sister, who is unwilling to interrupt her Conquests, comes into the Room before her with a familiar Run. *Dulcissa* takes Advantage of the Approach of the Winter, and has introduced a very pretty Shiver, closing up her Shoulders, and shrinking as she moves. All that are in this Mode carry their Fans between both Hands before them. *Dulcissa* herself, who is Author of this Air, adds the pretty Run to it; and has also, when she is in very good Humour, a taking Familiarity in throwing her self into the lowest Seat in the Room, and letting her hoop'd Petticoats fall with a lucky Decency about her. I know she practises this Way of sitting down in her Chamber; and indeed she does it as well as you may have seen an Actress fall down dead in a Tragedy: Not the least Indecency in her Posture. If you have observ'd what pretty Carcasses are carry'd off at the End of a Verse at the Theatre, it will give you a Notion how *Dulcissa* plumps into her Chair. Here's a little Country Girl, that's very cunning, that makes her Use of being young and unbred, and outdoes the Insnarers, who are almost twice her Age. The Air that she takes is to come into Company after a Walk, and is very successfully out of Breath upon Occasion. Her Mother is in the Secret, and calls her Romp, and then looks round to see what young Men stare at her.

'It would take up more than can come into one of your Papers, to enumerate all the particular Airs of the younger Company in this

---

[1] This has not been identified.

Place. But I cannot omit *Dulceorella,* whose Manner is the most indolent imaginable, but still as watchful of Conquest as the busiest Virgin among us. She has a peculiar Art of staring at a young Fellow, till she sees she has got him, and inflamed him by so much Observation. When she sees she has him, and he begins to toss his Head upon it, she is immediately short-sighted, and labours to observe what he is at a Distance with her Eyes half shut. Thus the Captive that thought her first struck, is to make very near Approaches, or be wholly disregarded. This Artifice has done more Execution than all the Ogling of the rest of the Women here, with the utmost Variety of half Glances, attentive Heedlessnesses, childish Inadvertencies, haughty Contempts, or artificial Oversights. After I have said thus much of Ladies among us who fight thus regularly, I am to complain to you of a Set of familiar Romps,[1] who have broken through all common Rules, and have thought of a very effectual Way of shewing more Charms than all of us. These, Mr. SPECTATOR, are the Swingers. You are to know these careless pretty Creatures are very Innocents again; and it is to be no Matter what they do, for 'tis all harmless Freedom. They get on Ropes, as you must have seen the Children, and are swung by their Men Visitants. The Jest is, that Mr. Such-a-one can name the Colour of Mrs. Such-a-one's Stockings; and she tells him, he is a lying Thief, so he is, and full of Roguery; and she'll lay a Wager, and her Sister shall tell the Truth if he says right, and he can't tell what Colour her Garters are of. In this Diversion there are very many pretty Shreaks, not so much for fear of falling, as that their Petticoats should unty: For there is great Care had to avoid Improprieties; and the Lover who swings the Lady, is to tye her Cloaths very close with his Hatband before she admits him to throw up her Heels.

'Now, Mr. SPECTATOR, except you can note these Wantonnesses in their Beginnings, and bring us sober Girls into Observation, there is no Help for it, we must swim with the Tide, the Coquets are too powerful a Party for us. To look into the Merit of a regular and well-behaved Woman, is a slow thing. A loose trivial Song gains the Affections, when a wise Homily is not attended to. There is no other way but to make War upon them, or we must go over to them. As for my Part, I will shew all the World it is not for want of Charms that I stand so long unasked; and if you do not take

[1] See No. 71 (vol. i).

Measures for the immediate Redress of us Rigids,[1] as the Fellows call us, I can move with a speaking Mein, can look significantly, can lisp, can trip, can loll, can start, can blush, can rage, can weep, if I must do it, and can be frighted, as agreeably as any She in *England*. All which is humbly submitted to your Spectatorial Consideration with all Humility, by

> *Your most humble Servant,*
> Matilda Mohair.'[2]
>
> T

No. 493

[STEELE]

Thursday, September 25, 1712[3]

Qualem commendes etiam atque etiam adspice, ne mox Incutiant aliena tibi peccata pudorem.

Hor.

IT is no unpleasant matter of Speculation to consider the recommendatory Epistles that pass round this Town from Hand to Hand, and the Abuse People put upon one another in that Kind. It is indeed come to that Pass, that instead of being the Testimony of Merit in the Person recommended, the true Reading of a Letter

---

[1] This is the first example in *OED* of the word in this sense, 'a strict or precise person'.

[2] This letter, and the four short letters on the subject in No. 496, are printed in *The Tunbridge-Miscellany: consisting of Poems, &c. Written at Tunbridge-Wells this Summer: By Several Hands*, published by Curll on 21 Oct. 1712 (advertised in No. 515). The letters are headed, 'The Swingers describ'd: in the following Letters to the Spectator', and introduced by the following lines:

> Since You, Great CENSOR, bear *Britannia*'s Weight,
> Sole, unsupported, since thy daily Care
> Brightens with Morals her Decaying Age,
> The suff'ring Public justly might complain,
> Shou'd we too long detain her CENSOR's Ear.

The letters are printed on pp. 21–25, and following them (pp. 26–27) is a short poem entitled 'Upon Sight of Chloris Swinging', which begins:

> A Pretty New Diversion this!
> An upstart Kind of Fairy Bliss!
> A Banquet merely for the View!
> *Platonick Lovers*! 'Tis for you.

Motto. Horace, *Epistles*, I. 18. 76–77:

> Commend not, till a man is throughly known:
> A rascal prais'd, you make his faults your own.

of this sort is, *The Bearer hereof is so uneasie to me, that it will be an Act of Charity in you to take him off my Hands; whether you prefer him or not it is all one, for I have no manner of Kindness for him, or Obligation to him or his; and do what you please as to that.* As negligent as Men are in this respect, a Point of Honour is concerned in it, and there is nothing a Man should be more ashamed of, than passing a worthless Creature into the Service or Interests of a Man who has never injured you. The Women indeed are a little too keen in their Resentments, to trespass often this Way: But you shall sometimes know that the Mistress and the Maid shall quarrel, and give each other very free Language, and at last the Lady shall be pacified to turn her out of Doors, and give her a very good Word to any body else. Hence it is that you see, in a Year and half's time, the same Face a Domestick in all Parts of the Town. Good-breeding and Good-nature lead People in a great Measure to this Injustice: When Suitors of no Consideration will have Confidence enough to press upon their Superiors, those in Power are tender of speaking the Exceptions they have against them, and are mortgaged into Promises out of their Impatience of Importunity. In this latter Case, it would be a very useful Enquiry to know the History of Recommendations: There are, you must know, certain Abettors of this Way of Torment who make it a Profession to manage the Affairs of Candidates: These Gentlemen let out their Impudence to their Clients, and supply any defective Recommendation, by informing how such and such a Man is to be attacked. They will tell you, get the least Scrap from Mr. such a one, and leave the rest to them. When one of these Undertakers have your Business in Hand, you may be sick, absent, in Town or Country, and the Patron shall be worried, or you prevail. I remember to have been shown a Gentleman, some Years ago, who punish'd a whole People for their Facility in giving their Credentials.[1] This Person had belonged to a Regiment which did Duty in the *West Indies*, and by the Mortality of the Place

---

[1] N. Darnell Davis, *The Spectator's Essays relating to the West Indies*, pp. 14–15, suggests that Sir Richard Dutton may have been the governor referred to here. 'Sir Richard Dutton was an unpopular governor; apparently, from thinking more of the interests of the Royal African Company than of the welfare of the colonists.' During the agitation over the question of the succession to the throne in 1681, he procured from the Grand Jury of the Island of Barbados an address of 'abhorrence' against the Whig attempts to oust the Duke of York from the succession. Again, when in 1683 Sir Richard was leaving Barbados, the Grand Jury drew up an address to be presented to the King by 'their noble and high deserving Governor', who had 'stifled and discountenanced faction and fanaticism in the very embrio'. As a result of this testimonial Sir Richard was returned to Barbados the following year.

happened to be commanding Officer in the Colony. He oppressed his Subjects with great Frankness till he became sensible that he was heartily hated by every Man under his Command. When he had carried his Point, to be thus detestable, in a pretended Fit of Dishumour,[1] and feigned Uneasiness of living where he found he was so universally unacceptable, he communicated to the Chief Inhabitants a Design he had to return for *England*, provided they would give him ample Testimonials of their Approbation. The Planters came into it to a Man, and in proportion to his deserving the quite contrary, the Words Justice, Generosity, and Courage were inserted in his Commission, not omitting the general Good-liking of People of all Conditions in the Colony. The Gentleman returns for *England*, and within few Months after came back to them their Governor on the strength of their own Testimonials.

Such a Rebuke as this cannot indeed happen to easie Recommenders, in the ordinary Course of things from one Hand to another; but how would a Man bear to have it said to him, The Person I took into Confidence on the Credit you gave him, has proved false, unjust, and has not answered any way the Character you gave me of him.

I cannot but conceive very good Hopes of that Rake *Jack Toper* of the *Temple*, for an honest Scrupulousness in this Point. A Friend of his meeting with a Servant that had formerly lived with *Jack*, and having a Mind to take him, sent to him to know what Faults the Fellow had, since he could not please such a careless Fellow as he was. His Answer was as follows.

SIR,

' *THOMAS* that lived with me was turned away because he was too good for me. You know I live in Taverns; he is an orderly sober Rascal, and thinks much to sleep in an Entry till Two in a Morning. He told me one Day when he was dressing me, that he wondered I was not dead before now, since I went to Dinner in the Evening, and went to Supper at two in the Morning. We were coming down *Essex-street*[2] one Night a little flustered, and I was giving him the Word to alarm the Watch; he had the Impudence to tell me it was against the Law. You that are Married, and live

---

[1] See Nos. 424 (vol. iii) and 479.
[2] This street ran south from the Strand near St. Clement Danes Church. The end from Devereux Court to the Thames was commonly called Essex Buildings (Hatton, p. 28).

one Day after another the same way, and so on the whole Week, I dare say will like him, and he will be glad to have his Meat in due season.[1] The Fellow is certainly very Honest. My Service to your Lady.

Yours, J. T.'

Now this was very fair Dealing. *Jack* knew very well, that tho' the Love of Order made a Man very awkard in his Equipage, it was a valuable Quality among the Queer People who live by Rule; and had too much good Sense and good Nature to let the Fellow starve, because he was not fit to attend his Vivacities.[2]

I shall end this Discourse with a Letter of Recommendation from *Horace* to *Claudius Nero*. You will see, in that Letter, a Slowness to ask a Favour a strong Reason for being unable to deny his good Word any longer, and that it is a Service to the Person to whom he recommends, to comply with what is asked: All which are necessary Circumstances, both in Justice and Good-breeding, if a Man would ask so as to have Reason to complain of a Denyal; and indeed a Man should not in strictness ask otherwise. In hopes the Authority of *Horace*, who perfectly understood how to live with great Men, may have a good effect towards amending this Facility in People of Condition, and the Confidence of those who apply to them without Merit, I have translated the Epistle.

To CLAUDIUS NERO.[3]

SIR,

' SEPTIMIUS, who waits upon you with this, is very well acquainted with the Place you are pleased to allow me in your Friendship. For when he beseeches me to recommend him to your Notice, in such a manner as to be received by you, who are delicate in the Choice of your Friends and Domesticks, he knows our Intimacy, and understands my Ability to serve him better than I do my self. I have defended my self against his Ambition to be yours as long as I possibly could, but fearing the Imputation of hiding my Power in you out of mean and selfish Considerations, I am at last prevailed upon to give you this Trouble. Thus, to avoid the Appearance of a greater Fault, I have put on this Confidence.

[1] Ps. cxlv. 15.
[2] Vivacity: 'a vivacious or lively act, expression, scene, etc. Usually in plural' (*OED*). Steele uses it also in No. 448, paragraph 2.
[3] Horace, *Epistles*, 1. 9. The recipient was Tiberius Claudius Nero, stepson of Augustus and later the emperor Tiberius.

If you can forgive this Transgression of Modesty in behalf of a Friend, receive this Gentleman into your Interests and Friendship, and take it from me that he is an Honest and a Brave Man.'

T

No. 494   *Friday, September 26, 1712*[1]

[ADDISON]

*Ægritudinem laudare, unam rem maximè detestabilem,
quorum est tandem Philosophorum?*

Cic.

ABOUT an Age ago it was the Fashion in *England*, for every one that would be thought religious, to throw as much Sanctity as possible into his Face, and in particular to abstain from all Appearances of Mirth and Pleasantry, which were looked upon as the Marks of a Carnal Mind. The Saint was of a sorrowful Countenance, and generally eaten up with Spleen and Melancholly. A Gentleman, who was lately a great Ornament to the Learned World, has diverted me more than once with an Account of the Reception which he met with from a very famous Independent Minister, who was Head of a Colledge in those times.[2] This Gentleman was then

---

[1] *Motto.* Cicero, *Tusculan Disputations*, 4. 25. 55: To what sect of philosophers does it belong, pray, to extol melancholy, the most detestable thing in nature?

[2] Nichols, followed by other editors, identifies the gentleman 'lately a great ornament to the learned world' as Anthony Henley (1666–1711) and the 'famous independent minister' as Dr. Thomas Goodwin (1600–79), President of Magdalen College; but Henley was not born until after Goodwin had left Oxford and did not matriculate at Oxford (at 15) until after Goodwin's death (Foster, *Alumni Oxonienses*, 1891, ii. 693). The problem is further complicated by J. R. Bloxam (*Register of Presidents, Fellows, Demies . . . of Magdalen College*, Oxford, 1857, ii, p. cix) who quotes the *Spectator* story apropos of Goodwin and tells the story as if he had other evidence that the gentleman was Henley. He brings forth no records, however; perhaps because, as Foster says, Henley matriculated not at Magdalen but Christ Church. The *DNB* also uses the *Spectator* as a source. All biographers of Henley seem to base their accounts on Le Neve's notice in *Memoirs British and Foreign of the Lives . . . who dy'd in the year 1711* (1712), pp. 531–7. Another candidate suggested is 'the famous Thomas, or, more familiarly, Tom Bradbury, the supposed author of the ballad "Of Bray the Vicar I have been" '. Lord Hailes is quoted to this effect in Granger's *Biographical History* (ed. 1824, v. 58 n.). The *DNB*, s.v. Goodwin, also follows Granger. Where Hailes said this is uncertain, and who Tom Bradbury was is equally uncertain. He was not the 'outspoken and facetious London Independent Minister', the Rev. Thomas Bradbury (1677–1759), as the *DNB* notes; nor was he any of the Bradburys listed by Foster; nor does Foster mention any Thomas that fits the

a young Adventurer in the Republic of Letters, and just fitted out for the University with a good Cargo of *Latin* and *Greek*. His Friends were resolved that he should try his Fortune at an Election which was drawing near in the College, of which the Independent Minister, whom I have before mentioned, was Governor. The Youth, according to Custom, waited on him in order to be examined. He was received at the Door by a Servant, who was one of that gloomy Generation that[a] were then in Fashion. He conducted him, with great Silence and Seriousness, to a long Gallery which was darkned at Noonday, and had only a single Candle burning in it. After a short Stay in this melancholly Apartment, he was led into a Chamber hung with Black, where he entertained himself for some time by the glimmering of a Taper, till at length the Head of the Colledge came out to him, from an inner Room, with half a Dozen Night-Caps upon his Head, and a religious Horror in his Countenance.[1] The young Man trembled; but his Fears encreased, when, instead of being asked what Progress he had made in Learning, he was examined how he abounded in Grace. His *Latin* and *Greek* stood him in little stead; he was to give an Account only of the State of his Soul, whether he was of the Number of the Elect; what was the Occasion of his Conversion; upon what Day of the Month, and Hour of the Day it happened; how it was carried on, and when compleated? The whole Examination was summed up with one short Question, Namely, *Whether he was prepared for Death?* The Boy, who had been bred up by honest Parents, was

---

[a] that] which *Fol.*

case. Finally, the author of the *Spectateur moderne* (Amsterdam, 1731) tentatively suggests Locke as the gentleman in question.

Dr. Thomas Goodwin was made President of Magdalen College by Cromwell in 1649. As Cromwell's chaplain he prayed with him in his last illness. At the Restoration he was deprived of his Oxford post and then preached in London to an assembly of Independents until his death in 1679. Stories of Goodwin's austere religion are common (see *Biographia Britannica*, ed. 1793, v. 505 n.). Two other Independent ministers (John Owen, Dean of Christ Church, and Thankful Owen, President of St. John's) were heads of Oxford colleges at the same time with Goodwin; but the circumstance of the 'half-dozen night-caps' agrees so well with the nickname mentioned by Anthony à Wood ('Nine-caps') that editors have taken it as certainty that Dr. Thomas Goodwin is intended.

[1] According to Robert Halley (*Works of Thomas Goodwin*, with Memoir by Halley, Edinburgh, 1861, ii, p. xxxii) Goodwin was to be recognized by his night-caps, 'for he had become especially careful in protecting his brains from the cold'. Cardinal Howard, in Rome, asked Goodwin's son about his father's work on a difficult text, and receiving an evasive answer about the difficulty of the work, replied, 'Yes, especially when a man has half-a-dozen nightcaps over his eyes' (*Biographia Britannica*, ed. 1793, v. 505 n.). Halley repeats the story, as does W. Wilson (*History of Dissenting Churches*, 1808–14, iii. 447).

frighted out of his Wits at the Solemnity of the Proceeding, and by the last dreadful Interrogatory; so that upon making his Escape out of this House of Mourning, he could never be brought a Second time to the Examination, as not being able to go through the Terrors of it.

Notwithstanding this general Form and Outside of Religion is pretty well worn out among us, there are many Persons, who, by a natural Unchearfulness of Heart, mistaken Notions of Piety, or Weakness of Understanding, love to indulge this uncomfortable way of Life, and give up themselves a Prey to Grief and Melancholly. Superstitious Fears, and groundless Scruples, cut them off from the Pleasures of Conversation, and all those Social Entertainments which are not only innocent but laudable; as if Mirth was made for Reprobates, and Chearfulness of Heart denied those who are the only Persons that have a proper Title to it.

Sombrius is one of these Sons of Sorrow. He thinks himself obliged in Duty to be sad and disconsolate. He looks on a sudden Fit of Laughter, as a Breach of his Baptismal Vow. An innocent Jest startles him like Blasphemy. Tell him of one who is advanced to a Title of Honour, he lifts up his Hands and Eyes; describe a Publick Ceremony, he shakes his Head; show him a gay Equipage, he blesses himself. All the little Ornaments of Life are Pomps and Vanities. Mirth is wanton, and Wit prophane. He is scandalized at Youth for being lively, and at Childhood for being playful. He sits at a Christening, or a Marriage-Feast, as at a Funeral; sighs at the Conclusion of a merry Story; and grows devout when the rest of the Company grow pleasant. After all, *Sombrius* is a religious Man, and would have behaved him self very properly, had he lived when Christianity was under a general Persecution.

I would by no means presume to tax such Characters with Hypocrisie, as is done too frequently, that being a Vice which I think none but He, who knows the Secrets of Mens Hearts, should pretend to discover in another, where the Proofs of it do not amount to a Demonstration. On the contrary, as there are many Excellent Persons, who are weighed down by this habitual Sorrow of Heart, they rather deserve our Compassion than our Reproaches. I think, however, they would do well to consider, whether such a Behaviour does not deter Men from a Religious Life, by representing it as an unsociable State, that extinguishes all Joy and Gladness, darkens the Face of Nature, and destroys the Relish of Being it self.

I have, in former Papers, shown how great a Tendency there is to Chearfulness in Religion, and how such a Frame of Mind is not only the most lovely, but the most commendable in a virtuous Person.[1] In short, those who represent Religion in so unamiable a Light, are like the Spies sent by *Moses* to make a Discovery of the Land of *Promise*, when by their Reports they discouraged the People from entering upon it.[2] Those who show us the Joy, the Chearfulness, the good Humour, that naturally spring up in this happy State, are like the Spies bringing along with them the Clusters of Grapes, and delicious Fruits, that might invite their Companions into the pleasant Country which produced them.

An Eminent Pagan Writer has made a Discourse, to show that the Atheist, who denies a God, does him less Dishonour than the Man who owns his Being, but at the same time believes him to be cruel, hard to please, and terrible to Human Nature.[3] For my own part, says he, I wou'd rather it should be said of me, that there was never any such Man as *Plutarch*, than that *Plutarch* was ill-natured, capricious or inhuman.

If we may believe our Logicians, Man is distinguished from all other Creatures, by the Faculty of Laughter.[4] He has an Heart capable of Mirth, and naturally disposed to it. It is not the Business of Virtue to extirpate the Affections of the Mind, but to regulate them. It may moderate and restrain, but was not designed to banish Gladness from the Heart of Man. Religion contracts the Circle of our Pleasures, but leaves it wide enough for her Votaries to expatiate in. The Contemplation of the Divine Being, and the Exercise of Virtue, are in their own Nature so far from excluding all Gladness of Heart, that they are perpetual Sources of it. In a word, the true Spirit of Religion cheers, as well as composes, the Soul; it banishes indeed all Levity of Behaviour, all vicious and dissolute Mirth, but in exchange fills the Mind with a perpetual Serenity, uninterrupted Chearfulness, and an habitual Inclination to please others, as well as to be pleased in it self.

O

[1] Nos. 381, 387 (vol. iii).
[2] Num. xiii.
[3] Plutarch, 'Of Superstition', 10 (*Moralia*, 170A).
[4] Cf. No. 249 (vol. ii). Patrick Hume's note to *Paradise Lost*, ix. 239, reads: 'Smiling is so great an Indication of Reason, that some Philosophers have alter'd the *Definition of Man*, from *Animal Rationale* to *Risibile*, affirming Man to be the only Creature endowed with the Power of Laughter. . . .'

> *Duris ut ilex tonsa bipennibus*
> *Nigræ feraci frondis in Algido*
> *Per damna, per cædes ab ipso*
> *Ducit opes animumque ferro.*
>   Hor.

As I am one who, by my Profession, am obliged to look into all kinds of Men, there are none whom I consider with so much Pleasure, as those who have any thing new or extraordinary in their Characters, or Ways of living. For this Reason I have often amused[2] my self with Speculations on the Race of People called *Jews*, many of whom I have met with in most of the considerable Towns which I have passed through in the Course of my Travels. They are, indeed, so disseminated through all the trading Parts of the World, that they are become the Instruments by which the most distant Nations converse with one another, and by which Mankind are knit together in a general Correspondence. They are like the Pegs and Nails in a great Building, which, though they are but little valued in themselves, are absolutely necessary to keep the whole Frame together.[3]

That I may not fall into any common beaten Tracks of Observation, I shall consider this People in three Views; First, with regard to their Number; Secondly, their Dispersion; and Thirdly their Adherence to their Religion; and afterwards endeavour to shew, first what Natural Reasons, and secondly what Providential Reasons may be assigned for these three remarkable Particulars.

---

[1] *Motto.* Horace, *Odes*, 4. 4. 57–60:

> Now like an Oak on some cold Mountain's Brow,
> At every Wound they sprout and grow,
> The Axe and Sword new Vigour give,
> And by their Ruins they revive.

[2] Here used in the obsolete sense of 'to engage, arrest, or occupy the attention of' (*OED*).

[3] Steele had used a similar figure in *Tatler* 85:

> These Under-Characters of Men are Parts of the sociable World by no Means to be neglected: They are like Pegs in a Building. They make no Figure in it, but hold the Structure together, and are as absolutely necessary as the Pillars and Columns.

The *Jews* are looked upon by many to be as numerous at present, as they were formerly in the Land of *Canaan*.[1]

This is wonderful, considering the dreadful Slaughter made of them under some of the *Roman* Emperors, which Historians describe by the Death of many Hundred Thousands in a Year,[a] and the innumerable Massacres and Persecutions they have undergone in *Turkey*, as well as in all Christian Nations of the World. Their *Rabbins*, to express the great Havock which has been sometimes made of them, tell us, after their usual manner of Hyperbole, that there were such Torrents of Holy Blood shed, as carried Rocks of an hundred Yards in Circumference above three Miles into the Sea.[2]

Their Dispersion is the second remarkable Particular in this People. They swarm over all the East, and are settled in the remotest Parts of *China*: They are spread through most of the Nations of *Europe* and *Africk*, and many Families of them are established in the *West Indies*. Not to mention whole Nations bordering on *Prester John*'s Country, and discovered in the inner Parts of *America*, if we may give any Credit to their own Writers.[3]

Their firm Adherence to their Religion, is no less remarkable than their Numbers and Dispersion, especially considering it as persecuted or contemned over the Face of the whole Earth. This is likewise the more remarkable, if we consider the frequent Apostacies of this People, when they lived under their Kings, in the Land of *Promise*, and within sight of their Temple.

If in the next place we examine, what may be the Natural Reasons

[a] Year,] War, *all edd.*

---

[1] Cf. Jacques Basnage de Beauval, *History of the Jews* (1708), p. 748: ' 'Tis impossible to fix the number of Persons this Nation is at present compos'd of. But yet we have reason to believe, there are still near three Millions of People, who profess this Religion. . . .' This book is advertised in No. 21:

The History of the Jews, from Jesus Christ to the Present Time: Containing their Antiquities, their Religion, their Rites, the Dispersion of the Ten Tribes in the East, and the Persecutions this Nation has suffer'd in the West; being a Supplement and Continuation of Josephus's History, by Mr. Basnage: Translated into English by Tho. Taylor, A.M. In Folio. Printed for James Round at Seneca's Head in Exchange Ally.

[2] Bayle, art. 'Barcochebas', Remark H, comments on some of the stories told by the Rabbins. 'They add, that the Blood run with such a force that it carried Stones of four pounds weight along with it, and that it run the space of four Miles into the Sea. . . . The Jews say that *Hadrian* destroy'd twice more People of their Nation, than *Moses* brought out of the Land of *Egypt*. . . .'

[3] Prester John (i.e. Presbyter John) was a fabulous Christian monarch believed to have made extensive conquests from the Moslems in the twelfth century and to have established a powerful empire somewhere in Asia or in Africa.

for these three Particulars, which we find in the *Jews*, and which are not to be found in any other Religion or People, I can in the first place attribute their Numbers to nothing, but their constant Employment, their Abstinence, their Exemption from Wars, and, above all, their frequent Marriages; for they look on Celibacy as an accursed State, and generally are married before Twenty, as hoping the *Messiah* may descend from them.

The Dispersion of the *Jews* into all the Nations of the Earth, is the second remarkable Particular of that People, though not so hard to be accounted for. They were always in Rebellions and Tumults while they had the Temple and Holy City in view, for which Reason they have often been driven out of their old Habitations in the Land of *Promise*. They have as often been banished out of most other Places where they have settled, which must very much disperse and scatter a People, and oblige them to seek a Livelihood where they can find it. Besides, the whole People is now a Race of such Merchants as are Wanderers by Profession, and, at the same time, are in most if not all Places incapable of either Lands or Offices, that might engage them to make any Part of the World their Home.

This Dispersion would probably have lost their Religion, had it not been secured by the Strength of its Constitution: For they are to live all in a Body, and generally within the same Enclosure, to marry among themselves, and to eat no Meats that are not killed or prepared their own way. This shuts them out from all Table Conversation, and the most agreeable Intercourses of Life; and, by consequence, excludes them from the most probable Means of Conversion.

If, in the last Place, we consider what Providential Reason may be assigned for these three Particulars, we shall find that their Numbers, Dispersion, and Adherence to their Religion, have furnished every Age, and every Nation of the World, with the strongest Arguments for the Christian Faith, not only as these very Particulars are foretold of them, but as they themselves are the Depositaries of these, and all the other Prophecies which tend to their own Confusion.[1] Their Number furnishes us with a sufficient

---

[1] 'One of the chiefest Designs of this Book', wrote Thomas Taylor in dedicating his translation of Basnage to Jonathan Trelawny, Bishop of Winchester, 'is to lay before the Scoffers and Despisers of our Religion, an Argument of its Truth in a Language they understand: An Argument which . . . would effectually convince [the Deist] that not a Tittle shall fail of all the Promises and Menaces of the Gospel.

If he demand a present Miracle for his Faith; Behold! here the greatest, of more than sixteen hundred Years Continuance, the *Jews* wandring, and dispersed into

Cloud of Witnesses, that attest the Truth of the old Bible. Their Dispersion spreads these Witnesses through all Parts of the World. The Adherence to their Religion, makes their Testimony unquestionable. Had the whole Body of *Jews* been converted to Christianity, we should certainly have thought all the Prophecies of the Old Testament, that relate to the Coming and History of our Blessed Saviour, forged by Christians, and have looked upon them, with the Prophecies of the *Sybils*, as made many Years after the Events they pretended to foretell. O

No. 496   *Monday, September 29, 1712*[1]
[STEELE]

Gnatum pariter uti his decuit aut etiam amplius
Quod illa ætas magis ad hæc utenda idonea est.
Terent. Heaut. A. 1. Sc. 1.

Mr. SPECTATOR,

'THOSE Ancients who were the most accurate in their Remarks on the Genius and Temper of Mankind, by considering the various Bent and Scope of our Actions throughout the Progress of Life, have with great Exactness allotted Inclinations and Objects of Desire particular to every Stage, according to the different Circumstances of our Conversation and Fortune, thro' the several

all Corners of the Earth, by the Malediction of Heaven: Often massacred and exil'd in as great Multitudes as came from *Egypt*; Despised, hated, persecuted by all Nations; and tho mingled and confounded with them, still distinguished in their Laws, Customs and Religion, remaining a standing Evidence of Divine Vengeance upon Unbelief, and an indelible Monument of the Truth of Christianity' (pp. iii–iv).

A letter signed T. S. and dated 9 Oct. 1712 (Lillie, ii. 347) comments on this paper:

A friend of mine, who, by living in a corner of the town where the people called Jews abound, having imbibed and indulged a too inhospitable temper, thought you dealt too favourably with them in a late paper, therefore importuned me to acquaint you with my observation of their playing at back-gammon on Friday-evening by the light of their lamp, which I presume, you know is the ceremony designed to usher in the solemnities of the ensuing day. But this I declined as a theme too insipid. . . .

[1] *Motto.* Terence, *Heautontimorumenos*, 131–3: My son should enjoy these things equally with me, or even more, because youth is more appropriate for these things.

Periods of it. Hence they were disposed easily to excuse those Excesses which might possibly arise from a too eager Pursuit of the Affections more immediately proper to each State: They indulged the Levity of Childhood with Tenderness, overlooked the Gayety of Youth with good Nature, tempered the forward Ambition and Impatience of ripened Manhood with Discretion, and kindly imputed the tenacious Avarice of old Men to their want of Relish for any other Enjoyment. Such Allowances as these were no less advantagious to common Society than obliging to particular Persons; for by maintaining a Decency and Regularity in the Course of Life, they supported the Dignity of humane Nature, which then suffers the greatest Violence when the Order of things is inverted; and in nothing is it more remarkably villified and ridiculous, than when Feebleness preposterously attempts to adorn it self with that outward Pomp and Lustre which serve only to set off the Bloom of Youth with better Advantage. I was insensibly carried into Reflections of this Nature, by just now meeting *Paulino* (who is in his Climacterick)[1] bedeck'd with the utmost Splendour of Dress and Equipage, and giving an unbounded Loose to all Manner of Pleasure, whilst his only Son is debarr'd all innocent Diversion, and may be seen frequently solacing himself in the *Mall*[2] with no other Attendance than one antiquated Servant of his Father's for a Companion and Director.

'It is a monstrous Want of Reflection, that a Man cannot consider that when he cannot resign the Pleasures of Life in his Decay of Appetite and Inclination to them, his Son must have a much uneasier Task to resist the Impetuosity of growing Desires. The Skill therefore should methinks be, to let a Son want no lawful Diversion, in proportion to his future Fortune, and the Figure he is to make in the World. The first Step towards Virtue that I have observed in young Men of Condition that have run into Excesses, has been that they had a Regard to their Quality and Reputation in the Management of their Vices. Narrowness in their Circumstances has made many Youths to supply themselves as Debauchees, commence Cheats and Rascals. The Father who allows his Son to his utmost Ability avoids this latter Evil, which as to the World is much greater than the former. But the contrary Practice

---

[1] See No. 295 (vol. iii).
[2] A gravel walk on the north side of St. James's Park, leading up to Buckingham House. Cf. No. 437.

has prevail'd so much among some Men, that I have known them deny them what was meerly necessary for Education suitable to their Quality. Poor young *Antonio* is a lamentable Instance of ill Conduct in this Kind. The young Man did not want natural Talents; but the Father of him was a Coxcomb, who affected being a fine Gentleman so unmercifully, that he could not endure in his Sight, or the frequent Mention of one, who was his Son growing into Manhood, and thrusting him out of the gay World. I have often thought the Father took a secret Pleasure in reflecting, that when that fine House and Seat came into the next Hands, it would revive his Memory, as a Person who knew how to enjoy them, from Observation of the Rusticity and Ignorance of his Successor. Certain it is, that a Man may, if he will, let his Heart close to the having no Regard to any thing but his dear Self, even with Exclusion of his very Children. I recommend this Subject to your Consideration, and am,

SIR,

Your most humble Servant,

T. B.'

Mr. SPECTATOR,

London, Sept. 26. 1712.

'I AM just come from *Tunbridge*, and have since my Return read Mrs. *Matilda Mohair's* Letter to you:[1] She pretends to make a mighty Story about the Diversion of swinging in that Place.[2] What was done, was only among Relations; and no Man swung any Woman who was not second Cousin at farthest. She is pleased to say, Care was taken that the Gallants tied the Ladies Legs before they were wafted into the Air. Since she is so spiteful I'll tell you the plain Truth; there was no such Nicety observed, since we were all, as I just now told you, near Relations; but Mrs. *Mohair* her self has been swung there, and she invents all this Malice because it was observed she has crooked Legs, of which I was an Eye-Witness.

Your humble Servant,

Rachel Shooestring.'

[1] No. 492.
[2] Cf. Gay, *Shepherd's Week* (1714), Monday, 103–6:

On two near elms, the slacken'd cord I hung,
Now high, now low my *Blouzelinda* swung.
With the rude wind her rumpled garment rose,
And show'd her taper leg, and scarlet hose.

Mr. SPECTATOR,

Tunbridge, Sept. 26. 1712.

'WE have just now read your Paper containing Mrs. *Mohair's* Letter. It is an Invention of her own from one End to the other; and I desire you would print the enclosed Letter by it self, and shorten it so as to come within the Compass of your Half-Sheet. She is the most malicious Minx in the World, for all she looks so innocent. Don't leave out that Part about her being in Love with her Father's Butler, which makes her shun Men; for that is the truest of it all.

Your Humble Servant,

Sarah Trice.

'*P. S.* She has crooked Legs.'

Mr. SPECTATOR,

Tunbridge, Sept. 26. 1712.

'ALL that Mrs. *Mohair* is so vex'd at against the good Company of this Place is, that we all know she has crooked Legs. This is certainly true. I don't care for putting my Name, because one would not be in the Power of the Creature.

Your Humble Servant unknown.'

Mr. SPECTATOR,

Tunbridge, Sept. 26. 1712.

'THAT insufferable Prude Mrs. *Mohair*, who has told such Stories of the Company here, is with Child, for all her nice Airs and her crooked Legs. Pray be sure to put her in for both those two Things, and you'll oblige every Body here, especially

Your humble Servant,

Alice Bluegarter.'[1]

T

---

[1] These four letters were reprinted in Oct. 1712 in Curll's *Tunbridge-Miscellany* (see above, p. 247).

No. 497
[STEELE]

Tuesday, September 30, 1712[1]

Οὗτός ἐστι γαλεώτης γέρων.
Menander.

A FAVOUR well bestowed, is almost as great an Honour to him who confers it as to him who receives it. What indeed makes for the superior Reputation of the Patron in this Case, is, that he is always surrounded with specious Pretences of unworthy Candidates, and is often alone in the kind Inclination he has towards the Well-deserving. Justice is the first Quality in the Man who is in a Post of Direction; and I remember to have heard an old Gentleman talk of the Civil Wars, and in his Relation give an Account of a General Officer, who with this one Quality, without any shining Endowments, became so popularly beloved and honoured, that all Decisions between Man and Man were laid before him by the Parties concern'd in a private Way, and they would lay by their Animosities implicitly if he bid them be Friends, or submit themselves in the Wrong without Reluctance, if he said it, without waiting the Judgment of Court-Marshals. His Manner was to keep the Dates of all Commissions in his Closet, and wholly dismiss from the Service such who were deficient in their Duty, and after that took Care to prefer according to the Order of Battle. His Familiars were his entire Friends, and could have no interested Views in courting his Acquaintance; for his Affection was no Step to their Preferment, though it was to their Reputation. By this means a kind Aspect, a Salutation, a Smile, and giving out his Hand, had the Weight of what is esteemed by vulgar Minds more substantial. His Business was very short, and he who had nothing to do but Justice, was never affronted with a Request of a familiar daily Visitant for what was due to a brave Man at a Distance. Extraordinary Merit he used to recommend to the King for some Distinction at home, till the Order of Battle made Way for his rising in the Troops. Add to this, that he had an excellent Manner of getting rid of such whom he observed were good at *an Halt*, as his Phrase was. Under this Description he comprehended all those who were contented to live without Reproach, and had no Promptitude in their Minds towards Glory. These Fellows were also recom-

[1] *Motto.* Menander, Εὐνοῦχος (Kock, *Fragments*, 188): This is Old Man Weasel.

mended to the King, and taken off of the General's Hands into Posts wherein Diligence and common Honesty were all that were necessary. This General had no weak Part in his Line; but every Man had as much Care upon him, and as much Honour to lose as himself. Every Officer could answer for what pass'd where he was, and the General's Presence was never necessary any where but where he had placed himself at the first Disposition, except that Accident happen'd from extraordinary Efforts of the Enemy which he could not foresee; but it was remarkable that it never fell out from Failure in his own Troops. It must be confess'd, the World is just so much out of Order, as an unworthy Person possesses what should be in the Direction of him who has better Pretensions to it.

Instead of such a Conduct as this old Fellow used to describe in his General, all the Evils which have ever happen'd among Mankind have arose from the wanton Disposition of the Favours of the Powerful. It is generally all that Men of Modesty and Virtue can do to fall in with some whimsical Turn in a Great Man, to make Way for Things of real and absolute Service. In the Time of Don *Sebastian* of *Portugal*, or some Time since, the first Minister would let nothing come near him but what bore the most profound Face of Wisdom and Gravity. They carried it so far, that, for the greater Shew of their profound Knowledge, a Pair of Spectacles, tied on their Noses with a black Ribband round their Heads, was what compleated the Dress of those who made their Court at his Levee, and none with naked Noses were admitted to his Presence. A blunt honest Fellow, who had a Command in the Train of Artillery, had attempted to make an Impression upon the Porter Day after Day in vain, till at length he made his Appearance in a very thoughtful dark Suit of Cloaths, and two Pair of Spectacles on at once. He was conducted from Room to Room with great Deference to the Minister, and carrying on the Farce of the Place, he told his Excellence, That he had pretended in this manner to be wiser than he really was, but with no ill Intention; but he was honest Such-a-one of the Train, and he came to tell him that they wanted Wheelbarrows and Pick-axes. The thing happened not to displease, the great Man was seen to smile, and the successful Officer was reconducted with the same profound Ceremony out of the House.[1]

When *Leo* the Tenth reigned Pope of *Rome*, his Holiness, tho' a Man of Sense, and of an excellent Taste of Letters, of all things

---

[1] The incident has not been identified.

affected Fools, Buffoons, Humourists, and Coxcombs:[1] Whether it were from Vanity, and that he enjoyed no Talents in other Men but what were inferior to him, or whatever it was, he carried it so far, that his whole delight was in finding out new Fools, and, as our Phrase is, playing them off,[2] and making them shew themselves to Advantage. A Priest of his former Acquaintance suffered a great many Disappointments in attempting to find Access to him in a regular Character, till at last in Despair he retired from *Rome*, and returned in an Equipage so very phantastical, both as to the Dress of himself and Servants, that the whole Court were in an Emulation who should first introduce him to his Holiness. What added to the Expectation his Holiness had of the Pleasure he should have in his Follies, was, that this Fellow, in a Dress the most exquisitely ridiculous, desired he might speak to him alone, for he had Matters of the highest Importance, upon which he wanted a Conference. Nothing could be denied to a Coxcomb of so great Hope; but when they were apart, the Impostor revealed himself, and spoke as follows.

DO not be surprized, most holy Father, at seeing, instead of a Coxcomb to laugh at, your old Friend, who has taken this Way of Access to admonish you of your own Folly. Can any thing shew your Holiness how unworthily you treat Mankind, more than my being put upon this Difficulty to speak with you? It is a Degree of Folly to delight to see it in others, and it is the greatest Insolence imaginable to rejoyce in the Disgrace of humane Nature. It is a criminal Humility in a Person of your Holiness's Understanding, to believe you cannot excel but in the Conversation of Half-wits, Humourists, Coxcombs, and Buffoons. If your Holiness has a Mind to be diverted like a rational Man, you have a great Opportunity for it, in disrobing all the Impertinents you have favoured of all their Riches and Trappings at once, and bestowing them on the Humble, the Vertuous, and the Meek. If your Holiness is not concerned for the Sake of Virtue and Religion, be pleased to reflect, that for the Sake of your own Safety it is not proper to be so very much in Jest. When the Pope is thus merry, the People will in Time begin to think many things, which they have hitherto beheld with great Veneration, are in themselves Objects of Scorn and Derision. If they once get a Trick of knowing how to laugh, your Holiness's

---

[1] Giovanni de' Medici, Pope from 1513 to 1521. See Bayle, art. 'Leo X', Remark F.
[2] See *OED*: 'to cause a person to exhibit himself disadvantageously'. This is the first example given of the phrase.

saying this Sentence in one Night-cap and t'other with the other, the Change of your Slippers, bringing you your Staff in the Midst of a Prayer, then stripping you of one Vest and clapping on a second during Divine Service, will be found out to have nothing in it. Consider, Sir, that at this Rate a Head will be reckoned never the wiser for being bald; and the Ignorant will be apt to say, that going barefoot does not at all help on in the Way to Heaven. The red Cap and the Coul will fall under the same Contempt; and the Vulgar will tell us to our Faces, that we shall have no Authority over them but from the Force of our Arguments and the Sanctity of our Lives.

T

No. 498   *Wednesday, October 1, 1712*[1]

[STEELE]

. . . Frustra retinacula tendens
Fertur equis Auriga, neque audit currus habenas.

To the SPECTATOR GENERAL *of* Great Britain.

From the farther End of the Widow's Coffee-house[2] *in* Devereaux-Court,[3]
Monday *Evening,* 28 *Minutes and a Half past Six.*

Dear Dumb,

'IN short, to use no further Preface, if I should tell you that I have seen a Hackney-Coachman,[4] when he has come to set down his

[1] *Motto.* Virgil, *Georgics,* 1. 513-14:

> Nor Reins, nor Curbs, nor threat'ning Cries they fear,
> But force along the trembling Charioteer. DRYDEN.

[2] In Ned Ward's *London Spy,* part 2, there is an account of a visit to this coffee-house (Casanova Society ed., pp. 27-32).

[3] A narrow street which led south from the Strand. After making five right-angled turns it led into Essex Street on the west and to an inner gate of the Temple on the east. The Grecian Coffee-house was also in this court, as well as John Sly's 'Observatory' (see Nos. 187 [vol. ii], 526).

[4] 'These Coaches', writes John Macky (*A Journey through England,* 1714),

> are very necessary Conveniences, not to be met with any where abroad; for you know that at *Paris, Brussels, Rome,* or *Vienna,* you must either hire a Coach by the Day, or take it at least by the Hour; but here you have Coaches at the Corner of every Street, which for a Shilling will carry you any where within a reasonable Distance, and for two, from one End of the City to the other. There are eight hundred of them licensed by Act of Parliament, and carry their Number on their Coaches; so that if you should chance to leave any thing in a Coach, and know but the Number of it, you know presently where to lay your Claim to it; and be you never so late at a Friend's House in any Place of this great City, your Friend by taking the Number of the Coach secures your Safety home (2nd ed., 1722, pp. 173-4).

Fare, which has consisted of two or three very fine Ladies, hand them out, and salute every one of them with an Air of Familiarity, without giving the least Offence, you would perhaps think me guilty of a Gasconade.[1] But to clear my self from that Imputation, and to explain this Matter to you, I assure you that there are many illustrious Youths within this City, who frequently recreate themselves by driving of a Hackney-Coach: But those whom, above all others, I would recommend to you, are the young Gentlemen belonging to our Inns of Court. We have, I think, about a dozen Coachmen, who have Chambers here in the *Temple*; and as it is reasonable to believe others will follow their Example, we may perhaps in Time, (if it shall be thought convenient) be drove to *Westminster* by our own Fraternity, allowing every fifth Person to apply his Meditations this Way, which is but a modest Computation as the Humour is now likely to take. It is to be hoped likewise, that there are in the other Nurseries of the Law to be found a proportionable Number of these hopeful Plants, springing up to the everlasting Renown of their native Country. Of how long standing this Humour has been, I know not; the first Time I had any particular Reason to take Notice of it was about this Time Twelvemonth, when, being upon *Hampstead-Heath* with some of these studious young Men, who went thither purely for the Sake of Contemplation, nothing would serve them but I must go thorough a Course of this Philosophy too; and being ever willing to embellish my self with any commendable Qualification, it was not long e'er they perswaded me into the Coach-box; nor indeed much longer before I underwent the Fate of my Brother *Phaeton*, for having drove about fifty Paces with pretty good Success, through my own natural Sagacity, together with the good Instructions of my Tutors, who, to give them their Due, were on all Hands encouraging and assisting me in this laudable Undertaking; I say, Sir, having drove about fifty Paces with pretty good Success, I must needs be exercising the Lash, which the Horses resented so ill from my Hands, that they gave a sudden Start, and thereby pitched me directly upon my Head, as I very well remembered about Half an Hour afterwards, which not only deprived me of all the Knowledge I had gain'd for fifty Yards before, but had like to have broken my Neck into the

---

[1] A fairly new word in English. The first example in *OED* is from *Tatler* 115, where Steele refers to Sir Hannibal's way of speaking as one 'commonly distinguish'd by the Name of Gasconade'.

Bargain. After such a severe Reprimand, you may imagine I was not very easily prevail'd with to make a second Attempt; and indeed, upon mature Deliberation, the whole Science seemed, at least to me, to be surrounded with so many Difficulties, that notwithstanding the unknown Advantages which might have accrued to me thereby, I gave over all Hopes of attaining it, and I believe had never thought of it more, but that my Memory has been lately refreshed by seeing some of these ingenious Gentlemen ply in the open Streets, one of which I saw receive so suitable a Reward to his Labours, that tho' I know you are no Friend to Story-telling, yet I must beg Leave to trouble you with this at large.

'About a Fortnight since, as I was diverting my self with a Pennyworth of Wall-nuts at the *Temple*-Gate, a lively young Fellow in a Fustian Jacket shot by me, beckon'd a Coach, and told the Coachman he wanted to go as far as *Chelsey*: They agreed upon the Price, and this young Gentleman mounts the Coach-box; the Fellow staring at him, desired to know if he should not drive till they were out of Town? No, no, reply'd he: He was then going to climb up to him, but receiv'd another Check, and was then ordered to get into the Coach, or behind it, for that he wanted no Instructors; but be sure, you Dog you, says he, don't you bilk me. The Fellow thereupon surrender'd his Whip, scratch'd his Head, and crept into the Coach. Having my self Occasion to go into the *Strand* about the same Time, we started both together; but the Street being very full of Coaches, and he not so able a Coachman as perhaps he imagined himself, I had soon got a little Way before him; often, however,[a] having the Curiosity to cast my Eye back upon him to observe how he behaved himself in this high Station, which he did with great Composure till he came to the Pass, which is a Military Term the Brothers of the Whip have given the Straight at St. *Clement*'s Church; when he was arrived near this Place, where are always Coaches in waiting, the Coachmen began to suck up the Muscles of their Cheeks, and to tip the Wink upon each other, as if they had some Roguery in their Heads, which I was immediately convinced of; for he no sooner came within Reach, but the first of them with his Whip took the exact Dimension of his Shoulders, which he very ingeniously call'd Endorsing; and indeed I must say that every one of them took due Care to endorse him as he came thro' their Hands. He seem'd at first a little uneasy under the

---

[a] before him; often, however,] before him often; however, *Fol.*

Operation, and was going in all haste to take the Numbers of their Coaches; but at length, by the Mediation of the worthy Gentleman in the Coach, his Wrath was asswaged, and he prevail'd upon to pursue his Journey; though indeed I thought they had clapt such a Spoke in his Wheel, as had disabled him from being a Coachman for that Day at least: For I am only mistaken, Mr. SPEC. if some of these Endorsements were not wrote in so strong a Hand, that they are still legible. Upon my enquiring the Reason of this unusual Salutation, they told me, that it was a Custom among them, whenever they saw a Brother tottering or unstable in his Post, to lend him a Hand in order to settle him again therein: For my part I thought their Allegations but reasonable, and so march'd off. Besides our Coachmen, we do[a] abound in divers other Sorts of ingenious robust Youth, who, I hope, will not take it ill if I refer[1] giving you an Account of their several Recreations to another Opportunity. In the mean time, if you would but bestow a little of your wholsome Advice upon our Coachmen, it might perhaps be a Reprieve to some of their Necks. As I understand you have several Inspectors under you, if you would but send one amongst us here in the *Temple*, I am perswaded he would not want Employment. But I leave this to your own Consideration, and am,

SIR,

Your very humble Servant,

Moses Greenbag.

'*P. S.* I have heard our Criticks in the Coffee-houses hereabout talk mightily of the Unity of Time and Place: According to my Notion of the Matter, I have endeavoured at something like it in the Beginning of my Epistle. I desire to be inform'd a little as to that Particular. In my next I design to give you some Account of excellent Watermen, who are bred to the Law, and far outdo the Land-Students abovemention'd.'

T

---

[a] Besides our Coachmen, we do] Besides, our Coachmen do *Fol.*

---

[1] Here used in the obsolete sense of 'defer, postpone'. Cf. *Daily Courant*, 14 Nov. 1711: 'The rest of this Piece is referred to another Opportunity.'

Thursday, October 2, 1712[1]

> *. . . nimis uncis*
> *Naribus indulges . . .*
> Pers.

MY Friend WILL HONEYCOMB has told me, for above this half Year, that he had a great Mind to try his Hand at a *Spectator*, and that he would fain have one of his writing in my Works. This Morning I received from him the following Letter, which, after having rectified some little Orthographical Mistakes, I shall make a Present of to the Publick.

Dear SPEC.

'I WAS, about two Nights ago, in Company with very agreeable young People of both Sexes, where talking of some of your Papers which are written on Conjugal Love, there arose a Dispute among us, whether there were not more bad Husbands in the World than bad Wives. A Gentleman, who was Advocate for the Ladies, took this Occasion to tell us the Story of a famous Siege in *Germany*, which I have since found related in my Historical Dictionary, after the following manner.[2] When the Emperor *Conrade* the Third had besieged *Guelphus*, Duke of *Bavaria*, in the City of *Hensberg*, the Women finding that the Town could not possibly hold out long, petitioned the Emperor that they might depart out of it, with so much as each of them could carry. The Emperor, knowing they could not convey away many of their Effects, granted them their Petition: When the Women, to his great Surprize, came out of the Place with every one her Husband upon her Back. The Emperor was so moved at the Sight, that he burst into Tears, and after having very much extolled the Women for their Conjugal Affection, gave the Men to their Wives, and received the Duke into his Favour.

---

[1] *Motto.* Persius, *Satires*, I. 40–41:
You drive the Jest too far. DRYDEN.

[2] The incident referred to is the famous legend of the *Weibertreue*, and is supposed to have taken place when Conrad III besieged the town of Weinsburg (Hensburg) in the year 1140. Guelphus, or Welf, was the brother of Henry the Proud, Conrad's powerful rival in Bavaria and Saxony, who had just died in the preceding year. The story has been often told. In *The History of Bavaria . . . collected from the best ancient historians . . .* by Capt. John Stevens (1706), it is related on p. 50.

'The Ladies did not a little triumph at this Story, asking us, at the same time, whether in our Consciences we believed that the Men of any Town in *Great Britain* would, upon the same Offer,[a] and at the same Conjuncture, have loaden themselves with their Wives; or rather, whether they would not have been glad of such an Opportunity to get rid of them? To this my very good Friend *Tom Dapperwit*, who took upon him to be the Mouth of our Sex, replied, that they would be very much to blame if they wou'd not do the same good Office for the Women, considering that their Strength would be greater, and their Burdens lighter.[1] As we were amusing our selves with Discourses of this Nature, in order to pass away the Evening, which now begins to grow tedious, we fell into that laudable and primitive Diversion of Questions and Commands.[2] I was no sooner vested with the Regal Authority, but I enjoined all the Ladies, under pain of my Displeasure, to tell the Company ingenuously,[b] in case they had been in the Siege abovementioned, and had the same Offers made them as the good Women of that Place, what every one of them would have brought off with her, and have thought most worth the saving? There were several merry Answers made to my Question, which entertained us till Bed-time. This filled my Mind with such an huddle of Ideas, that upon my going to sleep I fell into the following Dream.

'I saw a Town of this Island, which shall be nameless, invested on every side, and the Inhabitants of it so streightned as to cry for Quarter. The General refused any other Terms than those granted to the abovementioned Town of *Hensberg*, namely, that the married Women might come out with what they could bring along with them. Immediately the City Gates flew open, and a Female Procession appeared, Multitudes of the Sex following one another in a row, and staggering under their respective Burdens. I took my Stand upon an Eminence in the Enemies Camp, which was appointed for the general Rendezvous of these Female Carriers, being very desirous to look into their several Ladings. The first of them had an huge Sack upon her Shoulders, which she set down with

---

[a] Offer,] Offers, *Fol.*   [b] ingenuously,] ingeniously, *Fol.*

---

[1] Tom Dapperwit is mentioned in No. 482 as a correspondent who looks on marriage as a purgatory. He is referred to again in No. 511; and in No. 530 is suggested as Will Honeycomb's successor in the Club. Mr. Dapperwit is also mentioned as a correspondent in No. 619.

[2] See No. 245 (vol. ii).

great Care: Upon the opening of it, when I expected to have seen her Husband shot out of it, I found it was filled with China Ware. The next appeared in a more decent Figure, carrying an handsom young Fellow upon her Back: I could not forbear commending the young Woman for her Conjugal Affection, when, to my great Surprise, I found that she had left the good Man at home, and brought away her Gallant. I saw the third, at some distance, with a little withered Face peeping over her Shoulder, whom I could not suspect for any but her Spouse, till upon her setting him down I heard her call[a] him dear Pugg, and found him to be her Favourite Monkey. A fourth brought a huge Bale of Cards along with her; and the fifth a *Bolonia* Lapdog,[1] for her Husband it seems being a very Burly Man, she thought it would be less Trouble for her to bring away little *Cupid*. The next was the Wife of a rich Usurer, loaden with a Bag of Gold; she told us that her Spouse was very old, and by the Course of Nature could not expect to live long, and that to shew her tender regards for him she had saved that which the poor Man loved better than his Life. The next came towards us with her Son upon her Back, who, we were told, was the greatest Rake in the Place, but so much the Mother's Darling that she left her Husband behind, with a large Family of hopeful Sons and Daughters, for the sake of this Graceless Youth.

'It would be endless to mention the several Persons, with their several Loads, that appeared to me in this strange Vision. All the Place about me was covered with Packs of Ribbands, Brocades, Embroidery, and Ten thousand other Materials, sufficient to have furnish'd a whole street of Toy-shops. One of the Women, having an Husband who was none of the heaviest, was bringing him off upon her Shoulders, at the same time that she carried a great Bundle of *Flanders-Lace* under her Arm, but finding herself so over-loaden that she could not save both of them, she dropp'd the good Man, and brought away the Bundle. In short, I found but one Husband among this great Mountain of Baggage, who was a lively Cobler, that kicked and spurr'd all the while his Wife was carrying him on, and, as it was said, had scarce passed a Day in his Life without giving her the Discipline of the Strap.

[a] call] calling *Fol.*

---

[1] Cf. Guy Miege, *Present State of Great Britain* (1707), p. 13: 'Here are also *Dogs* of all sorts, for Fighting, Hunting, and Fowling, and others, (like *Bolonia* Dogs) for the Diversion of Ladies.'

'I cannot conclude my Letter, Dear SPEC, without telling thee one very odd Whim in this my Dream. I saw, methought, a dozen Women employed in bringing off one Man; I could not guess who it should be, till upon his nearer approach I discovered thy short Phiz. The Women all declared that it was for the sake of thy Works, and not thy Person, that they brought thee off, and that it was on condition that thou shouldst continue the *Spectator*. If thou thinkest this Dream will make a tolerable one, it is at thy Service, from,

Dear SPEC,

Thine, Sleeping and Waking,

WILL. HONEYCOMB.'

The Ladies will see, by this Letter, what I have often told them, that WILL. is one of those old-fashioned Men of Wit and Pleasure of the Town, that shews his Parts by Raillery on Marriage, and one who has often tryed his Fortune that way without Success. I cannot however dismiss his Letter, without observing, that the true Story on which it is built does Honour to the Sex, and that in order to abuse them, the Writer is obliged to have recourse to Dream and Fiction.

O[1]

No. 500   *Friday, October 3, 1712*[2]

[ADDISON]

. . . huc natas adjice septem,

Et totidem juvenes, & mox generósque nurúsque.

Quærite nunc, habeat quam nostra superbia causam:

Ov. Met.

SIR,

'YOU, who are so well acquainted with the Story of *Socrates*, must have read how, upon his making a Discourse concerning

---

[1] Beginning with this number Tonson's name is added to the imprint in the original sheets.

[2] *Motto.* Ovid, *Metamorphoses*, 6. 182–4:

> Seven are my daughters of a form divine,
> With seven fair sons, an indefective line.
> Go, fools, consider this, and ask the cause
> From which my pride its strong presumption draws. CROXAL.

Love, he pressed his Point with so much Success that all the Batchelors in his Audience took a Resolution to Marry by the first Opportunity, and that all the married Men immediately took Horse and
galloped home to their Wives.[1] I am apt to think your Discourses,
in which you have drawn so many agreeable Pictures of Marriage,
have had a very good Effect this way in *England*. We are obliged to
you at least, for having taken off that Senseless Ridicule, which for
many Years the Witlins of the Town have turned upon their Fathers
and Mothers. For my own part, I was born in Wedlock, and I don't
care who knows it: For which Reason, among many others, I should
look upon my self as a most Insufferable Coxcomb, did I endeavour
to maintain that Cuckoldom was inseparable from Marriage, or to
make use of *Husband* and *Wife* as Terms of Reproach. Nay, Sir, I will
go one Step further, and declare to you before the whole World,
that I am a married Man, and at the same time I have so much
Assurance as not to be ashamed of what I have done.

'Among the several Pleasures that accompany this State of Life,
and which you have described in your former Papers, there are two
you have not taken Notice of, and which are seldom cast into the
Account, by those who write on this Subject. You must have
observed, in your Speculations on Human Nature, that nothing is
more gratifying to the Mind of Man than Power or Dominion, and
this I think my self amply possessed of, as I am the Father of a
Family. I am perpetually taken up in giving out Orders, in prescrib-
ing Duties, in hearing Parties, in Administring Justice, and in
distributing Rewards and Punishments. To speak in the Language
of the Centurion, *I say unto one, go and he goeth, and to another come
and he cometh, and to my Servant do this and he doeth it.*[2] In short, Sir,
I look upon my Family as a Patriarchal Sovereignty, in which I am
my self both King and Priest. All great Governments are nothing
else but Clusters of these little private Royalties, and therefore
I consider the Masters of Families as small Deputy-Governors presiding over the several little Parcels and Divisions of their Fellow-
Subjects. As I take great Pleasure in the Administration of my
Government in particular, so I look upon my self not only as a more
useful, but as a much greater and happier Man than any Batchelor
in *England* of my own Rank and Condition.

---

[1] Xenophon, *Symposium*, 9, has this conclusion, not immediately following Socrates'
speech, however, but after a performance between Ariadne and Dionysus.
[2] Matt. viii. 9.

'There is another accidental Advantage in Marriage, which has likewise fallen to my Share, I mean the having a multitude of Children. These I cannot but regard as very great Blessings. When I see my little Troop before me, I rejoyce in the Additions which I have made to my Species, to my Country, and to my Religion, in having produced such a number of reasonable Creatures, Citizens, and Christians. I am pleased to see my self thus perpetuated, and as there is no Production comparable to that of an human Creature, I am more proud of having been the Occasion of ten such glorious Productions, than if I had built an hundred Pyramids at my own Expence, or published as many Volumes of the finest Wit and Learning. In what a beautiful Light has the Holy Scripture represented *Abdon*, one of the Judges of *Israel*, who had forty Sons and thirty Grandsons, that rode on Threescore and Ten Ass-Colts, according to the Magnificence of the Eastern Countries?[1] How must the Heart of the old Man rejoice, when he saw such a beautiful Procession of his own Descendents, such a numerous Cavalcade of his own raising? For my own part, I can sit in my Parlour with great Content, when I take a Review of half a dozen of my little Boys mounted upon Hobby-Horses, and of as many little Girls tutoring their Babies, each of them endeavouring to excell the rest, and to do something that may gain my Favour and Approbation. I cannot question but he who has blessed me with so many Children, will assist my Endeavours in providing for them. There is one thing I am able to give each of them, which is a virtuous Education. I think it is Sir *Francis Bacon*'s Observation, that in a numerous Family of Children the eldest is[a] often spoiled by the Prospect of an Estate, and the youngest by being the Darling of the Parent; but that some one or other in the middle, who has not perhaps been regarded, has made his Way in the World, and over-topp'd the rest.[2] It is my Business to implant in every one of my Children the same Seeds of Industry, and the same honest Principles. By this Means I think I have a fair Chance, that one or other of them may grow considerable in some or other way of Life, whether it be in the Army, or in the Fleet, in Trade, or any of the three learned Professions; for you must know, Sir, that from long Experience and

[a] is] are *Fol.*

---

[1] Judges xii. 13–14.
[2] Bacon, 'Of Parents and Children' (*Essays*, ed. W. A. Wright, p. 24).

Observation, I am perswaded of what seems a Paradox to most of those with whom I converse, namely, that a Man who has many Children, and gives them a good Education, is more likely to raise a Family, than he who has but one, notwithstanding he leaves him his whole Estate. For this Reason I cannot forbear amusing my self with finding out a General, an Admiral, or an Alderman of *London*, a Divine, a Physician, or a Lawyer, among my little People who are now perhaps in Petticoats; and when I see the Motherly Airs of my little Daughters when they are playing with their Puppets, I cannot but flatter my self that their Husbands and Children will be happy, in the possession of such Wives and Mothers.

'If you are a Father, you will not perhaps think this Letter impertinent; but if you are a single Man, you will not know the Meaning of it, and probably throw it into the Fire; whatever you determine of it, you may assure your self that it comes from one who is

Your most humble Servant,
and Well-wisher,
Philogamus.'

O

No. 501   *Saturday, October 4, 1712*[1]

[ADDISON; PARNELL]

Durum: sed levius fit patientiâ
Quicquid corrigere est nefas.
Hor.

AS some of the finest Compositions among the Ancients are in Allegory, I have endeavoured, in several of my Papers, to revive that way of Writing, and hope I have not been altogether unsuccessful in it: For I find there is always a great Demand for those particular Papers, and cannot but observe that several Authors have endeavoured of late to excell in Works of this Nature. Among these, I do not know any one who has succeeded better than

---

[1] *Motto.* Horace, *Odes*, I. 24. 19–20:
    'Tis hard: but when we needs must bear,
    Enduring Patience makes the Burthen light. CREECH.

a very ingenious Gentleman, to whom I am obliged for the following Piece, and who was the Author of the Vision in the CCCCLXth Paper.[1]   O[a]

HOW are we tortured with the Absence of what we covet to possess, when it appears to be lost to us! What Excursions does the Soul make in Imagination after it! and how does it turn into it self again, more foolishly fond and dejected, at the Disappointment! Our Grief, instead of having recourse to Reason, which might restrain it, searches to find a further Nourishment. It calls upon Memory to relate the several Passages and Circumstances of Satisfactions which we formerly enjoy'd; the Pleasures we purchased by those Riches that are taken from us; or the Power and Splendour of our departed Honours; or the Voice, the Words, the Looks, the Temper and Affections of our Friends that are deceased. It needs must happen from hence, that the Passion shou'd often swell to such a Size as to burst the Heart which contains it, if Time did not make these Circumstances less strong and lively, so that Reason should become a more equal Match for the Passion, or if another Desire which becomes more present did not overpower them with a livelier Representation. These are Thoughts which I had when I fell into a kind of Vision upon this Subject, and may therefore stand for a proper Introduction to a Relation of it.

I found my self upon a naked Shore, with Company whose afflicted Countenances witnessed their Conditions. Before us flowed a Water deep, silent, and called the River of *Tears*, which issuing from two Fountains on an upper Ground encompassed an Island that lay before us. The Boat which plied in it was old and shattered, having been sometimes overset by the Impatience and Haste of single Passengers to arrive at the other side. This immediately was brought to us by *Misfortune* who steers it, and we were all preparing to take our Places, when there appeared a Woman of a mild and composed Behaviour, who began to deter us from it, by representing the Dangers which would attend our Voyage. Hereupon some who knew her for *Patience*, and some of those too who till then cry'd the loudest, were perswaded by her, and return'd back. The rest of us went in, and she (whose Good-nature wou'd not suffer

[a] *Signature* O] *at end of paper in Fol.*

---

[1] Thomas Parnell. The 'vision' of the Grotto of Grief is reprinted in Parnell's *Poems on several Occasions* (1722), pp. 191–8.

her to forsake Persons in Trouble) desired leave to accompany us, that she might at least administer some small Comfort or Advice while we Sailed. We were no sooner Embarked but the Boat was pushed off, the Sheet was spread, and being filled with *Sighs*, which are the Winds of that Country, we made a Passage to the farther Bank, through several Difficulties of which the most of us seem'd utterly regardless.

When we landed, we perceived the Island to be strangely overcast with Fogs, which no Brightness cou'd pierce, so that a kind of gloomy Horror sat always brooding over it. This had something in it very shocking to easie Tempers, insomuch that some others, whom *Patience* had by this time gain'd over, left us here, and privily conveyed themselves round the Verge of the Island to find a Ford by which she told them they might escape.

For my Part, I still went along with those who were for piercing into the Centre of the Place; and joyning our selves to others whom we found upon the same Journey, we marched solemnly as at a Funeral, through bordering Hedges of Rosemary, and through a Grove of Yeugh-Trees, which love to over-shadow Tombs and flourish in Church-Yards. Here we heard on every side the Wailings and Complaints of several of the Inhabitants, who had cast themselves disconsolately at the Feet of Trees; and as we chanced to approach any of these, we might perceive them wringing their Hands, beating their Breasts, tearing their Hair, or after some other manner visibly agitated with Vexation. Our Sorrows were heightned by the Influence of what we heard and saw, and one of our Number was wrought up to such a pitch of Wildness, as to talk of hanging himself upon a Bough which shot temptingly across the Path we travelled in, but he was restrain'd from it by the kind Endeavours of our abovementioned Companion.

We had now gotten into the most dusky, silent Part of the Island, and by the redoubled Sounds of Sighs, which made a doleful Whistling in the Branches, the Thickness of Air which occasioned faintish Respiration, and the violent Throbbings of Heart which more and more affected us, we found that we approach'd the *Grotto of Grief*. It was a wide, hollow, and melancholly Cave, sunk deep in a Dale, and watered by Rivulets that had a Colour between red and black. These crept slow and half-congealed amongst its Windings, and mixed their heavy Murmur with the Eccho of Groans that rolled through all the Passages. In the most retired Part of it sat the

Doleful Being her self, the Path to her was strowed with Goads, Stings and Thorns, and her Throne on which she sat was broken into a Rock, with ragged Pieces pointing upwards for her to lean upon. A heavy Mist hung above her, her Head oppressed with it reclined upon her Arm, thus did she Reign over her disconsolate Subjects, full of her self to Stupidity, in eternal Pensiveness, and the profoundest Silence. On one side of her stood *Dejection* just dropping into a Swoon, and *Paleness* wasting to a Skeleton; on the other side were *Care* inwardly tormented with Imaginations, and *Anguish* suffering outward *Troubles* to suck the Blood from her Heart in the Shape of *Vultures*. The whole Vault had a genuine Dismallness in it, which a few scattered Lamps, whose blewish Flames arose and sunk in their Urns, discovered to our Eyes with Encrease. Some of us fell down, overcome and spent with what they suffered in the way, and were given over to those Tormentors that stood on either hand of the Presence; others, galled and mortified with Pain, recover'd the Entrance, where *Patience*, whom we had left behind, was still waiting to receive us.

With her (whose Company was now become more grateful to us by the want we had found of her) we winded round the Grotto, and ascended at the Back of it, out of the mournful Dale in whose Bottom it lay. On this Eminence we halted, by her Advice, to pant for Breath, and lifting our Eyes, which till then were fixed downwards, felt a sullen sort of Satisfaction in observing through the Shades what Numbers had entered the Island. This Satisfaction, which appears to have Ill-nature in it, was excusable, because it happened at a time when we were too much taken up with our own Concern to have respect to that of others, and therefore we did not consider them as suffering, but our selves as not suffering in the most forlorn Estate. It had also the ground-work of Humanity and Compassion in it, tho' the Mind was then too dark and too deeply engaged to perceive it; but as we proceeded onwards it began to discover itself, and from observing that others were unhappy, we came to question one another, when it was that we met, and what were the sad Occasions that brought us together. Then we heard our Stories, we compared them, we mutually gave and received Pity, and so by degrees became tollerable Company.

A considerable part of the troublesome Road was thus deceived,[1] at length the Openings among the Trees grew larger, the Air

---

[1] I.e. beguiled, wiled away. *OED* gives quotations from 1591 to 1841.

seemed thinner, it lay with less Oppression upon us, and we could now and then discern Tracts in it of a lighter Greyness, like the Breakings of Day, short in Duration, much enlivening, and called in that Country *Gleams of Amusement.* Within a short while these Gleams began to appear more frequent, and then brighter and of a longer Continuance; the *Sighs,* that hitherto filled the Air with so much Dolefulness, altered to the Sound of common Breezes, and in general the Horrors of the Island were abated.

When we had arrived at last at the Ford by which we were to pass out, we met with those fashionable Mourners who had been ferryed over along with us, and who being unwilling to go as far as we, had coasted by the Shoar to find the Place, where they waited our coming, that by shewing themselves to the World only at the time when we did, they might seem also to have been among the Troubles of the Grotto. Here the Waters, that rolled on the other Side so deep and silent, were much dryed up, and it was an easie matter for us to wade over.

The River being crossed, we were received upon the further Bank by our Friends and Acquaintance, whom *Comfort* had brought out to congratulate our appearance in the World again. Some of these blamed us for staying so long away from them, others advised us against all Temptations of going back again; every one was cautious not to renew our Trouble, by asking any Particulars of the Journey; and all concluded, that in a case of so much Melancholly and Affliction, we could not have made choice of a fitter Companion than *Patience.* Here *Patience,* appearing Serene at her Praises, delivered us over to *Comfort. Comfort* smiled at his receiving the Charge, immediately the Sky purpled on that side to which he turned, and double Day at once broke in upon me.

No. 502   *Monday, October 6, 1712*[1]
[STEELE]

Melius, Pejus, prosit, obsit, nil vident nisi quod lubet.
                                                    Ter.

WHEN Men read, they taste the Matter with which they are
entertained according as their own respective Studies and
Inclinations have prepared them, and make their Reflections
accordingly. Some perusing a *Roman* Writer, would find in them,
whatever the Subject of the Discourses were, Parts which implied
the Grandeur of that People in their Warfare or their Politicks. As
for my Part, who am a meer Spectator, I drew this Morning Conclusions of their Eminence in what I think great, to wit, in having
worthy Sentiments, from the reading a Comedy of *Terence*. The
Play was the *Self-Tormentor*.[2] It is from the Beginning to the End
a perfect Picture of humane Life, but I did not observe in the Whole
one Passage that could raise a Laugh. How well disposed must that
People be, who could be entertained with Satisfaction by so sober
and polite Mirth! In the first Scene of the Comedy, when one of
the old Men accuses the other of Impertinence for interposing in
his Affairs, he answers, *I am a Man, and cannot help feeling any Sorrow
that can arrive at Man.*[3] It is said this Sentence was received with an
universal Applause. There cannot be a greater Argument of the
general good Understanding of a People, than a sudden Consent to
give their Approbation of a Sentiment which has no Emotion in it.
If it were spoken with never so great Skill in the Actor, the Manner
of uttering that Sentence could have nothing in it which could
strike any but People of the greatest Humanity, nay People
elegant and skilful in Observations upon it. It is possible he might
have laid his Hand on his Breast, and with a winning Insinuation
in his Countenance, expressed to his Neighbour that he was a Man
who made his Case his own; yet I'll engage a Player in *Covent-
Garden* might hit such an Attitude a thousand times before he

---

[1] *Motto.* Terence, *Heautontimorumenos*, 643. Be it better or worse, for them or
against them, they see nothing but what they list.
[2] In addition to the motto for this number Steele drew on this play for mottoes
to Nos. 454, 496, 509, and 515.
[3] Lines 75–77. Menedemus is the accuser, and it is Chremes who answers with
the celebrated line, *Homo sum: humani nil a me alienum puto*. The present passage in
the *Spectator* (this sentence and the four following) is quoted in *Guardian* 59 apropos
of Addison's *Cato*: the warm reception given this play has removed from the English
'the Imputation which a late Writer had thrown upon them in his 502d *Speculation*'.

would have been regarded.[1] I have heard that the Minister of State in the Reign of Queen *Elizabeth* had all Manner of Books and Ballads brought to him, of what Kind soever, and took great Notice how much they took with the People; upon which he would, and certainly might, very well judge of their present Dispositions, and the most proper Way of applying them according to his own Purposes.[2] What passes on the Stage, and the Reception it meets from the Audience, is a very useful Instruction of this Kind. According to what you may observe there on our Stage, you see them often moved so directly against all common Sense and Humanity, that you would be apt to pronounce us a Nation of Savages. It cannot be called a Mistake of what is pleasant, but the very Contrary to it is what most assuredly takes with them. The other Night an old Woman carried off with a Pain in her Side, with all the Distortions and Anguish of Countenance which is natural to one in that Condition, was laughed and clapped off the Stage.[3] *Terence's* Comedy, which I am speaking of, is indeed written as if he hoped to please none but such as had as good a Taste as himself. I could not but reflect upon the natural Description of the innocent young Woman made by the Servant to his Master. *When I came to the House*, said he, *an old Woman opened the Door, and I followed her in, because I could by entering upon them unawares better observe what was your Mistress's ordinary Manner of spending her Time, the only Way of judging any ones Inclinations and Genius. I found her at her Needle in a sort of second Mourning, which she wore for an Aunt she had lately lost. She had nothing on but what shewed she dressed only for her self. Her Hair hung negligently about her Shoulders. She had none of the Arts with which others use to set themselves off, but had that Negligence of Person which is remarkable in those who are careful of their Minds*——*Then she had a Maid who was at Work near her, that was a Slattern, because her Mistress was careless; which I take to be another Argument of your Security in her; for the Go-betweens of Women of Intreague are rewarded too well to be dirty. When you were named, and I told her you desired to see her, she threw down her Work for Joy, covered her Face, and decently hid her Tears*——[4] He

---

[1] The allusion to '*Covent-Garden*' is to the general theatre district—to Drury Lane theatre near by, and possibly to Martin Powell's puppet theatre in the Piazzas. Covent Garden theatre was not built until 1732.

[2] Nichols refers to Andrew Fletcher of Saltoun, who is reported to have said: 'I knew a very wise man who believed, that if a man were permitted to make all the ballads, he need not care who should make the laws of a nation.'

[3] This incident has not been identified.

[4] Lines 274–307. The servant is Syrus (servant to Chremes), and he is reporting to Clinia.

must be a very good Actor, and draw Attention rather from his own Character than the Words of the Author, that could gain it among us for this Speech, though so full of Nature and good Sense.

The intolerable Folly and Confidence of Players putting in Words of their own, does in a great measure feed the absurd Taste of the Audience. But, however that is, it is ordinary for a Cluster of Coxcombs to take up the House to themselves, and equally insult both the Actors and the Company. These Savages, who want all manner of Regard and Deference to the rest of Mankind, come only to shew themselves to us, without any other Purpose than to let us know they despise us.

The Gross of an Audience is compos'd of two Sorts of People, those who know no Pleasure but of the Body, and those who improve or command corporeal Pleasures by the Addition of fine Sentiments of the Mind. At present the intelligent Part of the Company are wholly subdued by the Insurrections of those who know no Satisfactions but what they have in common with all other Animals.

This is the Reason that when a Scene tending to Procreation is acted, you see the whole Pit in such a Chuckle, and old Letchers, with Mouths open, stare at the loose Gesticulations on the Stage with shameful Earnestness, when the justest Pictures of Humane Life in its calm Dignity, and the properest Sentiments for the Conduct of it, pass by like meer Narration, as conducing only to somewhat much better which is to come after. I have seen the whole House at some Times in so proper a Disposition, that indeed I have trembled for the Boxes, and feared the Entertainment would end in the Representation of the Rape of the *Sabines*.

I would not be understood in this Talk to argue, that nothing is tolerable on the Stage but what has an immediate Tendency to the Promotion of Virtue. On the contrary, I can allow, provided there is nothing against the Interests of Virtue, and is not offensive to good Manners, that Things of an indifferent Nature may be represented. For this Reason I have no Exception to the well-drawn Rusticities in the *Country-Wake*; and there is something so miraculously pleasant in *Dogget's* acting the awkard Triumph and comick Sorrow of *Hob* in different Circumstances, that I shall not be able to stay away whenever it is acted.[1] All that vexes me is, that the

[1] *The Country-Wake*, by Doggett, was produced at Lincoln's Inn Fields theatre in 1696, with the author in the part of Young Hob. It was revived, in altered form,

Gallantry of taking the Cudgels for *Gloucestershire*, with the Pride of Heart in tucking himself up, and taking Aim at his Adversary, as well as the other's Protestation in the Humanity of low Romance, That he could not promise the Squire to break *Hob*'s Head, but he would, if he could, do it in Love; then flourish and begin: I say, what vexes me is, that such excellent Touches as these, as well as the Squire's being out of all Patience at *Hob*'s Success, and venturing himself into the Crowd, are Circumstances hardly taken Notice of, and the Height of the Jest is only in the very Point that Heads are broken. I am confident, were there a Scene written, wherein *Penkethman* should break his Leg by wrestling with *Bullock*, and *Dicky* come in to set it, without one Word said but what should be according to the exact Rules of Surgery in making this Extention, and binding up the Leg, the whole House should be in a Roar of Applause at the dissembled Anguish of the Patient, the Help given by him who threw him down, and the handy Address and arch Looks of the Surgeon.[1] To enumerate the Entrance of Ghosts, the Embattling of Armies, the Noise of Heroes in Love, with a thousand other Enormities, would be to transgress the Bounds of this Paper, for which Reason[a] it is possible they may have hereafter distinct Discourses; not forgetting any of the Audience who shall set up for Actors, and interrupt the Play on the Stage; and Players who shall prefer the Applause of Fools to that of the reasonable Part of the Company.   T[2]

[a] Reason] *12mo*; Reasons *Fol.*, *8vo*

as a farce at Drury Lane on 6 Oct. 1711 (advertisement in No. 189), with Doggett as Hob, Bullock as Sir Thomas Testy, Pack as Friendly, and Mrs. Santlow as Flora. It was frequently given thereafter, and had just been performed on the Thursday (2 Oct.) preceding the publication of this paper.

Thomas Doggett was an Irish actor, who came to England about 1690 with a travelling company, and in 1702 had a booth at Bartholomew Fair. Besides the part of Hob in his own play, he was famous for his playing of Fondlewife in *The Old Bachelor* and Ben in *Love for Love*, a part which Congreve is said to have written for him. In 1709–11 he was partner with Cibber, Wilks, and Swiney in the management of the Haymarket theatre. Cibber (chap. xiv) says 'he was the most an original, and the strictest observer of nature, of all his contemporaries. . . . His greatest success was in characters of lower life, which he improv'd, from the delight he took, in his observations of that kind, in the real world. In songs, and particular dances too, of humour, he had no competitor' (*Apology*, Everyman's Library ed., p. 252).

In spite of the similar title and similar characters, the two plays are different. The earlier play, *The Country-Wake*, is a comedy; *Hob* is a one-act farce. *Hob, or The Country Wake*, with 'the famous Song perform'd by Mr. Pack, call'd, London City's Triumph; or, my Lord Mayor's Show' was published on 15 Feb. 1714/15 (advertisement in *Post Boy*).

[1] Bullock played Sir Thomas Testy, while 'Dicky' Norris took the part of Dick.
[2] For a Postscript to this number see No. 521. Lillie (ii. 346–8) prints a letter

No. 503   *Tuesday, October* 7, 1712[1]
[STEELE]

Deleo omnes dehinc ex animo Mulieres.

Ter.

Mr. SPECTATOR,

'YOU have often mention'd with great Vehemence and Indignation the Misbehaviour of People at Church;[2] but I am at
present to talk to you on that Subject, and complain to you of one,
whom at the same Time I know not what to accuse of, except it be
looking too well there, and diverting the Eyes of the Congregation
to that one Object. However I have this to say, that she might have
stayed at her own Parish, and not come to perplex those who are
otherwise intent upon their Duty.

'Last *Sunday* was Sevenight I went into a Church not far from
London-Bridge; but I wish I had been contented to go to my own
Parish, I am sure it had been better for me: I say I went to Church
thither, and got into a Pew very near the Pulpit. I had hardly been
accommodated with a Seat, before there entered into the Isle a
young Lady in the very Bloom of Youth and Beauty, and dressed
in the most elegant Manner imaginable. Her Form was such, that
it engaged the Eyes of the whole Congregation in an Instant, and
mine among the rest. Tho' we were all thus fixed upon her, she
was not in the least out of Countenance, or under the least Disorder,
tho' unattended by any one, and not seeming to know particularly
where to place her self. However she had not in the least a confident
Aspect, but moved on with the most graceful Modesty, every one
making Way, till she came to a Seat just over-against that in which
I was placed. The Deputy of the Ward[3] sate in that Pew, and she
stood opposite to him; and at a Glance into the Seat, tho' she did
not appear the least acquainted with the Gentleman, was let in,
with a Confusion that spoke much Admiration at the Novelty of
the Thing. The Service immediately began, and she composed her

signed T. S. and dated 9 Oct. 1712 which comments on this paper and observes
'how great a share our vicious theatre contributes to the general debauchery of the
nation'.
    [1] *Motto.* Terence, *Eunuchus,* 296: From henceforth I blot the whole female sex
from my thoughts.
    [2] For earlier papers on this topic see Nos. 53 (vol. i), 158, 242, 259, 270, 282
(vol. ii), 284 (vol. iii), and 460.
    [3] In the City of London, a member of the Common Council who acts instead of
an alderman in his absence (*OED*).

self for it with an Air of so much Goodness and Sweetness, that the Confession, which she uttered so as to be heard where I sate, appeared an Act of Humiliation more than she had Occasion for. The Truth is, her Beauty had something so innocent, and yet so sublime, that we all gazed upon her like a Phantom. None of the Pictures which we behold of the best *Italian* Painters, have any Thing like the Spirit which appeared in her Countenance, at the different Sentiments expressed in the several Parts of divine Service: That Gratitude and Joy at a Thanksgiving, that Lowliness and Sorrow at the Prayers for the Sick and Distressed, that Triumph at the Passages which gave Instances of the divine Mercy, which appeared respectively in her Aspect, will be in my Memory to my last Hour. I protest to you, Sir, she suspended the Devotion of every one around her; and the Ease she did every Thing with, soon dispersed the churlish Dislike and Hesitation in approving what is excellent, too frequent amongst us, to a general Attention and Entertainment in observing her Behaviour. All the While that we were gazing at her she took Notice of no Object about her, but had an Art of seeming awkardly attentive, whatever else her Eyes were accidentally thrown upon. One Thing indeed was particular, she stood the whole Service, and never kneeled or sate; I do not question but that was to shew her self with the greater Advantage, and set forth to better Grace her Hands and Arms, lifted up with the most ardent Devotion, and her Bosom, the fairest that ever was seen, bare to Observation; while she, you must think, knew nothing of the Concern she gave others, any other than as an Example of Devotion, that threw her self out, without Regard to Dress or Garment, all Contrition, and loose of all worldly Regards, in Extasy of Devotion. Well, now the Organ was to play a Voluntary, and she was so skilful in Musick, and so touched with it, that she kept Time, not only with some Motion of her Head, but also with a different Air in her Countenance. When the Musick was strong and bold, she looked exalted, but serious; when lively and airy, she was smiling and gracious; when the Notes were more soft and languishing, she was kind and full of Pity. When she had now made it visible to the whole Congregation, by her Motion and Ear, that she could dance, and she wanted now only to inform us that she could sing too, when the Psalm was given out, her Voice was distinguished above all the rest, or rather People did not exert their own in order to hear her. Never was any heard so sweet and so strong. The Organist observed it, and he thought fit to play to her only, and she swelled every Note; when she found she had thrown us all out, and had the last Verse to herself in such a Manner, as the whole Congregation was intent upon her, in the same Manner as you see in Cathedrals they are on the Person who sings alone the Anthem. Well, it came at last to the Sermon, and our young Lady would not lose her Part in that neither; for she fixed her Eye upon the Preacher, and as he said any thing she approved, with one of *Charles Mathers*'s fine Tablets she set down the Sentence, at once shewing her fine Hand, the Gold-Pen, her Readiness in Writing, and her Judgment in chusing what to write.[1] To sum up what I intend by this long and particular Account, I mean to appeal to you, whether it is reasonable that such a Creature as this shall come from a janty[2] Part of the Town, and give herself such violent Airs, to the Disturbance of an innocent and inoffensive Congregation, with her Sublimities.[3] The Fact, I assure you, was as I have related; but I had like to have forgot another very considerable Particular. Assoon as Church was done, she immediately stept out of her Pew, and fell into the finest pitty-pat Air, forsooth, wonderfully out of Countenance, tossing her Head up and down as she swam along the Body of the Church. I, with several others of the Inhabitants, follow'd her out, and saw her hold up her Fan to an Hackney-Coach at a Distance, who immediately came up to her, and she whipp'd into it with great Nimbleness, pull'd the Door with a bowing Mein, as if she had been used to a better Glass. She said aloud, *You know where to go*, and drove off. By this Time the best of the Congregation was at the Church-Door, and I could hear some say, *A very fine Lady*; others, *I'll warrant ye, she's no better than she shou'd be*; and one very wise old Lady said, *She ought to have been taken up.* Mr. SPEC-TATOR, I think this Matter lies wholly before you; for the Offence does not come under any Law, tho' it is apparent this Creature came among us only to give herself Airs, and enjoy her full Swing in being admired. I desire you would print this, that she may be confin'd to her own Parish; for I can assure you, there is no attending any thing else in a Place where she is a Novelty. She has been talk'd of among us ever since under the Name of the *Phantom*: But

---

[1] For Mather see No. 328 (vol. iii).
[2] Here used in its original meaning of 'well-bred, genteel'.
[3] 'High dignity of office, vocation, or the like. 1594–a 1727' (*OED*).

I would advise her to come no more; for there is so strong a Party made by the Women against her, that she must expect they will not be excell'd a second Time in so outragious a Manner without doing her some Insult. Young Women, who assume after this rate, and affect exposing themselves to View in Congregations at t'other End of the Town, are not so mischievous, because they are rivall'd by more of the same Ambition, who will not let the rest of the Company be particular: But, in the Name of the whole Congregation where I was, I desire you to keep these agreeable Disturbances out of the City, where Sobriety of Manners is still preserv'd, and all Glaring and ostentatious Behaviour, even in Things laudable, discountenanc'd. I wish you may never see the Phantom, and am,

SIR,

Your most humble Servant,

Ralph Wonder.'

T

No. 504   *Wednesday, October 8, 1712*[1]

[STEELE]

Lepus tute es, & pulpamentum quæris.

Ter.

IT is a great Convenience to those who want Wit to furnish out a Conversation, that there is something or other in all Companies where it is wanted substituted in its Stead, which, according to their Taste does the Business as well. Of this Nature is the agreeable Pastime in Country-Halls of Cross-Purposes, Questions and Commands, and the like.[2] A little superior to these are those who can play at Crambo,[3] or cap Verses. Then above them are such as can make Verses, that is Rhime; and among those who have the Latin Tongue, such as used to make what they call golden Verses.[4]

---

[1] *Motto.* Terence, *Eunuchus,* 426: You are a hare yourself and yet are looking for game.   [2] See No. 245 (vol. ii).   [3] See No. 63 (vol. i).
[4] In Latin prosody a balanced line, with a pair of nouns, each with an adjective and connected with a single verb. Cf. Dryden, Preface to *Sylvia* (1685): 'that verse commonly which they call golden, or two substantives and two adjectives, with a verb betwixt them to keep the peace' (*Essays,* ed. Ker, i. 255). Leonard Welsted (*Remarks on Longinus,* 1712, p. 173) refers to 'what they call the *Golden* Verse' as 'at best but a *Monkish* Invention'.

Commend me also to those who have not Brains enough for any of these Exercises, and yet do not give up their Pretensions to Mirth. These can slap you on the Back unawares, laugh loud, ask you how you do with a Twang[1] on your Shoulders, say you are dull to Day, and laugh a Voluntary to put you in Humour; the laborious Way among the minor Poets, of making things come into such and such a Shape, as that of an Egg, an Hand, an Ax,[2] or any thing that no Body had ever thought on before for that Purpose, or which would have cost a great deal of Pains to accomplish it if they did. But all these Methods, tho' they are mechanical, and may be arrived at with the smallest Capacity, do not serve an honest Gentleman who wants Wit for his ordinary Occasions; therefore it is absolutely necessary that the Poor in Imagination should have something which may be serviceable to them at all Hours upon all common Occurrences. That which we call Punning is therefore greatly affected by Men of small Intellects.[3] These Men need not be concerned with you for the whole Sentence, but if they can say a quaint thing, or bring in a Word which sounds like any one Word you have spoken to them, they can turn the Discourse, or distract you so that you cannot go on, and by Consequence if they cannot be as witty as you are, they can hinder your being any wittier than they are. Thus if you talk of a Candle, he *can deal* with you; and if you ask to help you to some Bread, a Punster should think himself very ill *bred* if he did not; and if he is not as well *bred* as your self, he hopes for *Grains* of Allowance. If you do not understand that last Fancy, you must recollect that Bread is made of Grain; and so they go on for ever, without Possibility of being exhausted.

There are another Kind of People of small Faculties, who supply want of Wit with want of Breeding; and because Women are both by Nature and Education more offended at any thing which is immodest than we Men are, these are ever harping upon things they ought not to allude to, and deal mightily in double Meanings. Every one's own Observation will suggest Instances enough of this Kind, without my mentioning any; for your double Meaners are dispersed up and down through all Parts of Town or City where there are any to offend, in order to set off themselves. These Men

---

[1] 'A ringing or resounding blow' (*OED*). This is the first example given of this word.

[2] See No. 58 (vol. i).

[3] See No. 59 (vol. i). *Pinkethman's Jests* (2nd ed., 1721, i. 110-20) includes a collection of contemporary puns.

are mighty loud Laughers, and held very pretty Gentlemen with the sillier and unbred Part of Womankind. But above all already mentioned, or any who ever were, or ever can be in the World, the happiest and surest to be pleasant are a Sort of People whom we have not indeed lately heard much of, and those are your *Biters*.[1]

A Biter is one who tells you a thing you have no Reason to disbelieve in it self; and perhaps has given you, before he bit you, no Reason to disbelieve it for his saying it; and if you give him Credit, laughs in your Face, and triumphs that he has deceived you. In a Word, a Biter is one who thinks you a Fool, because you do not think him a Knave. This Description of him one may insist upon to be a just one, for what else but a Degree of Knavery is it, to depend upon Deceit for what you gain of another, be it in Point of Wit, or Interest, or any thing else?

This Way of Wit is called *Biting*, by a Metaphor taken from Beasts of Prey, which devour harmless and unarm'd Animals, and look upon them as their Food wherever they meet them. The Sharpers about Town very ingeniously understood themselves to be to the undesigning Part of Mankind what Foxes are to Lambs, and therefore used the Word *Biting* to express any Exploit wherein they had over-reach'd any innocent and inadvertent Man of his Purse. These Rascals of late Years have been the Gallants of the Town, and carry'd it with a fashionable haughty Air, to the Discouragement of Modesty and all honest Arts. Shallow Fops, who are govern'd by the Eye, and admire every thing that struts in Vogue, took up from the Sharpers the Phrase of *Biting*, and used it upon all Occasions, either to disown any nonsensical Stuff they should talk themselves, or evade the Force of what was reasonably said by others. Thus when one of these cunning Creatures was enter'd into a Debate with you, whether it was practicable in the present State of Affairs to accomplish such a Proposition, and you thought he had let fall what destroy'd his Side of the Question, as soon as you look'd with an Earnestness ready to lay hold of it, he immediately cry'd, *Bite*, and you were immediately to acknowledge all that Part was in Jest. They carry this to all the Extravagance imaginable, and if one of these Witlings knows any Particulars which may give Authority to what he says, he is still the more ingenious if he imposes upon your Credulity. I remember a remarkable Instance of this Kind. There came up a shrewd young

---

[1] See No. 47 (vol. i), and *Tatler* 12.

Fellow to a plain young Man, his Countryman, and taking him aside with a grave concern'd Countenance, goes on at this rate: I see you here, and have you heard nothing out of *Yorkshire*—You look so surpriz'd you could not have heard of it—and yet the Particulars are such, that it cannot be false: I am sorry I am got into it so far, that I now must tell you; but I know not but it may be for your Service to know—On *Tuesday* last, just after Dinner—you know his Manner is to smoke, opening his Box, your Father fell down dead in an Apoplexy. The Youth shew'd the filial Sorrow which he ought—Upon which the witty Man cry'd, *Bite, there was nothing in all this*—

To put an End to this silly, pernicious, frivolous Way at once, I will give the Reader one late Instance of a Bite, which no Biter for the future will ever be able to equal, tho' I heartily wish him the same Occasion. It is a Superstition with some Surgeons, who beg the Bodies of condemn'd Malefactors, to go to the Goal, and bargain for the Carkass with the Criminal himself. A good honest Fellow did so last Sessions, and was admitted to the condemn'd Men on the Morning wherein they died. The Surgeon communicated his Business, and fell into Discourse with a little Fellow, who refused Twelve Shillings, and insisted upon Fifteen for his Body. The Fellow, who kill'd the Officer of *Newgate*,[1] very forwardly, and like a Man who was willing to deal, told him, Look you, Mr. Surgeon, that little dry Fellow, who has been half-starv'd all his Life, and is now half-dead with Fear, cannot answer your Purpose. I have ever live high and freely, my Veins are full, I have not pined in Imprisonment; you see my Crest swells to your Knife, and after *Jack-Catch* has done, upon my Honour you'll find me as sound as e'er a Bullock in any of the Markets.[2] Come, for Twenty Shillings I am your Man—Says the Surgeon, Done, there's a Guinea—This witty Rogue took the Money, and assoon as he had it in his Fist, cries, *Bite, I am to be hang'd in Chains.*[3]

T

[1] The old prison for criminals and debtors, situated at the west end of Newgate street, opposite the Old Bailey.

[2] The original Jack Ketch, the hangman, had died in 1686. According to *OED* the popularity of the name (sometimes written *Catch* and *Kitch*) was owing to the fact that it was given to the hangman in the puppet-play of Punchinello, introduced from Italy shortly after Ketch's death.

[3] Hanging in chains, or 'gibbeting', though not recognized by statute until 1752, had long been the sentence for the worst cases of murder. By this practice the body of the criminal remained hanging in chains near the scene of his crime. By the act of 1752, 'in atrocious cases it was frequently usual for the court to direct the murderer,

[ADDISON]

Non habeo denique nauci Marsum Augurem,
Non vicanos Aruspices, non de Circo Astrologos,
Non Isiacos Conjectores, non Interpretes somniûm:
Non enim sunt ii aut scientiâ, aut arte Divini,
Sed superstitiosi vates, impudentesque harioli,
Aut inertes, aut insani, aut quibus egestas imperat:
Qui sui quæstûs causâ fictas suscitant sententias,
Qui sibi semitam non sapiunt, alteri monstrant viam,
Quibus divitias pollicentur, ab iis drachmam petunt;
De divitiis deducant drachmam, reddant cætera.

Ennius.

THOSE who have maintained that Men would be more miserable than Beasts, were their Hopes confined to this Life only;
among other Considerations take Notice, that the latter are only
afflicted with the Anguish of the present Evil, whereas the former
are very often pained by the Reflection on what is passed, and the
Fear of what is to come. This Fear of any Future Difficulties or
Misfortunes is so natural to the Mind, that were a Man's Sorrows
and Disquietudes summed up at the End of his Life, it would
generally be found that he had suffered more from the Apprehensions of such Evils as never happened to him, than from those Evils

---

after execution, to be hung upon a gibbet in chains, near the place where the fact
was committed' (Blackstone, *Commentaries*, book iv, chap. xiv (ed. Oxford, 1769, iv.
202)). The judge had the option of ordering the malefactor to be hung in chains or
given over to surgeons to be dissected.

   [1] *Motto*. Ennius, quoted in Cicero, *De divinatione*, i. 58. 132 (altered):
> I mind not this—for all your Marsian Augurs;
> Your Village, Market-hunting Fortune-Tellers;
> Astrologers, Divining-Priests of Isis,
> Or Dream Expounders: For they are not Men
> Inspir'd by Heav'n, or of superiour Knowledge;
> But superstitious, impudent Pretenders,
> Vile lazy Slaves, Madmen or needy Varlets,
> Whose counterfeit Predictions spring from want:
> Know not their own way, yet point out anothers,
> Promising Treasures at a Drachma's Price,
> Then by so much lessen their Client's Stock;
> And leave them all the rest in Expectation.

which had really befallen him. To this we may add, that among those Evils which befall us, there are many that have been more painful to us in the Prospect, than by their actual Pressure.

This natural Impatience to look into Futurity, and to know what Accidents may happen to us hereafter, has given Birth to many[a] ridiculous Arts and Inventions. Some found their Prescience on the Lines of a Man's Hand, others on the Features of his Face; some on the Signatures which Nature has impressed on his Body, and others on his own Hand Writing: Some read Mens Fortunes in the Stars, as others have searched after them in the Entrails of Beasts, or the Flights of Birds. Men of the best Sense have been touched, more or less, with these Groundless Horrors and Presages of Futurity, upon surveying the most indifferent Works of Nature. Can any thing be more surprising than to consider *Cicero*, who made the greatest Figure at the Bar, and in the Senate of the *Roman* Commonwealth, and, at the same time, outshined all the Philosophers of Antiquity in his Library and in his Retirements, as busying himself in the College of Augurs, and observing, with a religious Attention, after what manner the Chickens peckt the several Grains of Corn which were thrown to them?[1]

Notwithstanding these Follies are pretty well worn out of the Minds of the Wise and Learned in the present Age, Multitudes of weak and ignorant Persons are still Slaves to them. There are Numberless Arts of Prediction among the Vulgar, which are too trifling to enumerate, and infinite Observations of Days, Numbers, Voices, and Figures, which are regarded by them as Portents and Prodigies.[b] In short, every thing prophesies to the superstitious Man, there is scarce a Straw or a rusty piece of Iron that lies in his way by Accident.

It is not to be conceived how many Wizards, Gypsies and Cunning Men are dispersed through all the Countries and Market Towns of *Great Britain*, not to mention the Fortune-Tellers and Astrologers, who live very comfortably upon the Curiosity of several well-disposed Persons in the Cities of *London* and *Westminster*.[2]

Among the many pretended Arts of Divination, there is none which so universally amuses as that by Dreams. I have indeed

[a] many] a thousand *Fol*.　　[b] Prodigies.] Prodigies; *Fol*.

---

[1] Cicero, *De legibus*, 2. 13. 32–33; *De natura deorum* 2. 65. 163.
[2] See No. 131 (vol. ii).

observed in a late Speculation[1] that there have been sometimes, upon very Extraordinary Occasions, supernatural Revelations made to certain Persons by this means; but as it is the chief Business of this Paper to root out popular Errors, I must endeavour to expose the Folly and Superstition of those Persons, who, in the common and ordinary Course of Life, lay any stress upon things of so uncertain, shadowy and chimerical a Nature. This I cannot do more effectually than by the following Letter, which is dated from a Quarter of the Town[2] that has always been the Habitation of some prophetick *Philomath*;[3] it having been usual, Time out of Mind, for all such People as have lost their Wits, to resort to that Place either for their Cure or for their Instruction.

Moor-Fields,[4] October 4, 1712.

Mr. SPECTATOR,

'HAVING long considered whether there be any Trade wanting in this great City, after having surveyed very attentively all kinds of Ranks and Professions, I do not find in any Quarter of the Town an *Oneirocritick*,[5] or, in plain *English*, an Interpreter of Dreams. For want of so useful a Person, there are several good People who are very much puzled in this Particular, and dream a whole Year together without being ever the wiser for it. I hope I am pretty well qualified for this Office, having studied by Candle-light all the Rules of Art which have been laid down upon this Subject. My great Uncle by my Wife's side was a *Scotch* Highlander, and second-sighted.[6] I have four Fingers and two Thumbs upon one Hand, and was born on the longest Night of the Year. My Christian and Sirname begin and end with the same Letters. I am lodged in *Moorfields*, in a House that for this fifty Years has been always tenanted by a Conjuror.

'If you had been in Company, so much as my self, with ordinary Women of the Town, you must know that there are many of them who every Day in their Lives, upon seeing or hearing of any thing that is unexpected, cry *my Dream is out*; and cannot go to sleep in

---

[1] No. 487.   [2] Bedlam was then in Moorfields.
[3] Literally 'lover of learning', but popularly applied to an astrologer or prognosticator.
[4] Cf. No. 193 (vol. ii). Hatton (p. 57) describes it as marked by 'pleasant Walks and Green Fields of firm Ground, where is a good Air of no small Advantage to the Hospital of Lunaticks, called *Bedlam*'.
[5] Literally 'an interpreter of dreams'.
[6] Doubtless a reference to Duncan Campbell, the fortune-teller and 'dumb conjurer' of No. 31. See also No. 474.

quiet the next Night, 'till something or other has happened which has expounded the Visions of the preceding one. There are others who are in very great Pain for not being able to recover the Circumstances of a Dream, that made strong Impressions upon them while it lasted. In short, Sir, there are many whose waking Thoughts are wholly employed on their sleeping ones. For the Benefit therefore of this curious and inquisitive Part of my Fellow-Subjects, I shall in the first place tell those Persons what they dreamt of, who fancy they never dream at all. In the next place, I shall make out any Dream, upon hearing a single Circumstance of it; and in the last place, shall expound to them the good or bad Fortune which such Dreams portend. If they do not presage good Luck, I shall desire nothing for my Pains; not questioning at the same time that those who consult me will be so reasonable as to afford me a moderate Share out of any considerable Estate, Profit or Emolument which I shall thus discover to them. I Interpret to the Poor for nothing, on condition that their Names may be inserted in publick Advertisements, to attest the Truth of such my Interpretations. As for People of Quality or others who are indisposed, and do not care to come in Person, I can interpret their Dreams by seeing their Water. I set aside one Day in the Week for Lovers; and interpret by the Great[1] for any Gentlewoman who is turned of Sixty, after the rate of half a Crown *per* Week, with the usual Allowances for good Luck. I have several Rooms and Apartments fitted up, at reasonable Rates, for such as have not Conveniencies for dreaming at their own Houses.

'*N. B.* I am not dumb.

Titus Trophonius.'[2]

O

---

[1] This phrase, 'at a fixed price for the whole amount', is now only dialectal (*OED*). See No. 22 (vol. i).

[2] Trophonius was the builder of the first temple of Apollo at Delphi and himself the possessor of an oracle. See Fontenelle's *Dialogues des Morts* (1683) and *Histoire des Oracles* (1687). Cf. also Nos. 598 and 599 (vol. v).

> *Candida perpetuo reside, Concordia, lecto,*
> *Tamque pari semper sit Venus æqua jugo.*
> *Diligat illa senem quondam: Sed & ipsa marito,*
> *Tunc quoque cum fuerit, non videatur anus.*
> Mart.

THE following Essay is written by the Gentleman, to whom the World is obliged for those several Excellent Discourses which have been marked with the Letter X.[2]

I HAVE somewhere met with a Fable that made *Wealth* the Father of *Love*.[3] It is certain a Mind ought, at least, to be free from the Apprehensions of Want and Poverty, before it can fully attend to all the Softnesses and Endearments of this Passion. Notwithstanding we see Multitudes of married People, who are utter Strangers to this delightful Passion, amidst all the Affluence of the most plentiful Fortunes.

It is not sufficient to make a Marriage happy, that the Humours of two People should be alike; I could instance an hundred Pair, who have not the least Sentiment of Love remaining for one another, yet are so like in their Humours, that if they were not already married, the whole World would design them for Man and Wife.

The Spirit of Love has something so extreamly fine in it, that it is very often disturbed and lost, by some little Accidents which the careless and unpolite never attend to, till it is gone past Recovery.

Nothing has more contributed to banish it from a Married State, than too great a Familiarity, and laying aside the common Rules of Decency. Tho' I could give Instances of this in several Particulars, I shall only mention that of *Dress*.[4] The Beaus and Belles about Town, who dress purely to catch one another, think there is no farther Occasion for the Bait, when their first Design has succeeded.

---

[1] *Motto.* Martial, *Epigrams*, 4. 13. 7–10:
> Perpetual Concord bless their Nuptial State,
> And Love and Union make their Joys compleat;
> May she love him in Age, and he behold
> Her, tho' in Years, yet not believe her old.

[2] Steele in No. 555 identifies Eustace Budgell as the author of the papers signed X.

[3] Cf. Plato, *Symposium*, 203B–C.

[4] In No. 302 carelessness in dress had been noted as 'the Bane of conjugal Love'.

But besides the too common Fault in point of Neatness, there are several others which I do not remember to have seen touched upon, but in one of our Modern Comedies, where a *Frenchwoman* offering to undress and dress her self before the Lover of the Play, and assuring his Mistress that it was very usual in *France*, the Lady tells her, that's a Secret in Dress she never knew before, and that she was so unpolished an *Englishwoman*, as to resolve never to learn even to dress before her Husband.[1]

There is something so gross in the Carriage of some Wives, that they lose their Husbands Hearts for Faults, which, if a Man has either good-Nature, or good-Breeding, he knows not how to tell them of. I am afraid, indeed, the Ladies are generally most faulty in this Particular; who, at their first giving into Love, find the way so smooth and pleasant, that they fancy 'tis scarce possible to be tired in it.

There is so much Nicety and Discretion required to keep Love alive after Marriage, and make Conversation still new and agreeable after Twenty or Thirty Years, that I know nothing which seems readily to promise it, but an earnest Endeavour to please on both Sides, and superior good Sense on the part of the Man.

By a Man of Sense, I mean one acquainted with Business and Letters.

A Woman very much settles her Esteem for a Man, according to the Figure he makes in the World, and the Character he bears among his own Sex. As Learning is the chief Advantage we have over them, it is, methinks, as scandalous and inexcusable for a Man of Fortune to be illiterate, as for a Woman not to know how to behave her self on the most ordinary Occasions. It is this which sets the two Sexes at the greatest Distance; a Woman is vexed and surprised, to find nothing more in the Conversation of a Man, than in the Common Tattle of her own Sex.

Some small Engagement at least in Business, not only sets a Man's Talents in the fairest Light, and allots him a Part to Act, in which a Wife cannot well intermeddle, but gives frequent Occasions for those little Absences, which, whatever seeming Uneasiness they may give, are some of the best Preservatives of Love and Desire.

The Fair Sex are so conscious to themselves, that they have nothing in them which can deserve entirely to engross the whole

---

[1] In Steele's *Funeral, or Grief à la Mode* Mlle d'Epingle shocks Lady Harriot by offering to undress before her and Mr. Campley.

Man, that they heartily despise one, who, to use their own Expression, is always hanging at their Apron-Strings.

Lætitia is pretty, modest, tender, and has Sense enough; she married *Erastus*, who is in a Post of some Business, and has a general Taste in most Parts of Polite Learning.[1] *Lætitia*, where-ever she Visits, has the Pleasure to hear of something which was handsomly said or done by *Erastus*. *Erastus*, since his Marriage, is more gay in his Dress than ever, and in all Companies is as Complaisant to *Lætitia* as to any other Lady. I have seen him give her her Fan when it has dropped, with all the Gallantry of a Lover. When they take the Air together, *Erastus* is continually improving her Thoughts, and, with a turn of Wit and Spirit which is peculiar to him, giving her an Insight into things she had no Notions of before. *Lætitia* is transported at having a new World thus opened to her, and hangs upon the Man that gives her such agreeable Informations. *Erastus* has carried this Point still farther, as he makes her daily not only more fond of him, but infinitely more satisfied with her self. *Erastus* finds a Justness or Beauty in whatever She says or observes, that *Lætitia* her self was not aware of; and, by his Assistance, she has discovered an hundred good Qualities and Accomplishments in her self, which she never before once dreamed of. *Erastus*, with the most artful Complaisance[2] in the World, by several remote Hints, finds the Means to make her say or propose almost whatever he has a mind to, which he always receives as her own Discovery, and gives her all the Reputation of it.

Erastus has a perfect Taste in Painting, and carried *Lætitia* with him, the other Day, to see a Collection of Pictures: I sometimes visit this happy Couple. As we were last Week walking in the long Gallery before Dinner, *I have lately laid out some Mony in Paintings,*

---

[1] Lillie (ii. 37–40) prints a letter from an anonymous correspondent, dated 10 Nov. 1712, which praises the *Spectator*'s 'late ingenious essays on the married state' and describes two men who were unwilling 'to allow those many blessings your spectatorial dignity has assign'd, as the necessary consequences of that state, though an Erastus and a Laetitia were to be found in every couple'. The letter describes a tradesman who reprimanded his wife severely because she could not exactly calculate the advantages he might make in his ordinary course of trade.

This, Sir, as it is matter of fact, I presume will more readily claim a place in your daily and never too much to be admired speculations; and more especially to expose the vanity of some of our sex, whose too elated and fond conceit of themselves, have not only carried them beyond the bounds of discretion, but contumeliously to treat the fair sex, whose inward as well as external beauties, justly merit the veneration and esteem of all other created beings in the universe (p. 39).

[2] See No. 103 (vol. i).

says *Erastus*, *I bought that* Venus *and* Adonis *purely upon* Lætitia's *Judgment, it cost me Threescore Guineas, and I was this Morning offer'd an hundred for it.* I turned towards *Lætitia*, and saw her Cheeks glow with Pleasure, while at the same time she cast a Look upon *Erastus*, the most tender and affectionate I ever beheld.

Flavilla married *Tom Tawdry*; she was taken with his laced Coat and rich Sword-knot; she has the Mortification to see *Tom* despised by all the worthy Part of his own Sex. *Tom* has nothing to do after Dinner, but to determine whether he will pare his Nails at St. *James's*, *White's*, or his own House. He has said nothing to *Flavilla* since they were Married, which she might not have heard as well from her own Woman. He however takes great care to keep up the sawcy ill-natured Authority of an Husband. Whatever *Flavilla* happens to assert, *Tom* immediately contradicts with an Oath, by way of Preface; and, *My dear, I must tell you you talk most confoundedly silly. Flavilla* had an Heart naturally as well disposed for all the Tenderness of Love as that of *Lætitia*, but as Love seldom continues long after Esteem, it is difficult to determine, at present, whether the unhappy *Flavilla* hates or despises the Person most, whom she is obliged to lead her whole Life with.   X

No. 507   *Saturday, October* 11, 1712[1]
[ADDISON]

Defendit numerus, junctæque umbone phalanges.

Juv.

THERE is something very Sublime, tho' very Fanciful, in *Plato's* Description of the Supreme Being, that *Truth is his Body, and Light his Shadow.*[2] According to this Definition, there is nothing so contradictory to his Nature as Error and Falshood. The Platonists have so just a Notion of the Almighty's Aversion to every thing which is false and erroneous, that they looked upon *Truth* as no less necessary than *Virtue*, to qualifie an Human Soul for the Enjoyment of a separate State. For this Reason, as they

---

[1] *Motto.* Juvenal, *Satires,* 2. 46: They are protected by their numbers and the close shields of their phalanx.

[2] Cf. Plato, *Republic,* 507B–511E.

recommended Moral Duties to qualifie and season the Will for a future Life, so they prescribed several Contemplations and Sciences to rectifie the Understanding. Thus *Plato* has called Mathematical Demonstrations the Catharticks or Purgatives of the Soul, as being the most proper Means to cleanse it from Error, and to give it a Relish of Truth, which is the natural Food and Nourishment of the Understanding, as Virtue is the Perfection and Happiness of the Will.[1]

There are many Authors who have shewn wherein the Malignity of a *Lie* consists, and set forth, in proper Colours, the Heinousness of the Offence. I shall here consider one Particular Kind of this Crime, which has not been so much spoken to: I mean, that abominable Practice of *Party-lying*.[2] This Vice is so very predominant among us at present, that a Man is thought of no Principles, who does not propagate a certain System of Lies. The Coffee-Houses are supported by them, the Press is choaked with them, eminent Authors live upon them. Our Bottle-Conversation is so infected with them, that a Party-Lie is grown as fashionable an Entertainment, as a lively Catch or a merry Story: The Truth of it is, half the great Talkers in the Nation would be struck dumb, were this Fountain of Discourse dryed up. There is, however, one Advantage resulting from this detestable Practice; the very Appearances of Truth are so little regarded, that Lies are at present discharged in the Air, and begin to hurt no Body. When we hear a Party-story from a Stranger, we consider whether he is a Whig or a Tory that relates it, and immediately conclude they are Words of Course, in which the honest Gentleman designs to recommend his Zeal, without any Concern for his Veracity. A Man is looked upon as bereft of common Sense, that gives Credit to the Relations of Party-Writers, nay his[a] own Friends shake their Heads at him, and consider him in no other Light than as an officious Tool or a well-meaning Ideot. When it was formerly the Fashion to husband a Lie, and trump it up in some extraordinary Emergency, it generally

---

[a] Party-Writers, nay his] Party-Writers, his *Fol.*

---

[1] Plato, *Republic*, 527D–E.
[2] On the Thursday following the appearance of this number (16 Oct.) Arbuthnot's pamphlet is advertised in the *Post Boy* as 'this day published':

Proposals for Printing a very curious Discourse, in Two Vols. in 4to, entitled Ψευδολογία Πολετεκὴ. Or, A Treatise of the Art of POLITICAL LYING, with an Abstract of the First Vol. of the said Treatise. Printed for J. Morphew. 3d.

did Execution, and was not a little serviceable to the Faction that made use of it; but at present every Man is upon his Guard; the Artifice has been too often repeated to take Effect.

I have frequently[a] wondered to see Men of Probity, who would scorn to utter a Falshood for their own particular Advantage, give so readily into a Lie when it is become the Voice of their Faction, notwithstanding they are thoroughly sensible of it as such. How is it possible for those, who are Men of Honour in their Persons, thus to become Notorious Liars in their Party? If we look into the Bottom of this Matter, we may find, I think, three Reasons for it, and at the same time discover the Insufficiency of these Reasons to justifie so Criminal a Practice.

In the first place, Men are apt to think that the Guilt of a Lie, and consequently the Punishment, may be very much diminished, if not wholly worn out, by the Multitudes of those who partake in it. Though the Weight of a Falshood would be too heavy for *one* to bear, it grows light in their Imaginations, when it is shared among *many*. But in this Case a Man very much deceives himself; Guilt, when it spreads through Numbers, is not so properly divided as multiplied: Every one is criminal in proportion to the Offence which he commits, not to the Number of those who are his Companions in it. Both the Crime and the Penalty lie as heavy upon every Individual of an offending Multitude, as they would upon any single Person, had none shared with him in the Offence. In a Word, the Division of Guilt is like that of Matter, though it may be separated into infinite Portions, every Portion shall have the whole Essence of Matter in it, and consist of as many Parts as the whole did before it was divided.

But in the second place, though Multitudes, who join in a Lie, cannot exempt themselves from the Guilt, they may from the Shame of it. The Scandal of a Lie is in a manner lost and annihilated, when diffused among several Thousands; as a Drop of the blackest Tincture wears away and vanishes, when mixed and confused in a considerable Body of Water: The Blot is still in it, but is not able to discover it self. This is certainly a very great Motive to several Party-Offenders, who avoid Crimes, not as they are prejudicial to their Virtue, but to their Reputation. It is enough to shew the Weakness of this Reason, which palliates Guilt without removing it, that every Man, who is influenced by it, declares himself in

[a] frequently] often Fol.

effect an infamous Hypocrite, prefers the Appearance of Virtue to its Reality, and is determined in his Conduct neither by the Dictates of his own Conscience, the Suggestions of true Honour, nor the Principles of Religion.

The third and last great Motive for Mens joining in a popular Falshood, or, as I have hitherto called it, a Party-Lie, notwithstanding they are convinced of it as such, is the doing Good to a Cause which every Party may be supposed to look upon as the most meritorious. The Unsoundness of this Principle has been so often exposed, and is so universally acknowledged, that a Man must be an utter Stranger to the Principles, either of natural Religion or Christianity, who suffers himself to be guided by it. If a Man might promote the supposed Good of his Country by the blackest Calumnies and Falshoods, our Nation abounds more in Patriots than any other of the Christian World. When *Pompey* was desired not to set Sail in a Tempest that would hazard his Life, *It is necessary for me*, says he, *to Sail, but it is not necessary for me to Live:*[1] Every Man should say to himself, with the same Spirit, It is my Duty to speak Truth, tho' it is not my Duty to be in an Office. One of the Fathers has carried this Point so high, as to declare *he would not tell a Lie though he were sure to gain Heaven by it:*[2] However extravagant such a Protestation may appear, every one will own, that a Man may say very reasonably *he would not tell a Lie, if he were sure to gain Hell by it*; or, if you have a mind to soften the Expression, that he would not tell a Lie to gain any Temporal Reward by it, when he should run the hazard of losing much more than it was possible for him to gain.

O

---

[1] Plutarch, *Life of Pompey*, 50. 2.
[2] Cf. St. George Ash, *Two Sermons Preached at Tunbridge-Wells* (1714), p. 17: 'The Primitive Disciples would sooner Die than tell an Untruth . . .; then what a dismal Age of Christianity do we now live in, wherein neither Words, nor Oaths, nor the strictest Laws can bind Men up to Truth?'

No. 508   *Monday, October 13, 1712*[1]
[STEELE]

> *Omnes autem & habentur & dicuntur Tyranni, qui*
> *potestate sunt perpetua, in ea Civitate quæ libertate*
> *usa est.*
>
> Corn. Nepos.

THE following Letters complain of what I have frequently observed with very much Indignation; therefore I shall[a] give them to the Publick in the Words with which my Correspondents, who suffer under the Hardships mentioned in them, describe them.

Mr. SPECTATOR,

'IN former Ages all Pretensions to Dominion have been supported and submitted to, either upon Account of Inheritance, Conquest, or Election; and all such Persons who have taken upon 'em any Soveraignty over their Fellow-Creatures upon any other Account, have been always call'd Tyrants, not so much because they were guilty of any particular Barbarities, as because every Attempt to such a Superiority was in its Nature tyrannical. But there is another Sort of Potentates who may with greater Propriety be call'd Tyrants than those last mention'd, both as they assume a despotick Dominion over those as free as themselves, and as they support it by Acts of notable Oppression and Injustice; and these are the Rulers in all Clubs and Meetings. In other Governments, the Punishments of some have been alleviated by the Rewards of others; but what makes the Reign of these Potentates so particularly grievous, is, that they are exquisite in punishing their Subjects, at the same Time they have it not in their Power to reward 'em. That the Reader may the better comprehend the Nature of these Monarchs, as well as the miserable State of those that are their Vassals, I shall give an Account of the King of the Company I am fallen into, whom for his particular Tyranny I shall call *Dionysius*; as also of the Seeds that sprung up to this odd Sort of Empire.

---

[a] therefore I shall] *8vo*; therefore shall *Fol.*, *12mo*

---

[1] *Motto*. Cornelius Nepos, *De viris illustribus*, 1. 8. 3 (altered): But all are held and accounted tyrants, who hold continual power in that city which was formerly free.

'Upon all Meetings at Taverns, 'tis necessary some one of the Company should take it upon him to get all Things in such Order and Readiness, as may contribute as much as possible to the Felicity of the Convention; such as hastening the Fire, getting a sufficient Number of Candles, tasting the Wine with a judicious Smack, fixing the Supper, and being brisk for the Dispatch of it. Know then that *Dionysius* went thro' these Offices with an Air that seem'd to express a Satisfaction rather in serving the Publick, than in gratifying any particular Inclination of his own. We thought him a Person of an exquisite Palate, and therefore by Consent beseech'd him to be always our Proveditor; which Post, after he had handsomly denied, he could do no otherwise than accept. At first he made no other use of his Power than in recommending such and such Things to the Company, ever allowing these Points to be disputable; insomuch that I have often carried the Debate for Partridge, when his Majesty has given Intimation of the high Relish of Duck, but at the same Time has chearfully submitted, and devour'd his Partridge with most gracious Resignation. This Submission on his Side naturally produc'd the like on ours; of which he in a little Time made such barbarous Advantage, as in all those Matters, which before seem'd indifferent to him, to issue out certain Edicts as uncontroulable and unalterable as the Laws of the *Medes* and *Persians*. He is by turns outragious, peevish, froward, and jovial. He thinks it our Duty for the little Offices, as Proveditor, that in Return all Conversation is to be interrupted or promoted by his Inclination for or against the present Humour of the Company. We feel at present, in the utmost Extremity, the Insolence of Office; however, I being naturally warm, ventur'd to oppose him in a Dispute about a Haunch of Venison. I was altogether for Roasting, but *Dionysius* declared himself for Boiling with so much Prowess and Resolution, that the Cook thought it necessary to consult his own Safety, rather than the Luxury of my Proposition. With the same Authority that he orders what we shall eat and drink, he also commands us where to do it, and we change our Taverns according as he suspects any Treasonable Practices in the settling the Bill by the Master, or sees any bold Rebellion in point of Attendance by the Waiters. Another Reason for changing the Seat of Empire I conceive to be the Pride he takes in the Promulgation of our Slavery, tho' we pay our Club for our Entertainments even in these Palaces of our Grand Monarch. When he has a mind to take the Air, a

Party of us are commanded out by way of Life-Guard, and we march under as great Restrictions as they do. If we meet a neighbouring King, we give or keep the Way according as we are out-number'd or not; and if the Train of each is equal in Number, rather than give Battle, the Superiority is soon adjusted by a Desertion from one of 'em.

'Now, the Expulsion of these unjust Rulers out of all Societies would gain a Man as everlasting a Reputation, as either of the *Brutus*'s got from their Endeavours to extirpate Tyranny from among the *Romans*.[1] I confess my self to be in a Conspiracy against the Usurper of our Club; and to shew my Reading, as well as my merciful Disposition, shall allow him till the Ides of *March* to dethrone himself. If he seems to affect Empire till that Time, and does not gradually recede from the Incursions he has made upon our Liberties, he shall find a Dinner dress'd which he has no Hand in, and shall be treated with an Order, Magnificence, and Luxury, as shall break his proud Heart; at the same Time that he shall be convinced in his Stomach he was unfit for his Post, and a more mild and skilful Prince receive the Acclamations of the People, and be set up in his Room; but, as *Milton* says,

> *These Thoughts*
> *Full Counsel must mature. Peace is despair'd,*
> *And who can think Submission? War then, War*
> *Open, or understood, must be resolv'd.*[2]
>
> I am,
>
> SIR,
>
> Your most obedient humble Servant.'

Mr. SPECTATOR,

'I AM a young Woman at a Gentleman's Seat in the Country, who is a particular Friend of my Father's, and came hither to pass away a Month or two with his Daughters. I have been entertained with the utmost Civility by the whole Family, and nothing has been omitted which can make my Stay easy and agreeable on the Part of the Family: But there is a Gentleman here, a Visitant as I am, whose Behaviour has given me great Uneasinesses. When I first arrived here he used me with the utmost Complaisance;[3] but, for-

---

[1] L. Junius Brutus, the leader of the Romans in expelling the Tarquins, and M. Junius Brutus, who took part in the murder of Julius Caesar.
[2] *Paradise Lost*, i. 659–62 ('For who can think Submission?').
[3] See No. 103 (vol. i).

sooth, that was not with Regard to my Sex, and since he has no Designs upon me, he does not know why he should distinguish me from a Man in things indifferent. He is, you must know, one of those familiar Coxcombs, who have observed some well-bred Men with a good Grace converse with Women, and say no fine things, but yet treat them with that sort of Respect which flows from the Heart and the Understanding, but is exerted in no Professions or Compliments. This Puppy, to imitate this Excellence, or avoid the contrary Fault of being troublesome in Complaisance, takes upon him to try his Talent upon me, insomuch that he contradicts me upon all Occasions, and one Day told me I lied. If I had stuck him with my Bodkin, and behaved my self like a Man, since he won't treat me as a Woman, I had, I think, served him right. I wish, Sir, you would please to give him some Maxims of Behaviour in these Points, and resolve me if all Maids are not in Point of Conversation to be treated by all Batchelours as their Mistresses? If not so, are they not to be used as gently as their Sisters? Is it sufferable, that the Fop of whom I complain should say, as he would rather have such a one without a Groat, than me with the *Indies*? What Right has any Man to make Suppositions of things not in his Power, and then declare his Will to the dislike of one that has never offended him? I assure you these are things worthy your Consideration, and I hope we shall have your Thoughts upon them. I am, tho' a Woman justly offended, ready to forgive all this, because I have no Remedy but leaving very agreeable Company sooner than I desire. This also is an heinous Aggravation of his Offence, that he is inflicting Banishment upon me. Your printing this Letter may perhaps be an Admonition to reform him: Assoon as it appears I will write my Name at the End of it, and lay it in his Way; the making which just Reprimand I hope you will put in the Power of,

SIR,

Your constant Reader,
and humble Servant.'

T

No. 509
[STEELE]

Tuesday, October 14, 1712[1]

Hominis frugi & temperantis functus officium.
Ter.

THE useful Knowledge in the following Letter shall have a Place in my Paper, tho' there is nothing in it which immediately regards the Polite or the Learned World; I say Immediately, for upon Reflection every Man will find there is a remote Influence upon his own Affairs, in the Prosperity or Decay of the Trading Part of Mankind. My present Correspondent, I believe, was never in Print before; but what he says well deserves a general Attention, tho' delivered in his own homely Maxims, and a Kind of Proverbial Simplicity; which Sort of Learning has raised more Estates, than ever were, or will be, from Attention to *Virgil, Horace, Tully, Seneca, Plutarch,* or any of the rest, whom, I dare say, this worthy Citizen would hold to be indeed ingenious, but unprofitable Writers. But to the Letter.

Mr. WILLIAM SPECTATOR.

Broadstreet, Octob. 10. 1712.[2]

SIR,

'I ACCUSE you of many Discourses on the Subject of Money, which you have heretofore promised the Publick, but have not discharged your self thereof. But, forasmuch as you seemed to depend upon Advice from others what to do in that Point, have sate down to write you the Needful upon that Subject.[3] But, before I enter thereupon, I shall take this Opportunity to observe to you, that the thriving frugal Man shews it in every Part of his Expence, Dress, Servants, and House; and I must, in the first Place, complain to you, as SPECTATOR, that in these Particulars there is at this Time, throughout the City of *London,* a lamentable Change from that Simplicity of Manners, which is the true Source of Wealth and

---

[1] *Motto.* Terence. *Heautontimorumenos,* 579: You've done the part of a staid and reserved gentleman.

[2] Broad Street ran northward out of Threadneedle Street toward Gresham College. It is possible that this is a misprint for Bread Street—which would be an appropriate address for Hezekiah Thrift. Hatton (p. 11) says of it: 'This street is now inhabited, mostly with Rich Merchants and Wholesale Traders. . . .'

[3] In *Tatler* 78 'will advise the Needful' is one of the phrases in Lemuel Leger's letter, written in a style 'adapted for the Dispatch of Business, by leaving out insignificant Particles'.

Prosperity. I just now said the Man of Thrift shews Regularity in every thing; but you may, perhaps, laugh that I take Notice of such a Particular as I am going to do, for an Instance, that this City is declining, if their ancient Oeconomy is not restored. The Thing which gives me this Prospect, and so much Offence, is the Neglect of the *Royal Exchange*, I mean the Edifice so called, and the Walks appertaining thereunto.[1] The *Royal Exchange* is a Fabrick that well deserves to be so called, as well to express that our Monarchs highest Glory and Advantage consists in being the Patrons of Trade, as that it is commodious for Business, and an Instance of the Grandeur both of Prince and People. But, alas! at present it hardly seems to be set apart for any such Use or Purpose. Instead of the Assembly of honourable Merchants, substantial Tradesmen, and knowing Masters of Ships, the Mumpers,[2] the Halt, the Blind, and the Lame, your Venders of Trash, Apples, Plumbs, your Ragga-muffins, Rakeshames,[3] and Wenches, have justled the greater Number of the former out of that Place. Thus it is, especially on the Evening-Change; so that what with the Din of Squalings, Oaths, and Cries of Beggars, Men of greatest Consequence in our City absent themselves from the Place. This Particular, by the way, is of evil Consequence; for if the *Change* be no Place for Men of the highest Credit to frequent, it will not be a Disgrace to those of less Abilities to absent. I remember the Time when Rascally Company were kept out, and the unlucky Boys with Toys and Balls were whipped away by a Beadle. I have seen this done indeed of late, but then it has been only to chase the Lads from Chuck,[4] that the Beadle might seize their Copper.

'I must repeat the Abomination, that the Walnut Trade is carry'd on by old Women within the Walks, which makes the Place impassible by reason of Shells and Trash. The Benches around are so filthy, that no one can sit down, yet the Beadles and Officers have the Impudence at *Christmas* to ask for their Box, tho' they deserve the Strapado.[5] I do not think it impertinent to have

---

[1] In Ned Ward's *London Spy*, part iii, which contains an account of a visit to the Royal Exchange, the entrance is described as 'lin'd with *Hawkers, Gardeners, Mandrake-sellers*', and Porters', a '*Pippin-Mongers* Stall' is 'Surmounted with a *Chymists* Shop', and an unflattering picture is given of the various nationalities who frequent the walks (Casanova Society edition, pp. 67–74).
[2] I.e. beggars. *Obs. exc. dial.* or *slang* (*OED*).
[3] A general term of disparagement for disorderly persons. The last example in *OED* is dated *c.* 1840.
[4] Short for 'chuck-farthing'. See No. 466.
[5] Here used in the erroneous sense of 'chastisement by blows'. Cf. *OED*: properly,

mentioned this, because it speaks a Neglect in the Domestick Care of the City, and the Domestick is the truest Picture of a Man every where else.

'But I designed to speak on the Business of Money and Advancement of Gain. The Man proper for this, speaking in the general, is of a sedate plain good Understanding, not apt to go out of his Way, but so behaving himself at home, that Business may come to him. Sir *William Turner*, that valuable Citizen, has left behind him a most excellent Rule, and couched it in very few Words, suited to the meanest Capacity.[1] He would say, *Keep your Shop, and your Shop will keep you.* It must be confessed, that if a Man of a great Genius could add Steadiness to his Vivacities,[2] or substitute slower Men of Fidelity to transact the methodical Part of his Affairs, such a one would outstrip the rest of the World: But Business and Trade is not to be managed by the same Heads which write Poetry, and make Plans for the Conduct of Life in general. So, tho' we are at this Day beholden to the late witty and inventive Duke of *Buckingham*[3] for the whole Trade and Manufacture of Glass, yet I suppose there is no one will aver, that, were his Grace yet living, they would not rather deal with my diligent Friend and Neighbour, Mr. *Gumley*,

'a form of punishment or torture to extract confession in which the victim's hands were tied across his back and secured to a pulley; he was then hoisted from the ground and let down half way with a jerk'.

[1] Sir William Turner, an eminent woollen-draper in St. Paul's Churchyard, knighted in 1662, was Lord Mayor of London in 1669, and president of the two hospitals of Bethlehem and Bridewell; died 9 Feb. 1692/3. He is mentioned several times by Pepys. See Luttrell, i. 410–11, ii. 19, iii. 32; W. D. B. in the *Topographer and Genealogist*, i (1846), 506–7; and H. Askew in *N & Q*, cxlvi (1924), 260. The proverb, which I have not found associated with him, apparently dates from the early seventeenth century (Tilley S392 and Apperson).

[2] Steele had used this word in No. 448 (above, p. 75).

[3] Shortly after the Restoration the Duke took out a patent for manufacturing glass and set up a factory at Lambeth with glass-blowers imported from Venice. (See John Harold Wilson, *A Rake and his Times* [N.Y., 1954], p. 21.) Evelyn (19 Sept. 1676) mentions this in a visit to Lambeth: 'We also saw the *Duke* of *Bouckingams Glasse worke*, where they made huge *Vasas* of mettal as cleare & ponderous & thick as Chrystal; also *Looking-glasses* far larger & better than any that come from *Venice*' (*Diary*, ed. De Beer, iv. 98–99). The products are advertised in the *Post-Man*, 15 Feb. 1699/1700:

Large Looking-glass Plates, the like never made in England before, both for size and goodness, are now made at the old Glass house at Foxhall, known by the name of the Duke of Buckinghams House, Where all persons may be furnished with rough plates from the smallest sizes to those of six foot in length, and proportionable breadth, at reasonable rates.

In *The Lover* (No. 34) Steele estimated that England 'gains fifty thousand pounds a year by exporting this commodity for the service of foreign nations: the whole owing to the inquisitive and mechanic as well as liberal genius of the late Duke of Buckingham'.

for any Goods to be prepared and delivered on such a Day, than he would with that illustrious Mechanick above-mention'd.[1]

'No, No, Mr. SPECTATOR, you Wits must not pretend to be rich; and it is possible the Reason may be, in some Measure, because you despise, or at least you do not value it enough to let it take up your chief Attention; which the Trader must do, or lose his Credit, which is to him what Honour, Reputation, Fame, or Glory is to other Sort of Men.

'I shall not speak to the Point of Cash it self, till I see how you approve of these my Maxims in general: But, I think, a Speculation upon *Many a Little makes a Mickle, a Penny sav'd is a Penny got*,[2] *Penny wise and Pound foolish*,[3] *It is Need that makes the old Wife trot*, would be very useful to the World, and if you treated them with Knowledge would be useful to your self, for it would make Demands for your Paper among those who have no Notion of it at present. But of these Matters more hereafter. If you did this, as you excel many Writers of the present Age for Politeness, so you would outgo the Author of the true Strops of Razors for Use.[4]

'I shall conclude this Discourse with an Explanation of a Proverb, which by vulgar Errour is taken and used when a Man is reduced to an Extremity, whereas the Propriety of the Maxim is to use it when you would say, There is Plenty, but you must make such a Choice, as not to hurt another who is to come after you.

'Mr. *Tobias Hobson*, from whom we have the Expression, was a very honourable Man, for I shall ever call the Man so who gets an Estate honestly. Mr. *Tobias Hobson* was a Carrier, and being a Man of great Abilities and Invention, and one that saw where there might good Profit arise, tho' the duller Men overlooked it; this ingenious Man was the first in this Island who let out Hackney-Horses. He lived in *Cambridge*, and observing that the Scholars rid

[1] An advertisement in *The Lover* (No. 26) of 24 April 1714, advises
That John Gumley hath taken for a Ware-house, and furnished, all the Upper Part of the New Exchange in the Strand, against Half-Moon-street, with the largest and finest Looking-Glasses in Frames, and out of Frames. . . . Also John Gumley's House and Shop the Corner of Norfolk-street, is to be Lett, with the next House to it, having 2 Rooms on a Floor. Note, The said Ware-house is now open'd.

Steele describes it in *The Lover* (No. 34). In December 1714 Gumley's daughter married William Pulteney, afterwards Earl of Bath. Cf. the poem, 'The Looking Glass: On Mrs. Pulteney' (1717), formerly attributed to Pope:

> O could the sire renown'd in glass, produce
> One faithful mirror for his daughter's use!

[2] This was Sir Andrew Freeport's favourite maxim. Cf. No. 2 (vol. i).
[3] Cf. No. 295 (vol. iii).   [4] See No. 428.

hard, his Manner was to keep a large Stable of Horses, with Boots, Bridles, and Whips to furnish the Gentlemen at once, without going from College to College to borrow, as they have done since the Death of this worthy Man: I say, Mr. *Hobson* kept a Stable of forty good Cattle always ready and fit for travelling; but when a Man came for an Horse, he was led into the Stable, where there was great Choice, but he obliged him to take the Horse which stood next to the Stable-Door; so that every Customer was alike well served according to his Chance, and every Horse ridden with the same Justice: From whence it became a Proverb, when what ought to be your Election was forced upon you, to say, *Hobson's Choice.*[1] This memorable Man stands drawn in Fresco at an Inn (which he used) in *Bishopsgate-street*, with an hundred Pound Bag under his Arm, with this Inscription upon the said Bag,

The fruitful Mother of an hundred more.[2]

'Whatever Tradesman will try the Experiment, and begin the Day after you publish this my Discourse to treat his Customers all alike, and all reasonably and honestly, I will ensure him the same Success.

I am,
SIR,
Your loving Friend,
Hezekiah Thrift.'

T

[1] Apperson gives 1649 as the earliest date for the saying, 'Hobson's choice', in a speech by the Earl of Pembroke (*Somers Tracts*, vii. 87). It was well known by the time of the *Spectator*: it is cited by L'Estrange (*Fables and Stories Moraliz'd*, 1699, p. 231), 'The *Crow* had only *Hobson's Choyce* before him; *That, or* Nothing' (Fable 250). The *Flying-Post* of 4 Apr. 1700 advertises *Hobson's Choice: A Poem: In Answer to the Choice lately written by a Person of Quality* (Sold by John Nutt, near Stationers-Hall).
[2] William King, author of *The Art of Cookery*, in an undated letter to Dr. Lister, refers to the 'effigies of that worthy person' (i.e. Hobson) as still to be seen at the Bull-inn in Bishopsgate Street (Chalmers, *English Poets*, ix. 247).

. . . *Si sapis*
Neque præterquam quas ipse amor molestias
Habet, addas; & illas, quas habet, recte feras.
Ter.

I WAS the other Day driving in an Hack[2] thro' *Gerard-street*, when my Eye was immediately catch'd with the prettiest Object imaginable, the Face of a very fair Girl, between Thirteen and Fourteen, fixed at the Chin to a painted Sash, and made part of the Lanskip.[3] It seem'd admirably done, and upon throwing my self eagerly out of the Coach to look at it, it laugh'd, and flung from the Window. This amiable Figure dwelt upon me; and I was considering the Vanity of the Girl, and her pleasant Coquettry in acting a Picture till she was taken Notice of, and raised the Admiration of her Beholders. This little Circumstance made me run into Reflections upon the Force of Beauty, and the wonderful Influence the Female Sex has upon the other Part of the Species. Our Hearts are seized with their Enchantments, and there are few of us, but brutal Men, who by that Hardness lose the chief Pleasure in them, can resist their Insinuations, tho' never so much against our own Interest and Opinion. It is common with Women to destroy the good Effects a Man's following his own Way and Inclination might have upon his Honour and Fortune, by interposing their Power over him in Matters wherein they cannot influence him, but to his Loss and Disparagement. I do not know therefore a Task so difficult in humane Life, as to be Proof against the Importunities of a Woman a Man loves. There is certainly no Armour against Tears, sullen Looks, or at best constrain'd Familiarities in her whom you usually meet with Transport and Alacrity. Sir *Walter Rawleigh* was quoted in a Letter (of a very ingenious Correspondent of mine) on this Subject. That Author, who had lived in Courts, Camps, travell'd

---

[1] *Motto.* Terence, *Eunuchus*, 76–78: If you are wise, add no more troubles to those that love has brought on you, but bear what's already befallen you like a man.

[2] I.e. hackney-coach or carriage. *OED* (which marks this as 'now only *U.S.*') quotes from Steele's *Lying Lover*, III. ii, as the earliest example of the word. I do not find the word there.

[3] Gerard Street, built *c.* 1681, was near Soho, running from Princes Street to Grafton Street. At this time it was a residential district for people of gentility: Hatton (p. 33) calls it 'a regular and spacious street'.

through many Countries, and seen many Men under several Climates, and of as various Complections,[1] speaks of our Impotence to resist the Wiles of Women in very severe Terms. His Words are as follow:

What Means did the Devil find out, or what Instruments did his own Subtlety present him, as fittest and aptest to work his Mischief by? Even the unquiet Vanity of the Woman; so as by Adam's *hearkening to the Voice of his Wife, contrary to the express Commandment of the living God, Mankind by that her Incantation became the Subject of Labour, Sorrow, and Death; the Woman being given to Man for a Comforter and Companion, but not for a Counsellor. It is also to be noted by whom the Woman was tempted: Even by the most ugly and unworthy of all Beasts, into whom the Devil entered and perswaded. Secondly, What was the Motive of her Disobedience? Even a Desire to know what was most unfitting her Knowledge; an Affection which has ever since remained in all the Posterity of her Sex. Thirdly, What was it that moved the Man to yield to her Perswasions?[a] Even the same Cause which hath moved all Men since to the like Consent, namely, an Unwillingness to grieve her, or make her sad, lest she should pine, and be overcome with Sorrow. But if* Adam *in the State of Perfection, and* Solomon *the Son of* David, *God's chosen Servant, and himself a Man endued with the greatest Wisdom, did both of them disobey their Creator by the Perswasion and for the Love they bare to a Woman, it is not so wonderful as lamentable, that other Men in succeeding Ages have been allured to so many inconvenient and wicked Practices by the Perswasions of their Wives, or other beloved Darlings, who cover over and shadow many malicious Purposes with a counterfeit Passion of dissimulate Sorrow and Unquietness.[2]*

The Motions of the Minds of Lovers are no where so well described, as in the Works of skilful Writers for the Stage. The Scene between *Fulvia* and *Curius,* in the second Act of *Johnson's Catiline,* is an excellent Picture of the Power of a Lady over her Gallant.[3] The Wench plays with his Affections; and as a Man of all Places in the World wishes to make a good Figure with his Mistress, upon her upbraiding him with want of Spirit, he alludes to Enterprizes which

---

[a] *Perswasions?*] 8vo; *Perswasions;* Fol., 12mo

---

[1] See No. 373 (vol. iii).
[2] *History of the World,* book i, chap. iii, sec. 4 (ed. 1677, p. 41).
[3] *Catiline,* Act II, scene iii. It seems not to have been performed in 1711–12.

he cannot reveal but with the Hazard of his Life. When he is worked thus far, with a little Flattery of her Opinion of his Gallantry, and Desire to know more of it out of her overflowing Fondness to him, he brags to her till his Life is in her Disposal.

When a Man is thus liable to be vanquished by the Charms of her he loves, the safest Way is to determine what is proper to be done, but to avoid all Expostulation with her before he executes what he has resolved. Women are ever too hard for us upon a Treaty, and one must consider how senseless a thing it is to argue with one whose Looks and Gestures are more prevalent with you, than your Reason and Arguments can be with her. It is a most miserable Slavery to submit to what you disapprove, and give up a Truth for no other Reason, but that you had not Fortitude to support you in asserting it. A Man has enough to do to conquer his own unreasonable Wishes and Desires; but he does that in vain if he has those of another to gratify. Let his Pride be in his Wife and Family, let him give them all the Conveniences of Life in such a manner as if he were proud of them; but let it be his own innocent Pride, and not their exorbitant Desires, which are indulged by him. In this Case all the little Arts imaginable are used to soften a Man's Heart, and raise his Passion above his Understanding; but in all Concessions of this Kind, a Man should consider whether the Present he makes flows from his own Love, or the Importunity of his Beloved: If from the latter, he is her Slave; if from the former, her Friend. We laugh it off, and do not weigh this Subjection to Women with that Seriousness which so important a Circumstance deserves. Why was Courage given to Man, if his Wife's Fears are to frustrate it? When this is once indulged, you are no longer her Guardian and Protector, as you were designed by Nature; but, in Compliance to her Weaknesses, you have disabled your self from avoiding the Misfortunes into which they will lead you both, and you are to see the Hour in which you are to be reproached by herself for that very Complaisance to her. It is indeed the most difficult Mastery over our selves we can possibly attain, to resist the Grief of her who charms us; but let the Heart ake, be the Anguish never so quick and painful, it is what must be suffer'd and passed through, if you think to live like a Gentleman, or be conscious to your self that you are a Man of Honesty. The old Argument, that *You do not love me if you deny me this*, which first was used to obtain a Trifle, by habitual Success will oblige the unhappy Man who gives Way to it, to resign the Cause even of his Country and his Honour.

T[1]

No. 511
[ADDISON]

Thursday, October 16, 1712[2]

Quis non invenit turbâ quod amaret in illâ?

Ov.

Dear SPEC.

'FINDING that my last Letter took, I do intend to continue my Epistolary Correspondence with thee, on those dear confounded Creatures *Women*.[3] Thou knowest, all the little Learning I am Master of is upon that Subject: I never looked in a Book, but for their sakes. I have lately met with two pure[4] Stories for a *Spectator*, which I am sure will please mightily, if they pass through thy Hands. The first of them I found by chance in an *English* Book called *Herodotus*,[5] that lay in my Friend *Dapperwit*'s Window, as I visited him one Morning.[6] It luckily opened in the Place where I met with the following Account. He tells us that it was the Manner among the *Persians* to have several *Fairs* in the Kingdom, at which all the young unmarried Women were annually exposed to Sale. The Men who wanted Wives came hither to provide themselves: Every Woman was given to the highest Bidder, and the Mony which she fetched laid aside for the Publick Use, to be employed as thou shalt hear by and by. By this Means the richest People had the Choice of the Market, and culled out all the most extraordinary Beauties. As soon as the Fair was thus picked, the Refuse was to be distributed among the Poor, and among those who could not go to the Price of a *Beauty*. Several of these married the *Agreeables*, without paying a Farthing for them, unless somebody chanced to think it worth his while to bid for them, in which Case the best Bidder was

---

[1] Austin Dobson (*Selections from Steele*) thought that 'much of this paper reproduces difficulties Steele had experienced in his own domestic life'.

[2] *Motto.* Ovid, *Ars amatoria*, 1. 175: In such a crowd who has not found an object that he likes?

[3] See No. 499.　　　　　　　　　　　　　　　[4] See No. 182 (vol. ii).

[5] Herodotus, *History*, 1. 196. Herodotus relates it of the Babylonians, not the Persians.　　　　　　　　　　　　　　　[6] For Dapperwit see No. 499.

always the Purchaser. But now you must know, Spec. it happened in *Persia*, as it does in our own Country, that there were as many *ugly Women* as *Beauties* or *Agreeables*, so that by Consequence, after the Magistrates had put off a great many, there were still a great many that stuck upon their Hands. In order therefore to clear the Market, the Mony which the Beauties had sold for was disposed of among the Ugly; so that a poor Man, who could not afford to have a Beauty for his Wife, was forced to take up with a Fortune; the greatest Portion being always given to the most Deformed. To this the Author adds, that every poor Man was forced to live kindly with his Wife, or, in Case he repented of his Bargain, to return her Portion with her to the next publick Sale.

'What I would recommend to thee on this Occasion is, to establish such an Imaginary Fair in *Great Britain*; Thou couldst make it very pleasant, by matching Women of Quality with Coblers and Carmen, or describing Titles and Garters leading off in great Ceremony Shopkeepers and Farmers Daughters.[1] Tho' to tell thee the Truth, I am confoundedly afraid that as the Love of Mony prevails in our Island more than it did in *Persia*, we should find that some of our greatest Men would chuse out the Portions, and rival one another for the richest Piece of Deformity; and that on the contrary, the Toasts and Belles would be bought up by extravagant Heirs, Gamesters, and Spendthrifts. Thou couldst make very pretty Reflections upon this Occasion in Honour of the *Persian* Politicks,[2] who took care, by such Marriages, to beautifie the upper part of the Species, and to make the greatest Persons in the Government the most Graceful. But this I shall leave to thy judicious Pen.

'I have another Story to tell thee, which I likewise met with in a Book.[3] It seems the General of the *Tartars*, after having laid Siege to a strong Town in *China*, and taken it by Storm, would set to Sale all the Women that were found in it. Accordingly he put each of them into a Sack, and after having thoroughly considered the Value of the Woman who was inclosed, marked the Price that was demanded for her upon the Sack. There were a great Confluence of Chapmen, that resorted from every Part, with a design to purchase, which they were to do *unsight unseen*. The Book mentions a Merchant in particular, who observing one of the Sacks to be marked pretty

---

[1] As Gregory Smith points out, this may be taken as 'a premonition of the fastidious Will's own fate'.   [2] Here used in the obsolete sense of 'politicians'.
[3] This story is told in Louis Le Comte, *Memoirs and Observations...made in a late Journey through the Empire of China* (1697), pp. 296–8.

high, bargained for it, and carried it off with him to his House. As he was resting with it upon an half-way Bridge, he was resolved to take a survey of his Purchase: Upon opening the Sack, a little old Woman popped her Head out of it, at which the Adventurer was in so great a Rage, that he was going to shoot her out into the River. The old Lady however begged him first of all to hear her Story, by which he learned that she was Sister to a great *Mandarin,* who would infallibly make the Fortune of his Brother-in-Law, as soon as he should know to whose Lot she fell. Upon which the Merchant again tied her up in his Sack, and carryed her to his House, where she proved an excellent Wife, and procured him all the Riches from her Brother that she had promised him.

'I fancy, if I was disposed to dream a second time, I could make a tolerable Vision upon this Plan. I would suppose all the unmarried Women in *London* and *Westminster* brought to Market in Sacks, with their respective Prices on each Sack. The first Sack that is sold is marked with five thousand Pound: Upon the opening of it, I find it filled with an admirable Housewife, of an agreeable Countenance: The Purchaser, upon hearing her good Qualities, pays down her Price very chearfully. The second I would open should be a five hundred Pound Sack: The Lady in it, to our Surprise, has the Face and Person of a Toast: As we are wondering how she came to be set at so low Price, we hear that she would have been valued at ten thousand Pound, but that the Publick had made those Abatements for her being a Scold. I would afterwards find some beautiful, modest and discreet Woman, that should be the Top of the Market; and perhaps discover half a dozen Romps tyed up together in the same Sack, at one hundred Pound an Head. The Prude and the Coquet should be valued at the same Price, tho' the first should go off the better of the two. I fancy thou wouldst like such a Vision, had I Time to finish it; because, to talk in thy own way, there is a Moral in it. Whatever thou may'st think of it, prithee do not make any of thy queer Apologies for this Letter, as thou didst for my last. The Women love a gay lively Fellow, and are never angry at the Railleries of one who is their known Admirer. I am always bitter upon them, but well with them.

Thine,
HONEYCOMB.'

O[1]

For note [1] *see opposite page.*

Lectorem delectando pariterque monendo.
                                    Hor.

THERE is nothing which we receive with so much Reluctance as Advice. We look upon the Man who gives it us as offering an Affront to our Understanding, and treating us like Children or Ideots. We consider the Instruction as an implicit Censure, and the Zeal which any one shews for our Good on such an Occasion as a Piece of Presumption or Impertinence. The Truth of it is, the Person who pretends to advise, does, in that Particular, exercise a Superiority over us, and can have no other Reason for it, but that, in comparing us with himself, he thinks us defective either in our Conduct or our Understanding. For these Reasons, there is nothing so difficult as the Art of making Advice agreeable; and indeed all the Writers, both Ancient and Modern, have distinguished themselves among one another, according to the Perfection at which they have arrived in this Art. How many Devices have been made use of, to render this bitter Potion palatable? Some convey their Instructions to us in the best chosen Words, others in the most harmonious Numbers, some in Points of Wit, and others in short Proverbs.

But among all the different Ways of giving Counsel, I think the finest, and that which pleases the most universally, is *Fable*, in whatsoever Shape it appears.[2] If we consider this way of instructing or giving Advice, it excells all others, because it is the least

---

[1] *Motto.* Horace, *Ars poetica*, 344:
            That in one Line instructs and pleases all. CREECH.

[2] Cf. Addison's remarks on this genre in No. 183.

---

[1] A letter signed J. M. and printed in Lillie (ii. 355–7) points out another example of 'exposing women to publick sale':

> masquerades. where, by reason of the masks, the chapmen are as much disappointed as at China, for on the beauty or deformity of the face, depends the whole fate of the bargain, for you know that most livelily strikes the fancy of the Spectator. It frequently happens in these revels of love, that instead of an imagin'd beauty, which a gentleman flatters himself with, and which he thought lay concealed under the mask, to his great astonishment, after much address, he discovers a wither'd, toothless, wrinkled, face.

J. M. says that an earlier letter of his had been printed in the *Spectator*—probably the first letter in No. 296.

shocking, and the least subject to those Exceptions which I have before mentioned.

This will appear to us, if we reflect, in the first place, that upon the reading of a Fable we are made to believe we advise our selves. We peruse the Author for the sake of the Story, and consider the Precepts rather as our own Conclusions, than his Instructions. The Moral insinuates it self imperceptibly, we are taught by Surprise, and become wiser and better unawares. In short, by this Method a Man is so far over-reached as to think he is directing himself, whilst he is following the Dictates of another, and consequently is not sensible of that which is the most unpleasing Circumstance in Advice.

In the next Place, if we look into Human Nature, we shall find that the Mind is never so much pleased, as when she exerts her self in any Action that gives her an Idea of her own Perfections and Abilities. This natural Pride and Ambition of the Soul is very much gratified in the reading of a Fable; for in Writings of this Kind,[a] the Reader comes in for half of the Performance; Every thing appears to him like a Discovery of his own; he is busied all the while in applying Characters and Circumstances, and is in this respect both a Reader and a Composer. It is no wonder therefore that on such Occasions, when the Mind is thus pleased with it self, and amused[1] with its own Discoveries, that it is highly delighted with the Writing which is the Occasion of it. For this Reason the *Absalon* and *Achitophel* was one of the most popular Poems that ever appeared in *English*.[2] The Poetry is indeed very fine, but had it been much finer it would not have so much pleased, without a Plan which gave the Reader an Opportunity of exerting his own Talents.

This oblique manner of giving Advice is so inoffensive, that if we look into ancient Histories, we find[b] the wise Men of old very often chose to give Counsel to their Kings in Fables. To omit many which will occur to every ones Memory, there is a pretty Instance of this Nature in a *Turkish* Tale, which I do not like the worse for that little Oriental Extravagance which is mixed with it.[3]

---

[a] Kind,] nature, *Fol.*   [b] find] find that *Fol.*

[1] See No. 93 (vol. i).
[2] Quotations from Dryden's poem appear in Nos. 77, 162, and 222.
[3] The story told here is 'The Fable of the Two Owls' in the *Turkish Tales* (Tonson, 1708), pp. 174–6. Addison had quoted from this collection in No. 94.

We are told that the Sultan *Mahmoud,* by his perpetual Wars abroad, and his Tyranny at home, had filled his Dominions with Ruin and Desolation, and half-unpeopled the *Persian* Empire. The Visier to this great Sultan, (whether an Humourist or an Enthusiast we are not informed) pretended to have learned of a certain Dervise to understand the Language of Birds, so that there was not a Bird that could open his Mouth but the Visier knew what it was he said. As he was one Evening with the Emperor, in their Return from hunting, they saw a couple of Owls upon a Tree that grew near an old Wall out of an heap of Rubbish. *I would fain know,* says the Sultan, *what those two Owls are saying to one another; listen to their Discourse, and give me an account of it.* The Visier approached the Tree, pretending to be very attentive to the two Owls. Upon his Return to the Sultan, *Sir,* says he, *I have heard part of their Conversation, but dare not tell you what it is.* The Sultan would not be satisfied with such an Answer, but forced him to repeat Word for Word every thing the Owls had said. *You must know then,* said the Visier, *that one of these Owls has a Son, and the other a Daughter, between whom they are now upon a Treaty of Marriage. The Father of the Son said to the Father of the Daughter, in my hearing, Brother, I consent to this Marriage, provided you will settle upon your Daughter fifty ruined Villages for her Portion. To which the Father of the Daughter replied, Instead of fifty I will give her five hundred, if you please. God grant a long Life to Sultan* Mahmoud! *whilst he reigns over us we shall never want ruined Villages.*

The Story says, the Sultan was so touched with the Fable, that he rebuilt the Towns and Villages which had been destroyed, and from that time forward consulted the Good of his People.

To fill up my Paper, I shall add a most ridiculous Piece of natural Magick, which was taught by no less a Philosopher than *Democritus,* namely, that if the Blood of certain Birds, which he mentioned, were mixed together, it would produce a Serpent of such a wonderful Virtue that whoever did eat it should be skill'd in the Language of Birds, and understand every thing they said to one another.[1]

---

[1] Pliny, *Natural History,* 10. 137. See Bayle, art. 'Democritus', Remark H:

Here follow some other idle Fancies of *Democritus.* He said that the Blood of some Birds, which he named, being mixed together, would bring forth a Serpent of such an admirable virtue, that whosoever did eat it might understand what the Birds said to each other. *Pliny* is in the right to laugh at this Chimera.

Whether the Dervise abovementioned might not have[a] eaten such a Serpent, I shall leave to the Determinations of the Learned.

O[1]

No. 513
[ADDISON]

Saturday, *October* 18, 1712[2]

> . . . *afflata est numine quando*
> *Jam propiore Deo* . . .
>
> Virg.

THE following Letter comes to me from that Excellent Man in Holy Orders, whom I have mentioned more than once as one of that Society who assist me in my Speculations. It is a *Thought in Sickness*, and of a very serious Nature, for which Reason I give it a place in the Paper of this Day.

SIR,

'THE Indisposition which has long hung upon me, is at last grown to such an Head, that it must quickly make an End of me, or of it self. You may imagine, that whilst I am in this bad State of Health there are none of your Works which I read with greater Pleasure than your *Saturdays* Papers. I should be very glad if I could furnish you with any Hints for that Day's Entertainment. Were I able to dress up several Thoughts of a serious Nature, which have made great Impressions on my Mind during a long Fit of Sickness, they might not be an improper Entertainment for that Occasion.

'Among all the Reflections which usually rise in the Mind of a sick Man, who has Time and Inclination to consider his approaching End, there is none more natural than that of his going to appear Naked and Unbodied before him who made him. When a Man

---

[a] might not have] had not *Fol.*

[1] An Advertisement referring to this essay is appended to No. 514. See below, p.330.

[2] *Motto.* Virgil, *Aeneid,* 6. 50–51:
When all the God came rushing on her Soul. DRYDEN.

considers, that, as soon as the vital Union is dissolved, he shall see that Supreme Being, whom he now contemplates at a Distance, and only in his Works; or, to speak more Philosophically, when by some Faculty in the Soul he shall apprehend the Divine Being, and be more sensible of his Presence, than we are now of the Presence of any Object which the Eye beholds, a Man must be lost in Carelessness and Stupidity, who is not alarmed at such a Thought. Dr. *Sherlock*, in his excellent Treatise upon Death, has represented, in very strong and lively Colours, the State of the Soul in its first Separation from the Body, with regard to that Invisible World which every where surrounds us, tho' we are not able to discover it through this grosser World of Matter which is accommodated to our Senses in this Life.[1] His Words are as follow.

'That Death, which is our leaving this World, is nothing else but our putting off these Bodies, teaches us, that it is only our Union to these Bodies, which intercepts the sight of the other World: The other World is not at such a Distance from us, as we may imagine; the Throne of God indeed is at a great remove from this Earth, above the third Heavens, where he displays his Glory to those blessed Spirits which encompass his Throne; but as soon as we step out of these Bodies, we step into the other World, which is not so properly another World, (for there is the same Heaven and Earth still) as a new State of Life. To live in these Bodies is to live in this World; to live out of them, is to remove into the next: For while our Souls are confin'd to these Bodies, and can look only thro' these material Casements, nothing but what is material can affect us, nay, nothing but what is so gross, that it can reflect Light, and convey the shapes and colours of things with it to the Eye: So that though within this visible World, there be a more glorious Scene of Things than what appears to us, we perceive nothing at all of it: for this Vail of Flesh parts the visible and invisible World: But when we put off these Bodies, there are new and surprizing Wonders present themselves to our view; when these material Spectacles are taken off, the Soul with its own naked Eyes sees what was invisible before: And then we are in the other World, when we can see it, and converse with it: Thus St. Paul *tells us,* That when we are at home in the body, we are absent from the Lord; but when we are absent from the body, we are present with the Lord, 2. Cor. 5. 6, 8.[2] *And methinks this is enough to cure us of our Fondness for these Bodies, unless we think it more desirable to be confined to*

---

[1] *A Practical Discourse concerning Death* (1689). The passage quoted is from chap. i, sect. ii, subsect. iii (3d ed., 1690, pp. 46–48).
[2] A free version of 2 Cor. v. 6, 8.

a Prison, and to look through a Grate all our Lives, which gives us but a very narrow Prospect, and that none of the best neither, than to be set at liberty to view all the Glories of the World: What would we give now for the least Glimpse of that Invisible World, which the first step we take out of these Bodies will present us with? There are such things as eye hath not seen, nor ear heard, neither hath it entered into the heart of man to conceive;[1] *Death opens our Eyes, enlarges our Prospect, presents us with a new and more glorious World, which we can never see, while we are shut up in Flesh, which should make us as willing to part with this Veil, as to take the Film off of our Eyes, which hinders our sight.*

'As a thinking Man cannot but be very much affected with the Idea of his appearing in the Presence of that Being *whom none can see and live,*[2] he must be much more affected when he considers that this Being whom he appears before, will examine all the Actions of his past Life, and reward or punish him accordingly. I must confess that I think there is no Scheme of Religion, besides that of Christianity, which can possibly support the most virtuous Person under this Thought. Let a Man's Innocence be what it will, let his Virtues rise to the highest pitch of Perfection attainable in this Life, there will be still in him so many secret Sins, so many human Frailties, so many Offences of Ignorance, Passion, and Prejudice, so many unguarded Words and Thoughts, and in short, so many Defects in his best Actions, that, without the Advantages of such an Expiation and Attonement as Christianity has reveal'd to us, it is impossible that he should be cleared before his Soveraign Judge, or that he should be able *to stand in his Sight.*[3] Our Holy Religion suggests to us the only Means whereby our Guilt may be taken away, and our imperfect Obedience accepted.

'It is this Series of Thought that I have endeavoured to express in the following Hymn, which I have composed during this my Sickness.

I.

WHEN rising from the Bed of Death,
O'erwhelm'd with Guilt and Fear,
I see my Maker, Face to Face,
O how shall I appear?

---

[1] 1 Cor. ii. 9.
[2] Exod. xxxiii. 20.
[3] Ps. v. 5.

II.

If yet, while Pardon may be found,
And Mercy may be sought,
My Heart with inward Horrour shrinks,
And trembles at the Thought;

III.

When thou, O Lord, shalt stand disclos'd
In Majesty severe,
And sit in Judgment on my Soul,
O how shall I appear!

IV.

But thou hast told the troubled Mind,
Who does her Sins lament,
The timely Tribute of her Tears
Shall endless Woe prevent.

V.

Then see the Sorrows of my Heart
Ere yet it be too late;
And hear my Saviour's dying Groans,
To give those Sorrows weight.

VI.

For never shall my Soul despair
Her Pardon to procure,
Who knows thine only Son has dy'd
To make her Pardon sure.

'There is a noble Hymn in *French*, which Monsieur *Bayle* has celebrated for a *very fine one*, and which the famous Author of the *Art of Speaking* calls an *Admirable one*, that turns upon a Thought of the same Nature.[1] If I could have done it Justice in *English*, I would have sent it you translated; it was written by Monsieur *Des Barreaux*,

---

[1] By Jacques Vallée, Seigneur des Barreaux (1602–73). Bayle, art. 'Des Barreaux', Remark EΔ, calls it 'a Devout Sonnet which is known to every Body', and quotes it. The reference to the author of the *Art of Speaking* (Lamy) is also from Bayle: 'The Author of the *Art of Speaking* finds this Sonnet *admirable*.' An English translation, in quatrains, is printed in Lillie (ii. 360–2). It begins:

> Great God! thy judgments we confess,
> On whomsoe'er they fall,
> To be the laws of righteousness,
> And equitable all!

who had been one of the greatest Wits and Libertines in *France*, but in his last Years was as remarkable a Penitent.

> *GRAND Dieu, tes jugemens sont remplis d'équité;*
> *Toujours tu prens plaisir à nous être propice:*
> *Mais j'ai tant fait de mal, que jamais ta bonté*
> *Ne me pardonnera sans choquer ta Justice.*
>
> *Ouy, mon Dieu, la grandeur de mon impieté*
> *Ne laisse à ton pouvoir que le choix du suplice:*
> *Ton interest s'oppose à ma felicité;*
> *Et ta clemence même attend que je perisse.*
>
> *Contente ton desir puis qu'il t'est glorieux;*
> *Offense toy des pleurs qui coulent de mes yeux;*
> *Tonne, frappe, il est temps, rens moi guerre pour guerre.*
> *J'adore en perissant la raison qui t'aigrit:*
> *Mais dessus quel endroit tombera ton tonnerre,*
> *Qui ne soit tout couvert du sang de JESUS CHRIST.*

'If these Thoughts may be serviceable to you, I desire you will place them in a proper Light, and am ever, with great Sincerity,

SIR,

Your, &c.'

O

No. 514   *Monday, October* 20, 1712[1]

[STEELE]

> *Me Parnassi deserta per ardua, dulcis*
> *Raptat Amor; juvat ire jugis qua nulla priorum*
> *Castaliam molli divertitur Orbita Clivo.*

Virg.

Mr. SPECTATOR,

'I CAME home a little later than usual the other Night, and not finding my self inclined to Sleep, I took up *Virgil* to divert me

[1] *Motto.* Virgil, *Georgics*, 3. 291–3:

> But the commanding Muse my Chariot guides;
> Which o're the dubious Cliff securely rides:
> And pleas'd I am, no beaten Road to take:
> But first the way to new Discov'ries make. DRYDEN.

This 'dream-vision' of Parnassus is apparently a contribution; there is no clue to the authorship.

till I shou'd be more dispos'd to Rest. He is the Author whom I always chuse on such Occasions, no one writing in so divine, so harmonious, nor so equal a Strain, which leaves the Mind compos'd, and soften'd into an agreeable Melancholy, the Temper in which, of all others, I chuse to close the Day. The Passages I turn'd to were those beautiful Raptures in his *Georgicks*,[1] where he professes himself entirely given up to the Muses, and smit with the Love of Poetry, passionately wishing to be transported to the cool Shades and Retirements of the Mountain *Hæmus*.[2] I clos'd the Book and went to Bed. What I had just before been reading made so strong an Impression on my Mind, that Fancy seem'd almost to fulfil to me the Wish of *Virgil*, in presenting to me the following Vision.

'Methought I was on a sudden plac'd in the Plains of *Bœotia*, where at the End of the Horizon I saw the Mountain *Parnassus* rising before me. The Prospect was of so large an Extent, that I had long wander'd about to find a Path which shou'd directly lead me to it, had I not seen at some Distance a Grove of Trees, which in a Plain that had nothing else remarkable enough in it to fix my Sight, immediately determin'd me to go thither. When I arriv'd at it, I found it parted out into a great Number of Walks and Allies, which often widen'd into beautiful Openings, as Circles or Ovals, set round with Yews and Cypresses, with Nitches, Grotto's, and Caves plac'd on the Sides, encompass'd with Ivy. There was no Sound to be heard in the whole Place, but only that of a gentle Breeze passing over the Leaves of the Forest, everything beside was buried in a profound Silence. I was captivated with the Beauty and Retirement of the Place, and never so much before that Hour was pleas'd with the Enjoyment of my self. I indulg'd the Humour, and suffer'd my self to wander without Choice or Design. At length, at the End of a Range of Trees, I saw three Figures seated on a Bank of Moss, with a silent Brook creeping at their Feet. I ador'd them as the tutelar[a] Divinities of the Place, and stood still to take a particular View of each of them. The Middlemost, whose Name was *Solitude*, sate with her Arms across each other, and seem'd rather pensive and wholly taken up with her own Thoughts, than any ways griev'd or displeas'd. The only Companions which she

---

[a] tutelar] titular *Fol.*

[1] *Georgics*, 2. 475–89.
[2] A range of mountains separating Thrace and Moesia.

admitted into that Retirement, was the Goddess *Silence*, who sate on her right Hand with her Finger on her Mouth, and on her left *Contemplation*, with her Eyes fix'd upon the Heavens. Before her lay a Celestial Globe, with several Schemes of mathematical Theorems. She prevented my Speech with the greatest Affability in the World: Fear not, said she, I know your Request before you speak it; you would be led to the Mountain of the Muses: The only Way to it lies thro' this Place, and no one is so often employ'd in conducting Persons thither as my self. When she had thus spoken she rose from her Seat, and I immediately plac'd my self under her Direction; but whilst I pass'd thro' the Grove, I cou'd not help enquiring of her who were the Persons admitted into that sweet Retirement. Surely, said I, there can nothing enter here but Virtue and virtuous Thoughts: The whole Wood seems design'd for the Reception and Reward of such Persons as have spent their Lives according to the Dictates of their Conscience and the Commands of the Gods. You imagine right, said she; assure your self this Place was at first design'd for no other: Such it continu'd to be in the Reign of *Saturn*, when none enter'd here but holy Priests, Deliverers of their Country from Oppression and Tyranny, who repos'd themselves here after their Labours; and those whom the Study and Love of Wisdom had fitted for divine Conversation. But now it is become no less dangerous than it was before desirable: Vice has learn'd so to mimick Virtue, that it often creeps in hither under its Disguise. See there! just before you, *Revenge* stalking by, habited in the Robe of *Honour*. Observe not far from him *Ambition* standing alone; if you ask him his Name, he will tell you it is *Emulation* or *Glory*. But the most frequent Intruder we have is *Lust*, who succeeds now the Deity to whom in better Days this Grove was entirely devoted. *Virtuous Love*, with *Hymen*, and the Graces attending him, once reign'd over this happy Place; a whole Train of Virtues waited on him, and no dishonourable Thought durst presume for Admittance; but now! how is the whole Prospect chang'd? and how seldom renew'd by some few who dare despise sordid Wealth, and imagine themselves fit Companions for so charming a Divinity?

'The Goddess had no sooner said thus, but we were arriv'd at the utmost Boundaries of the Wood, which lay contiguous to a Plain that ended at the Foot of the Mountain. Here I kept close to my Guide, being sollicited by several Phantomes, who assur'd me they wou'd shew me a nearer Way to the Mountain of the Muses.

Among the rest *Vanity* was extremely importunate, having deluded infinite Numbers, whom I saw wandering at the Foot of the Hill. I turn'd away from this despicable Troop with Disdain, and addressing my self to my Guide, told her, That as I had some Hopes I shou'd be able to reach up Part of the Ascent, so I despair'd of having Strength enough to attain the Plain on the Top. But being inform'd by her that it was impossible to stand upon the Sides, and that if I did not proceed onwards I should irrecoverably fall down to the lowest Verge, I resolv'd to hazard any Labour and Hardship in the Attempt: So great a Desire had I of enjoying the Satisfaction I hop'd to meet with at the End of my Enterprize!

'There were two Paths, which led up by different Ways to the Summit of the Mountain; the one was guarded by the Genius which presides over the Moment of our Births. He had it in Charge to examine the several Pretensions of those who desir'd a Pass that Way, but to admit none excepting those only on whom *Melpomene*[1] had look'd with a propitious Eye at the Hour of their Nativity. The other Way was guarded by *Diligence*, to whom many of those Persons apply'd who had met with a Denial the other Way; but he was so tedious in granting their Request, and indeed after Admittance the Way was so very intricate and laborious, that many after they had made some Progress chose rather to return back than proceed, and very few persisted so long as to arrive at the End they propos'd. Besides these two Paths, which at length severally led to the Top of the Mountain, there was a third made up of these two, which a little after the Entrance joyn'd in one. This carried those happy Few, whose good Fortune it was to find it, directly to the Throne of *Apollo*. I don't know whether I should even now have had the Resolution to have demanded Entrance at either of these Doors, had I not seen a Peasant-like Man (followed by a numerous and lovely Train of Youth of both Sexes) insist upon Entrance for all whom he led up. He put me in mind of the Country Clown who is painted in the Map for leading Prince *Eugene* over the *Alps*:[2] He had a Bundle of Papers in his Hand, and producing several, which, he said, were given to him by Hands which he knew *Apollo* would allow as Passes, among which, methoughts, I saw some of my own Writing, the whole Assembly was admitted, and gave, by their Presence, a new Beauty and Pleasure to these happy Mansions. I found the Man did not pretend to enter himself, but served as

[1] The muse presiding over tragedy.   [2] See No. 340 (vol. iii).

a kind of Forester in the Lawns to direct Passengers, who by their own Merit, or Instructions he procured for them, had Virtue enough to travel that Way. I look'd very attentively upon this kind homely Benefactor, and forgive me, *Mr.* SPECTATOR, if I own to you I took him for your self. We were no sooner entered but we were sprinkled three times with the Water of the Fountain *Aganippe*,[1] which had Power to deliver us from all Harms, but only Envy, which reach'd even to the End of our Journey. We had not proceeded far in the middle Path when we arrived at the Summit of the Hill, where there immediately appeared to us two Figures, which extreamly engaged my Attention; the one was a young Nymph in the Prime of her Youth and Beauty; she had Wings on her Shoulders and Feet, and was able to transport herself to the most distant Regions in the smallest Space of Time. She was continually varying her Dress, sometimes into the most natural and becoming Habits in the World, and at others into the most wild and freakish Garb that can be imagined. There stood by her a Man full-aged, and of great Gravity, who corrected her Inconsistencies, by showing them in his[a] Mirror, and still flung her affected and unbecoming Ornaments down the Mountain, which fell in the Plain below, and were gathered up and wore with great Satisfaction by those that inhabited it. The Name of the Nymph was *Fancy*, the Daughter of *Liberty*, the most beautiful of all the Mountain Nymphs. The other was *Judgment*, the Offspring of *Time*, and the only Child he acknowledged to be his.[2] A Youth, who sate upon a Throne just between them, was their genuine Offspring; his Name was *Wit*, and his Seat was compos'd of the Works of the most celebrated Authors. I could not but see with a secret Joy, that though the *Greeks* and *Romans* made the Majority, yet our own Countrymen were the next both in Number and Dignity. I was now at Liberty to take a full Prospect of that delightful Region. I was inspir'd with new Vigour and Life, and saw every thing in nobler and more pleasing View than before; I breath'd a purer Æther in a Sky which was a continu'd Azure, gilded with perpetual

---

[a] his *M*; this *all edd.*

---

[1] In Boeotia, the haunt of the Muses.

[2] The pictorial representation of Fancy and Judgement is typical of the time. In Antoine Le Grand's *Entire Body of Philosophy* (1694) there is an engraving of the four 'faculties'—understanding, imagination, memory, and will—in which imagination is depicted as a woman with wings on her head to 'denote the swiftness of that Faculty' (Sig. c).

Sun-shine. The two Summits of the Mountain rose on each Side, and formed in the midst a most delicious Vale, the Habitation of the Muses, and of such as had composed Works worthy of Immortality. *Apollo* was seated upon a Throne of Gold, and for a Canopy an aged Lawrel spread its Boughs and its Shade over his Head. His Bow and Quiver lay at his Feet. He held his Harp in his Hand, whilst the Muses round about him celebrated with Hymns his Victory over the Serpent *Python*, and sometimes sung in softer Notes the Loves of *Leucothoe* and *Daphnis*.[1] *Homer*, *Virgil*, and *Milton* were seated the next to them. Behind were a great Number of others, among whom I was surprized to see some in the Habit of *Laplanders*, who, notwithstanding the Uncouthness of their Dress, had lately obtained a Place upon the Mountain.[2] I saw *Pindar* walking all alone, no one daring to accost him till *Cowley* joyn'd himself to him, but, growing weary of one who almost walk'd him out of Breath, he left him for *Horace* and *Anacreon*, with whom he seemed infinitely delighted.

'A little farther I saw another Groupe of Figures; I made up to them, and found it was *Socrates* dictating to *Xenophon* and the Spirit of *Plato*; but most of all *Musæus* had the greatest Audience about him. I was at too great a Distance to hear what he said, or to discover the Faces of his Hearers, only I thought I now perceived *Virgil*, who had joined them, and stood in a Posture full of Admiration at the Harmony of his Words.

'Lastly, At the very Brink of the Hill I saw *Boccalini* sending Dispatches to the World below of what happen'd upon *Parnassus*; but I perceived he did it without Leave of the Muses, and by Stealth, and was unwilling to have them revised by *Apollo*.[3] I could now from this Height and serene Sky behold the infinite Cares and Anxieties with which Mortals below sought out their Way through the Maze of Life. I saw the Path of Virtue lie straight before them, whilst Interest, or some malicious Demon, still hurry'd them out of the Way. I was at once touch'd with Pleasure at my own Happiness, and Compassion at the Sight of their inextricable Errors. Here the two contending Passions rose so high, that they were inconsistent with the sweet Repose I enjoy'd, and awaking with

[1] See Ovid, *Metamorphoses*, 4. 214–70; 1. 452–567. Both were loves of Phoebus Apollo.
[2] A reference to the two odes in Nos. 366 and 406 (vol. iii).
[3] Cf. Nos. 291 and 355 (vol. iii).

a sudden Start, the only Consolation I could admit of for my Loss, was the Hopes that this Relation of my Dream will not displease you.'

T[1]

No. 515   *Tuesday, October* 21, 1712[2]

[STEELE]

Pudet me & miseret qui harum mores cantabat mihi
Monuisse frustra . . .

Ter.

MR. SPECTATOR,

'I AM obliged to you for printing the Account I lately sent you of a Coquet who disturbed a sober Congregation in the City of *London*.[3] That Intelligence ended at her taking Coach, and bidding the Driver go where he knew. I could not leave her so, but dogged her, as hard as she drove, to *Paul's* Church-yard, where there was a Stop of Coaches attending Company coming out of the Cathedral. This gave me Opportunity to hold up a Crown to her Coachman, who gave me the Signal, that[a] he would hurry on, and make no Haste, as you know the Way is when they favour a Chase. By his many kind Blunders, driving against other Coaches, and slipping off some of his Tackle, I could keep up with him, and lodged my fine Lady in the Parish of St. *James's*. As I guessed when I first saw her at Church, her Business is to win Hearts and throw 'em away, regarding nothing but the Triumph. I have had the Happiness, by tracing her through all with whom I heard she was acquainted, to find one who was intimate with a Friend of mine, and to be

---

[a] Signal, that] *12mo*; Signal, and that *Fol.*, *8vo*

---

[1] The following Advertisement appears at the end of No. 514 in the Folio sheets (in italics in the original):

    A Letter written *October* 14, dated *Middle-Temple*, has been overlooked, by reason it was not directed to the *SPECTATOR* at the usual Places; and the Letter of the 18th, dated from the same Place is groundless, the Author of the Paper of *Friday* last not having ever seen the Letter of the 14th. In all Circumstances except the Place of Birth of the Person to whom the Letters were written, the Writer of them is misinformed.

[2] *Motto.* Terence, *Heautontimorumenos*, 260–1: Now I'm ashamed, and troubled to the soul, that he who read me so many good lectures upon the tricks of those creatures, lost all his advice.

This number seems to be made up of a genuine contribution.

[3] No. 503.

introduced to her Notice. I have made so good use of my Time, as to procure from that Intimate of hers one of her Letters, which she writ to her when in the Country. This Epistle of her own may serve to alarm the World against her in ordinary Life, as mine, I hope, did those who shall behold her at Church. The Letter was written last Winter to the Lady who gave it me; and I doubt not but you will find it the Soul of an happy self-loving Dame, that takes all the Admiration she can meet with, and returns none of it in love to her Admirers.

Dear Jenny,

"I am glad to find you are likely to be disposed of in Marriage so much to your Approbation as you tell me. You say you are afraid only of me, for I shall laugh at your Spouse's Airs. I beg of you not to fear it, for I am too nice a Discerner to laugh at any, but whom most other People think fine Fellows; so that your Dear may bring you hither as soon as his Horses are in Case enough to appear in Town, and you be very safe against any Raillery you may apprehend from me;[1] for I am surrounded with Coxcombs of my own making, who are all ridiculous in a manner: Your Good-man, I presume, can't exert himself. As Men who cannot raise their Fortunes, and are uneasy under the Incapacity of shining in Courts, rail at Ambition, so do awkard and insipid Women, who cannot warm the Hearts and charm the Eyes of Men, rail at Affection:[a] But she that has the Joy of seeing a Man's Heart leap into his Eyes at beholding her, is in no Pain for want of Esteem among a Crew of that Part of her own Sex who have no Spirit but that of Envy, and no Language but that of Malice. I do not in this, I hope, express my self insensible of the Merit of *Leodacia*, who lowers her Beauty to all but her Husband, and never spreads her Charms but to gladden him who has a Right in them: I say, I do Honour to those who can be Coquets, and are not such; but I despise all who would be so, and in Despair of arriving at it themselves, hate and villify all those who can. But, be that as it will, in Answer to your Desire of knowing my History: One of my chief present Pleasures is in Country Dances; and, in Obedience to me, as well as the Pleasure of coming up to me with a good Grace, shewing themselves in their Address

---

[a] Affection] *8vo*; Affectation, *Fol., 12mo*

---

[1] In case, i.e. in good physical condition. *OED* quotes Swift, *Battle of the Books* (1704): 'Their Horses large, but extremely out of Case.'

to others in my Presence, and the like Opportunities, they are all Proficients that Way: And I had the Happiness of being the other Night where we made six Couple, and every Woman's Partner a profess'd Lover of mine. The wildest Imagination cannot form to it self, on any Occasion, higher Delight than I acknowledge my self to have been in all that Evening. I chose out of my Admirers a Set of Men who most love me, and gave them Partners of such of my own Sex who most envy'd me.

"My Way is, when any Man who is my Admirer pretends to give himself Airs of Merit, as at this Time a certain Gentleman you know did, to mortify him by favouring in his Presence the most insignificant Creature I can find. At this Ball I was led into the Company by pretty Mr. *Fanfly*, who, you know, is the most obsequious well-shap'd well-bred Woman's Man in Town. I at first Entrance declared him my Partner if I danced at all; which put the whole Assembly into a Grin, as forming no Terrours from such a Rival. But we had not been long in the Room, before I over-heard the meritorious Gentleman above-mentioned say with an Oath, There is no Raillery in the thing, she certainly loves the Puppy. My Gentleman, when we were dancing, took an Occasion to be very soft in his Oglings upon a Lady he danced with, and whom he knew of all Women I love most to outshine. The Contest began who should plague the other most. I, who do not care a Farthing for him, had no hard Task to out-vex him. I made *Fanfly*, with a very little Encouragement, cut Capers *Coupee*,[1] and then sink with all the Air and Tenderness imaginable. When he performed this, I observed the Gentleman you know of fall into the same Way, and imitate as well as he could the despised *Fanfly*. I cannot well give you, who are so grave a Country Lady, the Idea of the Joy we have when we see a stubborn Heart breaking, or a Man of Sense turning Fool for our Sakes; but this happened to our Friend, and I expect his Attendance whenever I go to Church, to Court, to the Play, or the Park. This is a Sacrifice due to us Women of Genius, who have the Eloquence of Beauty, an easy Mein. I mean by an easy Mein, one which can be on Occasion easily affected: For I must tell you, dear *Jenny*, I hold one Maxim, which is an uncommon one, to wit, That our greatest Charms are owing to Affectation. 'Tis to That

---

[1] 'A dance step formerly much used; the dancer rests on one foot and passes the other forward or backward, making a sort of salutation; hence sometimes used for a bow made while advancing' (*OED*).

that our Arms can lodge so quietly just over our Hips, and the Fan can play without any Force or Motion but just of the Wrist. 'Tis to Affectation we owe the pensive Attention of *Deidamia* at a Tragedy, the scornful Approbation of *Dulciamara* at a Comedy, and the lowly Aspect of *Lanquicelsa* at a Sermon.

"To tell you the plain Truth, I know no Pleasure but in being admired, and have yet never failed of attaining the Approbation of the Man whose Regard I had a Mind to. You see all the Men who make a Figure in the World (as wise a Look as they are pleased to put upon the Matter) are moved by the same Vanity as I am. What is there in Ambition, but to make other People's Wills depend upon yours? This indeed is not to be aim'd at by one who has a Genius no higher than to think of being a very good Housewife in a Country Gentleman's Family. The Care of Poultrey and Piggs are great Enemies to the Countenance: The vacant Look of a fine Lady is not to be preserved, if she admits any thing to take up her Thoughts but her own dear Person. But I interrupt you too long from your Cares, and my self from my Conquests.

> *I am, Madam,*
> *Your most humble Servant.*"

'Give me Leave, Mr. SPECTATOR, to add her Friend's Answer to this Epistle, who is a very discreet ingenious Woman.

Dear Gatty,[1]
"I Take your Raillery in very good part, and am obliged to you for the free Air with which you speak of your own Gayeties. But this is but a barren superficial Pleasure; indeed,[a] *Gatty*, we are made for Man, and in serious Sadness I must tell you, whether you your self know it or no, all these Gallantries tend to no other End but to be a Wife and Mother as fast as you can.

> *I am, Madam,*
> *Your most obedient Servant.*" '

T

---

[a] Pleasure; indeed,] *8vo*; Pleasure; for indeed, *Fol., 12mo*

---

[1] A nickname for Gertrude. Cf. Etherege's *She Would if She Could*, Shadwell's *A True Widow* (III. i), &c. Mrs. Gatty is 'an Agreeable Beauty' in *Tatler* 24. Cf. Steele's *The Lover*, No. 3:

I must desire Aronces to give an exact relation of the airs and glances of the whole company, and particularly how Mrs. Gatty sits, when it happens that she is to pass by the Lover Vagabond, who, I find, is got into that company by the favour of his cousin Jenny.

No. 516   *Wednesday, October 22, 1712*[1]
[STEELE]

Immortale odium & nunquam sanabile vulnus.
Inde furor vulgo, quod Numina vicinorum
Odit uterque locus, quum solos credat habendos
Esse Deos quos ipse colit . . .

                                  Juv.

OF all the monstrous Passions and Opinions which have crept into the World, there is none so wonderful as that those who profess the common Name of *Christians* should pursue each other with Rancour and Hatred for Differences in their Way of following the Example of their Saviour. It seems so natural that all who pursue the Steps of any Leader should form themselves after his Manners, and that it is impossible to account for Effects so different from what we might expect from those who profess themselves Followers of the highest Pattern of Meekness and Charity, but by ascribing such Effects to the Ambition and Corruption of those who are so audacious, with Souls full of Fury, to serve at the Altars of the God of Peace.

The Massacres to which the Church of *Rome* has animated the ordinary People are dreadful Instances of the Truth of this Observation; and whoever reads the History of the *Irish* Rebellion, and the Cruelties which ensued thereupon, will be sufficiently convinced to what Rage poor Ignorants may be work'd up by those who profess Holiness, and become Incendiaries, and, under the Dispensation[a] of Grace, promote Evils abhorrent to Nature.

This Subject and Catastrophe, which deserve so well to be remarked by the Protestant World, will, I doubt not, be considered by the Reverend and Learned Prelate that preaches to Morrow before many of the Descendants of those who perished on that

[a] Dispensation] *8vo*; Dispensations *Fol.*, *12mo*

---

[1] *Motto.* Juvenal, *Satires,* 15. 34, 36–38:

       A Grutch in both, time out of Mind begun,
       And mutually bequeath'd from Sire to Son,
       Religious Spight, and pious Spleen bred first,
       This Quarrel which so long the Bigots nurst.
       Each calls the other's God a senseless Stock,
       His own Divine. . . .   TATE.

lamentable Day, in a Manner suitable to the Occasion, and worthy his own great Virtue and Eloquence.[1]

I shall not dwell upon it any further, but only transcribe out of a little Tract, called, *The Christian Hero*, published in 1701, what I find there in Honour of the Renowned Hero *William* III. who rescued that Nation from the Repetition of the same Disasters. His late Majesty, of glorious Memory, and the Most Christian King are considered at the Conclusion of that Treatise as Heads of the Protestant and Roman-Catholick World in the following Manner.[2]

'There were not ever, before the Entrance of the Christian Name into the World, Men who have maintain'd a more renown'd Carriage, than the two great Rivals who possess the full Fame of the present Age, and will be the Theme and Examination of the future. They are exactly form'd by Nature for those Ends to which Heaven seems to have sent them amongst us: Both animated with a restless Desire of Glory, but pursue it by different Means, and with different Motives: To one it consists in an extensive undisputed Empire over his Subjects, to the other in their rational and voluntary Obedience: One's Happiness is founded in their want of Power, the other's in their want of Desire to oppose him: The one enjoys the Summit of Fortune with the Luxury of a *Persian*, the other with the Moderation of a *Spartan*: One is made to oppress, the other to relieve the Oppressed: The one is satisfied with the Pomp and Ostentation of Power to prefer and debase his Inferiours, the other delighted only with the Cause and Foundation of it to cherish and protect 'em: To one therefore Religion is but a convenient Disguise, to the other a vigorous Motive of Action.

'For without such Ties of real and solid Honour, there is no Way of forming a Monarch, but after the Machiavilian Scheme,[a] by

---

[a] Scheme,] *Christian Hero*; Scene, *all edd.*

[1] St. George Ash, Bishop of Clogher, preached to the Irish Protestants in London, at St. Clement Danes Church, on 23 Oct. The sermon is advertised in No. 526:

This Day is Published,

A Sermon preached to the Protestants of Ireland, now in London, at the Parish-Church of St. Clement-Dane, October 23. 1712. being the Day appointed by Act of Parliament in Ireland for an Anniversary Thanksgiving for the Deliverance of the Protestants of that Kingdom from the bloody Massacre begun by the Irish Papists on the 23d of October, 1641. By St. George, Lord Bishop of Clogher. Printed for Sam. Buckley at the Dolphin in Little-Britain. Price 3d.

It is advertised also in Nos. 527 and 529; a second edition is advertised in No. 531.

[2] The passage here reprinted is from the concluding portion (chap. iv) of Steele's *Christian Hero* (*Tracts and Pamphlets*, ed. Blanchard, pp. 58–62).

which a Prince must ever seem to have all Virtues, but really to be Master of none, but is to be liberal, merciful, and just only as they serve his Interests; while, with the noble Art of Hypocrisy, Empire would be to be extended, and new Conquests be made by new Devices, by which prompt Address his Creatures might insensibly give Law in the Business of Life, by leading Men in the Entertainment of it.[1]

'Thus when Words and Show are apt to pass for the substantial things they[2] are only to express, there would need no more to enslave a Country but to adorn a Court; for while every Man's Vanity makes him believe himself capable of becoming Luxury, Enjoyments are a ready Bait for Sufferings, and the Hopes of Preferment Invitations to Servitude, which Slavery would be colour'd with all the Agreements, as they call it, imaginable. The noblest Arts and Artists, the finest Pens and most elegant Minds, jointly employ'd to set it off, with the various Embellishments of sumptuous Entertainments, charming Assemblies and polished Discourses: And those apostate Abilities of Men, the adored Monarch might profusely and skilfully encourage, while they flatter his Virtue, and gild his Vice at so high a Rate, that he, without Scorn of the one, or Love of the other, would alternately and occasionally use both, so that his Bounty should support him in his Rapines, his Mercy in his Cruelties.

'Nor is it to give Things a more severe Look than is natural, to suppose such must be the Consequences of a Prince's having no other Pursuit than that of his own Glory; for, if we consider an Infant born into the World, and beholding it self the mightiest Thing in it, its self the present Admiration and future Prospect of a fawning People, who profess themselves great or mean, according to the Figure he is to make amongst them, what Fancy would not be debauched to believe they were but what they professed themselves, his mere Creatures, and use them as such by purchasing with their Lives a boundless Renown, which he, for Want of a more just Prospect, would place in the Number of his Slaves,[3] and

---

[1] Steele omits the conclusion of the sentence:

And making their great Monarch the Fountain of all that's delicate and refin'd, and his Court the Model for Opinions in Pleasure, as well as the Pattern in Dress; which might prevail so far upon an undiscerning World as (to accomplish it for its approaching Slavery) to make it receive a superfluous Babble for an Universal Language.

[2] The 3rd edition reads 'we', an error corrected here.
[3] The 3rd edition reads 'of Slaves', an error corrected here.

the Extent of his Territories; such undoubtedly would be the tragical Effects of a Prince's living with no Religion, which are not to be surpassed but by his having a false one.

'If Ambition were spirited with Zeal, what would follow, but that his People should be converted into an Army, whose Swords can make Right in Power, and solve Controversy in Belief? And if Men should be stiff-necked to the Doctrine of that visible Church, let them be contented with an Oar and a Chain, in the Midst of Stripes and Anguish, to contemplate on him, whose Yoke is easy, and whose Burthen is light.

'With a Tyranny begun on his own Subjects, and Indignation that others draw their Breath independent of his Frown or Smile, why should he not proceed to the Seizure of the World? And if nothing but the Thirst of Sway were the Motive of his Actions, why should Treaties be other than meer Words, or solemn national Compacts be any thing but an Halt in the March of that Army, who are never to lay down their Arms, till all Men are reduced to the Necessity of hanging their Lives on his way-ward Will; who might supinely, and at Leisure, expiate his own Sins by other Mens Sufferings, while he daily meditates new Slaughter, and new Conquest?

'For meer Man, when giddy with unbridled Power, is an insatiate Idol, not to be appeased with Myriads offered to his Pride, which may be puffed up by the Adulation of a base and prostrate World, into an Opinion that he is something more than humane, by being something less: And, alass, what is there that mortal Man will not believe of himself, when complimented with the Attributes of God? He can then conceive Thoughts of a Power as *Omnipresent* as his: But should there be such a Foe of Mankind now upon Earth, have our Sins so far provoked Heaven, that we are left utterly naked to his Fury? Is there no Power, no Leader, no Genius, that can conduct and animate us to our Death, or our Defence? Yes, our great God never gave one to reign by his Permission, but he gave to another also to reign by his Grace.

'All the Circumstances of the illustrious Life of our Prince, seem to have conspired to make him the Check and Bridle of Tyranny; for his Mind has been strengthened and confirmed by one continued Struggle, and Heaven has educated him by Adversity to a quick Sense of the Distresses and Miseries of Mankind, which he was born to redress: In just Scorn of the trivial Glories and light Ostentations of Power, that glorious Instrument of Providence, moves like that, in a steady, calm, and silent Course, independent either of Applause or Calumny, which renders him, if not in a political, yet in a moral, a philosophick, an heroick, and a Christian Sense, an absolute Monarch: Who satisfied with this unchangeable, just, and ample Glory, must needs turn all his Regards from himself, to the Service of others; for he begins his Enterprizes with his own Share in the Success of them; for Integrity bears in it self its Reward, nor can that which depends not on Event ever know Disappointment.

'With the undoubted Character of a glorious Captain, and (what he much more values than the most splendid Titles) that of a sincere and honest Man, he is the Hope and Stay of *Europe*, an Universal Good not to be engrossed by us only; for distant Potentates implore his Friendship, and injured Empires court his Assistance. He rules the World, not by an Invasion of the People of the Earth, but the Address of its Princes; and if that World should be again rous'd from the Repose which his prevailing Arms had[1] given it, why should we not hope that there is an Almighty, by whose Influence the terrible Enemy, that thinks himself prepar'd for Battle, may find he is but ripe for Destruction, and that there may be in the Womb of Time great Incidents, which may make the Catastrophe of a prosperous Life as unfortunate as the particular Scenes of it were successful. For there does not want a skilful Eye and Resolute Arm to observe and grasp the Occasion: A Prince, who from

> ... *Fuit Ilium & ingens*
> *Gloria* ...   Virg.'[2]

T

---

[1] The 3rd edition reads 'have'.

[2] *Aeneid*, 2. 325–6: Troy is no more, nor its great glory. Steele has broken off at the beginning of the final paragraph: 'A Prince, who from a just Notion of his Duty to that Being, to whom he must be accountable, has in the service of his Fellow-Creatures, a noble contempt of Pleasures, and Patience of Labours ....' The Virgilian phrase is not syntactically joined to the rest of the sentence.

Heu pietas! heu prisca fides! . . .
Virg.

WE last Night received a piece of ill News at our Club, which
very sensibly afflicted every one of us.[2] I question not but
my Readers themselves will be troubled at the hearing of it. To
keep them no longer in Suspence, Sir ROGER DE COVERLY *is Dead.*
He departed this Life at his House in the Country, after a few
Weeks Sickness. Sir ANDREW FREEPORT has a Letter from one of
his Correspondents in those Parts, that informs him the old Man
caught a Cold at the County Sessions, as he was very warmly
promoting an Address of his own penning, in which he succeeded
according to his Wishes. But this Particular comes from a Whig-
Justice of Peace, who was always Sir ROGER's Enemy and Antagonist. I have Letters both from the Chaplain and Captain *Sentry*
which mention nothing of it, but are filled with many Particulars
to the Honour of the good old Man. I have likewise a Letter from
the Butler, who took so much care of me last Summer when I was
at the Knight's House. As my Friend the Butler mentions, in the
Simplicity of his Heart, several Circumstances the others have
passed over in Silence, I shall give my Reader a Copy of his Letter,
without any Alteration or Diminution.

Honoured Sir,

'KNOWING that you was my old Master's good Friend, I
could not forbear sending you the melancholy News of his

---

[1] *Motto.* Virgil, *Aeneid*, 6. 878:
> Alas for goodness! and alas for the faith of old!

[2] The death of Sir Roger de Coverley is one of the first intimations of the breaking-
up of the Spectator Club and the cessation of the paper. Some twenty years later
Eustace Budgell wrote in No. 1 of *The Bee* (Feb. 1733, p. 27):
> Mr. *Addison* was so fond of this Character, that a little before he laid down the
> *Spectator* (foreseeing that some nimble Gentleman would catch up his Pen the
> Moment he had quitted it) he said to an intimate Friend, with a certain *Warmth*
> in his Expression which he was not often guilty of, By G—d, *I'll* KILL *Sir* Roger,
> *that no Body else may* MURDER *him.* Accordingly, the whole *Spectator*, No. 517.
> consists of nothing else but an Account of the *Old Knight's Death*, and some *moving
> Circumstances* which attended it.

Johnson, in his Life of Addison (World's Classics ed., i. 425), and others have interpreted this as the result of Addison's anger at the Sukey episode in No. 410. Taken
literally, however, the statement merely means that Addison had already decided
on the cessation of the *Spectator* and was determined to have no 'nimble Gentleman'
attempting to continue the character of Sir Roger.

Death, which has afflicted the whole Country, as well as his poor
Servants, who loved him, I may say, better than we did our Lives.
I am affraid he caught his Death the last County Sessions, where he
would go to see Justice done to a poor Widow Woman, and her
Fatherless Children that had been wronged by a Neighbouring
Gentleman; for you know, Sir, my good Master was always the
poor Man's Friend. Upon his coming home, the first Complaint he
made was, that he had lost his Roast-Beef Stomach, not being able
to touch a Sirloin, which was served up according to Custom; and
you know he used to take great Delight in it. From that time forward he grew worse and worse, but still kept a good Heart to the
last. Indeed we were once in great Hopes of his Recovery, upon a
kind Message that was sent him from the Widow Lady whom he
had made Love to the Forty last Years of his Life; but this only
proved a Light'ning before Death. He has bequeathed to this Lady,
as a token of his Love, a great Pearl Necklace, and a couple of Silver
Bracelets set with Jewels, which belonged to my good old Lady his
Mother: He has bequeathed the fine white Gelding, that he used
to ride a hunting upon, to his Chaplain, because he thought he
would be kind to him, and has left you all his Books. He has, moreover, bequeathed to the Chaplain a very pretty Tenement with
good Lands about it. It being a very cold Day when he made his
Will, he left for Mourning, to every Man in the Parish a great Frize[1]
Coat, and to every Woman a black Riding-hood. It was a most
moving Sight to see him take leave of his poor Servants, commending us all for our Fidelity, whilst we were not able to speak a Word
for weeping. As we most of us are grown Gray-headed in our Dear
Master's Service he has left us Pensions and Legacies, which we
may live very comfortably upon, the remaining part of our Days.
He has bequeathed a great deal more in Charity, which is not yet
come to my Knowledge, and it is peremptorily said in the Parish,
that he has left Mony to build a Steeple to the Church; for he was
heard to say some time ago, that if he lived two Years longer
Coverly Church should have a Steeple to it. The Chaplain tells every
Body that he made a very good End, and never speaks of him without Tears. He was buried, according to his own Directions, among
the Family of the *Coverly's*, on the Left Hand of his Father Sir
Arthur. The Coffin was carried by Six of his Tenants, and the Pall
held up by Six of the *Quorum*:[2] The whole Parish followed the Corps

[1] I.e. frieze, a coarse woollen cloth, with nap.   [2] See No. 2 (vol. i).

with heavy Hearts, and in their Mourning Suits, the Men in Frize, and the Women in Riding hoods. Captain *Sentry*, my Master's Nephew, has taken Possession of the Hall-House, and the whole Estate. When my old Master saw him a little before his Death, he shook him by the Hand, and wished him Joy of the Estate which was falling to him, desiring him only to make a good use of it, and to pay the several Legacies, and the Gifts of Charity which he told him he had left as Quit-rents upon the Estate. The Captain truly seems a courteous Man, though he says but little. He makes much of those whom my Master loved, and shows great Kindness to the old House-dog, that you know my poor Master was so fond of. It wou'd have gone to your Heart to have heard the Moans the dumb Creature made on the Day of my Master's Death. He has ne'er joyed himself since; no more has any of us. 'Twas the melancholiest Day for the poor People that ever happened in *Worcestershire*. This being all from,

Honoured Sir,
Your most Sorrowful Servant,
Edward Biscuit.

P. S. 'My Master desired, some Weeks before he died, that a Book which comes up to you by the Carrier should be given to Sir *Andrew Freeport* in his Name.'

This Letter, notwithstanding the poor Butler's manner of writing it, gave us such an Idea of our good old Friend, that upon the reading of it there was not a dry Eye in the Club. Sir *Andrew* opening the Book found it to be a Collection of Acts of Parliament. There was in particular the Act of Uniformity,[1] with some Passages in it marked by Sir *Roger*'s own Hand. Sir *Andrew* found that they related to two or three Points, which he had disputed with Sir *Roger* the last time he appeared at the Club. Sir *Andrew*, who would have been merry at such an Incident on another Occasion, at the sight of the old Man's Hand-writing burst into Tears, and put the Book into his Pocket. Captain *Sentry* informs me, that the Knight has left Rings and Mourning for every one in the Club.

O

---

[1] See No. 3 (vol. i).

No. 518   *Friday, October* 24, 1712[1]

> *. . . miserum est alienæ incumbere famæ*
> *Ne collapsa ruant subductis tecta columnis.*
>   Juv.

THIS being a Day of Business with me, I must make the present Entertainment like a Treat at an House-Warming, out of such Presents as have been sent me by my Guests. The first Dish which I serve up is a Letter come fresh to my Hand.[2]

Mr. SPECTATOR,

'IT is with inexpressible Sorrow that I hear of the Death of good Sir *Roger*, and do heartily condole with you upon so melancholly an Occasion. I think you ought to have blacken'd the Edges of a Paper which brought us so ill News, and to have had it stamped likewise in Black. It is expected of you that you should write his Epitaph, and, if possible, fill his Place in the Club with as worthy and diverting a Member. I question not but you will receive many Recommendations from the Publick of such as will appear Candidates for that Post.

'Since I am talking of Death, and have mentioned an Epitaph, I must tell you, Sir, that I have made Discovery of a Church-Yard in which I believe you might spend an Afternoon, with great Pleasure to your self and to the Publick: It belongs to the Church of *Stebon-Heath*, commonly called *Stepney*. Whether or no it be that the People of that Parish have a particular Genius for an Epitaph,[3] or that there be some Poet among them who undertakes that Work by the Great,[4] I can't tell, but there are more remarkable Inscriptions in

---

[1] *Motto.* Juvenal, *Satires*, 8. 76–77 (altered):

> 'Tis Poor relying on another's Fame;
> For, take the Pillars but away, and all
> The Superstructure must in Ruins fall. STEPNEY.

[2] Since the account of Sir Roger's death was published only on the preceding day, it may be doubted whether this is a letter from a correspondent. This number is unsigned, and the author of this letter is probably Addison, who wrote Nos. 517 and 519. See *Modern Philology*, xlvii (1950), 174–5.

[3] St. Dunstan's, Stepney, a fifteenth-century church in the densely populated district in East London along the river, was well known for its curious epitaphs. Hatton (pp. 218–30) reproduces over twenty, including the first two quoted in this letter. Another epitaph from this church is given in *Tatler* 202.

[4] See No. 22 (vol. i).

that Place than in any other I have met with, and I may say without Vanity that there is not a Gentleman in *England* better read in Tomb-stones than my self, my Studies having laid very much in Church-yards. I shall beg leave to send you a Couple of Epitaphs, for a Sample of those I have just now mentioned. They are written in a different manner; the first being in the diffused and luxuriant, the second in the close contracted Stile. The first has much of the Simple and Pathetick; the second is something Light, but Nervous. The first is thus:

> *Here* Thomas Sapper *lyes interr'd, Ah why!*
> *Born in* New England, *did in* London *dye;*
> *Was the third Son of Eight, begot upon*
> *His Mother* Martha *by his Father* John.
> *Much favour'd by his Prince he 'gan to be,*
> *But nipt by Death at th' Age of Twenty Three.*
> *Fatal to him was that we Small-pox name,*
> *By which his Mother and two Brethren came*
> *Also to breath their last nine Years before,*
> *And now have left their Father to deplore*
> *The Loss of all his Children with his Wife,*
> *Who was the Joy and Comfort of his Life.*[1]

The Second is as follows,

> *Here lies the Body of* Daniel Saul,
> Spittle-fields *Weaver, and that's all.*[2]

I will not dismiss you, whilst I am upon this Subject, without sending a short Epitaph which I once met with, though I cannot possibly recollect the Place. The Thought of it is serious, and, in my Opinion, the finest that I ever met with upon this Occasion. You know, Sir, it is usual, after having told us the Name of the Person who lies interr'd, to launch out into his Praises. This Epitaph takes a quite contrary Turn, having been made by the Person himself some time before his Death.

> *Hic jacet* R. C. *in expectatione diei supremi. Qualis erat dies iste indicabit.*[3]

[1] The epitaph is given in Hatton, p. 224, with the name Thomas Saffin, deceas'd June 18, 1687. It lies on 'a gray Marble Tomb Stone, a pretty way Southward from the East end of the Church'. For Dr. Johnson's merriment over this epitaph (25 Oct. 1784) see Boswell's Life, ed. Hill–Powell, iv. 358–9. [2] Hatton, p. 228.
[3] A similar epitaph is said to have been in King's College Chapel, Cambridge. See *European Magazine and London Review*, July 1787, p. 9.

Here lieth *R. C.* in expectation of the last Day. What sort of a Man he was that Day will discover.

I am, SIR, &c.'ᵃ

ᵃ *No. 518 unsigned in Fol., 8vo, 12mo*

The following Letter is dated from *Cambridge.*

SIR,

'HAVING lately read, among your Speculations, an Essay upon Phisiognomy,[1] I cannot but think that if you made a Visit to this Ancient University, you might receive very considerable Lights upon that Subject, there being scarce a young Fellow in it who does not give certain Indications of his particular Humour and Disposition conformable to the Rules of that Art. In Courts and Cities every Body lays a Constraint upon his Countenance, and endeavours to look like the rest of the World; but the Youth of this Place, having not yet formed themselves by Conversation, and the Knowledge of the World, give their Limbs and Features their full Play.

'As you have considered Human Nature in all its Lights, you must be extremely well apprised, that there is a very close Correspondence between the Outward and the Inward Man; that scarce the least Dawning, the least Parturiency towards a Thought can be stirring in the Mind of Man, without producing a suitable Revolution in his Exteriors, which will easily discover it self to an Adept in the Theory of the Phiz. Hence it is, that the intrinsic Worth and Merit of a Son of *Alma Mater* is ordinarily calculated from the Cast of his Visage, the Contour of his Person, the Mechanism of his Dress, the Disposition of his Limbs, the Manner of his Gate and Air, with a number of Circumstances of equal Consequence and Information. The Practitioners in this Art often make use of a Gentleman's Eyes, to give 'em Light into the Posture of his Brains; take a handle from his Nose, to judge of the size of his Intellects; and interpret the over-much Visibility and Pertness of one Ear, as an infallible mark of Reprobation, and a Sign the Owner of so saucy a Member fears neither God nor Man. In Conformity to this Scheme, a contracted Brow, a lumpish[2] down-cast Look, a sober sedate Pace, with both Hands dangling quiet and steddy in Lines

---

[1] No. 86 is the only paper which can be called 'an essay upon physiognomy', although the subject is touched upon at the beginning of No. 206.

[2] See No. 440.

exactly parallel to each Lateral Pocket of the Galligaskins, is Logic, Metaphysics and Mathematics in Perfection. So likewise the *Belles Lettres* are typified by a Saunter in the Gate, a Fall of one Wing of the Peruke backward, an Insertion of one Hand in the Fobb, and a negligent swing of the other, with a Pinch of right and fine *Barcelona* between Finger and Thumb, a due Quantity of the same upon the upper Lip, and a Noddle-Case[1] loaden with Pulvil.[2] Again, a grave solemn stalking Pace is Heroic Poetry, and Politicks; an Unequal one, a Genius for the Ode, and the modern Ballad; and an open Breast, with an audacious Display of the Holland Shirt, is construed a fatal Tendency to the Art Military.

'I might be much larger upon these Hints, but I know whom I write to. If you can graft any Speculation upon them, or turn them to the Advantage of the Persons concerned in them, you will do a Work very becoming the *British Spectator*, and oblige,

Your very Humble Servant,
Tom. Tweer.'[3]

No. 519　　　　　*Saturday, October 25, 1712*[4]
[ADDISON]

Inde hominum, pecudumque genus, vitæque volantum,
Et quæ marmoreo fert monstra sub æquore pontus.

Virg.

THOUGH there is a great deal of Pleasure in contemplating the Material World, by which I mean that System of Bodies into which Nature has so curiously wrought the Mass of dead Matter, with the several Relations which those Bodies bear to one another; there is still, methinks, something more wonderful and surprizing in Contemplations on the World of Life, by which I mean

[1] I.e. a wig.

[2] 'Cosmetic or perfumed powder for powdering the wig or perfuming the person' (*OED*).

[3] 'The public is assured on good authority, that this last letter was written by *Orator* Henley, as he was commonly called' (Nichols). For John Henley see No. 396 (vol. iii).

[4] *Motto.* Virgil, *Aeneid*, 6. 728–9:
Hence Men and Beasts the Breath of Life obtain;
And Birds of Air, and Monsters of the Main. DRYDEN.

all those Animals with which every Part of the Universe is furnished. The Material World is only the Shell of the Universe: The World of Life are its Inhabitants.

If we consider those Parts of the Material World which lie the nearest to us, and are therefore subject to our Observations and Enquiries, it is amazing to consider the Infinity of Animals with which it is stocked.[1] Every part of Matter is peopled: Every green Leaf swarms with Inhabitants. There is scarce a single Humour in the Body of a Man, or of any other Animal, in which our Glasses do not discover Myriads of living Creatures. The Surface of Animals is also covered with other Animals, which are in the same manner the Basis of other Animals that live upon it; nay, we find in the most solid Bodies, as in Marble it self, innumerable Cells and Cavities that are crouded with such imperceptible Inhabitants, as are too little for the naked Eye to discover. On the other Hand, if we look into the more bulky Parts of Nature, we see the Seas, Lakes and Rivers teeming with numberless Kinds of living Creatures: We find every Mountain and Marsh, Wilderness and Wood, plentifully stocked with Birds and Beasts, and every part of Matter affording proper Necessaries and Conveniencies for the Livelihood of Multitudes which inhabit it.

The Author of the *Plurality of Worlds* draws a very good Argument from this Consideration, for the *peopling* of every Planet, as indeed it seems very probable from the Analogy of Reason, that if no part of Matter, which we are acquainted with, lies waste and useless, those great Bodies which are at such a Distance from us should not be desart and unpeopled, but rather that they should be furnished with Beings adapted to their respective Situations.[2]

Existence is a Blessing to those Beings only which are endowed with Perception, and is, in a manner, thrown away upon dead Matter, any further than as it is subservient to Beings which are

---

[1] The development of the microscope in the seventeenth century, especially through the work of Antony van Leeuwenhoek (1632–1723), had opened up a new world not only to the scientists but also to the cultivated public, a world rightly described by Addison as 'amazing'. For Leeuwenhoek and his discoveries see A. Wolf, *A History of Science . . . in the 16th & 17th Centuries* (New York, 1939), pp. 71–75, 420–2.

[2] Fontenelle's *Entretiens sur la pluralité des mondes* (1686) was translated by Mrs. Behn in 1688 and by John Glanvill in 1695. A later version by W. Gardiner, based on Glanvill's translation, appeared in 1715; to subsequent editions (1728, 1737, &c.) was added 'Mr. Addison's Defence of the Newtonian philosophy'. For a review of Fontenelle's arguments for the presence of inhabitants on other bodies of our system see A. O. Lovejoy, *The Great Chain of Being* (Cambridge, Mass., 1936), pp. 130–2.

conscious of their Existence. Accordingly we find, from the Bodies which lie under our Observation, that Matter is only made as the Basis and Support of Animals, and that there is no more of the one, than what is necessary for the Existence of the other.

Infinite Goodness is of so communicative a Nature, that it seems to delight in the conferring of Existence upon every degree of Perceptive Being. As this is a Speculation, which I have often pursued with great Pleasure to my self, I shall enlarge farther upon it, by considering that part of the Scale of Beings, which comes within our Knowledge.[1]

There are some living Creatures which are raised but just above dead Matter. To mention only that Species of Shell-fish, which are formed in the Fashion of a Cone, that grow to the Surface of several Rocks, and immediately die upon their being severed from the Place where they grow. There are many other Creatures but one Remove from these, which have no other Sense besides that of Feeling and Taste. Others have still an additional one of Hearing; others of Smell, and others of Sight. It is wonderful to observe, by what a gradual Progress the World of Life advances through a prodigious Variety of Species, before a Creature is formed that is compleat in all its Senses, and even among these there is such a different degree of Perfection in the Sense, which one Animal enjoys beyond what appears in another, that though the Sense in different Animals be distinguished by the same common Denomination, it seems almost of a different Nature. If after this we look into the several inward Perfections of Cunning and Sagacity, or what we generally call Instinct, we find them rising after the same manner, imperceptibly one above another, and receiving additional Improvements, according to the Species in which they are implanted. This Progress in Nature is so very gradual, that the most perfect of an inferior Species comes very near to the most imperfect, of that which is immediately above it.

The exuberant and overflowing Goodness of the Supreme Being, whose Mercy extends to all his Works, is plainly seen, as I have before hinted, from his having made so very little Matter, at least what falls within our Knowledge, that does not Swarm with Life:

---

[1] 'Next to the word' 'Nature"', writes Professor Lovejoy, ' "the great Chain of Being" was the sacred phrase of the eighteenth century, playing a part somewhat analogous to that of the blessed word "evolution" in the late nineteenth' (p. 184). For the history of the idea, and particularly Addison's role in popularizing the term, see Lovejoy, pp. 184–207.

Nor is his Goodness less seen in the Diversity, than in the Multitude of living Creatures. Had he only made one Species of Animals, none of the rest would have enjoyed the Happiness of Existence;[1] he has, therefore, *specified* in his Creation every degree of Life, every Capacity of Being. The whole Chasm in Nature, from a Plant to a Man, is filled up with diverse Kinds of Creatures, rising one over another, by such a gentle and easie Ascent, that the little Transitions and Deviations from one Species to another, are almost insensible. This intermediate Space is so well husbanded and managed, that there is scarce a degree of Perception which does not appear in some one part of the World of Life. Is the Goodness, or Wisdom of the Divine Being, more manifested in this his Proceeding?

There is a Consequence, besides those I have already mentioned, which seems very naturally deducible from the foregoing Considerations. If the Scale of Being rises by such a regular Progress, so high as Man, we may by a Parity of Reason suppose that it still proceeds gradually through those Beings which are of a Superior Nature to him, since there is an infinitely greater Space and Room for different Degrees of Perfection, between the Supreme Being and Man, than between Man and the most despicable Insect. This Consequence of so great a Variety of Beings which are superior to us, from that Variety which is inferior to us, is made by Mr. *Lock*, in a Passage which I shall here set down, after having premised, that notwithstanding there is such infinite room between Man and his Maker for the Creative Power to exert it self in, it is impossible that it should ever be filled up, since there will be still an infinite Gap or Distance between the highest created Being, and the Power which produced him.

That there should be more Species of intelligent Creatures above us, than there are of sensible and material below us, is probable to me from hence; That in all the visible corporeal World, we see no Chasms, or no Gaps. All quite down from us, the descent is by easie steps, and a continued series of

---

[1] For the principle of 'plenitude' see Lovejoy, pp. 208–26. A characteristic statement of the theory is to be found in Part II of John Scott's *The Christian Life*:

Was God obliged in Goodness to make all Kinds of Beings *equally perfect?* If *so*, there must have been but *one* Kind of Beings in the whole Universe, and consequently there must have been *infinite* Kinds of Beings that are *capable* of Happiness for ever *unmade*, or for ever *unprovided for*. Wherefore since the Goodness of God was so infinitely *fruitful* as to *communicate* it self in *different* Degrees of Perfection to all *Possibilities* of Being, that so there might be *no* Kind wanting to *compleat* the Universe, it was requisite that there should be a *mean* Degree of Perfection between *Angels* and *Brutes*; otherwise there would have been a *Gap* and *Chasm* in the World.... (vol. i, chap. iv (ed. 1700), pp. 244–5).

things, that in each remove, differ very little one from the other. There are Fishes that have Wings, and are not Strangers to the airy Region: and there are some Birds, that are Inhabitants of the Water; whose Blood is cold as Fishes, and their Flesh so like in taste, that the scrupulous are allowed them on Fish-days. There are Animals so near of kin both to Birds and Beasts, that they are in the middle between both: Amphibious Animals link the Terrestrial and Aquatique together; Seals live at Land and at Sea, and Porpoises have the warm Blood and Entrails of a Hog, not to mention what is confidently reported of Mermaids, or Sea-men. There are some Brutes, that seem to have as much Knowledge and Reason, as some that are called Men; and the Animal and Vegetable Kingdoms are so nearly joyn'd, that if you will take the lowest of one, and the highest of the other, there will scarce be perceived any great difference between them; and so on till we come to the lowest and the most inorganical parts of Matter, we shall find every where that the several Species are linked together, and differ but in almost insensible degrees. And when we consider the infinite Power and Wisdom of the Maker, we have reason to think, that it is suitable to the magnificent Harmony of the Universe, and the great Design and infinite Goodness of the Architect, that the Species of Creatures should also, by gentle degrees, Ascend upward from us toward his infinite Perfection, as we see they gradually descend from us downwards: Which if it be probable, we have reason then to be persuaded, that there are far more Species of Creatures above us, than there are beneath; we being in degrees of perfection, much more remote from the infinite Being of God, than we are from the lowest state of Being, and that which approaches nearest to nothing. And yet of all those distinct Species, we have no clear distinct Ideas.[1]

In this System of Being, there is no Creature so wonderful in its Nature, and which so much deserves our particular Attention, as Man, who fills up the middle Space between the Animal and Intellectual Nature, the visible and invisible World, and is that Link in the Chain of Beings which has been often termed the *nexus utriusque mundi*.[2] So that he, who in one Respect is associated with Angels and Arch-Angels, may look upon a Being of infinite Perfection as his Father, and the highest Order of Spirits as his Brethren, may in another Respect say to *Corruption, thou art my Father, and to the Worm, thou art my Mother and my Sister*.[3]   O

---

[1] Locke, *Essay concerning Human Understanding*, III. vi. 12.
[2] (The joining of both of two worlds.) Cf. Henry More, *Antidote against Atheism*, book ii, chap. xii: 'And then we acknowledging Man to dwell as it were in the borders of the Spiritual and Material World, (for he is *utriusque mundi nexus*, as *Scaliger* truly calls him). . .' (3rd ed., 1662, p. 84).   [3] Job xvii. 14.

No. 520   *Monday, October 27, 1712*[1]

[STEELE]

Quis desiderio sit pudor aut modus
Tam chari capitis!

                                        Hor.

Mr. SPECTATOR,

'THE just Value you have express'd for the Matrimonial State, is the Reason that I now venture to write to you, without Fear of being ridiculous, and confess to you, that though it is three Months since I lost a very agreeable Woman, who was my Wife, my Sorrow is still fresh; and I am often, in the midst of Company, upon any Circumstance that revives her Memory, with a Reflection what she would say or do on such an Occasion; I say, upon any Occurence of that Nature, which I can give you a Sense of, though I cannot express it wholly, I am all over Softness, and am obliged to retire, and give Way to a few Sighs and Tears, before I can be easy. I cannot but recommend the Subject of Male Widowhood to you, and beg of you to touch upon it by the first Opportunity. To those who have not liv'd like Husbands during the Lives of their Spouses, this would be a tasteless Jumble of Words; but to such (of whom there are not a few) who have enjoy'd that State with the Sentiments proper for it, you will have every Line, which hits the Sorrow, attended with a Tear of Pity and Consolation. For I know not by what Goodness of Providence it is, that every Gush of Passion is a Step towards the Relief of it; and there is a certain Comfort in the very Act of Sorrowing, which, I suppose, arises from a secret Consciousness in the Mind, that the Affliction it is under flows from a virtuous Cause. My Concern is not indeed so outragious

---

¹ *Motto.* Horace, *Odes*, I. 24. 1–2:

> And who can grieve too much? what time shall end
> Our mourning for so dear a Friend? CREECH.

In the folio sheets only the first line is used. These lines from Horace had served as motto for No. 133.

The original letter, requesting 'some few and speedy directions how to make the memory of such a wife not only deare but delightfull', is preserved at Blenheim Palace (No. 76 in Richmond P. Bond, *New Letters*). A comparison of it (see Appendix) with the text in the *Spectator* shows that Steele has rewritten the letter to express what 'F. J.' would like to have written. 'This admirable letter was written, it is said, by a Mr. Francham, of Norwich' (Nichols). A John Fransham, a linendraper of Norwich, is mentioned in the *DNB*, at the end of the article on John Fransham (1730–1810), the free-thinker. There is no positive evidence that he is the 'F. J.' whose appeal has resulted in this epistolary effort by Steele.

as at the first Transport; for I think it has subsided rather into a soberer State of Mind, than any actual Perturbation of Spirit. There might be Rules formed for Men's Behaviour on this great Incident, to bring them from that Misfortune into the Condition I am at present, which is, I think, that my Sorrow has converted all Roughness of Temper into Meekness, Good-nature, and Complacency: But indeed, when in a serious and lonely Hour I present my departed Consort to my Imagination, with that Air of Perswasion in her Countenance when I have been in Passion, that sweet Affability when I have been in good Humour, that tender Compassion when I have had any thing which gave me Uneasiness; I confess to you I am inconsolable, and my Eyes gush with Grief as if I had seen her but just then expire. In this Condition I am broken in upon by a charming young Woman, my Daughter, who is the Picture of what her Mother was on her Wedding-Day.[1] The good Girl strives to comfort me; but how shall I let you know that all the Comfort she gives me is to make my Tears flow more easily? The Child knows she quickens my Sorrow, and rejoices my Heart at the same Time. Oh, ye Learned, tell me by what Word to speak a Motion of the Soul for which there is no Name. When she kneels and bids me be comforted, she is my Child; when I take her in my Arms, and bid her say no more, she is my very Wife, and is the very Comforter I lament the Loss of. I banish her the Room, and weep aloud, that I have lost her Mother, and that I have her.

'Mr. SPECTATOR, I wish it were possible for you to have a Sense of these pleasing Perplexities; you might communicate to the guilty Part of Mankind, that they are incapable of the Happiness which is in the very Sorrows of the Vertuous.

'But pray spare me a little longer; give me Leave to tell you the Manner of her Death. She took Leave of all her Family, and bore the vain Application of Medicines with the greatest Patience imaginable. When the Physician told her she must certainly die, she desired, as well as she could, that all who were present, except my self, might depart the Room. She said she had nothing to say, for she was resigned, and I knew all she knew that concerned us in this World; but she desired to be alone, that in the Presence of God only she might, without Interruption, do her last Duty to me, of

---

[1] See *OED*, 'picture', 2g, where this quotation is given, the earliest in this special sense: 'A person so strongly resembling another as to seem a likeness or imitation of him or her.'

thanking me for all my Kindness to her; adding, That she hoped in my last Moments I should feel the same Comfort for my Goodness to her, as she did in that she had acquitted herself with Honour, Truth, and Virtue to me.

'I curb my self, and will not tell you that this Kindness cut my Heart in twain, when I expected an Accusation for some passionate Starts of mine in some Parts of our Time together, to say nothing, but thank me for the Good, if there was any Good suitable to her own Excellence! All that I had ever said to her, all the Circumstances of Sorrow and Joy between us, crowded upon my Mind in the same Instant; and when immediately after I saw the Pangs of Death come upon that dear Body which I had often embraced with Transport; when I saw those cherishing Eyes begin to be ghastly, and their last Struggle to be to fix themselves on me, how did I lose all Patience? She expired in my Arms, and in my Distraction I thought I saw her Bosom still heave. There was certainly Life yet still left; I cried she just now spoke to me: But, alas! I grew giddy, and all things moved about me from the Distemper of my own Head; for the best of Women was breathless, and gone for ever.

'Now the Doctrine I would, methinks, have you raise from this Account I have given you, is, That there is a certain Equanimity in those who are good and just, which runs into their very Sorrow, and disappoints the Force of it. Tho' they must pass through Afflictions in common with all who are in humane Nature, yet their conscious Integrity shall undermine their Affliction; nay, that very Affliction shall add Force to their Integrity, from a Reflection of the use of Virtue in the Hour of Affliction. I sate down with a Design to put you upon giving us Rules how to overcome such Griefs as these; but I should rather advise you to teach Men to be capable of them.

You Men of Letters have what you call the fine Taste in their Apprehensions of what is properly done or said: There is something like this deeply grafted in the Soul of him who is honest and faithful in all his Thoughts and Actions. Every thing which is false, vitious, or unworthy is despicable to him, tho' all the World should approve it. At the same Time he has the most lively Sensibility in all Enjoyments and Sufferings which it is proper for him to have, where any Duty of Life is concerned. To want Sorrow when you in Decency and Truth should be afflicted, is, I should think, a greater Instance of a Man's being a Blockhead, than not to know the Beauty of any Passage in *Virgil*. You have not yet observed, Mr. SPECTATOR, that the fine Gentlemen of this Age set up for Hardness of Heart, and Humanity has very little Share in their Pretences. He is a brave Fellow who is always ready to kill a Man he hates, but he does not stand in the same Degree of Esteem who laments for the Woman he loves. I should fancy you might work up a thousand pretty Thoughts, by reflecting upon the Persons most susceptible of the sort of Sorrow I have spoken of; and I dare say you will find upon Examination, that they are the wisest and the bravest of Mankind who are most capable of it.

<table>
<tr><td></td><td>I am,</td></tr>
<tr><td>Norwich,</td><td>SIR,</td></tr>
<tr><td>7°. Octobris,</td><td>Your most humble Servant,</td></tr>
<tr><td>1712.</td><td>F. J.'</td></tr>
</table>

T¹

No. 521

[STEELE]

Tuesday, October 28, 1712²

Vera redit facies, dissimulata perit.

Pe. Arb.

Mr. SPECTATOR,

'I HAVE been for many Years loud in this Assertion, That there are very few that can see or hear, I mean that can report what they have seen or heard; and this thro' Incapacity or Prejudice, one of which disables almost every Man who talks to you from representing things as he ought. For which Reason I am come to a Resolution of believing nothing I hear; and I contemn the Men given to Narration under the Appellation of a Matter of Fact Man: And according to me, a Matter of Fact³ Man is one whose Life and Conversation is spent in the Report of what is not Matter of Fact.

'I remember when Prince *Eugene* was here, there was no knowing

¹ A letter in Lillie (ii. 362–4) signed A. W. praises this number. 'Among the various fine thoughts in that paper, give me leave to remind you of one; which is, I banish her the room, and weep aloud, that I have lost her mother, and have her' (p. 362). After describing his own grief in the loss of a daughter, the writer concludes: 'There is nothing I wish for so much, as to have seen what Cicero had said on the like occasion. Now I am persuaded you can say whatever he could' (p. 364).

² *Motto.* Petronius Arbiter, *Satyricon*, 80 (altered): The real face appears, the false one's gone.

³ This is the first example in *OED* of the phrase used as attributive adjective.

his Height or Figure, till you, Mr. SPECTATOR, gave the Publick Satisfaction in that Matter.[1] In Relations, the Force of the Expression lies very often more in the Look, the Tone of Voice, or the Gesture, than the Words themselves; which being repeated in any other manner by the Undiscerning, bear a very different Interpretation from their original Meaning. I must confess, I formerly have turn'd this Humour of mine to very good Account; for whenever I heard any Narrations utter'd with extraordinary Vehemence, and grounded upon considerable Authority, I was always ready to lay any Wager that it was not so. Indeed I never pretended to be so rash, as to fix the Matter any particular Way in Opposition to theirs; but as there are an hundred Ways of any thing happening, besides that it has happen'd, I only controverted its falling out in that one Manner as they settled it, and left it to the Ninety nine other Ways, and consequently had more Probability of Success. I had arrived at a particular Skill in warming a Man so far in his Narration, as to make him throw in a little of the Marvelous, and then, if he has much Fire, the next Degree is the Impossible. Now this is always the Time for fixing the Wager. But this requires the nicest Management, otherwise very probably the Dispute may arise to the old Determination by Battle. In these Conceits I have been very fortunate, and have won some Wagers of those who have professedly valued themselves upon Intelligence, and have put themselves to great Charge and Expence to be misinform'd considerably sooner than the rest of the World.

'Having got a comfortable Sum by this my Opposition to publick Report, I have brought my self now to so great a Perfection in Inattention, more-especially to Party Relations, that at the same time I seem with greedy Ears to devour up the Discourse, I certainly don't know one Word of it, but pursue my own Course of Thought, whether upon Business or Amusement, with much Tranquility: I say Inattention, because a late Act of Parliament has secur'd all Party-Lyars from the Penalty of a Wager, and consequently made it unprofitable to attend to them.[2] However, good Breeding obliges a Man to maintain the Figure of the keenest Attention, the true Posture of which in a Coffee-house I take to consist in leaning over a Table, with the Edge of it pressing hard upon your Stomach; for

[1] See No. 340 (vol. iii).
[2] 7 Anne, cap. 17. By it all wagers laid upon a contingency relating to the war with France were declared to be void (Nichols).

the more Pain the Narration is received with, the more gracious is your bending over: Besides that, the Narrator thinks you forget your Pain by the Pleasure of hearing him.

'Fort *Knock* has occasioned several very perplex'd and inelegant Heats and Animosities; and there was one t'other Day in a Coffee-house where I was, that took upon him to clear that Business to me, for he said he was there.¹ I knew him to be that sort of Man that had not Strength of Capacity to be inform'd of any thing that depended merely upon his being an Eye-Witness, and therefore was fully satisfy'd he could give me no Information, for the very same Reason he believ'd he could, for he was there. However, I heard him with the same Greediness as *Shakespear* describes in the following Lines:

> *I saw a Smith stand on his Hammer, thus,*
> *With open Mouth swallowing a Taylor's News.*²

'I confess of late I have not been so much amaz'd at the Declaimers in Coffee-houses as I formerly was, being satisfied that they expect to be rewarded for their Vociferations. Of these Liars there are two Sorts. The Genius of the first consists in much Impudence and a strong Memory; the others have added to these Qualifications a good Understanding and smooth Language. These therefore have only certain Heads, which they are as eloquent upon as they can, and may be call'd Embellishers; the others repeat only what they hear from others as literally as their Parts or Zeal will permit, and are called Reciters. Here was a Fellow in Town some Years ago, who used to divert himself by telling a Lie at *Charing-Cross* in the Morning at eight of Clock, and then following it through all Parts of the Town till eight at Night; at which Time he came to a Club of his Friends, and diverted them with an Account what Censure it had at *Will's* in *Covent-Garden*, how dangerous it was believed to be at *Child's*, and what Inference they drew from it with Relation to

---

¹ Fort Knocke, an important post at the junction of the canals of Ypres and Furnes above Dixemude, was taken by surprise on 6 Oct. (N.S.) 1712 by Captain de la Rüe of the Allied army. A few days before the appearance of this number the *Post Boy* of 23 Oct. reported from The Hague:

> The Surprizing of Fort Knocke is by Prince Eugene judg'd of such Importance, that he has written to their High-Mightinesses, That he esteems the Commander of that bold Enterprize well worthy Consideration. By way of Recompence, the States have conferr'd on the said Commander, namely, Monsieur de la Rue, the Government of the Fort he took. . . .

² *King John*, IV. ii. 193, 195.

Stocks at *Jonathan*'s.[1] I have had the Honour to travel with this Gentleman I speak of in Search of one of his Falshoods; and have been present when they have described the very Man they have spoken to, as him who first reported it, tall or short, black or fair, a Gentleman or a Raggamuffin, according as they liked the Intelligence. I have heard one of our ingenious Writers of News say, that when he has had a Customer come with an Advertisement of an Apprentice or a Wife run away, he has desired the Advertiser to compose himself a little, before he dictated the Description of the Offender: For when a Person is put into a publick Paper by a Man who is angry with him, the real Description of such Person is hid in the Deformity with which the angry Man described him; therefore this Fellow always made his Customers describe him as he would the Day before he offended, or else he was sure he would never find him out. These and many other Hints I could suggest to you for the Elucidation of all Fictions; but I leave it to your own Sagacity to improve or neglect this Speculation.

I am, SIR,

Your most obedient,

Humble Servant.'

Postscript *to the* Spectator *Number* 502.

N.B. *There are in the Play of the* Self-Tormentor *of* Terence's, *which is allowed a most excellent Comedy, several Incidents which would draw Tears from any Man of Sense, and not one which would move his Laughter.*

T

---

[1] Will's, Child's, Jonathan's. For these see No. 1.

> *. . . Adjuro nunquam eam me deserturum,*
> *Non, si capiundos mihi sciam esse inimicos omnis homines.*
> *Hanc mihi expetivi, contigit: conveniunt mores: valeant*
> *Qui inter nos dissidium volunt: hanc, nisi mors,*
> *Mi adimet nemo.*
>
> Ter.

I SHOULD esteem my self a very happy Man, if my Speculations could in the least contribute to the rectifying the Conduct of my Readers in one of the most important Affairs of Life, to wit, their Choice in Marriage. This State is the Foundation of Community, and the chief Band of Society; and I do not think I can be too frequent on Subjects which may give Light to my unmarried Readers, in a Particular which is so essential to their following Happiness or Misery. A virtuous Disposition, a good Understanding, an agreeable Person, and an easy Fortune, are the Things which should be chiefly regarded on this Occasion. Because my present View is to direct a young Lady, who, I think, is now in Doubt whom to take of many Lovers, I shall talk at this Time to my female Reader. The Advantages, as I was going to say, of Sense, Beauty, and Riches, are what are certainly the chief Motives to a prudent young Woman of Fortune for changing her Condition;[2] but as she is to have her Eye upon each of these, she is to ask her self whether the Man who has most of these Recommendations in the Lump is not the most desirable. He that has excellent Talents, with a moderate Estate, and an agreeable Person, is preferable to him who is only rich, if it were only that good Faculties may purchase Riches, but Riches cannot purchase worthy Endowments. I do not mean that Wit, and a Capacity to entertain, is what should be highly valued, except it is founded upon Good-nature and Humanity. There are many ingenious Men, whose Abilities do little else but make themselves and those about them uneasy: Such are those who are far gone in the Pleasures of the Town, who cannot support Life without

---

[1] *Motto.* Terence, *Andria*, 694–7: I swear never to forsake her; no, though I were sure to make all men my enemies. Her I desired; her I have obtained; our humours agree. Perish all those who would separate us! Death alone shall deprive me of her.
[2] This is the first example in *OED* of this phrase as a locution for 'getting married'.

quick Sensations and gay Reflections, and are Strangers to Tranquility, to right Reason, and a calm Motion of Spirits without Transport or Dejection. These ingenious Men, of all Men living, are most to be avoided by her who would be happy in an Husband. They are immediately sated with Possession, and must necessarily fly to new Acquisitions of Beauty, to pass away the whiling Moments and Intervals of Life;[1] for with them every Hour is heavy that is not joyful. But there is a sort of Man of Wit and Sense, that can reflect upon his own Make, and that of his Partner, with the Eyes of Reason and Honour, and who believes he offends against both these, if he does not look upon the Woman (who chose him to be under his Protection in Sickness and Health) with the utmost Gratitude, whether from that Moment she is shining or defective in Person or Mind: I say there are those who think themselves bound to supply with good Nature the Failings of those who love them, and who always think those the Objects of Love and Pity, who came to their Arms the Objects of Joy and Admiration.

Of this latter sort is *Lysander*, a Man of Wit, Learning, Sobriety, and Good-nature, of Birth and Estate below no Woman to accept, and of whom it might be said, Should he succeed in his present Wishes his Mistress raised his Fortune, but not that she made it. When a Woman is deliberating with her self whom she shall chuse of many near each other in other Pretensions, certainly he of best Understanding is to be prefer'd. Life hangs heavily in the repeated Conversation of one who has no Imagination to be fired at the several Occasions and Objects which come before him, or who cannot strike out of his Reflections new Paths of pleasing Discourse. Honest *Will. Thrash* and his Wife, tho' not married above four Months, have scarce had a Word to say to each other this six Weeks; and one cannot form to one's self a sillier Picture, than these two Creatures in solemn Pomp and Plenty unable to enjoy their Fortunes, and at a full Stop among a Crowd of Servants, to whose Taste of Life they are beholden for the little Satisfactions by which they can be understood to be so much as barely in Being. The Hours of the Day, the Distinctions of Noon and Night, Dinner and Supper, are the greatest Notices they are capable of. This is perhaps representing the Life of a very modest Woman, joined to a dull Fellow, more insipid than it really deserves; but I am sure it is not to exalt the Commerce with an ingenious Companion too high, to

---

[1] See No. 448.

say that every new Accident or Object which comes into such a
Gentleman's Way, gives his Wife new Pleasures and Satisfactions.
The Approbation of his Words and Actions is a continual new Feast
to her; nor can she enough applaud her good Fortune in having her
Life varied every Hour; her Mind more improved, and her Heart
more glad from every Circumstance which they meet with. He will
lay out his Invention in forming new Pleasures and Amusements,
and make the Fortune she has brought him subservient to the
Honour and Reputation of her and her's. A Man of Sense who is
thus obliged, is ever contriving the Happiness of her who did him
so great a Distinction; while the Fool is ungrateful without Vice,
and never returns a Favour because he is not sensible of it. I would,
methinks, have so much to say for my self, that if I fell into the
Hands of him who treated me ill, he should be sensible when he
did so: His Conscience should be of my Side, whatever became of
his Inclination. I do not know but it is the insipid Choice which
has been made by those who have the Care of young Women, that
the Marriage State it self has been liable to so much Ridicule. But
a well-chosen Love, moved by Passion on both Sides, and perfected
by the Generosity of one Party, must be adorn'd with so many
handsome Incidents on the other Side, that every particular Couple
would be an Example in many Circumstances to all the rest of the
Species. I shall end the Chat upon this Subject with a Couple of
Letters, one from a Lover who is very well acquainted with the
Way of bargaining on these Occasions; and the other from his
Rival, who has a less Estate, but great Gallantry of Temper. As for
my Man of Prudence, he[a] makes Love, as he says, as if he were
already a Father, and laying aside the Passion, comes to the Reason
of the Thing.

Madam,

'**M**Y Council has perused the Inventory of your Estate, and
considered what Estate you have, which it seems is only
yours, and to the Male Heirs of your Body; but, in Default of such
Issue, to the right Heirs of your Uncle *Edward* for ever. Thus,
Madam, I am advised you cannot (the Remainder not being in you)
dock the Entail; by which means my Estate, which is Fee-Simple,
will come by the Settlement proposed to your Children begotten
by me, whether they are Males or Females; but my Children

<hr>

a he] *1723*; who *Fol., 8vo, 12 mo.*

begotten upon you will not inherit your Lands, except I beget a Son. Now, Madam, since Things are so, you are a Woman of that Prudence, and understand the World so well, as not to expect I should give you more than you can give me.

I am, Madam,
(with great Respect)
Your most obedient humble Servant,

T. W.'

The other Lover's Estate is less than this Gentleman's, but he express'd himself as follows.

Madam,

'I HAVE given in my Estate to your Council, and desir'd my own Lawyer to insist upon no Terms which your Friends can propose for your certain Ease and Advantage[1]: For indeed I have no Notion of making Difficulties of presenting you with what cannot make me happy without you.

I am, Madam,
Your most devoted humble Servant,

B. T.'

You must know the Relations have met upon this, and the Girl being mightily taken with the latter Epistle, she is laugh'd out, and Uncle *Edward* is to be dealt with to make her a suitable Match to the worthy Gentleman who has told her he does not care a Farthing for her. All I hope for is, that the Lady *Fair* will make use of the first light Night to show *B. T.* she understands a Marriage is not to be considered as a common Bargain.

T

---

[1] In No. 299 Sir John Enville had made a similar concession and desired his fiancée o 'write her own terms' (iii. 69). For other references to marriage-articles see i. 347 nd iii. 111 .

> ... *nunc augur Apollo,*
> *Nunc Lyciæ sortes, nunc & Jove missus ab ipso*
> *Interpres Divûm fert horrida jussa per auras.*
> *Scilicet is superis labor* ...
>
> Virg.

I AM always highly delighted with the Discovery of any rising Genius among my Countrymen. For this Reason I have read over, with great Pleasure, the late Miscellany published by Mr. *Pope*, in which there are many Excellent Compositions of that ingenious Gentleman.[2] I have had a Pleasure, of the same kind, in perusing a Poem that is just published *on the Prospect of Peace*, and which, I hope, will meet with such a Reward from its Patrons, as so noble a Performance deserves.[3] I was particularly well pleased to find that the Author had not amused himself with Fables out of the Pagan Theology, and that when he hints at any thing of this[a] nature, he alludes to it only as to a Fable.

Many of our Modern Authors, whose Learning very often extends no farther than *Ovid*'s *Metamorphosis*, do not know how to celebrate a Great Man, without mixing a parcel of School-boy Tales

---

[a] this] that *Fol.*

---

[1] *Motto.* Virgil, *Aeneid*, 4. 376–9:

> Now *Lycian* Lotts, and now the *Delian* God;
> Now *Hermes* is employ'd from *Jove*'s abode,
> To warn him hence; as if the peaceful State
> Of Heav'nly Pow'rs were touch'd with Humane Fate! DRYDEN.

[2] This is the volume containing 'The Rape of the Lock', the 'Epistle to Miss Blount, with the Works of Voiture', and other shorter pieces of Pope, advertised in No. 383 (20 May 1712) as 'This Day . . . Published':

> Miscellaneous Poems and Translations. By several Hands. Printed for Bernard Lintott, at the Cross Keys between the two Temple Gates in Fleetstreet.

[3] Tickell's poem is advertised in No. 521, two days before the publication of this number:

> This Day is Published,
> A Poem to his Excellency the Lord Privy-Seal, on the Prospect of PEACE. By Mr. Tickell. Printed for J. Tonson at Shakespear's-Head, over against Catherine street in the Strand.

The Lord Privy Seal at this time was Bishop John Robinson. Pope praises Tickell's poem in a letter to Caryll of 29 Nov. 1712 (*Correspondence*, ed. Sherburn, i. 156–8). The second edition was published on 6 Nov., the third on 10 Nov., and the fourth on 3 Dec. (advertisements in Nos. 529, 532, and 552).

with the Recital of his Actions.[1] If you read a Poem on a fine Woman, among the Authors of this Class, you shall see that it turns more upon *Venus* or *Helen*, than on the Party concerned. I have known a Copy of Verses on a great Hero highly commended, but upon asking to hear some of the beautiful Passages, the Admirer of it has repeated to me a Speech of *Apollo*, or a Description of *Polypheme*. At other times when I have searched for the Actions of a Great Man, who gave a Subject to the Writer, I have been entertained with the Exploits of a River-God, or have been forced to attend a Fury in her mischievous Progress, from one end of the Poem to the other. When we are at School it is necessary for us to be acquainted with the System of Pagan Theology, and may be allowed to enliven a Theme, or point an Epigram with an Heathen God; but when we would write a manly Panegyrick, that should carry in it all the Colours of Truth, nothing can be more ridiculous than to have recourse to our *Jupiter's* and *Juno's*.

No Thought is beautiful which is not just, and no Thought can be just which is not founded in Truth, or at least in that which passes for such.[2]

In Mock-Heroick Poems, the use of the Heathen Mythology is not only excusable but graceful, because it is the Design of such Compositions to divert, by adapting the fabulous Machines of the Ancients to low Subjects, and at the same time by ridiculing such kinds of Machinery in Modern Writers.[3] If any are of Opinion, that there is a necessity of admitting these Classical Legends into our Serious Compositions, in order to give them a more Poetical Turn; I would recommend to their Consideration the Pastorals of Mr. *Philips*.[4] One would have thought it impossible for this Kind of Poetry to have subsisted without Fawns and Satyrs, Wood-Nymphs and Water-Nymphs, with all the Tribe of Rural Deities. But we see

---

[1] Possibly a thrust at John Dennis. In the preface to *The Battle of Ramillia* (1706) Dennis had defended his adorning the Duke of Marlborough's actions with the 'machines' of fiction:

> To which I answer, that because what the Duke of *Marlborough* has done is in its self so wonderful that it appears incredible, and Truth it self has the Resemblance of Fable and of Fiction, for that very Reason I was encouraged to embellish it with the Ornaments of Poetry. This is the Defence that *Boileau* has made for himself in his fourth Epistle . . . (*Works*, ed. Hooker, i. 394).

[2] Cf. No. 62 (vol. i): '*Bouhours* . . . has taken Pains to shew, That it is impossible for any Thought to be beautiful which is not just, and has not its Foundation in the Nature of things. . . .'

[3] Perhaps a compliment to Pope's 'Rape of the Lock', first published in the *Miscellany* mentioned above.   [4] These had been praised earlier in No. 400.

he has given a new Life, and a more natural Beauty to this way of Writing, by Substituting in the Place of these Antiquated Fables, the superstitious Mythology which prevails among the Shepherds of our own Country.

Virgil and *Homer* might compliment their Heroes, by interweaving the Actions of Deities with their Atchievements; but for a Christian Author to write in the Pagan Creed, to make Prince *Eugene* a Favourite of *Mars*, or to carry on a Correspondence between *Bellona* and the Marshal *De Villars*, would be downright Puerility, and unpardonable in a Poet that is past Sixteen.[1] It is want of sufficient Elevation in a Genius to describe Realities, and place them in a shining Light, that makes him have recourse to such trifling antiquated Fables; as a Man may write a fine Description of *Bacchus* or *Apollo*, that does not know how to draw the Character of any of his Contemporaries.

In order, therefore, to put a stop to this absurd Practice, I shall publish the following Edict, by Vertue of that Spectatorial Authority with which I stand Invested.

'WHEREAS the Time of a General Peace is, in all appearance, drawing near; being informed that there are several ingenious Persons who intend to shew their Talents on so happy an Occasion, and being willing, as much as in me lies, to prevent that Effusion of Nonsense, which we have good Cause to apprehend; I do hereby strictly require every Person, who shall write on this Subject, to remember that he is a Christian, and not to Sacrifice his Catechism to his Poetry. In order to it, I do expect of him in the first place, to make his own Poem without depending upon *Phœbus* for any part of it, or calling out for Aid upon any one of the Muses by Name. I do likewise positively forbid the sending of *Mercury* with any particular Message or Dispatch relating to the Peace, and shall by no means suffer *Minerva* to take upon her the Shape of any Plenipotentiary concerned in this Great Work. I do further declare, that I shall not allow the Destinies to have had an Hand in the Deaths of the several Thousands who have been slain in the late War, being of Opinion that all such Deaths may be very well accounted for by the Christian System of Powder and Ball. I do therefore strictly forbid the Fates to cut the Thread of Man's Life

---

[1] For the Duc de Villars, the great general who saved his country by the victory at Denain in 1712, see Trevelyan, iii. 2–4.

upon any Pretence whatsoever, unless it be for the sake of the Rhime. And whereas I have good Reason to fear, that *Neptune* will have a great deal of Business on his Hands, in several Poems which we may now suppose are upon the Anvil, I do also prohibit his Appearance, unless it be done in Metaphor, Simile, or any very short Allusion, and that even here he be not permitted to enter, but with great Caution and Circumspection. I desire that the same Rule may be extended to his whole Fraternity of Heathen Gods, it being my Design to condemn every Poem to the Flames, in which *Jupiter* Thunders, or exercises any other Act of Authority, which does not belong to him: In short, I expect that no Pagan Agent shall be introduced, or any Fact related which a Man cannot give Credit to with a good Conscience. Provided always, that nothing herein contained shall extend, or be construed to extend, to several of the Female Poets in this Nation, who shall be still left in full Possession of their Gods and Goddesses, in the same manner as if this Paper had never been written.'

O

No. 524　　　　　　　　*Friday, October* 31, 1712[1]

Nos populo damus. . . .
Sen.

WHEN I first of all took it in my Head to write Dreams and Visions, I determined to Print nothing of that nature, which was not of my own Invention. But several laborious Dreamers have

[1] *Motto.* Seneca, *Epistulae morales*, 99. 17: We go with the crowd.

The introductory paragraph of this number is almost certainly by Addison. The letter which follows, writes Nichols,

has been ascribed to Professor Simpson, of Glasgow. It seems to rest on better authority, that it was the joint composition of Mr. Dunlop, then Greek Professor of that University, and a Mr. Montgomery, a gentleman in the mercantile line, of an amiable character, an enterprizing spirit, and great abilities. He traded to Sweden, and his business carrying him there, it is said that in consequence of something between him and Queen Christina, he was obliged to leave that kingdom abruptly. This event was supposed to have affected his intellects, much in the same manner as Sir Roger de Coverley is represented in these papers to have been injured by his passion for a beautiful widow.

It seems impossible now to know how much factual basis there is for these statements. Robert Simson (1687–1768) was elected professor of mathematics at Glasgow University on 11 Mar. 1711–12, after a year's study in London, where he made the

of late communicated to me Works of this nature, which, for their Reputations and my own, I have hitherto suppressed. Had I printed every one that came to my Hands, my Book of Speculations would have been little else but a Book of Visions. Some of my Correspondents have indeed been so very modest, as to offer at an Excuse for their not being in a Capacity to dream better. I have by me, for Example, the Dream of a Young Gentleman not past Fifteen. I have likewise by me the Dream of a Person of Quality, and another called the Ladies-Dream. In these, and other Pieces of the same nature, it is supposed the usual Allowances will be made to the Age, Condition and Sex of the Dreamer. To prevent this Inundation of Dreams, which daily flows in upon me, I shall apply to all Dreamers of Dreams, the Advice which *Epictetus* has couched after his manner in a very simple and concise Precept. *Never tell thy Dreams*, says that Philosopher, *for tho' thou thy self may'st take a Pleasure in telling thy Dream, another will take no Pleasure in hearing it.*[1] After this short Preface, I must do Justice to two or three Visions which I have lately published, and which I have owned to have been written by other Hands. I shall add a Dream to these, which comes to me from *Scotland*, by one who declares himself of that Country, and for all I know may be Second-sighted.[2] There is, indeed, something in it of the Spirit of *John Bunyan*; but at the same time a certain Sublime, which that Author was never Master of.[3] I shall publish it, because I question not but it will fall in with the Taste of all my popular Readers, and amuse[4] the Imaginations of those who are more profound; declaring, at the same time, that this is the last Dream which I intend to publish this Season.

SIR,

'I Was last *Sunday*, in the Evening, led into a serious Reflection on the Reasonableness of Virtue, and great Folly of Vice, from an Excellent Sermon I had heard that Afternoon in my Parish Church.

acquaintance of several eminent mathematicians, including Edmond Halley (*DNB*). Alexander Dunlop (1684–1747) was appointed professor of Greek at Glasgow about 1706 and was author of a Greek grammar published in 1736. I have not been able to discover more of Mr. Montgomery, the 'gentleman in the mercantile line'.

[1] Perhaps a reminiscence of *Enchiridion*, c. 33. 14: 'In talk with others let there be no long or immoderate mention of one's own deeds or dangers. For it is not the case, that as it is pleasant to you to mention your own dangers, so it is also pleasant to the others to hear what has happened to you.' I owe this suggestion to the kindness of Professor Benedict Einarson. Steele in *Tatler* 268 had also quoted this precept from Epictetus. [2] Probably another reference to Duncan Campbell.
[3] One of the few allusions to Bunyan at this period. [4] Cf. No. 495.

Among other Observations, the Preacher shewed us that the Temptations which the Tempter proposed, were all on a Supposition, that we are either Madmen or Fools, or with an Intention to render us such; that in no other Affair we would suffer our selves to be thus imposed upon, in a Case so plainly and clearly against our visible Interest. His Illustrations and Arguments carried so much Perswasion and Conviction with them, that they remained a considerable while fresh, and working in my Memory; 'till at last the Mind, fatigu'd with Thought, gave way to the forceable Oppressions of Slumber and Sleep, whilst Fancy, unwilling yet to drop the Subject, presented me with the following Vision.

'Methought I was just awoke out of a Sleep, that I could never remember the beginning of; the Place where I found my self to be was a wide and spacious Plain, full of People that wander'd up and down through several beaten Paths, whereof some few were streight, and in direct Lines; but most of them winding and turning like a Labyrinth; but yet it appeared to me afterwards, that these last all met in one Issue, so that many that seemed to steer quite contrary Courses, did at length meet and face one another, to the no little Amazement of many of them.

'In the midst of the Plain there was a great Fountain: they call'd it the Spring of *Self-Love*; out of it issued two Rivulets to the Eastward and Westward, the Name of the first was *Heavenly Wisdom*, its Water was wonderfully clear, but of a yet more wonderful Effect; the other's Name was *Worldly Wisdom*, its Water was thick, and yet far from being dormant or stagnating, for it was in a continual violent Agitation; which kept the Travellers, whom I shall mention by and by, from being sensible of the foulness and thickness of the Water, which had this Effect, that it intoxicated those that drunk it, and made 'em mistake every Object that lay before them; both Rivulets were parted near their Springs into so many others, as there were streight and crooked Paths, which they attended all along to their respective Issues.

'I observed from the several Paths many now and then diverting, to refresh and otherwise qualify themselves for their Journey, to the respective Rivulets that ran near them; they contracted a very observable Courage and Steadiness in what they were about, by drinking these Waters. At the End of the Perspective of every streight Path, all which did end in one Issue and Point, appeared a high Pillar, all of Diamond, casting Rays as bright as those of the

Sun into the Paths; which Rays had also certain simpathising and alluring Virtues in them, so that whosoever had made some considerable Progress in his Journey onwards towards the Pillar, by the repeated Impression of these Rays upon him, was wrought into an habitual Inclination and Conversion of his Sight towards it, so that it grew at last in a manner natural to him to look and gaze upon it, whereby he was kept steady in the streight Paths, which alone led to that Radiant Body, the beholding of which was now grown a Gratification to his Nature.

'At the Issue of the crooked Paths there was a great black Tower, out of the Centre of which streamed a long Succession of Flames, which did rise even above the Clouds; it gave a very great Light to the whole Plain, which did sometimes out-shine the Light, and opprest the Beams of the Adamantine Pillar; tho', by the Observation I made afterwards, it appeared that it was not for any Diminution of Light, but that this lay in the Travellers, who would sometimes step out of the streight Paths, where they lost the full Prospect of the Radiant Pillar, and saw it but sideways; but the great Light from the black Tower, which was somewhat particularly scorching to them, would generally light and hasten them to their proper Climate again.

'Round about the black Tower there was, methoughts, many Thousands of huge mis-shapen ugly Monsters; these had great Nets, which they were perpetually plying and casting towards the crooked Paths, and they would now and then catch up those that were nearest to them; these they took up streight, and whirled over the Walls into the Flaming Tower, and they were no more seen nor heard of.

'They would sometimes cast their Nets towards the right Paths to catch the Stragglers, whose Eyes for want of frequent drinking at the Brook that ran by them grew dim, whereby they lost their way; these would sometimes very narrowly miss being catched away, but I could not hear whether any of these had ever been so unfortunate, that had been before very hearty in the streight Paths.

'I considered all these strange Sights with great Attention, till at last I was interrupted by a Cluster of the Travellers in the crooked Paths, who came up to me, bid me go along with them, and presently fell to Singing and Dancing; they took me by the Hand, and so carryed me away along with them. After I had followed them a considerable while, I perceived I had lost the black Tower of Light, at which I greatly wondered; but as I looked and gazed round about me, and saw nothing, I begun to fancy my first Vision had been but a Dream, and there was no such thing in reality; but then I considered, that if I could fancy to see what was not, I might as well have an Illusion wrought on me at present, and not see what really was before me. I was very much confirmed in this Thought, by the Effect I then just observed the Water of *Worldly Wisdom* had upon me; for as I had drunk a little of it again, I felt a very sensible Effect in my Head; methought it distracted and disordered all there; this made me stop of a sudden, suspecting some Charm or Inchantment. As I was casting about within my self what I should do, and whom to apply to in this Case, I spyed at some distance off me a Man beckning, and making Signs to me to come over to him. I cryed to him, *I did not know the way.* He then called to me audibly, to step at least out of the Path I was in, for if I staid there any longer I was in danger to be catched in a great Net that was just hanging over me, and ready to catch me up; that he wondered I was so blind, or so distracted, as not to see so imminent and visible a Danger; assuring me, that as soon as I was out of that Way, he would come to me to lead me into a more secure Path. This I did, and he brought me his Palm full of the Water of *Heavenly Wisdom*, which was of very great use to me, for my Eyes were streight cleared, and I saw the great Black Tower just before me; but the great Net, which I spy'd so near me, cast me in such Terror, that I ran back as far as I could in one Breath, without looking behind me; then my Benefactor thus bespoke me,[1] You have made the wonderfullest Escape in the World, the Water you used to drink is of a bewitching Nature, you would else have been mightily shocked at the Deformities and Meanness of the Place; for beside the Sett of blind Fools, in whose Company you was, you may now observe many others, who are only bewitched after another no less dangerous manner. Look a little that way, there goes a crowd of Passengers, they have indeed so good a Head, as not to suffer themselves to be blinded by this bewitching Water; the Black Tower is not vanished out of their Sight, they see it whenever they look up to it; but see how they go side-ways, and with their Eyes downwards, as if they were mad, that they may thus rush into the Net, without being beforehand troubled at the Thought of so miserable a Destruction. Their Wills are so perverse, and their Hearts so fond of the Pleasures of the Place, that rather

[1] Bespoke, i.e. 'spoke to'. 'Now chiefly *poet*.' (*OED*.)

than forego them they will run all Hazards, and venture upon all the Miseries and Woes before them.

'See there that other Company, tho' they should drink none of the bewitching Water, yet they take a course bewitching and de-luding; see how they chuse the crookedest Paths, whereby they have often the Black Tower behind them, and sometimes see the radiant Column side-ways, which gives them some weak Glympse of it. These Fools content themselves with that, not knowing whether any other have any more of its Influence and Light than themselves; this Road is called that of *Superstition* or *Human Invention*; they grosly over-look that which the Rules and Laws of the Place prescribe to them, and contrive some other Scheme and Sett of Directions and Prescriptions for themselves, which they hope will serve their turn. He shewed me many other kind of Fools, which put me quite out of humour with the Place. At last he carry'd me to the right Paths, where I found true and solid Pleasure, which entertain'd me all the way, 'till we came in closer sight of the Pillar, where the Satisfaction increased to that measure that my Faculties were not able to contain it; in the straining of them I was violently waked, nor a little grieved at the vanishing of so pleasing a Dream.'[a]

Glascow. Sept. 29.

[a] *No. 524 unsigned in Fol., 8vo, 12mo*

No. 525   *Saturday, November 1, 1712*[1]
[HUGHES]

'Ο δ' εἰς τὸ σῶφρον ἐπ' ἀρετήν τ' ἄγων ἔρως,
Ζηλωτὸς ἀνθρώποισιν . . .   Eurip.

IT is my Custom to take frequent Opportunities[a] of enquiring, from time to time, what Success my Speculations meet with in the Town. I am glad to find, in particular, that my Discourses on Marriage have been well received. A Friend of mine gives me to understand, from *Doctor's Commons*, that more Licences have been taken out there of late than usual.[2] I am likewise informed of several pretty

[a] take frequent Opportunities] take Opportunities *Fol.*

[1] *Motto.* Euripides, *Fragment* 671 (Nauck, iii. 180): But Love, that leads to Temperance and Virtue, should be Mankind's Ambition.
[2] Doctors' Commons was situated about half-way between the west end of St. Paul's churchyard and the Thames, on the west side of St. Benet's Hill. Special permits issued there allowed immediate marriage.

Fellows, who have resolved to commence Heads of Families by the first favourable Opportunity. One of them writes me Word that he is ready to enter into the Bonds of Matrimony, provided I will give it him under my Hand (as I now do) that a Man may shew his Face in good Company after he is married, and that he need not be ashamed to treat a Woman with Kindness, who puts her self into his Power for Life.

I have other Letters on this Subject, which say that I am attempting to make a Revolution in the World of Gallantry, and that the Consequence of it will be, that a great deal of the sprightliest Wit and Satyr of the last Age will be lost. That a bashful Fellow, upon changing his Condition,[1] will be no longer puzzled how to stand the Raillery of his facetious Companions; that he need not own he married only to plunder an Heiress of her Fortune, nor pretend that he uses her ill, to avoid the ridiculous[a] Name of a fond Husband.

Indeed if I may speak my Opinion of great part of the Writings which once prevailed among us under the Notion of Humour, they are such as wou'd tempt one to think there had been an Association among the Wits of those Times to rally Legitimacy out of our Island. A State of Wedlock was the common Mark of all the Adventurers in Farce and Comedy, as well as the Essayers in Lampoon and Satyr, to shoot at; and nothing was a more standing Jest in all Clubs of fashionable Mirth and gay Conversation. It was determined among those[b] airy Criticks, that the Appellation of *a Sober Man* shou'd signify *a Spiritless Fellow*. And I am apt to think it was about the same time, that *Good-nature*, a Word so peculiarly elegant in our Language that some have affirmed it cannot well be expressed in any other, came first to be rendered Suspicious, and in danger of being transferred from its original Sense, to so distant an Idea as that of *Folly*.[2]

I must confess it has been my Ambition, in the Course of my Writings, to restore, as well as I was able, the proper Ideas of Things. And as I have attempted this already on the Subject of Marriage, in several Papers, I shall here add some further Observations which occur to me on the same Head.[3]

---

[a] ridiculous] scandalous *Fol.*   [b] those] these *Fol.*

[1] For this phrase see No. 522.
[2] Cf. Edward Chamberlayne, *Magnae Britanni Notitia* (ed. 1708), p. 37:
Good Nature is a qualification peculiar to the *English*, so peculiar, that as a noble Writer observes, there is no Word for it in any other Language.
[3] Nos. 33 (vol. i), 479, 490, 522, &c.

Nothing seems to be thought, by our fine Gentlemen, so indispensable an Ornament in fashionable Life, as Love. *A Knight Errant*, says *Don Quixot, without a Mistress, is like a Tree without Leaves*;[1] and a Man of Mode among Us, who has not some Fair One to sigh for, might as well pretend to appear dressed, without his Periwig. We have Lovers in Prose innumerable. All our Pretenders to Rhime are professed Inamorato's;[2] and there is scarce a Poet, good or bad, to be heard of, who has not some real or supposed *Sacharissa* to improve his Vein.

If Love be any Refinement, *Conjugal Love* must be certainly so in a much higher Degree. There is no Comparison between the frivolous Affectation of attracting the Eyes of Women with whom you are only captivated by Way of Amusement, and of whom perhaps you know nothing more than their Features, and a regular and uniform Endeavour to make your self valuable, both as a Friend and Lover, to one whom you have chosen to be the Companion of your Life. The first is the Spring of a thousand Fopperies, silly Artifices, Falshoods, and perhaps Barbarities; or at best arises no higher than to a kind of Dancing-School Breeding, to give the Person a more sparkling Air. The latter is the Parent of substantial Virtues and agreeable Qualities, and cultivates the Mind, while it improves the Behaviour. The Passion of Love to a Mistress, where it is most Sincere, resembles too much the Flame of a Feaver; that to a Wife is like the Vital Heat.

I have often thought, if the Letters written by Men of Good-nature to their Wives, were to be compared with those written by Men[a] of Gallantry to their Mistresses, the former, notwithstanding any Inequality of Stile, would appear to have the Advantage. Friendship, Tenderness and Constancy, drest in a Simplicity of Expression, recommend themselves by a more native Elegance, than passionate Raptures, extravagant Encomiums, and slavish Adoration. If we were admitted to search the Cabinet of the beautiful *Narcissa*, among heaps of Epistles from several Admirers which are there preserved with equal Care, how few should we find but would make any one Sick in the reading, except her who is flattered by them? But in how different a Stile must the wise *Benevolus*, who converses with that good Sense and Good-humour among all his

---

[a] Men] them *Fol.*

---

[1] *Don Quixote*, part i, chap. i.   [2] For this word see No. 30 (vol. i).

Friends, write to a Wife who is the worthy Object of his utmost Affection?[1] *Benevolus*, both in Publick and Private, on all Occasions of Life, appears to have every good Quality and desirable Ornament. Abroad he is reverenc'd and esteemed; at home beloved and happy. The Satisfaction he enjoys there settles into an habitual Complacency, which shines in his Countenance, enlivens his Wit, and seasons his Conversation. Even those of his Acquaintance, who have never seen him in his Retirement, are Sharers in the Happiness of it; and it is very much owing to his being the best and best beloved of Husbands, that he is the most stedfast of Friends, and the most agreeable of Companions.

There is a sensible Pleasure in contemplating such beautiful Instances of domestick Life. The Happiness of the Conjugal State appears heightened to the highest Degree it is capable of, when we see two Persons of accomplished Minds, not only united in the same Interests and Affections, but in their Taste of the same Improvements, Pleasures and Diversions. *Pliny*, one of the finest Gentlemen, and politest Writers of the Age in which he lived, has left us, in his Letter to *Hispulla* his Wife's Aunt, one of the most agreeable Family Pieces of this Kind I have ever met with.[2] I shall end this Discourse with a Translation of it; and I believe the Reader will be of my Opinion, that *Conjugal Love* is drawn in it with a Delicacy which makes it appear to be, as I have represented it, an Ornament as well as a Virtue.

PLINY *to* HISPULLA.

'AS I remember that great Affection which was between you and your excellent Brother, and know you love his Daughter as your own, so as not only to express the Tenderness of the best of Aunts, but even to supply that of the best of Fathers, I am sure it will be a Pleasure to you to hear, that she proves worthy of her Father, worthy of You, and of your and her Ancestors. Her Ingenuity is admirable; her Frugality extraordinary. She loves me, the surest Pledge of her Virtue; and adds to this a wonderful Disposition to Learning, which she has acquired from her Affection to me. She reads my Writings, studies them, and even gets them by Heart. You'd smile to see the Concern she is in when I have a Cause to

---

[1] 'Mr. John Hughes probably meant here to pay a compliment to his friend Steele, who was certainly one of the best of husbands' (Nichols).
[2] Pliny, *Letters*, 4. 19.

plead, and the Joy she shews when it is over. She finds Means to have the first News brought her of the Success I meet with in Court, how I am heard, and what Decree is made. If I recite any thing in Publick, she cannot refrain from placing her self privately in some Corner to hear, where with the utmost delight she feasts on my Applauses. Sometimes she sings my Verses, and accompanies them with the Lute, without any Master, except Love, the best of Instructors. From these Instances I take the most certain Omens of our perpetual and encreasing Happiness; since her Affection is not founded on my Youth and Person, which must gradually decay, but she is in Love with the immortal Part of me, my Glory and Reputation. Nor indeed could less be expected from one who had the Happiness to receive her Education from you; who in your House was accustomed to every thing that was virtuous and decent, and even began to love me by your Recommendation. For, as you had always the greatest Respect for my Mother, you were pleased from my Infancy to form me, to commend me, and kindly to presage I should be one Day what my Wife fancies I am. Accept therefore our united Thanks; mine, that you have bestowed her on me, and hers, that you have given me to her, as a mutual Grant of Joy and Felicity.'[1a]

[a] *No. 525 unsigned in Fol., 8vo, 12mo*

No. 526   *Monday, November 3, 1712*[2]
[STEELE]

. . . *Fortius utere Loris.*
Ovid.

I AM very loth to come to Extremities with the young Gentlemen mentioned in the following Letter, and do not care to chastise them with my own Hand, till I am forced by Provocations too great to be suffered without the absolute Destruction of my Spectatorial Dignity. The Crimes of these Offenders are placed under the Observation of one of my chief Officers, who is posted just

---

[1] Hughes's authorship of this number is revealed at the end of No. 537.
[2] *Motto.* Ovid, *Metamorphoses*, 2. 127: Stronger pull the reins.

at the Entrance of the Pass between *London* and *Westminster*.[1] As I have great Confidence in the Capacity, Resolution, and Integrity of the Person deputed by me to give an Account of Enormities, I doubt not but I shall soon have before me all proper Notices which are requisite for the Amendment of Manners in Publick, and the Instruction of each Individual of the humane Species in what is due from him, in respect to the whole Body of Mankind. The present Paper shall consist only of the above-mentioned Letter, and the Copy of a Deputation which I have given to my trusty Friend Mr. *John Sly*;[2] wherein he is charged to notify to me all that is necessary for my Animadversion upon the Delinquents mentioned by my Correspondent, as well as all others described in the said Deputation.

To the SPECTATOR-GENERAL of Great Britain.

'I grant it does look a little familiar, but I must call you

Dear Dumb,

'BEING got again to the farther End of the *Widow*'s Coffee-house,[3] I shall from hence give you some Account of the Behaviour of our Hackney-Coachmen since my last. These indefatigable Gentlemen, without the least Design, I dare say, of Self-Interest or Advantage to themselves, do still ply as Volunteers Day and Night for the Good of their Country. I will not trouble you with enumerating many Particulars, but I must by no Means omit to inform you of an Infant about six Foot high, and between twenty and thirty Years of Age, who was seen in the Arms of an Hackney-Coachman driving by *Will*'s Coffee-house in *Covent-Garden*, between the Hours of four and five in the Afternoon of that very Day wherein you published a Memorial against them. This impudent young Cur, tho' he cou'd not sit in a Coach-Box without holding, yet wou'd he venture his Neck to bid Defiance to your Spectatorial Authority, or to any thing that you countenanced. Who he was I know not, but I heard this Relation this Morning from a Gentleman who was an Eye-Witness of this his Impudence; and I was willing to take the first Opportunity to inform you of him, as holding it extreamly requisite that you shou'd nip him in the Bud. But I am my self most concerned for my Fellow-Templers, Fellow-Students, and Fellow-Labourers

[1] See No. 498.
[2] See No. 187 (vol. ii).   [3] See No. 498.

in the Law, I mean such of them as are dignify'd and distinguish'd under the Denomination of Hackney-Coachmen. Such aspiring Minds have these ambitious young Men, that they cannot enjoy themselves out of a Coach-Box. It is however an unspeakable Comfort to me, that I can now tell you that some of them are grown so bashful as to study only in the Night-time or in the Country. The other Night I spied one of our young Gentlemen very diligent at his Lucubrations in *Fleet-street*; and, by the Way, I shou'd be under some Concern, lest this hard Student shou'd one Time or other crack his Brain with studying, but that I am in Hopes Nature has taken Care to fortify him in Proportion to the great Undertakings he was designed for. Another of my Fellow-Templers, on *Thursday* last, was getting up into his Study at the Bottom of *Grays-Inn-Lane*, in order, I suppose, to contemplate in the fresh Air.[1] Now, Sir, my Request is, that the great Modesty of these two Gentlemen may be recorded as a Pattern to the rest; and if you wou'd but give them two or three Touches with your own Pen, tho' you might not perhaps prevail with them to desist entirely from their Meditations, yet I doubt not but you wou'd at least preserve them from being publick Spectacles of Folly in our Streets: I say two or three Touches with your own Pen; for I have really observed, Mr. SPEC. that those *Spectators* which are so prettily laced down the Sides with little c's,[2] how instructive or diverting soever they may be, do not carry with them that Authority as the others. I do again therefore desire, that, for the sake of their dear Necks, you will bestow one Penful of your own Ink upon them. I know you are loth to expose them; and it is, I must confess, a thousand Pities that any young Gentleman, who is come of honest Parents, should be brought to publick Shame: And indeed I should be glad to have them handled a little tenderly at the first; but if fair Means will not prevail, there is then no other Way to reclaim them but by making use of some wholsome Severities; and I think it is better that a Dozen or two of such good-for-nothing Fellows should be made Examples of, than that the Reputation of some Hundreds of as hopeful young Gentlemen as my self should suffer thro' their Folly. It is not, however, for me to direct you what to do; but, in short, if our Coachmen will drive on this Trade, the very first of

[1] Gray's Inn Lane ran northward from Holborn into the open country. It was noted for its fresh air; here Sir Roger loved to 'clear his pipes' (No. 269).
[2] In the original editions of the *Spectator* letters were printed with inverted commas at the beginning of each line—like 'little c's.'

them that I do find meditating in the Street, I shall make bold to take the Number of his Chambers, together with a Note of his Name, and dispatch them to you, that you may chastise him at your own Discretion.[1]

I am,
Dear SPEC.
For ever yours,
Moses Greenbag,
Esq; if you please.

P. S. 'Tom. Hammercloth, one of our Coachmen, is now pleading at the Bar at the other End of the Room, but has a little too much Vehemence, and throws out his Arms too much to take his Audience with a good Grace.'

To my Loving and Well-beloved John Sly, *Haberdasher of Hats and Tobacconist, between the Cities of* London *and* Westminster,

WHEREAS frequent Disorders, Affronts, Indignities, Omissions, and Trespasses, for which there are no Remedies by any Form of Law, but which apparently disturb and disquiet the Minds of Men, happen near the Place of your Residence; and that you are, as well by your commodious Situation as the good Parts with which you are endow'd, properly qualified for the Observation of the said Offences; I do hereby authorize and depute you, from the Hours of Nine in the Morning till Four in the Afternoon, to keep a strict Eye upon all Persons and Things that are convey'd in Coaches, carry'd in Carts, or walk on Foot from the City of *London* to the City of *Westminster,* or from the City of *Westminster* to the City of *London,* within the said Hours. You are therefore not to depart from your Observatory at the End of *Devereux-Court* during the said Space of each Day; but to observe the Behaviour of all Persons who are suddenly transported from stamping on Pebbles to sit at Ease in Chariots, what Notice they take of their Foot-Acquaintance, and send me the speediest Advice when they are guilty of over-looking, turning from, or appearing grave and distant to their old Friends. When Man and Wife are in the same Coach, you are to see whether they appear pleased or tired with each other, and whether they carry the due Mein in the Eye of the World between Fondness and

[1] 'An allusion to the usual and prudent precaution of *taking the number* of a hackney-coach before entrance' (Nichols).

Coldness. You are carefully to behold all such as shall have Addition of Honour or Riches, and report whether they preserve the Countenance they had before such Addition. As to Persons on Foot, you are to be attentive whether they are pleased with their Condition, and are dress'd suitable to it; but especially to distinguish such as appear discreet, by a low-heel'd Shooe, with the decent Ornament of a Leather-Garter.[1] To write down the Names of such Country Gentlemen as, upon the Approach of Peace, have left the Hunting for the Military Cock of the Hat: Of all who strut, make a Noise, and swear at the Drivers of Coaches to make Haste when they see it impossible they should pass: Of all young Gentlemen in Coach-Boxes, who labour at a Perfection in what they are sure to be excelled by the meanest of the People. You are to do all that in you lies that Coaches and Passengers give Way according to the Course of Business, all the Morning in Term Time towards *Westminster*, the rest of the Year towards the *Exchange*. Upon these Directions, together with other secret Articles herein inclosed, you are to govern your self, and give Advertisement thereof to me at all convenient and spectatorial Hours when Men of Business are to be seen. Hereof you are not to fail. Given under my Seal of Office.

The SPECTATOR.

T

No. 527   *Tuesday, November 4, 1712*[2]

Facile invenies, & pejorem, & pejus moratam,
Meliorem neque tu reperies, neque sol videt.

Plautus in Sticho.

I AM so tender of my Women-Readers, that I cannot defer the Publication of any thing which concerns their Happiness or Quiet. The Repose of a married Woman is consulted in the first of

---

[1] Nichols saw here an allusion to John Warner, the banker, who 'always wore black leather garters buckled under the knee' (*Literary Anecdotes*, iii. 74). Advertisements in Nos. 22, 23, and 24 refer to 'Mr. Warner, a Goldsmith without Temple-bar'. In an advertisement in the *Post Boy* of 25 May 1714 his place of business is given as 'the Anchor without Temple-Bar'. 'Mr. Warner, *Goldsmith*', was one of the subscribers to the collected edition of the *Spectator*.

[2] *Motto*. Plautus, *Stichus*, 109-10: You will easily find one more wicked and immoral—but a better neither will you find, nor does the Sun behold.

The introductory paragraph is by Steele, and the final poem is by Pope, together with, it would seem, the letter which introduces it.

the following Letters, and the Felicity of a Maiden Lady in the second. I call it a Felicity to have the Addresses of an agreeable Man; and I think I have not any where seen a prettier Application of a Poetical Story than that of his, in making the Tale of *Cephalus* and *Procris* the History-Picture of a Fan in so gallant a manner as he addresses it. But see the Letters.

Mr. SPECTATOR,

"'TIS now almost three Months since I was in Town about some Business; and the Hurry of it being over, took Coach one Afternoon, and drove to see a Relation, who marry'd about six Years ago a wealthy Citizen. I found her at home, but her Husband gone to the *Exchange*, and expected back within an Hour at the farthest. After the usual Salutations of Kindness, and a hundred Questions about Friends in the Country, we sat down to Picquet, play'd two or three Games, and drank Tea.[1] I should have told you that this was my second Time of seeing her since Marriage, but before she liv'd at the same Town where I went to School; so that the Plea of a Relation, added to the Innocence of my Youth, prevail'd upon her good Humour to indulge me in a Freedom of Conversation as often, and oftener, than the strict Discipline of the School would allow of. You may easily imagine after such an Acquaintance we might be exceeding merry without any Offence, as in calling to Mind how many Inventions I had been put to in deluding the Master, how many Hands forg'd for Excuses, how many Times been sick in perfect Health; for I was then never sick but at School, and only then because out of her Company. We had whil'd away three Hours after this Manner, when I found it past Five; and not expecting her Husband would return till late, rose up, told her I should go early next Morning for the Country: She kindly answer'd she was afraid it would be long before she saw me again; so I took my Leave and parted. Now, Sir, I had not been got home a Fortnight, when I receiv'd a Letter from a Neighbour of theirs, that ever since that fatal Afternoon the Lady had been most inhumanly treated, and the Husband publickly storm'd that he was made a Member of too numerous a Society. He had, it seems, listened most of the Time my Cousin and I were together. As jealous Ears always hear double, so he heard enough to make him mad; and as jealous

[1] For picquet see No. 434.

378

Eyes always see thro' Magnifying-Glasses, so he was certain it could not be I, whom he had seen a beardless Stripling, but fancy'd he saw a gay Gentleman of the *Temple* ten Years older than my self, and for that Reason, I presume, durst not come in, nor take any Notice when I went out. He is perpetually asking his Wife if she does not think the Time long (as she said she should) till she see her Cousin again. Pray, Sir, what can be done in this Case? I have writ to him to assure him I was at his House all that Afternoon expecting to see him: His Answer is, 'tis only a Trick of hers, and that he neither can nor will believe me. The parting Kiss I find mightily nettles him, and confirms him in all his Errors. *Ben. John-son*, as I remember, makes a Foreigner, in one of his Comedies, *admire the desperate Valour of the bold* English, *who let out their Wives to all Encounters.*[1] The general Custom of Salutation should excuse the Favour done me, or you should lay down Rules when such Distinctions are to be given or omitted. You cannot imagine, Sir, how troubled I am for this unhappy Lady's Misfortune; and beg you would insert this Letter, that the Husband may reflect upon this Accident coolly. It is no small Matter, the Ease of a virtuous Woman for her whole Life: I know she will conform to any Regularities (tho' more strict than the common Rules of our Country require) to which his particular Temper shall incline him to oblige her. This Accident puts me in Mind how generously *Pisistratus* the *Athenian* Tyrant behaved himself on a like Occasion, when he was instigated by his Wife to put to Death a young Gentleman, because, being passionately fond of his Daughter, he had kiss'd her in Publick as he met her in the Street; *What* (said he) *shall we do to those who are our Enemies, if we do thus to those who are our Friends?*[2] I will not trouble you much longer, but am exceedingly concern'd lest this Accident may cause a virtuous Lady to lead a miserable Life with a Husband, who has no Grounds for his Jealousy but what I have faithfully related, and ought to be reckon'd none. 'Tis to be fear'd too, if at last he sees his Mistake, yet People will be as slow and unwilling in disbelieving Scandal, as they are quick and forward in believing it. I shall

---

[1] Ben Jonson, *Volpone*, I. v. 100–2:

> 'Fore heauen, I wonder at the desperate valure
> Of the bold *English*, that they dare let loose
> Their wiues, to all encounters!

The speaker is Volpone himself.

[2] Plutarch, 'Apophthegmata' (*Moralia*, 189C). The young man's name was Thrasybulus.

endeavour to enliven this plain honest Letter with *Ovid*'s Relation about *Cybele*'s Image. The Ship wherein it was aboard was stranded at the Mouth of the *Tiber*, and the Men were unable to move it, till *Claudia*, a Virgin, but suspected of Unchastity, by a slight Pull hawl'd it in. The Story is told in the 4th Book of the *Fasti*.

> *Parent of Gods, began the weeping Fair,*
> *Reward or punish, but oh! hear my Pray'r.*
> *If Lewdness e'er Defil'd my Virgin Bloom,*
> *From Heav'n with Justice I receive my Doom:*
> *But if my Honour yet has known no Stain,*
> *Thou, Goddess, thou my Innocence maintain:*
> *Thou, whom the nicest Rules of Goodness sway'd,*
> *Vouchsafe to follow an unblemish'd Maid.*
> *She spoke, and touch'd the Cord with glad Surprize,*
> *(The Truth was witness'd by ten thousand Eyes)*
> *The pitying Goddess easily comply'd,*
> *Follow'd in Triumph, and adorn'd her Guide:*
> *While* Claudia, *blushing still for past Disgrace,*
> *March'd silent on with a slow solemn Pace:*
> *Nor yet from some was all Distrust remov'd,*
> *Tho' Heav'n such Virtue by such Wonders prov'd.*[1]

I am, Sir,

Your very humble Servant,

Philagnotes.'

Mr. SPECTATOR,

'YOU will oblige a languishing Lover if you will please to print the enclosed Verses in your next Paper. If you remember the *Metamorphosis*, you know *Procris*, the fond Wife of *Cephalus*, is said to have made her Husband, who delighted in the Sports of the Wood, a Present of an unerring Javelin. In Process of Time he was so much in the Forest, that his Lady suspected he was pursuing some Nymph, under the Pretence of following a Chace more innocent. Under this Suspicion she hid herself among the Trees to observe his Motions. While she lay concealed, her Husband, tired with the Labour of Hunting, came within her Hearing. As he was fainting with Heat, he cry'd out, *Aura veni; Oh charming Air approach.*

---

[1] Ovid, *Fasti*, 4. 319 ff. The translator has not been identified.

'The unfortunate Wife taking the Word *Air* to be the Name of a Woman, began to move among the Bushes, and the Husband believing it a Deer, threw his Javelin and kill'd her. This History painted on a Fan, which I presented to a Lady, gave Occasion to my growing poetical.'ᵃ

> *Come gentle Air! th' Eolian Shepherd said,*
> *While Procris panted in the secret Shade;*
> *Come gentle Air! the fairer Delia cries,*
> *While at her Feet her Swain expiring lies.*
> *Lo the glad Gales o'er all her Beauties stray,*
> *Breathe on her Lips, and in her Bosom play.*
> *In Delia's Hand this Toy is fatal found,*
> *Nor did that fabled Dart more surely wound.*
> *Both Gifts destructive to the Givers prove,*
> *Alike both Lovers fall by those they love:*
> *Yet guiltless too this bright Destroyer lives,*
> *At Random wounds, nor knows the Wounds she gives:*
> *She views the Story with attentive Eyes,*
> *And pities Procris while her Lover dies.*[1]

ᵃ *No. 527 unsigned in Fol., 8vo, 12mo*

---

[1] The lines are by Pope, and were reprinted in his *Works* (1717) with two minor changes (line 8, 'Nor could'; line 12, 'knows the Wound'). The passage in Ovid is from the *Metamorphoses*, 7. 796–862. In 1741 Pope reprinted the poem among his Imitations of English Poets, under the title, 'Waller: On a Fan of the Author's design, in which was painted the story of Cephalus and Procris with the Motto, *Aura Veni*'. See the *Minor Poems*, ed. Norman Ault and John Butt (Twickenham ed., vol. vi), pp. 45–47. The accompanying letter, which is apparently by Pope, is printed in vol. i of Pope's *Prose Works*, ed. Norman Ault (Oxford, 1936), p. 70; it is not in Professor Sherburn's edition of the *Correspondence*.

No. 528   *Wednesday, November 5, 1712*[1]
[STEELE]

Dum potuit solita gemitum virtute repressit.
                                        Ovid.

Mr. SPECTATOR,

'I WHO now write to you am a Woman loaded with Injuries; and the Aggravation of my Misfortune is, that they are such which are overlooked by the Generality of Mankind, and tho' the most afflicting imaginable, not regarded as such in the general Sense of the World. I have hid my Vexation from all Mankind; but have now taken Pen, Ink, and Paper, and am resolved to unbosome my self to you, and lay before you what grieves me and all the Sex. You have very often mentioned particular Hardships done to this or that Lady; but, methinks, you have not in any one Speculation directly pointed at the partial Freedom Men take, the unreasonable Confinement Women are obliged to, in the only Circumstance in which we are necessarily to have a Commerce with them, that of Love. The Case of Celibacy is the great Evil of our Nation; and the Indulgence of the vitious Conduct of Men in that State, with the Ridicule to which Women are exposed, tho' never so virtuous, if long un-married, is the Root of the greatest Irregularities of this Nation. To shew you, Sir, that tho' you never have given us the Catalogue of a Lady's Library as you promised,[2] we read good Books of our own chusing, I shall insert on this Occasion a Paragraph or two out of *Echard's Roman History.*[3] In the 44th Page of the second Volume the Author observes, That *Augustus,* upon his Return to *Rome* at the End of a War, received Complaints that too great a Number of the young Men of Quality were unmarried. The Emperor there-upon assembled the whole *Equestrian* Order; and having separated the Married from the Single, did particular Honours to the former; but he told the latter, that is to say, Mr. SPECTATOR, he told the Batchelors, "That their Lives and Actions had been so peculiar, that he knew not by what Name to call 'em; not by that of Men,

---

[1] *Motto.* Ovid, *Metamorphoses,* 9. 163:
       With wonted fortitude she bore the smart,
       And not a groan confessed her burning heart. GAY.

[2] See Nos. 37, 79, 92 (vol. i), 140 (vol. ii).

[3] *The Roman History, from the Settlement of the Empire by Augustus Caesar, to the Removal of the Imperial Seat by Constantine the Great,* by Laurence Echard, Prebendary of Lincoln, was published in 1698. The reference ('the 44th Page of the second Volume') is to the 4th edition (1706).

for they perform'd nothing that was manly; not by that of Citizens, for the City might perish notwithstanding their Care; nor by that of *Romans*, for they design'd to extirpate the *Roman* Name." Then proceeding to shew his tender Care and hearty Affection for his People, he further told 'em, "That their Course of Life was of such pernicious Consequence to the Glory and Grandeur of the *Roman* Nation, that he cou'd not chuse but tell 'em, that all other Crimes put together cou'd not equalize theirs: For they were guilty of Murder, in not suffering those to be born which shou'd proceed from them; of Impiety, in causing the Names and Honours of their Ancestors to cease; and of Sacrilege, in destroying their Kind, which proceed from the immortal Gods, and human Nature, the principal Thing consecrated to 'em: Therefore in this Respect they dissolv'd the Government, in disobeying its Laws; betray'd their Country, by making it barren and waste; nay, and demolish'd their City, in depriving it of Inhabitants. And he was sensible that all this proceeded not from any kind of Virtue or Abstinence, but from a Looseness and Wantonness, which ought never to be encourag'd in any Civil Government." There are no Particulars dwelt upon that let us into the Conduct of these young Worthies, whom this great Emperor treated with so much Justice and Indignation; but any one who observes what passes in this Town, may very well frame to himself a Notion of their Riots and Debaucheries all Night, and their apparent Preparations for them all Day. It is not to be doubted but these *Romans* never passed any of their Time innocently but when they were asleep, and never slept but when they were weary and heavy with Excesses, and slept only to prepare themselves for the Repetition of them. If you did your Duty as a SPECTATOR, you would carefully examine into the Number of Births, Marriages, and Burials; and when you had deducted out of your Deaths all such as went out of the World without marrying, then cast up the Number of both Sexes born within such a Term of Years last past, you might from the single People departed make some useful Inferences or Guesses how many there are left unmarried, and raise some useful Scheme for the Amendment of the Age in that Particular. I have not Patience to proceed gravely on this abominable Libertinism; for I cannot but reflect, as I am writing to you, upon a certain lascivious Manner which all our young Gentlemen use in Publick, and examine our Eyes with a Petulancy[1] in their own, which is a downright

---

[1] A variant of *petulance*, used in the obsolete sense of 'wantonness, immodesty'. The last quotation in *OED* is dated 1748.

Affront to Modesty. A disdainful Look on such an Occasion is returned with a Countenance rebuked, but by averting their Eyes from the Woman of Honour and Decency to some flippant Creature, who will, as the Phrase is, be kinder. I must set down things as they come into my Head, without standing upon Order. Ten thousand to one but the gay Gentleman who stared at the same Time is an House-keeper;[1] for you must know they have got into a Humour of late of being very regular in their Sins, and a young Fellow shall keep his four Maids and three Footmen with the greatest Gravity imaginable. There are no less than six of these venerable House-keepers of my Acquaintance. This Humour among young Men of Condition is imitated by all the World below them, and a general Dissolution[2] of Manners arises from the one Source of Libertinism without Shame or Reprehension in the Male Youth. It is from this one Fountain that so many beautiful helpless young Women are sacrificed, and given up to Lewdness, Shame, Poverty, and Disease: It is to this also that so many excellent young Women, who might be Patterns of conjugal Affection and Parents of a worthy Race, pine under unhappy Passions for such as have not Attention enough to observe, or Virtue enough to prefer them to their common Wenches. Now, Mr. SPECTATOR, I must be free to own to you, that I my self suffer a tasteless insipid Being, from a Consideration I have for a Man who would not, as he has said in my Hearing, resign his Liberty, as he calls it, for all the Beauty and Wealth the whole Sex is possessed of. Such Calamities as these would not happen, if it could possibly be brought about, that by fineing Batchelors as Papists, Convicts,[a] or the like, they were distinguished to their Disadvantage from the rest of the World, who fall in with the Measures of civil Society. Lest you should think I speak this as being, according to the senseless rude Phrase, a malicious old Maid, I shall acquaint you I am a Woman of Condition not now three and twenty, and have had Proposals from at least ten different Men, and the greater Number of them have upon the Upshot[3] refused me. Something or other is always amiss when the Lover takes to some new Wench: A Settlement is easily excepted against; and there is very little Recourse to avoid the vitious Part of our Youth, but throwing ones

---

[a] Papists, Convicts,] Papist's Convict, *Fol.*; Papists Convict, *8vo, 12mo*

[1] I.e. householder. 'Now *rare* or *Obs.*' (*OED*.)
[2] I.e. dissoluteness. See *OED*.
[3] This phrase is marked 'obsolete' by *OED*, with the last quotation dated 1796.

self away upon some lifeless Blockhead, who tho' he is without Vice, is also without Virtue. Now-a-days we must be contented if we can get Creatures which are not bad, good are not to be expected. Mr. SPECTATOR, I sat near you the other Day, and think I did not displease your Spectatorial Eye-sight; which I shall be a better Judge of when I see whether you take Notice of these Evils your own way, or print this Memorial dictated from the disdainful heavy Heart of,

SIR,
Your most obedient
Humble Servant,
Rachael Welladay.'¹

Tᵃ

ᵃ *At the end of No. 528 the following advertisement appears in Fol.:*

*Whereas there hath been lately published*² *a certain legendary Story of an unknown Theo-dosius concerning the Priesthood of Christ, translated out of Suidas, under the Title of A very* ancient, authentick, and remarkable Testimony concerning our blessed Lord and Saviour Jesus Christ; *which the Translator hath taken the Liberty not only to dedicate to me, but to use my Name in the Title Page, thereby giving Occasion to think I countenance the Authority of that Testimony: Now these are to certify, That the Person who published that Pamphlet is altogether a Stranger to me; and that I was no ways acquainted with his Design till I saw it in Print; for though the Passage produced may appear remarkable, yet I cannot think the Testimony either ancient or authentick.*

Nov. 4, 1712.   Rob. Nelson.

---

¹ A letter signed Bellmour and dated 'Middle Temple November 6', in reply to this of Mrs. Welladay, is in the Blenheim Palace papers. It was printed, somewhat inaccurately, in Aitken's edition. For the text see Appendix V.

² The book here referred to is advertised in the *Post Boy* of 30 Oct. as 'this day' published:

Dedicated to Robert Nelson.

A very ancient, authentick, and remarkable Testimony concerning our Blessed Lord and Saviour Jesus Christ: By Theodosius, a Jew, who liv'd in the Time of the Emperor Justinian. Now first made English from the original Greek; to which is added, Pliny's Letter to Trajan, concerning the Behaviour of the Primitive Christians. Printed for E. Curll; and sold by J. Morphew.

Nelson's disclaimer is also printed in the *Post Boy* of 6 Nov.

No. 529
[ADDISON]
Thursday, November 6, 1712[1]

Singula quæque locum teneant sortita decenter.
Hor.

UPON the hearing of several late Disputes concerning Rank and Precedence, I could not forbear amusing my self with some Observations, which I have made upon the Learned World, as to this great Particular.[2] By the Learned World I here mean at large, all those who are any way concerned in Works of Literature, whether in the Writing, Printing or Repeating Part. To begin with the Writers; I have observed that the Author of a *Folio,* in all Companies and Conversations, sets himself above the Author of a *Quarto*; the Author of a *Quarto* above the Author of an *Octavo*; and so on, by a gradual Descent and Subordination, to an Author in *Twenty-Fours.*[3] This Distinction is so well observed, that in an Assembly of the Learned, I have seen a *Folio* Writer place himself in an Elbow-chair, when the Author of a *Duo-decimo* has, out of a just Deference to his superior Quality, seated himself upon a Squabb.[4] In a Word, Authors are usually ranged in Company after the same manner as their Works are upon a Shelf.

The most Minute Pocket-Author, hath beneath him the Writers of all Pamphlets, or Works that are only stitched. As for the Pamphleteer, he takes place of none but of the Authors of single Sheets, and of that Fraternity who publish their Labours on certain Days, or on every Day of the Week. I do not find that the Precedency among the Individuals, in this latter Class of Writers, is yet setled.

For my own part, I have had so strict a Regard to the Ceremonial which prevails in the Learned World, that I never presumed to take Place of a Pamphleteer till my daily Papers were gathered into those

---

[1] *Motto.* Horace, *Ars poetica,* 92:
      Let ev'ry Thing have its due Place and Time. ROSCOMMON.

[2] For the quarrel between Count Rechteren and M. de Mesnager see No. 481.

[3] Peter Motteux had written in the *Gentleman's Journal,* Feb. 1692/3, pp. 37–38: Now some of us Book-wrights perhaps not unjustly measure the greatness of our Fame by that of our Volums: Thus your *Quarto* Author takes his Place in the Second Tire, and looks down as contemptibly on all your Octavo's and Decimo-sexto's, as a Fat Dean on a poor *sine Cure.* And 'tis indeed a greater happiness to some to have their Books thus plac'd among those of the Second Magnitude, than if they were First-Rate Authors in a less Volum: For as most Libraries have more Spectators than Readers, the larger Books being more observable, must also please a greater number than the smaller.

[4] A sofa, ottoman, or couch.

two first Volumes, which have already appeared.[1] After which, I naturally jumped over the Heads not only of all Pamphleteers, but of every *Octavo* Writer in *Great-Britain*, that had written but one Book. I am also informed by my Bookseller, that six *Octavo*'s have at all times been looked upon as an Equivalent to a *Folio*, which I take notice of the rather, because I would not have the Learned World surprized, if after the Publication of half a dozen Volumes I take my Place accordingly.[2] When my scattered Forces are thus rallied, and reduced into Regular Bodies, I flatter my self that I shall make no despicable Figure at the Head of them.

Whether these Rules, which have been received time out of Mind in the Common-Wealth of Letters,[3] were not originally established with an eye to our Paper Manufacture, I shall leave to the Discussion of others, and shall only remark further in this Place, that all Printers and Booksellers take the Wall[4] of one another, according to the above-mentioned Merits of the Authors to whom they respectively belong.

I come now to that Point of Precedency which is setled among the three Learned Professions, by the Wisdom of our Laws. I need not here take Notice of the Rank which is allotted to every Doctor in each of these Professions, who are all of them, tho' not so high as Knights, yet a Degree above Squires; This last Order of Men being the illiterate Body of the Nation, are consequently thrown together into a Class below the three Learned Professions. I mention this for the sake of several Rural 'Squires, who's Reading does not rise so high as to *the present State of England*,[5] and who are often apt to usurp that Precedency which by the Laws of their Country is not due to them. Their Want of Learning, which has planted them in this Station, may in some measure extenuate their Misdemeanour, and our Professors ought to pardon them when they offend in this Particular, considering that they are in a State of Ignorance, or, as we usually say, do not know their Right Hand from their Left.

---

[1] Volumes i and ii were published in January 1712.

[2] At this time volumes iii and iv were in the press; they were actually published during this month of November—by the 27th, as a reference in No. 547 shows (see *Studies in Bibliography*, v (1953), p. 111 n.). Addison is aware that the printing of the complete *Spectator* will fill at least six octavo volumes; actually seven were used—and an eighth for the continuation of 1714.

[3] Addison had used this phrase in Nos. 58 and 438 (vol. i).

[4] I.e. to take precedence. Cf. *Romeo and Juliet* I. i. 15.

[5] The subtitle of *Angliae Notitia*, an annual compilation begun by Edward Chamberlayne in 1669, and continued by his son John. In 1708 the title was altered to *Magnae Britanniae Notitia*. It contained lists of members of parliament, knights and peers, &c., and hence would be useful in determining 'precedency'.

There is another Tribe of Persons who are Retainers to the Learned World, and who regulate themselves upon all Occasions by several Laws peculiar to their Body. I mean the Players or Actors of both Sexes. Among these it is a standing and uncontroverted Principle, that a Tragedian always takes Place of a Comedian; and 'tis very well known the merry Drolls who[a] make us laugh are always placed at the lower end of the Table, and in every Entertainment give way to the Dignity of the Buskin. It is a Stage Maxim, Once a King and always a King. For this Reason it would be thought very absurd in Mr. *Bullock*, notwithstanding the Height and Gracefulness of his Person, to sit at the Right Hand of an Hero, though he were but five Foot high.[1] The same Distinction is observed among the Ladies of the Theatre. Queens and Heroines preserve their Rank in private Conversation, while those who are Waiting-Women and Maids of Honour upon the Stage, keep their Distance also behind the Scenes.

I shall only add, that by a Parity of Reason, all Writers of Tragedy look upon it as their due to be seated, served, or saluted before Comick Writers: Those who deal in Tragi-Comedy usually taking their Seats between the Authors of either side. There has been a long Dispute for Precedency between the Tragick and Heroick Poets. *Aristotle*[2] would have the latter yield the *Pas*[3] to the former, but Mr. *Dryden* and many others would never submit to this Decision. Burlesque Writers pay the same Deference to the Heroick, as Comick Writers to their Serious Brothers in the Drama.

By this short Table of Laws, Order is kept up, and Distinction preserved in the whole Republick of Letters.[4]   O

---

[a] who] that *Fol.*

---

[1] Bullock generally took low-comedy parts. He had appeared on 3 Nov. as Sir Harry Gubbin in Steele's *Tender Husband,* and on the day this paper appeared played Boniface in *The Beaux' Stratagem* of Farquhar.

[2] Aristotle, *Poetics,* 26. Dryden's defence of the epic as superior to tragedy will be found in the *Apology for Heroic Poetry* and the Dedication of the *Aeneis.* The opening sentence of the latter reads, 'A Heroic Poem, truly such, is undoubtedly the greatest work which the soul of man is capable to perform' (Ker, ii. 154).

[3] Another French importation (cf. No. 165, vol. ii): 'the right of going first; precedence'. The first occurrence in English listed in *OED* is dated 1707.

[4] See No. 445.

*Sic visum Veneri; cui placet impares
Formas atque animos sub juga ahenea
Sævo mittere cum joco.*

Hor.

IT is very usual for those who have been severe upon Marriage, in some part or other of their Lives to enter into the Fraternity which they have ridiculed, and to see their Raillery return upon their own Heads. I scarce ever knew a Woman-hater that did not, sooner or later, pay for it. Marriage, which is a Blessing to another Man, falls upon such an one as a Judgment. Mr. *Congreve*'s *Old Batchelor* is set forth to us with much Wit and Humour, as an Example of this kind.[2] In short those who have most distinguished themselves by Railing at the Sex in general, very often make an honourable Amends, by chusing one of the most worthless Persons of it, for a Companion and Yoke-fellow. *Hymen* takes his Revenge in kind, on those who turn his Mysteries into Ridicule.

My Friend *Will. Honeycomb,* who was so unmercifully witty[3] upon the Women, in a couple of Letters, which I lately communicated to the Publick, has given the Ladies ample Satisfaction by marrying a Farmer's Daughter; a piece of News which came to our Club by the last Post.[4] The *Templer* is very positive that he has married a Dairy-maid: But *Will,* in his Letter to me on this Occasion, sets the best Face upon the Matter that he can, and gives a more tollerable account of his Spouse. I must confess I suspected something more than ordinary, when upon opening the Letter I found that *Will* was fallen off from his former Gayety, having changed *Dear Spec.* which was his usual Salute at the Beginning of the Letter, into *My Worthy Friend,* and subscribed himself in the latter End of it at full length

---

[1] *Motto.* Horace, *Odes,* 1. 33. 10–12:

> Fair and ugly, false and true,
> All to great Venus' Yoke must bow:
> Such Pleasure in our Pains she takes,
> And laughs to see what Sport she makes.

[2] Congreve's *Old Batchelor,* in which 'is excellently represented the Reluctance of a Batter'd Debauchee to come into the Trammels of Order and Decency' (*Tatler* 9) had been recently given (10 Oct.) at Drury Lane, with Keen in the role of Heartwell.
[3] Here used in the obsolete sense of 'sharply critical, sarcastic'. The last example in *OED* is dated 1746.
[4] See Nos. 499 and 511.

William Honeycomb. In short, the gay, the loud, the vain *Will. Honeycomb,* who had made Love to every great Fortune that has appeared in Town for above[a] thirty Years together, and boasted of Favours from Ladies whom he had never seen, is at length wedded to a plain Country Girl.

His Letter gives us the Picture of a converted Rake. The sober Character of the Husband is dashed with the Man of the Town, and enlivened with those little Cant-phrases[1] which have made my Friend *Will* often thought very pretty Company. But let us hear what he says for himself.

My Worthy Friend,

'I Question not but you, and the rest of my Acquaintance, wonder that I, who have lived in the Smoak and Gallantries of the Town for thirty Years together, should all on a sudden grow fond of a Country-life. Had not my Dog of a Steward[b] run away as he did, without making up his Accounts, I had still been immersed in Sin and Sea-Coal. But since my late forced Visit to my Estate, I am so pleased with it, that I am resolved to live and dye upon it. I am every Day abroad among my Acres, and can scarce forbear filling my Letter with Breezes, Shades, Flowers, Meadows, and purling Streams. The Simplicity of Manners, which I have heard you so often speak of, and which appears here in Perfection, charms me wonderfully. As an Instance of it, I must acquaint you, and by your means the whole Club, that I have lately married one of my Tenants Daughters. She is born of honest Parents, and tho' she has no Portion she has a great deal of Virtue. The natural Sweetness and Innocence of her Behaviour, the Freshness of her Complection, the unaffected Turn of her Shape and Person, shot me through and through every time I saw her, and did more Execution upon me in Grogram, than the greatest Beauty in Town or Court had ever done in Brocade.[2] In short, she is such an one as promises me a good Heir to my Estate, and if by her means I cannot leave to my Children what are falsely called the Gifts of Birth; high Titles and Alliances: I hope to convey to them the more real and valuable Gifts of Birth;

---

[a] above] *8vo*; about *Fol., 12mo*   [b] my Dog of a Steward] my Dog the Steward *Fol.*

---

[1] See *OED*, Cant 5c. This is the earliest example in *OED* of the word used attributively.

[2] See No. 254 (vol. ii).

strong Bodies and healthy Constitutions. As for your fine Women, I need not tell thee that I know them. I have had my share in their Graces, but no more of that. It shall be my Business hereafter to live the Life of an honest Man, and to act as becomes the Master of a Family. I question not but I shall draw upon me the Raillery of the Town, and be treated to the Tune of *the Marriage-Hater matched*;[1] but I am prepared for it. I have been as witty upon others in my time. To tell thee truly, I saw such a Tribe of Fashionable young fluttering Coxcombs shot up, that I did not think my Post of an *homme de ruelle* any longer tenable.[2] I felt a certain Stiffness in my Limbs, which entirely destroyed that Jauntyness of Air I was once Master of. Besides, for I may now confess my Age to thee, I have been eight and forty above these twelve Years. Since my Retirement into the Country will make a Vacancy in the Club, I could wish you would fill up my Place with my Friend *Tom Dapperwitt*.[3] He has an infinite deal of Fire, and knows the Town. For my own part, as I have said before, I shall endeavour to live hereafter suitable to a Man in my Station, as a prudent Head of a Family, a good Husband, a careful Father (when it shall so happen), and as

Your most Sincere Friend
and Humble Servant,
WILLIAM HONEYCOMB.'[4]

O

[1] The title of a comedy by Thomas D'Urfey (1692).

[2] The ladies' fashion of 'receiving visits in their beds' had been satirized by Addison in No. 45.

[3] Tom Dapperwitt, who regarded marriage as purgatory (No. 482), appears also in Nos. 499 and 511.

[4] 'Philospec', writing from the Temple on 11 Nov. 1712 (Lillie, ii. 30–33), relates a visit to his prospective wife with this number of the *Spectator* in hand.

There is none of your spectators have had more influence upon me, than those many excellent discourses upon a marriage-life, which you have touch'd so finely, and have set that matter (which has been very little understood) in so clear a light, that a young fellow must be obstinately resolved to shut his eyes against his reason and common sense, that won't own, there may be made, and that it is in the power of any discerning person to make a married life the end of all happiness in the world (pp. 30–31).

No. 531   *Saturday, November 8, 1712*[1]
[ADDISON]

> *Qui mare & terras variisque mundum*
> *Temperat horis:*
> *Unde nil majus generatur ipso,*
> *Nec viget quicquam simile aut secundum.*
>
> Hor.

SIMONIDES being asked by *Dionysius* the Tyrant what God was, desired a Day's time to consider of it before he made his Reply.[2] When the Day was expired, he desired two Days; and afterwards, instead of returning his Answer, demanded still double the Time to consider of it. This great Poet and Philosopher, the more he contemplated the Nature of the Deity, found that he waded but the more out of his Depth; and that he lost himself in the Thought, instead of finding an End of it.

If we consider the Idea which wise Men, by the Light of Reason, have framed of the Divine Being, it amounts to this: That he has in him all the Perfection of a Spiritual Nature; And since we have no Notion of any kind of Spiritual Perfection but what we discover in our own Souls, we joyn Infinitude to each kind of these Perfections, and what is a Faculty in an Human Soul becomes an Attribute in God. *We* exist in Place and Time, the Divine Being fills the Immensity of Space with his Presence, and Inhabits Eternity. *We* are possessed of a little Power and a little Knowledge, the Divine Being is Almighty and Omniscient. In short, by adding Infinity to any kind of Perfection we enjoy, and by joyning all these different kinds of Perfections in one Being, we form our Idea of the great Sovereign of Nature.

Though every one who thinks must have made this Observation, I shall produce Mr. *Lock*'s Authority to the same purpose, out of

---

[1] *Motto.* Horace, *Odes,* I. 12. 15–18:

> Who guides the Earth, and Sea and fleeting Years :
> He claims the first and highest Place,
> Nothing so great, so wise above,
> None second is.

[2] Cicero, *De natura deorum,* I. 22. 60. A frequently cited anecdote; cf. Bayle, 'Simonides', Remark F; Lord Hervey, letter to Sir Thomas Hanmer, 20 Jan. 712/13: 'like him who undertook a definition of the Deity, desiring longer and longer time for the solution' (*Letter Books of John Hervey, First Earl of Bristol* [Wells, 1894], i. 346).

his Essay on Human Understanding.[1] 'If we examine the *Idea* we have of the incomprehensible supreme Being, we shall find, that we come by it the same Way; and that the complex *Ideas* we have both of God, and separate Spirits, are made up of the simple *Ideas* we receive from *Reflection*; *v. g.* having from what we experiment in our selves, got the *Ideas* of Existence and Duration; of Knowledge and Power; of Pleasure and Happiness; and of several other Qualities and Powers, which it is better to have, than to be without: When we would frame an *Idea* the most suitable we can to the supreme Being, we enlarge every one of these with our *Idea* of Infinity; and so putting them together, make our complex *Idea of God.*'

It is not impossible that there may be many kinds of Spiritual Perfection, besides those which are lodged in an human Soul; but it is impossible that we should have Ideas of any kinds of Perfection, except those of which we have some small Rays and short imperfect Strokes in our selves. It would be therefore a very high Presumption to determine whether the Supream Being has not many more Attributes than those which enter into our Conceptions of him. This is certain, that if there be any kind of Spiritual Perfection which is not marked out in an human Soul, it belongs, in its Fulness, to the Divine Nature.

Several eminent Philosophers have imagined that the Soul, in her separate State, may have new Faculties springing up in her, which she is not capable of exerting during her present Union with the Body; and whether these Faculties may not correspond with other Attributes in the Divine Nature, and open to us hereafter new Matter of Wonder and Adoration, we are altogether ignorant. This, as I have said before, we ought to acquiesce in, that the Sovereign Being, the great Author of Nature, has in him all possible Perfection, as well in *Kind* as in *Degree*: to speak according to our methods of conceiving.[a] I shall only add under this Head, that when we have raised our Notion of this Infinite Being as high as it is possible for the Mind of Man to go, it will fall infinitely short of what He really is. *There is no end of his Greatness*: The most exalted Creature[b] he has made is only capable of adoring it, none but himself can comprehend it.

[a] conceiving.] conceiving him. *Fol.*   [b] Creature] Creature which *Fol.*

---

[1] Locke, *Essay*, II. xxiii. 33.

The Advice of the Son of *Sirach* is very just and sublime in this Light.[1] *By his word all things consist. We may speak much, and yet come short: wherefore in sum, he is all. How shall we be able to magnifie him? for he is great above all his Works. The Lord is terrible and very great; and marvellous is his power. When you glorifie the Lord exalt him as much as you can; for even yet will he far exceed. And when you exalt him put forth all your strength, and be not weary; for you can never go far enough. Who hath seen him, that he might tell us? And who can magnifie him as he is? There are yet hid greater things than these be, for we have seen but a few of his Works.*

I have here only considered the Supreme Being by the Light of Reason and Philosophy. If we would see him in all the Wonders of his Mercy, we must have Recourse to Revelation, which represents him to us, not only as infinitely Great and Glorious, but as infinitely Good and Just in his Dispensations towards Man. But as this is a Theory which falls under every ones Consideration, though indeed it can never be sufficiently considered, I shall here only take notice of that habitual Worship and Veneration which we ought to pay to this Almighty Being. We should often refresh our Minds with the Thought of him, and annihilate our selves before him in the Contemplation of our own Worthlessness and of his transcendent Excellency and Perfection. This would imprint in our Minds such a constant and uninterrupted Awe and Veneration as that which I am here recommending, and which is in reality a kind of incessant Prayer, and a reasonable Humiliation of the Soul before him who made it.

This would effectually kill in us all the little Seeds of Pride, Vanity and Self-conceit, which are apt to shoot up in the Minds of such whose Thoughts turn more on those comparative Advantages which they enjoy over some of their Fellow-Creatures, than on that infinite Distance which is placed between them and the Supreme Model of all Perfection. It would likewise quicken our Desires and Endeavours of uniting our selves to him by all the Acts of Religion and Virtue.

Such an habitual Homage to the Supreme Being would, in a particular manner, banish from among us that prevailing Impiety of using his Name on the most trivial Occasions.

I find the following Passage in an excellent Sermon, preached at the Funeral of a Gentleman who was an Honour to his Country, and

[1] Ecclesiasticus. 43. 26–32.

394

a more diligent as well as successful Enquirer into the Works of Nature, than any other our Nation has ever produced.[1] 'He had the profoundest Veneration for the Great God of Heaven and Earth that I have ever observed in any Person. The very Name of God was never mentioned by him without a Pause and a visible Stop in his Discourse, in which one that knew him most particularly above twenty Years, has told me, that he was so exact that he does not remember to have observed him once to fail in it.'

Every one knows the Veneration which was paid by the *Jews* to a Name so great, wonderful and holy. They would not let it enter even into their religious Discourses. What can we then think of those who make use of so tremendous a Name in the ordinary Expressions of their Anger, Mirth, and most impertinent Passions? of those who admit it into the most familiar Questions and Assertions, ludicrous Phrases and Works of Humour? not to mention those who violate it by solemn Perjuries? It would be an Affront to Reason to endeavour to set forth the Horror and Prophaneness of such a Practice. The very Mention of it exposes it sufficiently to those in whom the Light of Nature, not to say Religion, is not utterly extinguished. O

No. 532
[STEELE]

Monday, November 10, 1712[2]

> . . . *Fungar vice cotis, acutum*
> *Reddere quæ ferrum valet, exsors ipsa secandi.*
> Hor.

IT is a very honest Action to be studious to produce other Men's Merit; and I make no Scruple of saying I have as much of this Temper as any Man in the World. It would not be a thing to be bragged of, but that it is what any Man may be Master of who will take Pains enough for it. Much Observation of the Unworthiness in being pained at the Excellence of another, will bring you to a Scorn

---

[1] By Gilbert Burnet, Bishop of Salisbury, *A Sermon preached at the Funeral of the Honourable Robert Boyle at St. Martins in the Fields, January 7, 1691/2* (1692), p. 24.
[2] *Motto.* Horace, *Ars poetica*, 304–5:
> I'le play the *Whet stone*, useless and unfit
> To cut my self, I'le sharpen others Wit. CREECH.

of your self for that Unwillingness: And when you have got so far, you will find it a greater Pleasure than you ever before knew, to be zealous in promoting the Fame and Welfare of the Praise-worthy. I do not speak this as pretending to be a mortified self-denying Man, but as one who has turned his Ambition into a right Channel. I claim to my self the Merit of having extorted excellent Productions from a Person of the greatest Abilities,[1] who would not have let them appeared by any other Means; to have animated a few young Gentlemen into worthy Pursuits, who will be a Glory to our Age;[2] and at all Times, and by all possible Means in my Power, undermined the Interests of Ignorance, Vice, and Folly, and attempted to substitute in their Stead Learning, Piety, and good Sense. It is from this honest Heart that I find my self honoured as a Gentleman-Usher to the Arts and Sciences. Mr. *Tickell* and Mr. *Pope* have, it seems, this Idea of me. The former has writ me an excellent Paper of Verses in Praise, forsooth, of my self; and the other enclosed for my Perusal an admirable Poem, which, I hope, will shortly see the Light.[3] In the mean Time I cannot suppress any Thought of his, but insert his Sentiment about the dying Words of *Adrian*. I won't determine in the Case he mentions; but have thus much to say in favour of his Argument, That many of his own Works which I have seen, convince me that very pretty and very sublime Sentiments may be lodged in the same Bosom without Diminution to its Greatness.

Mr. SPECTATOR,[4]

'I WAS the other Day in Company with five or six Men of some Learning; where chancing to mention the famous Verses which the Emperor *Adrian* spoke on his Death-bed, they were all agreed

[1] Steele's tribute to Addison.

[2] Steele here may have had in mind Ambrose Philips, John Hughes, Philip Frowde —and Pope.

[3] Pope's *Temple of Fame*, not published until 1715. On 12 Nov., two days after this number appeared, Steele writes to Pope: 'I have read over your *Temple of Fame* twice, and cannot find any thing amiss, of weight enough to call a fault, but see in it a thousand thousand beauties. Mr. *Addison* shall see it to-morrow: After his perusal of it, I will let you know his thoughts' (*Correspondence*, ed. Blanchard, p. 63).

[4] Pope's letter was reprinted by him with the date 7 Nov. 1712 in the 1735 edition of his correspondence, with three minor changes in phrasing. For the text see Sherburn, i. 149–50. In reprinting the letter in 1735 Pope added his translation of Hadrian's verses. For the letter dated 29 Nov. 1712 which Pope later printed as one which he had addressed to Steele see Sherburn, i. 158–9. It begins: 'I am sorry you publish'd that notion about *Adrian*'s *Verses* as mine; had I imagin'd you wou'd use my name, I shou'd have express'd my sentiments with more modesty and diffidence. I only sent it to have your opinion, and not to publish my own, which I distrusted.'

that 'twas a Piece of Gayety unworthy that Prince in those Circumstances. I could not but dissent from this Opinion: Methinks it was by no Means a gay, but a very serious Soliloquy to his Soul at the Point of his Departure; in which Sense I naturally took the Verses at my first reading them when I was very young, and before I knew what Interpretation the World generally put upon them.

> *Animula vagula, blandula,*
> *Hospes Comesque corporis,*
> *Quæ nunc abibis in loca?*
> *Pallidula, rigida, nudula,*
> *Nec (ut soles) dabis Joca!*

Alas, my Soul! thou pleasing Companion of this Body, thou fleeting Thing that art now deserting it! whither art thou flying? to what unknown Region? Thou art all trembling, fearful, and pensive. Now what is become of thy former Wit and Humour? thou shalt jest and be gay no more! I confess I cannot apprehend where lies the Trifling in all this; 'tis the most natural and obvious Reflection imaginable to a dying Man; and if we consider the Emperor was a Heathen, that Doubt concerning the future Fate of his Soul will seem so far from being the Effect of want of Thought, that 'twas scarce reasonable he should think otherwise; not to mention that here is a plain Confession included of his Belief in its Immortality. The diminutive Epithets of *Vagula, Blandula,* and the rest, appear not to me as Expressions of Levity, but rather of Endearment and Concern; such as we find in *Catullus,* and the Authors of *Hendeca-syllabi* after him, where they are used to express the utmost Love and Tenderness for their Mistresses—— If you think me right in my Notion of the last Words of *Adrian,* be pleased to insert this in the *Spectator*; if not, to suppress it.

I am, &c.'

To the supposed Author of the *Spectator.*[1]

> *IN Courts licentious, and a shameless Stage,*
> *How long the War shall Wit with Virtue wage:*
> *Enchanted by this prostituted Fair,*
> *Our Youth run headlong in the fatal Snare;*
> *In height of Rapture clasp unheeded Pains,*
> *And suck Pollution through their tingling Veins.*

---

[1] This is the first publication of Tickell's poem. It was reprinted in 1749 in volume ii of the *Works of the most celebrated minor poets* and again in 1750 in the *Works of Celebrated Authors* (ii. 249–50), with Tickell's name.

Thy spotless Thoughts unshock'd the Priest may hear,
And the pure Vestal in her Bosom wear.
To conscious Blushes, and diminish'd Pride,
Thy Glass betrays what treach'rous Love would hide;
Nor harsh thy Precepts, but infus'd by Stealth,
Please while they cure, and cheat us into Health.
Thy Works in Chloe's *Toilet gain a Part,*
And with his Tailor share the Fopling's Heart:
Lash'd in thy Satyr, the penurious Cit
Laughs at himself, and finds no Harm in Wit:
From Felon-Gamesters the raw Squire is free,[1]
And Britain *owes her rescued Oaks to thee.*
His Miss the frolick Viscount dreads to toast,[2]
Or his third Cure the shallow Templar boast;
And the rash Fool, who scorn'd the beaten Road,
Dares quake at Thunder, and confess his God.

The brainless Stripling, who, expell'd to Town,
Damn'd the stiff College and pedantick Gown,
Aw'd by thy Name, is dumb, and thrice a Week[3]
Spells uncouth Latin, *and pretends to* Greek.
A sauntring Tribe! such born to wide Estates,
With Yea and No in Senates hold Debates:
At length despis'd, each to his Fields retires,
First with the Dogs, and King amidst the Squires;
From Pert to Stupid sinks supinely down,
In Youth a Coxcomb, and in Age a Clown.

Such Readers scorn'd, thou wing'st thy daring Flight
Above the Stars, and tread'st the Fields of Light;
Fame, Heav'n, and Hell, are thy exalted Theme,
And Visions such as Jove *himself might dream;*

---

[1] Tickell here alludes to a story told by Hughes (in a letter signed Will Trusty, printed in *Tatler* 73) of the attempts made by sharpers to lure a young squire into their toils and get possession of his estate. The letter concludes with the warning 'to all young landed Knights and 'Squires, That whenever they are drawn to Play, they would consider it as calling 'em down to a Sentence already pronounc'd upon 'em, and think of the Sound of those Words, *His Oaks must be fell'd*'. See Duncombe's preface to Hughes's *Poems* (1735), vol. i, p. xxxiv.

[2] Nichols and Chalmers identify the viscount as Bolingbroke.

[3] The reference to the mottoes would apply to the *Tatler* rather than to the *Spectator*. Tickell, it is clear from lines 101–2, is addressing the poem to Steele as Mr. Spectator; like most of his contemporaries Tickell continued to identify Isaac Bickerstaff and Mr. Spectator with Steele.

Man sunk to Slav'ry, tho' to Glory born,
Heav'n's Pride when upright, and deprav'd his Scorn.

Such Hints alone could British Virgil[1] *lend,*
And Thou alone deserve from such a Friend:
A Debt, so borrow'd, is illustrious Shame,
And Fame when shar'd with him is double Fame.
So flush'd with Sweets, by Beauty's Queen bestow'd,
With more than mortal Charms Æneas glow'd.[2]
Such gen'rous Strifes Eugene *and* Marlbro' *try,*
And as in Glory, so in Friendship vie.

Permit these Lines by Thee to live—nor blame
A Muse that pants and languishes for Fame;
That fears to sink when humbler Themes she sings,
Lost in the Mass of mean forgotten Things.
Receiv'd by Thee, I prophesy, my Rhymes
The Praise of Virgins in succeeding Times;
Mix'd with thy Works, their Life no Bounds shall see,
But stand protected, as inspir'd by Thee.

So some weak Shoot, which else would poorly rise,[a]
Jove's Tree adopts, and lifts him to the Skies;
Through the new Pupil fost'ring Juices flow,
Thrust forth the Gems,[3] and give the Flow'rs to blow
Aloft; immortal reigns the Plant unknown,
With borrow'd Life, and Vigour not his own.

To the SPECTATOR GENERAL,

Mr. John Sly *humbly sheweth,[4]*

'THAT upon reading the Deputation given to the said Mr.
John Sly, all Persons passing by his Observatory behaved

---

[a] *Line not indented in Fol.*

[1] Addison.
[2] Tickell is probably influenced by Addison's description of Austria's young monarch in *The Campaign*, 421–4:

> Thus the great father of Almighty *Rome*
> (Divinely flusht with an immortal bloom
> That *Cytherea's* fragrant breath bestow'd)
> In all the charms of his bright mother glow'd.

[3] I.e. buds. The last example in *OED* of this use is dated 1813.
[4] See No. 526.

themselves with the same Decorum, as if your Honour your self had been present.

'That your said Officer is preparing, according to your Honour's secret Instructions, Hats for the several kind of Heads that make Figures in the Realms of *Great-Britain*, with Cocks significant of their Powers and Faculties.

'That your said Officer has taken due Notice of your Instructions and Admonitions concerning the Internals[1] of the Head from the outward Form of the same. His Hats for Men of the Faculties of Law and Physick do but just turn up, to give a little Life to their Sagacity; his Military Hats glare full in the Face; and he has prepared a familiar easy Cock for all good Companions between the above-mention'd Extreams. For this End he has consulted the most Learned of his Acquaintance for the true Form and Dimensions of the *Lepidum Caput*, and made a Hat fit for it.

'Your said Officer does further represent, That the young Divines about Town are many of them got into the Cock Military, and desires your Instructions therein.

'That the Town has been for several Days very well behaved; and further your said Officer saith not.'

T

No. 533   *Tuesday, November 11, 1712*[2]
[STEELE]

Immo duas dabo, inquit ille, una si parum est:
Et si duarum pœnitebit, addentur duæ.

Plaut.

To the SPECTATOR.

SIR,

'YOU have often given us very excellent Discourses against that unnatural Custom of Parents, in forcing their Children to marry contrary to their Inclinations. My own Case, without further Preface, I will lay before you, and leave you to judge of it. My Father

[1] 'The inward parts or organs' (*OED*, where the only example given is dated 1834).
[2] *Motto.* Plautus, *Stichus*, 550–1 (altered): Well, says he, if one is not enough, you shall have two; and if you are not content with those, e'en double them.

and Mother, both being in declining Years, would fain see me, their eldest Son, as they call it, settled. I am as much for that as they can be; but I must be settled, it seems, not according to my own, but their Liking. Upon this Account I am teiz'd every Day, because I have not yet fallen in Love, in spite of Nature, with one of a neighbouring Gentleman's Daughters; for, out of their abundant Generosity, they give me the Choice of Four. *Jack*, begins my Father, Mrs. *Katherine* is a fine Woman—Yes, Sir; but she is rather too old —She will make the more discreet Manager, Boy. Then my Mother plays her Part. Is not Mrs. *Betty* exceeding fair? Yes, Madam; but she is of no Conversation; she has no Fire, no agreeable Vivacity; she neither speaks nor looks with Spirit. True, Son; but for those very Reasons she will be an easy, soft, obliging, tractable Creature. After all, cries an old Aunt, (who belongs to the Class of those who read Plays with Spectacles on) what think you, Nephew, of proper Mrs. *Dorothy*? What do I think? Why I think she cannot be above six Foot two Inches high. Well, well, you may banter as long as you please, but Height of Stature is commending and majestick. Come, come, says a Cousin of mine in the Family, I'll fit him: *Fidelia* is yet behind—Pretty Miss *Fiddy* must please you—Oh! your very humble Servant, dear Cos. she is as much too young as her eldest Sister is too old. Is it so indeed, quoth she, good Mr. *Pert*? you, who are but barely turn'd of 22, and Miss *Fiddy* in half a Year's Time will be in her Teens, and she is capable of learning any thing: Then she will be so observant; she'll cry perhaps now and then, but never be angry. Thus they will think for me in this Matter, wherein I am more particularly concern'd than any Body else. If I name any Woman in the World, one of these Daughters has certainly the same Qualities. You see by these few Hints, Mr. SPECTATOR, what a comfortable Life I lead. To be still more open and free with you, I have been passionately fond of a young Lady (whom give me Leave to call *Miranda*) now for these three Years. I have often urged the Matter home to my Parents with all the Submission of a Son, but the Impatience of a Lover. Pray, Sir, think of three Years; what inexpressible Scenes of Inquietude, what Variety of Misery must I have gone through in three long whole Years? *Miranda*'s Fortune is equal to those I have mentioned, but her Relations are not Intimates with mine. Ah! there's the Rub. *Miranda*'s Person, Wit, and Humour, are what the nicest Fancy could imagine; and though we know you to be so elegant a Judge of Beauty, yet there is none among all your various Characters of fine Women preferable to *Miranda*. In a Word, she is never guilty of doing any thing but one amiss, (if she can be thought to do amiss by me) in being as blind to my Faults, as she is to her own Perfections.

I am, SIR,

Your very humble obedient Servant,
Deutererastus.'ª[1]

Mr. SPECTATOR,

'WHEN you spent so much Time as you did lately in censuring the ambitious young Gentlemen who ride in Triumph through Town and Country in Coach-boxes,[2] I wish'd you had employed those Moments in Consideration of what passes sometimes within Side of those Vehicles. I am sure I suffered sufficiently by the Insolence and ill Breeding of some Persons who travelled lately with me in a Stage-Coach out of *Essex* to *London*. I am sure, when you have heard what I have to say, you will think there are Persons under the Character of Gentlemen that are fit to be no where else but in the Coach-box. Sir, I am a young Woman of a sober and religious Education, and have preserved that Character; but on *Monday* was Fortnight it was my Misfortune to come to *London*. I was no sooner clapt in the Coach, but, to my great Surprize, two Persons in the Habit of Gentlemen attack'd me with such indecent Discourse as I can't repeat to you, so you may conclude not fit for me[b] to hear.[3] I had no Relief but the Hopes of a speedy End of my short Journey. Sir, form to your self what a Persecution this must needs be to a virtuous and a chaste Mind; and in order to your proper handling such a Subject, fancy your Wife or Daughter, if you had any, in such Circumstances, and what Treatment you would think then due to such Dragoons. One of them was called a Captain, and entertained us with nothing but filthy stupid Questions, or lewd Songs, all the Way. Ready to burst with Shame and Indignation, I repined that Nature had not allowed us as easily to shut our Ears as our Eyes. But was not this a kind of Rape? Why should there be Accessaries in Ravishment any more than Murther? Why should not every Contributor to the Abuse of Chastity suffer Death? I am sure these shameless Hell-hounds deserved it highly. Can you exert your self

---

^a Deutererastus] Dustererastus *all edd.*   ^b not fit for me] not for me *Fol.*

¹ Deutererastus—probably with reference to the account of Erastus and Laetitia in No. 506 (above, pp. 297–8). I owe this emendation to Miss F. M. Williams.
² Nos. 498, 526.   ³ Cf. No. 132 and No. 242 (vol. ii) (the first letter).

better than on such an Occasion? If you do not do it effectual, I'll read no more of your Papers. Has every impertinent Fellow a Privilege to torment me, who pay my Coach-hire as well as he? Sir, pray consider us in this Respect as the weakest Sex, and have nothing to defend our selves; and I think it is as Gentleman-like to challenge a Woman to fight, as to talk obscenely in her Company, especially when she has not Power to stir. Pray let me tell you a Story which you can make fit for publick View. I knew a Gentleman, who having a very good Opinion of the Gentlemen of the Army, invited ten or twelve of them to sup with him; and at the same Time invited two or three Friends, who were very severe against the Manners and Morals of Gentlemen of that Profession. It happened one of them brought two Captains of his Regiment newly come into the Army, who at first Onset engaged the Company with very lewd Healths and suitable Discourse. You may easily imagine the Confusion of the Entertainer, who finding some of his Friends very uneasy, desired to tell them a Story of a great Man, one Mr. *Lock*, (whom I find you frequently mention) That being invited to dine with the then Lords *Hallifax*, *Anglisey* and *Shaftsbury*, immediately after Dinner, instead of Conversation, the Cards were immediately called for, where the bad or good Success produced the usual Passions of Gaming. Mr. *Lock* retiring to a Window, and writing, my Lord *Anglisey* desired to know what he was writing:[1] *Why, my Lords* (answered he) *I could not sleep last Night for the Pleasure and Improvement I expected from the*

---

[1] The story is told by Jean Le Clerc in *The Life and Character of Mr. John Locke . . . done into English* by T. F. P. Gent. (1706), p. 6. According to Le Clerc, it was 'at my Lord *Ashley*'s' that the incident occurred.

Mr. *Locke* took notice of the Game for some time, and then taking out his Pocketbook, he set himself to write somewhat with very great Seriousness, one of the Lords having observ'd it asks him what it was that he was writing. My Lord, says he, I endeavour to get as much as I can in your good Company, and having waited with impatience the Honour of being present at a Meeting of the wisest and most ingenious men of the Age, and enjoying at length this Happiness; I thought it was best to write your Conversation, and I have accordingly set down the substance of what has been said within this hour or two. There was no need for Mr. *Locke* to read much of this Dialogue, these noble Lords perceiv'd the banter, and diverted themselves a while with improving the jest; they left their play and enter'd into Conversation more aggreable to their Character and so spent the rest of the day.

Le Clerc does not give the date of this incident or name the gentlemen present, though he had earlier mentioned Locke's association with Ashley, Buckingham, Halifax, 'and other Nobles'. The Lord Halifax mentioned in the *Spectator* would be George Savile, Marquis of Halifax (1633–95). It is not clear which Earl of Anglesey is meant. Arthur Annesley, Viscount Valentia, was created Earl of Anglesey in 1662 and died in 1686; his son James became the second Earl in 1686 and died four years later; he was succeeded by his son James the third Earl, who died in 1702 and was

Conversation of the greatest Men of the Age. This so sensibly stung them, that they gladly compounded to throw their Cards in the Fire if he would his Paper, and so a Conversation ensued fit for such Persons. This Story prest so hard upon the young Captains, together with the Concurrence of their superior Officers, that the young Fellows left the Company in Confusion. Sir, I know you hate long things, but if you like it you may contract it, or how you will; but I think it has a Moral in it.

'But, Sir, I am told you are a famous Mechanick as well as a Looker-on, and therefore humbly propose you would invent some Padlock, with full Power under your Hand and Seal for all modest Persons, either Men or Women, to clap upon the Mouths of all such impertinent impudent Fellows: And I wish you would publish a Proclamation, that no modest Person who has a Value for her Countenance, and consequently would not be put out of it, presume to travel after such a Day without one of them in their Pockets. I fancy a smart *Spectator* upon this Subject would serve for such a Padlock; and that publick Notice may be given in your Paper where they may be had, with Directions, Price 2*d.* and that Part of the Directions may be, when any Person presumes to be guilty of the above-mentioned Crime, the Party aggriev'd may produce it to his Face, with a Request to read it to the Company: He must be very much hardened that could outface that Rebuke; and his further Punishment I leave you to prescribe.

> *Your humble Servant,*
> Penance Cruel.'

T

---

succeeded by his brother John. Shaftesbury may refer to the first Earl, Anthony Ashley Cooper (1621–83), the Lord Chancellor under Charles II; his son the second Earl (d. 1699); or his grandson the third Earl (1671–1713), the author of the *Characteristicks.*

Rarus enim ferme sensus communis in illa
Fortuna . . .

                                   Juv.

Mr. SPECTATOR,

'I AM a young Woman of Nineteen, the only Daughter of very
wealthy Parents; and have my whole Life been used with a
Tenderness which did me no great Service in my Education. I have,
perhaps, an uncommon Desire for Knowledge of what is suitable to
my Sex and Quality; but, as far as I can remember, the whole Dispute about me has been, whether such a thing was proper for the
Child to do, or not? or whether such or such Food was the more
wholesome for the young Lady to eat? This was ill for my Shape,
that for my Complection, and t'other for my Eyes. I am not extravagant, when I tell you I do not know that I have trod upon the very
Earth since I was ten Years old: A Coach or Chair I am obliged to
for all my Motions from one Place to another ever since I can remember. All who had to do to instruct me, have ever been bringing
Stories of the notable things I have said, and the womanly Manner
of my behaving my self upon such and such an Occasion. This has
been my State till I came toward Years of Womanhood; and ever
since I grew towards the Age of Fifteen, I have been abused after
another Manner. Now, forsooth, I am so killing no one can safely
speak to me. Our House is frequented by Men of Sense, and I love
to ask Questions when I fall into such Conversation, but I am cut
short with something or other about my bright Eyes. There is, Sir,
a Language particular for talking to Women in; and none but those
of the very first good Breeding (who are very few, and who seldom
come into my Way) can speak to us without regard to our Sex.
Among the Generality of those they call Gentlemen, it is impossible
for me to speak upon any Subject whatsoever, without provoking
Somebody to say, *Oh! to be sure fine Mrs. such a one must be very par-*
ticularly acquainted with all that; all the World will contribute to her
Entertainment and Information. Thus, Sir, I am so handsome, that I

<hr/>

[1] *Motto.* Juvenal, *Satires,* 8. 73–74:
                  For we seldom find
    Much Sence with an exalted Fortune join'd. STEPNEY.

murther all who approach me; so wise, that I want no new Notices; and so well bred, that I am treated by all that know me like a Fool, for no one will answer as if I were their Friend or Companion. Pray, Sir, be pleased to take the Part of us Beauties and Fortunes into your Consideration, and do not let us be thus flattered out of our Senses. I have got an Hussey of a Maid, who is most craftily given to this ill Quality. I was at first diverted with a certain Absurdity the Creature was guilty of in every thing she said. She is a Country Girl, and in the Dialect of the Shire she was born in, would tell me that every Body reckoned her Lady had the purest Red and White in the World. Then she would tell me I was the most like one *Sisly Dobson* in their Town, who made the Miller make away with himself, and walk afterwards in the Corn-field where they used to meet. With all this, this cunning Hussey can lay Letters in my Way, and put a Billet in my Gloves, and then stand in it she knows nothing of it. I do not know, from my Birth to this Day, that I have been ever treated by any one as I ought; and if it were not for a few Books which I delight in, I should be at this Hour a Novice to all common Sense. Would it not be worth your While to lay down Rules for Behaviour in this Case, and tell People that we fair ones expect honest plain Answers as well as other People? Why must I, good Sir, because I have a good Air, a fine Complection, and am in the Bloom of my Years, be misled in all my Actions? and have the Notions of Good and Ill confounded in my Mind, for no other Offence but because I have the Advantages of Beauty and Fortune? Indeed, Sir, what with the silly Homage which is paid us by the sort of People I have above spoken of, and the utter Negligence which others have for us, the Conversation of us young Women of Condition is no other than what must expose us to Ignorance and Vanity, if not Vice. All this is humbly submitted to your Spectatorial Wisdom by,

SIR,

Your humble Servant,

Sharlot Wealthy.'

Mr. SPECTATOR, Will's *Coffee-House.*
'PRAY, Sir, it will serve to fill up a Paper, if you put in this; which is only to ask whether that Copy of Verses, which is a Paraphrase of *Isaiah,* in one of your Speculations is *not* written by

Mr. *Pope*?[1] Then you get on another Line, by putting in, with proper Distances, as at the End of a Letter,

> *I am, Sir,*
> *Your humble Servant,*
> Abraham Dapperwit.'

Mr. Dapperwit,

'I AM glad to get another Line forward, by saying that excellent Piece is Mr. *Pope*'s; and so, with proper Distances,

> *I am, Sir,*
> *Your humble Servant,*
> S——r.'

Mr. SPECTATOR,

'I WAS a wealthy Grocer in the City, and as fortunate as diligent; but I was a single Man, and you know there are Women. One in particular came to my Shop, who I wish'd might, but was afraid never wou'd make a Grocer's Wife. I thought, however, to take an effectual Way of Courting, and sold to her at less Price than I bought, that I might buy at less Price than I sold. She, you may be sure, often came, and help'd me to many Customers at the same Rate, fancying I was obliged to her. You must needs think this was a good living Trade, and my Riches must be vastly improved. In fine, I was nigh being declar'd Bankrupt, when I declared my self her Lover, and she herself married. I was just in a Condition to support my self, and am now in Hopes of growing rich by losing my Customers.

> *Yours,*
> Jeremy Comfitt.'

Mr. SPECTATOR,

'I AM in the Condition of the Idol you was once pleased to mention, and Bar-keeper of a Coffee-house.[2] I believe 'tis needless to tell you the Opportunities I must give, and the Importunities I suffer. But there is one Gentleman who besieges me as close as the *French* did *Bouchain*.[3] His Gravity makes him work cautious, and his regular Approaches denote a good Engineer. You need not doubt

---

[1] No. 378.

[2] See No. 87 (the last letter) (vol. i).

[3] This fortress, which had surrendered to Marlborough in Sept. 1711, was recaptured by Villars on 4 Oct. 1712, after only eight days' resistance. See Winston Churchill, *Marlborough*, vi. 561; Trevelyan, iii. 132–3, 222.

of his Oratory, as he is a Lawyer; and especially since he has had so little Use of it at *Westminster,* he may spare the more for me.

'What then can weak Woman do? I am willing to surrender, but he would have it at Discretion, and I with Discretion.[1] In the mean Time, whilst we parly, our several Interests are neglected. As his Siege grows stronger, my Tea grows weaker; and while he pleads at my Bar, none come to him for Counsel but in *Forma Pauperis.* Dear Mr. SPECTATOR, advise him not to insist upon hard Articles, nor by his irregular Desires contradict the well-meaning Lines of his Countenance. If we were agreed, we might settle to something, as soon as we could determine where we should get most, by the Law, at the Coffee-house, or at *Westminster.*

Your humble Servant,
Lucinda Parly.'

A Minuit from Mr. John Sly.[2]

'THE World is pretty regular for about forty Rod East, and ten West of the Observatory of the said Mr. *Sly;* but he is credibly inform'd, that when they are got beyond the Pass[3] into the *Strand,* or those who move Cityward are got within *Temple-Bar,* they are just as they were before. It is therefore humbly proposed, that Moving-Centries may be appointed all the busy Hours of the Day between the *Exchange* and *Westminster,* and report what passes to your Honour, or your subordinate Officers, from Time to Time.'

Ordered,

That Mr. *Sly* name the said Officers, provided he will answer for their Principles and Morals. T

[1] One of the French phrases mentioned in No. 165 (vol. ii). It is also used in No. 180 (paragraph 5).
[2] Cf. Nos. 526 and 532. [3] See No. 498.

Spem longam reseces . . .

Hor.

MY Four Hundred and Seventy First Speculation turned upon the Subject of Hope in general. I design this Paper as a Speculation upon that vain and foolish Hope, which is misemployed on Temporal Objects, and produces many Sorrows and Calamities in Human Life.

It is a Precept several times inculcated by *Horace,* that we should not entertain an Hope of any thing in Life which lies at a great Distance from us:[2] The Shortness and Uncertainty of our Time here makes such a kind of Hope unreasonable and absurd. The Grave lies unseen between us and the Object which we reach after: Where one Man lives to enjoy the Good he has in view, ten thousand are cut off in the Pursuit of it.

It happens likewise unluckily, that one Hope no sooner dies in us but another rises up in its stead. We are apt to fancy that we shall be happy and satisfyed, if we possess our selves of such and such particular Enjoyments; but either by reason of their Emptiness, or the natural Inquietude of the Mind, we have no sooner gained one Point but we extend our Hopes to another. We still find new inviting Scenes and Landskips lying behind those which at a distance terminated our View.

The natural Consequences of such Reflections are these; that we should take Care not to let our Hopes run out into too great a Length; that we should sufficiently weigh the Objects of our Hope, whether they be such as we may reasonably expect from them what we propose in their Fruition; and whether they are such as we are pretty sure of attaining, in case our Life extend it self so far. If we hope for things which are at too great a Distance from us, it is possible that we may be intercepted by Death in our Progress towards them. If we hope for things of which we have not thoroughly considered the Value, our Disappointment will be greater than our Pleasure in the Fruition of them. If we hope for what we are not likely to possess, we act and think in vain, and make Life a greater Dream and Shadow than it really is.

[1] *Motto.* Horace, *Odes,* I. II. 7: Contract thy hopes.
[2] Horace, *Odes,* I. 4. 15–16; I. 9. II; &c.

Many of the Miseries and Misfortunes of Life proceed from our want of Consideration, in one or all of these Particulars. They are the Rocks on which the sanguine Tribe of Lovers daily split, and on which the Bankrupt, the Politician, the Alchymist and Projector are cast away in every Age. Men of warm Imaginations and towring Thoughts are apt to overlook the Goods of Fortune which are[a] near them, for something that glitters in the Sight at a distance; to neglect solid and substantial Happiness, for what is showy and superficial; and to contemn that Good which lies within their reach, for that which they are not capable of attaining. Hope calculates its Schemes for a long and durable Life; presses forward to imaginary Points of Bliss; and grasps at Impossibilities: and consequently very often ensnares Men into Beggary, Ruine and Dishonour.

What I have here said may serve as a Moral to an *Arabian* Fable, which I find translated into *French* by Monsieur *Galland*.[1] The Fable has in it such a wild, but natural, Simplicity, that I question not but my Reader will be as much pleased with it as I have been, and that he will consider himself, if he reflects on the several Amusements of Hope which have sometimes passed in his Mind, as a near Relation to the *Persian* Glass-Man.

Alnaschar, says the Fable, was a very idle Fellow, that never would set his Hand to any Business during his Father's Life. When his Father died he left him to the value of an hundred Drachmas in *Persian* Mony.[2] *Alnaschar*, in order to make the best of it, laid it out in Glasses, Bottels, and the finest Earthen Ware. These he piled up in a large open Basket, and having made choice of a very little Shop placed the Basket at his Feet, and leaned his Back upon the Wall, in Expectation of Customers. As he sat in this Posture with his Eyes upon the Basket, he fell into a most amusing Train of Thought, and was over-heard by one of his Neighbours, as he talk'd to himself in the following manner. *This Basket*, says he, *cost me at the Wholesale Merchant's an Hundred Drachmas, which is all I have in the World. I shall quickly make two hundred of it, by selling it in Retail. These two hundred Drachmas will in a very little while rise to four Hundred, which of course*

[a] which are] that lie Fol.

[1] Antoine Galland's translation of the *Thousand and One Nights* was published at Paris in 12 volumes, 1704–17. See *Les Mille et une Nuits, contes arabes* (La Haye, 1706), v. 80. Volumes five and six were published in English translation (for A. Bell) in 1706 (advertised in *Post Boy*, 10 Dec.).
[2] According to Danet this ancient silver Greek coin was 'worth about Sevenpence Halfpenny of *English* Money'.

will amount in time to four Thousand. Four Thousand Drachmas cannot fail of making Eight Thousand. As soon as by this means I am Master of Ten Thousand, I will lay aside my Trade of a Glass-Man and turn Jeweller. I shall then deal in Diamonds, Pearls and all sorts of rich Stones. When I have got together as much wealth as I can well desire, I will make a Purchase of the finest House I can find, with Lands, Slaves, Eunuchs and Horses. I shall then begin to enjoy my self, and make a noise in the World. I will not, however, stop there, but still continue my Traffick till I have got together an Hundred Thousand Drachmas. When I have thus made my self Master of an hundred thousand Drachmas, I shall naturally set my self on the foot of a Prince, and will demand the Grand Visier's *Daughter in Marriage, after having represented to that Minister the Information which I have received of the Beauty, Wit, Discretion, and other high Qualities which his Daughter possesses. I will let him know, at the same time, that it is my Intention to make him a Present of a Thousand Pieces of Gold on our Marriage Night. As soon as I have married the Grand* Visier's *Daughter, I'll buy her ten black Eunuchs, the youngest and best that can be got for Mony. I must afterwards make my Father-in-Law a Visit with a great Train and Equipage. And when I am placed at his Right Hand, which he will do of Course, if it be only to Honour his Daughter, I will give him the thousand Pieces of Gold which I promised him, and afterwards, to his great Surprise, will present him another Purse of the same Value, with some short Speech,*[a] as,* Sir you see I am a Man of my Word. I always give more than I promise.

When I have brought the Princess to my House, I shall take particular care to breed in her a due Respect for me, before I give the Reins to Love and Dalliance. To this end I shall confine her to her own Apartment, make her a short Visit, and talk but little to her. Her Women will represent to me that she is inconsolable by Reason of my Unkindness, and beg me with Tears to caress her, and let her sit down by me; but I shall still remain inexorable, and will turn my Back upon her all the first Night. Her Mother will then come and bring her Daughter to me, as I am seated upon my Sofa. The Daughter, with Tears in her Eyes, will fling her self at my Feet, and beg of me to receive her into my Favour: Then will I, to imprint in her a thorough Veneration for my Person, draw up my Legs and spurn her from me with my Foot, in such a manner that she shall fall down several Paces from the Sofa.

Alnaschar was entirely swallowed up in this chimerical Vision, and could not forbear acting with his Foot what he had in his Thoughts: So that unluckily striking his Basket of Brittle Ware, which was the Foundation of all his Grandeur, he kicked his Glasses to a great

[a] *Speech,*] Compliment, Fol.

distance from him into the Street, and broke them into ten
thousand Pieces.   O

No. 536   *Friday, November 14, 1712*[1]
[ADDISON]

> *O veræ Phrygiæ neque enim Phryges!* . . .
>   Virg.

AS I was the other Day standing in my Bookseller's Shop, a pretty
young Thing, about Eighteen Years of Age, stept out of her
Coach, and brushing by me, beck'ned the Man of the Shop to the
further End of his Counter, where she whispered something to him
with an attentive Look, and at the same time presented him with
a Letter: After which pressing the End of her Fan upon his Hand,
she delivered the remaining Part of her Message, and withdrew.
I observed, in the midst of her Discourse, that she flushed, and cast
an Eye upon me over her Shoulder, having been informed, by my
Bookseller, that I was the Man of the short Face whom she had so
often read of. Upon her passing by me, the pretty blooming Creature
smiled in my Face, and dropp'd me a Curtsie. She scarce gave me
time to return her Salute, before she quitted the Shop with an easie
Scuttle,[2] and stepp'd again into her Coach, giving the Footmen
Directions to drive where they were bid. Upon her Departure my
Bookseller gave me a Letter, superscribed *To the ingenious Spectator*,
which the young Lady had desired him to deliver into my own
Hands, and to tell me that the speedy Publication of it would not
only oblige her self, but a whole Tea-Table of my Friends. I opened
it therefore, with a Resolution to Publish it whatever it should
contain, and am sure, if any of my Male Readers will be so severely
critical as not to like it, they would have been as well pleased with
it as my self, had they seen the Face of the pretty Scribe.

London Nov. 1712.

Mr. SPECTATOR,

'YOU are always ready to receive any Useful Hint or Proposal,
and such, I believe, you will think one that may put you in

---

[1] *Motto.* Virgil, *Aeneid*, 9. 617 (altered): O Phrygian women!—for ye are not
Phrygian men.   [2] See No. 323 (vol. iii).

a way to imploy the most idle Part of the Kingdom; I mean that Part of Mankind who are known by the Name of the Womens-Men,[1] or Beaus, &c. Mr. *Spectator*, You are sensible these pretty Gentlemen are not made for any Manly Imployments, and for want of Business are often as much in the Vapours as the Ladies. Now what I propose is this, that since Knotting[2] is again in Fashion, which has been found a very pretty Amusement, that you would recommend it to these Gentlemen as something that may make them useful to the Ladies they admire. And since 'tis not inconsistent with any Game, or other Diversion, for it may be done in the Play-House, in their Coaches, at the Tea-Table, and, in short, in all Places where they come for the sake of the Ladies (except at Church, be pleased to forbid it there to prevent Mistakes) it will be easily complyed with. 'Tis beside an Imployment that allows, as we see by the fair Sex, of many Graces, which will make the Beaus more readily come into it; it shews a White Hand and Diamond Ring to great Advantage; it leaves the Eyes at full Liberty to be imployed as before, as also the Thoughts, and the Tongue. In short, it seems in every Respect so proper, that 'tis needless to urge it further, by speaking of the Satisfaction these Male-Knotters will find, when they see their Work mix'd up in a Fringe, and worn by the Fair Lady for whom and with whom it was done. Truly, Mr. *Spectator*, I cannot but be pleased I have hit upon something that these Gentlemen are capable of; for 'tis sad so considerable a Part of the Kingdom (I mean for Numbers) should be of no manner of use. I shall not trouble you farther at this time, but only to say, that I am always your Reader, and generally your Admirer,

C. B.

'*P. S.* The sooner these fine Gentlemen are set to Work the better, there being at this time several fine Fringes that stay only for more Hands.'

I shall, in the next Place, present my Reader with the Description

---

[1] For the 'woman's man' see No. 130 (vol. ii).

[2] 'Fancy work done by knitting threads into knots, similar to tatting' (*OED*). The first example in *OED* is dated 1697; the word 'Knotter' used below is the earliest example in *OED* of the word. 'Phillis Knotting; a Song by Sir Ch. Sedley' appears in the *Gentleman's Journal*, Aug.–Sept. 1694 (p. 233). Cf. *Examiner*, 24 Apr. 1713 (vol. iii, no. 44): 'Lady *Char---te* is taken *Knotting* in St. *James*'s *Chapel*, during Divine Service, in the immediate Presence both of *God* and *Her Majesty*, who were affronted together.'

of a Sett of Men who are common enough in the World, tho' I do not remember that I have yet taken notice of them, as they are drawn in the following Letter.

Mr. SPECTATOR,

'SINCE you have lately, to so good Purpose, enlarged upon Conjugal Love,[1] it's to be hoped you'll discourage every Practice that rather proceeds from a Regard to Interest, than to Happiness. Now you cannot but observe, that most of our fine young Ladies readily fall in with the Direction of the Graver sort, to retain in their Service, by some small Encouragement, as great a Number as they can of supernumerary and insignificant Fellows, which they use like Whiflers,[2] and commonly call *Shoeing-Horns*.[3] These are never designed to know the length of the Foot,[4] but only when a good Offer comes to whet and spur him up to the Point. Nay 'tis the Opinion of that grave Lady, Madam *Matchwell*, that it's absolutely convenient for every prudent Family to have several of these Implements about the House, to clap on as occasion serves, and that every Spark ought to produce a Certificate of his being a Shoeing-Horn, before he be admitted as a Shoe. A certain Lady, whom I could name, if it was necessary, has at present more Shoeing-Horns of all Sizes, Countries, and Colours, in her Service, than ever she had new Shoes in her Life. I have known a Woman make use of a Shoeing-Horn for several Years, and finding him unsuccessful in that Function,

---

[1] See Nos. 525, 527, 528.

[2] Attendants who cleared the way for a procession or at some public spectacle; also supernumeraries, men of no consequence. Cf. *Hudibras*, II. ii. 649–50:

> Before the Dame, and round about,
> March'd Whifflers, and Staffiers on Foot.

In *Examiner* 19 Swift refers to the Whig journalists as Whifflers, who use 'little trifling Cavils and Carpings in the wrong Place' for arguments (*Prose Works*, ed. H. Davis, iii. 36). Steele's *Lover* No. 7 prints a letter signed Tom Whiffle. One of the poems in *Miscellanies in Prose and Verse, by a Person of Quality* [Edward Howard, 8th Earl of Suffolk] (1725) is called 'Upon a Whifler':

> If you frequent, the shining Theater,
> Where heav'nly Virgins in their Robes appear
> Vast Droves of Whiflers, thither do repair,
> The most on Foot, thô some in hackney Chair,
> Dispensing Ogles, to the blushing Fair. . . .   (p. 74)

[3] Shoeing-Horns, i.e. tools or decoys. Johnson's *Dictionary* quotes this passage and defines the word as 'any thing by which a transaction is facilitated: any thing used as a medium: in contempt'. Peter Motteux in the *Gentleman's Journal*, March 1691/2 (p. 2), speaks of a dedication full of quirks and flourishes as 'a *Rhetorical Shoeing Horn* to draw on the Reader's uneasy Attention'. There are many examples of the phrase in the popular literature of the first quarter of the eighteenth century.

[4] An old saying, dating from the sixteenth century (cf. *OED*, s.v. Foot, 26c).

convert him at length into a Shoe. I am mistaken if your Friend, Mr. WILLIAM HONEYCOMB, was not a cast Shoeing-Horn before his late Marriage. As for my self, I must frankly declare to you, that I have been an arrant Shoeing-Horn for above these Twenty Years. I served my first Mistress in that Capacity above Five of the Number before she was Shod. I confess, tho' she had many who made their Applications to her, I always thought my self the best Shoe in her Shop, and it was not, till a Month before her Marriage, that I discovered what I was. This had like to have broke my Heart, and raised such Suspicions in me, that I told the next I made Love to, upon receiving some unkind Usage from her, that I began to look upon my self as no more than her Shoeing-Horn. Upon which, my Dear, who was a Coquet in her Nature, told me I was Hypocondriacal, and that I might as well look upon my self to be an Egg or a Pipkin.[1] But in a very short time after she gave me to know that I was not mistaken in my self. It would be tedious to recount to you the Life of an unfortunate Shoeing-Horn, or I might entertain you with a very long and melancholy Relation of my Sufferings. Upon the whole, I think, Sir, it would very well become a Man in your Post, to determine in what Cases a Woman may be allowed, with Honour, to make use of a Shoeing-Horn, as also to declare whether a Maid on this side Five and Twenty, or a Widow who has not been Three Years in that State, may be granted such a Privilege, with other Difficulties which will naturally occur to you upon that Subject.

I am, SIR,

with the most profound Veneration,

Your, &c.'

O[a]

No. *536 not signed in Fol.*

---

[1] Well-recognized manifestations of the spleen. Cf. Pope's *Rape of the Lock*, iv. 47–54. The best general survey is 'The English Malady', by Cecil A. Moore, in his *Backgrounds of English Literature 1700–1760* (Minneapolis, 1953), pp. 179–235.

No. 537   *Saturday, November 15, 1712*[1]
[HUGHES]

Τοῦ μὲν γὰρ γένος ἐσμέν.... Arat.

To the SPECTATOR.

SIR,

'IT has been usual to remind Persons of Rank, on great Occasions in Life, of their Race and Quality, and to what Expectations they were born; that by considering what is worthy of them, they may be withdrawn from mean Pursuits, and encouraged to laudable Undertakings. This is turning Nobility into a Principle of Virtue, and making it Productive of Merit, as it is understood to have been originally a Reward of it.

'It is for the like Reason, I imagine, that you have in some of your Speculations asserted to your Readers the *Dignity of Human Nature*.[2] But you cannot be insensible that this is a controverted Doctrine; there are Authors who consider Human Nature in a very different View, and Books of Maxims have been written to shew the *Falsity of all Human Virtues*.[3] The Reflections which are made on this Subject usually take some Tincture from the Tempers and Characters of those that make them. Politicians can resolve the most shining Actions among Men into Artifice and Design; Others,[a] who are sowered by Discontent, Repulses, or ill Usage, are apt to mistake their Spleen for Philosophy;[b] Men of profligate[c] Lives, and such as

---

[a] Design; Others,] Design. Some, *Fol.*   [b] Philosophy;] Philosophy. *Fol.*
[c] profligate] vicious *Fol.*

[1] *Motto.* Aratus, *Phaenomena*, 5: For we are his offspring.
[2] A recurrent theme in both the *Tatler* and *Spectator*. *Tatler* 87 (by Steele) opens with the declaration, 'There is nothing which I contemplate with greater Pleasure than the Dignity of human Nature.' 'I must confess', writes Addison in *Tatler* 108, 'there is nothing that more pleases me, in all that I read in Books, or see among Mankind, than such Passages as represent human Nature in its proper Dignity.' He goes on to contrast the authors of antiquity, who 'cultivate the natural Grandeur of the Soul', with 'our modish *French* Authors' and their English imitators, who depreciate human nature. 'They give mean Interpretations and base Motives to the worthiest Actions: They resolve Virtue and Vice into Constitution. In short, they endeavour to make no Distinction between Man and Man, or between the Species of Men and that of Brutes.' He cites La Rochefoucauld as 'the great Philosopher for administring of Consolation to the Idle, the Envious, and worthless Part of Mankind'. Hughes, the author of the present essay, had dealt with the same theme earlier in the *Spectator* (No. 210).
[3] The reference may be, as Nichols thought, to La Rochefoucauld, but more probably to the *Traité de la Fausseté des vertus humaines* by Jacques Esprit (1678). The English translation, by W. Beauvoir, *Discourses on the Deceitfulness of Humane Virtues* appeared in 1706.

find themselves incapable of rising to any Distinction among their Fellow-Creatures, are for pulling down all Appearances of Merit which seem to upbraid them; and[a] Satyrists describe nothing but Deformity. From all these Hands we have such Draughts of Mankind as are represented in those burlesque Pictures, which the *Italians* call *Caracatura's*;[1] where the Art consists in preserving, amidst distorted Proportions and aggravated Features, some distinguishing Likeness of the Person, but in such a Manner as to transform the most agreeable Beauty into the most odious Monster.

'It is very disingenuous to level the best of Mankind with the worst, and for the Faults of Particulars to degrade the whole Species. Such Methods tend not only to remove a Man's good Opinion of others, but to destroy that Reverence for himself, which is a great Guard of Innocence, and a Spring of Virtue.

'It is true indeed that there are surprizing Mixtures of Beauty and Deformity, of Wisdom and Folly, Virtue and Vice, in the Human Make; such a Disparity is found among Numbers of the same Kind, and every Individual, in some Instances, or at some Times, is so unequal to himself, that *Man* seems to be the most wavering and inconsistent Being in the whole Creation.[2] So that the Question in Morality, concerning the Dignity of our Nature, may at first Sight appear like some difficult Questions in natural Philosophy, in which the Arguments on both Sides seem[b] to be of equal Strength. But as I began with considering this Point as it relates to Action, I shall here borrow an admirable Reflection from Monsieur *Pascal*, which I think sets it in its proper Light.

'*It is of dangerous Consequence,* says he, *to represent to Man how near he is to the Level of Beasts, without shewing him at the same time his* Greatness. *It is likewise dangerous to let him see his Greatness, without his* Meanness. *It is more dangerous yet to leave him ignorant of either; but very beneficial that he shou'd be made sensible of both.*[3]

[a] them; and] *8vo*; them. And *Fol.*; them; And *12mo*   [b] seem] appear *Fol.*

---

[1] This is the earliest quotation in *OED* to illustrate this meaning.

[2] Addison had devoted No. 162 to this theme.

[3] Pascal, *Pensées*, i. 7 (ed. Louis Lafuma, 1951, p. 81). In the translation by Basil Kennett (*Thoughts on Religion, and other Subjects*, 1704) the passage occurs in chap. xxiii (pp. 196–7):

It is dangerous to inform Man how near he stands to the Beasts, without shewing him at the same time, how infinitely he shines above them. Again, it is dangerous to let him see his Excellence, without making him acquainted with his Infirmity. And the greatest Danger of all is to leave him in utter Ignorance of the one, and of the other. But to have a just Representation of both, is his greatest Interest and Happiness.

'Whatever Imperfections we may have in our Nature, it is the Business of Religion and Virtue to rectify them, as far as is consistent with our present State. In the mean time, it is no small Encouragement to generous Minds[a] to consider that we shall put them all off with our Mortality. That sublime Manner of Salutation with which the *Jews* approach'd their Kings,

O King, *live for ever!*

may be addressed to the lowest and most despised Mortal among us, under all the Infirmities and Distresses with which we see him surrounded. And whoever believes the *Immortality of the Soul,* will not need a better Argument for the Dignity of his Nature, nor a stronger Incitement to Actions suitable to it.[b]

'I am naturally led by this Reflection to a Subject I have already touched upon in a former Letter, and cannot without Pleasure call to Mind the Thoughts of *Cicero* to this Purpose, in the Close of his Book concerning *Old Age*.[1] Every one who is acquainted with his Writings, will remember that the Elder *Cato* is introduced in that Discourse as the Speaker, and *Scipio* and *Lelius* as his Auditors. This venerable Person is represented looking forward as it were from the Verge of extream old Age, into a future State, and rising into a Contemplation on the unperishable Part of his Nature, and its Existence after Death. I shall collect Part of his Discourse. And as you have formerly offered some Arguments for the Soul's Immortality, agreeable both to Reason and the Christian Doctrine, I believe your Readers will not be displeased to see how the same great Truth shines in the Pomp of the *Roman* Eloquence.

' "This, says *Cato*, is my firm Persuasion, that since the human Soul exerts it self with so great Activity, since it has such a Remembrance of the Past, such a Concern for the Future, since it is enriched with so many Arts, Sciences and Discoveries, it is impossible but the Being which contains all these must be Immortal.

' "The elder *Cyrus*, just before his Death, is represented by XENOPHON speaking after this manner.[2] *Think not, my dearest Children, that when I depart from you I shall be no more, but remember that my Soul, even while I liv'd among you, was invisible to you; yet by my Actions you were sensible it existed in this Body. Believe it therefore Existing still, tho'*

---

[a] no small . . . Minds] an Encouragement to a generous Mind *Fol.*   [b] Actions suitable to it.] worthy Actions. *Fol.*

[1] Cicero, *De Senectute*, 21-23.   [2] Xenophon, *Cyropaedia*, 8. 7. 17-19.

it be still unseen. How quickly would the Honours of illustrious Men perish after Death, if their Souls performed nothing to preserve their Fame. For my own Part, I never could think that the Soul, while in a mortal Body, lives, but when departed out of it, dies; or that its Consciousness is lost when it is discharged out of an unconscious Habitation. But when it is freed from all corporeal Alliance, then it truly exists. Further, since the Human Frame is broken by Death, tell us what becomes of its Parts? It is visible whither the Materials of other Beings are translated, namely, to the Source from whence they had their Birth. The Soul alone, neither present nor departed, is the Object of our Eyes.'

' "Thus *Cyrus*. But to proceed. No One shall persuade me, *Scipio*, that your worthy Father, or your Grandfathers *Paulus* and *Africanus*, or *Africanus* his Father, or Unkle, or many other excellent Men whom I need not name, performed so many Actions to be remembred by Posterity, without being sensible that Futurity was their Right. And if I may be allowed an old Man's Privilege, to speak of my self, do you think I would have endured the Fatigue of so many wearisome Days and Nights both at home and abroad, if I imagined that the same Boundary which is set to my Life must terminate my Glory? Were it not more desirable to have worn out my Days in Ease and Tranquility, free from Labour, and without Emulation? But I know not how, my Soul has always raised it self, and looked forward on Futurity, in this View and Expectation, that when it shall depart out of Life, it shall then live for ever; and if this were not true, that the Mind is immortal, the Souls of the most worthy would not, above all others, have the strongest Impulse to Glory.

' "What besides this is the Cause that the wisest Men dye with the greatest Æquanimity, the ignorant with the greatest Concern? Does it not seem that those Minds which have the most extensive Views, foresee they are removing to a happier Condition, which those of narrower Sight do not perceive? I, for my part, am transported with the Hope of seeing your Ancestors, whom I have honoured and loved, and am earnestly desirous of meeting not only those excellent Persons whom I have known, but those too of whom I have heard and read, and of whom I my self have written. Nor would I be detained from so pleasing a Journey. O happy Day, when I shall escape from this Croud, this Heap of Pollution, and be admitted to that Divine Assembly of exalted Spirits! When I shall go not only to those great Persons I have named, but to my *Cato*, my Son, than whom a better Man was never born, and whose Funeral Rites I my self perform'd, whereas he ought rather to have attended mine. Yet has not his Soul deserted me, but seeming to cast back a Look on me, is gone before to those Habitations to which it was sensible I should follow him. And tho' I might appear to have born my Loss with Courage, I was not unaffected with it, but I comforted my self in the Assurance that it would not be long before we should meet again, and be divorced no more."

I am SIR, &c.'a

I question not but my Reader will be very much pleased to hear, that the Gentleman who has obliged the World with the foregoing Letter, and who was the Author of the 210th *Speculation on the Immortality of the Soul, the* 375th *on Virtue in Distress, the* 525th *on Conjugal Love,*b *and two or three other very fine ones among those which are not Lettered at the End, will soon publish a noble Poem, Intitled* An Ode to the Creator of the World, *occasioned by the Fragments of* Orpheus.[1]

No. 538
[ADDISON]

Monday, November 17, 1712[2]

> *. . . ultra*
> *Finem tendere opus*
> Hor.

SURPRIZE is so much the Life of Stories, that every one aims at it who endeavours to please by telling them. Smooth Delivery,

---

ᵃ *No. 537 unsigned in Fol., 8vo, 12mo*
ᵇ *the Soul, . . . Conjugal Love,*] *the Soul, that of* Saturday *was Sennight on Conjugal Love,* Fol.

---

[1] No. 540 announces this poem as soon to be published. It is advertised in No. 546:
This Day is publish'd,
A Poem intituled, An Ode to the Creator of the World, occasion'd by the Fragments of Orpheus. Printed for Jacob Tonson, at Shakespear's Head over-against Catherine-street in the Strand.

In an undated letter to Lord Chancellor Parker, Hughes says he wrote this poem several years ago and that it 'was published at the particular instance of Mr. Addison' (*Letters of several eminent persons*, ed. J. Duncombe, 1772, i. 143).

[2] *Motto.* Horace, *Satires,* 2. 1. 1–2 (altered): Beyond the End to spin the Work.
The motto in the Folio sheets was 'Aut famam sequere, aut sibi convenientia finge' (Horace, *Ars poetica,* 119):
> Keep to old Tales, or if you must have new,
> Feign things coherent, that may look like true. CREECH.

an elegant Choice of Words, and a sweet Arrangement, are all beauti-
fying *Graces*, but not the Particulars in this Point of Conversation
which either long command the Attention, or strike with the Violence of a sudden Passion, or occasion the Burst of Laughter which
accompanies Humour. I have sometimes fancy'd, that the Mind is
in this Case like a Traveller who sees a fine Seat in Haste; he acknowledges the Delightfulness of a Walk set with Regularity, but wou'd
be uneasy if he were oblig'd to pace it over, when the first View had
let him into all its Beauties from one End to the other.

However, a Knowledge of the Success which Stories will have
when they are attended with a Turn of Surprize, as it has happily
made the Characters of some, so has it also been the Ruine of the
Characters of others. There is a Sett of Men who outrage Truth,
instead of affecting us with a Manner in telling it; who over-leap the
Line of Probability, that they may be seen to move out of the common Road; and endeavour only to make their Hearers stare, by
imposing upon them with a kind of Nonsense against the Philosophy
of Nature, or such a Heap of Wonders told upon their own Knowledge, as it is not likely one Man shou'd ever have met with.

I have been led to this Observation by a Company into which I
fell accidentally. The Subject of *Antipathies* was a proper Field wherein such false Surprizers might expatiate, and there were those present
who appear'd very fond to shew it in its full Extent of traditional
History.[1] Some of them, in a learned Manner, offer'd to our Consideration the miraculous Powers which the Effluviums of Cheese
have over Bodies whose Pores are dispos'd to receive them in a
noxious Manner; others gave an Account of such who cou'd indeed
bear the Sight of Cheese, but not the Taste; for which they brought
a Reason from the Milk of their Nurses. Others again discours'd,
without endeavouring at Reasons, concerning an unconquerable
Aversion which some Stomachs have against a Joint of Meat when
it is whole, and the eager Inclination they have for it when, by its
being cut up, the Shape which had affected them is alter'd. From
hence they pass'd to Eels, then to Parsnips, and so from one Aversion
to another, till we had work'd up our selves to such a Pitch of Complaisance, that when the Dinner was to come in, we enquir'd the
Name of every Dish, and hop'd it wou'd be no Offence to any in
Company, before it was admitted. When we had sate down, this
Civility amongst us turn'd the Discourse from Eatables to other

[1] Cf. *The Turkish Spy*, book iv, letter xii (5th ed., 1703, iv. 280–1).

Sorts of Aversions; and the eternal Cat, which plagues every Conversation of this Nature, began then to engross the Subject. One had sweated at the Sight of it, another had smell'd it out as it lay conceal'd in a very distant Cupboard, and he who crown'd the whole Set of these Stories, reckon'd up the Number of Times in which it had occasion'd him to swound away: At last, says he, that you may all be satisfy'd of my invincible Aversion to a Cat, I shall give an unanswerable Instance; As I was going through a Street of *London*, where I never had been till then, I felt a general Damp and a Faintness all over me, which I could not tell how to account for, till I chanced to cast my Eyes upwards, and found that I was passing under a Sign-post on which the Picture of a Cat was hung.

The Extravagance of this Turn in the way of Surprize, gave a Stop to the Talk we had been carrying on: Some were silent because they doubted, and others because they were conquer'd in their own Way; so that the Gentleman had Opportunity to press the Belief of it upon us, and let us see that he was rather exposing himself than ridiculing others.

I must freely own that I did not all this while disbelieve every thing that was said; but yet I thought some in the Company had been endeavouring who should pitch the Bar farthest;[a] that it had for some Time been a measuring Cast,[1] and at last my Friend of the Cat and Sign-post had thrown beyond them all.

I then consider'd the Manner in which this Story had been received, and the Possibility that it might have pass'd for a Jest upon others, if he had not labour'd against himself. From hence, thought I, there are two Ways which the well-bred World generally takes to correct such a Practice, when they do not think fit to contradict it flatly.

The first of these is a general Silence, which I would not advise any one to interpret in his own Behalf. It is often the Effect of Prudence in avoiding a Quarrel, when they see another drive so fast, that there is no stopping him without being run against, and but very seldom the Effect of Weakness in believing suddenly. The Generality of Mankind are not so grosly ignorant as some overbearing Spirits would perswade themselves; and if the Authority of a Character or a Caution against Danger make us suppress our

---

[a] farthest;] furthest; *Fol.*

[1] 'A competitive throw at a mark in which the results are so close as to require measurement' (*OED*).

Opinions, yet neither of these are of Force enough to suppress our Thoughts of them. If a Man who has endeavoured to amuse his Company with Improbabilities could but look into their Minds, he would find that they imagine he lightly esteems of their Sense when he thinks to impose upon them, and that he is less esteemed by them for his Attempt in doing so. His Endeavour to glory at their Expence becomes a Ground of Quarrel, and the Scorn and Indifference with which they entertain it begins the immediate Punishment: And indeed (if we should even go no further) Silence, or a negligent Indifference, has a deeper Way of Wounding than Opposition; because Opposition proceeds from an Anger that has a Sort of generous Sentiment for the Adversary mingling along with it, while it shews that there is some Esteem in your Mind for him; in short, that you think him worth while to contest with: But Silence, or a negligent Indifference, proceeds from Anger, mixed with a Scorn that shews another he is thought by you too contemptible to be regarded.

The other Method which the World has taken for correcting this Practice of false Surprize, is to over-shoot such Talkers in their own Bow, or to raise the Story with further Degrees of Impossibility, and set up for a Voucher to them in such a Manner as must let them see they stand detected.[1] Thus I have heard a Discourse was once managed upon the Effects of Fear. One of the Company had given an Account how it had turned his Friend's Hair grey in a Night, while the Terrors of a Shipwreck encompass'd him. Another taking the Hint from hence, began, upon his own Knowledge, to enlarge his Instances of the like Nature to such a Number, that it was not probable he could ever have met with them; and as he still grounded these upon different Causes, for the sake of Variety, it might seem at last, from his Share of the Conversation, almost impossible that any one who can feel the Passion of Fear should all his Life escape so common an Effect of it. By this Time some of the Company grew negligent, or desirous to contradict him: But one rebuked the rest with an Appearance of Severity, and, with the known old Story in his Head, assured them they need not scruple to believe that the Fear of any thing can make a Man's Hair grey, since he knew one whose Perriwig had suffered so by it. Thus he stopp'd the Talk, and made them easy. Thus is the same Method taken to bring us to Shame which we fondly take to encrease our Character. It is indeed

[1] For 'vouchers' cf. No. 253 (ii. 482).

423

a kind of Mimickry by which another puts on our Air of Conversation to show us to our selves: He seems to look ridiculous before you, that you may remember how near a Resemblance you bear to him, or that you may know he will not lie under the Imputation of believing you. Then it is that you are struck dumb immediately with a conscientious Shame for what you have been saying: Then it is that you are inwardly grieved at the Sentiments which you cannot but perceive others entertain concerning you. In short, you are against your self; the Laugh of the Company runs against you; the censuring World is obliged to you for that Triumph which you have allow'd them at your own Expence; and Truth, which you have injured, has a near Way of being revenged on you, when by the bare Repetition of your Story you become a frequent Diversion for the Publick.[a]

Mr. SPECTATOR,

'THE other Day walking in *Pancras* Churchyard, I thought of your Paper wherein you mention Epitaphs, and am of Opinion this has a Thought in it worth being communicated to your Readers,[1]

> Here Innocence and Beauty lies, whose Breath
> Was snatch'd by early, not untimely Death.
> Hence did she go just as she did begin
> Sorrow to know, before she knew to sin.
> Death, that does Sin and Sorrow thus prevent,
> Is the next Blessing to a Life well spent.

I am, SIR,
Your Servant.'[bc]

---

[a] Publick.] Publick. *I am, Sir, your Servant.* Fol.   [b] *I am . . . Servant.*] om. in Fol.
[c] *No. 538 unsigned in Fol., 8vo, 12mo*

---

[1] No. 518. For St. Pancras Church see No. 452. The epitaph quoted here has not been identified.

Heteroclyta sunto. Quae Genus.

Mr. SPECTATOR,

'I AM a young Widow of a good Fortune and Family, and just come to Town; where I find I have Clusters of pretty Fellows come already to visit me, some dying with Hopes, others with Fears, tho' they never saw me. Now what I would beg of you, would be to know whether I may venture to use these pert Fellows with the same Freedom as I did my Country Acquaintance. I desire your Leave to use them as to me shall seem meet, without Imputation of a Jilt; for since I make Declaration that not one of them shall have me, I think I ought to be allowed the Liberty of insulting those who have the Vanity to believe it is in their Power to make me break that Resolution. There are Schools learning to use Foils, frequented by those who never design to fight; and this useless Way of aiming at the Heart, without Design to wound it on either Side, is the Play with which I am resolved to divert my self: The Man who pretends to win, I shall use like him who comes into a Fencing-School to pick a Quarrel. I hope, upon this Foundation, you will give me[a] the free Use of the natural and artificial Force of my Eyes, Looks, and Gestures. As for verbal Promises, I will make none, but shall have no Mercy on the conceited Interpreters of Glances and Motions. I am particularly skilled in the downcast Eye, and the Recovery into a sudden full Aspect, and away again, as you may have seen sometimes practised by us Country Beauties beyond all that you have observed in Courts and Cities. Add to this, Sir, that I have a ruddy heedless Look, which covers Artifice the best of any thing. Tho' I

---

[a] give me] *8vo*, give *Fol.*, *12mo*

[1] *Motto*. (Heteroclites, in Lily's Latin Grammar.)

'De Nominibus Heteroclitis. What are those Nouns called, which are Declined otherwise than according to Rule?

An. Quae genus, aut flexum variant, quaecunque novato Ritu deficiunt, superantve, Heteroclita sunto.'—William Walker, *The Royal Grammar* (1674), p. 140.

The three letters here printed seem to be genuine 'heteroclite' contributions arranged by Steele to form this number. There is no evidence for Nichols's suggestion that the second letter is by Eustace Budgell and the concluding letter by John Hughes. The original of the second letter, signed Eustace, is preserved at Blenheim Palace (*New Letters*, ed. Richmond P. Bond, No. 80). For the text see Appendix V. Steele has completely rewritten the letter, toning down some of the more flamboyant phrases. An earlier letter from the same correspondent on this topic will be found in Lillie, i. 32–33.

can dance very well, I affect a tottering untaught way of walking, by which I appear an easy Prey; and never exert my instructed Charms till I find I have engaged a Pursuer. Be pleased, Sir, to print this Letter, which will certainly begin the Chace of a rich Widow: The many Foldings, Escapes, Returns, and Doublings which I make, I shall from Time to Time communicate to you, for the better Instruction of all Females who set up, like me, for reducing the present exorbitant Power and Insolence of Man.

I am,

SIR,

Your faithful Correspondent,

Relicta Lovely.'

Dear Mr. SPECTATOR,

'I DEPEND upon your profess'd Respect for virtuous Love, for your immediate answering the Design of this Letter; which is no other than to lay before the World the Severity of certain Parents, who desire to suspend the Marriage of a discreet young Woman of Eighteen three Years longer, for no other Reason but that of her being too young to enter into that State. As to the Consideration of Riches, my Circumstances are such, that I cannot be suspected to make my Addresses to her on such low Motives as Avarice or Ambition. If ever Innocence, Wit, and Beauty united their utmost Charms, they have in her. I wish you would expatiate a little on this Subject, and admonish her Parents that it may be from the very Imperfection of Humane Nature it self, and not any personal Frailty of her or me, that our Inclinations baffled at present may alter; and while we are arguing with our selves to put off the Enjoyment of our present Passions, our Affections may change their Objects in the Operation. It is a very delicate Subject to talk upon; but if it were but hinted, I am in Hopes it would give the Parties concern'd some Reflection that might expedite our Happiness. There is a Possibility, and I hope I may say it without Imputation of Immodesty to her I love with the highest Honour; I say, there is a Possibility this Delay may be as painful to her as it is to me. If it be as much, it must be more, by reason of the severe Rules the Sex are under in being deny'd even the Relief of Complaint. If you oblige me in this, and I succeed, I promise you a Place at my Wedding, and a Treatment suitable to your Spectatorial Dignity.

Your most humble Servant,

Eustace.'

SIR,

'I YESTERDAY heard a young Gentleman, that look'd as if he was just come to the Town, and a Scarf,[1] upon Evil-speaking; which Subject, you know, Archbishop *Tillotson* has so nobly handled in a Sermon in his *Folio*.[2] As soon as ever he had nam'd his Text, and had open'd a little the Drift of his Discourse, I was in great Hopes he had been one of Sir ROGER's Chaplains. I have conceived so great an Idea of the charming Discourse above, that I should have thought one Part of my Sabbath very well spent in hearing a Repetition of it. But, alas! Mr. SPECTATOR, this Reverend Divine gave us his Grace's Sermon, and yet I don't know how; even I, that I am sure have read it at least twenty times, could not tell what to make of it, and was at a Loss sometimes to guess what the Man aim'd at. He was so just indeed as to give us all the Heads and the Sub-divisions of the Sermon; and farther, I think there was not one beautiful Thought in it but what we had. But then, Sir, this Gentleman made so many pretty Additions; and he could never give us a Paragraph of the Sermon, but he introduc'd it with something which, methought, look'd more like a Design to shew his own Ingenuity, than to instruct the People. In short, he added and curtail'd in such a Manner that he vex'd me; insomuch that I could not forbear thinking, (what, I confess, I ought not to have thought of in so holy a Place) that this young Spark was as justly blameable as *Bullock* or *Penkethman*[3] when they mend a noble Play of *Shakespear* or *Johnson*. Pray, Sir, take this into your Consideration; and if we must be entertain'd with the Works of any of those great Men, desire these Gentlemen to give them us as they find them, that so when we read them to our Families at home, they may the better remember that they have heard it at Church.

SIR,

Your humble Servant.'[a]

---

[a] *No. 539 unsigned in Fol., 8vo, 12mo*

---

[1] See No. 21 (vol. i).

[2] 'Against Evil-speaking' is the title of Sermon XLII, 'Preached before the King and Queen at Whitehall, February 25. 1693/4' (*Works*, 9th ed., 1728, i. 394–406).

[3] Cf. *Tatler* 89, where Steele comments on these two actors 'helping out Beaumont and Fletcher' by inserting words of their own.

No. 540   *Wednesday, November 19, 1712*[1]
[STEELE]

. . . Non Deficit Alter.
Virg.

Mr. SPECTATOR,

'THERE is no Part of your Writings which I have in more Esteem than your Criticism upon *Milton*. It is an honourable and candid Endeavour to set the Works of our Noble Writers in the graceful Light which they deserve. You will lose much of my kind Inclination towards you, if you do not attempt the Encomium of *Spencer* also, or at least indulge my Passion for that charming Author so far as to print the loose Hints I now give you on that Subject.[2]

'*Spencer*'s general Plan is the Representation of six Virtues, Holiness, Temperance, Chastity, Friendship, Justice, and Courtesy, in six Legends by six Persons. The six Personages are supposed under proper Allegories suitable to their respective Characters, to do all that is necessary for the full Manifestation of the respective Virtues which they are to exert.

'These one might undertake to shew, under the several Heads, are admirably drawn; no Images improper, and most surprizingly beautiful. The Red-cross Knight runs thro' the whole Steps of the Christian Life; *Guyon* does all that Temperance can possibly require; *Britomartis* (a Woman) observes the true Rules of unaffected Chastity; *Arthegal* is in every Respect of Life strictly and wisely just; *Calidore* is rightly courteous.

---

[1] *Motto.* Virgil, *Aeneid*, 6. 143: No lack of others.
The letter which makes up this entire number may have been contributed by Hughes, as Nichols and Aitken suggest. The only basis for this attribution is the fact that Hughes published an edition of Spenser in 1715. On the other hand, this number is not in Duncombe's list of Hughes's contributions to the *Spectator*, and Steele himself had already shown appreciation of Spenser in the *Tatler* (see below).

[2] There are several references to Spenser in the *Tatler*. He is praised in No. 90 (by Steele), and in Nos. 194 and 195 Steele uses book iv, canto x, 'in which Sir Scudamore relates the Progress of his Courtship to *Amoret* under a very beautiful Allegory', with reference to 'the State of Love in this Island'. In No. 229 Addison quotes two stanzas from book i, canto i, describing the 'Thousand monstrous Reptiles' attacking the Red Cross Knight.

When I see my self thus surrounded by such formidable Enemies, I often think of the Knight of the *Red-Cross* in *Spencer*'s *Den of Error*, who, after he has cut off the Dragon's Head, and left it wallowing in a Flood of Ink, sees a Thousand monstrous Reptiles making their Attempts upon him, one with many Heads, another with none, and all of them without Eyes.

He then quotes I. i. 22–23. In No. 254 the extraordinary relations of Sir John Mandeville and Ferdinand Mendez Pinto are compared to 'the Travels of *Ulysses* in *Homer*, or of the *Red-Cross* Knight in *Spencer*. All is Enchanted Ground, and Fairy Land'.

'In short, in *Fairy-Land*, where Knights-Errant have a full Scope to range, and to do even what *Ariosto's* or *Orlando's* could not do in the World without breaking into Credibility, *Spencer's* Knights have, under those six Heads, given a full and a truly Poetical System of Christian, Publick, and Low Life.

'His Legend of Friendship is more diffuse, and yet even there the Allegory is finely drawn, only the Heads various, one Knight could not there support all the Parts.

'To do Honour to his Country, Prince *Arthur* is an Universal Hero; in Holiness, Temperance, Chastity, and Justice super-excellent. For the same Reason, and to compliment Queen *Elizabeth*, *Gloriana*, Queen of Fairies, whose Court was the Asylum of the Oppressed, represents that glorious Queen. At her Commands all these Knights set forth, and only at her's the Red-Cross Knight destroys the Dragon, *Guyon* overturns the Bower of Bliss, *Arthegal* (i.e. *Justice*) beats down *Geryoneo* (i.e. *Phil.* II. King of *Spain*) to rescue *Belge* (i.e. *Holland*,) and he beats the *Grantorto* (the same *Philip* in another Light) to restore *Irena* (i.e. *Peace to* Europe.)

'*Chastity* being the first Female Virtue, *Britomartis* is a *Britain*; her Part is fine, tho' it requires Explication. His Stile is very Poetical; no Puns, Affectations of Wit, forced Antitheses, or any of that low Tribe.

'His old Words are all true *English*, and Numbers exquisite; and since of Words there is the *Multa Renascentur*,[1] since they are all proper, such a Poem should not (any more than *Milton's*) subsist all of it of common ordinary Words. See Instances of Descriptions.

Causless Jealousy in *Britomartis*, V. 6, 14. in
its Restlessness.

Like as a wayward Child, whose sounder Sleep
Is broken, with some fearful Dreams affright,
With froward Will doth set himself to weep,
Ne can be still'd for all his Nurse's Might,
But kicks, and squalls, and shrieks for fell Despight;
Now scratching her, and her loose Locks misusing,
Now seeking Darkness, and now seeking Light;
Then craving Suck, and then the Suck refusing;
Such was this Ladies Loves in her Love's fond accusing.[2]

[1] Horace, *Ars poetica*, 70 ('many shall be born again').
[2] *Faerie Queene*, V. vi. 14. The last line reads, 'Such was this Ladies fit, in her loues fond accusing'.

Curiosity occasioned by Jealousy, upon Occasion of
her Lover's Absence. *Ibid. St.* 8, 9.

Then as she looked long, at last she spy'd
One coming towards her with hasty Speed,
Well ween'd she then, e'er him she plain descry'd,
That it was one sent from her Love indeed:
Whereat her Heart was fill'd with Hope and Dread,
Ne wou'd she stay till he in Place cou'd come,
But ran to meet him forth to know his Tidings somme;
Even in the Door him meeting, she begun,
And where is he, thy Lord, and how far hence?
Declare at once; And hath he lost or won?[2]

Care and his *House* are described thus,
IV. 6. 33, 34, 35.

Not far away, not meet for any Guest,
They spy'd a little Cottage, like some poor Man's Nest.

34.

There entring in, they found the good Man self
Full busily unto his Work ybent,
Who was so weel a wretched wearish Elf,
With hollow Eyes and raw-bone Cheeks forspent,
As if he had in Prison long been pent.
Full black and griesly did his Face appear,
Besmeard with Smoak, that nigh his Eye-sight blent,
With rugged Beard and hoary shagged heare,
The which he never wont to comb, or comely shear.

35.

Rude was his Garment, and to Rags all rent,
Ne better had he, ne for better cared;
His blistred Hands amongst the Cinders brent,
And Fingers filthy, with long Nails prepared,
Right fit to rend the Food on which he fared.
His Name was Care; *a Blacksmith by his Trade,*
That neither Day nor Night from working spared,

---

[1] *Faerie Queene,* V. vi. 8 (lines 1–4, 7–9), 9 (lines 1–3). The first word in the first line
is 'There'.

But to small Purpose Iron Wedges made.
These be unquiet Thoughts that careful Minds invade.[1]

'*Homer*'s Epithets were much admired by Antiquity: See what great Justness and Variety there is in these Epithets of the Trees in the Forest where the Red-cross Knight lost *Truth*. B. 1. Cant. 1. St. 8, 9.

The sailing Pine, the Cedar proud and tall,
The Vine prop Elm, the Poplar never dry,
The Builder Oak, sole King of Forests all,
The Aspine good for Staves, the Cypress Funeral.

9.

The Lawrel Meed of mighty Conquerors,
And Poets sage; the Fir that weepeth still,
The Willow worn of forlorn Paramours,
The Eugh obedient to the Bender's Will,
The Birch for Shafts, the Sallow for the Mill;
The Myrrhe sweet, bleeding in the bitter Wound,
The warlike Beech, the Ash for nothing ill,
The fruitful Olive, and the Platane round,
The Carver Holm, the Maple seldom inward sound.[2]

'I shall trouble you no more, but desire you to let me conclude with these Verses, tho' I think they have already been quoted by you:[3] They are Directions to young Ladies opprest with Calumny. VI. 6, 14.'

The best (said he) *that I can you advise,*
Is to avoid the Occasion of the Ill;
For when the Cause whence Evil doth arise
Removed is, the Effect surceaseth still.
Abstain from Pleasure, and restrain your Will,
Subdue Desire, and bridle loose Delight,
Use scanted Diet, and forbear your Fill,
Shun Secrecy, and talk in open Sight,
So shall you soon repair your present evil Plight.[4]

T[5]

[1] *Faerie Queene*, IV. v. 32 (lines 8–9), 34, 35. (34. 3: 'Who was to weet'. 35. 4: 'with long nayles vnpared'. 35. 9: 'Those be vnquiet thoughts'.)
[2] Ibid. I. i. 8 (lines 6–9), 9.   [3] No. 390.
[4] *Faerie Queene*. VI. vi. 14.
[5] A letter signed M. R. (Monmouth-shire, 3 July) and printed in Lillie (ii. 189–90) praises the *Faerie Queene* and asks Mr. Spectator to write on the subject:

No. 541
[HUGHES]

Thursday, November 20, 1712[1]

> *Format enim Natura prius nos intus ad omnem*
> *Fortunarum habitum; juvat, aut impellit ad iram,*
> *Aut ad humum mærore gravi deducit & angit;*
> *Post effert animi motus interprete Lingua.*
>
> Hor.

MY Friend the *Templar*, whom I have so often mentioned in these Writings, having determined to lay aside his Poetical Studies, in order to a closer Pursuit of the Law, has put together, as a Farewell Essay, some Thoughts concerning *Pronunciation* and *Action*,[a] which he has given me leave to communicate to the Publick. They are chiefly collected from his Favourite Author, *Cicero*, who is known to have been an intimate Friend of *Roscius* the Actor, and a good Judge of Dramatical Performances, as well as the most Eloquent Pleader of the Time in which he liv'd.

CICERO concludes his celebrated Books *de Oratore* with some Precepts for Pronunciation and Action, without which Part he affirms that the best Orator in the World can never succeed; and an indifferent one, who is Master of this, shall gain much greater Applause. What could make a stronger Impression, says he, than those

---

[a] *Pronunciation* and *Action*,] *Action* and *Pronunciation*, Fol.

I am now in the country, and reading in Spencer's fairy-queen. Pray what is the matter with me? when the poet is sublime my heart burns, when he is compassionate I faint, when he is sedate my soul is becalm'd. This has provoked me to advise you (since you have gone through Milton) to begin Spencer, and that you would give us a Saturday on every stanza in the first book; and then that you would wait on the poet so far in print, in a letter like your own face, short but conspicuous; for I long to have the Spectator upon Spencer bound in my pocket together.

[1] *Motto.* Horace, *Ars poetica*, 108–11:

> For Nature forms, and softens us within,
> And writes our Fortunes Changes in our Face.
> Pleasure enchants, impetuous Rage transports,
> And Grief dejects, and wrings the tortur'd Soul,
> And these are all interpreted by Speech. ROSCOMMON.

Hughes's authorship of this number is revealed by Steele at the beginning of No. 554.

Exclamations of *Gracchus—Whither shall I turn? Wretch that I am! To what Place betake my self? Shall I go to the* Capitol?—*Alas! it is over-flowed with my Brother's Blood. Or shall I retire to my House? Yet there I behold my Mother plung'd in Misery, weeping and despairing!*[1] These Breaks and Turns of Passion, it seems, were so enforced by the Eyes, Voice and Gesture of the Speaker, that his very Enemies could not refrain from Tears. I insist, says *Tully,* upon this the rather, because our Orators, who are as it were Actors of the Truth it self, have quitted this manner of speaking, and the Players, who are but the Imitators of Truth, have taken it up.

I shall, therefore, pursue the Hint he has here given me, and for the Service of the *British* Stage I shall Copy some of the Rules which this great *Roman* Master has laid down; yet, without confining my self wholly to his Thoughts or Words; and to adapt this Essay the more to the Purpose for which I intend it, instead of the Examples he has inserted in his Discourse, out of the ancient Tragedies, I shall make use of parallel Passages out of the most Celebrated of our own.

The Design of Art is to assist Action as much as possible in the Representation of Nature; for the Appearance of Reality is that which moves us in all Representations, and these have always the greater Force, the nearer they approach to Nature, and the less they shew of Imitation.[2]

Nature her self has assigned, to every Emotion of the Soul, its peculiar Cast of the Countenance, Tone of Voice, and Manner of Gesture; and the whole Person, all the Features of the Face and Tones of the Voice answer, like Strings upon musical Instruments, to the Impressions made on them by the Mind.[3] Thus the Sounds of the Voice, according to the various Touches which raise them, form themselves into an Acute or Grave, Quick or Slow, Loud or Soft Tone. These too may be subdivided into various Kinds of Tones, as the gentle, the rough, the contracted, the diffused, the continued, the intermitted, the broken, abrupt, winding, softned, or elevated. Every one of these may be employed with Art and Judgment; and all supply the Actor, as Colours do the Painter, with an expressive Variety.

Anger exerts its peculiar Voice in an acute, raised, and hurrying

---

[1] Cicero, *De Oratore,* 3. 56. 214.
[2] Ibid. 3. 57. 215.
[3] Ibid. 3. 57. 216–17.

Sound. The passionate Character of King *Lear*, as it is admirably drawn by *Shakespear*, abounds with the strongest Instances of this kind.

> *Death! Confusion!*
> *Fiery?—what Quality?—why* Gloster, Gloster!
> *I'd speak with the Duke of* Cornwall *and his Wife.*
> *Are they inform'd of this? My Breath and Blood!*
> *Fiery? the fiery Duke? . . . &c.*[1]

Sorrow and Complaint demand a Voice quite different, flexible, slow, interrupted, and modulated in a mournful Tone; as in that pathetical Soliloquy of Cardinal *Wolsey* on his Fall.

> *Farewell!—A long Farewell to all my Greatness!*
> *This is the State of Man!—to day he puts forth*
> *The tender Leaves of Hopes; to-morrow Blossoms,*
> *And bears his blushing Honours thick upon him.*
> *The third Day comes a Frost, a killing Frost,*
> *And when he thinks, good easie Man, full surely*
> *His Greatness is a ripening, nips his Root,*
> *And then he falls as I do.*[2]

We have likewise a fine Example of this in the whole Part of *Andromache* in the *Distrest Mother*, particularly in these Lines,

> *I'll go, and in the Anguish of my Heart*
> *Weep o'er my Child—If he must dye, my Life*
> *Is wrapt in his, I shall not long survive.*
> *'Tis for his sake that I have suffer'd Life,*
> *Groan'd in Captivity, and outliv'd* Hector.
> *Yes, my* Astyanax, *we'll go together!*
> *Together to the Realms of Night we'll go;*
> *There to thy ravish'd Eyes thy Sire I'll show,*
> *And point him out among the Shades below.*[3]

Fear expresses it self in a low, hesitating and abject Sound.[4] If the Reader considers the following Speech of Lady *Macbeth*, while her Husband is about the Murder of *Duncan* and his Grooms, he will imagine her even affrighted with the Sound of her own Voice while she is speaking it.

---

[1] *King Lear*, II. iv. 96–98, 104–5.
[2] *Henry VIII*, III. ii. 351–8.
[3] Ambrose Philips, *The Distrest Mother*, I. v. 1–9.
[4] *De Oratore*, 3. 58. 218.

> *Alas! I am afraid they have awak'd*
> *And 'tis not done; th' Attempt and not the Deed*
> *Confounds us—Hark!—I laid the Daggers ready,*
> *He cou'd not miss them. Had he not resembled*
> *My Father as he slept, I had done it.*[1]

Courage assumes a louder Tone, as in that Speech of Don *Sebastian.*

> *Here satiate all your Fury;*
> *Let Fortune empty her whole Quiver on me,*
> *I have a Soul that like an ample Shield*
> *Can take in all, and Verge enough for more.*[2]

Pleasure dissolves into a luxurious, mild, tender and joyous Modulation; as in the following Lines in *Caius Marius,*

> *Lavinia! O there's musick in the Name,*
> *That softning me to infant Tenderness*
> *Makes my Heart spring, like the first Leaps of Life.*[3]

And Perplexity is different from all these, grave, but not bemoaning, with an earnest uniform Sound of Voice; as in that celebrated Speech of *Hamlet,*

> *To be, or not to be?—that is the Question.*
> *Whether 'tis nobler in the Mind to suffer*
> *The Slings and Arrows of outragious Fortune,*
> *Or to take Arms against a Sea of Troubles,*
> *And by opposing end them. To die, to sleep;*
> *No more; and by a Sleep to say we end*
> *The Heart-ake, and the thousand natural Shocks*
> *That Flesh is Heir to; 'Tis a Consummation*
> *Devoutly to be wish'd. To die, to sleep—*
> *To sleep, perchance to dream! Ay, there's the Rub.*
> *For in that Sleep of Death what Dreams may come,*
> *When we have shuffled off this Mortal Coil,*
> *Must give us pause.—There's the Respect*
> *That makes Calamity of so long Life;*
> *For who would bear the Whips and Scorns of Time,*
> *Th' Oppressor's Wrong, the proud Man's Contumely,*

[1] *Macbeth,* II. ii. 10–14.   [2] Dryden, *Don Sebastian,* I.
[3] Otway, *Caius Marius,* i. 305–7.

The Pangs of despis'd Love, the Laws Delay,
The Insolence of Office, and the Spurns
That patient Merit of th' unworthy takes,
When he himself might his Quietus make
With a bare Bodkin? who wou'd Fardles bear
To groan and sweat under a weary Life?
But that the Dread of something after Death,
The undiscover'd Country, from whose Bourn
No Traveller returns, puzzles the Will,
And makes us rather chuse those Ills we have,
Than fly to others that we know not of.[1]

As all these Varieties of Voice are to be directed by the Sense, so the Action is to be directed by the Voice, and with a beautiful Propriety, as it were, to enforce it. The Arm, which by a strong Figure *Tully* calls *the Orator's Weapon,*[2] is to be sometimes raised and extended, and the Hand, by its Motion, sometimes to lead, and sometimes to follow the Words, as they are uttered. The Stamping of the Foot too has its proper Expression in Contention, Anger, or absolute Command.[3] But the Face is the Epitome of the whole Man, and the Eyes are, as it were, the Epitome of the Face; for which Reason, he says, the best Judges among the *Romans* were not extreamly pleased, even with *Roscius* himself in his Masque. No Part of the Body, besides the Face, is capable of as many Changes as there are different Emotions in the Mind, and of expressing them all by those Changes. Nor is this to be done without the Freedom of the Eyes; therefore *Theophrastus* called one, who barely rehearsed his Speech with his Eyes fixt, an *absent Actor.*[4]

As the Countenance admits of so great Variety, it requires also great Judgment to govern it.[5] Not that the Form of the Face is to be shifted on every Occasion, lest it turn to Farce and Buffoonery; but it is certain, that the Eyes have a wonderful Power of marking the Emotions of the Mind, sometimes by a stedfast Look, sometimes by a careless one; now by a sudden Regard, then by a joyful Sparkling, as the Sense of the Words is diversifyed; for Action is, as it were, the Speech of the Features and Limbs, and must therefore conform it self always to the Sentiments of the Soul.[6] And it may

---

[1] *Hamlet,* III. i. 56–82.
[2] *De Oratore,* 3. 59. 220 (*quasi quoddam telum orationis*).
[3] Ibid. 3. 59. 221.
[4] Cicero names the actor as 'a certain Tauriscus'.
[5] *De Oratore,* 3. 59. 222.　　　　[6] Ibid. 3. 59. 223.

be observed, that in all which relates to the Gesture, there is a wonderful Force implanted by Nature; since the Vulgar, the Unskillful, and even the most Barbarous are chiefly affected by this. None are moved by the Sound of Words, but those who understand the Language; and the Sense of many things is lost upon Men of a dull Apprehension; but Action is a kind of Universal Tongue; all Men are subject to the same Passions, and consequently know the same Marks of them in others, by which they themselves express them.

Perhaps some of my Readers may be of Opinion, that the Hints I have here made use of, out of *Cicero*, are somewhat too refined for the Players on our Theatre; in answer to which I venture to lay it down, as a Maxim, that without Good Sense no one can be a good Player, and that he is very unfit to personate the Dignity of a *Roman* Hero, who cannot enter into the Rules for Pronunciation and Gesture delivered by a *Roman* Orator.

There is another thing which my Author does not think too minute to insist on, tho' it is purely mechanical; and that is the right *pitching* of the Voice. On this Occasion he tells the Story of *Gracchus*, who employed a Servant with a little Ivory Pipe to stand behind him, and give him the right Pitch, as often as he wandered too far from the proper Modulation.[1] Every Voice, says *Tully*, has its particular Medium and Compass, and the Sweetness of Speech consists in leading it thro' all the Variety of Tones naturally, and without touching any Extreme.[2] Therefore, says he, *Leave the Pipe at home, but carry the Sense of this Custom with you.*[a]

[a] *No. 541 unsigned in Fol., 8vo, 12 mo*

No. 542   *Friday, November 21, 1712*[3]
[ADDISON]

Et sibi præferri se gaudet . . .
Ov.

WHEN I have been present in Assemblies where my Paper has been talked of, I have been very well pleased to hear those

[1] Ibid. 3. 60. 225.   [2] Ibid. 3. 61. 227.
[3] *Motto.* Ovid, *Metamorphoses,* 2. 430:
He heard,
Well pleased, himself before himself preferred. ADDISON.

who would detract from the Author of it observe, that the Letters which are sent to the *Spectator* are as good, if not better, than any of his Works. Upon this Occasion many Letters of Mirth are usually mentioned, which some think the *Spectator* writ to himself, and which others Commend because they fancy he received them from his Correspondents: Such are those[a] from the *Valetudinarian*; the Inspector of the Sign-posts; the Master of the Fan Exercise: with that of the Hooped Petticoat; that of *Nicholas Hart* the annual Sleeper; that from Sir *John Envill*; that upon the *London* Cries;[1] with Multitudes of the same Nature. As I love nothing more than to mortifie the Ill-natured, that I may do it effectually, I must acquaint them, they have very often praised me when they did not design it, and that they have approved my Writings when they thought they had derogated from them. I have heard several of these unhappy Gentlemen proving, by undeniable Arguments, that I was not able to pen a Letter which I had written the Day before. Nay, I have heard some of them throwing out ambiguous Expressions, and giving the Company Reason to suspect that they themselves did me the Honour to send me such or such a particular Epistle, which happened to be talked of with the Esteem or Approbation of those who were present. These rigid Criticks are so afraid of allowing me any thing which does not belong to me, that they will not be positive whether the Lion, the wild Boar, and the Flower-pots in the Play-house did not actually write those Letters which came to me in their Names.[2] I must therefore inform these Gentlemen, that I often chuse this way of casting my Thoughts into a Letter, for the following Reasons; First, out of the Policy of those who try their Jest upon another, before they own it themselves. Secondly, because I would extort a little Praise from such who will never applaud any thing whose Author is known and certain. Thirdly, because it gave me an Opportunity of introducing a great variety of Characters into my Work, which could not have been done, had I always written in the Person of the *Spectator*. Fourthly, because the Dignity Spectatorial would have suffered, had I published as from my self those several ludicrous Compositions which I have ascribed to fictitious Names and Characters. And lastly, because they often serve

[a] those] these *Fol.*

---

[1] Nos. 25, 28, 102, 127, 184, 299, and 251. These all occur in numbers by Addison.
[2] Nos. 14 and 22 (both by Steele).

to bring in, more naturally, such additional Reflections as have been placed at the End of them.

There are others who have likewise done me a very particular Honour, though undesignedly. These are such who will needs have it, that I have translated or borrowed many of my Thoughts out of Books which are written in other Languages. I have heard of a Person, who is more famous for his Library than his Learning, that has asserted this more than once in his private Conversation.[1] Were it true, I am sure he could not speak it from his own Knowledge; but had he read the Books which he has collected, he would find this Accusation to be wholly groundless. Those who are truly learned will acquit me in this Point, in which I have been so far from offending, that I have been scrupulous perhaps to a Fault in quoting the Authors of several Passages which I might have made my own.[2] But as this Assertion is in reality an Encomium on what I have published, I ought rather to glory in it, than endeavour to confute it.

Some are so very willing to alienate from me that small Reputation which might accrue to me from any of these my Speculations, that they attribute some of the best of them to those imaginary Manuscripts with which I have introduced them. There are others, I must confess, whose Objections have given me a greater Concern, as they seem to reflect, under this Head, rather on my Morality than on my Invention. These are they who say an Author is guilty of Falsehood, when he talks to the Publick of Manuscripts which he never saw, or describes Scenes of Action or Discourse in which he was never engaged. But these Gentlemen would do well to consider, there is not a Fable or Parable which ever was made use of, that is not liable to this Exception; since nothing, according to this Notion, can be related innocently which was not once Matter of Fact. Besides, I think the most ordinary Reader may be able to discover, by my way of writing, what I deliver in these Occurrences as Truth, and what as Fiction.

Since I am unawares engaged in answering the several Objections which have been made against these my Works, I must take

[1] 'The person here alluded to was most probably Mr. Thomas Rawlinson, ridiculed by Addison under the name of Tom Folio in the Tatler, No. 158' (Nichols). Thomas Rawlinson, the book-collector, died at his house in Aldersgate Street on 6 Aug. 1725. His large collections of books and manuscripts were sold between 1722 and 1734.
[2] The same point is made by Steele at the beginning of No. 546.

Notice that there are some who affirm a Paper of this Nature should always turn upon diverting Subjects, and others who find Fault with every one of them that hath not an immediate Tendency to the advancement of Religion or Learning. I shall leave these Gentlemen to dispute it out among themselves, since I see one half of my Conduct patronized by each side. Were I serious on an improper Subject, or trifling in a serious one, I should deservedly draw upon me the Censure of my Readers; or were I conscious of any thing in my Writings that is not innocent at least, or that the greatest part of them were not sincerely designed to discountenance Vice and Ignorance, and support the Interest of true Wisdom and Virtue, I should be more severe upon my self than the Publick is disposed to be. In the mean while I desire my Reader to consider every particular Paper or Discourse as a distinct Tract by it self, and independant of every thing that goes before or after it.

I shall end this Paper with the following Letter, which was really sent me, as some[a] others have been which I have published, and for which I must own my self indebted to their respective Writers.

SIR,

'I Was this Morning in a Company of your Well-wishers, when we read over, with great Satisfaction, *Tully*'s Observations on Action adapted to the *British* Theatre:[1] Though, by the way, we were very sorry to find that you have disposed of another Member of your Club. Poor Sir *Roger* is dead, and the worthy Clergyman dying. Captain *Sentry* has taken Possession of a fair Estate, *Will. Honeycomb* has married a Farmer's Daughter, and the *Templar* withdraws himself into the Business of his own Profession. What will all this end in![2] We are afraid it portends no Good to the Publick. Unless you very speedily fix a Day for the Election of new Members, we are under Apprehensions of losing the *British Spectator*. I hear of a Party of Ladies who intend to address you on this Subject, and question not, if you do not give us the Slip very suddenly, that you will receive Addresses[b] from all Parts of the Kingdom to continue so

---

[a] some] several *Fol.* [b] Addresses] Petitions *Fol.*

---

[1] See the preceding number.
[2] The letter signed Philo-Spec, whether a genuine contribution or not, is a definite intimation that the *Spectator* is drawing to a close.

useful a Work. Pray deliver us out of this Perplexity, and among the Multitude of your Readers you will particularly oblige

Your most Sincere Friend and Servant,

Philo-Spec.'

O

No. 543
[ADDISON]

Saturday, November 22, 1712[1]

. . . facies non omnibus una
Nec diversa tamen . . .

Ov.

THOSE who were skillful in Anatomy among the Ancients, concluded from the outward and inward Make of an Human Body, that it was the Work of a Being transcendently Wise and Powerful. As the World grew more enlightened in this Art, their Discoveries gave them fresh Opportunities of admiring the Conduct of Providence in the Formation of an Human Body. *Galen*[2] was converted by his Dissections, and could not but own a Supreme Being upon a Survey of this his Handywork. There were, indeed, many Parts of which the old Anatomists did not know the certain Use, but as they saw that most of those which they examined were adapted with admirable Art to their several Functions, they did not question but those, whose Uses they could not determine, were contrived with the same Wisdom for respective Ends and Purposes. Since the Circulation of the Blood has been found out and many other great Discoveries have been made by our Modern Anatomists, we see new Wonders in the Human Frame, and discern several important Uses for those Parts, which Uses the Ancients knew nothing of. In short, the Body of Man is such a Subject as stands the utmost Test of Examination. Though it appears formed with the nicest Wisdom upon the most superficial Survey of it, it still mends upon the Search, and produces our Surprise and Amazement in Proportion as we pry into it. What I have here said of an Human Body, may

---

[1] *Motto.* Ovid, *Metamorphoses*, 2. 13–14: All are not like, nor yet altogether unlike.
[2] The Greek physician (d. A.D. 201), whose treatises served as the basis of the world's medical knowledge down to the time of the Renaissance.

be applied to the Body of every Animal which has been the Subject of Anatomical Observations.

The Body of an Animal is an Object adequate to our Senses. It is a particular System of Providence, that lies in a narrow Compass. The Eye is able to command it, and by successive Enquiries can search into all its Parts. Cou'd the Body of the whole Earth, or indeed the whole Universe, be thus submitted to the Examination of our Senses, were it not too big and disproportioned for our Enquiries, too unwieldy for the Management of the Eye and Hand, there is no Question but it would appear to us as curious and well-contrived a Frame as that of an human Body. We should see the same Concatenation and Subserviency, the same Necessity and Usefullness, the same Beauty and Harmony in all and every of its Parts, as what we discover in the Body of every single Animal.

The more extended our Reason is, and the more able to grapple with immense Objects, the greater still are those Discoveries which it makes of Wisdom and Providence in the Work of the Creation. A Sir *Isaac Newton*, who stands up as the Miracle of the present Age, can look through a whole Planetary System; consider it in its Weight, Number, and Measure; and draw from it as many Demonstrations of infinite Power and Wisdom, as a more confined Understanding is able to deduce from the System of an Human Body.[1]

But to return to our Speculations on Anatomy, I shall here consider the Fabrick and Texture of the Bodies of Animals in one particular View, which, in my Opinion, shews the Hand of a thinking and all-wise Being in their Formation, with the Evidence of a thousand Demonstrations. I think we may lay this down as an incontested Principle, that Chance never acts in a perpetual Uniformity and Consistence with it self. If one should always fling the same Number with ten thousand Dice, or see every Throw just five times less, or five times more in Number, than the Throw which immediately preceded it, who would not imagine there is some invisible Power which directs the Cast?[2] This is the Proceeding which we find in the Operations of Nature. Every kind of Animal is diversifyed by different Magnitudes, each of which gives rise to a different Species. Let a Man trace the Dog or Lion Kind, and he will observe how many of the Works of Nature are published, if I may use the Ex-

---

[1] Some of the arguments and examples in this paper follow those in Newton's *Opticks.* See A. D. Atkinson in *Notes & Queries,* 24 June 1950, p. 275.
[2] A favourite argument, deriving perhaps from Cicero, *De natura deorum,* 2. 27. 93.

pression, in a variety of Editions. If we look into the Reptile World, or into those different Kinds of Animals that fill the Element of Water, we meet with the same Repetitions among several Species, that differ very little from one another, but in Size and Bulk. You find the same Creature, that is drawn at large, copied out in several Proportions, and ending in Miniature. It would be tedious to produce Instances of this regular Conduct in Providence, as it would be superfluous to those who are versed in the Natural History of Animals. The magnificent Harmony of the Universe is such, that we may observe innumerable *Divisions* running upon the same *Ground*. I might also extend this Speculation to the dead Parts of Nature, in which we may find Matter disposed into many *similar* Systems, as well in our Survey of Stars and Planets, as of Stones, Vegetables, and other sublunary Parts of the Creation. In a Word, Providence has shewn the Richness of its Goodness and Wisdom, not only in the Production of many Original Species, but in the multiplicity of Descants which it has made on every Original Species in particular.

But to pursue this Thought still farther: Every living Creature, considered in it self, has many very complicated Parts that are exact Copies of some other Parts which it possesses, and which are complicated in the same manner. One *Eye* would have been sufficient for the Subsistence and Preservation of an Animal; but, in order to better his Condition, we see another placed with a Mathematical Exactness in the same most advantageous Situation, and in every Particular of the same Size and Texture. Is it possible for Chance to be thus delicate and uniform in her Operations? Should a Million of Dice turn up twice together the same Number, the Wonder would be nothing in Comparison with this. But when we see this Similitude and Resemblance in the Arm, the Hand, the Fingers; when we see one half of the Body entirely correspond with the other in all those minute Strokes, without which a Man might have very well subsisted; nay, when we often see a single[a] Part repeated an hundred times in the same Body, notwithstanding it consists of the most intricate weaving of numberless Fibres, and these Parts differing still in Magnitude, as the Convenience of their particular Situation requires, sure a Man must have a strange Cast of Understanding, who does not discover the Finger of God in so wonderful a Work. These Duplicates in those Parts of the Body, without which

[a] a single] one particular *Fol.*

443

a Man might have very well subsisted, tho' not so well as with them, are a plain Demonstration of an all-wise Contriver;[1] as those more numerous Copyings, which are found among the Vessels of the same Body, are evident Demonstrations that they could not be the Work of Chance. This Argument receives additional Strength, if we apply it to every Animal and Insect, within our Knowledge, as well as to those numberless living Creatures that are Objects too minute for an Human Eye; and if we consider how the several Species in this whole World of Life resemble one another in very many Particulars, so far as is convenient for their respective States of Existence. It is much more probable that an hundred Million of Dice should be casually thrown an hundred Million of Times in the same Number, than that the Body of any single Animal should be produced by the fortuitous Concourse of Matter. And that the like Chance should arise in innumerable Instances, requires a Degree of Credulity that is not under the direction of Common-Sense. We may carry this Consideration yet further, if we reflect on the two Sexes in every living Species, with their Resemblances to each other, and those particular Distinctions that were necessary for the keeping up of this great World of Life.[a]

There are many more Demonstrations of a Supreme Being, and of his transcendent Wisdom, Power and Goodness in the Formation of the Body of a living Creature, for which I refer my Reader to other Writings, particularly to the Sixth Book of the Poem Entitled *Creation*, where the Anatomy of the human Body is described with great Perspicuity and Elegance.[2] I have been particular on the Thought which runs through this Speculation, because I have not seen it enlarged upon by others. O

[a] We may . . . Life. *Added in 8vo, 12mo*

---

[1] Addison uses this epithet also in No. 121 (vol. i).
[2] *Creation: a philosophical poem in seven books*, by Sir Richard Blackmore, was published by Samuel Buckley and Jacob Tonson on 28 Feb. 1712 (advertisement in *London Gazette*). Book VI, which describes the wonders of the human frame, concludes:

> Who can this Field of Miracles survey,
> And not with *Galen* all in Rapture say,
> Behold a God, Adore him, and Obey!

Nunquam ita quisquam bene subducta ratione ad vitam fuit
Quin res, Ætas, usus semper aliquid apportet novi,
Aliquid moneat, ut illa, quæ te scire credas, nescias,
Et, quæ tibi putaris prima, in experiundo ut repudies.

                                             Ter.

THERE are, I think, Sentiments in the following Letter from my Friend Captain SENTRY, which discover a rational and equal Frame of Mind, as well prepared for an advantagious as an unfortunate Change of Condition.

SIR,   *Coverley-Hall, Nov. 15. Worcestershire.*
'I AM come to the Succession of the Estate of my honoured Kinsman Sir ROGER DE COVERLEY; and I assure you I find it no easy Task to keep up the Figure of Master of the Fortune which was so handsomely enjoyed by that honest plain Man. I cannot (with respect to the great Obligations I have, be it spoken) reflect upon his Character, but I am confirmed in the Truth which I have, I think, heard spoken at the Club, to wit, That a Man of a warm and well-disposed Heart with a very small Capacity, is highly superior in humane Society to him who with the greatest Talents is cold and languid in his Affections. But, alas! why do I make a Difficulty in speaking of my worthy Ancestor's Failings? his little Absurdities and Incapacity for the Conversation of the politest Men are dead with him, and his greater Qualities are even now useful to him. I know not whether by naming those Disabilities I do not enhance his Merit, since he has left behind him a Reputation in his Country which would be worth the Pains of the wisest Man's whole Life to arrive at. By the Way I must observe to you, that many of your Readers have mistook that Passage in your Writings, wherein Sir ROGER is reported to have enquired into the private Character of the young Woman at the Tavern.[2] I know you mentioned that Circumstance as an Instance of the Simplicity and Innocence of his

---

[1] *Motto.* Terence, *Adelphi,* 855–8: Never did man cast up the business of his life so exactly, but still experience, years, and custom will bring in some new particular, that he was not aware of, and show his ignorance of what he thought he knew, and after trial make him reject his former opinions.
[2] For Sir Roger's meeting with Sukey see No. 410 (vol. iii).

Mind, which made him imagine it a very easy thing to reclaim one of those Criminals, and not as an Inclination in him to be guilty with her. The less Discerning of your Readers cannot enter into that Delicacy of Description in the Character: But indeed my chief Business at this Time is to represent to you my present State of Mind, and the Satisfactions I promise to my self in the Possession of my new Fortune. I have continued all Sir ROGER's Servants, except such as it was a Relief to dismiss into little Beings[1] within my Mannor: Those who are in a List of the good Knight's own Hand to be taken Care of by me, I have quarter'd upon such as have taken new Leases of me, and added so many Advantages during the Lives of the Persons so quartered, that it is the Interest of those whom they are joined with to cherish and befriend them upon all Occasions. I find a considerable Sum of ready Money, which I am laying out among my Dependants at the common Interest, but with a Design to lend it according to their Merit rather than according to their Ability. I shall lay a Tax upon such as I have highly obliged, to become Security to me for such of their own poor Youth, whether Male or Female, as want Help towards getting into some Being in the World.[2] I hope I shall be able to manage my Affairs so, as to improve my Fortune every Year, by doing Acts of Kindness. I will lend my Money to the use of none but indigent Men, secured by such as have ceased to be indigent by the Favour of my Family or my self. What makes this the more practicable is, that if they will do any one Good with my Money, they are welcome to it upon their own Security: And I make no Exception against it, because the Persons who enter into the Obligations do it for their own Family. I have laid out four thousand Pounds this Way, and it is not to be imagined what a Crowd of People are obliged by it. In Cases where Sir ROGER has recommended I have lent Money to put out Children, with a Clause which makes void the Obligation, in Case the Infant dies before he is out of his Apprenticeship; by which Means the Kindred and Masters are extreamly careful of breeding him to Industry, that he may repay it himself by his Labour in three Years Journey-work after his Time is out for the use of his Securities. Opportunities

---

[1] Here used in the obsolete sense of 'living, subsistence'. In Steele's *Conscious Lovers* Bevil Junior's servant Tom says to his sweetheart, 'It will be nothing for them to give us a little being of our own, some small tenement, out of their large possessions.'

[2] *OED* quotes this sentence in illustration of *being* in the sense of 'position, standing in the world'. The meaning, however, seems identical with that in line 8.

of this Kind are all that have occurred since I came to my Estate; but I assure you I will preserve a constant Disposition to catch at all the Occasions I can to promote the Good and Happiness of my Neighbourhood.

'But give me Leave to lay before you a little Establishment which has grown out of my past Life, that, I doubt not, will administer great Satisfaction to me in that Part of it, whatever that is, which is to come.

'There is a Prejudice in favour of the Way of Life to which a Man has been educated, which I know not whether it would not be faulty to overcome: It is like a Partiality to the Interest of one's own Country before that of any other Nation. It is from an Habit of Thinking, grown upon me from my Youth spent in Arms, that I have ever held Gentlemen, who have preserv'd Modesty, Good-nature, Justice, and Humanity in a Soldier's Life, to be the most valuable and worthy Persons of the humane Race. To pass through imminent Dangers, suffer painful Watchings, frightful Alarms, and laborious Marches for the greater Part of a Man's Time, and pass the rest in a Sobriety conformable to the Rules of the most virtuous civil Life, is a Merit too great to deserve the Treatment it usually meets with among the other Part of the World. But I assure you, Sir, were there not very many who have this Worth, we could never have seen the glorious Events which we have in our Days. I need not say more to illustrate the Character of a Soldier, than to tell you he is the very contrary to him you observe loud, sawcy, and overbearing in a red Coat about Town. But I was going to tell you, that in Honour of the Profession of Arms, I have set apart a certain Sum of Money for a Table for such Gentlemen as have served their Country in the Army, and will please from Time to Time to sojourn all, or any Part of the Year at *Coverley.* Such of them as will do me that Honour shall find Horses, Servants, and all Things necessary for their Accommodation, and Enjoyment of all the Conveniencies of Life in a pleasant various Country. If Collonel *Camperfelt*[a] be in Town, and his Abilities are not employed another way in the Service, there is no Man would be more welcome here.[1] That Gentleman's thorough Knowledge in his Profession, together with the Simplicity of his Manners, and

---

[a] *Camperfelt*] Camporfelt *Fol.*

[1] 'A fine compliment to the father of the late worthy Admiral Kempenfelt who was drowned in the Royal George at Spithead, Aug. 29, 1782' (Nichols). For the connexion with Captain Sentry see No. 2 (vol. i).

Goodness of his Heart, would induce others like him to honour my Abode; and I should be glad my Acquaintance would take themselves to be invited or not, as their Characters have an Affinity to his.

'I would have all my Friends know, that they need not fear (though I am become a Country Gentleman) I will trespass against their Temperance and Sobriety. No, Sir, I shall retain so much of the good Sentiments for the Conduct of Life, which we cultivated in each other at our Club, as to contemn all inordinate Pleasures: But particularly remember, with our beloved *Tully*, that the Delight in Food consists in Desire, not Satiety. They who most passionately pursue Pleasure seldomest arrive at it. Now I am writing to a Philosopher, I cannot forbear mentioning the Satisfaction I took in the Passage I read Yesterday in the same *Tully*. A Nobleman of *Athens* made a Compliment to *Plato* the Morning after he had supped at his House, *Your Entertainments do not only please when you give them, but also the Day after.*[1]

> I am,
>
> My worthy Friend,
>
> Your most obedient humble Servant,
>
> WILLIAM SENTRY.'

T

No. 545   *Tuesday, November 25, 1712*[2]
[STEELE; GIGLI]

Quin potius Pacem Æternam pactosque Hymenæos Exercemus . . .

Virg.

I CANNOT but think the following Letter from the Emperor of *China*[3] to the Pope of *Rome*, proposing a Coalition of the *Chinese* and *Roman* Churches, will be acceptable to the Curious.[4] I must confess I my self being of Opinion that the Emperor has as much Authority to be Interpreter to him he pretends to expound, as the Pope has to be Vicar to the Sacred Person he takes upon him to represent, I was not a little pleased with their Treaty of Alliance. What Progress the Negotiation between his Majesty of *Rome* and his

[1] Cicero, *Tusculan Disputations*, 5. 35. 100.   [*For notes 2, 3 and 4 see opposite page.*

Holiness of *China* makes, (as we daily Writers say upon Subjects where we are at a Loss) Time will let us know. In the mean time, since they agree in the Fundamentals of Power and Authority, and differ only in Matters of Faith, we may expect the Matter will go on without Difficulty.

² *Motto.* Virgil, *Aeneid*, 4. 99–100:

> 'Tis better ended in a lasting Peace,
> And join'd for e'er in hymeneal Bands.

The Oriental epistle which occupies most of this number, with its exotic and florid language, has usually been taken as something concocted by Steele or, alternately, as an authentic letter by the Emperor of China. (It is accepted as genuine by René Fülöp-Miller in his *Macht und Geheimnis der Jesuiten* [Leipzig, 1929; English translation, 1930, pp. 254–5], with the statement that the original is in the Archives of the French Ministry of Foreign Affairs.) The writer, however, was the Italian journalist Girolamo Gigli (1660–1722), and the letter forms part of the 'Spedizione Prima' dated 8 Oct. 1712 of his satirical essays collected under the title of *Il Gazzettino* (ed. Ettore Allodoli [Lanciano, 1913], pp. 3–5). I am indebted for this discovery to my colleague, Dr. Hannibal Noce. Just how this reached the *Spectator* or who made the English translation (perhaps Addison?) is unknown. Steele was apparently unfamiliar with Italian, but the satirical tone of the letter matches his own anti-Catholic views.

The Italian text as printed in the *Spectator* contains so many errors, especially in spelling, that it has seemed better not to attempt listing all the deviations. It is printed here as Steele's readers saw it, and Gigli's own text is given in Appendix V.

The newspapers of 1710–12 contain frequent allusions to the embarrassment caused in Rome by the unorthodox experiments of the Jesuits in China at this time and to Pope Clement XI's decree concerning 'the Idolatrous Worship practised and taught in that vast Country by the Jesuits, who have framed a new Religion, . . . made up of some Doctrines of the Holy Scriptures, and some Tenets of Confucius, and other Heathen Authors' (*Post-Man*, 4 Oct. 1711).

Gigli himself said later in his *Dizionario Cateriniano* (quoted by Giulio Antimaco in the preface to L. Banchi's edition of *Il Gazzettino* [Milan, 1864, pp. xxix–xxxi]) that the supposed letter of 'Gionata Settimo imperatore della Cina' had diverted a number of persons but had also been accepted in many parts of Europe as a genuine document. About three weeks before this number of the *Spectator* appeared, the *Flying-Post* of 6 Nov. 1712 printed a dispatch from Vienna, dated 29 Oct., which refers to this supposed proposal of marriage:

> Some Letters from Rome say, the Emperor of China has sent to the Pope for one of his Nieces to be Empress, there being no Lady of their High Priest's Extraction in that Country for him to match with: But this needs Confirmation.

In Jan. 1713 the *Lettres Historiques* at The Hague, under the rubric, 'Affaires d'Italie', announced the proposal of marriage, and printed at length a French translation of the supposed letter from the Emperor (*Lettres historiques, contenant ce qui se passe de plus important en Europe; et les reflèxions nécessaires sur ce sujet* [A La Haye, Chez Adrian Moetjens, janvier 1713], pp. 3–10).

³ The Emperor of China at this time was K'ang-hsi, who reigned from 1662 to 1722, the first ruler of China in touch with European courts. It is not clear why he should be called 'Gionnata the VIIth' here. K'ang-hsi was the third son of his father, the fourth Manchu khan, and the ninth Manchu chieftain in the line of ancestors recognized by the nation. If we are to take 'the 4th year of our reign' literally, the letter would be dated 1665, at which time the emperor was but eleven years of age and China was governed by regents. Father Adam Schall von Bell, his tutor and friend, was at this time (1712) in prison, on trial for treason, together with other Jesuits in Peiping.

⁴ The Pope in 1665 was Alexander VII. At the time of the publication of this number the Pope was Clement XI, whose pontificate extended from 1700 to 1721.

Copia di Littera del Re della China al Papa, interpretata dal Padre
Segretario dell'India della Compagnia di Giesu.

*A Voi Benedetto sopra i benedetti PP, ed interpretatore grande de Pontifici e
Pastore Xmo dispensatore dell'* oglio de i Rè d'Europe Clemente XI.

'IL Favorito amico di Dio Gionata 7° Potentissimo sopra tutti i
potentissimi della terra, Altissmo sopra tutti gl'Altissmi sotto il
sole e la luna, che sude nella sede di smeraldo della China sopra cento
scalini d'oro, ad interpretare la lingua di Dio a tutti i descendenti
fedeli d'Abramo, che da la vita e la morte a cento quindici regni, ed
a cento settante Isole, scrive con la penna dello Struzzo vergine, e
manda salute ed accresimento di vecchiezza.

'Essendo arrivato il tempo in cui il fiore della reale nostro gioventu
deve maturare i Frutti della nostra vecctuezza, e confortare con
quell' i desiderii de i populi nostri divoti, e propogare il seme di
quella pianta che deve proteggerli, habbiamo Stabilito d'accom-
pagnarci con una virgine eccelsa ed amorosa allattata alla mamella
della leonessa forte e dell'Agnella mansueta. Percio essendoci stato
figurato sempre il vostro populo Europeo Romano per paese di
donne invitte, i forte, e chaste; allongiamo la nostra mano potente,
a stringere una di loro, e questa sara una vostra nipote, o nipote di
qualche altrograri Sacerdote Latino, che sia quardata dall' occhio
dritto di Dio, sara seminata in lei l'Autorita di Sarra, la Fedelta
d'Esther, e la sapienza di Abba; la vogliamo con l'occhio che guarda
il ciælo, e la terra e con la bocca della Conchiglia che si pasce della
ruggiada del matino. La sua eta non passi ducento corsi della Luna,
la sua statura sia alta quanto la spicca dritta del grano verde, e la,
sua grossezza quanto un manipolo di grano secco. Noi la manda-
remmo a vestire per li nostri mandatici Ambasciadori, e chi la
conduranno a noi, e noi incontraremmo alla riva del fiume grande
facendola salire sue nostro cocchio. Ella potra adorare appresso di
noi il suo Dio, con venti quatro altre a sua ellezzione, e potra cantare
con loro come la Tortora alla Primavera.

'Sodisfando noi Padre e amico nostro questa nostra brama, sarete
caggione di unire in perpetua amicitia cotesti vostri Regni d'Europa
al nostro dominante Imperio, e si abbracicranno le nostri leggi come
l'edera abbraccia la pianta, e noi medesemi Spargeremo del nostro
seme reale in coteste Provincei, riscaldando i letti di vostri Principi
con il fuoco amoroso delle nostre Amazoni, d'alcune delle quali i
nostri mandatici Ambasciadori vi porteranno le Somiglianza dipinte.

V. Confirmiamo di tenere in pace le due buone religiose famiglie delli Missionarii gli' Figlioli' d'Ignazio, e li bianchi e neri figlioli di Dominico il cui consiglio degl'uni e degl'altri ci serve di scorta nel nostro regimento e di lume ad interpretare le divine Legge come appuncto fa lume l'oglio che si getta in Mare. In tanto Alzandoci dal nostro Trono per Abbracciarvi, vi di chiariamo nostro conguinto e Confederato, ed ordiniamo che questo foglio sia segnato col nostro Segno Imperiale dalla nostra Citta, Capo del Mondo, il quinto giorno della terza lunatione l'anno quarto del nostro Imperio.

'Sigillo e un sole nelle cui faccia e anche quella della Luna ed intorno tra i Raggi vi sono traposte alcune Spada.

'Dico il Traduttore che secondo il Ceremonial di questo Lettere e recedentissimo specialmente Fessere scritto con la penna dello Struzzo virgine con la quelle non sogliosi scrivere quei Re che le pregiere a Dio e scrivendo a qualche altro Principe del Mondo, la maggior Finezza che usino, e scrivergli con la penna del Pavone.'

A Letter from the Emperor of *China* to the Pope, interpreted by a Father Jesuit, Secretary of the *Indies*.

To you blessed above the blessed, great Emperor of Bishops, and Pastor of Christians, Dispenser of the Oyl of the Kings of Europe, Clement XI.

"THE Favourite Friend of GOD *Gionnata* the VIIth, most powerful above the most powerful of the Earth, highest above the highest under the Sun and Moon, who sits on a Throne of Emerald of *China*, above a 100 Steps of Gold, to interpret the Language of GOD to the Faithful, and who gives Life and Death to 115 Kingdoms, and 170 Islands; he writes with the Quill of a Virgin *Ostrich*, and sends Health and Increase of old Age.

"Being arrived at the Time of our Age, in which the Flower of our Royal Youth ought to ripen into Fruit towards old Age, to comfort therewith the Desire of our devoted People, and to propagate the Seed of that Plant which must protect them: We have determined to accompany our selves with an high Amorous Virgin, suckled at the Breast of a wild Lioness, and a meek Lamb, and imagining with our selves that your *European* Roman People is the Father of many unconquerable and chaste Ladies, We stretch out our powerful Arm to embrace one of them, and she shall be one of your Nieces, or the Niece of some other great Latin Priest, the Darling of God's Right Eye. Let the Authority of *Sarah* be sown in her, the Fidelity of

Esther, and the Wisdom of *Abba*. We wou'd have her Eye like that of a *Dove*, which may look upon Heaven and Earth, with the Mouth of a Shel-Fish to feed upon the Dew of the Morning: Her Age must not exceed 200 Courses of the Moon; let her Stature be equal to that of an Ear of green Corn, and her Girth a Handful.

"We will send our *Mandarine*'s Embassadors to cloath her, and to conduct her to us, and we will meet her on the Bank of the great River, making her to leap up into our Chariot. She may with us worship her own God, together with 24 Virgins of her own Chusing, and she may Sing with them, as the *Turtle* in the Spring. You, O Father and Friend, complying with this our Desire, may be an Occasion of uniting in perpetual Friendship our high Empire with your *European* Kingdoms, and we may embrace your Laws, as the *Ivy* embraces the Tree; and we our selves may scatter our Royal Blood into your Provinces, warming the chief of your Princes with the amorous Fire of our *Amazons*, the resembling Pictures of some of which our said *Mandarine*'s Embassadors shall convey to you.

"We exhort you to keep in Peace two good Religious Families of *Missionaries*, the black Sons of *Ignatius*, and the white and black Sons of *Dominicus*, that the Counsel both of the one and the other may serve as a Guide to us in our Government, and a Light to interpret the Divine Law, as the Oyl cast into the Sea produces Light.[1]

"To conclude, we rising up in our Throne to embrace you, we declare you our Ally and Confederate; and have ordered this Leaf to be Sealed with our Imperial Signet, in our Royal City, the Head of the World, the 8th Day of the third Lunation, and the 4th Year of our Reign."

Letters from *Rome* say, the whole Conversation both among Gentlemen and Ladies has turned upon the Subject of this Epistle ever since it arrived. The Jesuit who translated it says, it loses much of the Majesty of the Original in the *Italian*. It seems there was an Offer of the same Nature made by a Predecessor of the present Emperor to *Lewis* the XIIIth of *France*, but no Lady of that Court would take the Voyage, that Sex not being at that Time so much used in politick Negociations. The Manner of Treating the Pope is according to the *Chinese* Ceremonial, very respectful. For the

[1] Actually during the reign of K'ang Hsi there were only Jesuits (sons of Ignatius) In Peiping. The Dominicans, who bitterly opposed the methods of the Jesuits, were in Chekiang. Dr. Charles O. Hucker and Father Leo Hotze have given me much helpful information on the Chinese background of this number.

Emperor writes to him with the Quill of a Virgin *Ostrich*, which was never used before but in Writing Prayers. Instructions are preparing for the Lady who shall have so much Zeal as to undertake this Pilgrimage, and be an Empress for the Sake of her Religion. The Principal of the *Indian* Missionaries has given in a List of the reigning Sins in *China*, in Order to prepare the Indulgencies necessary to this Lady and her Retinue, in advancing the Interests of the *Roman Catholick Religion* in those Kingdoms.

To the SPECTATOR-GENERAL.

May it please your Honour,
'I Have of late seen *French* Hats of a prodigious Magnitude pass by my Observatory.'

John Sly.[1]

T

No. 546   *Wednesday, November 26, 1712*[2]

[STEELE]

Omnia Patejacienda ut ne quid omnino quod venditor norit, emptor ignoret.   Tull.

IT gives me very great Scandal to observe, where-ever I go, how much Skill, in buying all Manner of Goods, there is necessary to defend your self from being cheated in whatever you see exposed to Sale. My Reading makes such a strong Impression upon me, that I should think my self a Cheat in my Way if I should translate any thing from another Tongue and not acknowledge it to my Readers.[3] I understood from common Report that Mr. *Cibber* was introducing a *French* Play upon our Stage, and thought my self concerned to let the Town know what was his and what foreign.[4] When I came to

---

[1] See Nos. 526, 532, and 534.
[2] *Motto.* Cicero, *De Officiis*, 3. 12. 51: Laying every thing open, so that what the Seller knows, the Buyer may by no means be ignorant of.
[3] Cf. No. 542 (above, p. 439).
[4] Cibber's *Ximena, or the Heroic Daughter*, founded on the *Cid* of Corneille, was first acted at Drury Lane on 28 Nov.; it was repeated on the following night and on 1, 2, 3, and 4 Dec. It was revived in 1718 and published the following year with a dedication to Steele.

the Rehearsal, I found the House so partial to one of their own
Fraternity, that they gave every thing which was said such Grace,
Emphasis, and Force in their Action, that it was no easy Matter to
make any Judgment of the Performance. Mrs. *Oldfield,* who, it seems,
is the heroick Daughter, had so just a Conception of her Part, that
her Action made what she spoke appear decent, just, and noble.
The Passions of Terrour and Compassion, they made me believe,
were very artfully raised, and the whole Conduct of the Play artful
and surprizing. We Authors do not much relish the Endeavours of
Players in this kind, but have the same Disdain as Physicians and
Lawyers have when Attornies and Apothecaries give Advice. *Cibber*
himself took the Liberty to tell me that he expected I would do him
Justice, and allow the Play well prepared for his Spectators, whatever it was for his Readers. He added very many Particulars not
uncurious concerning the Manner of taking an Audience, and laying
wait not only for their superficial Applause, but also for insinuating
into their Affections and Passions by the artful Management of
the Look, Voice, and Gesture of the Speaker. I could not but
consent that the heroick Daughter appeared in the Rehearsal
a moving Entertainment wrought out of a great and exemplary
Virtue.

The Advantages of Action, Show, and Dress on these Occasions
are allowable, because the Merit consists in being capable of imposing upon us to our Advantage and Entertainment. All that I was
going to say about the Honesty of an Author in the Sale of his Ware
was, that he ought to own all that he had borrowed from others, and
lay in a clear Light all that he gives his Spectators for their Money,
with an Account of the first Manufacturers. But I intended to give
the Lecture of this Day upon the common and prostituted Behaviour
of Traders in ordinary Commerce. The Philosopher made it a Rule
of Trade, that your Profit ought to be the common Profit; and it is
unjust to make any Step towards Gain, wherein the Gain of even
those to whom you sell is not also consulted.[1] A Man may deceive
himself if he thinks fit, but he is no better than a Cheat who sells
any thing without telling the Exceptions against it, as well as what
is to be said to its Advantage. The scandalous Abuse of Language
and hardening of Conscience which may be observed every Day in
going from one Place to another, is what makes a whole City to an

[1] The Philosopher was Antipater. Cicero, *De Officiis,* 3. 12. 52 (cf. the motto of
this paper).

unprejudiced Eye a Den of Thieves. It was no small Pleasure to me for this Reason to remark as I passed by *Cornhill*, that the Shop of that worthy honest, tho' lately unfortunate Citizen Mr. *John Moreton*, so well known in the Linnen Trade, is fitting up anew.[1] Since a Man has been in a distressed Condition, it ought to be a great Satisfaction to have passed through it in such a Manner as not to have lost the Friendship of those who suffered with him, but to receive an honourable Acknowledgment of his Honesty from those very Persons to whom the Law had consigned his Estate.

The Misfortune of this Citizen is like to prove of a very general Advantage to those who shall deal with him hereafter: For the Stock with which he now sets up being the Loan of his Friends, he cannot expose that to the Hazards of giving Credit, but enters into a Ready-Money[2] Trade, by which Means he will both buy and sell the best and cheapest. He imposes upon himself a Rule of affixing the Value of each Piece he sells to the Piece it self; so that the most ignorant Servant or Child will be as good a Buyer at his Shop as the most skilful in the Trade. For all which you have all his Hopes and Fortune for your Security. To encourage Dealing after this Way, there is not only the avoiding the most infamous Guilt in ordinary Bartering; but this Observation, That he who buys with ready Money saves as much to his Family, as the State exacts out of his Land for the Security and Service of his Country; that is to say, in plain *English*, Sixteen will do as much as Twenty Shillings.[3]

Mr. SPECTATOR,

'MY Heart is so swell'd with grateful Sentiments on Account of some Favours which I have lately received, that I must beg Leave to give them Utterance amongst the Crowd of other anonymous Correspondents; and Writing, I hope, will be as great a Relief to my forced Silence, as it is to your natural Taciturnity— My generous Benefactor will not suffer me to speak to him in any Terms of Acknowledgment, but ever treats me as if he had the greatest Obligations, and uses me with a Distinction that is not to be expected from one so much my Superior in Fortune, Years, and Understanding. He insinuates, as if I had a certain Right to his Favours from some Merit, which his particular Indulgence to me has discovered; but that is only a beautiful Artifice to lessen the Pain

---

[1] See No. 248 (vol. ii).
[2] This is the first example in *OED* of this phrase used attributively.
[3] Four shillings in the pound was the amount of the land tax.

an honest Mind feels in receiving Obligations, when there is no Probability of returning them.

'A Gift is doubled when accompany'd with such a Delicacy of Address; but what to me gives it an inexpressible Value, is its coming from the Man I most esteem in the World. It pleases me indeed as it is an Advantage and Addition to my Fortune; but when I consider it is an Instance of that good Man's Friendship, it over-joys, it transports me: I look on it with a Lover's Eye, and no longer regard the Gift, but the Hand that gave it. For my Friendship is so entirely void of any gainful Views, that it often gives me Pain to think it should have been chargeable to him; and I cannot at some melancholy Hours help doing his Generosity the Injury of fearing it should cool on this Account, and that the last Favour might be a Sort of Legacy of a departing Friendship.

'I confess these Fears seem very groundless and unjust; but you must forgive them to the Apprehension of one possess'd of a great Treasure, who is frighted at the most distant Shadow of Danger.

'Since I have thus far open'd my Heart to you, I will not conceal the secret Satisfaction I feel there of knowing the Goodness of my Friend will not be unrewarded. I am pleased with thinking the Providence of the Almighty hath sufficient Blessings in Store for him, and will certainly discharge the Debt, though I am not made the happy Instrument of doing it.

'However, nothing in my Power shall be wanting to shew my Gratitude; I will make it the Business of my Life to thank him, and shall esteem (next to him) those my best Friends, who give me the greatest Assistance in this good Work. Printing this Letter would be some little Instance of my Gratitude; and your Favour herein will very much oblige

Your most humble Servant, &c.

Novemb. 24.

W. C.'

T

Si vulnus tibi monstratâ radice vel herbâ
Non fieret levius, fugeres radice vel herbâ
Proficiente nihil curarier . . .

Hor.

IT is very difficult to praise a Man without putting him out of Countenance. My following Correspondent has found out this uncommon Art, and, together with his Friends, has celebrated some of my Speculations after such a concealed but diverting manner, that if any of my Readers think I am to blame in Publishing my own Commendations, they will allow I should have deserv'd their Censure as much, had I suppressed the Humour in which they are conveyed to me.

SIR,

'I AM often in a private Assembly of Wits of both Sexes, where we generally descant upon your Speculations, or upon the Subjects on which you have treated. We were last *Tuesday* talking of those two Volumes which you have lately Published.[2] Some were commending one of your Papers, and some another, and there was scarce a single Person in the Company that had not a favourite Speculation. Upon this a Man of Wit and Learning told us, he thought it would not be amiss if we paid the *Spectator* the same Compliment that is often made in our Publick Prints to Sir *William Read*, Dr. *Grant*, Mr. *Moor* the Apothecary, and other eminent Physicians, where it is usual for the Patients to Publish the Cures which have been made upon them, and the several Distempers under which they laboured.[3]

---

[1] *Motto.* Horace, *Epistles*, 2. 2. 149–51:

> Suppose You had a Wound, and One had show'd
> An Herb, which you apply'd but found no good,
> Would You be fond of this, increase your pain,
> And use the fruitless remedy again? CREECH.

[2] The reference is to volumes iii and iv in octavo, 'in large paper', which seem to have been published during November 1712, though the precise date is in doubt. In No. 529 Addison had speculated on the reputation to be gained by the publication of these two volumes.

[3] For Sir William Read and Dr. Roger Grant see No. 472. J. More, apothecary at the Pestle and Mortar in Abchurch Lane, frequently advertises his cures in the newspapers of the time, but not in the *Spectator*. One Michael Parot was cured of 'a Worm 16 Foot long, by taking the Medicines of J. More, Apothecary' (*Post Boy*,

The Proposal took, and the Lady where we visited having the two last Volumes in large Paper interleafed for her own private use, ordered them to be brought down, and laid in the Window, whither every one in the Company retired, and writ down a particular Advertisement in the Stile and Phrase of the like Ingenious Compositions which we frequently meet with at the end of our News Papers. When we had finished our Work, we read them with a great deal of Mirth at the Fireside, and agreed, *Nemine Contradicente*, to get them transcribed, and sent to the *Spectator*. The Gentleman who made the Proposal entered the following Advertisement before the Title Page, after which the rest succeeded in order.

'*Remedium efficax & universum*; or, An effectual Remedy adapted to all Capacities; shewing how any Person may Cure himself of Ill-Nature, Pride, Party-Spleen, or any other Distemper incident to the Human System, with an easie way to know when the Infection is upon him.[1] This Panacea is as innocent as Bread, agreeable to the Taste, and requires no Confinement. It has not its Equal in the Universe, as abundance of the Nobility and Gentry throughout the Kingdom have experienced.

'*N. B.* No Family ought to be without it.'

Over the two Spectators *on Jealousie, being the two first in the Third Volume,*[2]

'I *William Crazy,* aged Threescore and seven, having been for several Years afflicted with uneasie Doubts, Fears and Vapours, occasioned by the Youth and Beauty of *Mary* my Wife, aged Twenty five, do hereby for the Benefit of the Publick give Notice, that I have

---

11 Apr. 1710); Thomas Chiffinch, carpenter, was relieved of 'the Bloody-flux' (*Post-Man*, 11 Apr. 1710); Samuel Maynard of rheumatism and sciatica (*Tatler*, 11 Apr. 1710); Thomas Adin, weaver, of cough and consumption (*Tatler*, 22 Apr. 1710). In the *Post-Man* of 19 May 1711 More advertises that he cures the vertigo. See also Pope's poem, 'To Mr. John Moore, Author of the Celebrated Worm-Powder' (*Minor Poems*, ed. Ault and Butt, Twickenham ed., vi. 161–2).

[1] A parody of the advertisement which had appeared in the *Post Boy* of 11 and 15 Nov. 1712:

Remedium efficax & universum; or, An effectual Remedy adapted to all Capacities, shewing how any Person may cure himself of the Secret Disease, without advising with Physician, Surgeon, Quack, &c. Also an easy way to know when the Infection is upon him. Printed for Rob. Willoughby in Flower-de-lis-Court near Fetter-Lane, Fleetstreet.

[2] Nos. 170 and 171 (vol. ii).

found great Relief from the two following Doses, having taken them two Mornings together with a Dish of Chocolate. Witness my Hand, *&c.*'

For the Benefit of the Poor.

'In Charity to such as are troubled with the Disease of Levée-Haunting, and are forced to seek their Bread every Morning at the Chamber Doors of great Men, I *A. B.* do testifie, that for many Years past I laboured under this fashionable Distemper, but was cured of it by a Remedy which I bought of Mrs. *Baldwin*, contained in an Half Sheet of Paper, marked N° 193. where any one may be provided with the same Remedy at the price of a single Penny.'[1]

'An infallible Cure for *Hypocondriack Melancholy.* N° 173. 184. 191. 203. 209. 221. 233. 235. 239. 245. 247. 251.[2]

Probatum est.[3]

Charles Easy.'

'I *Christopher Query* having been troubled with a certain Distemper in my Tongue, which shewed it self in impertinent and superfluous Interrogatories, have not asked one unnecessary Question since my Perusal of the Prescription marked N° 228.'

'The *Britannick Beautifier*, being an Essay on Modesty N° 231, which gives such a delightful Blushing Colour to the Cheeks of those that are White or Pale, that it is not to be distinguished from a natural fine Complection, nor perceived to be artificial by the nearest Friend.[4] Is nothing of Paint, or in the least hurtful. It renders

---

[1] Mrs. Anne Baldwin in Warwick Lane, bookseller, was one of the agents in the distribution of the *Spectator*.

[2] These twelve numbers are all by Addison.

[3] *Probatum est* (it is tested), a legend frequently appearing on quack medicines and in medical advertisements.

[4] This advertisement appeared in Nos. 400, 438, and 480:

The Britannick Beautifier: Or, the greatest Cleanser of the Skin in Nature, for tho' a great Secret, yet well known by its Effects, for it takes away all Spots, Pimples, Freckles, Yellowness, Roughness, Wrinkles, Morphew, Scurf, Sun-burning, and the like, of a charming pretty Scent, and so safe that it may be taken inwardly without any Harm: For it is so friendly and kind, of such a noble Quality, that it makes those who before were wrinkled and discoloured, exceeding fair, fresh, plump, and smooth; and if used after the Small-Pox, assuredly takes away Pits or Marks, and renders the Skin smooth, soft and fair, as hath been happily experienced, and is therefore earnestly commended to all that would preserve or regain a fair Skin and fine Complection. Is sold at 2s. a Bottle, at Mrs. Dring's a Picture shop, next Door to the Leg-Tavern in Fleet-street, and at Mr. Halsey's,

the Face delightfully handsome; is not subject to be rubb'd off, and cannot be parallel'd by either Wash, Powder, Cosmetick, &c. It is certainly the best Beautifier in the World.

Martha Gloworm.'

'I, *Samuel Self,* of the Parish of St. *James*'s, having a Constitution which naturally abounds with Acids, made use of a Paper of Directions marked N° 177, recommending a healthful Exercise called *Good-Nature,* and have found it a most excellent Sweetner of the Blood.'

'Whereas I, *Elizabeth Rainbow,* was troubled with that Distemper in my Head, which about a Year ago was pretty Epidemical among the Ladies, and discovered it self in the Colour of their Hoods,[1] having made use of the Doctor's Cephalick Tincture, which he exhibited to the Publick in one of his last Year's Papers, I recovered in a very few Days.'[2]

'I, *George Gloom,* have for a long time been troubled with the Spleen, and being advised by my Friends to put my self into a Course of *Steele,* did for that end make use of Remedies conveyed to me several Mornings in short Letters, from the Hands of the invisible Doctor.[3] They were marked at the bottom *Nathaniel Henroost,*

Bookseller, at the Plough and Harrow near the Royal-Exchange in Cornhill (text of No. 480).

Martha Gloworm's testimonial also echoes the language of another advertisement in the *Spectator* (Nos. 124, 143, 162, 176, 197, 202, 233, 250, 276, 296, 318, 358, 398, 428, 438, 461, 517, and 545):

The famous Bavarian Red Liquor;

Which gives such a delightful blushing Colour to the Cheeks of those that are White or Pale, that it is not to be distinguished from a natural fine Complexion, nor perceived to be artificial by the nearest Friend. Is nothing of Paint, or in the least hurtful, but good in many Cases to be taken inwardly. It renders the Face delightfully handsome and beautiful, is not subject to be rubb'd off like Paint, therefore cannot be discovered by the nearest Friend. It is certainly the best Beautifier in the World: Is sold only at Mr. Payn's Toyshop, at the Angel and Crown in St. Paul's Churchyard near Cheapside, at 3s. 6d. a Bottle, with Directions.

[1] See No. 265 (vol. ii).

[2] This had long been a favourite patent medicine: 'Cephalick Tincture, for curing Convulsions and Vapours. 2s. 6d. and 5s. the bottles. At Mr. Thomas Alcraft's at the Sign of the Blue Coat Boy, a Toy-Shop, over against the Royal Exchange in Cornhill' (*Post-Man,* 11 Jan. 1705). It is advertised later in the *Spectator* of 1714 (Nos. 562, 570, 577, 588, 599, 603, and 620).

[3] The usual 'course of steel' refers to medicines containing iron, such as steel drops, lozenges, wine, &c. Swift writes to Stella on 17 Feb. 1712/13 of taking 'nasty steel drops' for the headache. The 'course of steel', with an allusion to the editor of the *Spectator,* occurs in *Examiner* 37 (see vol. i, pp. 17–18, note), and also in 'A Letter from a Dr. of Physick in Mijnheer-Borough, to a Dr. in Fickle-Borough', printed in

Alice Threadneedle, Rebecca Nettletop, Tom. Loveless, Mary Meanwell,
Thomas Smoaky, Anthony Freeman, Tom. Meggot, Rustick Sprightly, &c.
which have had so good an Effect upon me, that I now find my
self chearful, lightsome and easie, and therefore do recommend them
to all such as labour under the same Distemper.'[1]

Not having room to insert all the Advertisements which were
sent me, I have only picked out some few from the Third Volume,
reserving the Fourth for another Opportunity.   O

No. 548   *Friday, November 28, 1712*[2]

. . . Vitiis nemo sine nascitur, optimus ille
Qui minimis urgetur . . .

Hor.

Mr. SPECTATOR,   *Nov.* 27, 1712.
'I HAVE read this Day's Paper with a great deal of Pleasure, and
could send you an Account of several Elixirs and Antidotes in
your Third Volume, which your Correspondents have not taken

the *Flying-Post*, 23 Dec. 1712. This describes a new '*Pacifick Powder*', which quiets
turbulent spirits and makes people forget their own country, their names, and even
their near relations. 'It has already put the *Steel-course* out of Vogue, and will in a
little time, I think, discard it quite; which has, you know, for many Years, till this
last Summer, done Wonders, and strengthned us exceedingly.' So in *Tatler* 80
Mr. Bickerstaff prescribes 'the Cold Bath, with a Course of Steel', to a man suffering
from the spleen.

[1] The correspondents referred to here are Nathaniel Henroost (No. 176), Alice
Threadneedle (No. 182), Rebecca Nettletop (No. 190), Mary Meanwell (No. 208),
Thomas Smoaky (No. 202), Anthony Freeman (No. 212), Tom Meggot (No. 216),
and Rustic Sprightly (No. 240). No letter from Tom Loveless had appeared,
but there is one from Biddy Loveless in No. 196, one of whose lovers is Tom.

[2] *Motto.* Horace, *Satires*, I. 3. 68–69 (altered):

There's none but hath some fault, and he's the best,
Most Vertuous he, that's spotted with the least. CREECH.

This had been used (by Steele) as the motto of *Tatler* 246.
This paper, unsigned in all three of the earliest texts, is assigned to Addison by
both Morley and Aitken. (Gregory Smith makes no attribution.) The style and
subject-matter both sound like Addison, and it would be characteristic of him to
add the final paragraph, which was not in the original folio version. Though in the
form of a letter, it is purportedly written on the 27th, the preceding day, which is
unlikely for a genuine letter. Although it attacks Dennis's theory of poetic justice,
it has at least twice been attributed to Dennis himself—by Saintsbury (*History of
English Criticism*, 1911, p. 169) and by Mario M. Rossi (*L'estetica dell'empirismo
inglese*, vol. i (Florence, 1944), p. 234). It is much more probably to be taken as an
answer to Dennis's letter 'To the Spectator, Upon his Paper on the 16th of April'
(Hooker, ii. 18–22).

Notice of in their Advertisements; and at the same time must own to you, that I have seldom seen a Shop furnished with such a Variety of Medicaments, and in which there are fewer Soporifics. The several Vehicles you have invented for conveying your unacceptable Truths to us, are what I most particularly admire, as I am afraid they are Secrets which will die with you. I do not find that any of your Critical Essays are taken Notice of in this Paper, notwithstanding I look upon them to be excellent Cleansers of the Brain, and could venture to superscribe them with an Advertisement which I have lately seen in one of our News Papers, wherein there is an Account given of a Soveraign Remedy for restoring the Taste to all such Persons whose Palates have been vitiated by Distempers, unwholesome Food, or any the like Occasions.[1] But to let fall the Allusion, notwithstanding your Criticisms, and particularly the Candour which you have discovered in them, are not the least taking Part of your Works, I find your Opinion concerning *Poetical Justice*, as it is expressed in the first Part of your Fortieth *Spectator*, is controverted by some eminent Criticks;[2] and as you now seem, to our great Grief of Heart, to be winding up your Bottoms,[3] I hoped you would have enlarged a little upon that Subject. It is indeed but a single Paragraph in your Works, and I believe those who have read it with the same Attention I have done, will think there is nothing to be objected against it. I have however drawn up some Additional Arguments to strengthen the Opinion which you have there delivered, having endeavoured to go to the Bottom of that Matter, which you may either publish or suppress as you think fit.

'*Horace* in my Motto says, that all Men are vicious, and that they

---

[1] The following may be the advertisement referred to; it occurs frequently (23 times in all) in the *Spectator*, beginning in No. 75 and ending in No. 543:

> An Incomparable pleasant Tincture to restore the Sense of Smelling, tho' lost for many Years. A few Drops of which being snuff'd up the Nose, infallibly Cures those who have lost their Smell, let it proceed from what Cause soever: it admirably opens all manner of Obstructions of the Olfactory, or smelling Nerves, comforts and strengthens the Head and Brain, and revives the Smelling Faculty to a Miracle, effectually removing whatever is the Cause of the Disorder of that Sense, and perfectly Cures, so as to cause the Person to smell as quick and well, as any one in the World. Price 2s. 6d. a Bottle. Sold only at Mr. Payne's Toyshop at the Angel and Crown in St. Paul's Church Yard near Cheapside, with Directions.

[2] John Dennis is undoubtedly the chief of the 'eminent Criticks' referred to here.
[3] 'Bottom' is defined in *OED* as 'a clew or nucleus on which to wind thread; also a skein or ball of thread'. Cf. Prior, 'An Epitaph', 47–48:

> Each *Christmas* They Accompts did clear;
> And wound their Bottom round the Year.

differ from one another, only as they are more or less so. *Boileau* has given the same Account of our Wisdom, as *Horace* has of our Virtue.

> *Tous les hommes sont fous et, malgré tous leurs soins,*
> *Ne different entre eux, que du plus et du moins.*[1]

All Men, says he, are Fools,[a] and in spight of their Endeavours to the contrary, differ from one another only as they are more or less so.

'Two or three of the old *Greek* Poets have given the same turn to a Sentence which describes the Happiness of Man in this Life;

> Τὸ ζῆν ἀλύπως, ἀνδρός ἐστιν εὐτυχοῦς.[2]

That Man is most happy who is the least miserable.

It will not perhaps be unentertaining to the Polite Reader, to observe how these three beautiful Sentences are formed upon different Subjects by the same way of thinking; but I shall return to the first of them.

'Our Goodness being of a comparative, and not an absolute Nature, there is none who in strictness can be called a Virtuous Man. Every one has in him a natural Alloy, tho' one may be fuller of Dross than another: For this reason I cannot think it right to introduce a perfect or a faultless Man upon the Stage; not only because such a Character is improper to move Compassion, but because there is no such a thing in Nature. This might probably be one reason why the *Spectator* in one of his Papers took notice of that late invented Term called *Poetical Justice*, and the wrong Notions into which it has led some Tragick Writers. The most perfect Man has Vices enough to draw down Punishments upon his Head, and to justifie Providence in regard to any Miseries that may befal him. For this reason I cannot think, but that the Instruction and Moral are much finer, where a Man who is[b] virtuous in the main of his Character falls into Distress, and sinks under the Blows of Fortune at the end of a Tragedy, than when he is represented as Happy and Triumphant. Such an Example corrects the Insolence of Human Nature, softens the Mind of the Beholder with Sentiments of Pity and Compassion, comforts him under his own private

---

[a] All Men, says he, are Fools,] All Men are Fools, *Fol.*
[b] a Man who is] a Man is *Fol.*

---

[1] Boileau, *Satires*, iv. 39–40 ('du plus ou du moins').

[2] Menander, *Gnomai Monostichoi*, 509 (Meineke, *Fragmenta Comicorum Graecorum*, iv (1841), 354). It is included among the 'Sententiae singulis versibus contentae, e diversis Poetis' in Winterton (Cambridge, 1677), pp. 505, 517.

Affliction, and teaches him not to judge of Mens Virtues by their Successes. I cannot think of one real Hero in all Antiquity so far raised above Human Infirmities, that he might not be very naturally represented in a Tragedy as plunged in Misfortunes and Calamities. The Poet may still find out some prevailing Passion or Indiscretion in his Character, and shew it in such a manner, as will sufficiently acquit the Gods of any Injustice in his Sufferings. For as *Horace* observes in my Text, the best Man is faulty, tho' not in so great a degree as those whom we generally call vicious Men.

'If such a strict Poetical Justice, as some Gentlemen insist upon, were to be observed in this Art, there is no manner of reason why it should not extend to Heroic Poetry, as well as Tragedy. But we find it so little observed in *Homer*, that his *Achilles* is placed in the greatest point of Glory and Success, though his Character is Morally Vicious, and only Poetically Good, if I may use the Phrase of our Modern Criticks.[1] The *Æneid* is fill'd with Innocent unhappy Persons. *Nisus* and *Eurialus*, *Lausus* and *Pallas* come all to unfortunate ends. The Poet takes Notice in particular, that in the Sacking of *Troy*, *Ripheus* fell, who was the most just Man among the *Trojans*,

> ... *cadit et Ripheus justissimus unus*
> *Qui fuit in Teucris et servantissimus Æqui.*
> *Dijs aliter visum est* . . .[2]

and that *Pantheus* could neither be preserved by his transcendent Piety, nor by the holy Fillets of *Apollo*, whose Priest he was,

> ... *nec Te tua plurima Pantheu*
> *Labentem pietas, nec Apollinis infula texit.* Æn. l. 2.[3]

[1] Cf. Cowley, note to *Davideis*, ii. 725: 'Weeping seems to depend so much upon the Eyes, as to make the expression *Poetically true*, though not *Literally*' (*Poems*, ed. Waller, p. 320); Dryden, Dedication of *Aeneis*: 'By this example [Achilles], the critics have concluded that it is not necessary the manners of the hero should be virtuous. They are poetically good, if they are of a piece . . .' (Ker, ii. 159); Dacier, note to his translation of *Aristotle's Art of Poetry* (1705): when Aristotle speaks of the goodness of the manners ' 'tis not a Moral, but a Poetical Goodness; which consists in expressing the Manners, and so well making them known, that we may be able at the same time to perceive what they will produce' (p. 243).

[2] *Aeneid*, 2. 426–8:

> Then *Ripheus* follow'd, in th' unequal Fight;
> Just of his Word, observant of the right;
> Heav'n thought not so.   DRYDEN.

Addison had quoted these lines from Virgil in No. 74.

[3] *Aeneid*, 2. 429–30:

> Nor *Pantheus*, thee, thy Mitre nor the Bands
> Of awful *Phoebus*, sav'd from impious Hands. DRYDEN.

I might here mention the Practice of ancient Tragick Poets, both *Greek* and *Latin,* but as this Particular is touched upon in the Paper above-mentioned, I shall pass it over in Silence. I could produce Passages out of *Aristotle* in favour of my Opinion, and if in one Place he says that an absolutely Virtuous Man should not be represented as unhappy, this does not justifie any one who shall think fit to bring in an absolutely virtuous Man upon the Stage.[1] Those who are acquainted with that Author's way of writing know very well, that to take the whole Extent of his Subject into his Divisions of it, he often makes use of such Cases as are imaginary, and not reducible to Practice: He himself declares that such Tragedies as ended unhappily bore away the Prize in Theatrical Contentions, from those which ended happily;[2] and for the Fortieth Speculation, which I am now considering, as it has given Reasons why these are more apt to please an Audience, so it only proves that these are generally preferable to the other, tho' at the same time it affirms that many excellent Tragedies have and may be written in both kinds.

[a]'I shall conclude with observing, that tho' the *Spectator* above-mentioned is so far against the Rule of Poetical Justice as to affirm that good Men may meet with an unhappy Catastrophe in Tragedy, it does not say that ill Men may go off unpunish'd. The Reason for this Distinction is very plain, namely, because the best of Men are vicious enough to justifie Providence for any Misfortunes and Afflictions which may befall them, but there are many Men so Criminal that they can have no Claim or Pretence to Happiness. The best of Men may deserve Punishment, but the worst of Men cannot deserve Happiness.'[b]

---

[a] *Final paragraph om. in Fol. (text of 8vo)*   [b] *No. 548 unsigned in Fol., 8vo, 12mo*

---

[1] Aristotle, *Poetics*, 13. 2.
[2] Ibid. 13. 6.

No. 549
[ADDISON]

Saturday, November 29, 1712[1]

Quamvis digressu veteris confusus amici,
Laudo tamen . . .

Juv.

I BELIEVE most People begin the World with a Resolution to withdraw from it into a serious kind of Solitude or Retirement, when they have made themselves easie in it. Our Unhappiness is, that we find out some Excuse or other for deferring such our good Resolutions till our intended Retreat is cut off by Death. But among all kinds of People there are none who are so hard to part with the World, as those who are grown old in the heaping up of Riches. Their Minds are so warped with their constant Attention to Gain, that it is very difficult for them to give their Souls another Bent, and convert them towards those Objects, which, though they are proper for every Stage of Life, are so more especially for the last. *Horace* describes an old Usurer as so charmed with the Pleasures of a Country Life, that in order to make a Purchase he called in all his Mony; but what was the event of it? Why in a very few Days after he put it out again.[2] I am engaged in this Series of Thought by a Discourse which I had last Week with my worthy Friend Sir ANDREW FREEPORT, a Man of so much natural Eloquence, good Sense, and Probity of Mind, that I always hear him with a particular Pleasure. As we were sitting together, being the sole remaining Members of our Club, Sir ANDREW gave me an Account of the many busie Scenes of Life in which he had been engaged, and at the same time reckoned up to me abundance of those lucky Hits, which at another time he would have called pieces of good Fortune; but in the Temper of Mind he was then, he termed them Mercies, Favours of Providence, and Blessings upon an honest Industry.[3] Now, says he, you must know, my good Friend, I am so used to consider my self as Creditor and Debtor, that I often state my

[1] *Motto.* Juvenal, *Satires*, 3. 1–2: Although confounded by the departure of my old Friend, I cannot but commend him.

[2] Horace, *Epodes*, 2. 67–70.

[3] Cf. Pope, *Moral Essays*, iii. 375–8:

> Behold Sir Balaam, now a man of spirit,
> Ascribes his gettings to his parts and merit,
> What late he call'd a Blessing, now was Wit,
> And God's good Providence, a lucky Hit.

Accounts after the same manner, with regard to Heaven and my own Soul. In this case, when I look upon the Debtor-side, I find such innumerable Articles, that I want Arithmetick to cast them up; but when I look upon the Creditor-side, I find little more than blank Paper. Now tho' I am very well satisfied that it is not in my power to ballance Accounts with my Maker, I am resolved however to turn all my future Endeavours that way. You must not therefore be surprized, my Friend, if you hear that I am betaking my self to a more thoughtful kind of Life, and if I meet you no more in this Place.

I could not but approve so good a Resolution, notwithstanding the Loss I shall suffer by it. Sir ANDREW has since explained himself to me more at large in the following Letter, which is just come to my Hands.

Good Mr. SPECTATOR,

'NOTWITHSTANDING my Friends at the Club have always rallied me, when I have talked of retiring from Business, and repeated to me one of my own Sayings, *that a Merchant has never enough till he has got a little more,* I can now inform you that there is one in the World who thinks he has enough, and is determined to pass the Remainder of his Life in the Enjoyment of what he has. You know me so well, that I need not tell you, I mean, by the Enjoyment of my Possessions, the making of them useful to the Publick. As the greatest Part of my Estate has been hitherto of an unsteady and volatile Nature, either tost upon Seas or fluctuating in Funds; it is now fixt and settled in Substantial Acres and Tenements. I have removed it from the Uncertainty of Stocks, Winds and Waves, and disposed of it in a considerable Purchase. This will give me great Opportunity of being charitable in my way, that is in setting my poor Neighbours to Work, and giving them a comfortable Subsistence out of their own Industry. My Gardens,[a] my Fishponds, my Arable and Pasture Grounds[b] shall be my several Hospitals, or rather Work-houses, in which I propose to maintain a great many indigent Persons, who are now starving in my Neighbourhood. I have got a fine Spread of improveable Lands, and in my own Thoughts am already plowing up some of them, fencing others; planting Woods, and draining Marshes. In fine, as I have my Share in the Surface of this Island, I am resolved to make it as beautiful

---

[a] Gardens,] Garden, *Fol.* [b] Grounds] Ground *Fol.*

a Spot as any in Her Majesty's Dominions; at least there is not an Inch of it which shall not be cultivated to the best Advantage, and do its utmost for its Owner. As in my Mercantile Employment, I so disposed of my Affairs, that from whatever Corner of the Compass the Wind blew, it was bringing home one or other of my Ships; I hope, as a Husband-man, to contrive it so, that not a Shower of Rain, or a Glimpse of Sunshine, shall fall upon my Estate without bettering some part of it, and contributing to the Products of the Season. You know it has been hitherto my Opinion of Life, that it is thrown away when it is not some way useful to others. But when I am riding out by my self, in the fresh Air on the open Heath that lies by my House, I find several other Thoughts growing up in me. I am now of Opinion, that a Man of my Age may[a] find Business enough on himself, by setting his Mind in order, preparing it for another World, and reconciling it to the Thoughts of Death. I must, therefore, acquaint you, that besides those usual Methods of Charity, of which I have before spoken, I am at this very Instant finding out a convenient Place where I may build an Alms-house, which I intend to endow very handsomly, for a Dozen superannuated Husbandmen. It will be a great Pleasure to me to say my Prayers twice a Day with Men of my own Years,[b] who all of them, as well as my self, may have their Thoughts taken up how they shall die, rather than how they shall live. I remember an excellent Saying, that I learned at School, *Finis coronat opus.*[1] You know best whether it be in *Virgil* or in *Horace*, it is my business to apply it. If your Affairs will permit you to take the Country Air with me sometimes, you shall find an Apartment fitted up for you, and shall be every Day entertained with Beef or Mutton of my own feeding; Fish out of my own Ponds; and Fruit out of my own Gardens.[c] You shall have free Egress and Regress about my House, without having any Questions asked you, and in a Word such an hearty Welcome as you may expect from

> *Your most sincere Friend*
> *and humble Servant,*
> ANDREW FREEPORT.'

The Club of which I am a Member being entirely dispersed, I

[a] a Man of my Age may] a Man may *Fol.*   [b] Years,] Age, *Fol.*   [c] Gardens.] Garden. *Fol.*

[1] Cf. Ovid, *Heroides*, 2. 85.

shall consult my Reader next Week, upon a Project relating to the Institution of a new one. O

No. 550 *Monday, December 1, 1712*[1]

[ADDISON]

Quid dignum tanto feret hic promissor HIATU?
Hor.

SINCE the late Dissolution of the Club whereof I have often declared my self a Member, there are very many Persons who by Letters, Petitions, and Recommendations, put up for the next Election. At the same Time I must complain, that several indirect and underhand Practices have been made use of upon this Occasion. A certain Country Gentleman begun to *tapp*[2] upon the first Information he received of Sir ROGER's Death, when he sent me up Word, that if I would get him chosen in the Place of the Deceased, he would present me with a Barrel of the best *October*[3] I had ever drank in my Life. The Ladies are in great Pain to know whom I intend to elect in the Room of WILL. HONEYCOMB. Some of them indeed are of Opinion that Mr. HONEYCOMB did not take sufficient Care of their Interests in the Club, and are therefore desirous of having in it hereafter a Representative of their own Sex. A Citizen, who sub-scribes himself *Y. Z.* tells me that he has one and twenty Shares in the *African* Company,[4] and offers to bribe me with the odd one in

[1] *Motto.* Horace, *Ars poetica*, 138:
  What did he worth a *Gape* so large produce? CREECH.

In the original folio sheets the motto was from Horace, *Epistles*, 1. 14. 36: *Nec usisse pudet, sed non incidere ludum*, which was transferred to No. 553.

[2] In the obsolete slang sense, 'To "turn on the tap" of gifts; to open the purse or pocket; to spend or "bleed" freely' (*OED*). This is the first example of this figurative use in *OED*. [3] I.e. October ale.

[4] This joint-stock company exported cloth and other goods from England, pur-chased negroes in Africa for sale in the new world, and imported sugar from the West Indies. For its history see David Ogg, *England in the Reigns of James II and William III* (Oxford, 1955), pp. 312–13. On 27 and 29 Nov., shortly before this number appeared, the following advertisement was published in the *Daily Courant*:

 The Indenture of Agreement between the Royal African Company of England and their Creditors, pursuant to the late Act of Parliament for that purpose, being now subscribed by more than Two thirds in Value; The said Company desire that all Persons that have Subscribed and not Registred their Orders, do forthwith bring or send their Bonds to the African House to be Registred, that it may

case he may succeed Sir ANDREW FREEPORT, which he thinks would raise the Credit of that Fund. I have several Letters, dated from *Jenny Man*'s,[1] by[a] Gentlemen who are Candidates for Capt. SENTRY's Place, and as many from a Coffee-house[2] in *Paul*'s Church-yard of such who would fill up the Vacancy occasioned by the Death of my worthy Friend the Clergyman, whom I can never mention but with a particular Respect.

Having maturely weighed these several Particulars, with the many Remonstrances that have been made to me on this Subject, and considering how invidious an Office I shall take upon me if I make the whole Election depend upon my single Voice, and being unwilling to expose my self to those Clamours, which, on such an Occasion, will not fail to be raised against me for Partiality, Injustice, Corruption, and other Qualities which my Nature abhors, I have formed to my self the Project of a Club as follows.

I have Thoughts of issuing out Writs to all and every of the Clubs that are established in the Cities of *London* and *Westminster*, requiring them to choose out of their respective Bodies a Person of the greatest Merit, and to return his Name to me before *Lady-day*, at which Time I intend to sit upon Business.

By this Means I may have Reason to hope, that the Club over which I shall preside will be the very Flower and Quintescence of all other Clubs. I have communicated this my Project to none but a particular Friend of mine, whom I have celebrated twice or thrice for his Happiness in that kind of Wit which is commonly known by the Name of a Punn. The only Objection he makes to it is, that I shall raise up Enemies to my self if I act with so regal an Air; and that my Detractors, instead of giving me the usual Title of SPEC-TATOR, will be apt to call me the *King of Clubs*.

But to proceed on my intended Project: It is very well known that I at first set forth in this Work with the Character of a silent Man; and I think I have so well preserved my Taciturnity, that I do not remember to have violated it with three Sentences in the Space of almost two Years. As a Monosyllable is my Delight, I have

---

[a] by] from *Fol.*

---

appear the Company have Two thirds in Number and Value according to the aforesaid Act. And those that have not already subscribed are desired to do it, in order to have the benefit of the Act of Parliament made for that purpose, and also that they may be qualified to elect or be elected of the next Court of Assistants

[1] See No. 403 (vol. iii).   [2] Probably Child's.

made very few Excursions in the Conversations which I have related beyond a Yes or a No. By this Means my Readers have lost many good things which I have had in my Heart, though I did not care for uttering them.

Now in order to diversify my Character, and to shew the World how well I can talk if I have a Mind, I have Thoughts of being very loquacious in the Club which I have now under Consideration. But that I may proceed the more regularly in this Affair, I design upon the first Meeting of the said Club to have *my Mouth opened* in Form, intending to regulate my self in this Particular by a certain Ritual which I have by me, that contains all the Ceremonies which are practised at the opening the Mouth of a Cardinal.[1] I have likewise examined the Forms which were used of old by *Pythagoras*, when any of his Scholars, after an Apprenticeship of Silence, was made free of his Speech.[2] In the mean Time, as I have of late found my Name in foreign Gazettes upon less Occasions, I question not but in their next Articles from *Great Britain*, they will inform the World that *the* SPECTATOR'*s Mouth is to be opened on the twenty fifth of* March *next.* I may perhaps publish a very useful Paper at that Time of the Proceedings in that Solemnity, and of the Persons who shall assist at it. But of this more hereafter.   O

No. 551   *Tuesday, December 2, 1712*[3]

Sic Honor & Nomen divinis vatibus atque Carminibus venit.

Hor.

Mr. SPECTATOR,

'WHEN Men of worthy and excelling Genius's have obliged the World with beautiful and instructive Writings, it is in the

[1] See No. 452.
[2] Diogenes Laertius, *Lives of the Philosophers*, 8. 10. See André Dacier, *Life of Pythagoras*, published by Tonson in 1707, pp. 24–26.
[3] *Motto.* Horace, *Ars poetica*, 400–1:
> So great was the Divinity of Verse,
> And such Observance to a Poet paid. ROSCOMMON.

In the original folio sheets this number consisted of the opening essay on epitaphs and the closing letter signed Philonicus. Both appear to be contributed pieces. In the 8vo and 12mo reprints the contribution of G. R., with introductory and concluding paragraphs by Steele, was added.

Nature of Gratitude that Praise shou'd be return'd them, as one proper consequent Reward of their Performances. Nor has Mankind ever been so degenerately sunk but they have made this Return, and even when they have not been wrought up by the generous Endeavour so as to receive the Advantages design'd by it. This Praise, which arises first in the Mouth of particular Persons, spreads and lasts according to the Merit of Authors; and when it thus meets with a full Success, changes its Denomination, and is called *Fame*. They who have happily arriv'd at this, are, even while they live, enflam'd by the Acknowledgments of others, and spurr'd on to new Undertakings for the Benefit of Mankind, notwithstanding the Detraction which some abject Tempers wou'd cast upon them: But when they decease, their Characters being freed from the Shadow which *Envy* laid them under, begin to shine out with greater Splendour; their Spirits survive in their Works; they are admitted into the highest Companies, and they continue pleasing and instructing Posterity from Age to Age. Some of the best gain a Character, by being able to shew that they are no Strangers to them; and others obtain a new Warmth to labour for the Happiness and Ease of Mankind, from a Reflection upon those Honours which are paid to their Memories.

'The Thought of this took me up as I turn'd over those Epigrams which are the Remains of several of the *Wits* of *Greece*, and perceiv'd many dedicated to the Fame of those who had excell'd in beautiful poetick Performances. Wherefore, in Pursuance to my Thought, I concluded to do something along with them to bring their Praises into a new Light and Language, for the Encouragement of those whose modest Tempers may be deterr'd by the Fear of Envy or Detraction from fair Attempts to which their Parts might render them equal. You will perceive them as they follow to be conceiv'd in the Form of Epitaphs, a sort of Writing which is wholly set apart for a short pointed Method of Praise.

On *Orpheus*, written by *Antipater*.

No longer, Orpheus, *shall thy sacred Strains*
Lead Stones and Trees and Beasts along the Plains;
No longer sooth the boistrous Wind to sleep,
Or still the Billows of the raging Deep:
For thou art gone, the Muses mourn'd thy Fall
In solemn Strains, thy Mother most of all.

Ye Mortals, idly for your Sons ye moan,
If thus a Goddess cou'd not save her own.[1]

'Observe here, that if we take the Fable for granted, as it was believ'd to be in that Age when the Epigram was written, the Turn appears to have Piety to the Gods, and a resigning Spirit in its Application: But if we consider the Point with Respect to our present Knowledge, it will be less esteem'd; tho' the Author himself, because he believ'd it, may still be more valu'd than any one who shou'd now write with a Point of the same Nature.

On *Homer*, by *Alpheus* of *Mytilene.*

Still in our Ears Andromache *complains,*
And still in Sight the Fate of Troy *remains,*
Still Ajax *fights, still* Hector's *dragg'd along,*
Such strange Enchantment dwells in Homer's *Song;*
Whose Birth cou'd more than one poor Realm adorn,
For all the World is proud that he was born.[2]

'The Thought in the first Part of this is natural, and depending upon the Force of Poesy: In the latter Part it looks as if it wou'd aim at the History of seven Towns contending for the Honour of *Homer*'s Birth-place; but when you expect to meet with that common Story, the Poet slides by, and raises the whole *World* for a kind of *Arbiter*, which is to end the Contention amongst its several Parts.

On *Anacreon*, by *Antipater.*

This Tomb be thine, Anacreon; *all around*
Let Ivy wreath, let Flourets[a] *deck the Ground,*
And from its Earth, enrich'd by such a Prize,
Let Wells of Milk and Streams of Wine arise:
So will thine Ashes yet a Pleasure know,
If any Pleasure reach the Shades below.[3]

'The Poet here written upon is an easy gay Author, and he who writes upon him has fill'd his own Head with the Character of his Subject. He seems to love his Theme so much, that he thinks of nothing but pleasing him as if he were still alive by entring into his libertine Spirit; so that the Humour is easy and gay, resembling *Anacreon* in its Air, rais'd by such Images, and pointed with such

---

[a] *Flourets*] *Flowers* Fol.

[1] By Antipater [of Sidon]. *Greek Anthology*, 7. 8.
[2] By Alpheius of Mitylene. Ibid. 9. 97.   [3] By Antipater [of Sidon]. Ibid. 7. 23.

a Turn as he might have us'd. I give it a Place here, because the Author may have design'd it for his Honour; and I take an Opportunity from it to advise others, that when they wou'd praise, they cautiously avoid every looser Qualification, and fix only where there is a real Foundation in Merit.

On *Euripides*, by *Ion*.

Divine Euripides, *this Tomb we see*
So fair, is not a Monument for thee
So much as thou for it, since all will own
Thy Name and lasting Praise adorns the Stone.[1]

'The Thought here is fine, but its Fault is that it is general, that it may belong to any great Man, because it points out no particular Character. It wou'd be better, if when we light upon such a Turn, we joyn it with something that circumscribes and bounds it to the Qualities of our Subject. He who gives his Praise in gross, will often appear either to have been a Stranger to those he writes upon, or not to have found any thing in them which is Praise-worthy.

On *Sophocles*, by *Simonides*.

Winde, gentle Ever-green, to form a Shade
Around the Tomb where Sophocles *is laid;*
Sweet Ivy winde thy Boughs, and intertwine
With blushing Roses and the clustring Vine:
Thus will thy lasting Leaves with Beauties hung,
Prove grateful Emblems of the Lays he sung;
Whose Soul, exalted like a God of Wit,
Among the Muses *and the* Graces *writ.*[2]

'This Epigram I have open'd more than any of the former: The Thought towards the latter End seem'd closer couched, so as to require an Explication. I fancy'd the Poet aim'd at the Picture which is generally made of *Apollo* and the *Muses*, he sitting with his Harp in the Middle, and they around him. This look'd beautiful to my Thought, and because the Image arose before me out of the Words of the Original as I was reading it, I venture to explain them so.

On *Menander*, the Author unnamed.

The very Bees, O sweet Menander, *hung*
To taste the Muses *Spring upon thy Tongue;*

---

[1] Ion's epigram on Euripides = *Greek Anthology*, 7. 43 and 44. But the epigram quoted here seems to be rather No. 46, which is anonymous.
[2] *Greek Anthology*, 7. 22 [by Simias].

The very Graces *made the Scenes you writ*
Their happy Point of fine Expression hit.
Thus still you live, you make your Athens *shine,*
And raise its Glory to the Skies in thine.[1]

'This Epigram has a Respect to the Character of its Subject; for *Menander* writ remarkably with a Justness and Purity of Language. It has also told the Country he was born in, without either a set or a hidden Manner, while it twists together the Glory of the Poet and his Nation, so as to make the Nation depend upon his for an Encrease of its own.

'I will offer no more Instances at present to shew that they who deserve Praise have it return'd them from different Ages. Let these which have been laid down shew Men that Envy will not always prevail. And to the End that Writers may more successfully enliven the Endeavours of one another, let them consider, in some such Manner as I have attempted, what may be the justest Spirit and Art of Praise. It is indeed very hard to come up to it. Our Praise is trifling when it depends upon Fable; it is false when it depends upon wrong Qualifications; it means nothing when it is general; it is extreamly difficult to hit when we propose to raise Characters high, while we keep to them justly. I shall end this with transcribing that excellent Epitaph of Mr. *Cowley,* wherein, with a kind of grave and philosophick Humour, he very beautifully speaks of himself, (withdrawn from the World, and dead to all the Interests of it) as of a Man really deceased. At the same Time it is an Instruction how to leave the Publick with a good Grace.'

Epitaphium Vivi Authoris.

Hic, O Viator, sub Lare parvulo
Couleius *hic est conditus, hic jacet*
  Defunctus humani Laboris
  Sorte, supervacuaque Vita,
Non Indecora pauperie nitens,
Et non inerti Nobilis Otio,
  Vanoque dilectis popello
  Divitiis animosus hostis.
Possis ut illum dicere mortuum
En Terra jam nunc Quantula sufficit?

[1] *Greek Anthology,* 9. 187.

Exempta sit Curis, Viator,
Terra sit illa levis, precare.
Hic sparge Flores, sparge breves Rosas,
Nam Vita gaudet Mortua Floribus,
Herbisque Odoratis Corona
Vatis adhuc Cinerem Calentem.[1]

The Publication of these Criticisms having procured me the following Letter from a very Ingenious Gentleman, I cannot forbear inserting it in the Volume, tho' it did not come soon enough to have a Place in any of my single Papers.

Mr. SPECTATOR,

'HAVING read over, in your Paper, N° 551, some of the Epigrams, made by the *Grecian* Wits, in Commendation of their celebrated Poets; I could not forbear sending you another, out of the same Collection, which I take to be as great a Compliment to *Homer,* as any that has yet been paid him.[2]

Τίς ποθ' ὁ τὸν Τροίης πόλεμον, &c.[3]

Who first transcrib'd the famous Trojan *War,*
And wise Ulysses' *Acts, O* Jove *make known:*
For, since 'tis certain, Thine those Poems are,
No more let Homer *boast, they are his own.*

'If you think it worthy of a Place in your Speculations, for ought

---

[1] From the essay No. 11, 'Of My Self' (*Essays,* ed. Waller, pp. 461–2). The translation formerly attributed to Addison (Chalmers, *English Poets,* ix. 536) reads:

From life's superfluous cares enlarg'd,
His debt of human toil discharg'd,
Here Cowley lies! beneath this shed,
To every worldly interest dead;
With decent poverty content,
His hours of ease not idly spent;
To fortune's goods a foe profest,
And hating wealth by all carest.
'Tis true he's dead; for oh! how small
A spot of earth is now his all:
Oh! wish that earth may lightly lay,
And every care be far away;
Bring flowers; the short-liv'd roses bring,
To life deceas'd, fit offering:
And sweets around the poet strow,
Whilst yet with life his ashes glow.

[2] The letter and translation from G. R., together with the two paragraphs by Steele, were added in the first collected 8vo and 12mo editions (text of 8vo).

[3] *Greek Anthology,* 16. 293 (from the Planudean Anthology).

I know (by that means) it may in time be Printed as often in *English*, as it has already been in *Greek*. I am (like the rest of the World)

SIR,

4th *Decemb.*   *Your great Admirer,*

G. R.'

The Reader may observe that the Beauty of this Epigram is different from that of any in the foregoing. An Irony is looked upon as the finest Palliative of Praise; and very often conveys the noblest Panegyric under the Appearance of Satire. *Homer* is here seemingly accused and treated as a Plagiary, but what is drawn up in the form of an Accusation is certainly, as my Correspondent observes, the greatest Compliment that could have been paid to that Divine Poet.

Dear Mr. SPECTATOR,

'I AM a Gentleman of a pretty good Fortune, and of a Temper impatient of any thing which I think an Injury; however, I always quarrell'd according to Law, and instead of attacking my Adversary by the dangerous Method of Sword and Pistol, I made my Assaults by that more secure one of Writ or Warrant. I cannot help telling you, that, either by the Justice of my Causes, or the Superiority of my Counsel, I have been generally successful; and, to my great Satisfaction I can say it, that by three Actions of Slander, and half a Dozen Trespasses, I have for several Years enjoy'd a perfect Tranquility in my Reputation and Estate. By these means also I have been made known to the Judges, the Serjeants of our Circuit are my intimate Friends, and the Ornamental Counsel pay a very profound Respect to one who has made so great a Figure in the Law. Affairs of Consequence having brought me to Town, I had the Curiosity t'other Day to visit *Westminster-Hall*; and having placed my self in one of the Courts, expected to be most agreeably entertain'd. After the Court and Counsel were, with due Ceremony, seated, up stands a Learned Gentleman and began, When this *Matter* was last *stirr'd* before your Lordship: The next humbly moved to *quash* an *Indictment*; another complain'd that his Adversary had *snapp'd* a *Judgment*; the next inform'd the Court that his Client was *stripp'd* of his *Possession*; another begg'd Leave to acquaint his Lordship, that they had been *saddled* with Costs.[1] At last up got

---

[1] Of the 'illiberal cant' objected to by Philonicus, *stirr'd* and *stripp'd* are marked

a grave Serjeant, and told us, his Client had been *hung up* a whole Term by a *Writ of Error*. At this I could bear it no longer, but came hither, and resolv'd to apply my self to your Honour to interpose with these Gentlemen, that they would leave off such low and un-natural Expressions: For surely though the Lawyers subscribe to hideous *French* and false *Latin*, yet they should let their Clients have a little decent and proper *English* for their Money. What Man that has a Value for a good Name would like to have it said in a publick Court, that Mr. such-a-one was *stripp'd, saddled*, or *hung up*? This being what has escaped your Spectatorial Observation, be pleased to correct such an illiberal Cant among profess'd Speakers, and you'll infinitely oblige

Joe's *Coffee-house*,[1]   *Your humble Servant,*
Novemb. 28.   Philonicus.'

No. 552   *Wednesday, December 3, 1712*[2]
[STEELE]

... *Qui prægravat artes*
Infra se positas extinctus amabitur idem.
Hor.

AS I was tumbling about the Town the other Day in an Hackney-Coach, and delighting my self with busy Scenes in the Shops of each side of me, it came into my Head, with no small Remorse, that I had not been frequent enough in the Mention and Recom-mendation of the industrious Part of Mankind. It very naturally, upon this Occasion, touched my Conscience in particular, that I had not acquitted my self to my Friend Mr. *Peter Motteux*.[3] That industrious Man of Trade, and formerly Brother of the Quill, has dedicated to me a Poem upon Tea.[4] It would injure him, as a Man

by *OED* as 'now *rare*', though common in the eighteenth century; *quash* dates from *c.* 1330, and *hung up* from 1623. The earliest example of *saddled with* used figuratively dates from 1728. To *snap a judgment* does not seem to have been in common use.

[1] 'Joe's, alias, the Blue-Coat Coffee-house in Sweething's Alley' appears in an advertisement in the *Daily Courant* of 29 Aug. 1712.

[2] *Motto.* Horace, *Epistles*, 2. 1. 13–14:
For those are hated that excell the rest,
Altho when dead they are belov'd, and blest. CREECH.

[3] See No. 288 (vol. iii).

[4] Motteux's *Poem upon Tea* had been published by Tonson on 26 July, with a

of Business, if I did not let the World know that the Author of so good Verses writ them before he was concerned in Traffick. In order to expiate my Negligence towards him, I immediately resolved to make him a Visit. I found his spacious Warehouses filled and adorned with Tea, China, and Indian Ware. I could observe a beautiful Ordonnance[1] of the Whole, and such different and considerable Branches of Trade carried on in the same House, I exulted in seeing disposed by a Poetical Head. In one Place were exposed to view Silks of various Shades and Colours, rich Brocades, and the wealthiest Products of foreign Looms. Here you might see the finest Laces held up by the fairest Hands; and there examined by the beauteous Eyes of the Buyers the most delicate Cambricks, Muslins, and Linnens. I could not but congratulate my Friend on the humble, but, I hoped, beneficial use he had made of his Talents, and wished I could be a Patron to his Trade, as he had been pleased[a] to make me of his Poetry. The honest Man has, I know, that modest Desire of Gain which is peculiar to those who understand better Things than Riches; and I dare say he would be contented with much less than what is called Wealth in that Quarter of the Town which he inhabits, and will oblige all his Customers with Demands agreeable to the Moderation of his Desires.

Among other Omissions of which I have been also guilty with relation to Men of Industry of a superiour Order, I must acknowledge my Silence towards a Proposal frequently enclosed to me by Mr. *Renatus Harris, Organ-Builder*.[2] The Ambition of this Artificer

---

[a] had been pleased] *12mo*; had pleased *Fol., 8vo*

dedication to the *Spectator*. In the preface Motteux refers to his being engrossed in his China and Indian trade. The poem is advertised as 'just published' in No. 475 (4 Sept.).

[1] 'Plan or method of composition' (*OED*).

[2] Harris, who came from a family of organ-builders, is chiefly remembered for his rivalry with Father Bernard Smith over the contract for building the organ in the Temple Church in the 1680's. The organ in the choir of St. Paul's Cathedral, also built by Father Smith, was first used on 2 Dec. 1697 at the service of thanksgiving for the Peace of Ryswick (cf. the poem by John Hughes). Owing to a quarrel with Wren over the position of the organ, Smith decided to omit certain ranks of pipes, and the effect was not entirely satisfactory. A broadside in the British Museum, headed 'Queries about St. Paul's Organ', poses twelve questions regarding Smith's workmanship, and though not mentioning Harris by name probably emanated from him or his friends. Query VIII reads:

Whether there been't Organs in the City lowder, sweeter, and of more variety than St. *Paul's*, (which cost not one 3d. of the Price) And particularly, whether *Smith* at the *Temple* has not out-done *Smith* at St. *Paul's*? And whether St. *Andrew's Undershaft* has not out-done them both?

Harris, who had unsuccessfully competed with Smith for the contract for the organ

is to erect an Organ in St. *Paul's* Cathedral over the West Door at the Entrance into the Body of the Church, which in Art and Magnificence shall transcend any Work of that Kind ever before invented. The Proposal in perspicuous Language sets forth the Honour and Advantage such a Performance would be to the *British* Name, as well as that it would apply the Power of Sounds in a Manner more amazingly forcible than, perhaps, has yet been known, and I am sure to an End much more worthy. Had the vast Sums which have been laid out upon Opera's without Skill or Conduct, and to no other Purpose but to suspend or vitiate our Understandings, been disposed this Way, we should now, perhaps, have had an Engine so formed as to strike the Minds of half a People at once in a Place

at the Temple, had built the organ at St. Andrew's Undershaft in 1696. The broadside is undated but was certainly issued before Smith's death, which took place in February 1708.

About 1712 Harris issued *A Proposal (by Renatus Harris, Organ Builder) for the Erecting of an Organ in St. Paul's Cathedral, over the West Door, at the Entrance into the Body of that Church*. This pamphlet, referred to here by Steele, is rare, but the Library of St. Paul's Cathedral possesses a copy. In it Harris proposes an organ of six manuals, one of which is to be a 'swell', and a 32-foot stop on the pedals. The *Proposal* begins:

> As VOCAL MUSICK is the most perfect, so that sort of Instrumental which most resembles it, in its highest Perfection, must claim the Precedence of all others: In which Respect, the ORGAN is justly stil'd the *King of Instruments*; which has of late Years receiv'd many Improvements, particularly by representing all Wind and String'd Musick; to which Improvements the Proposer presumes he has in some measure contributed: And upon this Occasion, thinks it necessary to give an Account how he came to the Knowledge of swelling the Notes upon an ORGAN, because to this is owing the following Proposal.

The principal feature of Harris's plan is the experiment of a swell organ, 'capable of emitting Sounds to express Passion, by swelling any Note, as if inspir'd by Human Breath', which he says he first demonstrated before an assembly of musicians in his workshop on Tuesday in Whitsun week 1700. On this manual 'the Notes will be loud or soft, by swelling on a long Note or Shake, at the Organist's Pleasure. Sounds will come surprizing and harmoniously, as from the Clouds, or distant Parts, pass, and return again, or quick or slow as Fancy can suggest; and be in Tune in all Degrees of Loudness and Softness.'

Harris proposes that his organ be placed at a great distance from the choir, in order not to interfere with the present organ in the performance of the service.

The Use of it will be for the Reception of the Queen on all publick Occasions of Thanksgiving for the good Effects of Peace or War, upon all State-Days, St. *Cecilia's*-Day, the Entertainment of Foreigners of Quality and Artists, and on all Times of greatest Concourse, &c. And by the Advice and Assistance of Sir *Christopher Wren*, the external Figure and Ornaments may be contriv'd so proportionable to the Order of the Building, as to be a Decoration to that part of the Edifice, and no Obstruction to any of the rest.

The proposal, whereby Harris hoped to secure a grant from Parliament for the building of his organ, apparently came to nothing, in spite of the support given here by Steele. W. L. Sumner (*A History and Account of the Organs of St. Paul's Cathedral*, London, 1931) writes: 'As Harris was nearly Smith's equal in voicing, and probably his superior in the matter of mechanism, it is a pity that he was not allowed to realise his project in a practical form' (p. 13).

of Worship with a Forgetfulness of present Care and Calamity, and an Hope of endless Rapture, Joy, and Hallelujah hereafter.

When I am doing this Justice, I am not to forget the best Mechanick of my Acquaintance, that useful Servant to Science and Knowledge, Mr. *John Rowley*; but think I lay a great Obligation on the Publick, by acquainting them with his Proposals for a Pair of new Globes.[1] After his Preamble, he promises in the said Proposals that,

In the Celestial Globe,

'Care shall be taken that the Fixed Stars be placed according to their true Longitude and Latitude, from the many and correct Observations of *Hevelius, Cassini*, Mr. *Flamsteed*, Reg. Astronomer, Dr. *Halley, Savilian* Professor of Geometry in *Oxon*; and from whatever else can be procured to render the Globe more exact, instructive, and useful.[2]

'That all the Constellations be drawn in a curious, new, and particular Manner; each Star in so just, distinct, and conspicuous a Proportion, that its true Magnitude may be readily known by bare Inspection, according to the different *Light* and *Sizes* of the Stars. That the Tract or Way of such Comets as have been well observed, but not hitherto expressed in any Globe, be carefully delineated in this.

---

[1] John Rowley, the instrument-maker, was later appointed Master of Mechanicks to George I, and died in 1728. He is described in the *Daily Courant* of 2 June 1715 as 'the ingenious Author of the incomparable Instrument (commonly known by the Name of the Orrery) whereby the Motions of the Planets are occularly shewn in a most excellent Manner'. Steele praises Rowley in *The Englishman* (No. 11) as the inventor of the orrery; the machine was actually invented earlier by George Graham and took its name from Charles Boyle, 4th Earl of Orrery, for whom the instrument was made.

[2] The scientists named here were all concerned in astronomical measurements. Johannes Hevelius (1611–87), the Polish astronomer of Danzig, catalogued some 1,500 stars but in a less accurate fashion than Halley. Giovanni Domenico Cassini (1625–1712) was Director of the Observatory at Paris and noted as the discoverer of four of the satellites of Saturn. He died on 14 Sept. 1712 and was succeeded by his son Jacques Cassini (1677–1756), chiefly known for his efforts to determine the figure of the earth. The reference here is probably to the elder Cassini. John Flamsteed (1646–1719), the first astronomer royal, is referred to in No. 620. His astronomical observations, *Historia Coelestis*, had been published this year (1712), but in a shortened form which seriously diminished their scientific value (see A. Wolf, *History of Science . . . in the 16th & 17th Centuries*, 1939, p. 180). Edmond Halley (1656–1742), best known for his prediction of the return of the comet of 1682 which bears his name, became Savilian professor of geometry at Oxford in 1703 and succeeded Flamsteed as astronomer royal in 1720.

In the Terrestrial Globe.

'That by reason the Descriptions formerly made, both in the *English* or *Dutch* great Globes, are Erroneous, *Asia*, *Africa*, and *America* be drawn in a Manner wholly new; by which Means it is to be noted, that the Undertakers will be obliged to alter the Latitude of some Places in 10 Degrees, the Longitude of others in 20 Degrees: Besides which great and necessary Alterations, there be many remarkable Countries, Cities, Towns, Rivers, and Lakes, omitted in other Globes, inserted here according to the best Discoveries made by our late Navigators. Lastly, That the Course of the Trade-Winds, the *Monsoons*, and other Winds periodically shifting between the Tropicks, be visibly expressed.

'Now in Regard that this Undertaking is of so universal Use, as the Advancement of the most necessary Parts of the Mathematicks, as well as tending to the Honour of the *British* Nation, and that the Charge of carrying it on is very expensive, it is desired that all Gentlemen who are willing to promote so great a Work, will be pleased to subscribe the following Conditions.

'I. The Undertakers engage to furnish each Subscriber with a Celestial and Terrestrial Globe, each of 30 Inches Diameter, in all Respects curiously adorn'd, the Stars gilded, the Capital Cities plainly distinguished, the Frames, Meridians, Horizons, Hour-Circles and Indexes so exactly finished up and accurately divided, that a Pair of these Globes will really appear, in the Judgment of any disinterested and intelligent Person, worth Fifteen Pounds more than will be demanded for them by the Undertakers.

'II. Whosoever will be pleased to Subscribe, and pay Twenty Five Pounds in the Manner following for a Pair of these Globes, either for their own Use, or to present them to any College in the Universities, or any publick Library or School, shall have his Coat of Arms, Name, Title, Seat, or Place of Residence, *&c.* inserted in some convenient Place of the Globe.

'III. That every Subscriber do at first pay down the Sum of Ten Pounds, and Fifteen Pounds more upon the Delivery of each Pair of Globes perfectly fitted up: And that the said Globes be delivered within Twelve Months after the Number of Thirty Subscribers be compleated; and that the Subscribers be served with Globes in the Order in which they subscribed.

'IV. That a Pair of these Globes shall not hereafter be sold to any Person but the Subscribers under Thirty Pounds.

'V. That if there be not thirty Subscribers within four Months after the first of *December*, 1712, the Money paid shall be return'd on Demand by Mr. *John Warner*, Goldsmith, near *Temple-Bar*, who shall receive and pay the same according to the above-mentioned Articles.'[1]

T

No. 553

[ADDISON]

Thursday, December 4, 1712[2]

Nec lusisse pudet, sed non incidere ludum.

Hor.

THE Project which I published on *Monday* last, has brought me in several Packets of Letters. Among the rest I have received one from a certain Projector, wherein after having represented, that in all probability the Solemnity of *opening my Mouth* will draw together a great Confluence of Beholders, he proposes to me the hiring of *Stationer's-Hall* for the more convenient exhibiting of that Publick Ceremony.[3] He undertakes to be at the Charge of it himself, provided he may have the erecting of Galleries on every side, and the letting of them out upon that Occasion. I have a Letter also from a Bookseller, petitioning me in a very humble manner, that he may have the Printing of the Speech which I shall make to the Assembly upon the first opening of my Mouth. I am informed from all Parts, that there are great Canvassings in the several Clubs about Town, upon the chusing of a proper Person to sit with me on those arduous Affairs to which I have summoned them. Three Clubs have already proceeded to Election, whereof one has made a double Return. If I find that my Enemies shall take Advantage of my Silence to begin Hostilities upon me, or if any other Exigency of Affairs may so require, since I see Elections in so great a forwardness,

[1] For Warner see No. 526.
[2] *Motto.* Horace, *Epistles*, 1. 14. 36:

Once to be wild is no such foul disgrace,
But 'tis so still to run the frantick Race. CREECH.

In the folio sheets the motto was Horace, *Ars poetica* 138, afterwards used as the motto for No. 550.
[3] Stationers' Hall is described by Hatton as 'a handsome Brick Building, situate near the North end of *Cock Ally* in *Ludgate Street*' (p. 619).

we may possibly meet before the Day appointed; or if Matters go on to my Satisfaction, I may perhaps put off the Meeting to a further Day; but of this Publick Notice shall be given.

In the mean time, I must confess that I am not a little gratified and obliged by that Concern which appears in this great City, upon my present Design of laying down this Paper. It is likewise with much Satisfaction, that I find some of the most outlying Parts of the Kingdom alarmed upon this Occasion, having receiv'd Letters to expostulate with me about it, from several of my Readers of the remotest Boroughs of *Great Britain*. Among these I am very well pleased with a Letter dated from *Berwick upon Tweed*, wherein my Correspondent compares the Office which I have for some time executed in these Realms, to the Weeding of a great Garden; which, says he, it is not sufficient to weed once for all, and afterwards to give over, but that the Work must be continued daily, or the same Spots of Ground which are cleared for a while, will in a little time be over-run as much as ever. Another Gentleman lays before me several Enormities that are already sprouting, and which he believes will discover themselves in their full growth immediately after my Disappearance. There is no doubt, says he, but the Ladies Heads will shoot up as soon as they know they are no longer under the *Spectator*'s Eye;[1] and I have already seen such monstrous broad-brimm'd Hats under the Arms of Foreigners, that I question not but they will overshadow[a] the Island within a Month or two after the dropping of your Paper. But among all the Letters which are come to my Hands, there is none so handsomely written as the following one, which I am the more pleased with, as it is sent me from Gentlemen who belong to a Body which I shall always Honour, and where (I cannot speak it without a secret Pride) my Speculations have met with a very kind Reception. It is usual for Poets upon the Publishing of their Works, to Print before them such Copies of Verses as have been made in their Praise. Not that you must imagine they are pleased with their own Commendations, but because the elegant Compositions of their Friends should not be lost. I must make the same Apology for the Publication of the ensuing Letter, in which I have suppress'd no part of those Praises that are given my Speculations with too lavish and good-natur'd

[a] overshadow] overshade *Fol.*

---

[1] Addison had used a similar phrase in his discussion of head-dresses in No. 98.

an Hand, though my Correspondents can witness for me, that at other times I have generally blotted out those Parts in the Letters which I have receiv'd from them.

O[a]

Mr. SPECTATOR, *Oxford, Nov.* 25.

'IN spight of your Invincible Silence you have found out a Method of being the most agreeable Companion in the World: That kind of Conversation which you hold with the Town, has the good Fortune of being always pleasing to the Men of Taste and Leisure, and never offensive to those of Hurry and Business. You are never heard, but at what *Horace* calls *dextro tempore*,[1] and have the Happiness to observe the Politick Rule, which the same discerning Author gave his Friend, when he enjoyn'd him to deliver his Book to *Augustus.*

Si validus, si lætus erit, si denique poscet.[2]

You never begin to talk, but when People are desirous to hear you; and I defie any one to be out of Humour till you leave off. But I am led unawares into Reflections, foreign to the Original Design of this Epistle; which was to let you know, that some unfeigned Admirers of your inimitable Papers, who could, without any Flattery, greet you with the Salutation used to the Eastern Monarchs, viz. O *Spec. live for ever*,[3] have lately been under the same Apprehensions with Mr. *Philo-Spec;*[4] that the haste you have made to dispatch your best Friends, portends no long Duration to your own short Visage. We could not, indeed, find any just Grounds for Complaint in the Method you took to dissolve that venerable Body; No, the World was not worthy of your Divine. *Will Honeycomb* could not, with any Reputation, live single any longer. It was high time for the *Templar* to turn himself to *Cook.*[5] And Sir *Roger's* dying was the wisest thing he ever did in his Life. It was, however, Matter of great Grief to us, to think that we were in danger of losing so Elegant and Valuable an Entertainment. And we could

---

[a] *Signature added here in 8vo and 12mo; no signature here or at end of paper in Fol.*

[1] *Satires,* 2. 1. 18, rendered by Creech as 'a happy Time'.
[2] *Epistles,* 1. 13. 3:
If well, if merry, if he asks to read. CREECH.
[3] Cf. No. 537 ('That sublime Manner of Salutation with which the *Jews* approach'd their Kings').   [4] No. 542.
[5] Cook, i.e. Coke. See No. 2 (vol. i).

not, without Sorrow, reflect that we were likely to have nothing to interrupt our Sips in a Morning, and to suspend our Coffee in mid-air, between our Lips and right Ear, but the ordinary Trash of News-papers. We resolved, therefore, not to part with you so. But since, to make use of your own Allusion, the Cherries began now to crowd the Market, and their Season was almost over, we consulted our future Enjoyments, and endeavoured to make the exquisite Pleasure that delicious Fruit gave our Taste as lasting as we could, and by drying them protract their Stay beyond its natural Date. We own that thus they have not a Flavour equal to that of their juicy Bloom; but yet, under this Disadvantage, they pique the Palate, and become a Salver better than any other Fruit at its first Appearance. To speak plain, there are a number of us who have begun your Works afresh, and meet two Nights in the Week in order to give you a Rehearing. We never come together without drinking your Health, and as seldom part without general Expressions of Thanks to you for our Night's Improvement. This we conceive to be a more useful Institution than any other Club whatever, not excepting even that of *ugly Faces*.[1] We have one manifest Advantage over that renowned Society, with respect to Mr. *Spectator's* Company. For though they may brag that you sometimes make your personal Appearance amongst them, it is impossible they should ever get a Word from you. Whereas you are with us the Reverse of what *Phædria* would have his Mistress be in his Rival's Company, *Present in your Absence*.[2] We make you talk as much and as long as we please, and let me tell you, you seldom hold your Tongue for the whole Evening. I promise my self you will look with an Eye of Favour upon a Meeting which ows its Original to a mutual Emulation among its Members, who shall shew the most profound Respect for your Paper; not but we have a very great Value for your Person; and I dare say you can no where find four more sincere Admirers, and humble Servants, than

T F. G S. J T. E T.'

[1] No. 17 (vol. i).
[2] Terence, *Eunuchus*. Phaedria's request to his mistress was that 'when you are with your soldier in person don't be with him at heart'. See the quotation in No. 170 (vol. ii).

> *. . . tentanda Via est, quâ me quoque possim*
> *Tollere humo, Victorque virûm volitare per Ora.*
> Virg.

I AM obliged for the following Essay, as well as for that which lays down Rules out of *Tully* for Pronunciation and Action,[2] to the Ingenious Author of a Poem just Published, Entitled *An Ode to the Creator of the World, occasioned by the Fragments of* Orpheus.[3]

IT is a Remark made, as I remember, by a celebrated *French* Author, that *no Man ever pushed his Capacity as far as it was able to extend.*[4] I shall not enquire whether this Assertion be strictly true. It may suffice to say, that Men of the greatest Application and Acquirements can look back upon many vacant Spaces, and neglected Parts of Time, which have slipped away from them unemployed; and there is hardly any one considering Person in the World, but is apt to fancy with himself, at some time or other, that if his Life were to begin again, he could fill it up better.

The Mind is most provoked to cast on it self this ingenuous Reproach, when the Examples of such Men are presented to it, as have far outshot the generality of their Species, in Learning, Arts, or any valuable Improvements.

One of the most extensive and improved Genius's we have had any Instance of in our own Nation, or in[a] any other, was that of Sir *Francis Bacon* Lord *Verulam*. This great Man, by an extraordinary Force of Nature, Compass of Thought, and indefatigable Study, had amassed to himself such Stores of Knowledge as we cannot look upon without Amazement. His Capacity seems to have grasped All

---

[a] or in] or perhaps in *Fol.*

[1] *Motto.* Virgil, *Georgics,* 3. 8–9:
> New ways I must attempt, my groveling Name
> To raise aloft, and wing my flight to Fame. DRYDEN.

[2] No. 541.

[3] John Hughes. His poem is referred to at the end of No. 537.

[4] Hughes is probably recalling the passage in his own translation of Fontenelle's *Dialogues of the Dead* (1708), p. 103: ' 'Tis fit that in every thing Men shou'd propose a Point of Perfection beyond their reach. They wou'd never put themselves in the Road, if they expected to arrive only where they actually arrive: They must have in view an imaginary Stage to animate 'em' (Raymond Lully to Artemisia).

that was revealed in Books before his Time; and not satisfied with that, he began to strike out[1] new Tracks of Science, too many to be travelled over by any one Man, in the Compass of the longest Life. These, therefore, he could only mark down, like imperfect Coastings in Maps, or supposed Points of Land, to be further discovered, and ascertained by the Industry of After-Ages, who should proceed upon his Notices or Conjectures.

The Excellent Mr. *Boyle* was the Person, who seems to have been designed by Nature to succeed to the Labours and Enquiries of that extraordinary Genius I have just mentioned. By innumerable Experiments He, in a great Measure, filled up those Plans and Out-Lines of Science, which his Predecessor had sketched out. His Life was spent in the Pursuit of Nature, through a great Variety of Forms and Changes, and in the most rational, as well as devout Adoration of its Divine Author.[2]

It would be impossible to name many Persons, who have extended their Capacities so far as these two, in the Studies they pursued; but my learned Readers, on this Occasion, will naturally turn their Thoughts to a *Third*, who is yet living, and is likewise the Glory of our own Nation.[3] The Improvements which others had made in Natural and Mathematical Knowledge have so vastly increased in his Hands, as to afford at once a wonderful Instance how great the Capacity is of an Human Soul, and how inexhaustible the Subject of its Enquiries; so true is that Remark in Holy Writ, that, *tho' a wise Man seek to find out the Works of God from the Beginning to the End, yet shall he not be able to do it.*[4]

I cannot help mentioning here one Character more, of a different kind indeed from these, yet such a one as may serve to shew the wonderful Force of Nature and of Application, and is the most singular Instance of an Universal Genius I have ever met with. The Person I mean is *Leonardo da Vinci*, an *Italian* Painter, descended from a noble Family in *Tuscany*, about the beginning of the Sixteenth Century.[5] In his Profession of History-Painting he was so

---

[1] This is the first example in *OED* of this phrase used in a figurative sense.
[2] For Boyle's devotion see Nos. 389 (vol. iii) and 531, and *Guardian* 175.
[3] Identified by Nichols as Sir Isaac Newton. [4] Eccles. viii. 17.
[5] The substance of the material here is derived from Vasari. The anecdote of Leonardo's dying in the arms of Francis I is apocryphal. Leonardo had moved to France in 1517 at the invitation of the French king, who gave him a little country house at Amboise on the Loire, where he died on 2 May 1519. Francis I at that time was not at Amboise but with the Court at Saint-Germain-en-Laye. See Ludwig Goldscheider, *Leonardo da Vinci* (Phaedon Press, 1944), p. 13.

great a Master, that some have[a] affirmed he excelled all who went
before him. It is certain that he raised[b] the Envy of *Michael Angelo,*
who was his Contemporary, and that from the Study of his Works
Raphael himself learned his best Manner of Designing. He was a
Master too in Sculpture and Architecture, and skillful in Anatomy,
Mathematicks, and Mechanicks. The Aquæduct from the River
Adda to *Milan,* is mentioned as a Work of his Contrivance. He had
learned several Languages, and was acquainted with the Studies of
History, Philosophy, Poetry, and Musick. Tho' it is not necessary
to my present Purpose, I cannot but take Notice, that all who have
writ of him mention likewise his Perfections of Body. The Instances
of his Strength are almost incredible. He is described to have been
of a well-formed Person, and a Master of all genteel Exercises. And
lastly, we are told that his moral Qualities were agreeable to his
natural and intellectual Endowments, and that he was of an honest
and generous Mind, adorned with great Sweetness of Manners.
I might break off the Account of him here, but I imagine it will
be an Entertainment to the Curiosity of my Readers, to find so
remarkable a Character distinguish'd by as remarkable a Circumstance at his Death. The Fame of his Works having gained him an
universal Esteem, he was invited to the Court of *France,* where,
after some time, he fell sick; and *Francis the First* coming to see[c] him,
he raised himself in his Bed to acknowledge the Honour which was
done him by that Visit. The King embraced him, and *Leonardo*
fainting at the same Instant, expired in the Arms of that great
Monarch.

It is impossible to attend to such Instances as these without being
raised into a Contemplation on the wonderful Nature of an Human
Mind, which is capable of such Progressions in Knowledge, and can
contain such a Variety of Ideas without Perplexity or Confusion.
How reasonable is it from hence to infer its Divine Original? And
whilst we find unthinking Matter indued with a Natural Power
to last for ever, unless annihilated by Omnipotence, how absurd
wou'd it be to imagine, that a Being so much Superior to it shou'd
not have the same Privilege?

At the same time it is very surprizing, when we remove our
Thoughts from such Instances as I have mentioned, to consider
those we so frequently meet with in the Accounts of barbarous

a some have] it is *Fol.*   b before . . . raised] before him, that he raised *Fol.*
c see] visit *Fol.*

Nations among the *Indians*; where we find Numbers of People who scarce shew the first Glimmerings of Reason, and seem to have few Ideas above those of Sense and Appetite. These, methinks, appear like large Wilds, or vast uncultivated[a] Tracts of Human Nature; and when we compare them with Men of the most exalted Characters in Arts and Learning, we find it difficult to believe that they are Creatures of the same Species.

Some are of Opinion that the Souls of Men are all naturally equal, and that the great Disparity we so often observe, arises from the different Organization or Structure of the Bodies to which they are United. But whatever constitutes this first Disparity, the next great Difference which we find between Men in their several Acquirements is owing to accidental Differences in their Education, Fortunes, or Course of Life. The Soul is a kind of rough Diamond, which requires Art, Labour, and Time to polish it. For want of which, many a good Natural Genius is lost, or lies unfashioned, like a Jewel in the Mine.

One of the strongest Incitements to excel in such Arts and Accomplishments as are in the highest Esteem among Men, is the natural Passion which the Mind of Man has for Glory; which, though it may be faulty in the Excess of it, ought by no means to be discouraged. Perhaps some Moralists are too severe in beating down this Principle, which seems to be a Spring implanted by Nature to give Motion to all the latent Powers of the Soul, and is always observ'd to exert itself with the greatest Force in the most generous Dispositions. The Men, whose Characters have shone the brightest among the ancient *Romans*, appear to have been strongly animated by this Passion. *Cicero*, whose Learning and Services to his Country are so well known, was inflamed by it to an extravagant Degree, and warmly presses *Lucceius*, who was composing a History of those Times, to be very particular and zealous in relating the Story of his Consulship; and to execute it speedily, that he might have the Pleasure of enjoying in his Life-time some Part of the Honour[b] which he foresaw wou'd be paid to his Memory.[1] This was the Ambition of a great Mind; but he is faulty in the Degree of it, and cannot refrain from solliciting the Historian upon this Occasion to neglect the strict Laws of History, and in praising him, *even to exceed the Bounds of Truth*. The younger *Pliny* appears to have had

[a] or vast uncultivated] or uncultivated *Fol*.   [b] Honour] Glory *Fol*.

[1] *Epistulae ad familiares*, 5. 12.

the same Passion for Fame, but accompanied with greater Chastness and Modesty. His Ingenuous manner of owning it to a Friend, who had prompted him to undertake some great Work, is exquisitely beautiful, and raises him to a certain Grandeur above the Imputation of Vanity. *I must confess*, says he, *that nothing employs my Thoughts more than the Desire I have of perpetuating my Name, which in my Opinion is a Design worthy of a Man, at least of such a one, who being conscious of no Guilt, is not afraid to be remember'd by Posterity.*[1]

I think I ought not to conclude, without interesting all my Readers in the Subject of this Discourse. I shall therefore lay it down as a Maxim, that tho' all are not capable of shining in Learning or the Politer Arts, yet *every one is capable of excelling in something*. The Soul has in this Respect a certain vegetative Power, which cannot lie wholly idle. If it is not laid out and cultivated into a regular and beautiful Garden, it will of itself shoot up in Weeds or Flowers of a wilder Growth.

No. 555   *Saturday, December 6, 1712*[2]
[STEELE]

Respue quod non es . . .
Pers.

ALL the Members of the imaginary Society, which were described in my First Papers, having disappeared one after another, it is high time for the *Spectator* himself to go off the Stage. But, now I am to take my Leave I am under much greater Anxiety than I have known for the Work of any Day since I undertook this Province. It is much more difficult to converse with the World in a real than a personated Character. That might pass for Humour, in the *Spectator*, which would look like Arrogance in a Writer who sets his Name to his Work. The Fictitious Person might contemn those who disapproved him, and extoll his own Performances, without giving Offence. He might assume a mock-Authority, without being looked upon as vain and conceited. The Praises or Censures of himself fall only upon the Creature of his Imagination, and if any one finds fault with him, the Author may reply with the

---

[1] *Epistulae*, 5. 8 (to Titinius Capito). In this passage Pliny quotes the lines of Virgil which are used as the motto for this number.
[2] *Motto*. Persius, *Satires*, 4. 51. Lay the fictitious character aside.

Philosopher of old, *Thou dost but beat the Case of* Anaxarchus.[1] When
I speak in my own private Sentiments, I cannot but address my self
to my Readers in a more submissive manner, and with a just
Gratitude, for the kind Reception which they have given to these
Dayly Papers that have been published for almost the space of
Two Years last past.

I hope the Apology I have made as to the Licence allowable to a
feigned Character, may excuse any thing which has been said in
these Discourses of the *Spectator* and his Works; but the Imputation
of the grossest Vanity would still dwell upon me, if I did not give
some Account by what Means I was enabled to keep up the Spirit
of so long and approved a Performance. All the Papers marked with
a C, an L, an I, or an O, that is to say, all the Papers which I have
distinguished by any Letter in the name of the Muse *C L I O*,[2] were
given me by the Gentleman, of whose Assistance I formerly boasted
in the Preface and concluding Leaf of my *Tatlers*.[3] I am indeed much
more proud of his long continued Friendship, than I should be of
the Fame of being thought the Author of any Writings which he
himself is capable of producing. I remember when I finished the
Tender Husband, I told him there was nothing I so ardently wished,

---

[1] Anaxarchus, the philosopher of Abdera, was condemned by Nicocrean, tyrant
of Cyprus, to be pounded to death with iron pestles, but he suffered the torment
by making light of it, saying, 'Pound, pound the bag containing Anaxarchus; ye
pound not Anaxarchus' (Diogenes Laertius, *Lives of the Philosophers*, 9. 59). Cf. *Ovid's
Invective or Curse against Ibis*, trans. John Jones (Oxford, 1658), p. 138; Quevedo,
Visions, trans. R. L'Estrange (9th ed., 1702), p. 232.

[2] 'The Letters C, L, I, O, seem to have suggested the name of the muse to Steele
currente calamo; but it does not appear that he had either the least intention or
authority to explain the meaning of Addison's signatures' (Nichols).

[3] In the Preface, prefixed to Vol. iv of the *Tatler*, Steele writes of Addison:

But I have only one Gentleman, who will be nameless, to thank for any frequent
Assistance to me, which indeed it would have been barbarous in him to have
denied to one with whom he has lived in an Intimacy from Childhood, considering
the great Ease with which he is able to dispatch the most entertaining Pieces of
this Nature. This good Office he performed with such Force of Genius, Humour,
Wit, and Learning, that I fared like a distressed Prince who calls in a powerful
Neighbour to his Aid; I was undone by my Auxiliary; when I had once called him
in, I could not subsist without Dependance on him.

In the concluding *Tatler* (No. 271) Steele acknowledges that

the most approved Pieces in it were written by others, and those which have been
most excepted against by my self. The Hand that has assisted me in those noble
Discourses upon the Immortality of the Soul, the glorious Prospects of another
Life, and the most sublime Idea's of Religion and Virtue, is a Person who is too
fondly my Friend ever to own them; but I should little deserve to be his, if I
usurped the Glory of them. I must acknowledge at the same Time, that I think
the finest Strokes of Wit and Humour in all Mr. *Bickerstaff*'s Lucubrations are
those for which he is also beholden to him.

as that we might some time or other publish a Work written by us both, which should bear the Name of *the Monument*, in Memory of our Friendship.[1] I heartily wish what I have done here, were as Honorary to that Sacred Name, as Learning, Wit and Humanity render those Pieces which I have taught the Reader how to distinguish for his. When the Play above-mentioned was last Acted, there were so many applauded Stroaks in it which I had from the same Hand, that I thought very meanly of my self that I had never publickly acknowledged them. After I have put other Friends upon importuning him to publish Dramatick, as well as other Writings he has by him, I shall end what I think I am obliged to say on this Head, by giving my Reader this Hint for the better judging of my Productions, that the best Comment upon them would be an Account when the Patron to the *Tender Husband* was in *England*, or Abroad.

The Reader will also find some Papers which are marked with the Letter X, for which he is obliged to the Ingenious Gentleman who diverted the Town with the Epilogue to the *Distressed Mother*.[2] I might have owned these several Papers with the free Consent of these Gentlemen, who did not write them with a design of being known for the Authors. But as a candid and sincere Behaviour ought to be preferred to all other Considerations, I would not let my Heart reproach me with a Consciousness of having acquired a Praise which is not my Right.

The other Assistances which I have had have been conveyed by Letter, sometimes by whole Papers, and other times by short Hints from unknown Hands. I have not been able to trace Favours of this kind, with any Certainty, but to the following Names, which I place in the Order wherein I received the Obligation, tho' the first I am going to Name can hardly be mentioned in a List wherein he would not deserve the Precedence.[3] The Persons to whom I am

---

[1] *The Tender Husband* was given at Drury Lane on 23 Apr. 1705. In the Dedication to Addison, who wrote the prologue and gave Steele some help in the play itself, Steele writes:

My Purpose, in this Application, is only to show the Esteem I have for You, and that I look upon my Intimacy with You as one of the most valuable Enjoyments of my Life. At the same time I hope I make the Town no ill Compliment for their kind Acceptance of this Comedy, in acknowledging that it has so far rais'd my Opinion of it, as to make me think it no improper Memorial of an Inviolable Friendship.

[2] Eustace Budgell. For the Epilogue to *The Distressed Mother* see No. 338 (vol. iii).

[3] Steele is evidently thinking of Addison and Budgell, whom he has just discussed,

to make these Acknowledgments are Mr. *Henry Martyn*, Mr. *Pope*, Mr. *Hughs*, Mr. *Carey* of *New-College* in *Oxford*, Mr. *Tickell* of *Queen*'s in the same University, Mr. *Parnelle*, and Mr. *Eusden* of *Trinity* in *Cambridge*.[1] Thus, to speak in the Language of my late Friend Sir ANDREW FREEPORT, I have Ballanced my Accounts with all my Creditors for Wit and Learning. But as these Excellent Performances would not have seen the Light without the means of this Paper, I may still arrogate to my self the Merit of their being communicated to the Publick.

I have nothing more to add, but having swelled this Work to Five hundred and fifty five Papers, they will be disposed into seven Volumes, four of which are already publish'd, and the three others in the Press. It will not be demanded of me why I now leave off, tho' I must own my self obliged to give an Account to the Town of my Time hereafter, since I retire when their Partiality to me is so great, that an Edition of the former Volumes of *Spectators*[2] of above Nine thousand each Book is already sold off, and the Tax on each half Sheet has brought into the Stamp-Office one Week with another above 20 *l.* a Week arising from this single Paper, notwithstanding it at first reduced it to less than half the number that was usually Printed before this Tax was laid.[3]

I humbly beseech the Continuance of this Inclination to favour what I may hereafter produce, and hope I have in many Occurrences of Life tasted so deeply of Pain and Sorrow, that I am proof against much more prosperous Circumstances than any Advantages to which my own Industry can possibly exalt me.

I am,

My Good-natured Reader,

Your most Obedient,

Most Obliged

Humble Servant,

Richard Steele.

as heading the list. The high praise given to 'the first I am going to Name' scarcely applies to Martyn, but it does to Addison.

[1] For these see Introduction, pp. xliii–lv.

[2] This must apply to volumes i and ii, published in January 1712, although it is not clear whether Steele is referring to 8vo or 12mo volumes, or both.

[3] Taken literally this statement would mean a printing of between 1,600 and 1,700 *Spectators* after the imposition of the tax in August 1712. Johnson, in his life of Addison, taking a figure of £21 a week, or £3. 10*s*. a day, estimates 1,680 as the number of sheets printed daily. Aitken (*Life of Steele*, i. 319–20) makes much the same computation, and concludes that the daily circulation before the imposition of the tax would be nearly 4,000. See also 'The First Printing of the *Spectator*', *Modern Philology*, xlvii (1950), 167.

Vos valete & plaudite. Ter.[a, 1]

The following Letter regards an ingenious Sett of Gentlemen, who have done me the Honour to make me one of their Society.[b]

Mr. SPECTATOR,   *Dec.* 4. 1712.

'THE Academy of *Painting*, lately established in *London*, having done you, and themselves, the Honour to chuse you one of their Directors, that Noble and Lovely Art, which before was entitled to your Regards, as a *Spectator*, has an additional Claim to you, and you seem to be under a double Obligation to take some care of her Interests.[2]

'The Honour of our Country is also concerned in the matter I am going to lay before you; we (and perhaps other Nations as well as we) have a National false Humility as well as a National Vain-Glory; and tho' we boast our selves to excell all the World in things wherein we are outdone abroad; in other things we attribute to others a Superiority which we our selves possess. This is what is done, particularly, in the Art of *Portrait* or *Face-Painting*.[3]

'*Painting* is an Art of a vast Extent, too great by much for any mortal Man to be in full Possession of, in all its Parts; 'tis enough if any one succeed in painting Faces, History, Battels, Landscapes, Sea-pieces, Fruit, Flowers, or Drolls, *&c*. Nay no Man ever was

---

[a] *Vos valete & plaudite.* Ter.] *In Fol. this motto is placed at the end of the following letter (p. 497).*
[b] The following . . . Society.] *P. S.* Give me leave, before I conclude, to insert a Letter which regards an Ingenious Sett of Gentlemen, who have done me the Honour to make me one of their Society. *Fol.*

---

[1] *Vos valete & plaudite.* (Farewell, and clap your hands.) The closing sentence in Terence's *Self-Tormentor, Eunuch,* and *Phormio.* The other plays end simply with *Plaudite.*
[2] Although Evelyn had sketched a plan for an Academy in 1682, it was not until the autumn of 1711 that the first Academy of drawing and painting from life was founded in England, by Sir Godfrey Kneller, Michael Dahl, Antonio Pellegrini, Louis Laguerre, Jonathan Richardson, and James Thornhill. Subscriptions at a guinea each were collected, and suitable premises were found in Great Queen Street, near Kneller's house. On St. Luke's Day (18 Oct.) 1711 over sixty men met to elect a Governor and twelve directors. Kneller at this time was unanimously chosen Governor, and remained in this office until 1716. Among the twelve new members who joined the Academy in the autumn of 1712 was Sir Richard Steele, who later became one of the Directors. See William T. Whitley, *Artists and their Friends in England 1700–1799* (Medici Society, 1928), i. 7–10.
[3] Face-painting, i.e. portrait-painting. The following notice appears among the advertisements in No. 251:

Whereas it hath been maliciously reported, that Mr. Benj. Ferrers, Face Painter, who is Deaf and Dumb, hath left off Painting; this is to inform the Publick, that he doth still continue his Profession of Painting, and that the said Report is villanous and false. N.B. He lives in Duke street, York Buildings.

excellent in all the Branches (tho' many[a] in Number) of these several Arts, for a distinct Art I take upon me to call every one of those several Kinds of Painting.

'And as one Man may be a good Landscape-Painter, but unable to paint a Face, or a History tollerably well, and so of the rest; one Nation may excell in some kinds of Painting, and other kinds may thrive better in other Climates.

'*Italy* may have the Preference of all other Nations for History-Painting; *Holland* for Drolls, and a neat finished manner of Working; *France*, for Gay, Janty, Fluttering Pictures; and *England* for Portraits; but to give the Honour of every one of these kinds of Painting to any one of those Nations on account of their Excellence in any of these parts of it, is like adjudging the Prize of Heroick, Dramatick, Lyrick or Burlesque Poetry, to him who has done well in any one of them.

'Where there are the greatest Genius's, and most Helps and Encouragements, 'tis reasonable to suppose an Art will arrive to the greatest Perfection: By this Rule let us consider our own Country with respect to Face-Painting. No Nation in the World delights so much in having their own, or Friends or Relations Pictures; whether from their National Good-Nature, or having a Love to Painting, and not being encouraged in that great Article of Religious Pictures, which the Purity of our Worship refuses the free use of, or from whatever other Cause. Our Helps are not inferior to those of any other People, but rather they are greater; for what the Antique Statues and Bas-reliefs which *Italy* enjoys are to the History-Painters, the beautiful and noble Faces with which *England* is confessed to abound, are to Face-Painters; and besides, we have the greatest number of the Works of the best Masters in that kind of any People, not without a competent number of those of the most excellent in every other part of Painting. And for Encouragement, the Wealth and Generosity of the *English* Nation affords that in such a degree, as Artists have no reason to complain.

'And accordingly in fact, Face-Painting is no where so well performed as in *England*: I know not whether it has lain in your way to observe it, but I have, and pretend to be a tolerable Judge. I have seen what is done Abroad, and can assure you that the Honour of that Branch of Painting is justly due to us. I appeal to the judicious Observers for the Truth of what I assert. If Foreigners have often-

[a] many] few *Fol.*

times, or even for the most part, excelled our Natives, it ought to be imputed to the Advantages they have met with *here*, join'd to their own Ingenuity and Industry, nor has any one Nation distinguished themselves so as to raise an Argument in favour of their Country; but 'tis to be observed, that neither *French* nor *Italians*, nor any one of either Nation, notwithstanding all our Prejudices in their Favour, have, or ever had, for any considerable time, any Character among us as Face-Painters.

'The Honour is due to our own Country; and has been so for near an Age: So that instead of going to *Italy*, or elsewhere, one that designs for Portrait Painting ought to study in *England*. Hither such should come from *Holland*, *France*, *Italy*, *Germany*, &c. as he that intends to Practise any other kind of Painting, should go to those Parts where 'tis in greatest Perfection. 'Tis said the Blessed Virgin descended from Heaven to Sit to S. *Luke*;[1] I dare venture to affirm, that if she should desire another *Madonna* to be Painted by the Life, she would come to *England*; and am of Opinion that your present President, Sir *Godfrey Kneller*, from his Improvement since he Arrived in this Kingdom, would perform that Office better than any Foreigner living.[2] I am with all possible Respect,

SIR,

Your most Humble, and
most Obedient Servant, &c.[3]

The Ingenious Letters sign'd the Weather-glass, *with several others, were receiv'd, but came too late.*

POSTSCRIPT.

It had not come to my Knowledge, when I left off the *Spectator*, that I owe several excellent Sentiments and agreeable Pieces in this Work to Mr. *Ince* of *Grey's-Inn*.[4]

R. STEELE.

---

[1] The ultimate source for this legend is the work on church history by Theodorus Lector, *Anagnostes* (*c.* 530), surviving only in excerpts (Migne, *Pat. Gr.* cxlvi. 1061–2). See Dorothee Klein, *St. Lukas als Maler der Maria* (Berlin, 1933), pp. 8, 93.

[2] Godfrey Kneller (1646–1723) came to England from Germany about 1675 and became the first President of the Academy of Painting in 1711. For his somewhat excessive vanity see Whitley, ii. 19–22.

[3] The quotation from Terence (above, p. 495) appeared at the end of this letter in the Folio edition.

[4] The Postscript was added in the 8vo and 12mo editions. For Ince see Introduction, p. lv.

No. 556   *Friday, June 18, 1714*[1]
[ADDISON]

> *Qualis ubi in lucem coluber, mala gramina pastus,*
> *Frigida sub terra tumidum quem bruma tegebat;*
> *Nunc positis novus exuviis, nitidusque juventa,*
> *Lubrica convolvit sublato pectore terga*
> *Arduus ad solem, et linguis micat ore trisulcis.*[a]
>
>   Virg.

UPON laying down the Office of SPECTATOR, I acquainted the World with my Design of electing a new Club, and of opening my Mouth in it after a most solemn Manner.[2] Both the Election and the Ceremony are now past; but not finding it so easy as I at first imagined, to break through a fifty Years Silence, I would not venture into the World under the Character of a Man who pretends to talk like other People, till I had arrived at a full Freedom of Speech.

I shall reserve for another time the History of such Club or Clubs of which I am now a Talkative, but unworthy Member; and shall here give an Account of this surprising Change which has been produced in me, and which I look upon to be as remarkable an Accident as any recorded in History, since that which happened to the Son of *Crœsus,* after having been many Years as much Tongue-tied as my self.[3]

Upon the first opening of my Mouth, I made a Speech consisting of about half a Dozen well turned Periods; but grew so very hoarse upon it, that for three Days together, instead of finding the Use of my Tongue, I was afraid that I had quite lost it. Besides, the un-usual Extention of my Muscles on this Occasion, made my Face ake on both Sides to such a Degree, that nothing but an invincible

---

[a] *After motto.* To be continued every *Monday, Wednesday,* and *Friday.* Fol.

[1] *Motto.* Virgil, *Aeneid,* 2. 471–5:

> So shines, renew'd in Youth, the crested Snake,
> Who slept the Winter in a thorny Brake:
> And casting off his Slough, when Spring returns,
> Now looks aloft, and with new Glory burns:
> Restor'd with pois'nous Herbs, his ardent sides
> Reflect the Sun, and rais'd on Spires he rides:
> High o're the Grass, hissing he rowls along,
> And brandishes by fits his forky Tongue. DRYDEN.

[2] See No. 550.   [3] Herodotus, *History,* 1. 85

Resolution and Perseverance, could have prevented me from falling back to my Monosyllables.

I afterwards made several Essays towards Speaking; and that I might not be startled at my own Voice, which has happened to me more than once, I used to read aloud in my Chamber, and have often stood in the Middle of the Street to call a Coach, when I knew there was none within Hearing.

When I was thus grown pretty well acquainted with my own Voice, I laid hold of all Opportunities to exert it. Not caring however to speak much by my self, and to draw upon me the whole Attention of those I conversed with, I used, for some time, to walk every Morning in the *Mall*, and talk in Chorus with a Parcel of *Frenchmen*. I found my Modesty greatly relieved by the communicative Temper of this Nation, who are so very sociable, as to think they are never better Company than when they are all opening at the same time.[1]

I then fancied I might receive great Benefit from Female Conversation, and that I should have a Convenience of talking with the greater Freedom, when I was not under any Impediment of thinking: I therefore threw my self into an Assembly of Ladies, but could not for my Life get in a Word among them; and found that if I did not change my Company, I was in Danger of being reduced to my primitive Taciturnity.

The Coffee-houses have ever since been my chief Places of Resort, where I have made the greatest Improvements; in order to which I have taken a particular Care never to be of the same Opinion with the Man I conversed with. I was a Tory at *Button*'s[2] and a Whig at *Childe*'s;[3] a Friend to the *Englishman*[4] or an Advocate for the *Examiner*, as it best served my Turn:[5] Some fancy me a great Enemy to the *French* King, though, in reality, I only make use of

---

[1] Addison's constant view of the French: in an early letter to John Hough, Bishop of Lichfield, he speaks of 'their National Fault of being so very Talkative' (October 1699; *Letters*, ed. Graham, p. 8).

[2] This coffee-house, established by Daniel Button, a former servant of the Countess of Warwick, was, of course, a great centre of the Whigs. It had been set up apparently since the first series of the *Spectator* had concluded in December 1712. The *Guardian* (1713) received letters at Button's, and it was here that Addison's 'little Senate' held forth, much to the annoyance of the Tories.

[3] For Child's coffee-house see No. 16 (vol. i).

[4] The *Englishman* was the Whig paper conducted by Steele as a sequel to the *Guardian*. The first series ran from 6 Oct. 1713 to 15 Feb. 1714 (57 numbers). A second series of 38 numbers was to appear later, from 11 July to 21 Nov. 1715. See the edition by Rae Blanchard (Oxford, 1955).

[5] For the *Examiner*, the chief party paper of the Tories, see No. 367 (vol. iii).

him for a Help to Discourse. In short, I wrangle and dispute for Exercise; and have carried this Point so far, that I was once like to have been run through the Body for making a little too free with my Betters.

In a Word, I am quite another Man to what I was.

> . . . *Nil fuit unquam*
> *Tam dispar sibi* . . .[1]

My old Acquaintance scarce know me; nay I was asked the other Day by a Jew at *Jonathan's*, whether I was not related to a dumb Gentleman who used to come to that Coffee-house?[2] But I think I never was better pleased in my Life than about a Week ago, when, as I was battling it across the Table with a young Templar, his Companion gave him a Pull by the Sleeve, begging him to come away, for that the old Prig would talk him to Death.

Being now a very good Proficient in Discourse, I shall appear in the World with this Addition to my Character, that my Country-men may reap the Fruits of my new acquired Loquacity.

Those who have been present at publick Disputes in the University, know that it is usual to maintain Heresies for Argument's sake. I have heard a Man a most impudent Socinian for Half an Hour, who has been an Orthodox Divine all his Life after.[3] I have taken the same Method to accomplish my self in the Gift of Utterance, having talked above a Twelve-month not so much for the Benefit of my Hearers as of my self. But since I have now gained the Faculty I have been so long endeavouring after, I intend to make a right Use of it, and shall think my self obliged, for the future, to speak always in Truth and Sincerity of Heart. While a Man is learning to fence, he practises both on Friend and Foe; but when he is a Master in the Art, he never exerts it but on what he thinks the right Side.

That this last Allusion may not give my Reader a wrong Idea of my Design in this Paper, I must here inform him, that the Author of it is of no Faction, that he is a Friend to no Interests but those

---

[1] Horace, *Satires*, 1. 3. 18, altered. (Nothing was ever so unlike itself.) This had been used as the motto of No. 338.

[2] For Jonathan's see No. 1 (vol. i).

[3] One of the anti-Trinitarian sect founded by Laelius and Faustus Socinus, two Italian theologians (uncle and nephew) of the sixteenth century. According to Pope the freedom of William III's government 'Did all the dregs of bold Socinus drain' (*Essay on Criticism*, 545).

of Truth and Virtue, nor a Foe to any but those of Vice and Folly. Tho' I make more Noise in the World than I used to do, I am still resolved to act in it as an indifferent SPECTATOR. It is not my Ambition to increase the Number either of Whigs or Tories, but of wise and good Men; and I could heartily wish there were not Faults common to both Parties, which afford me sufficient Matter to work upon, without descending to those which are peculiar to either.

If in a Multitude of Counsellors there is Safety,[1] we ought to think our selves the securest Nation in the World. Most of our Garrets are inhabited by Statesmen, who watch over the Liberties of their Country, and make a Shift to keep themselves from starving by taking into their Care the Properties of their[a] Fellow-Subjects.

As these Politicians of both Sides have already worked the Nation into a most unnatural Ferment, I shall be so far from endeavouring to raise it to a greater Height, that, on the contrary, it shall be the chief Tendency of my Papers to inspire my Countrymen with a mutual Good-will and Benevolence.[2] Whatever Faults either Party may be guilty of, they are rather inflamed than cured by those Reproaches which they cast upon one another. The most likely Method of rectifying any Man's Conduct, is, by recommending to him the Principles of Truth and Honour, Religion and Virtue; and so long as he acts with an Eye to these Principles, whatever Party he is of, he cannot fail of being a good *Englishman*, and a Lover of his Country.

As for the Persons concerned in this Work, the Names of all of them, or at least of such as desire it, shall be published hereafter: Till which time I must entreat the courteous Reader to suspend his Curiosity, and rather to consider what is written, than who they are that write it.

Having thus adjusted all necessary Preliminaries with my

a of their] of all their *Fol.*

---

[1] Prov. xi. 14, xxiv. 6.

[2] Party spirit was at a high pitch during the summer of 1714, with apprehensions of the Queen's death and uncertainty over the succession to the throne. On the day following the publication of this number Thomas Harley wrote to Swift:

But, seriously, you never heard such bellowing about the town of the state of the nation, especially among the sharpers, sellers of bear-skins [i.e. stock-jobbers], and the rest of that kind: nor such crying . . . and squalling among the ladies; insomuch that it has at last reached the House of Commons; which I am sorry for, because it is hot and uneasy sitting there in this season of the year (Swift, *Correspondence*, ed. Ball, ii. 156).

Reader, I shall not trouble him with any more prefatory Discourses, but proceed in my old Method, and entertain him with Speculations on every useful Subject that falls in my Way.[a] [1]

No. 557

[ADDISON]

Monday, June 21, 1714 [2]

Quippe domum timet ambiguam, Tyriosque bilingues.[b]

Virg.

THERE is nothing, says *Plato*, *so delightful, as the hearing or the speaking of Truth.*[3] For this Reason there is no Conversation so agreeable as that of the Man of Integrity, who hears without any Intention to betray, and speaks without any Intention to deceive.

Among all the Accounts which are given of *Cato*, I do not remember one that more redounds to his Honour than the following Passage related by *Plutarch*.[4] As an Advocate was pleading the Cause of his Client before one of the Prætors, he could only produce a single Witness in a Point where the Law required the Testimony of two Persons; upon which the Advocate insisted on the Integrity of that Person whom he had produced: But the Prætor told him, That where the Law required two Witnesses he would not accept of one, tho' it were *Cato* himself. Such a Speech from a Person who sat at the Head of a Court of Justice, while *Cato* was still living, shews us more than a thousand Examples the high Reputation this great Man had gained among his Contemporaries upon the Account of his Sincerity.

[a] At the end of No. 556: *Letters for the SPECTATOR, will be taken in (as formerly) by S. Buckley in Amen-Corner, and J. Tonson in the Strand.* Fol.[5]
[b] *Below Motto.* To be continued every *Monday, Wednesday,* and *Friday.* Fol.

---

[1] Lillie (i. 293) prints a letter signed Philander, dated from 'Fernival's Inn', 26 June 1714, expressing the 'unspeakable delight that I find you have again begun to resume the thread of your former discourses in those ingenious papers which have so much obliged the town; I mean, your spectators.
[2] *Motto.* Virgil, *Aeneid*, I. 661:
> For much she fear'd the *Tyrians*, double tongu'd,
> And knew the Town to *Juno*'s care belong'd. DRYDEN.
[3] Diogenes Laertius, *Lives of the Philosophers*, 3. 39.
[4] Plutarch, *Cato the Younger*, 19. 4.
[5] Buckley had moved, in February of this year, from the Dolphin in Little Britain to Amen Corner (announcement in *Daily Courant*, 27 Feb. 1714).

When such an inflexible Integrity is a little softened and qualified by the Rules of Conversation and Good-breeding, there is not a more shining Virtue in the whole Catalogue of Social Duties. A Man however ought to take great Care not to polish himself out of his Veracity, nor to refine his Behaviour to the Prejudice of his Virtue.

This Subject is exquisitely treated in the most elegant Sermon of the great *British* Preacher.[1] I shall beg leave to transcribe out of it two or three Sentences, as a proper Introduction to a very curious Letter which I shall make the chief Entertainment of this Speculation.

'The old *English* Plainness and Sincerity, that generous Integrity of Nature, and Honesty of Disposition, which always argues true Greatness of Mind, and is usually accompanied with undaunted Courage and Resolution, is in a great Measure lost among us.

'The Dialect[2] of Conversation is now-a-days so swelled with Vanity and Compliment, and so surfeited (as I may say) of Expressions of Kindness and Respect, that if a Man that lived an Age or two ago should return into the World again, he would really want a Dictionary to help him to understand his own Language, and to know the true intrinsick Value of the Phrase in fashion; and would hardly, at first, believe at what a low Rate the highest Strains and Expressions of Kindness imaginable do commonly pass in current Payment; and when he should come to understand it, it would be a great while before he could bring himself with a good Countenance and a good Conscience, to converse with Men upon equal Terms in their own Way.'

I have by me a Letter which I look upon as a great Curiosity, and which may serve as an Exemplification to the foregoing Passage cited out of this most excellent Prelate. It is said to have been written in King *Charles* II's Reign by the Ambassador of *Bantam*, a little after his Arrival in *England*.[3]

---

[1] For Addison, as always, this is Archbishop Tillotson. The sentences here quoted are from the sermon, 'Of Sincerity towards God and Man', preached on 29 July 1694 (*Works*, ed. 1728, ii. 6), and had been quoted earlier by Steele in No. 103.

[2] Here in the primary meaning of 'language, speech'.

[3] Bantam was formerly an important trading station and seaport in the northwest extremity of the island of Java, about fifty miles west of Batavia. The visit of the Ambassador took place in May 1682. Luttrell (i. 182) describes the entry:

The 9th, the ambassador from the king of Bantam made his publick entry: he landed at the Tower, and was conducted in his majesties coach, with a numerous train of coaches and six horses, and many gentlemen of the East India company on horseback: his own retinue, being about 30 persons, with spears and targets,

Master,

'THE People where I now am have Tongues further from their Hearts than from *London* to *Bantam*, and thou knowest the Inhabitants of one of these Places does not know what is done in the other. They call thee and thy Subjects Barbarians, because we speak what we mean; and account themselves a civilized People, because they speak one thing and mean another: Truth they call Barbarity, and Falshood Politeness. Upon my first landing, one who was sent from the King of this Place to meet me told me, *That he was extreamly sorry for the Storm I had met with just before my Arrival.* I was troubled to hear him grieve and afflict himself upon my Account; but in less than a Quarter of an Hour he smiled, and was as merry as if nothing had happened. Another who came with him told me by my Interpreter, *He should be glad to do me any Service that lay in his Power.* Upon which I desired him to carry one of my Portmantaus for me; but instead of serving me according to his Promise, he laughed, and bid another do it. I lodged the first Week at the House of one who desired me *to think my self at home, and to consider his House as my own.* Accordingly, I the next Morning began to knock down one of the Walls of it, in order to let in the fresh Air, and had packed up some of the Houshold-Goods, of which I intended to have made thee a Present: But the false Varlet no sooner saw me falling to work, but he sent Word to desire me to give over, for that he would have no such Doings in his House. I had not been long in this Nation, before I was told by one for whom I had asked a certain Favour from the chief of the King's Servants, whom they here call the Lord-Treasurer, That I had *eternally obliged him.* I was so surprized at his Gratitude, that I could not forbear saying, What Service is there which one Man can do for another, that can oblige him to all Eternity! However I only asked him for my Reward, that he would lend me his eldest Daughter during my Stay in this Country; but I quickly found that he was as treacherous as the rest of his Countrymen.

'At my first going to Court, one of the great Men almost put me out of Countenance, by asking *ten thousand Pardons* of me for only treading by Accident upon my Toe. They call this kind of Lye a

clad in Indian stuffs, with sculp caps on their heads, were in the coaches; so they passed on in great order to the house prepared for him at Charingcrosse, where the Russian ambassador formerly lay.

See also Sir William Foster, *John Company* (1926), pp. 97–120.

Compliment; for when they are civil to a great Man, they tell him Untruths, for which thou wouldest order any of thy Officers of State to receive a hundred Blows upon his Foot. I do not know how I shall negotiate any thing with this People, since there is so little Credit to be given to 'em. When I go to see the King's Scribe, I am generally told that he is not at home, tho' perhaps I saw him go into his House almost the very Moment before. Thou wouldest fancy that the whole Nation are Physicians, for the first Question they always ask me, is, *how I do?* I have this Question put to me above a hundred times a Day. Nay, they are not only thus inquisitive after my Health, but wish it in a more solemn Manner with a full Glass in their Hands every time I sit with them at Table, tho' at the same time they wou'd perswade me to drink their Liquors in such Quantities, as I have found by Experience will make me sick. They often pretend to pray for thy Health also in the same Manner; but I have more Reason to expect it from the Goodness of thy Constitution, than the Sincerity of their Wishes. May thy Slave escape in Safety from this double-tongued Race of Men, and live to lay himself once more at thy Feet in thy Royal City of *Bantam*.'

No. 558   *Wednesday, June 23, 1714*[1]

[ADDISON]

> *Qui fit, Mæcenas, ut nemo, quam sibi sortem*
> *Seu ratio dederit, seu fors objecerit, illa*
> *Contentus vivat: laudet diversa sequentes?*
> *O Fortunati mercatores, gravis annis*
> *Miles ait, multo jam fractus membra labore!*
> *Contra mercator, navim jactantibus austris,*
> *Militia est potior. Quid enim? concurritur? horæ*
> *Momento cita mors venit, aut victoria læta.*
> *Agricolam laudat juris legumque peritus,*
> *Sub galli cantum consultor ubi ostia pulsat.*
> *Ille, datis vadibus, qui rure extractus in urbem est,*
> *Solos felices viventes clamat in urbe.*

[*For note 1 see the following page.*

Cætera de genere hoc (adeo sunt multa) loquacem
Delassare valent Fabium. Ne te morer, audi
Quo rem deducam. Si quis Deus, en ego dicat,
Jam faciam quod vultis: eris tu, qui modo miles,
Mercator: tu consultus modo, rusticus. Hinc vos,
Vos hinc mutatis discedite partibus. Eja,
Quid statis? Nolint. Atqui licet esse beatis....

Hor.

IT is a celebrated Thought of *Socrates*, that if all the Misfortunes of Mankind were cast into a publick Stock, in order to be equally distributed among the whole Species, those who now think themselves the most unhappy, would prefer the share they are already possess'd of, before that which would fall to them by such a Division.[2] *Horace* has carried this Thought a great deal further in the Motto of my Paper, which implies that the Hardships or Misfortunes we lie under, are more easy to us than those of any

---

[1] *Motto.* Horace, *Satires,* I. I. I–19:

> Whence comes, *my Lord,* this general discontent? }
> Why all dislike the *State* that *Chance* hath sent, }
> Or their own *Choice* procur'd? why All repent? }
> The weary *Souldier* now grown old in Wars,
> With bleeding Eyes looks o're his Wounds and Scars;
> *Curse that E're I the trade of War began,*
> *Ah me! the Merchant is a happy Man:*
> The *Merchant*, when the Waves and Winds are high, }
> Crys, happy happy *Men at Arms*; for why, }
> You fight, and streight comes Death, or joyful Victory. }
> The *Lawyer* that's disturb'd before 'tis light
> By restless Clients, or that wakes all night,
> Grows sick; and when He finds his rest is gone,
> Crys, happy *Farmers* that can sleep till Noon:
> The weary *Client* thinks the *Lawyer* blest,
> And craves a *City Life*, for that's the best.
> So many Instances in every state, }
> That mourn their own, but praise their Neighbours fate, }
> 'Twould tire even bawling *Fabius* to relate. }
> But to be short, see I'le adjust the Thing:
> Suppose some *God* should say I'le please you now,
> You *Lawyer* leave the *Bar* and take the *Plough*;
> You *Souldier* too shall be a *Merchant* made,
> Go, Go, and follow each his *proper* trade:
> How? what refuse? and discontented still? CREECH.

[2] Plutarch, 'A Letter to Apollonius', *Moralia,* 106B; cf. Herodotus, *History,* 7. 152. Attributed to Solon by Valerius Maximus, 7. 2. 2. It is cited by Burton (*Anatomy of Melancholy*, II. III. i. 1) who also quotes Horace, *Satires,* I. I. 17–20, the concluding lines of the passage which forms the motto of this number.

other Person would be, in case we could change Conditions with him.

As I was ruminating on these two Remarks, and seated in my Elbow-Chair, I insensibly fell asleep; when, on a sudden, methought there was a Proclamation made by *Jupiter*, that every Mortal should bring in his Griefs and Calamities, and throw them together in a Heap. There was a large Plain appointed for this purpose. I took my Stand in the Center of it, and saw with a great deal of Pleasure the whole human Species marching one after another, and throwing down their several Loads, which immediately grew up into a prodigious Mountain that seemed to rise above the Clouds.

There was a certain Lady of a thin airy Shape, who was very active in this Solemnity. She carried a magnifying Glass in one of her Hands, and was cloathed in a loose flowing Robe, embroidered with several Figures of Fiends and Spectres, that discovered themselves in a Thousand chimerical Shapes as her Garment hovered in the Wind. There was something wild and distracted in her Look. Her name was *FANCY*.[1] She led up every Mortal to the appointed Place, after having very officiously[2] assisted him in making up his Pack, and laying it upon his Shoulders. My Heart melted within me to see my Fellow-Creatures groaning under their respective Burthens, and to consider that prodigious Bulk of human Calamities which lay before me.

There were however several Persons who gave me great Diversion upon this Occasion. I observed one bringing in a Fardel very carefully concealed under an old embroidered Cloak, which, upon his throwing it into the Heap, I discovered to be Poverty. Another, after a great deal of puffing, threw down his Luggage; which, upon examining, I found to be his Wife.

There were Multitudes of Lovers saddled with very whimsical Burthens, composed of Darts and Flames; but, what was very odd, tho' they sighed as if their Hearts would break under these Bundles of Calamities, they could not perswade themselves to cast them into the Heap when they came up to it; but after a few faint efforts, shook their Heads and marched away as heavy loaden as they came. I saw Multitudes of old Women throw down their Wrinkles, and several young ones who stripped themselves of a tawny Skin. There were very great Heaps of red Noses, large Lips and rusty

[1] Cf. the picture of Fancy in No. 514.
[2] I.e. obligingly, courteously.

Teeth. The Truth of it is, I was surprized to see the greatest Part of the Mountain made up of bodily Deformities. Observing one advancing towards the Heap with a larger Cargo than ordinary upon his Back, I found upon his near Approach, that it was only a natural Hump, which he disposed of with great Joy of Heart among this Collection of humane Miseries. There were likewise Distempers of all Sorts, tho' I could not but observe that there were many more imaginary than real. One little Packet I could not but take Notice of, which was a Complication of all the Diseases incident to human Nature, and was in the Hand of a great many fine People: This was called the Spleen.[1] But what most of all surprized me, was a Remark I made, that there was not a single Vice or Folly thrown into the whole Heap: At which I was very much astonished, having concluded within my self that every one would take this Opportunity of getting rid of his Passions, Prejudices, and Frailties.

I took Notice in particular of a very profligate Fellow, who I did not Question came loaden with his Crimes, but upon searching into his Bundle, I found that instead of throwing his Guilt from him, he had only laid down his Memory. He was followed by another worthless Rogue, who flung away his Modesty instead of his Ignorance.

When the whole Race of Mankind had thus cast their Burthens, the *Phantome* which had been so busy on this Occasion, seeing me an idle Spectator of what passed, approached towards me. I grew uneasy at her Presence, when of a sudden she held her magnifying Glass full before my Eyes. I no sooner saw my Face in it, but was startled at the Shortness of it, which now appeared to me in its utmost Aggravation. The immoderate Breadth of the Features made me very much out of Humour with my own Countenance, upon which I threw it from me like a Mask. It happened very luckily, that one who stood by me had just before thrown down his Visage, which, it seems, was too long for him. It was indeed extended to a most shameful length; I believe the very Chin was, modestly speaking, as long as my whole Face. We had both of us an Opportunity of mending our selves, and, all the Contributions being now brought in, every Man was at Liberty to exchange his Misfortune for those of another Person. But as there arose many new Incidents in the Sequel of my Vision, I shall reserve them for the Subject of my next Paper.

[1] See No. 53 (vol. i).

Quid causæ est, meritò quin illis Jupiter ambas
Iratus buccas inflet: neque se fore posthac
Tam facilem dicat, votis ut præbeat aurem?

                                                    Hor.

IN my last Paper, I gave my Reader a Sight of that Mountain of Miseries which was made up of those several Calamities that afflict the Minds of Men. I saw, with unspeakable Pleasure, the whole Species thus delivered from its Sorrows, though, at the same time, as we stood round the Heap, and surveyed the several Materials of which it was composed, there was scarce a Mortal in this vast Multitude who did not discover what he thought Pleasures and Blessings of Life; and wonderd how the Owners of them ever came to look upon them as Burthens and Grievances.

As we were regarding very attentively this Confusion of Miseries, this Chaos of Calamity, *Jupiter* issued out a second Proclamation, that every one was now at Liberty to exchange his Affliction, and to return to his Habitation with any such other Bundle as should be delivered to him.

Upon this, *FANCY* began again to bestir her self, and, parcelling out the whole Heap with incredible Activity, recommended to every one his particular Packet. The Hurry and Confusion at this time was not to be expressed. Some Observations, which I made upon the Occasion, I shall communicate to the Publick. A venerable grey-headed Man, who had laid down the Cholick, and who I found wanted an Heir to his Estate, snatched up an undutiful Son that had been thrown into the Heap by his angry Father. The graceless Youth, in less than a quarter of an Hour, pulled the old Gentleman by the Beard, and had like to have knocked his Brains out; so that meeting the true Father, who came towards him in a Fit of the Gripes, he begged him to take his Son again, and give him back his Cholick; but they were incapable either of them to recede from the Choice they had made. A poor Gally-Slave, who

---

[1] *Motto.* Horace, *Satires*, I. I. 20–22:

> Now would not this vex *Jove*, and make him rage?
> Hath he not reason now to scourge the Age?
> And puff and swear He'd never hear again? CREECH.

had thrown down his Chains, took up the Gout in their stead, but made such wry Faces, that one might easily perceive he was no great Gainer by the Bargain. It was pleasant enough to see the several Exchanges that were made, for Sickness against Poverty, Hunger against want of Appetite, and Care against Pain.

The Female World were very busie among themselves in bartering for Features; one was trucking[1] a Lock of grey Hairs for a Carbuncle, another was making over a short Waste for a pair of round Shoulders, and a third cheapning a bad Face for a lost Reputation: But on all these Occasions, there was not one of them who did not think the new Blemish, as soon as she had got it into her Possession, much more disagreeable than the old one. I made the same Observation on every other Misfortune or Calamity which every one in the Assembly brought upon himself, in lieu of what he had parted with; whether it be that all the Evils which befall us are in some Measure suited and proportioned to our Strength, or that every Evil becomes more supportable by our being accustomed to it, I shall not determine.

I could not for my Heart forbear pitying the poor hump-back'd Gentleman mentioned in the former Paper, who went off a very well-shaped person with a Stone in his Bladder; nor the fine Gentleman who had struck up this Bargain with him that limped through a whole Assembly of Ladies who used to admire him, with a Pair of Shoulders peeping over his Head.

I must not omit my own particular Adventure. My Friend with the long Visage had no sooner taken upon him my short Face, but he made such a grotesque Figure in it, that as I looked upon him I could not forbear laughing at my self, insomuch that I put my own Face out of Countenance. The poor Gentleman was so sensible of the Ridicule, that I found he was ashamed of what he had done: On the other side I found that I my self had no great Reason to triumph, for as I went to touch my Forehead I missed the Place and clapped my Finger upon my upper Lip. Besides, as my Nose was exceeding prominent, I gave it two or three unlucky Knocks as I was playing my Hand about my Face, and aiming at some other part of it. I saw two other Gentlemen by me, who were in the same ridiculous Circumstances. These had made a foolish Swop between a couple of thick bandy Legs, and two long Trapsticks[2] that had

---

[1] Here used in the sense of exchanging commodities for profit.
[2] Sticks used in the game of trap or trap-ball.

no Calfs to them. One of these looked like a Man walking upon Stilts, and was so lifted up into the Air above his ordinary Height, that his Head turned round with it, while the other made such awkward Circles, as he attempted to walk, that he scarce knew how to move forward upon his new Supporters: Observing him to be a pleasant kind of Fellow, I stuck my Cane in the Ground, and told him I would lay him a Bottle of Wine, that he did not march up to it on a Line, that I drew for him, in a quarter of an Hour.

The Heap was at last distributed among the two Sexes, who made a most piteous Sight as they wandered up and down under the Pressure of their several Burthens. The whole Plain was filled with Murmurs and Complaints, Groans and Lamentations. *Jupiter* at length, taking Compassion on the poor Mortals, ordered them a second time to lay down their Loads, with a Design to give every one his own again. They discharged themselves with a great deal of Pleasure, after which, the Phantome, who had led them into such gross Delusions, was commanded to disappear. There was sent in her stead a Goddess of a quite different Figure. Her Motions were steady and composed, and her Aspect serious but cheerful. She every now and then cast her Eyes towards Heaven, and fixed them upon *Jupiter*: Her Name was *PATIENCE*. She had no sooner placed her self by the Mount of Sorrows, but, what I thought very remarkable, the whole Heap sunk to such a Degree, that it did not appear a third part so big as it was before. She afterwards returned every Man his own proper Calamity, and, teaching him how to bear it in the most commodious Manner, he marched off with it contentedly, being very well pleased that he had not been left to his own Choice, as to the kind of Evils which fell to his Lot.

Besides the several Pieces of Morality to be drawn out of this Vision, I learnt from it, never to repine at my own Misfortunes, or to envy the Happiness of another, since it is impossible for any Man to form a right Judgment of his Neighbours Sufferings; for which Reason also I have determined never to think too lightly of another's Complaints, but to regard the Sorrows of my Fellow Creatures with Sentiments of Humanity and Compassion.

No. 560   *Monday, June 28, 1714*[1]
[BUDGELL]

> *. . . Verba intermissa retentat.*
> Ov. Met.

EVERY one has heard of the famous Conjurer, who, according
to the Opinion of the Vulgar, has studied himself *dumb*; for
which Reason, as it is believed, he delivers out all his Oracles in
Writing.[2] Be that as it will, the blind *Tiresias*[3] was not more famous
in *Greece*, than this dumb Artist has been for some Years last past
in the Cities of *London* and *Westminster*. Thus much for the profound Gentleman who honours me with the following Epistle.

SIR,   *From my Cell*, June 24, 1714.
'BEING informed that you have lately got the Use of your
Tongue, I have some Thoughts of following your Example,
that I may be a *Fortune-teller* properly speaking. I am grown weary
of my Taciturnity, and having served my Country many Years
under the Title of the dumb Doctor, I shall now Prophesie by
Word of Mouth, and (as Mr. *Lee* says of the Magpie, who you know
was a great Fortune-teller among the Ancients) *chatter* Futurity.[4]
I have hitherto chosen to receive Questions and return Answers
in Writing, that I might avoid the Tediousness and Trouble of
Debates; my Querists being generally of a Humour to think, that

---

[1] *Motto*. Ovid, *Metamorphoses*, 1. 746: Reiterates the broken sounds and strives
to speak.

This number has been generally attributed to Addison, although Tickell did not
include it in the *Works*. Notes for the first letter and for the letter from Oxford in
this number exist among the Tickell papers in Addison's hand (Hodgart, pp. 376,
382); these portions may be assigned to Addison; the rest consists of genuine
contributions or matter prepared by Budgell.

[2] Duncan Campbell. See No. 31 (vol. i).

[3] The Theban soothsayer.

[4] Dryden and Lee's *Oedipus*, Act IV. In Act IV, written by Lee, Oedipus addresses
Tiresias:

> Now, Dotard; now, thou blind old wizard Prophet,
> Where are your boding Ghosts, your Altars now;
> Your Birds of knowledge, that, in dusky Air,
> Chatter Futurity. . . .

It does not appear that the magpie was 'a great Fortune-teller among the Ancients'.
The magpie (Latin *pica*) is associated with talkativeness, but not prophecy; the
similarity of the word to *picus* (woodpecker) or *Picus* (a woodland god) may account
for the confusion. The sixth-century *Etymologiae* of Isidore of Seville (12. 7. 46–47)
distinguishes between *pica*, the fabulous talker and imitator of the human voice,
and *picus Martius* (cf. Ovid, *Metamorphoses*, 14. 320 ff.), the bird with an air of the
supernatural and prophetic about it: 'Iste est picus Martius; nam alia est pica.'

they have never Predictions enough for their Mony. In short, Sir, my Case has been something like that of those discreet Animals the Monkeys, who, as the *Indians* tell us, can speak if they wou'd, but purposely avoid it that they may not be made to Work. I have hitherto gained a Livelyhood by holding my Tongue, but shall now open my Mouth in order to fill it. If I appear a little Word-bound in my first Solutions and Responses, I hope it will not be imputed to any want of Foresight, but to the long Disuse of Speech. I doubt not by this Invention to have all my former Customers over again, for if I have promised any of them Lovers or Husbands, Riches or good Luck, it is my Design to confirm to them *vivâ voce* what I have already given them under my Hand. If you will honour me with a Visit, I will compliment you with the first opening of my Mouth, and if you please you may make an entertaining Dialogue out of the Conversation of two Dumb Men. Excuse this Trouble, worthy Sir, from one who has been a long time

> *Your Silent Admirer,*
> Cornelius Agrippa.'[1]

I have received the following Letter, or rather *Billet-doux*, from a pert young Baggage, who congratulates with me upon the same Occasion.

Dear Mr. Prate-apace, *June* 23, 1714.

'I AM a Member of a Female Society who call our selves the *Chit-Chat* Club, and am ordered, by the whole Sisterhood, to congratulate you upon the Use of your Tongue.[2] We have all of us a mighty Mind to hear you talk, and if you will take your Place among us for an Evening, we have unanimously agreed to allow you one Minute in ten, without Interruption.

> *I am, SIR,*
> *Your Humble Servant,*
> S. T.'

P. S. '*You may find us at my Lady* Betty Clack's, *who will leave Orders with her Porter, that if an elderly Gentleman, with a short Face, enquires for her, he shall be admitted and no Questions asked.*'

---

[1] Cornelius Agrippa (1486–1535), the German philosopher and alchemist, author of *De occulta philosophia, De incertitudine et vanitate scientiarum,* and other works.
[2] The periodical essay *Chit-Chat,* of which three numbers (6 to 16 Mar. 1716) are extant, has been attributed to Steele. See Aitken (*Life,* ii. 87–91) and John Loftis (*Huntington Library Quarterly,* xiv (1950), 57–60, and *PMLA,* lxvi (1951), 197–210).

As this particular Paper shall consist wholly of what I have received from my Correspondents, I shall fill up the remaining part of it with other congratulatory Letters of the same Nature.

SIR, *Oxford, June 25, 1714.*
'WE are here wonderfully pleas'd with the Opening of your Mouth, and very frequently open ours in Approbation of your Design; especially since we find you are resolved to preserve your Taciturnity, as to all Party matters. We do not Question but you are as great an Orator as Sir *Hudibras*, of whom the Poet sweetly Sings,

> . . . *He could not ope*
> *His Mouth, but out there flew a Trope.*[1]

If you will send us down the Half-dozen well-turned Periods, that produced such dismal Effects in your Muscles, we will deposite them near an old Manuscript of *Tully*'s Orations, among the Archives of the University, for we all agree with you that there is not a more remarkable Accident recorded in History, since that which happened to the Son of *Crœsus*,[2] nay, I believe you might have gone higher, and have added *Balaam*'s Ass.[3] We are impatient to see more of your Productions, and expect what Words will next fall from you, with as much Attention as those who were set to watch the speaking Head which *Fryer Bacon* formerly erected in this Place.[4] We are,

> *Worthy SIR,*
> *Your most Humble Servants,*
> B. R. T. D. &c.'

Honest SPEC, *Middle-Temple, June 24.*
'I AM very glad to hear that thou beginnest to Prate; and find, by thy Yesterday's Vision, thou art so used to it, that thou canst not forbear talking in thy Sleep. Let me only advise thee to speak like other Men, for I am afraid thou wilt be very Queer, if thou dost not intend to use the Phrases in Fashion, as thou callest them

[1] *Hudibras,* I. i. 81–82. [2] Herodotus, *History,* I. 85. Cf. No. 556.
[3] Num. xxii. 28.
[4] Roger Bacon, who had a reputation for necromancy, was thought to have constructed a brazen head capable of speech. See Robert Greene's comedy, *Friar Bacon and Friar Bungay* (1594). One of the puppet shows of Powell was called *The Comical History of Fryar Bacon, Bungy and their Man Miles*; the *Daily Courant* advertises performances 'at Punch's Theatre in the Little Piazza, Covent Garden', on 19, 20, 21, 22, 23, and 24 Nov. 1711, and on 21 and 22 Dec. 1711.

in thy Second Paper. Hast thou a Mind to pass for a *Bantamite*,[1] or
to make us all *Quakers?* I do assure thee, Dear SPEC, I am not
Polished out of my Veracity, when I subscribe my self

> *Thy Constant Admirer,*
> *and Humble Servant,*
> Frank Townly.'

No. 561   *Wednesday, June 30, 1714*[2]

[ADDISON]

> *. . . Paulatim abolere Sichæum*
> *Incipit, & vivo tentat prævertere amore*
> *Jampridem resides animos desuetaque corda.*
> Virg.

SIR,

'I AM a tall, broad-shoulderd, impudent, black Fellow, and, as
I thought, every way qualified for a rich Widow: But, after
having tried my Fortune for above three Years together, I have not
been able to get one single Relict in the Mind. My first Attacks
were generally successful, but always broke off as soon as they came
to the Word *Settlement*. Though I have not improved my Fortune
this way, I have my Experience, and have learnt several Secrets
which may be of Use to those unhappy Gentlemen who are commonly distinguished by the Name of Widow-hunters, and who do
not know that this Tribe of Women are, generally speaking, as
much upon the Catch[3] as themselves. I shall here communicate to
you the Mysteries of a certain Female Cabal of this Order, who call
themselves the *Widow-Club*.[a] This Club consists of nine experienced

---

[a] *Widow-Club.*] *Italics added in 8vo, 12mo*

[1] See No. 557.
[2] *Motto.* Virgil, *Aeneid*, I. 720–2:

> Works in the pliant Bosom of the Fair;
> And moulds her Heart anew, and blots her former Care.
> The dead is to the living Love resign'd. DRYDEN.

Tickell included No. 561 in his edition of Addison's *Works*, but it is not listed in
the Tickell manuscript among the numbers 'by Mr Addison'. It may be a genuine
contribution from an anonymous correspondent, revised and worked over by
Addison.
[3] *OED* gives examples of this obsolete phrase ('to lie in wait') from 1630.

Dames, who take their Places once a Week round a large oval Table.

'I. Mrs. President is a Person who has disposed of six Husbands, and is now determined to take a seventh, being of Opinion, that there is as much Vertue in the Touch of a seventh Husband as of a seventh Son.[1] Her Comrades are as follow.

'II. Mrs. *Snapp*, who has four Jointures by four different Bed-fellows of four different Shires. She is at present upon the Point of Marriage with a *Middlesex* Man, and is said to have an Ambition of extending her Possessions through all the Counties in *England* on this side the *Trent*.

'III. Mrs. *Medlar*, who after two Husbands and a Gallant, is now wedded to an old Gentleman of sixty. Upon her making her Report to the Club after a Week's Cohabitation, she is still allowed to sit as a Widow, and accordingly takes her Place at the Board.

'IV. The Widow *Quick*, married within a Fortnight after the Death of her last Husband. Her *Weeds* have served her thrice, and are still as good as New.

'V. Lady *Catherine Swallow*. She was a Widow at eighteen, and has since buried a second Husband and two Coach-men.

'VI. The Lady *Waddle*. She was married in the 15th Year of her Age to Sir *Simon Waddle* Knight, aged threescore and twelve, by whom she had Twinns nine Months after his Decease. In the 55th Year of her Age she was married to *James Spindle*, Esq; a Youth of one and twenty, who did not out-live the Honey-Moon.

'VII. *Deborah Conquest*. The Case of this Lady is something particular. She is the Relict of Sir *Sampson Conquest*, sometime Justice of the *Quorum*. Sir *Sampson* was seven Foot high and two Foot in Breadth, from the tip of one Shoulder to the other. He had married three Wives, who all of them died in Child-bed. This terrified the whole Sex, who none of them durst venture on Sir *Sampson*. At length Mrs. *Deborah* undertook him, and gave so good an Account of him, that in three Years time she very fairly laid him out, and measured his Length upon the Ground. This Exploit has gained her so great a Reputation in the Club, that they have added Sir *Sampson*'s three Victories to hers, and give her the Merit of a fourth Widowhood; and she takes her Place accordingly.

'VIII. The Widow *Wildfire*, Relict of Mr. *John Wildfire*, Fox-hunter, who broke his Neck over a six Bar Gate. She took his Death

---

[1] Cf. *Tatler* 11: '*Tipstaff*, being a Seventh Son, us'd to cure the *King's Evil*.'

so much to Heart, that it was thought it would have put an End to her Life, had she not diverted her Sorrows by receiving the Addresses of a Gentleman in the Neighbourhood, who made Love to her in the second Month of her Widowhood. This Gentleman was discarded in a Fortnight for the sake of a young *Templar*, who had the Possession of her for six Weeks after, till he was beaten out by a broken Officer, who likewise gave up his Place to a Gentleman at Court. The Courtier was as short-lived a Favourite as his Predecessors, but had the Pleasure to see himself succeeded by a long Series of Lovers, who followed the Widow *Wildfire* to the 37th Year of her Age, at which time there ensued a Cessation of ten Years, when *John Felt*, Haberdasher, took it in his Head to be in love with her, and it is thought will very suddenly carry her off.

'IX. The last is pretty Mrs. *Runnet*, who broke her First Husband's Heart before she was Sixteen, at which time she was entered of the Club; but soon after left it, upon Account of a Second whom she made so quick a Dispatch of, that she returned to her Seat in less than a Twelve-month. This young Matron is looked upon as the most rising Member of the Society, and will probably be in the President's Chair before she Dies.

'These Ladies, upon their first Institution, resolved to give the Pictures of their Deceased Husbands to the Club Room, but Two of them bringing in their Dead at full Length, they covered all the Walls:[1] Upon which they came to a second Resolution, that every Matron should give her own Picture, and set it round with her Husbands in Miniature.

'As they have most of them the Misfortune to be troubled with the Cholick, they have a Noble Celler of Cordials and strong Waters. When they grow Maudlin they are very apt to commemorate their former Partners with a Tear. But ask them which of their Husbands they Condole,[2] they are not able to tell you, and discover plainly, that they do not Weep so much for the loss of a Husband, as for the want of One.

'The principal Rule, by which the whole Society are to govern themselves is this, To cry up the Pleasures of a single Life, upon all Occasions, in order to deter the rest of their Sex from Marriage, and Engross the whole Male World to themselves.

---

[1] Gregory Smith sees in this a humorous reference to the portraits of the Kit-Cat Club.

[2] I.e. 'grieve over'. The last example in *OED* is dated 1788.

'They are obliged, when any one makes Love to a Member of the Society, to communicate his Name, at which time the whole Assembly sit upon his Reputation, Person, Fortune, and good Humour; and if they find him qualified for a Sister of the Club, they lay their Heads together how to make him sure. By this means they are acquainted with all the Widow-hunters about Town, who often afford them great Diversion. There is an honest *Irish* Gentleman it seems, who knows nothing of this Society, but at different times has made Love to the whole Club.[1]

'Their Conversation often turns upon their former Husbands, and it is very diverting to hear them relate their several Arts and Stratagems, with which they amused the Jealous, pacified the Cholerick, or wheedled the Good-natured Man, 'till at last, to use the Club-phrase, *They sent him out of the House with his Heels foremost.*

'The Politicks, which are most cultivated by this Society of She-*Machiavils*,[2] relate chiefly to these two Points: How to treat a Lover, and How to manage a Husband. As for the first Set of Artifices, they are too Numerous to come within the compass of your Paper, and shall therefore be reserved for a second Letter.

'The Management of a Husband is built upon the following Doctrines, which are Universally assented to by the whole Club. Not to give him his Head at first. Not to allow him too great Freedoms and Familiarities. Not to be treated by him like a Raw Girl, but as a Woman that knows the World. Not to Lessen any thing of her former Figure. To celebrate the Generosity, or any other Vertue of a deceased Husband, which she would recommend to his Successor. To turn away all his old Friends and Servants, that she may have the Dear Man to her self. To make him disinherit the undutiful Children of any former Wife. Never to be thoroughly convinced of his Affection, 'till he has made over to her all his Goods and Chattels.

'After so long a Letter, I am without more Ceremony,

Your Humble Servant, &c.'

---

[1] The Irish fortune-hunter becomes a familiar figure in eighteenth-century literature. Cf. Nos. 20 (vol. i) and 282 (vol. ii).

[2] 'Young Machiavils' are mentioned in No. 305 (vol. iii).

No. 562   *Friday, July 2, 1714*[1]

[ADDISON]

. . . Præsens, absens ut sies.

Ter.

I T *is a hard and nice Subject for a Man to speak of himself, says* Cowley;
it grates his own Heart to say any thing of Disparagement, and the
Reader's Ears to hear any thing of Praise from him.[2] Let the Tenour of
his Discourse be what it will upon this Subject, it generally proceeds from *Vanity*. An ostentatious Man will rather relate a Blunder
or an Absurdity he has committed, than be debarred from talking
of his own dear Person.

Some very great Writers have been guilty of this Fault. It is
observed of *Tully* in particular, that his Works run very much in
the First Person, and that he takes all Occasions of doing himself
Justice.[3] 'Does he think, says *Brutus*, that his Consulship deserves
more Applause than my putting *Cæsar* to Death, because I am not
perpetually talking of the Ides of *March*, as he is of the Nones of
December?' I need not acquaint my learned Reader, that in the
Ides of *March*, *Brutus* destroyed *Cæsar*, and that *Cicero* quashed the
Conspiracy of *Catiline* in the Calends of *December*. How shocking
soever this great Man's talking of himself might have been to his
Contemporaries, I must confess I am never better pleased than
when he is on this Subject. Such Openings of the Heart give a Man
a thorough Insight into his personal Character, and illustrate
several Passages in the History of his Life: Besides, that there is
some little Pleasure in discovering the Infirmity of a great Man,
and seeing how the Opinion he has of himself agrees with what the
World entertains of him.

The Gentlemen of *Port-Royal*, who were more eminent for their
Learning and their Humility than any other in *France*, banished
the way of speaking in the First Person out of all their Works, as
arising from Vain-glory and Self-conceit. To shew their particular
Aversion to it, they branded this Form of Writing with the Name of

---

[1] *Motto*. Terence, *Eunuchus*, 192: That you may be absent while present. This
saying is referred to near the close of No. 553.
[2] The opening of Essay 11, 'Of My Self' (It is a hard and nice Subject for a man to
write of himself . . .) (*Essays*, ed. Waller, p. 455).
[3] Plutarch, *Life of Cicero*, 24. 1-2.

an *Egotism*:[1] a Figure not to be found among the ancient Rhetoricians.

The most violent Egotism which I have met with in the Course of my Reading, is that of Cardinal *Woolsey, Ego et Rex meus, I and my King*;[2] as perhaps the most eminent Egotist that ever appeared in the World, was *Montagne* the Author of the celebrated Essays.[3] This lively old *Gascon* has woven all his bodily Infirmities into his Works, and after having spoken of the Faults or Virtues of any other Man, immediately publishes to the World how it stands with himself in that Particular. Had he kept his own Counsel he might have passed for a much better Man, tho' perhaps he would not have been so diverting an Author. The Title of an Essay promises perhaps a Discourse upon *Virgil* or *Julius Cæsar*; but when you look into it, you are sure to meet with more upon Monsieur *Montagne* than of either of them. The younger *Scaliger*, who seems to have been no great Friend to this Author, after having acquainted the World that his Father sold Herrings, adds these Words; *La grande fadaise de Montagne, qui a escrit, qu'il aimoit mieux le vin blanc — que diable a-t-on à faire de sçavoir ce qu'il aime?*[4] For my Part, says *Montagne*, *I am a great Lover of your White Wines—What the Devil signifies it to the Publick*, says *Scaliger*, *whether he is a Lover of White Wines or of Red Wines?*

I cannot here forbear mentioning a Tribe of Egotists for whom I have always had a mortal Aversion, I mean the Authors of Memoirs, who are never mentioned in any Works but their own, and who raise all their Productions out of this single Figure of Speech.[5]

---

[1] The first example of the word in *OED*, which accepts Addison's statement with some hesitation. The earliest example of the English form *egoism* in *OED* is dated 1785.

[2] Cf. Shakespeare's *Henry VIII*, III. ii. 315. 'This egotism', writes A. F. Pollard, 'exceeded even Tudor arrogance, and it was exhibited in more than Tudor ostentation' (*Wolsey*, 1929, p. 320). Addison had used the illustration in the *Whig-Examiner* No. 2 (21 Sept. 1710) as an example of impudence. Cf. also Richard Bentley, *Dissertation upon the Epistles of Phalaris* (1699), preface, p. xl; John Tutchin, *Observator* 95 (20 Mar. 1702/3); &c. For the historicity of the phrase see A. F. Pollard, *Henry VIII* (1905), p. 110; and the same author's *Wolsey* (1929), p. 103.

[3] In *Tatler* 83 Steele uses the authority of Montaigne on this point: 'it being a Privilege asserted by Monsieur *Montaigne* and others, of vain-glorious Memory, That we Writers of Essays may talk of our selves. . . .'

[4] Joseph Justus Scaliger (1540–1609). See *Scaligerana, sive excerpta ex ore Josephi Scaligeri* (2nd ed., revised, Leyden, 1668), p. 230.

[5] *Tatler* 84 makes the same charge against

some merry Gentlemen of the *French* Nation, who have written very advantagious Histories of their Exploits in War, Love and Politicks, under the Title of Memoirs. I am afraid I shall find several of these Gentlemen tardy, because I hear of them in no Writings but their own. To read the Narrative of one of these Authors, you

Most of our modern Prefaces savour very strongly of the Egotism. Every insignificant Author fancies it of Importance to the World, to know that he writ his Book in the Country, that he did it to pass away some of his idle Hours, that it was published at the Importunity of Friends, or that his natural Temper, Studies or Conversations, directed him to the Choice of his Subject.

. . . Id populus curat scilicet.[1]

Such Informations cannot but be highly improving to the Reader.

In Works of Humour, especially when a Man writes under a fictitious Personage, the talking of one's self may give some Diversion to the Publick; but I would advise every other Writer never to speak of himself, unless there be something very considerable in his Character: Tho' I am sensible this Rule will be of little use in the World, because there is no Man who fancies his Thoughts worth publishing, that does not look upon himself as a considerable Person.

I shall close this Paper with a Remark upon such as are Egotists in Conversation: These are generally the vain or shallow Part of Mankind, People being naturally full of themselves when they have nothing else in them. There is one Kind of Egotists which is very common in the World, tho' I do not remember that any Writer has taken notice of them; I mean those empty conceited Fellows, who repeat as Sayings of their own, or some of their particular Friends, several Jests which were made before they were born, and which every one who has conversed in the World has heard a hundred times over. A forward young Fellow of my Acquaintance was very guilty of this Absurdity: He would be always laying a new Scene for some old Piece of Wit, and telling us, that as he and *Jack* such-a-one were together, one or t'other of them had such a Conceit on such an Occasion; upon which he would laugh very heartily, and wonder the Company did not join with him. When his Mirth was over I have often reprehended him out of *Terence, Tuumne, obsecro te, hoc dictum erat? vetus credidi.*[2] But finding him still incorrigible, and having a Kindness for the young Coxcomb, who was otherwise a

would fancy there was not an Action in a whole Campaign, which he did not contrive or execute. . . .

[1] Terence, *Andria*, 185 ('Oh, to be sure, the world makes that its business'). Burton (*Anatomy*, II. v. 1. vi) quotes this apropos of bashfulness.

[2] *Eunuchus*, 428 ('Gracious! Is that repartee yours? I thought it was old'). This is said to Thraso, the captain, by Gnatho, his dependant and flatterer.

good-natured Fellow, I recommended to his Perusal the *Oxford*[1] and *Cambridge* Jests,[2] with several little Pieces of Pleasantry of the same Nature. Upon the Reading of them he was under no small Confusion to find that all his Jokes had passed through several Editions, and that what he thought was a new Conceit, and had appropriated to his own Use, had appeared in Print before he or his ingenious Friends were ever heard of. This had so good an Effect upon him, that he is content at present to pass for a Man of plain Sense in his ordinary Conversation, and is never facetious but when he knows his Company.

No. 563   *Monday, July 5, 1714*[3]

. . . *Magni nominis Umbra.*
Lucan.

I SHALL entertain my Reader with two very curious Letters. The first of them comes from a chimerical Person, who I believe never writ to any Body before.

SIR,

'I AM descended from the ancient Family of the *Blanks*, a Name well known among all Men of Business.[4] It is always read in those little white Spaces of Writing which want to be filled up, and which for that Reason are called *blank* Spaces, as of Right appertaining to our Family: For I consider my self as the Lord of a

---

[1] *Oxford Jests, being a collection of witty jests, merry tales, and pleasant joques, collected by Captain William Hickes, native of Oxford* (London: S. Miller, 1669) is advertised in *Term Catalogues* for November 1669 and ran through many editions. The 8th edition is tentatively marked in the British Museum Catalogue as 1700.

[2] A 6th edition of *Cambridge Jests for Merry Spirits* appeared in 1700, with the title *Ingenii Fructus; or, the Cambridge Jests* (Aitken).

[3] *Motto.* Lucan, *Pharsalia,* I. 135: The mere shadow of a mighty name.
The two letters which make up this number are probably genuine contributions from unknown correspondents.

[4] One of the announced purposes of the *Spectator* had been to be of use to 'the Blanks of Society', persons at a stand for ideas (No. 4). David Lewis's *Miscellaneous Poems* (1730) contains a poem entitled 'On the Family of the Blanks' (pp. 289–90). It begins:

> Your *Blanks* are antient, num'rous Folks,
> There's *John a Stiles,* and *John a Nokes.*

Mannor, who lays his Claim to all Wastes or Spots of Ground that are unappropriated. I am a near Kinsman to *John a Styles* and *John a Nokes*;[1] and they, I am told, came in with the Conquerour. I am mentioned oftner in both Houses of Parliament than any other Person in *Great Britain.* My Name is written, or more properly speaking, not written, thus,   . I am one that can turn my Hand to every thing, and appear under any Shape whatsoever. I can make my self Man, Woman, or Child. I am sometimes metamorphosed into a Year of our Lord, a Day of the Month, or an Hour of the Day. I very often represent a Sum of Money, and am generally the first Subsidy that is granted to the Crown. I have now and then supplied the Place of several Thousands of Land Soldiers, and have as frequently been employed in the Sea Service.

'Now, Sir, my Complaint is this, that I am only made use of to serve a Turn, being always discarded as soon as a proper Person is found out to fill up my Place.

'If you have ever been in the Play-house before the Curtain rises, you see most of the front Boxes filled with Men of my Family, who forthwith turn out, and resign their Stations upon the Appearance of those for whom they are retained.[2]

'But the most illustrious Branch of the *Blanks* are those who are planted in high Posts, till such time as Persons of greater Consequence can be found out to supply them. One of these *Blanks* is equally qualified for all Offices: He can serve in time of Need for a Soldier, a Politician, a Lawyer, or what you please. I have known in my Time many a Brother *Blank* that has been born under a lucky Planet, heap up great Riches, and swell into a Man of Figure and Importance, before the Grandees of his Party could agree among themselves which of them should step into his Place: Nay, I have known a *Blank* continue so long in one of these vacant Posts, (for such it is to be reckoned all the Time a *Blank* is in it) that he has grown too formidable and dangerous to be removed.

'But to return to my self, since I am so very commodious a Person, and so very necessary in all well regulated Governments, I desire you will take my Case into Consideration, that I may be no longer made a Tool of, and only employed to stop a Gap. Such

---

[1] Fictitious names for parties in a legal action.
[2] It was customary for footmen to hold places for their masters until the play began (cf. No. 168, vol. ii).

Usage, without a Pun, makes me look very blank. For all which Reasons I humbly recommend my self to your Protection, and am

Your most obedient Servant,

Blank.'

P. S. 'I herewith send you a Paper, drawn up by a Country Attorney employed by two Gentlemen, whose Names he was not acquainted with, and who did not think fit to let him into the Secret which they were transacting. I heard him call it a Blank Instrument, and read it after the following manner. You may see by this single Instance of what Use I am to the busy World.

'*I T.* Blank, *Esq; of* Blank *Town, in the County of* Blank, *do own my self indebted in the Sum of* Blank *to Goodman* Blank, *for the Service he did me in procuring for me the Goods following,* Blank: *And I do hereby promise the said* Blank *to pay unto him the said Sum of* Blank, *on the* Blank *Day of the Month of* Blank *next ensuing, under the Penalty and Forfeiture of* Blank.'

I shall take Time to consider the Case of this my imaginary Correspondent, and in the mean while shall present my Reader with a Letter which seems to come from a Person that is made up of Flesh and Blood.

Good Mr. SPECTATOR,

'I AM married to a very honest Gentleman that is exceedingly good-natured, and at the same time very cholerick. There is no standing before him when he is in a Passion; but as soon as it is over he is the best humour'd Creature in the World. When he is angry he breaks all my China-Ware that chances to lie in his Way, and the next Morning sends me in twice as much as he broke the Day before. I may positively say, that he has broke me a Child's Fortune since we were first marry'd together.

'As soon as he begins to fret, down goes every thing that is within Reach of his Cane. I once prevailed upon him never to carry a Stick in his Hand, but this saved me nothing; for upon seeing me do something that did not please him, he kick'd down a great Jarr, that cost him above Ten Pound but the Week before. I then laid the Fragments together in a Heap, and gave him his Cane again, desiring him that if he chanced to be in Anger, he would spend his Passion upon the China that was broke to his Hand. But the very next Day, upon my giving a wrong Message to one of the Servants, he flew into such a Rage, that he swept down a Dozen Tea-Dishes which, to my Misfortune, stood very convenient for a Side-Blow.

'I then removed all my China into a Room which he never frequents; but I got nothing by this neither, for my Looking-Glasses immediately went to Rack.

'In short, Sir, whenever he is in a Passion he is angry at every thing that is brittle; and if on such Occasions he had nothing to vent his Rage upon, I do not know whether my Bones would be in Safety. Let me beg of you, Sir, to let me know whether there be any Cure for this unaccountable Distemper; or if not, that you will be pleased to publish this Letter: For my Husband having a great Veneration for your Writings, will by that means know you do not approve of his Conduct.

> I am,
> Your most humble Servant, &c.'

No. 564
[BUDGELL]

Wednesday, July 7, 1714[1]

. . . Adsit
Regula, peccatis quæ pœnas irroget æquas:
Ne Scutica dignum horribili sectere flagello.
> Hor.

IT is the Work of a Philosopher to be every Day subduing his Passions, and laying aside his Prejudices. I endeavour at least to look upon Men and their Actions only as an impartial Spectator, without any Regard to them as they happen to advance or cross my own private Interest. But while I am thus employed my self, I cannot help observing how those about me suffer themselves to be blinded by Prejudice and Inclination, how readily they pronounce

---

[1] *Motto.* Horace, *Satires*, I. 3. 117–19:

> Let *Rules* be fixt that may our Rage contain,
> And punish faults with a *Proportion'd* pain:
> And do not flea him, do not run him through,
> That only doth deserve a kick or two. CREECH.

The Tickell MS. identifies this as the first of nine papers in the 1714 *Spectator* 'written by Mr Budgell'.

on every Man's Character, which they can give in two Words, and make him either good for nothing, or qualified for every thing. On the contrary, those who search thoroughly into humane Nature, will find it much more difficult to determine the Value of their Fellow-Creatures, and that Mens Characters are not thus to be given in general Words. There is indeed no such thing as a Person entirely good or bad; Virtue and Vice are blended and mixed together in a greater or less Proportion in every one; and if you would search for some particular good Quality in its most eminent Degree of Perfection, you will often find it in a Mind where it is darkened and eclipsed by an hundred other irregular Passions.

Men have either no Character at all, says a celebrated Author, or it is that of being inconsistent with themselves.[1] They find it easier to join Extremities, than to be uniform and of a Piece. This is finely illustrated in *Xenophon*'s Life of *Cyrus* the Great.[2] That Author tells us, That *Cyrus* having taken a most beautiful Lady, named *Panthea*, the Wife of *Abradatas*, committed her to the Custody of *Araspas*, a young *Persian* Nobleman, who had a little before maintained in Discourse, that a Mind truly virtuous was incapable of entertaining an unlawful Passion. The young Gentleman had not long been in Possession of his fair Captive, when a Complaint was made to *Cyrus* that he not only sollicited the Lady *Panthea* to receive him in the Room of her absent Husband, but that finding his Entreaties had no Effect, he was preparing to make use of Force. *Cyrus*, who loved the young Man, immediately sent for him, and in a gentle manner representing to him his Fault, and putting him in mind of his former Assertion, the unhappy Youth, confounded with a quick Sense of his Guilt and Shame, burst out into a Flood of Tears, and spoke as follows.

Oh Cyrus, *I am convinced that I have two Souls. Love has taught me this Piece of Philosophy. If I had but one Soul, it could not at the same time pant after Virtue and Vice, wish and abhor the same thing. It is certain therefore we have two Souls: When the good Soul rules, I undertake noble and virtuous Actions; but when the bad Soul predominates, I am forced to*

[1] La Bruyère, 'Of Man', in his *Characters* (3rd ed., 1702), p. 256:
Men have no certain Characters; or if they have any, they have none which they always pursue, which never change, and by which they may be known. . . . Extreams are more easie to them, than regular and natural conduct; Enemies to moderation, excessive in all things, in good as well as evil, and when they cannot support, they ease themselves by changing.

[2] *Cyropaedia*, 5. 1. 2–18, 6. 1. 31–41.

do Evil. All I can say at present is, that I find my good Soul, encouraged
by your Presence, has got the Better of my bad.

I know not whether my Readers will allow of this Piece of
Philosophy; but if they will not, they must confess we meet with
as different Passions in one and the same Soul as can be supposed in
two.[1] We can hardly read the Life of a great Man who lived in
former Ages, or converse with any who is eminent among our
Contemporaries, that is not an Instance of what I am saying.

But as I have hitherto only argued against the Partiality and
Injustice of giving our Judgment upon Men in gross, who are such
a Composition of Virtues and Vices, of Good and Evil; I might
carry this Reflection still farther, and make it extend to most of
their Actions. If, on the one Hand, we fairly weighed every Circumstance, we should frequently find them obliged to do that Action
we at first Sight condemn, in order to avoid another we should have
been much more displeased with. If on the other hand we nicely
examined such Actions as appear most dazzling to the Eye, we
should find most of them either deficient and lame in several Parts,
produced by a bad Ambition, or directed to an ill End. The very
same Action may sometimes be so oddly circumstanced, that it is
difficult to determine whether it ought to be rewarded or punished.[2]
Those who compiled the Laws of *England* were so sensible of this,
that they have laid it down as one of their first Maxims, *It is better*
suffering a Mischief, than an Inconvenience; which is as much as to say
in other Words, That since no Law can take in or provide for all
Cases, it is better private Men should have some Injustice done
them, than that a publick Grievance should not be redressed.[3]

[1] Cf. Pascal, *Thoughts on Religion, and other Subjects,* trans. by Basil Kennett (1704),
p. 43:

How surprizing is it, that so numerous Contradictions should be found in one and
the same Subject! This double Temper and Disposition of Man is so visible, that
there have not been wanting those who imagin'd him to have two Souls; one single
Subject appearing to them incapable of so great and sudden Variety, from an
unmeasurable Presumption to a dreadful Abatement and Abjectness of Spirit.

[2] Pope's *Epistle to Cobham*, the first of the Moral Essays, develops some of the ideas
expressed here.

[3] The maxim is given in William Walker, *Parœmiologia Anglo-Latina* (1672), p. 46
(Adagia miscellanea, No. 25):

Better once a mischief, than alwayes an inconvenience. *Præstat semel malum, quàm*
semper incommodum.

'By a Mischief is meant, when one Man or some few men suffer by the Hardship
of a Law, which Law is yet useful for the Publick. But an Inconvenience is to have
a publick Law disobeyed or broken, or an Offence to go unpunished' (Sir Robert
Atkyns, *Parliamentary and Political Tracts* [before 1709], ed. 1734, p. 199, quoted
in *OED*).

This is usually pleaded in Defence of all those Hardships which fall on particular Persons in particular Occasions, which could not be foreseen when a Law was made. To remedy this however as much as possible, the Court of Chancery was erected, which frequently mitigates and breaks the Teeth of the Common Law, in Cases of Men's Properties, while in criminal Cases there is a Power of pardoning still lodged in the Crown.

Notwithstanding this, it is perhaps impossible in a large Government to distribute Rewards and Punishments strictly proportioned to the Merits of every Action. The *Spartan* Common-wealth was indeed wonderfully exact in this Particular; and I do not remember in all my Reading, to have met with so nice an Example of Justice as that recorded by *Plutarch*, with which I shall close my Paper for this Day.

The City of *Sparta* being unexpectedly attacked by a powerful Army of *Thebans*, was in very great Danger of falling into the Hands of their Enemies. The Citizens suddenly gathering themselves into a Body, fought with a Resolution equal to the Necessity of their Affairs; yet no one so remarkably distinguished himself on this Occasion, to the Amazement of both Armies, as *Isadas*, the Son of *Phœbidas*, who was at that time in the Bloom of his Youth, and very remarkable for the Comeliness of his Person. He was coming out of the Bath when the Alarm was given, so that he had not time to put on his Cloaths, much less his Armour; however transported with a Desire to serve his Country in so great an Exigency, snatching up a Spear in one Hand, and a Sword in the other, he flung himself into the thickest Ranks of his Enemies. Nothing could withstand his Fury: In what Part soever he fought he put the Enemies to Flight without receiving a single Wound. Whether, says *Plutarch*, he was the particular Care of some God, who rewarded his Valour that Day with an extraordinary Protection, or that his Enemies struck with the Unusualness of his Dress and Beauty of his Shape, supposed him something more than Man, I shall not determine.

The Gallantry of this Action was judged so great by the *Spartans*, that the *Ephori*, or chief Magistrates, decreed he should be presented with a Garland; but as soon as they had done so, fined him a thousand Drachmas for going out to the Battle unarmed.[1]

[1] Plutarch, *Life of Agesilaus*, 34. 6–8. Budgell repeats this story in his *Letter to Cleomenes* (1731), p. 101, using many of the phrases in this number of the *Spectator*. A thousand drachmas he explains in a footnote as 'about Thirty Pounds *English* Money'.

No. 565
[ADDISON]

Friday, July 9, 1714[1]

... *Deum namque ire per omnes*
Terrasque, tractusque maris, cœlumque profundum.
Virg.[a]

I WAS Yesterday about Sun-set walking in the open Fields, till the Night insensibly fell upon me. I at first amused my self with all the Richness and Variety of Colours which appeared in the Western Parts of Heaven: In Proportion as these faded away and went out, several Stars and Planets appeared one after another, till the whole Firmament was in a Glow. The Blewness of the *Æther*[2] was exceedingly heightened and enlivened by the Season of the Year, and by the Rays of all those Luminaries that passed through it. The *Galaxy*[3] appeared in its most beautiful White. To compleat the Scene, the full Moon rose at length in that clouded Majesty, which *Milton* takes Notice of, and opened to the Eye a new Picture of Nature, which was more finely shaded, and disposed among softer Lights than that which the Sun had before discovered to us.[4]

As I was surveying the Moon walking in her Brightness, and taking her Progress among the Constellations, a Thought rose in me which I believe very often perplexes and disturbs Men of serious and contemplative Natures. *David* himself fell into it in that Reflection, *When I consider the Heavens the work of thy Fingers, the Moon and the Stars which thou hast ordained; what is man that thou art mindful of him, and the son of man that thou regardest him?*[5] In the same manner, when I considered that infinite Hoste of Stars, or, to speak more Philosophically, of Suns, which were then shining upon me, with those innumerable Sets of Planets or Worlds, which were moving round their respective Suns; When I still enlarged the Idea, and supposed another Heaven of Suns and Worlds rising still above this which we discovered, and these still enlightened by a superior Firmament of Luminaries, which are planted at so great a Distance

[a] *Motto. Virg. om. in Fol.*

---

[1] *Motto.* Virgil, *Georgics,* 4. 221–2:
For God the whole created Mass inspires;
Thro' Heav'n, and Earth, and Oceans depth he throws
His Influence round, and kindles as he goes. DRYDEN.

[2] The clear sky; the upper regions of space beyond the clouds. Now *poet.* or *rhetorical* (*OED*).   [3] The Milky Way.

[4] Milton, *Paradise Lost,* iv. 607.   [5] Ps. viii. 3, 4 (slightly altered).

that they may appear to the Inhabitants of the former as the Stars do to us; In short, whilst I pursued this Thought I could not but reflect on that little insignificant Figure which I my self bore amidst the Immensity of God's Works.[1]

Were the Sun, which enlightens this part of the Creation, with all the Host of Planetary Worlds, that move about him, utterly extinguished and annihilated, they would not be miss'd more than a grain of Sand upon the Sea-shore. The Space they possess is so exceedingly little, in Comparison of the whole, that it would scarce make a *Blank* in the Creation. The Chasm would be imperceptible to an Eye, that could take in the whole Compass of Nature, and pass from one End of the Creation to the other, as it is possible there may be such a Sense in our selves hereafter, or in Creatures which are at present more exalted than our selves. We see many Stars by the help of Glasses, which we do not discover with our naked Eyes; and the finer our Telescopes are, the more still are our Discoveries. *Huygenius* carries this Thought so far, that he does not think it impossible there may be Stars whose Light is not yet travelled down to us, since their first Creation.[2] There is no Question but the Universe has certain Bounds set to it; but when we consider that it is the Work of infinite Power, prompted by infinite Goodness, with an infinite Space to exert it self in, how can our Imagination set any Bounds to it?

To return therefore to my first Thought, I could not but look upon my self with secret Horror as a Being, that was not worth the smallest Regard of one who had so great a Work under his Care and Superintendency. I was afraid of being overlooked amidst the Immensity of Nature, and lost among that infinite Variety of Creatures, which in all Probability swarm through all these immeasurable Regions of Matter.

In order to recover my self from this mortifying Thought, I considered that it took its rise from those narrow Conceptions, which we are apt to entertain of the Divine Nature. We our selves cannot attend to many different Objects at the same time. If we are careful to inspect some Things, we must of Course neglect

---

[1] The language here is reminiscent of Pascal, *Pensées* 72 (Brunschvicg, i. 70).

[2] Christian Huygens (1629–95), the Dutch physicist and astronomer, who developed the wave-theory of light. His *Cosmotheoros* was translated into English in 1698 as *The Celestial Worlds discover'd: or, Conjectures concerning the Inhabitants, Plants and Productions of the Worlds in the Planets*. I do not find Huygens's speculation here, however.

others. This Imperfection which we observe in our selves, is an Imperfection that cleaves in some Degree to Creatures of the highest Capacities, as they are Creatures, that is, Beings of finite and limited Natures. The Presence of every created Being is confined to a certain Measure of Space, and consequently his Observation is stinted to a certain number of Objects. The Sphere in which we move, and act, and understand, is of a wider Circumference to one Creature than another, according as we rise one above another in the Scale of Existence.[1] But the widest of these our Spheres has its Circumference. When therefore we reflect on the Divine Nature, we are so used and accustomed to this Imperfection in our selves, that we cannot forbear in some Measure ascribing it to him in whom there is no shadow of Imperfection. Our Reason indeed assures us, that his Attributes are Infinite, but the Poorness of our Conceptions is such, that it cannot forbear setting Bounds to every thing it contemplates, till our Reason come again to our Succour, and throws down all those little Prejudices which rise in us unawares, and are natural to the Mind of Man.

We shall therefore utterly extinguish this melancholy Thought, of our being overlooked by our Maker in the Multiplicity of his Works, and the Infinity of those Objects among which he seems to be incessantly employed, if we consider, in the first place, that he is Omnipresent; and, in the second, that he is Omniscient.

If we consider him in his Omnipresence: His Being passes through, actuates and supports the whole Frame of Nature. His Creation, and every Part of it, is full of him. There is nothing he has made, that is either so distant, so little, or so inconsiderable, which he does not essentially inhabit. His Substance is within the Substance of every Being, whether material or immaterial, and as intimately present to it as that Being is to it self. It would be an Imperfection in him, were he able to remove out of one Place into another, or to withdraw himself from any thing he has created, or from any part of that Space which is diffused and spread abroad to Infinity. In short, to speak of him in the Language of the old Philosopher, he is a Being whose Centre is every where, and his Circumference no where.[2]

---

[1] For the revolutionary theses in cosmography which gained acceptance in the seventeenth century see A. O. Lovejoy, *The Great Chain of Being*, chap. iv: 'The Principle of Plenitude and the New Cosmography'.

[2] Cf. Pascal, *Pensées*, 72. For earlier examples of the saying see W. A. Nitze, 'Pascal and the Medieval Definition of God', *Modern Language Notes*, lvii (1942), 552–8.

In the second Place, he is Omniscient as well as Omnipresent. His Omniscience indeed necessarily and naturally flows from his Omnipresence; he cannot but be conscious of every Motion that arises in the whole material World, which he thus essentially pervades, and of every Thought that is stirring in the intellectual World, to every part of which he is thus intimately united. Several Moralists have considered the Creation as the Temple of God, which he has built with his own Hands, and which is filled with his Presence. Others have considered infinite Space as the Receptacle, or rather the Habitation of the Almighty: But the noblest and most exalted way of considering this infinite Space is that of Sir *Isaac Newton*, who calls it the *Sensorium*[1] of the Godhead. Brutes and Men have their *Sensoriola*,[2] or little *Sensoriums*, by which they apprehend the Presence, and perceive the Actions of a few Objects that lie contiguous to them. Their Knowledge and Observation turns within a very narrow Circle. But as God Almighty cannot but perceive and know every thing in which he resides, Infinite Space gives room to Infinite Knowledge, and is, as it were, an Organ to Omniscience.

Were the Soul separate from the Body, and with one Glance of Thought should start beyond the Bounds of the Creation, should it for Millions of Years continue its Progress through Infinite Space with the same Activity, it would still find it self within the Embrace of its Creator, and encompassed round with the Immensity of the Godhead. Whilst we are in the Body he is not less present with us, because he is concealed from us. *O that I knew where I might find him!* says *Job. Behold I go forward, but he is not there; and backward, but I cannot perceive him. On the left hand, where he does work, but I cannot behold him: he hideth himself on the right hand, that I cannot see him.*[3] In short, Reason as well as Revelation assures us, that he can not be absent from us, notwithstanding he is undiscovered by us.

In this Consideration of God Almighty's Omnipresence and Omniscience, every uncomfortable Thought vanishes. He cannot but regard every thing that has Being, especially such of his Creatures who fear they are not regarded by him. He is privy to all their Thoughts, and to that Anxiety of Heart in particular, which

---

[1] The seat of sensation; the percipient centre by which sense-impressions are transmitted by the nerves (*OED*).

[2] *Sensoriolum*, in the sense of a small sensorium, is a diminutive apparently coined by Addison. This is the earliest example in *OED*.

[3] Job xxiii. 3, 8–9.

is apt to trouble them on this Occasion: For as it is impossible he should overlook any of his Creatures, so we may be confident that he regards, with an Eye of Mercy, those who endeavour to recommend themselves to his Notice, and in an unfeigned Humility of Heart think themselves unworthy that he should be mindful of them.

No. 566   *Monday, July* 12, 1714[1]
[BUDGELL]

Militiæ Species Amor est. . . .
Ovid.

AS my Correspondents begin to grow pretty numerous, I think my self obliged to take some Notice of them, and shall therefore make this Paper a Miscellany of Letters. I have, since my reassuming the Office of SPECTATOR, received abundance of Epistles from Gentlemen of the Blade, who, I find, have been so used to Action that they know not how to lie still: They seem generally to be of Opinion, that the Fair at home ought to reward them for their Services abroad, and that, till the Cause of their Country calls them again into the Field, they have a sort of Right to Quarter themselves upon the Ladies. In order to favour their Approaches, I am desired by some to enlarge upon the Accomplishments of their Profession, and by others to give them my Advice in the carrying on of their Attacks. But let us hear what the Gentlemen say for themselves.

Mr. SPECTATOR,

'THO' it may look somewhat perverse, amidst the Arts of Peace, to talk too much of War, it is but Gratitude to pay the last Office to its *Manes*, since even Peace it self is, in some Measure, obliged to it for its Being.

'You have, in your former Papers, always recommended the Accomplished to the Favour of the Fair; and, I hope, you will allow me to represent some part of a Military Life not altogether unnecessary to the forming a Gentleman. I need not tell you that in

---

[1] *Motto.* Ovid, *Ars amatoria*, 2. 233: Love is a kind of warfare.
This number is assigned to Budgell in the Tickell MS.

France, whose Fashions we have been formerly so fond of, almost every one derives his Pretences to Merit from the Sword; and that a Man has scarce the Face to make his Court to a Lady, without some Credentials from the Service to recommend him. As the Profession is very ancient, we have reason to think some of the greatest Men, among the old *Romans*, derived many of their Virtues from it, their Commanders being frequently, in other Respects, some of the most shining Characters of the Age.

'The Army not only gives a Man Opportunities of exercising those two great Virtues *Patience* and *Courage*, but often produces them in Minds where they had scarce any footing before. I must add, that it is one of the best Schools in the World to receive a general Notion of Mankind in, and a certain Freedom of Behaviour, which is not so easily acquired in any other Place. At the same time I must own, that some Military Airs are pretty extraordinary, and that a Man, who goes into the Army a Coxcomb, will come out of it a sort of Publick Nuisance: But a Man of Sense, or one who before had not been sufficiently used to a mixed Conversation, generally takes the true Turn. The Court has in all Ages been allowed to be the Standard of Good-breeding; and, I believe, there is not a juster Observation in Monsieur *Rochefoucault*, than that *A Man, who has been bred up wholly to Business, can never get the Air of a Courtier at Court, but will immediately catch it in the Camp.*[1] The Reason of this most certainly is, that The very Essence of Good-breeding and Politeness consists in several Niceties, which are so minute that they escape his Observation, and he falls short of the Original he would copy after; but when he sees the same things charged and aggravated to a Fault, he no sooner endeavours to come up to the Pattern which is set before him, than, tho' he stops somewhat short of that, he naturally rests where in reality he ought. I was, two or three Days ago, mightily pleased with the Observation of an humorous Gentleman upon one of his Friends, who was in other Respects every way an accomplished Person, that *He wanted nothing but a Dash of the Coxcomb in him*; by which he understood a little of that Alertness and Unconcern in the common Actions of Life, which is usually so visible among Gentlemen of the Army, and which a Campaign or two would infallibly have given him.

[1] Maxim 392: 'The Air of a *Citizen* is sometimes lost in an *Army*, but never in a *Court*' (*Moral Maxims and Reflections*, 1706, p. 70).

'You will easily guess, Sir, by this my Panegyrick upon a Military Education, that I am my self a Soldier, and indeed I am so; I remember, within three Years after I had been in the Army, I was ordered into the Country a Recruiting. I had very particular Success in this part of the Service, and was over and above assured, at my going away, that I might have taken a young Lady, who was the most considerable Fortune in the County, along with me. I preferred the Pursuit of Fame at that time to all other Considerations, and tho' I was not absolutely bent on a Wooden Leg, resolved at least to get a Scar or two for the good of *Europe*. I have at present as much as I desire of this Sort of Honour, and if you could recommend me effectually, should be well enough contented to pass the Remainder of my Days in the Arms of some dear kind Creature, and upon a pretty Estate in the Country: This, as I take it, would be following the Example of *Lucius Cincinnatus*, the Old *Roman* Dictator, who at the end of a War left the Camp to follow the Plow.[1] I am, Sir, with all imaginable Respect,

Your most Obedient,
Humble Servant,
Will. Warly.'

Mr. SPECTATOR,

'I AM an Half-pay Officer, and am at present with a Friend in the Country. Here is a rich Widow in the Neighbourhood, who has made Fools of all the Fox-hunters within fifty Miles of her. She declares she intends to marry, but has not yet been asked by the Man she could like. She usually admits her humble Admirers to an Audience or two, but after she has once given them Denial will never see them more. I am assured, by a Female Relation, that I shall have fair Play at her; but as my whole Success depends on my first Approaches, I desire your Advice, whether I had best *Storm* or proceed by way of *Sap*.

I am, SIR,
Yours, &c.'

P. S. 'I had forgot to tell you, that I have already carried one of her Out-works, that is, secured her Maid.'

---

[1] The Roman captain (d. 439 B.C.?) made dictator by the people of Rome. 'He accepted of that Dignity unwillingly, and having settled the Publick Affairs in Seventeen Days, he left it freely, and returned to his Plough as before' (Danet).

Mr. SPECTATOR,

'I HAVE assisted in several Sieges in the *Low-Countries*, and being still willing to employ my Talents, as a Soldier and Engineer, I lay down this Morning at Seven a Clock before the Door of an obstinate Female, who had for some time refused me Admittance. I made a Lodgment in an outer Parlour about Twelve: The Enemy retired to her Bed-Chamber, yet I still pursued, and about two a Clock this Afternoon she thought fit to Capitulate. Her Demands are indeed somewhat high, in Relation to the Settlement of her Fortune. But being in Possession of the House I intend to insist upon *Carte Blanche*,[1] and am in hopes, by keeping off all other Pretenders for the Space of twenty four Hours, to starve her into a Compliance. I beg your speedy Advice, and am,

SIR, *Yours,*

Peter Push.'

From my Camp in *Red-Lion* Square, *Saturday* 4 in the Afternoon.[2]

No. 567
[ADDISON]

Wednesday, July 14, 1714[3]

> . . . *Inceptus clamor frustratur hiantes.*
>
> Virg.

I HAVE received private Advice from some of my Correspondents, that if I would give my Paper a general Run, I should take care to season it with Scandal. I have indeed observed of late, that few Writings sell which are not filled with great Names and illustrious Titles. The Reader generally casts his Eye upon a new Book, and if he finds several Letters separated from one another by a Dash, he buys it up and peruses it with great Satisfaction. An *M* and an *h*, a *T* and an *r*, with a short Line between them, has sold many an

---

[1] This is one of the French terms censured in No. 165.

[2] Hatton describes it as 'a pleasant Square, of good Buildings; it is in Form near a parallellagram, and lies between *High holbourn* South and the Fields North . . .' (p. 68).

[3] *Motto.* Virgil, *Aeneid,* 6. 493:

But the weak Voice deceiv'd their gasping Throats. DRYDEN.

insipid Pamphlet.[1] Nay I have known a whole Edition go off by vertue of two or three well-written &c—'s.

A sprinkling of the Words *Faction, Frenchman, Papist, Plunderer,* and the like significant Terms, in an Italick Character, have also a very good Effect upon the Eye of the Purchaser; not to mention *Scribler, Lier, Rogue, Rascal, Knave,* and *Villain,* without which it is impossible to carry on a Modern Controversie.

Our Party-writers are so sensible of the secret Vertue of an Innuendo to recommend their Productions, that of late they never mention the Q——n or P————t at length, tho' they speak of them with Honour, and with that Deference which is due to them from every private Person. It gives a secret Satisfaction to a Peruser of these mysterious Works, that he is able to decipher them without help, and, by the Strength of his own natural Parts, to fill up a Blank-Space, or make out a Word that has only the first or last Letter to it.

Some of our Authors indeed, when they would be more Satyrical than ordinary, omit only the Vowels of a great Man's Name, and fall most unmercifully upon all the Consonants. This way of writing was first of all introduced by *T—m Br—wn,* of facetious Memory, who, after having gutted a Proper Name of all its intermediate Vowels, used to plant it in his Works, and make as free with it as he pleased, without any danger of the Statute.[2]

That I may imitate these celebrated Authors, and publish a Paper which shall be more taking than ordinary, I have here drawn up a very curious Libel, in which a Reader of Penetration will find a great deal of concealed Satyr, and if he be acquainted with the present Posture of Affairs, will easily discover the Meaning of it.[3]

'If there are *four* Persons in the Nation who endeavour to bring

---

[1] An *M* and an *h,* a *T* and an *r,* i.e. 'Marlborough' and 'Treasurer'.

[2] Tom Brown, the satirist, had died just ten years before, in 1704. His *Amusements serious and comical* appeared in 1700.

[3] This is referred to in the *Wentworth Papers* (p. 401), in a letter dated July 1714:
Having very little news to write and yet being loth that this should come empty to your Lordship, I have enclosed the Q—'s speech and a Spectatour, the former of which, the Whiggs very much exclaim against, as having not soe much mentioned the House of Hanover and as being (as they are pleased to say) more than a little too severe in the last Paragraph; the latter is thought to be wrote as a Banter upon those blank AB's and CD's mentioned in the H. of Lords in last Thursday's Debate, as to be sharers of the Fourth part belonging to her M— of wch debate I reckon your Lordship has already had a more exact account than I can write.

The proceedings referred to are apparently those of Thursday, 8 July (*Journals of the House of Lords,* xix. 755):
Mr. *Lownds* and Mr. *Taylor* attending, were called in, and examined as to their

all things into Confusion and ruin their native Country, I think every honest *Engl–shm–n* ought to be upon his Guard. That there are such every one will agree with me, who hears me name * * * with his first Friend and Favourite * * * not to mention * * * nor * * *. These People may cry Ch—rch, Ch—rch, as long as they please, but, to make use of a homely Proverb, The Proof of the P—dd—ng is in the eating. This I am sure of, that if a *certain Prince* should concur with a *certain Prelate*, (and we have Monsieur Z—n's Word for it) our Posterity would be in a sweet P—ckle. Must the *British* Nation suffer forsooth, because my Lady *Q—p—t—s* has been disobliged? Or is it reasonable that our *English* Fleet, which used to be the Terror of the Ocean, should lie[a] Wind-bound for the sake of a —. I love to speak out and declare my Mind clearly, when I am talking for the good of my Country. I will not make my Court to an ill Man, tho' he were a *B—y* or a *T—t*. Nay, I would not stick to call so wretched a Politician a Traitor, an Enemy to his Country, and a *Bl—nd—r—b—ss, &. &c.*'[b]

The remaining part of this Political Treatise, which is written after the manner of the most celebrated Authors in *Great Britain*, I may communicate to the Publick at a more convenient Season. In the mean while I shall leave this with my curious Reader, as some ingenious Writers[c] do their Enigmas, and if any sagacious Person can fairly unriddle it, I will print his Explanation, and, if he pleases, acquaint the World with his Name.

I hope this short Essay will convince my Readers, it is[d] not for want of Abilities that I avoid State-tracts, and that if I would apply my Mind to it, I might in a little time be as great a Master of the Political Scratch as any the most eminent Writer of the Age. I shall only add, that in order to outshine all this Modern Race of *Syncopists*,[e][1] and throughly content my *English* Readers, I intend shortly to[f] publish a SPECTATOR that shall not have a single Vowel in it.

[a] should lie] should now lie *Fol.*   [b] *&c. &c.* om. in Fol.   [c] Writers] Authors *Fol.*   [d] it is] that it is *Fol.*   [e] *Syncopists*,] *Italics added in 8vo, 12mo*   [f] intend shortly to] intend to *Fol.*

being Trustees for Her Majesty's Quarter Part of the Assiento Contract. . . . Also, Mr. *Shepherd,* Sir *Samuel Clark,* Sir *Theodore Jansen,* Mr. *Harcourt Masters,* Mr. *Chapman,* and Mr. *Blunt,* Directors of the *South Sea* Company, were called in; and examined, upon Oath, in relation to Her Majesty's Quarter Part of the Assiento Contract.

In this imaginary libel drawn up by Addison does 'my Lady Q–p–t–s' recall 'Her Majesty's Quarter Part'? Wendell and Greenough (*Selections from the Writings of Joseph Addison,* 1905) suggest that Q–p–t–s stands for 'quem putas'.

[1] This is the only example given in *OED* for this nonce-word.

> ... *Dum recitas, incipit esse Tuus.*
> Mart.

I WAS Yesterday in a Coffee-House not far from the *Royal Exchange*, where I observed three Persons in close Conference over a Pipe of Tobacco; upon which, having filled one for my own use, I lighted it at the little Wax Candle that stood before them; and after having thrown in two or three Whiffs amongst them, sat down, and made one of the Company. I need not tell my Reader, that lighting a Man's Pipe at the same Candle, is looked upon among Brother-smokers as an Overture to Conversation and Friendship. As we here lay our Heads together in a very amicable Manner, being intrenched under a Cloud of our own raising, I took up the last SPECTATOR, and casting my Eye over it, *The* SPECTATOR, says I, *is very witty to Day*; upon which a lusty lethargick old Gentleman who sat at the Upper-end of the Table, having gradually blown out of his Mouth a great deal of Smoke, which he had been collecting for some Time before, *Ay*, says he, *more witty than wise I am afraid*. His Neighbour who sat at his right Hand immediately coloured, and being an angry Politician, laid down his Pipe with so much Wrath that he broke it in the Middle, and by that Means furnished me with a Tobacco-stopper. I took it up very sedately, and looking him full in the Face, made use of it from Time to Time all the while he was speaking: *This Fellow*, says he, *can't for his Life keep out of Politicks. Do you see how he abuses* four *great Men here?* I fix'd my Eye very attentively on the Paper, and asked him if he meant those who were represented by Asterisks. *Asterisks*, says he, *do you call them? They are all of them Stars. He might as well have put Garters to 'em. Then pray do but mind the two or three next Lines! Ch–rch and P–dd–ng in the same Sentence! Our Clergy are very much beholden to him.* Upon this the third Gentleman, who was of a mild Disposition, and, as I found, a Whig in his Heart, desired him not to be too severe upon the SPECTATOR neither; *For*, says he, *you find he is very cautious of giving Offence, and has therefore put two Dashes into his Pudding. A Fig for his Dash*, says the angry Politician. *In his next*

---

[1] *Motto.* Martial, *Epigrams*, 1. 38. 2 (altered): When you rehearse my verse, it is not mine but thine.

Sentence he gives a plain Innuendo, that our Posterity will be in a sweet P–ckle. What does the Fool mean by his Pickle? Why does not he write it at length if he means honestly? I have read over the whole Sentence, says I; *but I look upon the Parenthesis in the Belly of it to be the most dangerous Part, and as full of Insinuations as it can hold. But who,* says I, *is my Lady Q–p–t–s? Ay, Answer that if you can, Sir,* says the furious Statesman to the poor Whig that sat over against him. But without giving him Time to reply, *I do assure you,* says he, *were I my Lady Q–p–t–s, I would sue him for* Scandalum Magnatum. *What is the World come to? Must every Body be allowed to —?* He had by this time filled a new Pipe, and applying it to his Lips, when we expected the last Word of his Sentence, put us off with a Whiff of Tobacco; which he redoubled with so much Rage and Trepidation that he almost stifled the whole Company. After a short Pause, I owned that I thought the SPECTATOR had gone too far in writing so many Letters of my Lady *Q–p–t–s's* Name; *but however,* says I, *he has made a little Amends for it in his next Sentence, where he leaves a blank Space without so much as a Consonant to direct us; I mean,* says I, *after those Words,* The Fleet, that used to be the Terrour of the Ocean, should be Wind-bound for the Sake of a —; *after which ensues a Chasm, that, in my Opinion, looks modest enough. Sir,* says my Antagonist, *you may easily know his Meaning by his Gaping; I suppose he designs his Chasm, as you call it, for an Hole to creep out at, but I believe it will hardly serve his Turn. Who can endure to see the great Officers of State, the* B—y's *and* T—t's, *treated after so scurrilous a Manner? I can't for my Life,* says I, *imagine who they are the* SPECTATOR *means? No!* says he, *— Your humble Servant Sir!* Upon which he flung himself back in his Chair after a contemptuous Manner, and smiled upon the old lethargick Gentleman on his Left Hand, who I found was his great Admirer. The Whig however had begun to conceive a Good-will towards me, and seeing my Pipe out, very generously offered me the use of his Box; but I declined it with great Civility, being obliged to meet a Friend about that Time in another Quarter of the City.

At my leaving the Coffee-house, I could not forbear reflecting with my self upon that gross Tribe of Fools who may be termed the *Over-wise,* and upon the Difficulty of writing any thing in this censorious Age, which a weak Head may not construe into private Satyr and personal Reflection.[1]

---

[1] Cf. No. 170 (vol. ii): 'No Men see less of the Truth . . . than these great Refiners upon Incidents, who are so wonderfully subtile and over-wise in their Conceptions.'

A Man who has a good Nose at an Innuendo, smells Treason and Sedition in the most innocent Words that can be put together, and never sees a Vice or Folly stigmatized, but finds out one or other of his Acquaintance pointed at by the Writer. I remember an empty pragmatical Fellow in the Country, who upon reading over *the whole Duty of Man*, had written the Names of several Persons in the Village at the Side of every Sin which is mention'd by that excellent Author; so that he had converted one of the best Books in the World[1] into a Libel against the 'Squire, Church-wardens, Overseers of the Poor, and all other the most considerable Persons in the Parish. This Book with these extraordinary marginal Notes fell accidentally into the Hands of one who had never seen it before; upon which there arose a current Report that Some-body had written a Book against the 'Squire and the whole Parish. The Minister of the Place having at that Time a Controversy with some of his Congregation upon the Account of his Tythes, was under some Suspicion of being the Author, till the good Man set his People right by shewing them that the satyrical Passages might be applied to several others of two or three neighbouring Villages, and that the Book was writ against all the Sinners in *England*.

No. 569

[ADDISON]

Monday, July 19, 1714

Reges dicuntur multis urgere culullis
Et torquere mero, quem perspexisse laborant,
An sit amicitia dignus . . .

Hor.

NO Vices are so incurable as those which Men are apt to glory in. One would wonder how Drunkenness should have the good Luck to be of this Number. *Anacharsis*, being invited to

---

[1] *The Whole Duty of Man* (1658). For Richard Allestree's authorship of this popular work see Paul Elmen in *The Library*, 5th ser., vi (1951), 19–27.
[2] *Motto*. Horace, *Ars poetica*, 434–6:
> Kings (thus says Story) that of old design'd,
> To raise a *Favourite* to a *Bosome Friend*;
> Did ply him hard with wine, unmaskt his thoughts,
> And saw him Naked, and with all his Faults. CREECH.

a Match of Drinking at *Corinth*, demanded the Prize very humour-
ously, because he was drunk before any of the rest of the Company;
for, says he, when we run a Race, he who arrives at the Goal first
is entitled to the Reward.[1] On the contrary, in this thirsty Generation the Honour falls upon him who carries off the greatest Quantity
of Liquour, and knocks down the rest of the Company. I was the
other Day with honest *Will*. *Funnell* the *West Saxon*, who was reckoning up how much Liquor had past through him in the last twenty
Years of his Life, which, according to his Computation, amounted to
twenty three Hogsheads of October, four Ton of Port, half a Kilder-
kin of small Beer, nineteen Barrels of Cider, and three Glasses of
Champaign; besides which, he had assisted at four hundred Bowls
of Punch, not to mention Sips, Drams, and Whets without Number.[2]
I question not but every Reader's Memory will suggest to him
several ambitious young Men, who are as vain in this Particular as
Will. *Funnell*, and can boast of as glorious Exploits.

Our modern Philosophers observe, that there is a general Decay
of Moisture in the Globe of the Earth. This they chiefly ascribe
to the Growth of Vegetables, which incorporate into their own
Substance many fluid Bodies that never return again to their former
Nature: But, with Submission, they ought to throw into their
Account those innumerable rational Beings which fetch their
Nourishment chiefly out of Liquids; especially when we consider
that Men, compared with their Fellow-Creatures, drink much more
than comes to their Share.

But however highly this Tribe of People may think of themselves, a drunken Man is a greater Monster than any that is to be
found among all the Creatures which God has made, as indeed
there is no Character which appears more despicable and deformed
in the Eyes of all reasonable Persons than that of a Drunkard.
Bonosus, one of our own Countrymen, who was addicted to this Vice,
having set up for a Share in the *Roman* Empire, and being defeated
in a great Battle, hang'd himself.[3] When he was seen by the Army

---

[1] Plutarch, 'Dinner of the Seven Wise Men' (*Moralia*, 156A).
[2] See No. 72 (vol. i).
[3] See 'Firmus, Saturninus, Proculus, and Bonosus', by Flavius Vopiscus of Syracuse
(*Scriptores Historiae Augustae*, 14–15). Bonosus, while not strictly 'one of our own
Countrymen', since he was a Spaniard by birth, was a Briton in descent. After his
defeat by Probus at Cologne, *c.* 280, he hanged himself, 'which gave rise to the jest
that it was not a man that was being hanged but a wine-jug'. The jest is frequently
quoted, e.g. in the 'Apophthegmata Latina' of G. Tuningius (*Apophthegmata Graeca,
Latina, Italica, Gallica, Hispanica,* Leyden, 1519, p. 31).

in this melancholy Situation, notwithstanding he had behaved himself very bravely, the common Jest was, That the Thing they saw hanging upon the Tree before them, was not a Man but a Bottle.

This Vice has very fatal Effects on the Mind, the Body, and Fortune of the Person who is devoted to it.

In regard to the Mind, it first of all discovers every Flaw in it. The sober Man, by the Strength of Reason, may keep under and subdue every Vice or Folly to which he is most inclined; but Wine makes every latent Seed sprout up in the Soul, and shew it self. It gives Fury to the Passions, and Force to those Objects which are apt to produce them. When a young Fellow complained to an old Philosopher that his Wife was not handsome, Put less Water in your Wine, says the Philosopher, and you'll quickly make her so.[1] Wine heightens Indifference into Love, Love into Jealousy, and Jealousy into Madness. It often turns the Good-natured Man into an Ideot, and the Cholerick into an Assassin. It gives Bitterness to Resentment, it makes Vanity insupportable, and displays every little Spot of the Soul in its utmost Deformity.

Nor does this Vice only betray the hidden Faults of a Man, and shew them in the most odious Colours, but often occasions Faults to which he is not naturally subject. There is more of Turn than of Truth in a Saying of *Seneca*, That Drunkenness does not produce but discover Faults.[2] Common Experience teaches us the[a] contrary. Wine throws a Man out of himself, and infuses Qualities into the Mind, which she is a Stranger to in her sober Moments. The Person you converse with, after the third Bottle, is not the same Man who at first sat down at Table with you. Upon this Maxim is founded one of the prettiest Sayings I ever met with, which is ascribed to *Publius Syrus*, *Qui ebrium ludificat lædit absentem; He, who jests upon a Man that is drunk, injures the Absent.*[3]

Thus does Drunkenness act in direct Contradiction to Reason, whose Business it is to clear the Mind of every Vice which is crept into it, and to guard it against all the Approaches of any that endeavours to make its Entrance. But besides these ill Effects which

---

[a] us the] us to the *Fol.*

[1] See L'Estrange, *Fables and Stories Moraliz'd* (1699), Fable 183:

It was a Pleasant Put-off, of a Droll when one told him he had gotten a very Plain Woman to his Wife. *Yes, yes*, says he, *I know I have, but I am now drinking to make her Handsom* (p. 171).

[2] *Epistulae morales*, 83. 20 (Non facit ebrietas vitia, sed protrahit).

[3] Publilius Syrus, 3.

this Vice produces in the Person who is actually under its Dominion, it has also a bad Influence on the Mind even in its sober Moments, as it insensibly weakens the Understanding, impairs the Memory, and makes those Faults habitual which are produced by frequent Excesses.

I should now proceed to shew the ill Effects which this Vice has on the Bodies and Fortunes of Men; but these I shall reserve for the Subject of some future Paper.

No. 570
[BUDGELL]

Wednesday, July 21, 1714[1]

> . . . *Nugæque canoræ.*
> Hor.

THERE is scarce a Man living who is not actuated by Ambition. When this Principle meets with an honest Mind and great Abilities, it does infinite Service to the World; on the contrary, when a Man only thinks of distinguishing himself, without being thus qualified for it, he becomes a very pernicious or a very ridiculous Creature. I shall here confine my self to that petty kind of Ambition, by which some Men grow eminent for odd Accomplishments and trivial Performances. How many are there whose whole Reputation depends upon a Punn or a Quibble? You may often see an Artist in the Streets gain a Circle of Admirers, by carrying a long Pole upon his Chin or Forehead in a perpendicular Posture. Ambition has taught some to write with their Feet, and others to walk upon their Hands.[2] Some *tumble* into Fame, others grow immortal by throwing themselves through a Hoop.

> *Cætera de genere hoc adeò sunt multa, loquacem*
> *Delassare valent Fabium . . .*[3]

[1] *Motto.* Horace, *Ars poetica,* 322: Noisy trifles.
   Notes for this number in Addison's hand are contained in the Tickell MS., which lists this paper as by Addison. It was not reprinted, however, by Tickell in Addison's *Works* and probably represents Budgell's reworking of Addison's notes.
[2] Cf. No. 220.
[3] Horace, *Satires,* I. I. 13–14:
> So many Instances in every state, . . .
> 'Twould tire even bawling *Fabius* to relate. CREECH.
Addison had used the beginning lines of this Satire as the motto for No. 558 a month earlier.

I am led into this Train of Thought by an Adventure I lately met with.

I was the other Day at a Tavern, where the Master of the House accommodating us himself with every thing we wanted, I accidentally fell into a Discourse with him;[1] and talking of a certain great Man, who shall be nameless, he told me, That he had sometimes the Honour *to treat him with a Whistle*; (adding by the way of Parenthesis) *For you must know, Gentlemen, that I whistle the best of any Man in* Europe.[a] This naturally put me upon desiring him to give us a Sample of his Art; upon which he called for a Case-Knife, and applying the Edge of it to his Mouth, converted it into a musical Instrument, and entertained me with an *Italian* Solo. Upon laying down the Knife, he took up a Pair of clean Tobacco-Pipes; and after having slid the small End of them over the Table in a most melodious Trill, he fetched a Tune out of them, whistling to them at the same time in Consort. In short, the Tobacco-Pipes became *Musical Pipes* in the Hands of our Virtuoso; who confessed to me ingenuously, he had broke such Quantities of them, that he had almost broke himself before he had brought this Piece of Musick to any tolerable Perfection. I then told him I would bring a Company of Friends to dine with him the next Week, as an Encouragement to his Ingenuity; upon which he thanked me, saying, That he would provide himself with a new Frying-Pan against that Day. I replied, That it was no Matter; Roast and Boiled would serve our Turn. He smiled at my Simplicity, and told me, That it was his Design to give us a Tune upon it. As I was surprised at such a Promise, he sent for an old Frying-Pan, and grating it upon the Board, whistled to it in such

---

[a] *For . . .* Europe. *Italics added in 8vo, 12mo*

[1] Nichols reported his name as Daintry. 'He was in the trained bands, and commonly known by the name of *Captain* Daintry.' According to Nichols this information had been given to 'the annotator' [i.e. John Calder] by 'old Mr. Heywood'. Nathan Drake (iii. 25) adds: 'He was celebrated for whistling on the edge of a knife, or with a pair of tobacco-pipes, and could convert a frying-pan or a gridiron into a very respectable musical instrument.' Drake also quotes the notice of his death from the *London Magazine*, April 1738:

Near Fishmongers' Hall, the celebrated Mr. *John Dentry*, better known by the appellation of *Signior Denterino*, which, by way of honour, he assumed, and put upon his sign. He kept a public-house, not only at the time of his death, but when the Spectators were writing; and from the odd talents he was possessed of, and his whimsical ways of entertaining his customers, furnished a subject for one of those excellent papers. Among many other surprising endowments, the Signior had that of whistling by the help of a knife to so great a perfection, that he became as famous for that, as most of the Italian Signiors have been for singing, who excel likewise in that way *by the help of a knife*.

a melodious Manner, that you could scarce distinguish it from a Base-Viol. He then took his Seat with us at the Table, and hearing my Friend that was with me humm over a Tune to himself, he told him if he would sing out he would accompany his Voice with a Tobacco-Pipe. As my Friend has an agreeable Base, he chose rather to sing to the Frying-Pan; and indeed between them they made up a most extraordinary Consort. Finding our Landlord so great a Proficient in Kitchen-Musick, I asked him if he was Master of the Tongs and Key. He told me that he had laid it down some Years since, as a little unfashionable; but that if I pleased he would give me a Lesson upon the Gridiron. He then informed me that he had added two Bars to the Gridiron, in order to give it a greater Compass of Sound; and I perceived was as well pleased with the Invention, as *Sappho* could have been upon adding two Strings to the Lute. To be short, I found that his whole Kitchen was furnished with musical Instruments; and could not but look upon this Artist as a kind of Burlesque Musician.

He afterwards of his own Accord fell into the Imitation of several Singing-Birds. My Friend and I toasted our Mistresses to the Nightingale, when all of a sudden we were surprised with the Musick of the Thrush. He next proceeded to the Sky-Lark, mounting up by a proper Scale of Notes, and afterwards falling to the Ground with a very easy and regular Descent. He then contracted his Whistle to the Voice of several Birds of the smallest Size. As he is a Man of a larger Bulk and higher Stature than ordinary, you would fancy him a Giant when you looked upon him, and a Tom Tit when you shut your Eyes. I must not omit acquainting my Reader, that this accomplished Person was formerly the Master of a Toy-shop near *Temple-Bar*; and that the famous *Charles Mathers* was bred up under him.[1] I am told that the Misfortunes which he has met with in the World, are chiefly owing to his great Application to his Musick; and therefore cannot but recommend him to my Readers as one who deserves their Favour, and may afford them great Diversion over a Bottle of Wine, which he sells at the Queen's Arms, near the End of the little Piazza in *Covent-Garden*.[2]

[1] See No. 328 (vol. iii).
[2] There are several 'Queen's Arms' advertised in the *Spectator,* but none in Covent-Garden. Nichols notes 'Mr. James Heywood likewise informed the editor, that the tavern here mentioned was much frequented by Steele and Addison'.

No. 571   *Friday, July 23, 1714*[1]
[ADDISON]

. . . *Cœlum quid quærimus ultra?*
Luc.

AS the Work I have engaged in will not only consist of Papers of Humour and Learning, but of several Essays Moral and Divine, I shall publish the following one, which is founded on a former SPECTATOR,[2] and sent me by a particular Friend, not questioning but it will please such of my Readers as think it no Disparagement to their Understandings to give way sometimes to a serious Thought.[3]

SIR,
'IN your Paper of *Friday* the 9th Instant, you had Occasion to consider the Ubiquity of the Godhead, and, at the same time, to shew, that as he is present to every thing, he cannot but be attentive to every thing, and privy to all the Modes and Parts of its Existence; or, in other Words, that his Omniscience and Omnipresence are co-existent, and run together through the whole Infinitude of Space. This Consideration might furnish us with many Incentives to Devotion and Motives to Morality, but as this Subject has been handled by several excellent Writers, I shall consider it in a Light wherein I have not seen it placed by others.

'*First*, How disconsolate is the Condition of an intellectual Being who is thus present with his Maker, but, at the same time, receives no extraordinary Benefit or Advantage from this his Presence!

'*Secondly*, How deplorable is the Condition of an intellectual Being who feels no other Effects from this his Presence but such as proceed from Divine Wrath and Indignation!

'*Thirdly*, How happy is the Condition of that intellectual Being who is sensible of his Maker's Presence from the secret Effects of his Mercy and Loving-kindness!

'*First*, How disconsolate is the Condition of an intellectual Being,

---

[1] *Motto.* Lucan, *Pharsalia,* 9. 579: Beyond Heaven what would we seek?
[2] No. 565.
[3] The letter which occupies the major part of this number was printed in the folio sheets without inverted commas. It forms, with Nos. 565, 580, and 590, a series of four essays upon 'infinitude'. For Addison's authorship of these see Introduction, pp. lxxvi–lxxvii.

who is thus present with his Maker, but, at the same time, receives no extraordinary Benefit or Advantage from this his Presence! Every Particle of Matter is actuated by this Almighty Being which passes through it. The Heavens and the Earth, the Stars and Planets, move and gravitate by Vertue of this great Principle within them. All the dead parts of Nature are invigorated by the Presence of their Creator, and made capable of exerting their respective Qualities. The several Instincts, in the brute Creation, do likewise operate and work towards the several Ends which are agreeable to them by this Divine Energy. Man only, who does not co-operate with this holy Spirit, and is unattentive to his Presence, receives none of those Advantages from it, which are perfective of his Nature and necessary to his Well-being. The Divinity is with him, and in him, and every where about him, but of no Advantage to him. It is the same thing to a Man without Religion, as if there were no God in the World. It is indeed impossible for an infinite Being to remove himself from any of his Creatures, but tho' he cannot withdraw his Essence from us, which would argue an Imperfection in him, he can withdraw from us all the Joys and Consolations of it. His Presence may perhaps be necessary to support us in our Existence; but he may leave this our Existence to it self, with regard to its Happiness or Misery. For, in this Sense, he may cast us away from his Presence, and take his Holy Spirit from us. This single Consideration one would think sufficient to make us open our Hearts to all those Infusions of Joy and Gladness which are so near at Hand, and ready to be poured in upon us; especially when we consider, *Secondly*, the deplorable Condition of an intellectual Being who feels no other Effects from his Maker's Presence, but such as proceed from Divine Wrath and Indignation!

'We may assure our selves, that the great Author of Nature will not always be as one, who is indifferent to any of his Creatures. Those who will not feel him in his Love, will be sure at length to feel him in his Displeasure. And how dreadful is the Condition of that Creature who is only sensible of the Being of his Creator by what he suffers from him! He is as essentially present in Hell as in Heaven, but the Inhabitants of those accursed Places behold him only in his Wrath, and shrink within their Flames to conceal themselves from him. It is not in the Power of Imagination to conceive the fearful Effects of Omnipotence incensed.

'But I shall only consider the Wretchedness of an intellectual

Being, who, in this Life, lies under the Displeasure of him, that at all Times and in all Places is intimately united with him. He is able to disquiet the Soul, and vex it in all its Faculties. He can hinder any of the greatest Comforts of Life from refreshing us, and give an Edge to every one of its slightest Calamities. Who then can bear the Thought of being an Out-cast from his Presence, that is, from the Comforts of it, or of feeling it only in its Terrors? How pathetick is that Expostulation of *Job*, when, for the Trial of his Patience, he was made to look upon himself in this deplorable Condition! *Why hast thou set me as a Mark against thee, so that I am become a burden to my self?*[1] But, *Thirdly*, how happy is the Condition of that intellectual Being, who is sensible of his Maker's Presence from the secret Effects of his Mercy and Loving-kindness!

'The Blessed in Heaven behold him Face to Face, that is, are as sensible of his Presence as we are of the Presence of any Person, whom we look upon with our Eyes. There is doubtless a Faculty in Spirits, by which they apprehend one another, as our Senses do material Objects; and there is no Question but our Souls, when they are disembodied, or placed in glorified Bodies, will by this Faculty, in whatever part of Space they reside, be always *sensible* of the Divine Presence. We, who have this Veil of Flesh standing between us and the World of Spirits, must be Content to know that the Spirit of God is present with us, by the Effects which he produceth in us. Our outward Senses are too gross to apprehend him; we may however taste and see how Gracious he is, by his Influence upon our Minds, by those Virtuous Thoughts, which he awakens in us, by those secret Comforts and Refreshments, which he conveys into our Souls, and by those ravishing Joys and inward Satisfactions, which are perpetually springing up, and diffusing themselves among all the Thoughts of good Men. He is lodged in our very Essence; and is as a Soul within the Soul, to irradiate its Understanding, rectifie its Will, purifie its Passions, and enliven all the Powers of Man. How happy therefore is an intellectual Being, who, by Prayer and Meditation, by Virtue and good Works, opens this Communication between God and his own Soul! Tho' the whole Creation frowns upon him, and all Nature looks black about him, he has his Light and Support within him, that are able to cheer his Mind, and bear him up, in the midst of all those Horrors which encompass him. He knows that his Helper is at Hand, and is always

[1] Job vii. 20.

nearer to him than any thing else can be, which is capable of Annoying or Terrifying him: In the midst of Calumny or Contempt, he attends to that Being who whispers better things within his Soul, and whom he looks upon as his Defender, his Glory, and the Lifter up of his Head. In his deepest Solitude and Retirement, he knows that he is in Company with the greatest of Beings; and perceives within himself such real Sensations of his Presence, as are more delightful than any thing that can be met with in the Conversation of his Creatures. Even in the Hour of Death, he considers the Pains of his Dissolution to be nothing else but the breaking down of that Partition, which stands betwixt his Soul, and the sight of that Being, who is always present with him, and is about to manifest it self to him in fullness of Joy.

'If we would be thus Happy, and thus Sensible of our Maker's Presence, from the secret Effects of his Mercy and Goodness, we must keep such a Watch over all our Thoughts, that, in the Language of the Scripture, his Soul may have Pleasure in us.[1] We must take care not to grieve his Holy Spirit, and endeavour to make the Meditations of our Hearts always acceptable in his Sight, that he may delight thus to reside and dwell in us. The Light of Nature could direct *Seneca* to this Doctrine, in a very remarkable Passage among his Epistles. *Sacer inest in nobis spiritus bonorum malorumque custos, et Observator, et quemadmodum nos illum tractamus, ita et ille nos.*[2] There is a Holy Spirit residing in us, who watches and observes both Good and Evil Men, and will treat us after the same manner that we treat him. But I shall conclude this Discourse with those more emphatical Words in divine Revelation, *If a Man love me, he will keep my Word, and my Father will love him, and we will come unto him, and make our Abode with him.*'[3]

[1] Heb. x. 38.
[2] *Epistulae morales*, 41. 2: 'Sacer intra nos spiritus sedet, malorum bonorumque nostrorum observator et custos. Hic prout a nobis tractatus est, ita nos ipse tractat.'
[3] John xiv. 23.

Quod medicorum est
Promittunt medici . . .
Hor.

I AM the more pleased with these my Papers, since I find they
have encouraged several Men of Learning and Wit to become
my Correspondents: I Yesterday received the following Essay
against Quacks, which I shall here communicate to my Readers for
the Good of the Publick,[2] begging the Writer's Pardon for those
Additions and Retrenchments which I have made in it.

THE Desire of Life is so natural and strong a Passion, that I have
long since ceased to wonder at the great Encouragement which the
Practise of Physick finds among us. Well-constituted Governments
have always made the Profession of a Physician both honourable
and advantageous. *Homer*'s *Machaon* and *Virgil*'s *Japis* were Men of
Renown, Heroes in War, and made at least as much havock among
their Enemies as among their Friends.[3] Those who have little or
no Faith in the Abilities of a Quack will apply themselves to him,
either because he is willing to sell Health at a reasonable Profit, or
because the Patient, like a drowning Man, catches at every Twig,
and hopes for Relief from the most ignorant, when the most able
Physicians give him none.[4] Tho' Impudence and many Words are

---

[1] *Motto.* Horace, *Epistles*, 2. I. 115–16:
And only *Doctors* will pretend to heal. CREECH.

Nos. 572 and 633 are by Zachary Pearce (1690–1774), at this time a Cambridge
undergraduate, and later Bishop of Rochester. They are named by him in a letter
to Dr. Birch of 5 June 1764 (Add. MS. 4316. f. 179) as the only contributions to the
Spectator 'that I can remember'. Nichols, followed by later editors, names Pearce as
author of these two essays, 'with alterations by Addison'. Since No. 572 is assigned
in the Tickell MS. to Budgell it is probable that the 'additions and retrenchments'
mentioned in the opening paragraph represent editorial revision by Budgell rather
than by Addison.

[2] A favourite phrase of the quack doctors. It heads the advertisement in No. 563
of 'an experienced Midwife,

dwelling now at the Sign of the Queen's-Arms, a Goldsmith's, near Exeter Exchange in the Strand, who perform'd a Cure upon a Lady at the Bath, after she
was given over by Physicians, and since has cured several Gentlewomen and
others in the City and Suburbs of London.'

[3] Machaon (*Iliad*, 2. 732, II. 512–15), son of Asclepius, the god of medicine, was
surgeon to the Greeks in the Trojan war. For Iapis see below, p. 555.

[4] Cf. No. 444, on the subject of medical quacks.

as necessary to these Itinerary *Galens*[1] as a laced Hat or a merry *Andrew*, yet they would turn very little to the Advantage of the Owner, if there were not some inward Disposition in the sick Man to favour the Pretensions of the Mountebank. Love of Life in the one, and of Mony in the other, creates a good Correspondence between them.

There is scarce a City in *Great Britain* but has one of this Tribe, who takes it into his Protection, and on the Market Day harangues the good People of the Place with Aphorisms and Receipts. You may depend upon it, he comes not there for his own private Interest, but out of a particular Affection to the Town. I remember one of these Publick-spirited Artists at *Hammersmith*, who told his Audience, 'that he had been born and bred there, and that having a special Regard for the Place of his Nativity, he was determined to make a Present of five Shillings to as many as would accept of it.' The whole Crowd stood agape, and ready to take the Doctor at his Word; when putting his Hand into a long Bag, as every one was expecting his Crown-Piece, he drew out an handful of little Packets, each of which he informed the Spectators was constantly sold at five Shillings and six Pence, but that he would bate the odd five Shillings to every Inhabitant of that Place: The whole Assembly immediately closed with this generous Offer, and took off all his Physick, after the Doctor had made them vouch for one another, that there were no Foreigners among them, but that they were all *Hammersmith-Men*.[2]

There is another Branch of Pretenders to this Art, who, without either Horse or Pickle-Herring, lye snug in a Garret, and send down Notice to the World of their extraordinary Parts and Abilities by Printed Bills and Advertisements.[3] These seem to have derived their Custom from an *Eastern* Nation which *Herodotus* speaks of,

---

[1] Used jocularly for a physician since 1598 (*OED*).
[2] A similar story is told in L'Estrange's 'The Mountebank's Treat' (*Fables and Stories Moraliz'd*, 1699, Fable 231, p. 214):

A *Mountebank*, that was just about to change his Quarter, gave Notice of it to his Customers and Benefactors: that so many of them as would be pleas'd to take their Leaves of him the Next Morning, he would make them a *Present of Eighteen-Pence a piece, for a Parting Acknowledgment*. The Company met at the appointed Time, and Place: and immediately out comes the *Doctor*, with a Glass in his Hand. *Look ye my Worthy Friends*, says he, *I am now about to be as good as my Word. This Glass is my* Never-failing-Cordial: you paid me *Half a Crown* a Bottle for it before, and you shall have it now, for a *Shilling*, so that there's the *Eighteen Pence apiece* I promis'd you.

[3] For Pickle-Herring see No. 47 (vol. i).

among whom it was a Law, that whenever any Cure was performed, both the method of the Cure, and an account of the Distemper, should be fixed in some publick Place;[1] but as Customs will corrupt, these our Moderns provide themselves of Persons to attest the Cure before they publish or make an Experiment of the Prescription. I have heard of a Porter, who serves as a Knight of the Post[2] under one of these Operators, and tho' he was never sick in his Life has been cured of all the Diseases in the Dispensary. These are the Men whose Sagacity has invented Elixirs of all sorts, Pills and Lozenges, and take it as an Affront if you come to them before you are given over by every body else. Their Medicines *are infallible, and never fail of Success*,[3] that is, of enriching the Doctor, and setting the Patient effectually at Rest.

I lately dropt into a Coffee-house at *Westminster*, where I found the Room hung round with Ornaments of this Nature. There were Elixirs, Tinctures, the *Anodine Fotus*, *English* Pills, Electuaries, and in short, more Remedies than I believe there are Diseases.[4] At the Sight of so many Inventions, I could not but imagine my self in a kind of Arsenal or Magazine, where store of Arms was reposited[5] against any sudden Invasion. Should you be attack'd by the Enemy Side-ways, here was an infallible Piece of defensive Armour to cure the Pleurisie: Should a Distemper beat up your Head-Quarters, here you might purchase an impenetrable Helmet, or in the Language of the Artist, a Cephalic Tincture: If your main Body be assaulted, here are various kinds of Armour in Case of various Onsets.[6] I began to Congratulate the present Age upon the

---

[1] Herodotus, *History*, I. 197. The eastern nation referred to was Babylonia.

[2] The ordinary phrase for a perjurer, one who got his living by giving false evidence.

[3] The usual language of the quacks. The following advertisement had appeared shortly before this (in Nos. 562 and 567):

An infallible Medicine for Weakness in Men, and more especially for Women. . . . The Symptoms are these; the Weariness of the Limbs, pale Face, Weakness, Inability to move, hollow Eyes, Diminution of Sight, Inaptency, Trembling, Pensiveness or Sadness, Thickness of Urine, and a Tendency to Consumption. Prepared by John Moore, Apothecary, at the Pestle and Mortar in Abchurch-Lane, London.

[4] 'Dr. Stoughton's great Cordial Elixir' is advertised frequently (first in No. 50). Fotus is a fomentation (*OED* gives this quotation and one earlier). Electuaries 'for Coughs and Colds', 'for Loss of Memory', and for other ills are often advertised in the *Spectator*.   [5] I.e. deposited (cf. *OED*).

[6] The 'Cephalic Tincture, So long celebrated for curing Convulsions, Apoplexies, Palsies, Head Pains, Vapours, and all Nervous Distempers, Infants Fits instantly', is advertised in Nos. 562, 570, 577, 588, 599, 603, and 620:

It is of admirable Use to refine the Blood to a due Circulation, to free it from

happiness Men might reasonably hope for in Life, when Death was thus in a manner Defeated; and when Pain it self would be of so short a Duration, that it would but just serve to enhance the Value of Pleasure. While I was in these Thoughts, I unluckily call'd to mind a Story of an Ingenious Gentleman of the last Age, who lying violently afflicted with the Gout, a Person came and offer'd his Service to Cure him by a Method, which he assured him was Infallible; the Servant who receiv'd the Message carried it up to his Master, who enquiring whether the Person came on Foot or in a Chariot; and being informed that he was on Foot; *Go*, says he, *send the Knave about his Business: Was his method as Infallible as he pretends, he would long before now have been in his Coach and Six.* In like manner I concluded, that had all these Advertisers arriv'd to that Skill they pretend to, they would have had no need for so many Years successively to publish to the World the place of their Abode, and the Virtues of their Medicines. One of these Gentlemen indeed pretends to an Effectual Cure for Leanness:[1] What Effects it may have had upon those who have try'd it I cannot tell; but I am credibly inform'd, that the Call for it has been so great that it has effectually cured the Doctor himself of that Distemper. Could each of them produce so good an Instance of the Success of his Medicines, they might soon persuade the World into an Opinion of them.

I observe that most of the Bills agree in one Expression, *viz.* that (*with Gods Blessing*) they perform such and such Cures:[2] This

Stagnation, and sudden Death, fit for hard Drinkers and those that use little Exercise. It is sold in 5 Shilling and Half-Crown Bottles, with a Book of its Vertues and Directions, from Markham's under St. Dunstan's Church, and Allcroft's in Corn-hill, Toyshops, and no where else.

[1] A frequently advertised remedy (No. 125, &c.):

An assured Cure for Leanness; which proceeds from a Cause that few know, but easily remov'd by an unparallel'd Specifick Tincture, which fortifies the Stomach, purifies the Blood, takes off Fretfulness in the Mind, occasions rest and easy Sleep, and as certainly disposes and causes the Body to thrive and become plump and fleshy, if no manifest Distemper afflicts the Patient, as Water will quench Fire; 'tis also the best Remedy in Nature for all Chronick Diseases that take their Rise from a bad Digestion in the Stomach, which this Specifick Tincture Infallibly rectifies and thereby Cures. It is pleasant to taste, and is sold only at Mr. Payn's Toy-shop at the Angel and Crown in St. Paul's Church-yard near Cheapside. Price 3s. 6d. a Bottle with Directions.

[2] Robert Norris, at the Pestle and Mortar on Snow-Hill, 'having been many Years successful in the Cure of Lunaticks', announces in No. 603 his removal to the Pestle and Mortar near the Middle of Hatton-Garden, 'where he hath a very convenient large House and Garden, airy, and fit to receive Persons of the best Rank of either Sex, with suitable Attendance. Any Persons applying themselves as above, may there be satisfied, that the Cure shall be industriously endeavoured (and by God's Blessing effected) on reasonable Terms, And likewise those incurable boarded.'

Expression is certainly very proper and emphatical, for that is all they have for it. And if ever a Cure is perform'd on a Patient where they are concern'd, they can claim no greater share in it than *Virgil*'s *Japis* in the curing of *Æneas*; he try'd his Skill, was very Assiduous about the Wound, and indeed was the only visible Means that relieved the Heroe; but the Poet assures us it was the particular Assistance of a Deity that speeded the Operation. An *English* Reader may see the whole Story in Mr. *Dryden*'s Translation.[1]

> *Prop'd on his Lance the pensive Heroe stood,*
> *And heard, and saw unmov'd, the mourning Crowd.*
> *The fam'd Physician tucks his Robes around,*
> *With ready Hands, and hastens to the Wound,*
> *With gentle Touches he performs his part,*
> *This way and that, solliciting the Dart,*
> *And exercises all his Heav'nly Art.*
> *All softning Simples, known of Sov'reign Use,*
> *He presses out, and pours their noble Juice;*
> *These first infus'd, to lenifie the Pain,*
> *He tugs with Pincers, but he tugs in vain.*
> *Then, to the Patron of his Art he pray'd;*
> *The Patron of his Art refus'd his Aid.*
>
> *But now the Goddess Mother, mov'd with Grief,*
> *And pierc'd with Pity, hastens her Relief.*
> *A branch of healing* Dittany *she brought,*
> *Which in the* Cretan *Fields with Care she sought:*
> *Rough is the Stem, which wooly Leafs surround;*
> *The Leafs with Flow'rs, the Flow'rs with Purple crown'd:*
> *Well known to wounded Goats; a sure Relief*
> *To draw the pointed Steel, and ease the Grief.*
> *This* Venus *brings, in Clouds involv'd; and brews*
> *Th' extracted Liquor with* Ambrosian *Dews,*
> *And od'rous* Panacee: *Unseen she stands,*
> *Temp'ring the mixture with her Heav'nly Hands:*
> *And pours it in a Bowl, already crown'd*
> *With Juice of medc'nal herbs, prepar'd to bathe the Wound.*
> *The Leech, unknowing of superior Art,*
> *Which aids the Cure, with this foments the part;*
> *And in a Moment ceas'd the raging smart.*

[1] *Aeneid*, xii. 585-97, 607-33 (in Virgil, lines 398-406, 411-29).

Stanch'd is the Blood, and in the bottom stands:
The Steel, but scarcely touch'd with tender Hands,
Moves up, and follows of its own Accord;
And Health and Vigour are at once restor'd.
Iäpis first perceiv'd the closing Wound;
And first the footsteps of a God he found.
Arms, Arms, he cries, the Sword and Shield prepare,
And send the willing Chief, renew'd to War.
This is no Mortal Work, no cure of mine,
Nor Art's effect, but done by Hands Divine:

No. 573   *Wednesday, July 28, 1714*[1]

[LADY MARY WORTLEY MONTAGU]

. . . Castigata remordent.
Juv.

MY Paper on the Club of Widows,[2] has brought me in several Letters; and, among the rest, a long one from Mrs. President, as follows.

Smart SIR,

'YOU are pleased to be very Merry, as you imagine, with us Widows: And you seem to ground your Satyr on our receiving Consolation so soon after the Death of our Dears, and the Number we are pleased to admit for our Companions; but you never reflect what Husbands we have bury'd, and how short a Sorrow the loss of them was capable of occasioning. For my own Part, Mrs. President as you call me, my First Husband I was Marry'd to at Fourteen, by my Uncle and Guardian, (as I afterwards discovered) by way of Sale, for the Third part of my Fortune. This Fellow looked upon me as a meer Child, he might breed up after his own Fancy; if he kissed my Chamber-Maid before my

---

[1] *Motto.* Juvenal, *Satires*, 2. 35: When reproved they bite back.
Assigned to Lady Mary Wortley Montagu in the Tickell MS., an attribution accepted by Professor Robert Halsband in his biography of Lady Mary (Oxford, 1956), pp. 37–38, who suggests that the name Edward Waitfort in the essay is 'a glance at a husband whose courtship had been long and querulous' and that Dr. Gruel is 'perhaps a jibe at her old friend Dr. Garth'.
[2] No. 561.

Face, I was supposed so ignorant, how could I think there was any hurt in it? When he came home Roaring Drunk at five in the Morning, 'twas the Custom of all Men that live in the World. I was not to see a Penny of Mony, for, poor Thing, how could I manage it? He took a handsome Cousin of his into the House, (as he said) to be my House-keeper, and to govern my Servants; for how should I know how to rule a Family? and while she had what Money she pleased, which was but reasonable for the Trouble she was at for my good, I was not to be so Censorious as to dislike Familiarity and Kindness between near Relations. I was too great a Coward to contend, but not so ignorant a Child to be thus impos'd upon. I resented his Contempt as I ought to do, and as most poor passive blinded Wives do, till it pleased Heaven to take away my Tyrant, who left me free possession of my own Land, and a large Jointure. My Youth and Money brought me many Lovers, and several endeavour'd to Establish an Interest in my Heart while my Husband was in his last Sickness; the Honourable *Edward Waitfort* was one of the First who Addressed to me, advised to it by a Cousin of his that was my intimate Friend, and knew to a Penny what I was worth. Mr. *Waitfort* is a very agreeable Man, and every Body would like him as well as he does himself, if they did not plainly see that his Esteem and Love is all taken up, and by such an Object as 'tis impossible to get the better of, I mean himself. He made no doubt of marrying me within Four or Five Months, and begun to proceed with such an assured easie Air, that piqued my Pride not to banish him; quite contrary, out of pure Malice, I heard his first Declaration with so much innocent Surprise, and blushed so prettily, I perceived it touched his very Heart, and he thought me the best-natured Silly poor thing upon Earth. When a Man has such a Notion of a Woman, he loves her better than he thinks he does. I was overjoyed to be thus revenged on him, for designing on my Fortune; and finding 'twas in my Power to make his Heart ake, I resolved to compleat my Conquest, and entertained several other Pretenders. The first Impression of my undesigning Innocence was so strong in his Head, he attributed all my Followers to the inevitable force of my Charms, and from several Blushes, and side Glances, concluded himself the Favourite; and when I used him like a Dog for my Diversion, he thought it was all Prudence and Fear, and pitied the Violence I did my own Inclinations, to comply with my Friends, when I marryed Sir *Nicholas Fribble* of sixty Years

THE SPECTATOR

of Age. You know Sir, the Case of Mrs. *Medlar*, I hope you would not have had me cry out my Eyes for such a Husband.[1] I shed Tears enough for my Widowhood a Week after my Marriage, and when he was put in his Grave, reckoning he had been two Years Dead, and my self a Widow of that standing, I married three Weeks afterwards *John Sturdy* Esq; his next Heir. I had indeed some Thoughts of taking Mr. *Waitfort*, but I found he could stay, and besides he thought it indecent to ask me to Marry again till my Year was out; so privately resolving him for my Fourth, I took Mr. *Sturdy* for the Present. Would you believe it Sir, Mr. *Sturdy* was just Five and Twenty, about six Foot high, and the stoutest Fox-hunter in the County, and I believe I wished Ten thousand times for my Old *Fribble* again; he was following his Dogs all the Day, and all the Night keeping them up at Table with him and his Companions; however I think my self obliged to them for leading him a Chase in which he broke his Neck. Mr. *Waitfort* begun his Addresses anew, and I verily believe I had Married him now, but there was a young Officer in the Guards, that had Debauched two or three of my Acquaintance, and I could not forbear being a little Vain of his Courtship. Mr. *Waitfort* heard of it, and read me such an insolent Lecture upon the Conduct of Women, I Married the Officer that very Day, out of pure Spite to him. Half an Hour after I was Married I received a Penitential Letter from the Honourable Mr. *Edward Waitfort*, in which he begged Pardon for his Passion, as proceeding from the violence of his Love: I triumphed when I Read it, and could not help, out of the pride of my Heart, shewing it to my new Spouse; and we were very merry together upon it. Alas! my Mirth lasted a short time; my young Husband was very much in Debt when I marryed him, and his first Action afterwards was to set up a gilt Chariot and Six, in fine Trappings before and behind. I had married so hastily, I had not the Prudence to reserve my Estate in my own Hands; my ready Mony was lost in two Nights at the Groom Porters; and my Diamond Necklace, which was Stole I did not know how, I met in the Street upon *Jenny Wheadle*'s Neck.[2] My Plate vanished piece by piece, and I had been reduced to downright Pewter, if my Officer had not been deliciously

[1] Mrs. Medlar is the widow in No. 561, 'now wedded to an old Gentleman of Sixty'.
[2] The Groom Porter was an official appointed by the Lord Chamberlain for the control of gaming; he had his own gaming-house, which was much frequented by the nobility. Cf. Farquhar, *The Constant Couple*, I. i. According to an advertisement in the *Daily Courant* of 30 Mar. 1711 it was located in Scotland Yard.

killed in a Duel, by a Fellow that had cheated him of Five hundred Pounds, and afterwards, at his own Request, satisfied him and me too, by running him through the Body. Mr. *Waitfort* was still in Love, and told me so again; to prevent all Fears of ill Usage, he desired me to reserve every thing in my own Hands; but now my Acquaintance begun to wish me Joy of his Constancy, my Charms were declining, and I could not resist the Delight I took in shewing the young Flirts about Town, it was yet in my Power to give pain to a Man of Sense: This and some private hopes he would hang himself, and what a Glory would it be for me, and how I should be envy'd, made me accept of being third Wife to my Lord *Friday*. I proposed, from my Rank and his Estate,[1] to live in all the Joys of Pride, but how was I mistaken? He was neither extravagant, nor ill-natured, nor debauched; I suffered however more with him than with all my others. He was splenatick. I was forced to sit whole Days harkening to his imaginary Ails; it was impossible to tell what would please him; what he liked when the Sun shined, made him sick when it rained; he had no Distemper, but lived in constant Fear of them all; my good Genius dictated to me to bring him acquainted with Doctor *Gruel*; from that Day he was always contented, because he had Names for all his Complaints; the good Doctor furnished him with Reasons for all his Pains, and Prescriptions for every Fancy that troubled him; in hot Weather he lived upon Juleps, and let Blood to prevent Feavers; when it grew cloudy, he generally apprehended a Consumption; to shorten the History of this wretched part of my Life, he ruined a good Constitution by endeavouring to mend it, and took several Medicines, which ended in taking the grand Remedy, which cured both him and me of all our Uneasinesses. After his Death, I did not expect to hear any more of Mr. *Waitfort*, I knew he had renounced me to all his Friends, and been very witty upon my Choice, which he affected to talk of with great Indifferency; I gave over thinking of him, being told that he was engaging[2] with a pretty Woman and a great Fortune; it vexed me a little, but not enough to make me neglect the Advice of my Cousin *Wishwell*, that came to see me, the Day my Lord went into the Country with *Russel*; she told me experimentally, nothing put an unfaithful Lover and a dead Husband

---

[1] Apparently a slip for 'his Rank and my Estate'.
[2] Here used in the intransitive sense, 'to betroth oneself', marked *Obs.* and *rare* by *OED*, which gives but one example, dated 1722.

so soon out of ones Head, as a new one, and, at the same time, proposed to me a Kinsman of hers; you understand enough of the World (said she) to know Mony is the most valuable Consideration, he is very rich, and I'm sure, cannot live long; he has a Cough that must carry him off soon. I knew afterwards she had given the self same Character of me to him; but however I was so much persuaded by her, I hastened on the Match, for fear he should die before the time came; he had the same Fears, and was so pressing, I married him in a Fortnight, resolving to keep it private a Fortnight longer. During this Fortnight Mr. *Waitfort* came to make me a Visit, he told me he had waited on me sooner, but had that Respect for me, he would not interrupt me in the first Day of my Affliction for my dead Lord; that as soon as he heard I was at Liberty to make another Choice, he had broke off a Match very advantagious for his Fortune just upon the Point of Conclusion, and was forty times more in Love with me than ever. I never received more Pleasure in my Life than from this Declaration, but I composed my Face to a grave Air, and said the News of his Engagement had touched me to the Heart, that in a rash jealous Fit, I had married a Man I could never have thought on if I had not lost all Hopes of him. Good-natured Mr. *Waitfort* had like to have dropped down dead at hearing this, but went from me with such an Air as plainly shewed me he laid all the Blame upon himself, and hated those Friends that had advised him to the fatal Application; he seemed as much touched by my Misfortune as his own, for he had not the least Doubt I was still passionately in Love with him. The truth of the Story is, my new Husband gave me reason to repent I had not staid for him; he had married me for my Mony, and I soon found he lov'd Mony to Distraction; there was nothing he would not do to get it, nothing he would not suffer to preserve it; the smallest Expence kept him awake whole Nights, and when he paid a Bill, 'twas with as many Sighs, and after as many Delays, as a Man that endures the loss of a Limb. I heard nothing but Reproofs for Extravagancy, whatever I did. I saw very well that he would have starved me, but for losing my Jointures; and he suffered Agonies between the Grief of seeing me have so good a Stomach, and the Fear that if he made me fast it might prejudice my Health. I did not doubt he would have broke my Heart, if I did not break his, which was allowable by the Law of Self-defence; the way was very easie. I resolved to spend as much Mony as I could, and before he was aware of the Stroke, appeared before him in a two thousand Pound Diamond Necklace; he said nothing, but went quietly to his Chamber, and, as it is thought, composed himself with a Dose of Opium. I behaved my self so well upon the Occasion, that to this Day I believe he died of an Apoplexy. Mr. *Waitfort* was resolved not to be too late this time, and I heard from him in two Days. I am almost out of my Weed at this present Writing, and very doubtful whether I'll marry him or no; I do not think of a Seventh, for the ridiculous Reason you mention,[1] but out of pure Morality that I think so much Constancy should be rewarded, tho' I may not do it after all perhaps. I do not believe all the unreasonable Malice of Mankind can give a Pretence why I should have been constant to the Memory of any of the deceased, or have spent much time in grieving for an insolent, insignificant, negligent, extravagant, splenatick, or covetous Husband; my first insulted me, my second was nothing to me, my third disgusted me, the fourth would have ruined me, the fifth tormented me, and the sixth would have starved me. If the other Ladies you name would thus give in their Husbands Pictures, at length, you would see, they have had as little Reason as my self to lose their Hours in weeping and wailing.'

No. 574
[ADDISON]

Friday, *July* 30, 1714[2]

Non possidentem multa vocaveris
Rectè Beatum, rectiùs occupat
Nomen Beati, qui Deorum
Muneribus sapienter uti
Duramque callet pauperiem pati.
Hor.

I WAS once engaged in Discourse with a *Rosicrusian*[a] about *the great Secret*. As this kind of Men (I mean those of them who are

[a] *Rosicrusian*] Rosicrusian Philosopher *Fol. Corrected in Errata (No. 575)*

---

[1] See No. 561, paragraph 2.   [*For note 2 see following page.*

not professed Cheats) are over-run with Enthusiasm and Philosophy, it was very amusing to hear this religious Adept descanting
on his pretended Discovery. He talked of the Secret as of a Spirit
which lived within an Emerald, and converted every thing that
was near it to the highest Perfection it is capable of. It gives a
Lustre,[a] says he, to the Sun and Water to the Diamond. It irradiates
every Metal, and enriches Lead with all the Properties of Gold. It
heightens Smoke into Flame, Flame into Light, and Light into
Glory. He further added, that a single Ray of it dissipates Pain, and
Care, and Melancholy from the Person on whom it falls. In short,
says he, its Presence naturally changes every Place into a kind of
Heaven. After he had gone on for some Time in this unintelligible
Cant, I found that he jumbled natural and moral Ideas together
into[b] the same Discourse, and that his great Secret was nothing
else but *Content*.

This Virtue does indeed produce, in some Measure, all those
Effects which the Alchymist usually ascribes to what he calls the
Philosopher's Stone; and if it does not bring Riches, it does the
same thing, by banishing the Desire of them.[1] If it cannot remove
the Disquietudes arising out of a Man's Mind, Body, or Fortune,
it makes him easy under them. It has indeed a kindly Influence
on the Soul of Man, in respect of every Being to whom he stands
related. It extinguishes all Murmur, Repining, and Ingratitude
towards that Being who has allotted him his Part to act in this
World. It destroys all inordinate Ambition, and[c] every Tendency
to Corruption, with regard to the Community wherein he is
placed. It gives Sweetness to his Conversation, and a perpetual
Serenity to all his Thoughts.

Among the many Methods which might be made use of for the
acquiring of this Virtue, I shall only mention the two following.

---

[a] a Lustre] Lustre *Fol.*   [b] into] in *Fol.*
[c] and] with *Fol. Corrected in Errata (No. 575)*

---

[1] Addison may be thinking of Steele's interest in alchemy (see Aitken, *Life*, i.
141–5).

---

[2] *Motto.* Horace, *Odes*, 4. 9. 45–49:
> He is not number'd with the blest
>   To whom the Gods large Stores have giv'n;
> But he who of enough possest,
>   Can wisely use the Gifts of Heav'n,
> Who Fortune's Frowns with Patience bears,
> And the worst Ills the Gods can send.

First of all, a Man should always consider how much he has more than he wants; and secondly, how much more unhappy he might be than he really is.

First of all, A Man should always consider how much he has more than he wants. I am wonderfully pleased with the Reply which *Aristippus* made to one who condoled him upon the Loss of a Farm, *Why,* said he, *I have three Farms still, and you have but one; so that I ought rather to be afflicted for you than you for me.*[1] On the contrary, foolish Men are more apt to consider what they have lost than what they possess; and to fix their Eyes upon those who are richer than themselves, rather than on those who are under greater Difficulties. All the real Pleasures and Conveniencies of Life lie in a narrow Compass; but it is the Humour of Mankind to be always looking forward, and straining after one who has got the Start of them[a] in Wealth and Honour. For this Reason, as there are none can be properly called rich, who have not more than they want; there are few rich Men in any of the politer Nations but among the middle Sort of People, who keep their Wishes within their Fortunes, and have more Wealth than they know how to enjoy. Persons of a higher Rank live in a kind of splendid Poverty, and are perpetually wanting, because instead of acquiescing in the solid Pleasures of Life, they endeavour to outvie one another in Shadows and Appearances. Men of Sense have at all times beheld with a great deal of Mirth this silly Game that is playing over their Heads, and by contracting their Desires, enjoy all that secret Satisfaction which others are always in quest of. The Truth is, this ridiculous Chase after imaginary Pleasures cannot be sufficiently exposed, as it is the great Source of those Evils which generally undo a Nation. Let a Man's Estate be what it will, he is a poor Man if he does not live within it, and naturally sets himself to Sale to any one that can give him his Price. When *Pittacus,* after the Death of his Brother, who had left him a good Estate, was offered a great Sum of Money by the King of *Lydia;* he thanked him for his Kindness, but told him he had already more by Half than he knew what to do with.[2] In short, Content is equivalent to Wealth, and Luxury to Poverty, or to give the Thought a more agreeable Turn, *Content is natural*

---

[a] them] him *Fol. Corrected in Errata (No. 575)*

[1] Plutarch, 'On Tranquillity' (*Moralia* 469C).
[2] Plutarch, 'On Brotherly Love' (*Moralia* 484C).

Wealth, says *Socrates*;[1] to which I shall add, *Luxury is artificial Poverty*. I shall therefore recommend to the Consideration of those who are always aiming after superfluous and imaginary Enjoyments, and will not be at the Trouble of contracting their Desires, an excellent Saying of *Bion* the Philosopher; namely, *That no Man has so much Care, as he who endeavours after the most Happiness*.[2]

In the second place, Every one ought to reflect how much more unhappy he might be than he really is. The former Consideration took in all those who are sufficiently provided with the Means to make themselves easy; this regards such as actually lie under some Pressure or Misfortune. These may receive great Alleviation from such a Comparison as the unhappy Person may make between himself and others, or between the Misfortune which he suffers, and greater Misfortunes which might have befallen him.

I like the Story of the honest *Dutch* Man, who, upon breaking his *Leg* by a Fall from the Mainmast, told the Standers-by, It was a great Mercy that 'twas not his *Neck*.[3] To which, since I am got into Quotations, give me leave to add the Saying of an old Philosopher, who, after having invited some of his Friends to dine with him, was ruffled by his Wife that came into the Room in a Passion, and threw down the Table that stood before them; *Every one*, says he, *has his Calamity, and he is a happy Man that has no greater than this*.[4] We find an Instance to the same purpose in the Life of Doctor *Hammond*, written by Bishop *Fell*. As this good Man was troubled with a Complication of Distempers, when he had the Gout upon him, he used to thank God that it was not the Stone; and when he had the Stone, that he had not both these Distempers on him at the same time.[5]

---

[1] Cf. Plato, *Apology* 30B: 'Virtue does not come from money, but from virtue comes money and all other good things to man. . . .'

[2] Diogenes Laertius, *Lives of the philosophers*, 4. 48: 'Being once asked who suffers most from anxiety, he replied, "He who is ambitious of the greatest prosperity." '

[3] Tom Brown's 'Letter to Monsieur des A—', describing the Dutch (one of the 'Letters from the best French Authors') observes:

Certainly, no People in the World receive Misfortunes with less Emotion. Let what Accidents soever befal them, they comfort themselves, that something worse might have happen'd to them. If they chance to break a Leg or an Arm, they think themselves favourably dealt with, that they did not break their Necks (*Works*, 4th ed., 1715, i. 368).

[4] Plutarch, 'On Tranquillity of Mind' (*Moralia* 471B). The story is told of Pittacus.

[5] See *The Life of the most learned, reverend and pious Dr. H. Hammond, written by John Fell* (1661), p. 188:

And even then when on the wrack of torture, would he be observing every circumstance of allay: *When 'twas the Gout, he would give thanks 'twas not the Stone*

I cannot conclude this Essay without observing, that there was never any System, besides that of Christianity, which could effectually produce in the Mind of Man the Virtue I have been hitherto speaking of. In order to make us content with our present Condition, many of the ancient Philosophers tell us that our Discontent only hurts our selves, without being able to make any Alteration in our Circumstances; others, that whatever Evil befalls us is derived to us by a fatal Necessity, to which the Gods themselves are subject; whilst others very gravely tell the Man who is miserable, that it is necessary he should be so, to keep up the Harmony of the Universe, and that the *Scheme* of Providence would be troubled and perverted were he otherwise.[1] These, and the like Considerations, rather silence than satisfy a Man. They may show him that his Discontent is unreasonable, but are by no means sufficient to relieve it. They rather give Despair than Consolation. In a word, a Man might reply to one of these Comforters, as *Augustus* did to his Friend who advised him not to grieve for the Death of a Person whom he loved, because his Grief could not fetch him again.[a] *It is for that very Reason*, said the Emperor, *that I grieve.*[2]

On the contrary, Religion bears a more tender Regard to humane Nature. It prescribes to every miserable Man the Means of bettering his Condition; nay, it shews him, that the bearing of his Afflictions as he ought to do will naturally end in the Removal of them: It makes him easy here, because it can make him happy hereafter.

Upon the Whole, a contented Mind is the greatest Blessing a Man can enjoy in this World;[b] and if in the present Life his Happiness arises from the subduing of his Desires, it will arise in the next from the Gratification of them.[3]

---

[a] fetch him again.] fetch him back again. *Fol.*   [b] World;] Life; *Fol. Corrected in Errata (No. 575)*

---

or Cramp, when 'twas the Stone, he then would say 'twas not so sharp as others felt, accusing his impatience that it appear'd so bad to him as it did.

[1] See Seneca, *Dialogues*, 11. 1. 4 ('De consolatione').
[2] The saying is not that of Augustus but of Solon. See Diogenes Laertius, *Lives of the philosophers*, I. 63. Bayle quotes it in the art. Foulques, Remark E.
[3] Cf. No. 634 (vol. v).

No. 575
[ADDISON]

Monday, August 2, 1714[1]

. . . Nec morti esse locum . . .
Virg.

A lewd young Fellow seeing an aged Hermit go by him barefoot, *Father*, says he, *you are in a very miserable Condition if there is not another World.*[2] *True, Son*, said the Hermit; *but what is thy Condition if there is?*[a] Man is a Creature designed for two different States of Being, or rather, for two different Lives. His first Life is short and transient; his second permanent and lasting. The Question we are all concerned in is this, In which of these two Lives it is our chief Interest to make our selves happy? or, in other Words, Whether we should endeavour to secure to our selves the Pleasures and Gratifications of a Life which is uncertain and precarious, and at its utmost Length of a very inconsiderable Duration; or to secure to our selves the Pleasures of a Life which is fixed and settled, and will never end? Every Man, upon the first hearing of this Question, knows very well which Side of it he ought to close with. But however right we are in Theory, it is plain that in Practice we adhere to the wrong Side of the Question. We make Provisions for this Life as tho' it were never to have an End, and for the other Life as tho' it were never to have a Beginning.

Should a Spirit of superior Rank, who is a Stranger to human Nature, accidentally alight upon the Earth, and take a Survey of its Inhabitants; what would his Notions of us be? Would not he think that we are a Species of Beings made for quite different Ends and Purposes than what we really are? Must not he imagine that we were placed in this World to get Riches and Honours? Would not he think that it was our Duty to toil after Wealth, and Station, and Title? Nay, would not he believe we were forbidden Poverty by

[a] *Father, . . . is?* Italics added in 8vo, 12mo

[1] *Motto.* Virgil, *Georgics*, 4. 226: No room is left for Death. DRYDEN.
[2] The story is told, 'from Sir Thomas More's Works', in Camden's *Remains concerning Britain* (ed. 1674), p. 368:

When a lusty gallant saw a Fryar going barefoot in a great Frost and Snow, he asked him why he did take such pain. He answered, that it was very little pain, if a man would remember Hell: Yea Fryar (quoth the Gallant) but what and if there be no Hell? Then thou art a great fool: Yea Master (quoth the Fryar) but what if there be hell, then is your Mastership much more fool.

The story is also told in John Scott, *The Christian Life*, part ii, chap. iii, 'Of the Folly of Atheism' (ed. 1700, ii. 139), where the hermit's interlocutors are two cardinals.

Threats of eternal Punishment, and enjoined to pursue our Pleasures under Pain of Damnation? He would certainly imagine that we were influenced by a Scheme of Duties quite opposite to those which are indeed prescribed to us. And truly, according to such an Imagination, he must conclude that we are a Species of the most obedient Creatures in the Universe; that we are constant to our Duty; and that we keep a steddy Eye on the End for which we were sent hither.

But how great would be his Astonishment, when he learnt that we were Beings not designed to exist in this World above threescore and ten Years? and that the greatest Part of this busy Species fall short even of that Age? How would he be lost in Horrour and Admiration, when he should know that this Sett of Creatures, who lay out all their Endeavours for this Life, which scarce deserves the Name of Existence; when, I say, he should know that this Sett of Creatures are to exist to all Eternity in another Life, for which they make no Preparations? Nothing can be a greater Disgrace to Reason, than that Men, who are perswaded of these two different States of Being, should be perpetually employed in providing for a Life of threescore and ten Years, and neglecting to make Provision for that, which after many Myriads of Years will be still new, and still beginning; especially when we consider that our endeavours for making our selves great, or rich, or honourable, or whatever else we place our Happiness in, may after all prove unsuccesful; whereas if we constantly and sincerely endeavour to make our selves happy in the other Life, we are sure that our Endeavours will succeed, and that we shall not be disappointed of our Hope.

¹ The following Question is started by one of the Schoolmen.

¹ This paragraph has often been attributed to Swift, and is included in Swift's *Prose Works*, ed. Herbert Davis, vol. ii (Oxford, 1939), p. 268. John Nichols seems to have been the first to attribute it to Swift. In his revision of Thomas Sheridan's edition of Swift (1801), Nichols prints in vol. v only *Spectator* 50, but in vol. xviii (p. 215) he prints this paragraph from No. 575, with the following introductory sentence: 'In the Spectator, No. 575, August 2, 1714, the following article was proposed by Dr. Swift.' (Sheridan's edition, 1784, 17 vols., does not include it.) Beyond Swift's statement in 1735 that he had 'writ several Tatlers, and some Spectators; and furnished Hints for many more', there is no evidence for his authorship. It is, moreover, unlikely that in the summer of 1714 Swift would be contributing to the *Spectator*.

The idea, of course, is common in theological writing, and the symbol itself—a mass of sand being annihilated at the rate of one grain in a thousand years—occurs in several works which Addison probably knew. It is to be found in *The Considerations of Drexelius upon Eternitie*, trans. Ralph Winterton (1658), pp. 106-7; and in *A Treatise of the Difference betwixt the Temporal and Eternal*, composed in Spanish by Juan Eusebio Nieremberg, S.J., and translated into English by Sir Vivian Mullineaux (1672), pp. 45-46, a work in Addison's library. For parallels to the idea see Archer Taylor, 'Locutions for Never', *Romance Philology*, ii (1948-9), 105 n.

Supposing the whole Body of the Earth were a great Ball or Mass of the finest Sand, and that a single Grain or Particle of this Sand should be annihilated every thousand Years. Supposing then that you had it in your Choice to be happy all the while this prodigious Mass of Sand was consuming by this slow Method till there was not a Grain of it left, on Condition you were to be miserable for ever after; or, supposing that you might be happy for ever after, on Condition you would be miserable till the whole Mass of Sand were thus annihilated at the Rate of one Sand in a thousand Years: Which of these two Cases would you make your Choice?

It must be confessed in this Case, so many Thousands of Years are to the Imagination as a kind of Eternity, tho' in reality they do not bear so great a Proportion to that Duration which is to follow them, as a Unite does to the greatest Number which you can put together in Figures, or as one of those Sands to the supposed Heap. Reason therefore tells us, without any Manner of Hesitation, which would be the better Part in this Choice. However, as I have before intimated, our Reason might in such a Case be so overset by the Imagination, as to dispose some Persons to sink under the Consideration of the great Length of the first Part of this Duration, and of the great Distance of that second Duration which is to succeed it. The Mind, I say, might give it self up to that Happiness which is at hand, considering that it is so very near, and that it would last so very long. But when the Choice we actually have before us is this, Whether we will choose to be happy for the Space of only threescore and ten, nay perhaps of only twenty or ten Years, I might say of only a Day or an Hour, and miserable to all Eternity; or, on the contrary, miserable for this short Term of Years, and happy for a whole Eternity: What Words are sufficient to express that Folly and want of Consideration which in such a Case makes a wrong Choice?

I here put the Case even at the worst, by supposing (what seldom happens) that a Course of Virtue makes us miserable in this Life: But if we suppose (as it generally happens) that Virtue would make us more happy even in this Life than a contrary Course of Vice; how can we sufficiently admire[1] the Stupidity or Madness of those Persons who are capable of making so absurd a Choice?[2]

[1] Here used of course in the archaic sense 'to wonder or marvel at'.
[2] Cf. Locke, *Essay concerning Human Understanding*, II. xxi. 70 (ed. 1700, p. 151): But when infinite Happiness is put in one Scale, against infinite Misery in the other; if the worst, that comes to the pious Man, if he mistakes, be the best

Every wise Man therefore will consider this Life only as it may conduce to the Happiness of the other, and chearfully sacrifice the Pleasures of a few Years to those of an Eternity.

No. 576   *Wednesday, August 4, 1714*[1]

[ADDISON]

Nitor in adversum; nec me, qui cætera, vincit
Impetus; & rapido contrarius evehor Orbi.
Ovid.

I REMEMBER a young Man of very lively Parts, and of a sprightly Turn in Conversation, who had only one Fault, which was an inordinate Desire of appearing fashionable. This ran him into many Amours, and consequently into many Distempers. He never went to Bed till two a-clock in the Morning, because he would not be a queer Fellow; and was every now and then knocked down by a Constable, to signalize his Vivacity. He was initiated into Half a Dozen Clubs before he was One and twenty, and so improved in them his natural Gayety of Temper, that you might frequently trace him to his Lodgings by a Range of broken Windows, and other the like Monuments of Wit and Gallantry. To be short, after having fully established his Reputation of being a very agreeable Rake, he died of old Age at Five and twenty.

There is indeed nothing which betrays a Man into so many Errors and Inconveniencies, as the Desire of not appearing singular; for which Reason it is very necessary to form a right Idea of Singularity, that we may know when it is laudable, and when it is vicious.[2] In the first Place, every Man of Sense will agree with me, that Singularity is laudable, when, in Contradiction to a Multitude, it adheres to the Dictates of Conscience, Morality, and Honour. In these Cases we ought to consider, that it is not Custom, but Duty, which is the Rule of Action; and that we should be only so far *sociable*, as we are reasonable Creatures. Truth is never the less so,

that the wicked can attain to, if he be in the right, Who can without madness run the venture?

[1] *Motto.* Ovid, *Metamorphoses,* 2. 72–73:

> I steer against their motions, nor am I
> Borne back by all the current of the sky. ADDISON.

Steele had used these lines for the motto of *Tatler* 159.

[2] Addison had treated this subject earlier in No. 458.

for not being attended to; and it is the Nature of Actions, not the Number of Actors, by which we ought to regulate our Behaiour. Singularity in Concerns of this Kind is to be looked upon as heroick Bravery, in which a Man leaves the Species only as he soars above it. What greater Instance can there be of a weak and pusillanimous Temper, than for a Man to pass his whole Life in Opposition to his own Sentiments? or not to dare to be what he thinks he ought to be?

Singularity therefore is only vicious when it makes Men act contrary to Reason, or when it puts them upon distinguishing themselves by Trifles. As for the first of these, who are singular in any thing that is irreligious, immoral, or dishonourable, I believe every one will easily give them up. I shall therefore speak of those only who are remarkable for their Singularity in things of no Importance, as in Dress, Behaviour, Conversation, and all the little Intercourses of Life. In these Cases there is a certain Deference due to Custom; and notwithstanding there may be a Colour of Reason to deviate from the Multitude in some Particulars, a Man ought to sacrifice his private Inclinations and Opinions to the Practice of the Publick. It must be confessed that good Sense often makes a Humourist;[1] but then it unqualifies him for being of any Moment in the World, and renders him ridiculous to Persons of a much inferior Understanding.

I have heard of a Gentleman in the North of *England*, who was a remarkable Instance of this foolish Singularity. He had laid it down as a Rule within himself, to act in the most indifferent Parts of Life according to the most abstracted Notions of Reason and good Sense, without any Regard to Fashion or Example. This Humour broke out at first in many little Oddnesses: He had never any stated Hours for his Dinner, Supper, or Sleep; because, said he, we ought to attend the Calls of Nature, and not set our Appetites to our Meals, but bring our Meals to our Appetites. In his Conversation with Country-Gentlemen, he would not make Use of a Phrase that was not strictly true: He never told any of them, that he was his humble Servant, but that he was his Well-wisher; and would rather be thought a Malecontent, than drink the King's Health when he was not a-dry. He would thrust his Head out of his Chamber-Window every Morning, and after having gaped for fresh

---

[1] 'Humorists' (persons subject to 'humours' or fancies) and their eccentricities are mentioned in No. 24 (i. 102), No. 251 (ii. 477) and elsewhere. Mr. Spectator himself is called in No. 101 'a great Humourist' (i. 425) and Sir Roger is also described as 'something of an Humourist,' whose 'Virtues, as well as Imperfections, are as it were tinged by a certain Extravagance' (No. 106; i. 440). No. 477 consists of a letter from 'an Humorist in Gardening' (iv. 188–82).

Air about half an Hour, repeat fifty Verses as loud as he could bawl them for the Benefit of his Lungs; to which End he generally took them out of *Homer*; the *Greek* Tongue, especially in that Author, being more deep and sonorous, and more conducive to Expectoration, than any other. He had many other Particularities, for which he gave sound and philosophical Reasons. As this Humour still grew upon him, he chose to wear a Turban instead of a Perriwig; concluding very justly, that a Bandage of clean Linnen about his Head was much more wholsome, as well as cleanly, than the Caul of a Wig, which is soiled with frequent Perspirations. He afterwards judiciously observed, that the many Ligatures in our *English* Dress must naturally check the Circulation of the Blood; for which Reason, he made his Breeches and his Doublet of one continued Piece of Cloth, after the Manner of the *Hussars*.[1] In short, by following the pure Dictates of Reason, he at length departed so much from the rest of his Countrymen, and indeed from his whole Species, that his Friends would have clapped him into *Bedlam*, and have begged his Estate; but the Judge being informed that he did no Harm, contented himself with issuing out a Commission of Lunacy against him, and putting his Estate into the Hands of proper Guardians.[2]

The Fate of this Philosopher puts me in Mind of a Remark in Monsieur *Fontenelle's* Dialogue of the Dead.[3] *The Ambitious and the Covetous* (says he) *are Madmen to all Intents and Purposes, as much as those who are shut up in dark Rooms; but they have the good Luck to have Numbers on their Side; whereas the Frenzy of one who is given up for a Lunatick, is a Frenzy* hors d'œuvre; *that is, in other Words, something which is singular in its Kind, and does not fall in with the Madness of a Multitude.*

The Subject of this Essay was occasioned by a Letter which I received not long since, and which, for want of Room at present, I shall insert in my next Paper.

---

[1] The light cavalry regiments of the Hungarian army; they first appeared in western Europe in 1694.

[2] Boswell (30 Sept. 1769) quotes Johnson's comment on this passage:

But consider how easy it is to make people stare, by being absurd. I may do it by going into a drawing-room without my shoes. You remember the gentleman in 'The Spectator,' who had a commission of lunacy taken out against him for his extreme singularity, such as never wearing a wig, but a night-cap. Now, Sir, abstractedly, the night-cap was best; but, relatively, the advantage was overbalanced by his making the boys run after him (ed. Hill–Powell, ii. 75).

[3] Dialogue IV (Guillaume de Cabestan and Albert Frideric de Brandebourg) in the 'Dialogues des morts modernes' (*Nouveaux Dialogues des Morts*, Londres, 1707, p. 58). (The translation is not that of Hughes.)

No. 577
[BUDGELL]

Friday, August 6, 1714[1]

> *. . . Hoc tolerabile, si non*
> *Et furere incipias . . .*
>
> Juv.

THE Letter mentioned in my last Paper is as follows.

SIR,

'YOU have so lately decryed that Custom, too much in use among most People, of making themselves the Subjects of their Writings and Conversation,[2] that I had some Difficulty to perswade my self to give you this Trouble, till I had considered that tho' I should speak in the First Person, yet I could not be justly charged with Vanity, since I shall not add my Name; as also, because what I shall write will not, to say the best, redound to my Praise; but is only designed to remove a Prejudice conceived against me, as, I hope, with very little Foundation. My short History is this.

'I have lived for some Years last past altogether in *London,* till about a Month ago an Acquaintance of mine, for whom I have done some small Services in Town, invited me to pass Part of the Summer with him at his House in the Country. I accepted his Invitation, and found a very hearty Welcome. My Friend, an honest plain Man, not being qualified to pass away his Time without the Reliefs of Business, has grafted the Farmer upon the Gentleman, and brought himself to submit even to the servile Parts of that Employment, such as inspecting his Plough, and the like. This necessarily takes up some of his Hours every Day; and as I have no Relish for such Diversions, I used at these Times to retire either to my Chamber, or a shady Walk near the House, and entertain my self with some agreeable Author. Now you must know, Mr. SPECTATOR, that when I read, especially if it be Poetry, it is very usual with me, when I meet with any Passage or Expression which strikes me

---

¹ *Motto.* Juvenal, *Satires,* 6. 614–15.

This might be borne with, if you did not also rave.

The first part of this number is probably a genuine letter from a contributor; the 'humble petition of John a Nokes and John a Stiles' exists in the Tickell MS. and may well be, as Mr. Hodgart suggests, by Addison.

² See No. 562.

much, to pronounce it aloud, with that Tone of the Voice which I think agreeable to the Sentiments there expressed; and to this I generally add some Motion or Action of the Body. It was not long before I was observed by some of the Family in one of these heroick Fits, who thereupon received Impressions very much to my Disadvantage. This however I did not soon discover, nor should have done probably, had it not been for the following Accident: I had one Day shut my self up in my Chamber, and was very deeply engaged in the Second Book of *Milton*'s *Paradise lost*. I walked to and fro with the Book in my Hand, and, to speak the Truth, I fear I made no little Noise; when presently coming to the following Lines,

> . . . *On a sudden open fly,*
> *With impetuous Recoil and jarring Sound,*
> *Th'infernal Doors, and on their Hinges grate*
> *Harsh Thunder,* &c.[1]

I in great Transport threw open the Door of my Chamber, and found the greatest Part of the Family standing on the Outside in a very great Consternation. I was in no less Confusion, and begged Pardon for having disturbed them; addressing my self particularly to comfort one of the Children, who received an unlucky Fall in this Action, whilst he was too intently surveying my Meditations through the Key-hole. To be short, after this Adventure I easily observed that great Part of the Family, especially the Women and Children, looked upon me with some Apprehensions of Fear; and my Friend himself, tho' he still continued his Civilities to me, did not seem altogether easy: I took Notice, that the Butler was never after this Accident ordered to leave the Bottle upon the Table after Dinner. Add to this, that I frequently over-heard the Servants mention me by the Name of the crazed Gentleman, the Gentleman a little touched, the mad *Londoner*, and the like. This made me think it high Time for me to shift my Quarters, which I resolved to do the first handsom Opportunity; and was confirmed in this Resolution by a young Lady in the Neighbourhood who frequently visited us, and who one Day, after having heard all the fine Things I was able to say, was pleased with a scornful Smile to bid me go to sleep.

'The first Minute I got to my Lodgings in Town, I set Pen to Paper to desire your Opinion, whether, upon the Evidence before

[1] *Paradise Lost*, ii. 879–82.

you, I am mad or not. I can bring Certificates that I behave my self soberly before Company, and I hope there is at least some Merit in withdrawing to be mad. Look you, Sir, I am contented to be esteemed a little touched, as they phrase it,[1] but should be sorry to be madder than my Neighbours; therefore, pray let me be as much in my Senses as you can afford. I know I could bring your-self as an Instance of a Man who has confessed talking to himself; but yours is a particular Case, and cannot justify me, who have not kept Silence any Part of my Life. What if I should own my self in Love? You know Lovers are always allowed the Comfort of Soliloquy——But I will say no more upon this Subject, because I have long since observed, the ready Way to be thought mad is to contend that you are not so; as we generally conclude that Man drunk, who takes Pains to be thought sober. I will therefore leave my self to your Determination; but am the more desirous to be thought in my Senses, that it may be no Discredit to you when I assure you that I have always been very much

Your Admirer.

'P. S. *If I must be mad, I desire the young Lady may believe it is for her.*'

The humble Petition of John a Nokes *and* John a Stiles,[2]

Sheweth,

'THAT your Petitioners have had Causes depending in *Westminster-Hall* above five hundred Years, and that we despair of ever seeing them brought to an Issue; That your Petitioners have not been involved in these Law Suits out of any litigious Temper of their own, but by the Instigation of contentious Persons; That the young Lawyers in our Inns of Court are continually setting us together by the Ears, and think they do us no Hurt, because they plead for us without a Fee; That many of the Gentlemen of the Robe have no other Clients in the World besides us two; That when they have nothing else to do, they make us Plaintiffs and Defendants, tho' they were never retained by either of us; That they traduce, condemn or acquit us, without any Manner of Regard to our Reputations and good Names in the World. Your Petitioners therefore (being thereunto incouraged by the favourable Reception

[1] The expression was actually a new one, according to *OED*, which gives 1704 as the date of the earliest quotation.
[2] See No. 563.

which you lately gave to our Kinsman *Blank*)[1] do humbly pray, that you will put an End to the Controversies which have been so long depending between us your said Petitioners, and that our Enmity may not endure from Generation to Generation; it being our Resolution to live hereafter as it becometh Men of peaceable Dispositions.

> *And your Petitioners (as in Duty bound)*
> *shall ever pray, &c.'*

No. 578   *Monday, August 9, 1714*[2]
[BUDGELL]

> *. . . Eque feris humana in corpora transit,*
> *Inque feras Noster . . .*
>
>   Ovid.

THERE has been very great Reason on several Accounts, for the learned World to endeavour at settling what it was that might be said to compose, *personal Identity*.

Mr. *Lock*, after having premised that the Word *Person* properly signifies a thinking intelligent Being that has Reason and Reflection, and can consider it self as it self; concludes, That it is Consciousness alone, and not an Identity of Substance, which makes this personal Identity or Sameness. Had I the same Consciousness (says that Author) that I saw the Ark and *Noah*'s Flood, as that I saw an Overflowing of the *Thames* last Winter, or as that I now write; I could no more doubt that I who write this now, that saw the *Thames* overflowed last Winter, and that view'd the Flood at the general Deluge, was the same *Self*, place that *Self* in what Substance you please, than that I who write this am the same *My self* now whilst I write, (whether I consist of all the same Substance material or immaterial or no) that I was Yesterday: For

---

[1] No. 563.
[2] *Motto.* Ovid, *Metamorphoses,* 15. 167–8:
> Th' unbodied spirit flies—
> And lodges where it lights in man or beast. DRYDEN.

Cf. also the motto for No. 343. This is marked in the Tickell MS. as one of the nine papers contributed by Budgell to the last volume.

as to this Point of being the same *Self*, it matters not whether this present *Self* be made up of the same or other Substances.[1]

I was mightily pleased with a Story in some Measure applicable to this Piece of Philosophy, which I read the other Day in *The Persian Tales*, as they are lately very well translated by Mr. *Philips*; and with an Abridgment whereof I shall here present my Readers.[2]

I shall only premise that these Stories are writ after the Eastern Manner, but somewhat more correct.

'*Fadlallah*, a Prince of great Virtues, succeeded his Father, *Bin-Ortoc*, in the Kingdom of *Mousel*. He reigned over his faithful Subjects for some Time, and lived in great Happiness with his beauteous Consort Queen *Zemroude*; when there appeared at his Court a young Dervis of so lively and entertaining a Turn of Wit, as won upon the Affections of every one he conversed with. His Reputation grew so fast every Day, that it at last raised a Curiosity in the Prince himself to see and talk with him. He did so, and far from finding that common Fame had flattered him, he was soon convinced that every thing he had heard of him fell short of the Truth.

'*Fadlallah* immediately lost all Manner of Relish for the Conversation of other Men; and as he was every Day more and more satisfied of the Abilities of this Stranger, offered him the first Posts in his Kingdom. The young Dervis, after having thanked him with a very singular Modesty, desired to be excused, as having made a Vow never to accept of any Employment, and preferring a free and independant State of Life to all other Conditions.

'The King was infinitely charmed with so great an Example of Moderation; and tho' he could not get him to engage in a Life

---

[1] Locke, *Essay concerning Human Understanding*, II. xxvii. 16.
[2] In No. 564 (7 July 1714) is advertised:

This Day is published, in a neat Pocket-Volume, The Thousand and One Days Persian Tales. Translated from the French by Mr. Philips. Printed for Jacob Tonson at Shakespear's-Head against Catherine-street in the Strand: Where may be had, Pastorals, and Distrest Mother, written by the same Author.

A rival translation, 'by the late Learned Dr. King, and several other Hands', was also published in 1714, 'Printed for W. Mears at the Lamb and J. Browne at the Black Swan, both without Temple Bar'. Both derive from the French of Pétis de la Croix. The version quoted in the *Spectator* is that of Ambrose Philips. The story told here, a portion of the History of Prince Fadlallah, son of Bin-Ortock, King of Mousel, is in vol. i, Days LVII–LX. (According to an advertisement quoted by R. H. Griffith in the *Times Literary Supplement*, 16 Nov. 1935, p. 752, the rival Mears translation was not published until 18 August.)

of Business, made him however his chief Companion and first Favourite.

'As they were one Day hunting together, and happened to be separated from the rest of the Company, the Dervis entertained *Fadlallah* with an Account of his Travels and Adventures. After having related to him several Curiosities which he had seen in the *Indies, It was in this Place,* says he, *that I contracted an Acquaintance with an old Brachman, who was skilled in the most hidden Powers of Nature: He died within my Arms, and with his parting Breath communicated to me one of the most valuable of his Secrets, on Condition I should never reveal it to any Man.* The King immediately reflecting on his young Favourite's having refused the late Offers of Greatness he had made him, told him he presumed it was the Power of making Gold. *No, Sir,* says the Dervis, *it is somewhat more wonderful than that; it is the Power of reanimating a dead Body, by flinging my own Soul into it.*

'While he was yet speaking a Doe came bounding by them; and the King, who had his Bow ready, shot her through the Heart; telling the Dervis that a fair Opportunity now offered for him to show his Art. The young Man immediately left his own Body breathless on the Ground, while at the same Instant that of the Doe was reanimated, she came to the King, fawned upon him, and after having played several wanton Tricks, fell again upon the Grass; at the same Instant the Body of the Dervis recovered its Life. The King was infinitely pleased at so uncommon an Operation, and conjured his Friend by every thing that was sacred to communicate it to him. The Dervis at first made some Scruple of violating his Promise to the dying Brachman; but told him at last that he found he could conceal nothing from so excellent a Prince; after having obliged him therefore by an Oath to Secrecy, he taught him to[a] repeat two Cabalistick Words, in pronouncing[b] of which the whole Secret consisted. The King, impatient to try the Experiment, immediately repeated them as he had been taught, and in an Instant found himself in the Body of the Doe. He had but little Time to contemplate himself in this new Being; for the treacherous Dervis shooting his own Soul into the royal Corps, and bending the Prince's own Bow against him, had laid him dead on the Spot, had not the King, who perceived his Intent, fled swiftly to the Woods.

'The Dervis, now triumphant in his Villany, returned to *Mousel,* and filled the Throne and Bed of the unhappy *Fadlallah.*

[a] to] how to *Fol.*   [b] in pronouncing] in the pronouncing *Fol.*

'The first thing he took Care of, in order to secure himself in the Possession of his new-acquired Kingdom, was to issue out a Proclamation, ordering his Subjects to destroy all the Deer in the Realm. The King had perished among the rest, had he not avoided his Pursuers by reanimating the Body of a Nightingale which he saw lie dead at the Foot of a Tree. In this new Shape he winged his Way in Safety to the Palace, where perching on a Tree which stood near his Queen's Apartment, he filled the whole Place with so many melodious and melancholy Notes as drew her to the Window. He had the Mortification to see, that instead of being pitied, he only moved the Mirth of his Princess, and of a young Female Slave who was with her. He continued however to serenade her every Morning, till at last the Queen, charmed with his Harmony, sent for the Bird-catchers, and ordered them to employ their utmost Skill to put that little Creature into her Possession. The King, pleased with an Opportunity of being once more near his beloved Consort, easily suffered himself to be taken; and when he was presented to her, tho' he shewed a Fearfulness to be touched by any of the other Ladies, flew of his own accord, and hid himself in the Queen's Bosom. *Zemroude* was highly pleased at the unexpected Fondness of her new Favourite, and ordered him to be kept in an open Cage in her own Apartment. He had there an Opportunity of making his Court to her every Morning, by a thousand little Actions which his Shape allowed him. The Queen passed away whole Hours every Day in hearing and playing with him. *Fadlallah* could even have thought himself happy in this State of Life, had he not frequently endured the inexpressible Torment of seeing the Dervis enter the Apartment, and caress his Queen even in his Presence.

'The Usurper, amidst his toying with the Princess, would often endeavour to ingratiate himself with her Nightingale; and while the enraged *Fadlallah* pecked at him with his Bill, beat his Wings, and shewed all the Marks of an impotent Rage, it only afforded his Rival and the Queen new Matter for their Diversion.

'*Zemroude* was likewise fond of a little Lap-Dog which she kept in her Apartment, and which one Night happened to die.

'The King immediately found himself inclined to quit the Shape of the Nightingale, and enliven this new Body. He did so, and the next Morning *Zemroude* saw her favourite Bird lie dead in the Cage. It is impossible to express her Grief on this Occasion, and when she called to mind all its little Actions, which even appeared to have somewhat in them like Reason, she was inconsolable for her Loss.

'Her Women immediately sent for the Dervis to come and comfort her, who, after having in vain represented to her the Weakness of being grieved at such an Accident, touched at last by her repeated Complaints; *Well, Madam,* says he, *I will exert the utmost of my Art to please you. Your Nightingale shall again revive every Morning, and serenade you as before.* The Queen beheld him with a Look which easily shewed she did not believe him; when laying himself down on a Sofa, he shot his Soul into the Nightingale, and *Zemroude* was amazed to see her Bird revive.

'The King, who was a Spectator of all that passed, lying under the Shape of a Lap-Dog in one Corner of the Room, immediately recovered his own Body, and running to the Cage with the utmost Indignation, twisted off the Neck of the false Nightingale.

'*Zemroude* was more than ever amazed and concerned at this second Accident, till the King entreating her to hear him, related to her his whole Adventure.

'The Body of the Dervis, which was found dead in the Wood, and his Edict for killing all the Deer, left her no Room to doubt of the Truth of it: But the Story adds, That out of an extream Delicacy, (peculiar to the Oriental Ladies) she was so highly afflicted at the innocent Adultery in which she had for some time lived with the Dervis, that no Arguments even from *Fadlallah* himself could compose her Mind. She shortly after died with Grief, begging his Pardon with her last Breath for what the most rigid Justice could not have interpreted as a Crime.

'The King was so afflicted with her Death, that he left his Kingdom to one of his nearest Relations, and passed the rest of his Days in Solitude and Retirement.'

No. 579
[ADDISON]

Wednesday, August 11, 1714[1]

> . . . *Odora canum vis.*
> Virg.

IN the Reign of King *Charles* I, the Company of Stationers, into whose Hands the Printing of the Bible is committed by Patent, made a very remarkable *Erratum* or Blunder in one of their Editions: For instead of *Thou shalt not commit Adultery*, they printed off several thousands of Copies with *Thou shalt commit Adultery*. Archbishop *Laud*, to punish this their Negligence, laid a considerable Fine upon that Company in the *Star-Chamber*.[2]

By the Practice of the World, which prevails in this degenerate Age, I am afraid that very many young Profligates, of both Sexes, are possessed of this spurious Edition of the Bible, and observe the Commandment according to that faulty Reading.

Adulterers, in the first Ages of the Church, were excommunicated for ever, and unqualified all their Lives from bearing a part in Christian Assemblies, notwithstanding they might seek it with Tears, and all[a] the Appearances of the most unfeigned Repentance.

I might here mention some antient Laws among the Heathens which punished this Crime with Death;[3] and others of the same Kind, which are now in Force among several Governments that have embraced the Reformed Religion. But because a Subject of this Nature may be too serious for my ordinary Readers, who are very apt to throw by my Papers, when they are not enlivened with something that is diverting or uncommon; I shall here publish the Contents of a little Manuscript lately fallen into my Hands, and which pretends to great Antiquity, tho' by Reason of some modern Phrases and other Particulars in it, I can by no means allow it to be genuine, but rather the Production of a Modern Sophist.

It is well known by the Learned, that there was a Temple upon Mount *Ætna* dedicated to *Vulcan*, which was guarded by Dogs of so

---

[a] and all] and with all *Fol.*

[1] *Motto.* Virgil, *Aeneid,* 4. 132: Keen-scented pack of hounds.
[2] The so-called 'Wicked Bible' was printed 'by Robert Barker and the Assigns of John Bill' in 1631. For omitting the word *not* in the Seventh Commandment the printers were fined £300 and the whole impression was called in.
[3] See Danet, art. 'Adulterium'. 'The *Athenian* Laws allow'd the Father of the Woman, the Husband, and even the Brother, to kill a Man taken in Adultery, with Impunity.'

exquisite a Smell, (say the Historians) that they could discern whether the Persons who came thither were chast or otherwise. They used to meet and faun upon such as were chast, caressing them as the Friends of their Master *Vulcan*; but flew at those who were polluted, and never ceased barking at them till they had driven them from the Temple.[1]

My Manuscript gives the following Account of these Dogs, and was probably designed as a Comment upon this Story.

'These Dogs were given to *Vulcan* by his Sister *Diana*, the Goddess of Hunting and of Chastity, having bred them out of some of her Hounds, in which she had observed this natural Instinct and Sagacity. It was thought she did it in Spight to *Venus*, who, upon her Return home, always found her Husband in a good or bad Humour, according to the Reception which she met with from his Dogs. They lived in the Temple several Years, but were such snappish Curs that they frighted away most of the Votaries. The Women of *Sicily* made a solemn Deputation to the Priest, by which they acquainted him, that they would not come up to the Temple with their annual Offerings unless he muzzled his Mastiffs; and at last compromised the Matter with him, that the Offering should always be brought by a Chorus of young Girls, who were none of them above seven Years old. It was wonderful (says the Author) to see how different the Treatment was which the Dogs gave to these little Misses, from that which they had shown to their Mothers. It is said that a Prince of *Syracuse*, having married a young Lady, and being naturally of a jealous Temper, made such an Interest with the Priests of this Temple, that he procured a Whelp from them of this famous Breed. The young Puppy was very troublesome to the fair Lady at first, insomuch that she sollicited her Husband to send him away, but the good Man cut her short with the old *Sicilian* Proverb, *Love me, love my Dog*.[2] From which Time she lived very peaceably with both of them. The Ladies of *Syracuse* were very much annoyed with him, and several of very good Reputation refused to come to Court till he was discarded. There were indeed some of them that defied his Sagacity, but it was observed tho' he did not actually bite them, he would growle at them most

---

[1] The story is told by Claudius Aelianus in the second century A.D. See Aelianus, *De natura animalium*, ed. Frederick Jacobs (Jena, 1832), book xi, chap. iii.

[2] The proverb, needless to say, is not Sicilian. Apperson ('Love', verb, 10) traces it back to a Latin version of the twelfth century.

confoundedly. To return to the Dogs of the Temple: After they had lived here in great Repute for several Years, it so happened, that as one of the Priests, who had been making a charitable Visit to a Widow who lived on the Promontory of *Lilybeum*,[1] returned home pretty late in the Evening, the Dogs flew at him with so much Fury, that they would have worried him if his Brethren had not come in to his Assistance: Upon which, says my Author, the Dogs were all of them hanged, as having lost their original Instinct.'

I cannot conclude this Paper without wishing, that we had some of this Breed of Dogs in *Great Britain*, which would certainly do *Justice*, I should say *Honour*, to the Ladies of our Country, and shew the World the difference between Pagan Women and those who are instructed in sounder Principles of Virtue and Religion.

No. 580
[ADDISON]

Friday, August 13, 1714[2]

. . . Si verbo audacia detur
Non metuam magni dixisse palatia Cœli.
Ov. Met.

SIR,

'I CONSIDERED in my two last Letters that awful and tremendous Subject, the Ubiquity or Omnipresence of the Divine Being.[3] I have shewn that he is equally present in all Places throughout the whole Extent of Infinite Space. This Doctrine is so agreeable to Reason, that we meet with it in the Writings of the enlightened Heathens, as I might show at large, were it not already done by other Hands. But tho' the Deity be thus essentially present through all the Immensity of Space, there is one Part of it in which he discovers himself in a most transcendent and visible Glory. This is that Place which is marked out in Scripture under the different

---

[1] Now Cape Boèo, at the western extremity of Sicily.
[2] *Motto.* Ovid, *Metamorphoses*, I. 175–6 (altered):
       This place, the brightest mansion of the sky,
       I'll call the palace of the Deity. DRYDEN.
[3] The reference is undoubtedly to Nos. 565 and 571. Since No. 565 is not in the form of a letter, this seems to confirm Addison's authorship of the series, Nos. 565, 571, 580, and 590.

Appellations of *Paradise, the third Heaven, the Throne of God,* and *the Habitation of his Glory.*[1] It is here where the glorified Body of our Saviour resides, and where all the celestial Hierarchies, and the innumerable Hosts of Angels, are represented as perpetually surrounding the Seat of God, with *Halleluiahs* and Hymns of Praise. This is that Presence of God which some of the Divines call his Glorious, and others his Majestatick[2] Presence. He is indeed as essentially present in all other Places as in this, but it is here where he resides in a sensible Magnificence, and in the midst of all those Splendors which can affect the Imagination of created Beings.

'It is very remarkable that this Opinion of God Almighty's Presence in Heaven, whether discovered by the Light of Nature, or by a general Tradition from our first Parents, prevails among all the Nations of the World, whatsoever different Notions they entertain of the Godhead. If you look into *Homer,* that is, the most ancient of the *Greek* Writers, you see the supreme Powers seated in the Heavens, and encompassed with inferior Deities, among whom the Muses are represented as singing incessantly about his Throne.[3] Who does not here see the main Strokes and Outlines of this great Truth we are speaking of? The same Doctrine is shadowed out in many other Heathen Authors, tho' at the same time, like several other revealed Truths, dashed and adulterated with a mixture of Fables and human Inventions. But to pass over the Notions of the *Greeks* and *Romans,* those more enlightened Parts of the Pagan World, we find there is scarce a People among the late discovered Nations who are not trained up in an Opinion, that Heaven is the Habitation of the Divinity whom they worship.

'As in *Solomon's* Temple there was the *Sanctum Sanctorum,* in which a visible Glory appeared among the Figures of the Cherubins, and into which none but the High-Priest himself was permitted to enter, after having made an Atonement for the Sins of the People;[4] so if we consider the whole Creation as one great Temple, there is in it this Holy of Holies, into which the High-Priest of our Salvation entered, and took his Place among Angels and Archangels, after having made a Propitiation for the Sins of Mankind.

'With how much Skill must the Throne of God be erected? With

---

[1] For Paradise see 2 Cor. xii. 4; the third Heaven, 2 Cor. xii. 2; the Throne of God, Rev. vii. 15. The Habitation of his Glory does not appear; cf. Habitation of thy Holiness, Isa. lxiii. 15.
[2] For earlier examples of this form see *OED.*
[3] *Iliad,* 2. 484, &c.   [4] 1 Kings viii. 6-11.

what glorious Designs is that Habitation beautified, which is contrived and built by him who inspired *Hyram* with Wisdom?[1] How great must be the Majesty of that Place, where the whole Art of Creation has been employed, and where God has chosen to show himself in the most magnificent manner? What must be the Architecture of Infinite Power under the Direction of Infinite Wisdom? A Spirit cannot but be transported, after an ineffable manner, with the sight of those Objects, which were made to affect him by that Being who knows the inward Frame of a Soul, and how to please and ravish it in all its most secret Powers and Faculties. It is to this majestick Presence of God, we may apply those beautiful Expressions in holy Writ: *Behold even to the Moon, and it shineth not; yea the Stars are not pure in his sight.*[2] The Light of the Sun, and all the Glories of the World in which we live, are but as weak and sickly Glimmerings, or rather Darkness it self, in Comparison of those Splendors which encompass the Throne of God.

'As the *Glory* of this Place is transcendent beyond Imagination, so probably is the *Extent* of it. There is Light behind Light, and Glory within Glory. How far that Space may reach, in which God thus appears in perfect Majesty, we cannot possibly conceive. Tho' it is not infinite, it may be indefinite; and tho' not immeasurable in its self, it may be so with regard to any created Eye or Imagination. If he has made these lower Regions of Matter so inconceivably wide and magnificent for the Habitation of mortal and perishable Beings, how great may we suppose the Courts of his House to be, where he makes his Residence in a more especial manner, and displays himself in the Fullness of his Glory, among an innumerable Company of Angels, and Spirits of just Men made perfect?[3]

'This is certain, that our Imaginations cannot be raised too high, when we think on a Place where Omnipotence and Omniscience have so signally exerted themselves, because that they are able to produce a Scene infinitely more great and glorious than what we are able to imagine. It is not impossible but at the Consummation of all things, these outward Apartments of Nature, which are now suited to those Beings who inhabit them, may be taken in and added to that glorious Place of which I am here speaking; and by that means made a proper Habitation for Beings who are exempt from Mortality, and cleared of their Imperfections: For so the Scripture

[1] 1 Kings v. 7–11.   [2] Job. xxv. 5.
[3] Heb. xii. 23.

seems to intimate, when it speaks of new Heavens and of a new Earth, wherein dwelleth Righteousness.[1]

'I have only considered this Glorious Place, with Regard to the Sight and Imagination, though it is highly probable that our other Senses may here likewise enjoy their highest Gratifications. There is nothing which more ravishes and transports the Soul, than Harmony; and we have great Reason to believe, from the Descriptions of this Place in Holy Scripture, that this is one of the Entertainments of it. And if the Soul of Man can be so wonderfully affected with those Strains of Musick, which Human Art is capable of producing, how much more will it be raised and elevated by those, in which is exerted the whole Power of Harmony! The Senses are Faculties of the Human Soul, though they cannot be employ'd, during this our vital Union, without proper Instruments in the Body. Why therefore should we exclude the Satisfaction of these Faculties, which we find by Experience are Inlets of great Pleasure to the Soul, from among those Entertainments which are to make up our Happiness hereafter? Why should we suppose that our Hearing and Seeing will not be gratify'd with those Objects which are most agreeable to them, and which they cannot meet with in these lower Regions of Nature; Objects, *which neither Eye hath seen, nor Ear heard, nor can it enter into the Heart of Man to conceive?*[2] *I knew a Man in Christ,* (says St. *Paul,* speaking of himself,) *above fourteen Years ago, (whether in the Body, I cannot tell, or whether out of the Body, I cannot tell: God knoweth) such a one caught up to the third Heaven. And I knew such a Man (whether in the Body, or out of the Body, I cannot tell: God knoweth,) How that he was caught up into Paradise, and heard unspeakable Words, which it is not possible for Man to utter.*[3] By this is meant, that what he heard was so infinitely different from any Thing which he had heard in this World, that it was impossible to express it in such Words as might convey a Notion of it to his Hearers.

'It is very natural for us to take Delight in Enquiries concerning any Foreign Country, where we are some Time or other to make our Abode; and as we all hope to be admitted into this Glorious Place, it is both a laudable and useful Curiosity, to get what Informations we can of it, whilst we make Use of Revelation for our Guide. When these everlasting Doors shall be open to us, we may be sure that the Pleasures and Beauties of this Place will infinitely transcend our

[1] 2 Pet. iii. 13.   [2] 1 Cor. ii. 9.
[3] 2 Cor. xii. 2–4 (A.V. 'not lawful for a man to utter').

present Hopes and Expectations, and that the Glorious Appearance of the Throne of God will rise infinitely beyond whatever we are able to conceive of it. We might here entertain our selves with many other Speculations on this Subject, from those several Hints which we find of it in the Holy Scriptures; as whether there may not be different Mansions and Apartments of Glory, to Beings of different Natures; whether as they excel one another in Perfection, they are not admitted nearer to the Throne of the Almighty, and enjoy greater Manifestations of his Presence; whether there are not Solemn Times and Occasions, when all the Multitude of Heaven celebrate the Presence of their Maker in more extraordinary Forms of Praise and Adoration; as *Adam*, though he had continued in a State of Innocence, would, in the Opinion of our Divines, have kept Holy the Sabbath Day, in a more particular Manner than any other of the Seven.[1] These, and the like Speculations, we may very innocently indulge, so long as we make Use of them to inspire us with a Desire of becoming Inhabitants of this delightful Place.

'I have in this, and in two foregoing Letters, treated on the most serious Subject[a] that can employ the Mind of Man, the Omnipresence of the Deity; a Subject, which if possible, should never depart from our Meditations. We have considered the Divine Being, as he inhabits Infinitude, as he dwells among his Work, as he is present to the Mind of Man, and as he discovers himself in a more Glorious Manner among the Regions of the Blest. Such a Consideration should be kept awake in us at all Times, and in all Places, and possess our Minds with a perpetual Awe and Reverence. It should be interwoven with all our Thoughts and Perceptions, and become One with the Consciousness of our own Being. It is not to be reflected on in the Coldness of Philosophy, but ought to sink us into the lowest Prostration before him, who is so astonishingly Great, Wonderful and Holy.'

[a] Subject] Subjects *Fol*.

---

[1] Seventeenth-century divines had debated the question whether Adam knew of and kept holy the Sabbath. The problem arose from a controversy concerning the nature of the Fourth Commandment, whether it was a natural or a ceremonial law—whether derived from the law of nature or from an explicit commandment. The second chapter of Peter Heylyn's *History of the Sabbath* (1636) quotes extensively from the Church Fathers to show that Adam did not keep the Sabbath (pp. 33–35). See also Francis White, *A Treatise of the Sabbath-Day* (1636), and Thomas Shepard, *Theses Sabbaticae* (1655).

Sunt bona, sunt quædam Mediocria, sunt mala plura
Quæ legis . . .

Mart.

I AM at present sitting with a Heap of Letters before me, which I have received under the Character of SPECTATOR; I have Complaints from Lovers, Schemes from Projectors, Scandal from Ladies, Congratulations, Compliments, and Advice in abundance.

I have not been thus long an Author, to be insensible of the natural Fondness every Person must have for their own Productions; and I begin to think I have treated my Correspondents a little too uncivilly in Stringing them all together on a File, and letting them lye so long unregarded. I shall therefore, for the future, think my self at least obliged to take some Notice of such Letters as I receive, and may possibly do it at the end of every Month.

In the mean time, I intend my present Paper as a short Answer to most of those which have been already sent me.

The Publick however is not to expect I should let them into all my Secrets, and though I appear abstruse to most People, it is sufficient if I am understood by my particular Correspondents.

My Well-wisher *Van Nath* is very arch, but not quite enough so to appear in Print.

Phyladelphus will, in a little time, see his Query fully answered by a Treatise which is now in the Press.

It was very improper at that time to comply with Mr. *G.*

Miss *Kitty* must excuse me.

The Gentleman who sent me a Copy of Verses on his Mistresses Dancing, is I believe too thoroughly in Love to compose correctly.

I have too great a Respect for both the Universities, to Praise one at the Expence of the other.

Tom Nimble is a very honest Fellow, and I desire him to present my Humble Service to his Cousin *Fill. Bumper.*

[1] *Motto.* Martial, *Epigrams*, I. 16. 1-2: Amongst what you now read, there are some good, some but so-so, but more bad.

No. 581 is assigned to Addison by both Morley and Aitken, but it is not included in the Tickell edition of Addison's *Works* (1721). According to the Tickell MS. it is one of the nine papers in the last volume written by Budgell. The two letters at the end may be genuine contributions.

I am obliged for the Letter upon Prejudice.

I may in due time animadvert on the Case of *Grace Grumble*.

The Petition of *P. S. granted*.

That of *Sarah Loveit, refused*.

The Papers of *A. S*. are returned.

I thank *Aristippus* for his kind Invitation.

My Friend at *Woodstock* is a bold Man, to undertake for all within Ten Miles of him.

I am afraid the Entertainment of *Tom Turnover* will hardly be relished by the good Cities of *London* and *Westminster*.

I must consider further of it, before I indulge *W. F.* in those Freedoms he takes with the Lady's Stockings.

I am obliged to the Ingenious Gentleman, who sent me an Ode on the Subject of a late SPECTATOR, and shall take particular Notice of his last Letter.

When the Lady who wrote me a Letter, dated *July* the 20th, in Relation to some Passages in a *Lover*,[1] will be more particular in her Directions, I shall be so in my Answer.

The poor Gentleman, who fancies my Writings could reclaim an Husband who can abuse such a Wife as he describes, has I am afraid too great an Opinion of my Skill.

Philanthropos is, I dare say, a very well-meaning Man, but is a little too prolix in his Compositions.

Constantius himself must be the best Judge in the Affair he mentions.

The Letter dated from *Lincoln* is receiv'd.

Arethusa and her Friend may hear further from me.

Celia is a little too hasty.

Harriot is a good Girl, but must not Curtsie to Folks she does not know.

I must ingeniously confess my Friend *Sampson Bentstaff* has quite puzzled me, and writ me a long Letter which I cannot comprehend one Word of.

Collidan must also explain what he means by his *Drigelling*.[2]

I think it beneath my *Spectatorial* Dignity, to concern my self in the Affair of the boild Dumpling.

---

[1] The periodical conducted by Steele from 25 Feb. to 27 May 1714, under the pseudonym of Marmaduke Myrtle, Gent. Of the forty numbers Addison contributed two (Nos. 10 and 39).

[2] *OED* gives *dridge* as an obsolete form of *dredge*, but the word used by Collidan may have no meaning.

I shall consult some *Litterati* on the Project sent me for the Discovery of the Longitude.[1]

I know not how to conclude this Paper better, than by inserting a couple of Letters which are really genuine, and which I look upon to be two of the smartest Pieces I have received from my Correspondents of either Sex.

Brother SPEC.

'WHILE you are surveying every Object that falls in your way, I am wholly taken up with one. Had that Sage, who demanded what Beauty was, lived to see the dear Angel I love, he would not have asked such a Question.[2] Had another seen her, he would himself have loved the Person in whom Heaven has made Virtue visible; and were you your self to be in her Company, you could never, with all your Loquacity, say enough of her good Humour and Sense. I send you the Outlines of a Picture, which I can no more finish than I can sufficiently admire the dear Original. I am,

Your most Affectionate Brother,
Constantio Spec.'

Good Mr. Pert,

'I WILL allow you nothing till you resolve me the following Question. Pray what's the Reason that while you only talk now upon *Wednesdays*, *Fridays* and *Mondays*, you pretend to be a greater Tatler, than when you spoke every Day as you formerly used to do? If this be your plunging out of your Taciturnity, pray let the length of your Speeches compensate for the Scarceness of them.

I am,
Good Mr. Pert,
Your Admirer, if you will be long enough for Me,
Amanda Lovelength.'

---

[1] The project of William Whiston and Humphry Ditton had been publicized by Addison in *Guardian* 107 (14 July, 1713). Among the bills signed by Queen Anne on 9 July 1714 was 'An Act for providing a publick Reward for such Person or Persons as shall discover the Longitude at Sea' (*Political State*, viii. 19).

[2] This may refer to some of the definitions at the beginning of No. 144.

No. 582   *Wednesday, August 18, 1714*[1]
[ADDISON]

> . . . *Tenet insanabile multos*
> *Scribendi Cacoethes . . .*
>
>   Juv.

THERE is a certain Distemper, which is mentioned neither by *Galen* nor *Hippocrates*, nor to be met with in the *London Dispensary*. *Juvenal*, in the Motto of my Paper, terms it a *Cacoethes*; which is a hard Word for a Disease called in plain *English, the Itch of Writing*. This *Cacoethes* is as Epidemical as the Small-Pox, there being very few who are not seized with it some time or other in their Lives. There is however this Difference in these two Distempers, that the first, after having indisposed you for a time, never returns again; whereas this I am speaking of, when it is once got into the Blood, seldom comes out of it. The *British* Nation is very much afflicted with this Malady, and tho' very many Remedies have been applied to Persons infected with it, few of them have ever proved successful. Some have been cauterized with Satyrs and Lampoons, but have received little or no Benefit from them; others have had their Heads fastened for an hour together between a cleft Board, which is made use of as a Cure for the Disease, when it appears in its greatest Malignity. There is indeed one kind of this Malady which has been sometimes removed, like the biting of a *Tarantula*,[2] with the sound of a musical Instrument, which is commonly known by the Name of a Cat-call.[3] But if you have a Patient of this kind under your Care, you may assure your self there is no other way of recovering him effectually, but by forbidding him the Use of Pen, Ink and Paper.

But to drop the Allegory before I have tired it out, there is no Species of Scriblers more offensive, and more incurable, than your Periodical Writers, whose Works return upon the Publick on certain Days and at stated times. We have not the Consolation in the Perusal of these Authors, which we find at the reading of all

---

[1] *Motto.* Juvenal, *Satires*, 7. 51–52:
> The Charms of Poetry our Souls bewitch,
> The Curse of Writing is an endless Itch.

[2] In *Tatler* 47 Steele had compared the spleen to the tarantula, 'the Effects of whose malignant Poison are to be prevented by no other Remedy but the Charms of Musick'.   [3] See No. 361 (vol. iii).

others, (namely) that we are sure if we have but Patience we may come to the End of their Labours. I have often admired a humorous Saying of *Diogenes*, who reading a dull Author to several of his Friends, when every one began to be tired, finding he was almost come to a blank Leaf at the end of it, cried, *Courage, Lads, I see Land.*[1] On the contrary, our Progress through that kind of Writers I am now speaking of is never at an End. One Day makes work for another, we do not know when to promise our selves Rest.

It is a melancholy thing to consider that the Art of Printing, which might be the greatest Blessing to Mankind, should prove detrimental to us, and that it should be made use of to scatter Prejudice and Ignorance through a People, instead of conveying to them Truth and Knowledge.

I was lately reading a very whimsical Treatise, entitled, *William Ramsey's Vindication of Astrology.*[a][2] This profound Author, among

ᵃ *Vindication of Astrology.* Italics added in 12mo

---

[1] Diogenes Laertius, *Lives of the philosophers*, 6. 38–39. The saying is quoted in *Menagiana* (3rd ed., 1715, i. 323).

[2] The running title of Ramsey's *Astrologia restaurata . . ., an introduction to the knowledge of the stars . . .*, 1653. The passage here quoted has never been found in any of the works of Ramsey, 'nor does it tally with his ideas' (*DNB*). The reason is that the passage is not from Ramsey. The quotation comes from an almanac for 1712, Richard Saunders's *Apollo Anglicanus: The English Apollo* (Printed by J. Wilde, for the Company of Stationers, 1712), where it will be found on the page facing the entry for December. The passage is part of a longer series of quotations, the authors of which are given on the preceding page facing the entry for November. In turning back to this page, Addison has seen, near the top of the page, 'W. Ramsey, in his forecited Vindication of *Astrology, cap.* 6', and has failed to notice, farther down, '*Paracelsus,* in his Book *De Meteoris, cap.* 3', which is the source. The connected passage follows:

[facing November 1712:]

which is wholly caused by the Sun. Thus *W. Ramsey,* in his forecited Vindication of *Astrology, cap.* 6. telling us of Infirmities, and vehemency of Heat caused by the Dog-star, and offering to shew a Reason why all Summers are not alike contagious, he says, It happens according to the Configurations of the Luminaries with the other Planets and fixed Stars, according to their Intentions and Remissions, (and then thus absurdly goes on) Neither Cold nor Heat proceeding from the absence or presence of the Sun, as some weakly conceive; agreeing with that Fancy of (the so much admired) *Paracelsus,* in his Book *De Meteoris, cap.* 3. That the Variety of the Altitudes of the Sun, do not cause Summer and Winter, because the Sun has the same Heat, be he higher or lower; but that there are

[facing December 1712:]

Æstival and Hibernal Stars that are the grand cause of those Seasons. But what follows is more absurd, if it may be, That the absence of the Sun is not the cause of Night, forasmuch as his Light is so great, that it may illuminate the Earth all over at once as clear as broad day; but that there are tenebrificous or dark Stars, by whose influence Night is brought on, for that they do ray out Darkness and Obscurity upon the Earth, as the Sun does Light.

The word *tenebrificous* is quoted as from Ramsey in *OED* on the authority of this passage in the *Spectator.*

many mystical Passages, has the following one. 'The Absence of the Sun is not the Cause of Night, forasmuch as his Light is so great that it may illuminate the Earth all over at once as clear as broad Day, but there are tenebrificous and dark Stars, by whose Influence Night is brought on, and which do ray out Darkness and Obscurity upon the Earth, as the Sun does Light.'

I consider Writers in the same View this Sage Astrologer does the heavenly Bodies. Some of them are Stars that scatter Light as others do Darkness: I could mention several Authors who are tenebrificous Stars of the first Magnitude, and point out a knott of Gentlemen who have been dull in Consort, and may be looked upon as a dark Constellation. The Nation has been a great while benighted with several of these Antiluminaries.[1] I suffered them to ray out their Darkness as long as I was able to endure it, till at length I came to a Resolution of rising upon them, and hope in a little time to drive them quite out of the *British* Hemisphere.

No. 583   *Friday, August* 20, 1714[2]

[ADDISON]

> *Ipse thymum pinosque ferens de montibus altis,*
> *Tecta serat latè circum, cui talia Curæ:*
> *Ipse labore manum duro terat, ipse feraces*
> *Figat humo plantas, et amicos irriget Imbres.*
>
>   Virg.

EVERY Station of Life has Duties which are proper to it. Those who are determined by Choice to any particular kind of Business, are indeed more happy than those who are determined by Necessity, but both are under an equal Obligation of fixing on Employments which may be either useful to themselves or beneficial to others. No one of the Sons of *Adam* ought to think himself exempt from that Labour and Industry which were denounced to our first Parent, and in him to all his Posterity. Those to

---

[1] This is the only example in *OED* of this special combination.

[2] *Motto*, Virgil, *Georgics*, 4. 112–15:

> With his own hand, the Guardian of the Bees,
> For Slips of Pines, may search the Mountain Trees:
> And with wild Thyme and Sav'ry, plant the Plain,
> 'Till his hard horny Fingers ake with Pain:
> And deck with fruitful Trees the Fields around,
> And with refreshing Waters drench the Ground. DRYDEN.

A draft of this essay is contained in the Tickell MS. See Hodgart, pp. 381–2.

whom Birth or Fortune may seem to make such an Application unnecessary, ought to find out some Calling or Profession for themselves, that they may not lie as a Burden on the Species, and be the only useless Parts of the Creation.

Many of our Country Gentlemen in their busie Hours apply themselves wholly to the Chase, or to some other Diversion which they find in the Fields and Woods. This gave occasion to one of our most eminent *English* Writers to represent every one of them as lying under a kind of Curse pronounced to them in the Words of *Goliah, I will give thee to the fowles of the air and to the beasts of the field.*[1]

Tho' Exercises of this kind, when indulged with Moderation, may have a good Influence both on the Mind and Body, the Country affords many other Amusements of a more noble kind.

Among these I know none more delightful in it self, and beneficial to the Publick, than that of *PLANTING.* I could mention a Nobleman whose Fortune has placed him in several Parts of *England,* and who has always left these visible Marks behind him, which show he has been there: He never hired a House in his Life, without leaving all about it the Seeds of Wealth, and bestowing Legacies on the Posterity of the Owner. Had all the Gentlemen of *England* made the same Improvements upon their Estates, our whole Country would have been at this time as one great Garden. Nor ought such an Employment to be looked upon as too inglorious for Men of the highest Rank. There have been Heroes in this Art, as well as in others. We are told in particular of *Cyrus* the Great, that he planted all the Lesser *Asia.*[2] There is indeed something truly magnificent in this kind of Amusement: It gives a nobler Air to several Parts of Nature; it fills the Earth with a Variety of beautiful Scenes, and has something in it like Creation. For this Reason the Pleasure of one who plants is something like that of a Poet, who, as *Aristotle* observes, is more delighted with his Productions than any other Writer or Artist whatsoever.[3]

Plantations have one Advantage in them which is not to be

---

[1] The reference is to 1 Sam. xvii. 44. I have not identified the eminent English writer.

[2] Xenophon, *Cyropaedia,* 8. 1. 39; *Oeconomicus,* 4. 8. 20–24.

[3] Cf. *Nicomachean Ethics,* 9. 7 (1168ª 1–3):

But persons who have bestowed benefits love and cherish those on whom they have been bestowed, even if these persons are of no use (to the benefactors) and are not likely ever to become of use to them. This sort of thing is seen in the arts as well: for every man loves his own product more than he would be loved by it if it should come to life. And perhaps this is seen most of all in poets: for these are surpassingly fond of their own poems, cherishing them as if they were children.

found in most other Works, as they give a Pleasure of a more lasting Date, and continually improve in the Eye of the Planter. When you have finished a Building, or any other Undertaking of the like Nature, it immediately decays upon your Hands; you see it brought to its utmost point of Perfection, and from that time hastening to its Ruin. On the contrary, when you have finished your Plantations, they are still arriving at greater degrees of Perfection as long as you live, and appear more delightful in every succeeding Year than they did in the foregoing.

But I do not only recommend this Art to Men of Estates as a pleasing Amusement, but as it is a kind of Virtuous Employment, and may therefore be inculcated by moral Motives; particularly from the Love which we ought to have for our Country, and the Regard which we ought to bear to our Posterity. As for the first, I need only mention what is frequently observed by others, that the Increase of Forest-Trees does by no means bear a Proportion to the Destruction of them, insomuch that in a few Ages the Nation may be at a Loss to supply it self with Timber sufficient for the Fleets of *England*.[1] I know when a Man talks of Posterity in Matters of this Nature, he is looked upon with an Eye of Ridicule by the cunning and selfish part of Mankind. Most People are of the Humour of an old Fellow of a Colledge, who when he was pressed by the Society to come into something that might redound to the good of their Successors, grew very peevish, *We are always doing*, says he, *something for Posterity, but I would fain see Posterity do something for us.*

But I think Men are inexcusable, who fail in a Duty of this Nature, since it is so easily discharged. When a Man considers, that the putting a few Twigs into the Ground, is doing good to one who will make his appearance in the World about Fifty Years hence, or that he is perhaps making one of his own Descendants, easie or rich, by so inconsiderable an Expence, if he finds himself averse to it, he must conclude that he has a poor and base Heart, void of all generous Principles and Love to Mankind.

There is one Consideration, which may very much enforce what I have here said. Many honest Minds that are naturally disposed to do good in the World, and become Beneficial to Mankind, complain within themselves that they have not Talents for it. This therefore is a good Office, which is suited to the meanest Capacities,

[1] Cf. Trevelyan, i. 6, on the widespread concern over this matter in the reign of Queen Anne.

and which may be performed by Multitudes, who have not Abilities sufficient to deserve well of their Country and to recommend themselves to their Posterity, by any other Method. It is the Phrase of a Friend of mine, when any useful Country Neighbour dies, that *you may Trace him*; which I look upon as a good Funeral Oration, at the Death of an honest Husband man, who has left the Impressions of his Industry behind him, in the Place where he has lived.

Upon the foregoing Considerations, I can scarce forbear representing the Subject of this Paper as a kind of Moral Virtue; which, as I have already shown, recommends it self likewise by the Pleasure that attends it. It must be confessed, that this is none of those turbulent Pleasures which is apt to gratifie a Man in the Heats of Youth; but if it be not so Tumultuous, it is more lasting. Nothing can be more delightful, than to entertain our selves with Prospects of our own making, and to walk under those Shades which our own Industry has raised. Amusements of this Nature compose the Mind, and lay at Rest all those Passions which are uneasie to the Soul of Man, besides, that they naturally engender good Thoughts, and dispose us to laudable Contemplations. Many of the old Philosophers passed away the greatest parts of their Lives among their Gardens. *Epicurus* himself could not think sensual Pleasure attainable in any other Scene.[1] Every Reader who is acquainted with *Homer, Virgil* and *Horace*, the greatest Genius's of all Antiquity, knows very well with how much Rapture they have spoken on this Subject; and that *Virgil* in particular has written a whole Book on the Art of Planting.[2]

This Art seems to have been more especially adapted to the Nature of Man in his Primæval State, when he had Life enough to see his Productions flourish in their utmost Beauty, and gradually decay with him. One who lived before the Flood, might have seen a Wood of the tallest Oakes in the Accorn. But I only mention this Particular, in order to introduce in my next Paper, a History which I have found among the Accounts of *China*, and which may be looked upon as an Antediluvian Novel.

[1] See Sir William Temple, 'Upon the Gardens of Epicurus', in *Miscellanea*, part ii (*Works*, 1720, i. 175).
[2] For Addison's essay on the *Georgics*, first printed in Dryden's *Virgil* (1697), see Guthkelch, ii. 3–11.

No. 584
[ADDISON]

Monday, August 23, 1714[1]

Hic gelidi fontes, hic mollia prata, Lycori,
Hic Nemus, hic toto tecum consumerer ævo.
Virg.

HILPA was one of the 150 Daughters of Zilpah, of the Race of Cohu, by whom some of the Learned think is meant Cain. She was exceedingly beautiful, and when she was but a Girl of threescore and ten Years of Age, received the Addresses of several who made Love to her. Among these were two Brothers, Harpath and Shalum; Harpath, being the First-born, was Master of that fruitful Region which lies at the Foot of Mount Tirzah, in the Southern Parts of China. Shalum (which is to say the Planter, in the Chinese Language) possessed all the neighbouring Hills, and that great Range of Mountains which goes under the Name of Tirzah. Harpath was of a haughty contemptuous Spirit; Shalum was of a gentle Disposition, beloved both by God and Man.

It is said that, among the Antediluvian Women, the Daughters of Cohu had their Minds wholly set upon Riches; for which Reason the beautiful Hilpa preferred Harpath to Shalum, because of his numerous Flocks and Herds, that covered all the low Country which runs along the Foot of Mount Tirzah, and is watered by several Fountains and Streams breaking out of the Sides of that Mountain.

Harpath made so quick a Dispatch in his Courtship, that he married Hilpa in the hundredth Year of her Age; and being of an insolent Temper, laughed to Scorn his Brother Shalum for having pretended to the beautiful Hilpa, when he was Master of nothing but a long Chain of Rocks and Mountains. This so much provoked Shalum

---

[1] Motto. Virgil, Eclogues, 10. 42–43 (altered):
  Come, see what Pleasures in our Plains abound;
  The Woods, the Fountains, and the flow'ry ground.
  As you are beauteous, were you half so true,
  Here cou'd I live, and love, and dye with only you. DRYDEN.

'Shalum and Hilpa: or, the antediluvian novel, by Mr. Price', appeared in the London Magazine, May and June 1739 (viii. 248, 304–5). Charlotte Ramsay, afterwards Mrs. Lennox, included 'Shallum to Hilpa, an Epistle: from the Spectator' in her Poems on Several Occasions (1747), pp. 86–88.

that he is said to have cursed his Brother in the Bitterness of his Heart, and to have pray'd that one of his Mountains might fall upon his Head, if ever he came within the Shadow of it.

From this Time forward *Harpath* would never venture out of the Vallies, but came to an untimely End in the 250th Year of his Age, being drowned in a River as he attempted to cross it. This River is called to this Day, from his Name who perished in it, the River *Harpath*; and, what is very remarkable, issues out of one of those Mountains which *Shalum* wished might fall upon his Brother, when he cursed him in the Bitterness of his Heart.

Hilpa was in the 160th Year of her Age at the Death of her Husband, having brought him but 50 Children, before he was snatched away as has been already related. Many of the Antediluvians made Love to the young Widow, tho' no one was thought so likely to succeed in her Affections as her first Lover *Shalum*, who renew'd his Court to her about ten Years after the Death of *Harpath*; for it was not thought decent in those Days, that a Widow should be seen by a Man within ten Years after the Decease of her Husband.

Shalum falling into a deep Melancholy, and resolving to take away that Objection which had been raised against him when he made his first Addresses to *Hilpa*, began immediately after her Marriage with *Harpath*, to plant all that mountainous Region which fell to his Lot in the Division of this Country. He knew how to adapt every Plant to its proper Soil, and is thought to have inherited many traditional Secrets of that Art from the first Man. This Employment turned at length to his Profit as well as to his Amusement: His Mountains were in a few Years shaded with young Trees, that gradually shot up into Groves, Woods, and Forests, intermix'd with Walks, and Launs, and Gardens; insomuch that the whole Region, from a naked and desolate Prospect, began now to look like a second Paradise. The Pleasantness of the Place, and the agreeable Disposition of *Shalum*, who was reckoned one of the mildest and wisest of all who lived before the Flood, drew into it Multitudes of People, who were perpetually employed in the sinking of Wells, the digging of Trenches, and the hollowing of Trees, for the better Distribution of Water through every Part of this spacious Plantation.

The Habitations of *Shalum* looked every Year more beautiful in the Eyes of *Hilpa*, who, after the space of 70 Autumns, was wonderfully pleased with the distant Prospect of *Shalum*'s Hills, which were then covered with innumerable Tufts of Trees and gloomy Scenes that gave a Magnificence to the Place, and converted it into one of the finest Landskips the Eye of Man could behold.

The *Chinese* record a Letter which *Shalum* is said to have written to *Hilpa*, in the eleventh Year of her Widow-hood. I shall here translate it, without departing from that noble Simplicity of Sentiments, and Plainness of Manners, which appears in the Original. *Shalum* was at this time 180 Years old, and *Hilpa* 170.

Shalum, *Master of Mount* Tirzah, *to* Hilpa,
Mistress of the Vallies.

In the 788th Year of the Creation.

'WHAT have I not suffered, O thou Daughter of *Zilpah*, since thou gavest thy self away in Marriage to my Rival? I grew weary of the Light of the Sun, and have been ever since covering my self with Woods and Forests. These threescore and ten Years have I bewailed the Loss of thee on the Tops of Mount *Tirzah*, and soothed my Melancholy among a thousand gloomy Shades of my own raising. My Dwellings are at present as the Garden of God; every Part of them is filled with Fruits, and Flowers, and Fountains. The whole Mountain is perfumed for thy Reception. Come up into it, O my Beloved, and let us People this Spot of the new World with a beautiful Race of Mortals; let us multiply exceedingly among these delightful Shades, and fill every Quarter of them with Sons and Daughters. Remember, O thou Daughter of *Zilpah*, that the Age of Man is but a thousand Years; that Beauty is the Admiration but of a few Centuries. It flourishes as a Mountain Oak, or as a Cedar on the Top of *Tirzah*, which in three or four hundred Years will fade away, and never be thought of by Posterity, unless a young Wood springs from its Roots. Think well on this, and remember thy Neighbour in the Mountains.'

Having here inserted this Letter, which I look upon as the only Antediluvian *Billet-doux* now extant, I shall in my next Paper give the Answer to it, and the Sequel of this Story.